THE RENASCENCE OF SOCIOLOGICAL THEORY

classical and contemporary

THE RENASCENCE
OF SOCIOLOGICAL
THEORY

GENERAL EDITORS

Henry Etzkowitz *State University of New York at Purchase*

Ronald M. Glassman *The William Paterson College of New Jersey*

F. E. PEACOCK PUBLISHERS, INC. • Itasca, Illinois

Cover illustration by Elihu Vedder
from Edward Fitzgerald's translation
of the *Rubáiyát of Omar Khayyám,*
Houghton, Mifflin & Co., 1886

Library of Congress
Catalog Card No. 90-63132
ISBN 0-87581-344-5
Printed in the U.S.A.
Printing 10 9 8 7 6 5 4 3 2 1
Year 95 94 93 92 91

CONTENTS

Contributors   ix

Introduction: The Renascence of Sociological Theory   1
   Henry Etzkowitz and Ronald M. Glassman

Sociology at the Turn of a New Century   1
Two Great Traditions   5
Sociological Theory in the United States after World War II   27
The End of a Century and a New Beginning for Sociology   50

PART ONE | **CLASSICAL TRADITIONS**

Essay 1   **Émile Durkheim and the Sociological Enterprise**   69
   Rosa Haritos and Ronald M. Glassman

Introduction   69
Durkheim and the Establishment of Sociology   72
The Cohesion of Modern Society: Organic Solidarity   77
Durkheim and the Ghost of Marx   83

Case Study:
   *The Positive and Negative Effects of Anomie
   in Science: The Case of the Discovery of the AIDS Virus*   88

Cultural Goals and Institutional Means: Robert K. Merton   89
An Application of Anomie Theory: The Race for Priority   90
A Modern Plague   91

The Negative Consequences of Anomie 93
Scientific Discovery and the Positive Role of Anomie 94
Conclusions 94

Essay 2   **On Marxism**   99
            Tom Mayer

An Interpretation of Marxism 99
Dialectics 101
Historical Materialism 103
Capitalism 106
Communism 111
A Marxist Analysis of the Russian Revolution 114

Essay 3   **Max Weber, the Modern World, and Modern Sociology**   125
            Ronald M. Glassman

Rationalization and Conception of the Modern World 125
Irrational Elements in Society: Charisma and Legitimacy 128
Weber's Theory of History, Social Change, and Social Structure 131
Epistemology, Methodology, and Scientific Objectivity 136
A Weberian Analysis of China in Transition 139

            **PART TWO │ NEW DIRECTIONS IN
            SYMBOLIC THEORY**

Essay 4   **Symbolic Interaction**   151
            Barbara Katz Rothman

What Is Symbolic Interaction? 151
The Basic Premises 152
Mind 154
Self 155
Society 156
Socialization 158
The Definition of the Situation 160
Research Implications 161
Using the Interactionist Perspective in Research 162

Essay 5   **Phenomenological Sociology**   167
            Myron Orleans

Introduction 167
The Founders of Phenomenological Theory 167
The Phenomenological Approach to Social Analysis 169
The Phenomenological Method of Social Analysis 175
Applying Phenomenology to Social Life 180

Essay 6 **Hermeneutics and Sociology**   187
            Janet Wolff

            Hermeneutic Theory 188
            The Problem of Relativism 190
            Structuralist Hermeneutics 192
            Critical Hermeneutics 193
            Hermeneutics and Sociology 194
            The Limits of Objectivity 196

Essay 7 **"Surrender-and-Catch" and Sociology**   201
            Kurt H. Wolff

            1. The Place and Time of Surrender-and-Catch 201
            2. The Concrete Origin of Surrender-and-Catch 203
            3. What, Then, Is Surrender-and-Catch? 203
            4. Man as a Mixed Phenomenon 208
            5. Surrender-and-Catch and Sociology 209
            6. Surrender-and-Catch and Some Related Contemporary
               Concerns 219

Essay 8 **Cultural Resistance to Rationalization: A Study of an Art
            Avant-Garde**   227
            Jeffrey A. Halley

            Introduction to the Problem 227
            Concepts 228
            The Example of the Dada Art Avant-Garde 236
            Conclusion 240

            **PART THREE │ NEW DIRECTIONS IN
            STRUCTURAL THEORY**

Essay 9 **Feminist Theories**   249
            Pauline B. Bart

            Socialist/Marxist Feminism 250
            Radical Feminist Theorists 256
            Liberal Feminism 260
            Conclusion 262

Essay 10 **Neofunctionalism and Modern Sociology**   267
            Jeffrey C. Alexander

Essay 11 **Critical Theory**   277
            Zygmunt Bauman

            The Project 277
            Basic Concepts 284

Sociological Applications 296
Bibliographical Note 301

Essay 12 **Structuralism in France**   305
            Edith Kurzweil

Influence of Saussurean Linguistics 306
Claude Lévi-Strauss 307
Louis Althusser 310
Michel Foucault 312
Conclusions 315

Essay 13 **New Directions in Neo-Marxism: A Marxist Social Psychology**   321
            Michael Brown

Introduction 321
Ways of Thinking under Capitalism 322
Social Psychology of Protest Movements 327

Essay 14 **Sociobiology: Theory and Controversy**   335
            Walda Katz Fishman

Introduction 335
The Theory of Sociobiology 336
Evaluation of Sociobiology: Science or Ideology? 345

Essay 15 **Technology and Social Change: Alternative Paths**   355
            Henry Etzkowitz

Introduction 355
Definitions 357
Historical Background of Ideas about Technology 358
Explanations of Technological Development 362
Social Effects of Technology 367
Conclusion 372

Name Index 375

Subject Index 377

CONTRIBUTORS

Jeffrey A. Alexander
Department of Sociology, University of California at Los Angeles

Pauline B. Bart
Department of Psychiatry, University of Illinois at Chicago

Zygmunt Bauman
Department of Sociology, University of Leeds, Leeds, United Kingdom

Michael Brown
Department of Sociology, Northeastern University, Boston, Massachusetts

Henry Etzkowitz
Department of Sociology, State University of New York at Purchase

Walda Katz Fishman
Department of Sociology, Howard University, Washington, D.C.

Ronald M. Glassman
Department of Sociology, William Paterson College of New Jersey, Wayne

Jeffrey A. Halley
Department of Sociology, University of Texas at San Antonio

Rosa Haritos
Department of Sociology, Columbia University, New York, New York

Edith Kurzweil
Department of Sociology, Rutgers University, Newark, New Jersey

Tom Mayer
Department of Sociology, University of Colorado at Boulder

Myron Orleans
Department of Sociology, California State University at Fullerton

Barbara Katz Rothman
Department of Sociology, City University of New York, Bernard M. Baruch College, New York

Janet Wolff
Department of Art and Art History, University of Rochester, Rochester, New York

Kurt H. Wolff
Department of Sociology, Brandeis University, Waltham, Massachusetts

The Renascence of Sociological Theory

Henry Etzkowitz and Ronald M. Glassman

INTRODUCTION

SOCIOLOGY AT THE TURN OF A NEW CENTURY

As we close upon the centennial of the founding of the first sociology department in the United States at the University of Chicago in the early 1890s, sociology is still in many ways a discipline in formation—an uneasy alliance of older elements of philosophy, statistics, and social work as well as newer elements of women's studies, black studies, and increasingly independent subfields, such as the sociology of organizations, medicine, and science. Nevertheless, as we move toward a new century, sociological theory is undergoing a renascence: a renewal and revival of purpose. Moving from a concentration on the critique of received work, sociological theorists are currently engaged in formulating a plethora of apparently competing frameworks. We believe that we can discern a significant degree of convergence and even synthesis among these trends.

Two decades ago Alvin W. Gouldner prophesied a "coming crisis in sociology." [1] Not only had functionalist sociology failed to predict the major fault lines that would characterize American society in the 1960s and 1970s, but Marxism had failed to predict the basic changes that began to occur in the Soviet Union, eastern Europe, and China during this same era. For Gouldner, both functionalism and Marxism were deficient as sociological theories. Furthermore, there were two Marxisms—structural Marxism and critical theory—pulling Marxism in differing theoretical directions. At the same time functionalism was becoming entrapped in its own methodology—the micro-mathematical focus of positivism turning functionalist sociology away from the study of the broader trends which would shake American society to its foundations in the 1960s.

Gouldner was correct. Sociology did plummet into a major theoretical crisis. Debates raged over whether the basic theoretical systems in sociology were adequate to the task of analyzing modern society. New theories were devised and old theories were revived to fill the gaps left by functional and Marxian analysis. This essay will focus on those debates and on the theoretical outpouring that followed in their wake. We shall argue that sociology is, at this moment in its history, at a unique juncture. For the first time the entire sociological tradition, both classical and modern, is fully visible to all of us. The relative calm of the 1980s in the United States allows for a reasonable assessment of our tradition, and with the revival of sociology all across Europe, and its efflorescence in Africa, Asia, and Latin America, a reintegration of the field of sociology and an expansion of sociological analysis may very well occur—a renascence of sociological theory by the turn of the new century.

Is Sociology Preparadigmatic?

The sociological tradition is rich and complex, yet it remains conflicted in its theory, method, and especially its political ideology. The conflicts within the tradition have led to differing schools of thought, and these schools of thought continue to be at war with one another.[2] Academic warfare is perhaps not the ideal process by which a social science discipline is supposed to develop, though, as Thomas S. Kuhn has suggested, this is the way scientific disciplines often do evolve.

Following Kuhn's model, some philosophers of science consider sociology an "immature" social science.[3] They suggest that sociology is preparadigmatic, that is, that sociology has not developed a consistent, systematic epistemology, methodology, and theoretical system.[4] Sociology, however, is *not* preparadigmatic. The problem is that it has developed *two* epistemologies, numerous methodologies, and a plethora of theoretical systems.

The two epistemologies—positivism and phenomenology—though dramatically different in their philosophical foundations and involved in two centuries of academic conflict—have interpenetrated. That is, the proponents of the one or the other have been influenced by the opposing view. From the days of David Hume[5] and Immanuel Kant[6] to the days of Karl Popper[7] and Alfred Schutz,[8] the argument has raged. Yet grudgingly, slowly, painfully, a more sophisticated epistemology *is* emerging.

Popper, formerly a staunch advocate of the positivist epistemology, in his last writings compromised greatly with the phenomenologists, incorporating much of the core of their position into his formulation—without giving up his empirical orientation.[9] While at the same time, contemporary German sociologists, though basically phenomenologists in their philosophical orientation, have expanded their empirical activities—thus absorbing what had been a positivist orientation.[10]

In fact, though sociology has since its birth existed with two essentially different philosophical traditions, these traditions have always been in contact with each other—either negatively through hostile argumentation or positively through interpenetration and partial synthesis. We shall describe both the hostilities and syntheses in detail later on. We shall also analyze the two epistemologies and their divergent origins.

At this point we wish to establish that the two traditions of sociology can perhaps be better viewed as *one warring tradition*. The reason for viewing sociology in this way is that both sides have always been aware of each other's positions, and both sides have intermittently been influenced by the other's position.

Syntheses and attempted syntheses have been as commonly produced in sociology—as we shall show—as isolated, separated development. The war goes on, but the two epistemologies are closer today than they ever have been.

Is Sociology Multiparadigmatic?

Robert K. Merton, in despair, has characterized sociology as multiparadigmatic, meaning that sociology has produced many different theoretical frameworks through which society can be viewed.[11] Merton prefers, of course, the functionalist theoretical paradigm, but recognizes that there are other basic theoretical systems through which society can be analyzed, such as the Marxist system, the Weberian system, the symbolic interactionist system, etc.

Again, however, if we look closely, there is an infinite number of sociological theories. In fact, there are a small number of *basic theoretical systems* out of which many subtheoretical systems are developed. We shall describe these subtheories and their basic theoretical origins shortly. But the point is that the various theories we use can be easily traced to their core theoretical foundations.

Variations on positivist and phenomenological themes flower anew; offshoots of Marxian, Weberian, and Durkheimian sociology continue to abound; new forms of functionalist analysis (and nonorganic systems analysis) have appeared intermittently; and new historical approaches emerge in parallel fashion.

Although sociology has not unified and may never unify, there are a few *basic traditions* from which the variations germinate. Further, *it is possible to utilize the concepts and insights of one tradition without rejecting the other.* One can, for instance, do a role analysis of contemporary marriage and divorce—leaning on functionalist and symbolic interactionist concepts—and a class analysis of the same marriage and divorce situation—leaning on Marxian and Weberian concepts (set in a historical frame of reference). The two sets of analyses have *both* proven fruitful in this regard, with such concepts as *role overload* (from the functionalist, symbolic interactionist traditions) and *women's liberation* (from the Marxian tradition) *both* becoming central to the contemporary analytical program of understanding gender issues.

The analyses derived from the basic sociological theories (and their subtheories) can be used *in consonance,* where they shed *differing* light on the same subject matter. It is also the case, however, that the differing theories often produce contradictory views of the same social phenomenon. In such cases, the theories *cannot* be used in consonance. The Marxian and Weberian analyses of capitalism, for instance, differ so basically that we simply cannot use them consonantly. Weber emphasizes the efficiency and rational cost-accounting methods of capitalist production; Marx emphasized the inequality engendered by capitalism and its inherent tendency toward monopoly and political domination by an economic elite.

Still, in so many cases *it is possible to use the insights of differing theories to enhance the total analysis of a given social phenomenon.* For example, though the stratification analysis of functionalism is very different from the Marxian class analysis, insights into the integrational effects of the former, and the conflict effects of the latter, are so well known as to be almost sociological clichés. Thus, we reiterate, it is possible to utilize the concepts and insights of differing theoretical systems together—either in synthesis or in parallel analysis.

Furthermore, *where one tradition is more useful, use it.* For instance, a modern Marxist who wishes to analyze the power of the state will use a Weberian approach. Or a modern functionalist, armed with a comprehensive Durkheimian-derived theory of crime, can use a Marxian approach when studying the outpouring of crime and violence from the contemporary lower class.[12]

And *where the traditions are in conflict—show it.* Here, for instance, the Marxian and functionalist analyses of the American consumer-oriented lifestyle or the character of the American upper class and its role in politics may be so different that they cannot be used together.[13] Although insights can still be gained from the differing perspectives, the theories cannot be used in synthesis but rather in parallel fashion.

Finally, *where the theoretical traditions converge*—rejoice in the synchronized analysis.

The above sounds so easy, so utopian. The truth is that sociology, though at a new plateau from which it may rise to new heights of theoretical sophistication (and a new clarity of societal analysis), may fall into the abyss and shatter into fragmented segments. Sociology may drift into a dark age of unlearned insignificance rather than a renascence.

Before predicting a renascence or a dark age for sociology—and the title of this book shows the authors' optimistic bias—we should answer the following questions. How did sociology become a discipline at war with itself? Over what, when, and where were the major battles fought? Why are we now at a strained truce from which peace and reintegration may emerge?

TWO GREAT TRADITIONS

Sociology emerged *twice* in history, once modeled after the natural sciences, once modeled after the humanities. The British and French traditions emphasized sociology's affinity with the natural sciences, while the German and Central European tradition emerged from a broader concept of science that included the study of history and philosophy.

Science and Sociology

The French were enthralled with science, and the potentiality within it for controlling nature. They believed that science—since it unlocked the secrets of the natural world—could unlock the secrets of the social world as well. Therefore, social science, modeled after natural science, could provide us with the knowledge that could help us perfect society and produce a better life.

Such was the optimism emanating from the liberated intellectuals of the French Revolution. Neither the violence nor the disorder resulting from the revolutionary (and counterrevolutionary) activity dampened their enthusiasm for the restructuring of society.

The Positivism of Comte. Auguste Comte epitomized French thinking in regard to the social sciences and their positive role in the renovation of society.[14] He encouraged social analysts to go beyond religion and philosophy toward the creation of a science of society. The new science, sociology, would follow the method of physics in its analysis of the social world. Empirical observation, mathematization, and verification of findings would characterize sociology.

This emphasis on empiricism and mathematicism in the analysis of the social world Comte called *positivism*.[15] For Comte and his followers positivism was the equivalent of the scientific method as applied to the social sciences. He believed that the new science, sociology, armed with the positivist methodology, would help create a better society for humans to live their lives in.

Comte's positivist sociology would come under heavy criticism, both from philosophers and from natural scientists, and we shall explain these criticisms shortly. For now, let it be established that Comte's idea of a scientific sociology created great enthusiasm in France, where some years later Durkheim would develop it into a viable school of sociology.

British Empiricism. Comte's scientific sociology was well received in Britain as well as France. The British had a long tradition of *empiricism,* dating back before Locke and Hume.[16] British empiricism as a philosophical tradition had much in common with Comte's positivism. And further, emanating from the excitement over Isaac Newton's work on the laws of motion, there was much enthusiasm for both the scientific method and the mathematical analysis of the natural world.[17] With empiricism and mathematization holding center stage in Britain, the idea of a scientific sociology, as Comte had suggested, was very well received.

Yet the British intellectual world was to be moved in a different direction. Before a positivist British sociology could emerge, Charles Darwin captured the British imagination—Puritan as it was at the time—with the notion of the essential connection of human to animal life.[18] Darwin's evolutionary biology produced a raging reaction in Britain—both positive and negative. Its graphic image that "Nature is writ red in tooth and claw . . . only the fit survive," [19] was congruent with the unbridled capitalism of that era, which was competitive at home and imperialist abroad. These and other Darwinian ideas, including evolution and natural selection from the animal and plant worlds, focused the British mentality on biology. The realm of organic life became the model from which British social science would emerge.

Social Darwinism, as developed by Herbert Spencer, postulates that society could best be understood as an organic system.[20] Like a living organism, society could be studied as a whole, something greater than the sum of its parts. Just as with an organism, we could study the specialized functions of its organs (the heart, the lungs, etc.). In the case of society, however, the organs are its social institutions, such as the family, the church, and the state.

Spencer's organic analogy would be better developed by Durkheim and the British anthropologists influenced by him. Spencer, however, made a major contribution to sociology, for his conception of society as a cultural whole, the institutions of which could be analyzed as they interrelated, became one of the mainstays of sociological theory.[21]

However, unfortunately for British sociology (and unfortunately for the world), Spencer's social Darwinism developed some ominous overtones. Darwin's theory of the survival of the fittest was carried over into the social realm. Some societies, said the social Darwinists, were more fit to survive than others—the British used this to justify their domination of "inferior" races (such as the Australian aborigines, the East Indians, the Africans, and of course the Irish). The social Darwinists went on to characterize their own English poor as "unfit," and therefore not worthy of help.

The racism, classism, and overt imperialist justification of social Darwinism discredited it eventually in Britain and elsewhere. Because of this peculiar British offshoot, sociology as a scientific discipline did not really emerge in Britain. The reverence for empiricism and mathematicism continued, but unfortunately was overridden by the intriguing but tainted theories of social Darwinism.

The scientific school of sociology would finally come to fruition in France (and then become reestablished in Britain). It was Durkheim who would create the first scientifically oriented sociology.

The French School.   The French school founded by Émile Durkheim fused the teachings of Comte with those of Spencer into a new scientifically oriented science of society. Comte had already named the new social science *sociology*, but it was Durkheim who would generate its first great studies.

From Comte, Durkheim borrowed the idea that sociology should utilize the scientific method to study social facts and that, like the natural sciences, sociology should aim at constructing the fundamental laws of social interaction that would hold for all time—transhistorically and cross-culturally.

Durkheim adapted the scientific method to sociological analysis. Observation and mathematization—the scientific method—became in Durkheim's hands the observation of society for the empirical determination of social facts, the use of statistical analysis for evaluation of empirically collected data, the building of theoretical laws of social interaction from such statistically organized data, and the transhistorical and cross-cultural comparison of such data to determine variations and regularities which might lead to emendation and modification of the original theory.

Despite his devotion to the scientific model, Durkheim never suggested experimentation. He grounded sociology on the desire to study society as it exists (and existed), without altering it artificially by creating an experimental situation.

In *The Rules of Sociological Method*, Durkheim established the scientific orientation of sociology by encouraging us to focus on social facts and the theoretically constructed social laws derived from them.[22] In *Suicide* Durkheim presented us with our first great cross-cultural study of a social phenomenon (previously thought to be a phenomenon of individual psychology).[23] From the study of social causalities of suicide, Durkheim developed his now famous laws of interaction: *nomos* (social cohesion or order) and *anomie* (social disorganization and loss of norms); *egoistic isolation* (separation of the individual from community, family, and church); and *altruistic overintegration* (total enmeshment of the individual with community, family, and church).

Durkheim carefully compared cross-cultural data on suicide—in one European society and another, within one religious group and another, and transhistorically—studying tribal data as well as data from modern urbanindustrial societies. He expanded his theory of suicide through his comparative method. Thus, Durkheim created the laws of suicide that would hold for all time; at the same time he took historical, structural, and cultural variations as givens in the study of human society.

Durkheim's avoidance of artificial experimental situations foreshadowed some of the problems involved in modeling sociology on a purely natural science base. Nonetheless, Durkheim's empirical-statistical orientation and his theoretical mirroring of the natural sciences in creating universal laws of social interaction bore fruit. *Suicide, The Elementary Forms of Religious Life,*[24] and *The Division of Labor in Society*[25] stand as monuments to his method and theory.

Durkheim thus borrowed from the Comtian version of the natural sciences. However, he also borrowed from Spencer and Albert Schaffle, Durkheim's German mentor, who held common views of society as an organic entity.

The British school of thought was heavily influenced by the exciting work of Darwin, and emphasized biological descriptions of reality. Extending the biological analogy to the social world, Spencer and Schaffle characterized human societies as organic wholes greater than the sum of their parts—the way a living organism is greater than the sum of its parts. Each part has a distinct function that is coordinated with other parts; taken together, the parts make up an entity beyond themselves. The heart, brain, and lungs, for instance, all have distinct functions; taken together, they make up a living, breathing, thinking, active being.

Durkheim, though rejecting biological reductionism, was enthralled with this organic analogy.[26] Taking it beyond Spencer (whom he criticized) Durkheim focused sociology on the institutions and norms which make up the organic whole of society and regulate its individual interactions.[27] Durkheim's view—and here he gave sociology another of its major orientations—was that the basic institutions of each society must be studied, and the function of each institution identified as it relates to the whole society. Family and church, for instance, could be identified as basic social institutions, and then their functions in the organic whole described (and then cross-culturally and transhistorically compared).

The functional analysis of social institutions became so basic for Durkheimian sociology that functionalism became its later title.

Durkheim, however, did not stop there. Taking the organic analogy further, he postulated that since humans, unlike bees or ants, have few instincts, humans create learned, shared norms for the regulation of social life. Society would be chaotic if it were made up of spontaneous individual human actions. Therefore, humans evolved systems of shared, learned, normatively regulated social action patterns.

The theory of norms and the normative regulation of social behavior is another great Durkheimian contribution to sociology. The theory of learned, shared norms, however, suggests a conception of humans in intersubjective interaction, and society as a collectivity of conscious human beings interacting in a learned, variable, changeable pattern of action. This latter is not "organic" in Spencer's sense. But then as R. Nisbet points out, Durkheim was a better sociologist than that, and his sociology transcended its own theoretical origins, providing an opening to the historical, cultural, and phenomenological schools of thought that would emerge to extend functionalism or to criticize it.[28]

Another of Durkheim's great contributions comes from his *Division of Labor*, in which he developed his theory of the organic solidarity of modern society.[29] Actually, it is not his organic analogy that proved great and lasting, but his theory of roles that became fundamental for sociological analysis.

Durkheim postulated that the growing specialization of occupational roles in modern society had produced a remarkable differentiation of functions. This differentiation of roles, however, produced a growing dependence of each specially trained individual on other specialists. The result is a role interdependence which binds the modern individual with all other individuals into an organic solidarity—organic because the different, specialized roles, taken together, make up a complex society which is greater than any of its parts. Modern society holds together as an entity through the process of role interdependence. The physicist cannot live without the farmer, the farmer without the clothing manufacturer, the tailor without the teacher, the teacher without the autoworker, etc.

Ferdinand Tönnies, in *Gemeinschaft und Gesellschaft,* had previously presented a pessimistic picture of modern society.[30] Durkheim did not wholly disagree with Tönnies, who after all had analyzed in depth the anomic, isolatory, and deviant trends of modern society. Durkheim, however, went beyond Tönnies by theorizing on why modern society, despite these structural tendencies, remains cohesive.[31] Tönnies had failed to do this.

In his *Division of Labor* Durkheim also debated with the ghost of Karl Marx, who had theorized that the modern division of labor would lead to heightened class conflict and ultimately to revolution. Durkheim did warn of the divisive potential within what he called the forced and/or *anomic division of labor.*[32] For Durkheim, however, the role of interdependence produced by the specialization of occupational tasks in the modern world engendered an organic linkage within society, which, when expanded to include a majority of the population, produced an interdependent cohesiveness that would override the potential for class conflict and revolution.

We shall discuss such debates later. For now, let us assert that Durkheim's theory of the differentiation, specialization, and role integration of modern society stands as one of the lasting contributions of his legacy. Role theory was *not* fully developed by Durkheim, but, along with his theory of institutions and norms, it would become one of the basic constructs through which functionalist sociology would analyze the social world.

Durkheim's sociology is nowhere better displayed than in his *Elementary Forms of Religious Life.*[33] In that work he begins by attempting to establish the functions of religion in society, and ends by establishing a theory of religion which could hold for all societies. Remarkably, he very nearly succeeded in his quest. No one today can study religion—any religion in any culture—without referring to Durkheim's insights.

In this endeavor, however, Durkheim was studying human, symbolic, abstract ideas—ideas with no organic base and no biological origin.[34] Yet, using the functionalist organic model, he described the function of church and ritual in the production of collective beliefs and collective activities that engender social cohesion and the sanctification of norms. These beliefs and activities make for the sacred conception of mores and the magical-mystical integration of individuals into the social whole.

The function of religion in the cohesive integration of society was thus brilliantly analyzed by Durkheim. Then—as only a genius can—he leaped beyond his own biologized theory to the realm of humans as humans. For he postulated that humans create a collective set of beliefs and values—*the collec-*

tive conscience or *collective consciousness*—a world of human symbols and human intersubjectivity.[35] Durkheim never used these terms, but certainly subsumed them in his analysis of the function of the collective beliefs.

Having established the symbolic nature of the collective belief system, he then fell back upon his functionalist analysis, describing the laws of the collective conscience. Where it is unified, social cohesion is powerful; where it is diverse or weak, social cohesion gives way to *social disorganization*, which engenders a high rate of *deviance*. A diverse or weak collective consciousness diminishes the sacred nature of the norms. With the hold of the norms thus loosened, nonnormative or deviant behavior increases dramatically.

If the collective beliefs are shattered entirely, social disintegration may result—or what Durkheim calls a condition of *anomie*, engendering what he terms a pathological rate of deviance. The society would be "sick" (pathological), but from this sickness something wonderful could emerge. For with the collective beliefs weakened or shattered, and the norms demystified, new moral values may emerge, and thus human societies may change, and sometimes for the better.

Thus from this, the human, symbolic side of his conception of society, Durkheim developed his theory of social change. How do we get from one organic whole to another? You cannot determine such social causality from an organic analogy. Societies do not mutate. Therefore, Durkheim leans to the nonorganic or symbolic side of his analytical framework to describe his theory of social change.

Through population increase (and here Durkheim assumes the Marxian and Weberian causalities for such an increase, which we will describe later but which are based on material and politico-military advances), human societies come to overlap and interact. Their symbolic collective belief systems come into jarring contact. The insights gained from such cross-cultural interchanges weaken the sacred quality of the collective beliefs and norms.

Durkheim calls this condition of overlapping and competing collective beliefs a situation of *moral density*. In this situation the competing collective beliefs may collapse altogether (or at least become greatly weakened in their hold on the populace). This precipitates social disorganization and anomie. Under such circumstances deviation from the competing norms and beliefs increases dramatically, and eventually new collective beliefs and new norms emerge, producing a reintegration of society—a new organic whole (whose new institutions and roles need to be identified and functionally analyzed).

This theory of social change based on population increase and moral density is not an organic theory. Nor is it functionalist. In fact, from Durkheim's theory of population increase and competing collective beliefs a higher synthesis of sociological theory could eventually emerge. But such a synthesis would be delayed by world wars and ideological and epistemological struggles that would last for decades.

In the meantime, the students of Durkheim, such as Marcel Mauss,[36] Maurice Halbwachs,[37] Bronislaw Malinowski,[38] and Claude Lévi-Strauss[39] continued to develop the functional analysis established by Durkheim. In anthropology as well as in sociology they expanded the functionalist conceptual framework.

Eventually, the anthropological theory derived from Durkheim and his followers became influential in Britain as well as in France. The British anthropologists, already familiar with Spencer's teachings (but rejecting social Darwinism), were excited by Durkheim's functionalism, which held no negative racial stereotypes.

Radcliffe-Brown and other British anthropologists extended Durkheim's analysis by developing the concept of the *role* beyond Durkheim's beginnings.[40] Role analysis and normative analysis came to characterize their work, along with the conception of status within small-group societies.

Radcliffe-Brown and Malinowski also helped develop the concept of *culture,* which became *the* basis of the anthropological discipline.[41] The British anthropologists concentrated on cultural wholes and cultural unities rather than organic wholes, as Spencer had emphasized. This took functionalist analysis to a new dimension, divorcing it from a biological analogy that had become embarrassing and was now unnecessary.

Within the cultural unity of a given society, the structures (institutions) were identified, and the functions of these institutions described. The norms, roles, and statuses within these cultural wholes were then analyzed (completing the functionalist analysis of the social relations of a given group).

To sum up, French and British sociology and anthropology would develop functional theory to its near perfection; its full fruition occurred later in the United States, as we shall see. And the *epistemology of positivism*—with its empirical, mathematical orientation—would undergird the functionalist theory of integration of social institutions.

The history of sociology would be simple to describe, had it consisted of only this one line of development. There would have been few conflicts and no complexities. However, sociology developed twice. Even though this dual development has produced much confusion and conflict in the discipline, it has also given us a deeper set of insights into the social world.

To understand the other great sociological tradition, let us now shift the scene from France and Britain to Germany.

History, Philosophy, and Society

The Germans, like the French and the British, were impressed by science and its remarkable accomplishments. The Germans also contributed greatly to the scientific enterprise, but they were obsessed with a different problem: the problem of Germany itself and its place in the world.

Germanic tribes became the dominant power in Europe after the fall of Rome. Germanic legions inherited Europe; it was Charles the Great—Charlemagne—who was crowned king of the Franks and emperor of the West in 800 A.D.[42] Germanic tribes gave their names to France and the provinces of northern Italy, and fought the Moslems to a standstill in Spain. Germanic tribes brought the Anglo-Saxon language to England and their military training to the rest of Europe.

Of course, the Germans had been barbarians, and their lack of civilized culture ushered in the Dark Ages. But in the end they unified Europe and made it a strong new force in the world. After the decline of the Frankish Empire founded by Charlemagne, another Germanic leader—Otto the Great—established in the tenth century the Holy Roman Empire, which claimed to be the successor state to the Roman Empire in the West. The German emperors ruled over most of present-day Germany, central Europe, and northern and central Italy.

Toward the end of the Middle Ages, however, German hegemony over Europe was challenged by the Italian city-states and principalities, the monarchies of England and France, and the rise of the Spanish Empire. In the eighteenth century Italian, Spanish, and British merchants far surpassed the Germans in commercial activity. At times the Germans, who remained split into a number of states, were challenged militarily by the French. During the nineteenth century Britain became the great industrial nation of Europe. Germany remained a backward collection of rival states until Otto von Bismarck, the powerful chancellor of Prussia, defeated the Austrians in 1866 and the French in 1870. As a result, the Germans finally achieved national unity in the German Empire, which lasted until 1918.

This brief historical summary helps explain the fascination German intellectuals have had with history—the history of Europe as a whole and the history of Germany in particular.[43] Searching for the meaning of history, they looked to the outpouring of scholarship on classical Rome and Greece that emerged during the Italian Renaissance and the English and French Enlightenment. But the Germans were distrustful of the democratic and libertarian ideas promulgated by the English and French. They preferred a more elitist philosophy of life and social organization.[44] Whereas the British exalted Aristotle (to Thomas Hobbes's chagrin), and the French revived the spirited words of Pericles, the German political thinkers were attracted to Plato's elitist theories, which, emphasizing the natural aristocracy of the most intelligent and wise members of a polity, granted them the right to rule.[45]

Plato's criticisms of the excesses and instability of Athenian democracy sat well with the German intellectuals, who were frightened by the French Revolution and repulsed by its disorder. Platonism became an obsession in Germany, and the extension of Plato's ideas formed the major thrust of German philosophizing for almost a century.

Ironically, the major German philosopher of the Enlightenment, Immanuel Kant, was a fully committed democrat who welcomed the rights of man proclaimed by the French revolutionaries! Yet Kant's political ideology was not influential in Germany, whereas his extension and reformulation of Plato's theory of ideas became the foundation for all subsequent German philosophizing.[46]

British philosophy tended to emphasize pre-Socratic Greek scientific, logical, and mathematical teachings, focusing on empirical observations and their logical ordering.[47] But German philosophy tended to emphasize post-Socratic Greek philosophy, which focused on human ideas, human irrationalities, and the instability of the social world.[48] These two different trends in philosophy led to two different trends in sociology. Let us now look at the German tradition.

As mentioned, the German school of sociology was not stimulated by the natural sciences, which were flourishing in Germany, but by Kantian and Hegelian philosophy.

The Influence of Kant and Hegel. Kant revived Plato's theory of ideas.[49] Plato had thought that abstract ideas, such as *circle, unicorn, democracy, communism, justice,* and *honor,* which have no existence in the perceptual world, still motivate human action. Kant was writing in reaction to the British school of philosophy, whose practitioners believed that the objective empirical perception of the natural and social world was not only possible, but the basis for all scientific inquiry. The human mind, they held, was a tabula rasa (blank slate) that functioned simply as a recorder of objectively perceived, empirically verifiable reality.[50] (In modern terms, the mind is like the film of a camera that faithfully reproduces the perceptual world.)

In his philosophy of positivism Comte had enshrined the British empiricist position as the core of the scientific method. We shall analyze this position shortly. Here we wish to establish that the German philosophers led by Kant rejected the view that the human mind was merely a photographic device. For Kant, following Plato, the mind was also a producer of ideas—and human ideas, once created, could not only motivate human behavior but could also intervene in the perception of the natural and social world as well.

On the simple level, for instance, when we look at a rectangular object with legs holding it up, we see a table. Having learned the idea *table,* we then see round tables, square tables, large tables, small tables, pink tables, etc. Furthermore, we can imagine tables that do not exist, and we can impute meaning to the perceived objects we have learned are tables (in terms of their use or function or their usual location).

On the more complex side, the idea *circle* has no empirical perceptual reality at all. Unlike table, which exists in variations from the idea, *circle* cannot exist at all, except in the human mind. A circle is a two-dimensional figure in a three-dimensional world. Spheres and rings can exist, but these are not circles. Furthermore, spheres and rings are always imperfect, yet we always see them as perfect or circular (though three-dimensional). Thus, *circle* is a human idea, with no actual, empirical representation; yet we use the idea *circle* as easily as we use the idea *table.*

And now we get to the real cases, wherein Kant's revival of Plato's philosophy impacts directly on sociology. The idea of *God,* for instance, though completely unverifiable empirically, has motivated humans to a wide range of social behavior. Sometimes this behavior is altruistic and humanistic, sometimes demonic and murderous. From the saving of souls to human sacrifice, humans have acted on the idea of *God*—an idea which is unverifiable empirically, but for which humans are willing to die.

Kant's philosophy of ideas had direct relevance for the emergence of German sociology. For it we were to study humans in society, then we had to study humans *as humans,* and not as electrons or ants.

The human mind, for Kant, was more than a recorder of objective reality. If this was so, then the understanding of human social actions should encompass more than the empirical observation of social behavior—it should also include an attempt at understanding the ideas[51] and shared meanings[52] created by humans, and an attempt at uncovering the motivations and social interactions engendered by these ideas.

The German sociologists insisted that humans live in a world of human ideas and human institutions, characterized by human motivations and values. Therefore, the scientific understanding of human behavior would have to include the study of human subjective, value-loaded actions.[53] Objective observation and mathematical analysis were not enough. Without an understanding of the ideational context, the sociological analysis of human actions would be incomplete and often misleading.

A dialogue among British empiricists, French positivists, and German idealists (who later were called phenomenologists) was begun. But at the same time, since the French and German schools of sociology were moving in two different directions, the battle lines were also being drawn. To make things worse, the epistemological gulf would widen before it would narrow.

Hegel took Kant's revival of Plato's theory of ideas much further. And though Hegel was pro-state, antidemocratic, antihumanistic, and possessed by German ethnocentricity, he made some remarkable contributions to the study of human society. Hegel developed phenomenological epistemology beyond Plato and Kant. He initiated the understanding of history in terms of structured stages,[54] and he focused attention on the emergence of the progressive development of human self-consciousness or "spiritual" evolution, as the motivating cause of historical change.[55]

All of these concepts were better developed by Marx, Weber, Georg Simmel, Tönnies, and other German sociologists. But it was Hegel who generated the ideas that the others would react against and perfect. Hegel carried to an extreme Kant's revival of Plato's ideas. For Hegel, ideas became the central focus for social analysis, and spiritual ideas became the basic motivating force for the progressive development of human societies. Armed with Kant's version of Platonic idealism, Hegel revived and expanded Heraclitus's theory of change.[56]

Heraclitus—a Greek philosopher who lived before Plato's time and heavily influenced Plato's thought—had established the centrality of change in the natural and social sciences. Heraclitus was the first thinker to establish that all matter in the universe was in a constant state of flux, that all living organisms were born, grew, and died, and that all human societies were established, developed, and then degenerated.

"You cannot step twice into the same river; for other and yet other waters are ever flowing on." This was Heraclitus's famous saying, and it still intrigues the mind today. Just look at your own childhood pictures and try to determine whether you are the same person or different. Or study the United States at its bicentennial to determine whether it is the same nation now as it was in 1776. The universe itself, if it is exploding from its "big bang" origin, is ever changing, ever in motion, ever in flux.

Heraclitus's theory of change is paradoxical: it is absolutely essential for the understanding of the natural and social worlds, yet it makes the analysis of those worlds so much more complicated.

Heraclitus extended the study of change—natural and social—in one further brilliant, but maddening, way. He did not believe that change occurs as a linear, logical process. Rather he believed that change occurs through a *dialectical* process, which engenders completely new phenomena—not given by a logical extension of past phenomena, yet containing elements from the past. In simplistic terms Heraclitus referred to the dialectical process as a "fusion of opposites" producing something completely new.[57] But his dialectic is more complicated than this.

We have but a few "cosmic fragments" of Heraclitus's work, but from them we can describe his dialectical process of change in this way: from the existing structure, which seems to be stable during a finite moment in time (but which is actually always changing), new elements emerge.[58] These new elements fuse with the still existing older structure to produce a completely new structure, which seems to exist as stable during a finite period of time (but which of course is actually changing). Thus the new structure is totally new, but yet made up of elements of the old and new combined in a unique way.

This sounds unduly complicated, but the point is extremely important. Neither the course of the natural universe nor that of human history can be predicted through the use of mathematical logic alone, because new elements emerge, not included in the logical equation, and these new factors alter the direction of change. This is why the future is never fully predictable through scientific endeavor, no matter how precise its mathematics or how formal its logic.

Hegel built on the work of Heraclitus and Plato by establishing the theory of the dialectical nature of human social change. Hegel insisted that social change must be built into our study of human beings in society—that sociology and history were, therefore, *one*.[59]

Hegel then took a giant leap beyond Heraclitus and Plato. He asserted that the *totality* of history could be understood, and it was the job of the social scientist to explain history in its totality. Hegel offered such an explanation. For Hegel, history could be understood as a series of progressive stages, achieved and organized around the causal mechanism of human spiritual development. This spiritual development encompassed the human quest for understanding ourselves in the universe.

Hegel divided history into a series of spiritual stages beginning with primitive religion, moving to Oriental religion, then to Jewish monotheism, Greek rationalism, and culminating in German Protestant individualism and science. Each stage represented a progressive improvement in human self-consciousness, self-worth, and dominance over the natural world.

According to Hegel, in the primitive stage of history humans were afraid of nature and tormented by the spirits, gods, and demons of the natural world who brought them death and birth, famine and feast, flood and sunshine—all beyond their control. Driven by the desperation of their helplessness, primitives sacrificed animals and even humans to the spirits of the natural world, whom they could neither understand nor escape.

Oriental religion was a great epochal improvement, for the spirits became one single mystical force in the universe—a force that was neither good nor evil. Humans were one with the universe, though separated from it by their mindful fears and bodily needs. However, through meditation humans could transcend themselves—transcend their minds and their bodies—and become one with the universal mystical force.

In Hegel's view, this Oriental conception represented great spiritual progress over the primitive stage. However, transcendental meditation produced a loss of individual self and eventuated in the withdrawal of the individual from the struggle to gain mastery over nature. Therefore, though far better than the primitive stage of fear and trembling, the Oriental stage still left much to be done in terms of human progress and self-development.

For Hegel, the stages of Jewish monotheism and Greek rationalism represented the first great stages of human ascendance.

Because Jewish monotheism was anthropomorphic, and technically speaking a regression from the pure mysticism of the Orient, it was nonetheless a progressive stage because God was characterized as a human being, and returning this favor, humans were seen as godlike.

The Jewish God, though meant to be conceived in purely mystical terms, in fact was described as a patriarch—the "father-God" of the "chosen people." While this seems primitive, in fact it raises humans up in their own eyes—for if God were a human being then humans were made in God's image and, therefore, godlike, holy, sacred, above nature. According to Hegel, humans in the Jewish world were valued in and for themselves. Human sacrifices were forbidden. Suicide was forbidden. Social caring was demanded for each individual, rich or poor, fortunate or unfortunate. God was the center of the universe, but his children were on center stage as well.

The Greeks, emerging from a period of primitive religion and confused by the plethora of religious systems surrounding them, began to lose religious beliefs altogether. Thrown into a state of existential anxiety about life in a seemingly hostile universe, they were influenced by the study of Egyptian, Persian, Cretan, Jewish, and Phoenician thought, often through cultic groups. As a result, the Greeks developed the secular orientation to the world we now call science. Greek science and mathematics were at first shrouded in cultic-religious fanaticism, but they developed eventually into a spiritual orientation which encouraged the rational, logical, empirical analysis of the natural and social world.

For Hegel, the gain in the Greek era was the feeling for the first time in history that humans could understand and control the natural world, that they could harness the powers of nature for their own benefit. Hegel concluded that the progressive development of these two lines of human history—the anthropomorphized God of the Jews and the rational, scientific orientation of the Greeks—represented the two great lines of human development and progress. Christianity's anthropomorphized view of God and the development of the sciences in Europe produced the next higher stages of historical development. The Christian designation of Jesus—a historical person—as God (the second person of the Trinity) seemed to represent a regression in mystical purity from Judaism, just as Judaism was a regression from the pure mysticism of the Orient. Still for Hegel Christianity represented a progression because now God was an actual man. Humanity was not only created in God's image, but humanity and God were merged as one.

According to Hegel, the image of Jesus as both God and man heightened the self-consciousness of humans and elevated their self-concept to an even more godlike proportion. This spiritual self-consciousness came to its ultimate fruition in the German Protestant conception of the individual covenant between God and the individual Christian. This made it possible for the layman or laywoman to live out the "exemplary life of Christ," which was no longer reserved for the monk or nun, as had been the case during the Catholic Middle Ages.

German Protestant individualism, wherein the individual looks to no one but himself or herself and Jesus—the human-God and God-human—raises human self-awareness and the human spirit to the center of history and the universe. As such, it represents the highest stage of human spiritual development—the end of history, according to Hegel.

Along with German Protestantism, the development of European science, mathematics, and rational philosophy raised the human spirit beyond its own ontology.[60] This sums up the theory of history and social change that was to drive German intellectuals mad with excitement and argumentation. But the French, British, and American social scientists regarded this development as simply mad—that is, as warped, racist, and incoherent.

Marx's Theories. Karl Marx not only restructured Hegel's theory by emphasizing the material rather than the spiritual causalities in the stages of history; he also created a viable system of sociology out of what had been a rambling philosophy of history. Marx retained Hegel's dialectical logic, but rejected his emphasis on the spiritual causality of change. Marx believed that humans turned their conscious efforts toward material survival, which, after all, is the basic fact from which we humans cannot escape. Having secured survival, humans could then turn their consciousness to other aspects of existence (such as the spiritual realm to which Hegel referred). But material survival would still remain the basic concern of humans in groups.[61]

From his focus on material survival, Marx then generated his conception of the totality of history. Following Hegel, he presented his version of the stages of history. Standing Hegel on his head, Marx based his stages on the organization of humans for material survival. The key factor for Marx in the process of material survival was the mode of production. The stages of history, according to Marx, represented a progressive development of the forces of production that led to an ever improving mode of production.

The first stage of history was the stage of primitive communism, in which hunting and gathering was the basic mode of production. Marx called this stage *primitive communism* because the hunting-gathering effort was cooperatively organized and because the food, shelter, and clothing produced from this effort were shared rather equitably.

Marx was aware from anthropological studies, such as that of Lewis Henry Morgan on the Iroquois Indians, that the hunting-gathering economies were not pure communism; there were some private possessions.[62] But Marx was essentially correct in thinking that communal sharing was definitely the basic social ethic—not because hunter-gatherers were ideological communists but because they could not survive without a full cooperative effort, and because there was no surplus of goods which anybody could hoard or selfishly accumulate.

In any case, though most modern social scientists are cautious about designating this first stage of history as primitive communism, all modern social scientists accept the mode of production category—hunter-gatherers—as a useful conceptual category.

The second stage of history—and here Marx follows Hegel again—is the Oriental mode of production, which was based on large-scale agricultural production. The Oriental mode of production was characterized by Marx as consisting of village-peasant agriculture, organized from the top down by the emperor, aristocrats, and imperial bureaucrats. With the "divine king" at the top, the peasants toiled in squalor—the major portion of the fruits of their labor being taken away for the luxurious life-style of the aristocrats.

Marx spent his lifetime analyzing why the peasants throughout the world rarely revolted.[63] After all, they made up the vast majority in the Oriental empires. We shall shortly present his explanation for peasant passivity.

Continuing with his stage theory and focusing on agricultural production, Marx, like Hegel, turned to the Greek and Roman epochs. These civilizations differed from the Oriental empires in their mode of production. Being basically military, they developed a mode of production based on slave labor. The slaves were war captives. Therefore, Marx called this stage of history the ancient slave–agricultural mode of production. The Romans brought slave production to its ultimate development. Yet slave production was less efficient than peasant production and dependent on continuous military victories.[64]

Marx then added a regressive stage of history, feudalism, to his theory. Feudalism represented a degeneration of the Roman slave system and a superimposition of the German tribal-military system onto the knight-serf manorial system.[65] Little surplus was produced, and in the subsistence economy of feudalism the quality of life declined for both the upper and the lower classes.

Finally, Marx turned to the industrial era of history, dividing it into two segments: the capitalist stage and the socialist stage.

Marx's theory of industrial capitalism was his greatest contribution to historical sociology. According to Marx, this system emerged from its trade-capitalist origins in the merchant-trading cities of Italy, Germany, Holland, and England of the late Renaissance. It ripped apart the bonds of feudal life, destroyed feudal relationships, engendered a new class (the bourgeoisie or city business class), and established a new commercial-industrial world that became the basis of modern society in all its aspects. Modern cities, scientific agriculture, machine production, democratic political institutions, and ideas—all flow from the capitalist-industrial base.[66]

Although industrial capitalism ushered in a new and better era than feudalism, it left the majority of the population in poverty. For the second new class which capitalist industrialism engendered—the workers—resembled the peasants of the Oriental empires, the slaves of ancient civilizations, and the serfs of feudalism; they still lived in poverty and under political oppression.

Remember that Marx, an exile from Germany, was writing in Charles Dickens's England—a time when the conditions of all the workers were wretched, and employers were free to exploit the labor of children and women in the factories and mills. Moreover, workers could not vote or run for office because a property qualification reserved these rights for the rich.[67]

Therefore, Marx projected a further stage of development based on the socialist-industrial mode of production. Under socialist industrialism, the workers were to run the factories in cooperative fashion, and the fruits of their labor were to be equally distributed. The motto of this theory was as follows: "From each according to his ability, to each according to his need." [68] Women would work alongside the men and be liberated from their subservient household role. The "state would wither away" because government repression would no longer be necessary. Religion—especially superstitions and messianic promises of an afterlife—would evaporate. Eventually, the final stage of history—pure communism—would be attained. In this stage an individual might be a bricklayer or peasant in the morning, a poet in the afternoon, and a musician at night. Humanity would reach its full potential as a species. Marx believed this stage of existence to be the fullest expression of human nature—*species being*.[69]

Of course, this last stage, mitigating the Durkheimian division of labor, is as yet far from being realized in any contemporary society. Only partial models, such as the Israeli kibbutzim with their rotation of jobs and company job-sharing schemes that allow individuals the time to pursue more than one serious vocation, can be pointed to as exemplifications of the Marxian ideal. Nevertheless, the idea of people fully realizing their various capacities and sharing the essential dirty work is a powerful one. It has become part of the feminist conception of equality in marriage and other interpersonal relationships and, through the feminist initiative, may well become the most important socialist principle to infiltrate capitalist societies.

The other stages of history as conceptual categories have had to be amended and extended by social scientists to include, for instance, such stages of primitive agriculture as horticulture or small-plot farming as opposed to large-scale grain production. Yet basically modern social scientists use Marx's materialist mode of production categories to understand the totality of history.[70] Anthropologists routinely use mode of production categories, while political scientists and sociologists refer to the industrial world, or to the Third World as "developing" industrially.

Marx did not offer just his global philosophy of history. He also presented the world with a system of sociology based on his theory of history. Marx's theory of social organization flowed from his theory of history. The mode of production became the basic organizing factor from which the social relationships of society flowed. Marx's theory of social organization was very different from that of Durkheim (but not so incompatible with it as some American sociologists believe, as we shall shortly show).

According to Marx, the mode of production gave rise to a set of social relationships. These relationships were not simply a specialized set of economic roles, as Durkheim later characterized them.[71] For Marx, these relationships were the various social classes caused by the fact that the wealth, power and status of the different economic groups were unequal. Slaveholder and slave, lord and serf, capitalist and worker, man and woman, etc.—these are not occupational roles, but relations of domination and subordination.[72]

Each mode of production in history engendered class relations, so that for Marx history was basically the record of these class relationships. Obviously, if these class relationships were based on domination and subordination, then history was a tale of class conflict.[73]

Why, then, were there long periods in human history in which such conflict was not evident and society was very stable? Why did the lower classes, who usually made up the vast majority of a society, not simply rise up and overwhelm their overlords?

To answer these questions, Marx offered his theory of social cohesion—which is quite different in spirit from that of the functionalists who would write later on.

In Marx's system, society held together because the upper class (the ruling class) developed an ideology to justify its usurpation of power and wealth. These ideologies have usually been religious in nature throughout most of history, although secular ideologies also abound. If the lower classes believed the ideology, which defined them as lesser beings or spiritually undeserving, while defining the upper class as "divine" or carrying "royal blood" or more "fit" to rule as a result of intellectual or moral superiority, then they did not revolt because they believed they deserved their lower place in society. Marx called this condition of downtrodden acceptance of fate by the lower classes *false consciousness*—false because the lower classes believed the manipulative ideology of the upper class.[74]

Who can deny that the lower classes believed such false ideologies? When Emperor Hirohito died in 1989, most of the older generation of Japanese mourned him as if he were divine. After World War II, when General Douglas MacArthur paraded Hirohito around in a business suit, with loudspeakers blaring "Hirohito is an ordinary man," many Japanese threw themselves on the ground, covered their eyes, and cried out in disbelief.[75]

If this was true in 1945 and 1989, imagine the ancient Egyptian or Chinese peasants' acceptance of false consciousness in the Oriental stage! Today in the United States homeless people lie in the streets with million-dollar condominiums towering above them. Yet many Americans accept this condition out of a belief in the Protestant work ethic—the concept that the poor are damned and deserve their fate as punishment for their "sloth," while the rich deserve their billions as "God's stewards on earth" since their wealth is a "sign" of grace.[76]

Thus the belief in a false ideology inhibited the lower classes from revolt and legitimated the wealth, power, and status of the upper class. This is why society has held together. This is also why Marx opposed religion. Since he held that religion was the "opiate of the people," breaking down religious belief was one way to liberate the lower classes from their oppression.[77]

Here we can see the affinity between Durkheim's notion of the collective conscience and the sacred nature of the norms as a major force for cohesion and Marx's notion of religion as a false, but effective, unifier of society. Whereas Marx believed that the breakdown of religion would liberate people from class domination and superstition, Durkheim warned that such a development would engender a pathological rate of deviance.

In any case, the analysis of classes, class conflict, and false consciousness became the Marxian analysis of social organization along with Marx's conception of the modes of production and the stages of history. The structure of society was derived from the mode of production and historical changes, not from an organic analogy.[78]

Marx's conception of social structure also had ominous overtones, for cohesion was achieved through domination and manipulation. The upper class gained control over the means of production and then foisted its false ideology onto the lower classes.

Durkheim also dealt with class conflict in his *Division of Labor*.[79] In it he seemed to imply that role interdependence applied to the middle-class strata, while the lower classes of workers, if too poor and chronically unemployed, might not be integrated into the interdependent set of occupational role relations. As a result, they might exhibit anomic tendencies such as crime, violence, and other forms of deviance. (Robert K. Merton would later develop this theme.[80])

Nevertheless, the conceptions of social organization of Marx and Durkheim are essentially different, and place the two great traditions on different planes of analysis: the one emphasizing conflict, the other cohesion. This, of course, is the way they are usually presented in sociology textbooks. But let us go on with Marx's contributions. After developing a theory of social organization that went beyond Hegel's theory, Marx then turned to the problem of social change. He began with human consciousness, as did Hegel, but Marx believed that human consciousness was essentially focused on material survival. Human consciousness—when turned toward material survival—collectively and creatively invented new forces of production; that is, a new technology plus improved forms of productive organization.

So, for instance, the bow and arrow became a critical piece of technological development in the hunting process. At the same time large-scale hunting also required careful organization, such as dividing the group of hunters into two subgroups: (1) the noisemakers who drove the animals toward the place of ambush and (2) the people waiting in ambush.

Improvements in the forces of production caused the older mode of production to become outmoded. When the old mode of production became a hindrance, it had to make way for the new mode of production. Once established, the new mode of production engendered new and different social relationships. The classes and ideology that emerged imprinted their characteristics on a new stage of history until new forces of production were invented, thus starting the process all over again.

The basic causal factor in social change was the invention of material improvements that progressively altered the mode of production. When a monumental change in the mode of production changed relationships in society, it would rip asunder the previous set of social relationships. The lower classes would break out of their false consciousness, and a period of class conflict would ensue. This revolutionary period would be full of violent conflicts and counterrevolutions creating terrible upheavals in society. A period of violent revolution would last until the new mode of production was fully established and until a new ruling class had established its ideology to such a degree that society would then drift into a new period of quiescence and coalescence around a new, more productive material base.

During the revolutionary period, however, the new classes engendered by the new mode of production would fight the old, and the old classes would fight amongst themselves. Varying class alliances would occur between the old and the new classes, sometimes in bewildering and unexpected combinations. The end result of this class warfare might be: (1) the establishment of the new classes and the defeat of the old; (2) a stalemate between the old and the new; or (3) a regression, wherein the old classes might emerge triumphant. Eventually, however, a progressive stage of history based on the new mode of production was usually attained in the long run.

To illustrate, in the movement to capitalist industrialism from feudalism in Britain, the new classes defeated the feudal classes, even though the kingship and feudal style in the countryside were retained.[81] In France such a stalemate developed between the capitalist and feudal classes that the revolutionary and counterrevolutionary violence continued for a long time.[82] In Germany the feudal classes continued to dominate the capitalist classes right up to World War II (though they encouraged the capitalists to create the industrial mode of production), and fascism—a regressive if temporary form of society—emerged with the feudal holdovers.[83]

One last point should be kept in mind on Marx's theory of social change. Marx believed that social change could be brought about through *praxis,* that is, through a direct intervention by intellectually prepared revolutionaries whose task it was to break the lower classes away from their false consciousness. Without waiting for the tide of history to do the job, the revolutionaries would do it on their own.[84]

Socialist intellectuals, of course, with Marx as their spiritual leader, have attempted to overthrow capitalist society wherever they could. And this made Marx more than a sociologist; it made him also a leader of world revolution. We shall come back to this point, which is critical not only for the history of the modern world but also for the history of sociology. For sociology has never known how to absorb Marxian ideas, while separating them from their revolutionary content. The Marxists have not wanted to make this separation, yet sociology, as a social science, must somehow do so. Can one be a Marxian sociologist without being a revolutionary? Can we separate Marx's sociology from Marx's politics? While it is difficult, we have to do it in order to retain his insights for the foundation of the discipline.

Sociology, of course, has often absorbed Marxian ideas, while denying their revolutionary intent. Most Marxist sociologists have not wanted to make this separation, and one of the fault lines in the discipline has been whether analysts can participate in movements for social change—either revolutionary or reformist—without losing their objectivity. Various socialist, liberal, and conservative sociologists have alternatively taken activist and observer stances toward their societies and, as we shall see, the role of sociology in policy-making is a controversial issue.

Again, can we separate Marx's sociology from Marx's politics? This has been attempted by some, while others have kept them fused. The question of the relationship of sociology to Marxism also raises, by implication, the issue of the relationship of sociology to society. While at times it may be intellectually helpful to pursue a line of analysis as if it existed apart from society, the Marxian notion that consciousness is connected to social life is as true for sociology as for other social enterprises. Indeed, sociology has developed a subdiscipline, the sociology of knowledge, to analyze this phenomenon.

Weber and the German Sociological Tradition. If Hegel's work was difficult in the extreme and too Germanic, and if Marx's work was brilliant, but loaded with political dynamite, Weber's work made the German tradition acceptable to the sociological world. Weber virtually founded the German school of sociology, taking the insights of Hegel and Marx, taming them, and adding his own ideas to the mix.

Weber was preceded by Simmel,[85] Tönnies,[86] and other German sociologists whose work on the urbanization, modernization, and capitalization of society has become part of the classical tradition of sociology. Weber synthesized the German tradition of historical sociology and idealist philosophy into a theoretical framework for the analysis of contrasting civilizations.

Separating his political beliefs from the sociological endeavor as Durkheim had done, Weber engendered a more academic atmosphere in which the German school could operate with less controversy. Looking back on the work of Hegel and Marx, Weber sought to create *a more balanced view* in which to analyze both the material and spiritual aspects of human social life. In *The Protestant Ethic and the Spirit of Capitalism,* he analyzed the causal significance of religion in the process of social change.[87] In *The Agrarian Sociology of Ancient Civilizations* and *The General Economic History,* he gave primary significance to economic causes in social change and social structure.

Recognizing that Marx had had to overemphasize material causes in contradistinction to Hegel, Weber sought to balance these factors in his interpretation of the totality of history.[88] Weber also insisted that Marx's stages of history were too rigid, too teleological. History sometimes moved in peculiar ways, creating civilizational uniqueness that didn't fit in with the stage theory. For instance, India stands out as a most peculiar case; its caste system cohesion makes it unlike other Oriental civilizations.[89] Greek civilization was also unique[90]—Marx had recognized this fact in giving it a separate category as a culture based on slave production. According to Weber, even though Marx's theory of stages in history is intriguing, it doesn't always fit historical reality nor would history move toward socialism as its final stage. Socialism, in Weber's view, would fail because of its overly bureaucratic and centralized state.[91]

Furthermore, Weber believed that Marx had underemphasized the power of the modern state and the political sphere in general in the causal process of social change and in social organization. Therefore, he added to Marx's mode of production theory the theory of the mode of administration (monarchical, bureaucratic, or parliamentary-bureaucratic),[92] the theory of political power, and the conception of the *charismatic leader,* who could make history as well as be a part of history.[93]

Finally, Weber utilized a sophisticated class analysis that was more complex than the Marxian analysis.[94] He added to it an analysis of status groups, such as priests and bureaucrats, and an analysis of the political parties and political organizations these groups utilized in order to express their political power.[95]

Weber's work firmly established the German school of sociology, and a dialogue—albeit a hostile one—began with the French school of sociology.

This dialogue could have shed light on the strange dual tradition that was emerging under the rubric of sociology. A great deal of profound work was done in both Germany and France to try to reconcile the enormous differences between the two traditions. But World War I, the fascist movement, and World War II intervened. The two great traditions never really got the chance to confront each other, never really became fully aware of each other's brilliant works.

The work of Weber had many points of consonance with that of Durkheim, especially in their analysis of religion. But their differences were even greater, and these differences have remained unreconciled from the 1930s to the present day.

Two Different Epistemologies

From Kant and Hegel the German school developed an epistemology based on Plato's theory of ideas and Heraclitus's theory of change. This philosophical foundation for sociology reached its fullest development in Weber's theory of social action and his methodology of *Verstehen*, or understanding.

Since human ideas and values, such as democracy, socialism, and God, were accepted as the motivating forces for human behavior, and since it was essential to understand these ideas in specific historical contexts, which change over time, German sociologists believed that true social scientists must immerse themselves in the value-oriented context in which they live; they must also study history meticulously.

German epistemology came to be called *phenomenology*, a discipline that entailed the blending of empirical observation with the categories of the mind: the perception of the real world was a process of mind and sense perception in interaction.

The methodology derived from this was *Verstehen*, or the understanding, of the social world of which the sociologist is necessarily a part. This does not in any way preclude empirical observation, but it sets such observation in a framework of ideas, values, and historical currents.

The French and British schools (and as we shall soon see, the American school) developed positivism as their epistemology or philosophical foundation. British empiricism and the French reverence for the methods of the natural sciences combined to produce an epistemology that emphasized data collection through the empirical observation of society in an "objective" fashion—that is, by avoiding the value-loaded enmeshment we have as members of society. This was to be accomplished by stepping beyond such values and historical currents to a world of scientific and mathematical objectivity that could bring a higher level of truth to sociology.

British empiricism, which was established by Locke and Hume and could be traced back to Francis Bacon, rejected the intrusion of categories of the mind into the empirical process and continued to insist on the possibility of an objective observation of social reality. This trend reached its peak in the 1950s in the United States.

Further, along with empiricism British epistemology also established another process that became a part of the foundation of positivism and an integral part of its methodology. That was *mathematicism* or the extension of mathematical logic to the analysis of social relationships.

This trend reached its philosophical peak in Britain with the establishment of logical positivism as the basic school of British philosophy. Alfred North Whitehead and Bertrand Russell took mathematicism to its extreme in *Principia Mathematica,* which attempted to reduce all knowledge to mathematical symbols analyzed through mathematical logic.[96]

In sociology this mathematical trend reached its pinnacle in the United States as quantitative sociology, which used mathematical models to analyze society; in this school statistical analysis reached its greatest complexity. Data collection and mathematical analysis became the dominant methodology arising from the positivist epistemology. The confrontation between these two philosophical foundations and their differing methodologies engendered the great sociology war, which is still raging. We were in a period of truce in the 1980s, but the war is, unfortunately, not over.

Beyond epistemology, two differing ideologies have also fueled the feud, generating heat where light is needed. Let's now consider this development.

Warring Ideologies

Perhaps worse than the philosophical gulf separating the two traditions is the ideological gulf. The French and British tradition projects democracy as the best form of government, accepting its commercial, capitalist base as the only form of economy supportive of legal democracy.[97]

The rejection of democracy by the Germans in favor of monarchism by Hegel, utopianized *Gemeinschaft* feudalism by Tönnies, communism by Marx, or worst of all, fascism by Robert Michels[98] produced a chasm that could not be bridged.

German sociology always remained tinged with an antidemocratic spirit. This German mind-set, which was epitomized by Fichte, Nietzsche, and Hegel, would always be regarded with antipathy by the British and Americans. The events of World War II, when the Holocaust was perpetrated by the Germans, reinforced the British and American rejection of German thought in general and German sociology in particular.

Despite the epistemological and ideological wars, proponents of the two great traditions developed their epistemologies, theories, and substantive studies in a grand way. They were aware of the critiques of each other's traditions, and there was interpenetration of theory and substantive analysis between the differing schools of thought. In fact, though the criticisms increased in intensity, some cross-fertilization did occur, as with the comparative-historical and symbolic portions of Durkheim's work or with the early development of systems theory in Germany.

Weber's work was much influenced by Marxian scholarship, and the works of the Marxists were influenced by Weber, as we will later see from Georg Lukac's explicit debt to Weber and Herbert Marcuse's implicit one. Furthermore, German historical and phenomenological ideas began to gain great currency in France, where a literature of phenomenological philosophy and historically oriented sociology emerged. Finally, in Germany, though positivism was excoriated as a simplistic misreading of the scientific process, the universities and state agencies began to utilize social research for the analysis of contemporary trends.

The process of critique and cross-fertilization, however, was stopped dead in its tracks. World War I, the fascist takeovers in Italy, Germany, Spain, and almost in France, the communist revolution in Russia, and the cataclysm of World War II—all these developments crushed the spirit of free inquiry in Europe and prevented a further development of the two traditions. Both the growing differences and increased interpenetrations of the theoretical schools of thought were suspended. So crushed was Europe by war, fascism, and communism that the whole sociological enterprise disintegrated and was unable to revitalize itself until two decades after the end of World War II. Sociology, however, continued to develop in the United States.

SOCIOLOGICAL THEORY IN THE UNITED STATES
AFTER WORLD WAR II

American sociology, which began before the turn of this century, has had a distinguished and interesting history. Its high points include: (1) the Chicago schools oriented to social problems and urban sociology[99]; and (2) the independent development by George Herbert Mead, his contemporaries, and his followers of a variation of neo-Kantian, protophenomenological sociology known as *symbolic interactionism*.[100] From Mead to Erving Goffman this school of thought has continued its expansive, creative development.[101]

American sociology's main thrust developed after World War II when functionalism and positivism embodied American sociology and generated its basic features. Of course, there were other sociologists like C. Wright Mills, Robert and Helen Lynd, and Alvin W. Gouldner, who went beyond functionalist-positivist sociology. They would, however, be the first to acknowledge that this was the main effort of American sociology against which they had to defend their work.

In the 1940s and 1950s American sociology emerged in a self-conscious way with a peculiar naiveté due to both a lack of sophistication about the European traditions and a distrust of them. This distrust had been generated by the horrors of the fascist movement, the Nazi Holocaust against the Jews, and the Stalinist repression in the Soviet Union. It also reflected resentment over our own reluctant participation in World War II, a conflict caused by the irrational actions of the Europeans.

American scholars of the 1940s and 1950s did not admire the German thinkers, whom they blamed for their role in forming the nation that had inflicted the worst horrors in the history of humanity. Who could look up to Hegel, a philosopher claiming that "the German world" was the ultimate stage of human history? What American scholar could forget that Nietzsche's *Übermensch* had been corrupted by the Nazis into the "blond-beast superman"?[102] Nor could Americans show much enthusiasm for epistemology or phenomenology of Martin Heidegger, who had turned Nazi.[103]

How could American scholars take Marx's work seriously when his ideal of the "worker's democracy" and the "withering away of the state" had led to a Stalinist dictatorship and the takeover of eastern Europe? Marx's jibes at bourgeois democracy seemed strangely out of place in a world where bourgeois democracy was the last bastion of civilization and humanism in a world gone mad with barbarism and hate.

As for Max Weber, had he not propounded the theory of the charismatic leader and called for a *Führer democracy* in Germany?[104] Weber had criticized the "Anglo-Saxon tradition," and wondered in letters to Michels (who later became an ardent supporter of Mussolini) whether Germany could copy England's parliamentary democracy.[105] Years later Weber was at least partially vindicated, as his unyielding support for democracy became better understood.[106] So too could the works of Marx be understood in a more sophisticated way. But this was not the case in the 1940s and 1950s.

Even Kant, one of Germany's purest exponents of parliamentary democracy, was rejected at that time—because he was a German, writing in a difficult style, and because he seemed opposed to empiricism, objectivity, and the scientific process.

To sum up, no sophisticated analysis or absorption of the German tradition could occur in the climate of the 1940s and 1950s—and of course the McCarthy investigations ushered in an era when the works of Marx and Marxists were looked upon as treasonous.

French sociology, especially the work of Durkheim, was held in a better light; it was even extended substantively by Merton and Nisbet.[107] However, knowledge of French sociology was quite fragmented and incomplete, and its incorporation into American sociology at that time was not sophisticated or theoretically complex.[108]

How did American sociology develop, given these ideologically charged circumstances?

American Positivism

First let us look at the methodology developed by American sociology. The major objective of American sociologists was to escape European subjectivism, historicism, and fanaticism. Proponents of American sociology, therefore, turned to what they saw as scientific objectivity—*pure empiricism* with *mathematical calculation* and *value-free analysis*. Such a methodology became a patriotic objective for American sociologists, who deeply believed it was the only road to sociological truth.[109]

American sociologists dismissed Kantian and Hegelian criticisms of positivism as the rantings of ideologically deluded maniacs whose ideas had nearly destroyed the world. To the credit of American sociology, empiricism was developed to its utmost potential. Interview techniques were standardized; questionnaires were made complex (yet calculable); statistical analysis became mathematically sophisticated; and computer compilation was perfected in order to organize all the data collected through the use of mass questionnaires.

Even *participant observation*—an empirical technique developed by British and American anthropologists—was expanded and systematized by the symbolic interactionists of the Chicago school.

The rejection of historical and ideational analysis was accomplished with a self-righteous air, while the establishment of the positivist methodology was carried out in order to reestablish scientific objectivity in a sociological discipline thought to have gone astray. American patriotism was deeply enmeshed in sociological epistemology and methodology.

As we shall see, the creed of American positivism after the era of Talcott Parsons became: just collect data, wherever it is available. Don't theorize—this will get in the way of objective data collection and its statistical analysis.

In fact, the mathematical coalescence of collected data became an American obsession, as opposed to the sociological analysis of data.[110] Increasingly, narrow microstudies were encouraged by the American positivists, whose empirical methodology demanded microprecision and mathematical virtuosity rather than in-depth sociological analysis or broad comparative studies.

So far did this positivist trend proceed that in the end, gathering data for the sake of gathering data superseded sociological theorizing and sociological analysis as the main thrust of American sociology.[111] There were sociologists like Seymour M. Lipset and James S. Coleman who did excellent survey research, and brought a comparative-historical approach to their research. Comparisons, however, were often limited to cross-national and older surveys as legitimate data.[112] Paul F. Lazarsfeld created an instrument for the analysis of latent functions.[113] American sociology made a major contribution to sociological methodology by perfecting computer compilation and statistical analysis of mass-survey data. In the end, however, the discipline lost too much in America by its virtually complete rejection of the study of history and human ideas, and by its failure to use theory to guide its empirical efforts.[114] The sociologists of the 1950s failed to predict a single major trend of the 1960s—not the black movement, the youth rebellion, the sexual revolution, the women's movement, the religious decline, or the rise of cults. Yet some of these trends were predicted by maverick sociologists like C. Wright Mills and the social philosopher Herbert Marcuse.[115]

Before we discuss the new trends of the 1960s and the theoretical and epistemological outpouring they engendered, let us first look at the sociological theory developed in America during the 1940s and 1950s, along with the empiricist-positivist methodology. The theory here parallels the methodology in its attempt to eliminate historicism and ideology while developing an overarching framework for the analysis of human society.

American Structural Functionalism

It is ironic to note that Talcott Parsons, the father of American functionalism, had studied extensively in Germany. He was especially familiar with what the Germans called *systems theory*, an ahistorical form of sociological theory different from Marxian and Weberian theories.[116] Though the German systems theory was "nonorganic" in its terminology, it analyzed a given social system in nonhistorical and noncultural terms, and therefore shared some common features with French functional analysis. Parsons was also familiar with Weberian social action theory, but tended to interpret it in a much less symbolic, less Kantian (that is, less phenomenological) way than Weber had.

Despite the fact that Parsons had studied in Germany, he was increasingly influenced, while teaching at Harvard, by the organic analogy theories of such British anthropologists as Radcliffe-Brown[117] and by the homeostasis theory of L. J. Henderson.[118] In the end Parson's system resembled the organic theories of the British sociologists and anthropologists, but retained elements of the more abstract German systems theory.[119]

The form of analysis undertaken by Parsons also represented a distinctive synthesis of German formalism and French functionalism. In his substantive work Parsons tended toward functionalist analysis. This is important because his influence—through his substantive work and that of his students—tended to promulgate functionalism, rather than his own more remote, formal, and abstract systems approach.[120]

Parsons's work is paradoxical. Although the beginnings of a synthesis of the two great traditions might have emerged from it, precisely the opposite happened. Drifting away from the German tradition, Parsons and his students developed an amalgamation of the British and French traditions. But this amalgamation moved in a very different direction from that of Durkheim. While Durkheim developed his functional analysis with a growing in-depth understanding of the intersubjective symbolic ties between humans, and while he always verified his empirical and statistical analyses with remarkable cross-cultural and transhistorical comparisons, American sociologists, led by Parsons and his students, moved instead toward an increasingly ahistorical, organicist model of society, and toward an abstract context in which to analyze empirically collected data.

It is worth mentioning again that Parsons himself embodied a theoretical background that cut across the two great traditions. He could have provided a bridge between them, but he abandoned his background, and his theory became increasingly abstract. Parsons's theory eliminated the symbolic, inter-subjective thrust of the action orientation borrowed from Weber, and em-phasized the formal categories of systems theory. At the same time, Parsons's analyses leaned increasingly toward functionalism. He began to emphasize homeostasis theory, with its organic analysis of the "absorption of change" and system's "adjustments to such change." Rather than focusing on social change and its causes, Parsons focused on the system's ability to absorb change and conflict, and then to return to a situation of cohesion, order, and calm. This reflected the hope of 1950s America that society could return to normal after the terrible period of disruption that began with the Great De-pression of 1929 and ended with World War II.

In fact, Parsons became increasingly America-oriented and fascinated with the America of the 1950s. Convinced that this America represented the future for a better world, he did not encourage cross-cultural analysis or transhistorical comparisons. Rather he joyously celebrated America and Americanism—as did much of the world at that time—and sought to show that corporate America and suburban America were the vanguard society destined for world emulation. In this he was not completely wrong, for the American-style corporation and the life-style of suburban America did, in fact, become the models the world tried to emulate.

There was trouble in paradise, however. Hostile takeovers, insider trad-ing, and the suburban life-style of the 1980s are very different from the cor-porate and personal styles of the 1950s. When Parsons projected suburban America in the fifties as the world model, he did not have in mind the follow-ing developments: the dual-career couple—divorced, remarried, and combin-ing stepchildren from differing households; young couples living together unmarried; gay couples adopting children; rampant drug use and an increas-ing rate of teen suicide; and in our urban-suburban regions the highest crime rate of any industrial nation in the world. Nor did he expect American corpo-rations to move toward financial manipulations and to stray from industrial production. This was not Parsons's America.

Nor would American sociology really follow Parsonsian theory. In fact, Merton's functionalism rather than Parsons's "dark" and complicated syn-thesis set the style for American sociological theory. Merton, who had stud-ied with Parsons at Harvard, became the most influential sociologist on the American scene. Although Merton absorbed Parsons's theories, Merton himself was more fascinated by Durkheim's functionalism. As a result, Mer-ton moved American sociology firmly toward functional analysis[121] and to-ward a microempiricist bent tied to a series of core concepts.[122]

At Columbia, where he pursued his career, Merton expanded on Durkheim's theories and those of the British anthropologists. In fact, Mer-ton created the sociology we now think of as American sociology. He focused American sociology on the study of *roles and norms, statuses and institutions, an-omie and deviance.* He moved American sociology away from Parsons's systems theory and toward Durkheim's more usable functionalist theory.[123]

Emanating from the work of Merton and others of his generation, the concept of roles was developed far beyond Durkheim's constructs. The study of role sets, role-interaction patterns, roles as embedded in institutions, and the status connected to different social roles—all of this emanated from the Mertonian era.[124] Functional analysis in this American form became status and role sociology.[125] The study of normative behavior patterns and the functional interrelation of institutions dominated analysis during this period.

Merton himself made a number of major contributions, some of which extended Durkheimian theory, while others extended functionalist analysis. Perhaps his essay "Social Structure and Anomie" was his most formidable contribution.[126] It extended Durkheim's theory of anomie into a general theory of deviance, focusing it on American society in particular in order to explain America's very high rate of crime and *retreatism* (withdrawal from society through the use of alcohol and drugs). Merton even transformed the functional analysis of Durkheim to include a theory of rebellion and revolution.

Of course, we might say that this theory was not developed in dialogue with the ghost of Marx, but with the living Marxists of America's 1940s and 1950s. In fact, Merton's efforts at replacing the Marxian theory of social conflict and revolution with his Durkheimian-functionalist framework led to repeated efforts at this enterprise by a whole generation of his students.

So it was that Lewis A. Coser developed a functionalist theory of conflict.[127] S. N. Eisenstadt set forth a functionalist conception of the structure of ancient empires.[128] Suzanne Keller propounded a functionalist conception of the structure of social organization in ancient empires as a replacement for the Marxian ruling-class analysis.[129] Finally, Gabriel Almond extended this enterprise toward a theory of Third World modernization that was derived from the functionalist categories found in Durkheim's *Division of Labor*.[130] Almond's theory came to dominate both political sociology and political science in the United States. Categories such as *urbanization, specialization of roles,* and *differentiation and integration* were utilized to analyze Third World development rather than the historical stage theories used by the Marxists or the traditional-versus-modern model used by the Weberians.

The functional analysis of the United States, the Third World, and the world of ancient empires thus emerged as the dominant mode of sociological analysis in the Mertonian era. Although Parsons's aura was still real, his theory was too abstract, and as a result the mantle of authority was passed to Merton and his students.

Along with these remarkable accomplishments, Merton added another crucial insight. In his manifest and latent functions theory Merton takes us below the surface of everyday phenomena, and asks the sociologist to find deeper meanings behind human institutional behavior.[131] What are the non-obvious, yet socially significant functions[132] of institutional arrangements and role-sets and status behavior?

Uncovering the latent functions of institutions beyond their manifest or everyday obvious functions was for Merton the sociologist's true job. He believed that this is what elevated sociology to the realm of a sophisticated social science analysis—beyond mere journalistic or commonsense explanations of human social behavior.

Merton's achievement was great theorizing in the Durkheimian tradition, but ironically it also inadvertently undermined the positivist-empiricist microstudy methodology developed by American sociologists in the 1950s. If we had to uncover the latent functions of institutions, how could we deduce these functions entirely from questionnaire and interview data that tended to call forth the everyday or commonsense responses of ordinary citizens who were queried?

For Merton, the *critical* step of sociological analysis was the logical *third* step, which came after the first step—data collection—and the second step—statistical compilation of the data. Unfortunately, many American sociologists of that era avoided, or at least minimized, the third step, whereas they monumentally overemphasized the first two steps.

This third step—the process of sociologically analyzing society in order to uncover the hidden, nonobvious, or latent functions of institutions, roles, and normative actions—could have provided an intellectual bridge between functionalist analysis and the phenomenological neo-Kantian epistemology. For the third step demanded more than a positivist-empiricist presentation of data. Such a bridge, however, would only be crossed in a later era when *neo*functionalists* and *neo*-Kantians of various strands encountered each other's work.[133] (Lazarsfeld worked on this problem through his analysis of latent functions[134]; and others, like Lipset, followed all the steps of analysis.[135])

In the 1950s and 1960s, the students of Parsons and Merton gained influence in sociology departments all across America. They pushed for empirical data collection, highly developed statistical analysis, functionalist theoretical constructs, the bare minimum of sociological analysis of the collected data, and the outright rejection of theory development beyond that already promulgated by Parsons and Merton. Merton had set forth this trend—declaring a moratorium on theory development—in his influential essay "Theories of the Middle Range." [136] In it he encouraged sociologists to create hypotheses focusing on specific problem areas, but insisted that "grand theorizing" was not appropriate to the development of sociology at that time.

If theorizing had come to an end, then the theories of Parsons and Merton were "biblical"; they had been written down and were now the "law." [137] Although Merton did not close himself off from alternative trends—he brought C. Wright Mills to Columbia University and maintained ties to his Marxian former student, Alvin Gouldner—some of the followers of Merton and Parsons became "true believers." Anyone who differed with them was considered a "heretic." This is hardly a situation for developing scientific objectivity, but this was the atmosphere of the period when the influence of Parsons and Merton dominated American sociology.

---

*See Essay 10 in this volume, "Neofunctionalism and Modern Sociology."

The theories of Parsons and Merton might have remained "sacred" had not the predictions derived from these theories gone awry. Because they did not offer a theory of history and social change, and because their theory of conflict proved inadequate, American structural-functionalism was unprepared, and almost unwilling, to analyze the 1960s. Surprised by the disruptive quality of the movements of the 1960s and by their radical nature, American functionalists shrank back into a shell. They rejected the social events of the 1960s and the sociological theories engendered by them.

Parsonsian and Mertonian sociology worked as long as society remained stable and cohesive, and as long as America remained preeminent in the world. But the sixties happened, and Europe and Japan became prosperous again. Was the United States really cohesive and stable during the 1950s? Did the feminist, civil rights, new left, and racial movements of the 1960s not have their roots in the earlier suffragette, abolitionist, socialist, and progressive movements?

The sociology of the 1950s reflected the American scene. Although women and minorities, who had gained new freedoms and access to the industrial economy as a result of wartime labor shortages, did not with to return to the *status quo ante*, most of the people of the United States wished to return to normalcy after the disruption of World War II. They wanted to restore the family, bring white males back to the workplace, and return women to their traditional place in the home. In general, they wanted to go back to life as usual, or at least as it was imagined to be, absent the disruption of the depression of the thirties and the new life-styles of the twenties. In addition, a middle-class way of life was being fashioned that would become the model for the world. A new suburbia was under construction.

As the soldiers flooded back home from the war, there was a housing shortage. Thanks to the availability of low-interest mortgage loans, American builders were able to create a new phenomenon emblematic of U.S. ascendency in the world. We were presented with the split-level home, a quarter acre of lawn, and a two-car garage. This represented the highest standard of living of any middle class in history and symbolized America's superiority over fascism and communism.

Although some American sociologists, including David Riesman, William H. Whyte, and John R. Seeley, were critical of the new life-style, Parsons saw it as the vanguard achievement of the United States that would be emulated by Europeans and the rest of the world. Probably the major reason for the acceptance of American sociology in the 1950s was the expansive optimism generated by the move of Americans to the suburban world, and the envious eyes cast at that world by the war-torn Europeans, who were astonished by the suburban affluence portrayed in American movies and desired to achieve that same goal.

Suburban life, of course, proved to be more problematical than expected. Fathers were absent from the home because of increased time spent commuting to work. Women, who became isolated from the extended family and from neighborhood networks, soon discovered the difficulties of one-on-one child care and the boredom of school days as the children grew older. Children found too few children on the block, so that "play dates" had to be arranged and team sports had to be formally organized by adults. Teens would wander about aimlessly because there were few central meeting places and few sources of community integration apart from sports teams.

Further, we might ask whether the 1950s really were so quiescent. Was the suburban Garden of Eden the only living space of 1950s America? The 1950s were the McCarthy era when the constitutional rights of American leftists were destroyed. The Korean War was raging. Poverty still existed in the inner cities. Leather-jacketed gangs hung out in the streets with chains and switchblade knives, and city high schools were "blackboard jungles." Finally, blacks in the South, who had no constitutional rights, felt liberated by their military service in World War II, and decided to protest against their postwar situation. To sum up, the 1950s were not so quiescent and stable. But the move to the suburbs did seem a wonderful compromise of city and country, a fulfillment of the American Dream in astonishingly affluent terms. New infrastructures were created in former countrysides, whereas older infrastructures were abandoned in the cities.

American functionalism mirrored the optimism of the suburban dream, and joined in the rejection of the American left. It studied the inner-city turbulence as deviance, spawning a whole literature on juvenile delinquency and viewing it as an aberration outside the suburban mainstream.

Functionalist sociology believed that the suburban institutions would become the long-term institutional arrangement for the industrial world in general. The nuclear family, with its three children, mother-housewife, father-breadwinner, and dog, corporate and professional career lines for men, established church of your choice for weekend services, and moderate to liberal political ideology—these were the models functionalist sociology believed would be typical for a long time to come.[138]

But the sixties happened—and the seventies' reaction to the sixties happened as well.

The 1960s and American Sociology

Sociology—especially sociology modeled after the scientific tradition—prided itself on its ability to predict as well as to analyze. Yet the functionalist sociologists of the 1950s were so enthralled with the suburbs, so disenchanted with the leftists and their criticisms of American capitalist society, and so sure that inner-city deviance and racism in the North and South would recede that they idealized rather than analyzed America.

Functionalism's chief exponents, Parsons and Merton, were not conservatives. They were American liberals who believed that the urban and southern poor would and should rise up on the social scale. Nonetheless, they were completely caught by surprise by the monumental changes that erupted in the 1960s. Their functionalist-positivist sociology failed to predict a single major trend of the 1960s. As mentioned, it did not predict the black civil rights movement or the violence and hatred that would be turned against it in the North as well as in the South. It predicted neither the youth rebellion nor the sexual revolution as its major thrust. Rock music, disenchantment with Western world religion (and especially with Puritan up-tight, antisexual Christianity), the turn to Oriental religion and strange cults (ranging from humanistic ones to devil worship)—none of these developments was even vaguely envisioned by the stunned and horrified functionalist sociologists. Blue jeans, long hair, and nude oneness with nature were simply not part of the clean-cut suburban look the functionalists had predicted as the world suburban style.

The women's movement was especially embarrassing to functionalism since the suburban family, with the housewife-mother at its core, was held up as a model for the future. The women's movement, which encouraged women to leave the household and enter the career world—along with the soon-to-emerge and utterly unthinkable 45 percent divorce rate—broke the role set of the suburban family and obliterated the tranquility that supposedly characterized the suburban world. Drug use by middle-class youth, the rise of ultraradical politics during the Vietnam War, the descent into cultic religion and hippiedom, mass demonstrations, and another terrible war—none of this had been predicted by the 1950s functionalists. Therefore, a new generation of American sociologists sought answers elsewhere.

Now Weber *had* predicted that sensualism would emerge with the decline of Puritanism, and Marcuse had reiterated this prophecy. Marx had predicted the women's movement, and Durkheim had theorized that the decline of religion would engender pathological deviance and anomie. As a result, there was a return to the sociological classics.

C. Wright Mills's work foreshadowed that of the 1960s in general.[139] Studying with Hans Gerth,[140] who, as a German émigré was familiar with the German historical tradition and with Weber's work in particular, Mills absorbed the German tradition and applied it to the American scene.

In *White Collar* Mills produced a brilliant Marxian-Weberian synthesis describing the emergence in America of the *new* middle class or salaried white-collar workers locked into the status hierarchies of giant corporations or government bureaus.[141] "Yuppyism" of a kind was predicted by Mills. Would such a middle class continue to be the basis for democracy that the independent, small-business old middle class had been?

Taking his Marxian-Weberian synthesis further in *The Power Elite*, Mills predicted the decline of representative democracy and the rise of the elite managers of corporate, military, and governmental bureaucracies.[142] This, too, had been Weber's great worry.[143]

In terms of sociological theory, Mills's characterization of American positivism as *abstract empiricism* and his complete rejection of Parsons's system theory (as formalistic, empty, and casuist) projected Mills onto center stage.

This made him the charismatic leader of the rebellion against the American sociology of the 1950s.

Liberated by Mills's attack on American sociology, books such as Arthur Vidich and Maurice Stein's *Sociology on Trial*[144] and Alvin Gouldner's attacks on value-free sociology began to appear.[145]

In *The Sociological Imagination* Mills suggested a return to the classical tradition of sociology in order to rekindle sociological imagination, which he felt had been lost by a lapse into organic analogies and a mania for data collection and statistical analysis, which he called *abstract empiricism*.[146] The study of the macrotrends of history and the basic organizational foundations of society were, for Mills, the reason for sociology as a social science. Furthermore, Mills believed that *individuals* existed in history as influential beings—that society was not made up of such reified structures as institutions and roles or classes. People were not to be viewed as robots who simply acted in categorical fashion. Individual biographies *were* meaningful. *History, biography, and social structure* became the rallying cry of Mills's sociology.

Mills became quite radical in the early sixties, and his last works, *Listen Yankee* and *The Causes of World War III*, contained strong criticisms of American cold war policies.[147] A generation of young sixties radicals followed his lead, though often mistaking his work for a vulgar Marxism that Mills rejected. In fact, Mills's work represented a sophisticated blend of Weberian and Marxian theories, and, as such, foreshadowed an epoch of sociology in which the theories of Marx and Weber would be rediscovered, and various syntheses of their theories (with other theories) would produce new theoretical systems. Critical theory, neo-Marxism, world systems theory, and others which we will shortly describe, all owe a debt to Mills's spirit.

Mills's work thus represented a bridge between the fifties and the sixties. Whether one acknowledged Mills's role or not, a new era in sociological theorizing was beginning.

Sociological Theory in the 1960s

Because American sociology needed a theory of social change and social conflict, the revival of Marxism could easily be explained. But American hostility against Marxist political thought was still overwhelming. The revival of Marxian sociology was, therefore, greeted with anger and rejection by old-guard functionalists (even though some of them protected Marxist scholars at the old guard's universities).[148] They had, after all, set out to create a sociology that did not need Marx's insights. Admitting that Marx's insights were necessary to sociology meant that they had to admit to failure. Furthermore, the older functionalists were genuinely upset by the antidemocratic strain in Marx's thought, which was the reason that some of them had accepted the 1950s attack on the American left.

Like it or not, Marxism was established in American sociology in the 1960s. And the Marxians provided American sociology with the study of history and the material causes for social change—elements lacking in functionalist analysis. After all, America's history of oppression against blacks had resulted in violent confrontations, and it had to be studied in order to understand the further course of black-white relations. After all, hadn't Marx written on women as an oppressed class?[149] And hadn't he predicted that the bourgeois family—to a degree unknown in the peasant family—would degrade and disempower women by limiting them to household labor? And further, had not the change in the mode of production from machine-factory work to computer-automated office work created a situation wherein women became both needed and wanted in the work force (and wherein the unskilled labor of poor blacks was not needed or wanted any more)? Later, of course, feminist sociologists would go beyond Marx, but we are speaking here of an early trend in feminism.[150]

The Marxian emphasis on the study of history—in macro stages—and of social change were absolutely essential for sociology, and in the 1960s became a major focus of younger sociologists. The study of social conflict, which was also central to Marxian sociology, was reestablished in the 1960s. Marx had written on the black problem in America in a series of articles for the *New York Herald-Tribune* during the 1860s. He had prophetically asserted that if the United States failed to solve its race problem, the proletarian movement would split; white workers would direct their hatred toward black workers with whom they would be in job competition instead of toward the capitalist owners of the big firms. During the late 1960s the white backlash against blacks was especially evident among working-class whites—a development that demonstrated the relevance of the Marxian model of conflict.

When the revolt of the youth and women occurred, the Marxian model was extended to analyze these new conflicts in the same class-oriented manner.[151] The analysis of conflict and change and history were brought firmly into American sociology by this Marxian revival.[152] But the functionalists continued to reject Marx's work without managing to analyze these trends adequately in their own terms.[153] Before the functionalists could group in their embattled position, another Marxian revival emerged through the rediscovered works of the Frankfurt school, especially those of Herbert Marcuse.[154] While the Frankfurt school had been known for years, and the works of Erich Fromm and others were popular, the school only became central for sociological theory in the sixties.[155]

The sociologists of the Frankfurt school blended the work of Marx and Freud (and later of Weber) in order to explain the extraordinary outpouring of sadism, hatred, violence, and mass genocide that characterized fascism (and especially Nazism) all over Europe.[156]

As Marxists first attempted to explain the failure of the working class to remain cohesive during World War I, they added to Marxism the theory of Freud on id aggression (and the obliteration of ego and superego controls) during periods of war and extreme social conflict. This theory became popular in America during the 1960s, as young idealists saw, or heard of, the Ku

Klux Klan in the South and brutal lynchings perpetrated by them. This was reinforced as the students encountered in the North mob hatred, violence from the white working class of "hard hats," and even violence from the police intervening during the riots.

In *Eros and Civilization* Marcuse theorized on the repression of the id aggression (Thanatos) and the liberation of the id sensuality (Eros).[157] "Make love, not war" became the Marcusian motto of the 1960s youth generation. And with this motto the Frankfurt school became one of the vibrant theoretical trends of the 1960s.

In the 1970s the Frankfurt school was extended. Renamed *critical theory,* it turned its analysis to systems crises and interpersonal communication patterns. But in the 1960s the celebration of sensuality linked with the Marxian conflict orientation also popularized Frankfurt school theory.

Freud, however, had warned that the liberation of id drives could make civilization impossible; for sensuality as well as aggression had to be at least partially repressed. By the late 1960s Marcuse's "Make love" motto had become perverted to "If it feels good, do it." This new motto was different in intent. "If it feels good, do it" included every version of human sexuality, some of which can be hurtful or harmful; others can be destructive of love relationships or destructive of marital stability and family life. Further, "if it feels good" came to include drug highs and hallucinatory drug experiences along with sexuality.

Marcuse himself was shocked by the results of his own utopian ideas, and his last introduction to *Eros and Civilization* reflected this dismay.[158]

And what of the Marxists? Having brought sociology back to the theory of social change, history, and conflict that American sociology sorely needed, they then revived the Marxian critique of capitalism and the socialist ideal. Both these developments backfired in the American context.

The total rejection of corporate capitalism, no matter how accurate the critique may have been, left the youth of the late 1960s with few alternatives. Humanistic career lines were acceptable, but limited in numbers (and cut back drastically during the Nixon era). Given this situation, many young people simply dropped out of the career market, and "turned on" to the world of drugs. "Hippieness" became a new reference group in modern society, characterized by a retreat into an anomic, drug-oriented street culture or withdrawal into idealistic farming and craft communes in the countryside.

But these trends failed because the hippie subculture created a downward spiral of mobility and individual self-development which most Americans rejected. In terms of the communes, these trends failed because farming is very difficult; when not mechanized, it is economically uncompetitive.[159] The communes also failed because group life without social rules governing sexuality, power, child rearing, and economic productivity becomes chaotic and destructive of human relationships. Life in the communes ended up as economically meager, politically degrading, and psychologically disturbing. The 1960s communes did not last long. Unlike the Israeli kibbutzim, which were carefully structured, they never became models of small-scale democratic-socialist idealism. Nevertheless, the counterculture has influenced American society through the advocacy of organic farming. It has also encouraged the environmental movement and the development of new styles in poetry, music, and art.*

One last problem generated by the Marxists created a reaction against their ideology. Their dream of romantic socialism led them to idealize Mao Zedong, Fidel Castro, and Ho Chi Minh. Yet Stalin had been denounced by Kruschchev, and Mao Zedong had disrupted China drastically with his Great Leap Forward and Cultural Revolution. Though Castro modernized Cuba and raised up the lower class, especially the black lower class, he had failed to keep his promises on democratic reforms. Finally, though the regime the Americans had attempted to prop up in Saigon was corrupt and murderous, the regime in Hanoi, nationalistic and arrogant, was dictatorial in the totalitarian extreme.

The sixties came to a tumultuous end with the shooting of the students at Kent State University and Jackson State University, and with the Nixon administration's decision to withdraw from Vietnam. The new trends in sociological theory were both firmly established and under heavy attack, while the old trends in American sociology continued, but struggled under the criticism generated by a new generation of sociologists influenced by the events of the sixties.

One other sociological trend of the 1960s must be discussed before we can analyze the seventies. The disruptive—and unpredicted—events of the 1960s brought not only the theory of the American functionalists into question, but their positivist methodology as well. If positivism, with its empiricist bent, had failed to predict a monumental social revolution (not political revolution) brewing under its supposed scrutiny, then perhaps its epistemology—its very root—had been misconceived.

Phenomenology: The Epistemology of the Sixties

Perhaps Mills was correct that American empiricism was "abstract empiricism" or the collection of data with no purpose.[160] And perhaps the development of sophisticated statistical analysis was a cover for the lack of sociological analysis—functionalist or otherwise—which had so often characterized the studies of the 1950s. How often had not the methodically meticulous and mathematically complex studies published in American journals of sociology, especially in the *American Sociological Review,* ended with the statement, "More research is necessary"? Perhaps the research had not been properly grounded theoretically and epistemologically.

Some members of the younger generation of sociologists rejected positiv-

---

*See Essay 8 in this volume, "Cultural Resistance to Rationalization: A Study of an Art Avant-Garde."

ism, abstract empiricism, and statistical analysis. Searching for a new epistemology and methodology, they found it in the works of Alfred Schutz, who had brought phenomenology with him from Germany.[161] Schutz taught that intersubjectivity was the key to the understanding of human behavior. After the dissemination of Schutz's ideas, the basis of the German tradition of sociology was brought to America—humans would be studied as humans, and society would be studied as a symbolic connection of humans in intersubjective interaction rather than the study of institutions and roles in "organic" relationship.

Harold Garfinkel spread phenomenological epistemology on the West Coast,[162] while on the East Coast Peter Berger popularized and expanded upon Schutz's ideas.[163] Phenomenology did not have a major influence on American methodology (though Garfinkel tried to influence it with his ethnomethodology), but it certainly brought the positivist methodology into question.

Furthermore and tangentially to sociology, in the mid-1960s when non-Western religions were being avidly studied, phenomenology gained widespread appeal as a Western version of "mind-oriented" philosophies. The phenomenologists were rigorous proponents of sociological inquiry, not cultic theologians, and their work had a permanent impact on social theory and method, opening it to new directions and insights. In the 1980s that work was renewed under the rubric *hermeneutic sociology*—a term used by Heidegger but eschewed by Schutz.[164]

Resistance by functionalists to both the phenomenological epistemology and methodology, however, was fierce. The functionalists believed—falsely—that empirical analysis was impossible through, or even rejected by, phenomenological methodology.[165]. This was not actually the case. Phenomenologists encouraged the empirical observation of society, but insisted that sociologists should try to do so by first suspending their preconceived ideas about the world they were observing. Having suspended all mentally constructed frameworks, sociologists could then try to observe human action as it actually occurred, not as it was supposed to occur (according to role or class or some other preconceived category of action).* Whether we can do this fully is unlikely. Certainly phenomenologists tried to do it, and produced some intriguing work.[166] However, most sociologists agree that all observations are theory-laden, including Marxist, functionalist, and Weberian sociologists.

In any case the phenomenologists brought the German epistemology to America.[167] This would be critical for sociological theory in its modern development. But its methodology of *epoche* (the suspension of learned, constructed frameworks during the empirical process), has been found wanting. This is because—like abstract empiricism (though philosophically more sophisticated)—this methodology discourages the use of theoretical categories in the empirical observation process. A reaction against phenomenology,

---

*See Essay 5 in this volume, "Phenomenological Sociology."

called *structuralism,* emerged later in France and gained widespread acceptance among functionalists, including Marxists and Weberians, all of whom recognized the need for theoretically constructed categories to analyze empirically observed events.*

Phenomenology thus received a mixed reception. Even though it did not become part of the mainstream, it opened sociology to a *metatheoretical search* for its own origins and destiny.

Phenomenology and the Revival of Symbolic Interactionism.

The rise of phenomenology brought with it a renewed interest in symbolic interactionism. Although symbolic interactionism never disappeared, it had been eclipsed by functionalism as the major trend in American sociological theory. Its central methodological technique—*participant observation*—had become suspect as too subjectivist during the era of positivist domination.

It is fascinating to note that American symbolic interactionism arose on its own, independently of German neo-Kantianism, though influenced by Kant's philosophy. George Herbert Mead[168] and the American pragmatist philosophers John Dewey and William James developed their own specifically American brand of idealism, but they shared a humanistic orientation with neo-Kantianism, which they were familiar with as philosophers.[169]

The symbolic connections between humans became the main focus of their philosophical orientation. But, unlike the Germans, the Americans focused *not* on history, ideology, and epistemology, but on the social-psychological bonds between human beings. Thus Mead theorized about the socialization of children, focusing on the *significant others* who influence a child's self-image and the child's identification with socially defined role models (such as the police officer, president, baseball player, nurse, etc.). Mead called such a model the *generalized other.*[170]

The whole idea of the influence of *social* forces on the development of the *self* was brilliantly analyzed by Mead and Charles H. Cooley. Cooley's notion of the *looking-glass self* (the self-image "reflected" in the eyes of the group one interacts with) was a great contribution to sociology's intellectual history.[171]

The symbolic interactionists developed another concept, the *reference group,* which has become standard in sociological literature.[172] Reference group identification helps mold one's self-image. For instance, if two modern individuals are both middle-class and from the same ethnic background, but one looks toward hippies, while the other aligns herself with yuppies, their life-styles, values, and social behavior may become dramatically different. The reference group, in this case, is the key causal factor.

Symbolic interactionism was further developed by Muzafer Sherif[173] and Erving Goffman, with Goffman's books becoming especially popular in the early sixties. Goffman's work was a high point in this theory's development. His *Presentation of Self in Everyday Life* and *Asylums* became classics of sociol-

---

*See Essay 12 in this volume, "Structuralism in France."

ogy.[174] Goffman's concept of the *total institution* and its effect on identity and day-to-day behavior became influential not only within sociology but also in shaping public policy toward mental hospitals and the deinstitutionalization of mental patients.

As American symbolic interactionism developed, it became more American. That is, the practitioners of the 1950s and early 1960s synthesized their symbolic work with American functionalism. They analyzed role behavior, status hierarchies, and nonnormative social situations (like job interviews, walking in an urban crowd, or interactions at a cocktail party). In these studies they pointed the way to a higher level of functional analysis, which included a *micro*-level symbolic, subjectivist approach. They extended functional analysis at the *macro*-level as well by engaging in studies of professional role socialization, such as the socialization provided for doctors, soldiers, psychologists, and even mental patients.[175]

Thus, at both the micro and macro levels, the blend of symbolic interactionist humanism with functionalism's structuralism raised American sociology to a more sophisticated plateau.[176] But American sociologists—especially American positivists—did not really understand the epistemological implications of symbolic interactionism. In fact, it was Berger, who had emigrated as a youth to America, who pointed out this important point. Berger made the connection between European phenomenology and American symbolic interactionism.[177] Because Berger had studied with Schutz, he was familiar with German phenomenology. He was also aware of Durkheim's symbolic orientation embodied in the concept of the collective consciousness. Berger blended Durkheim's conceptions with those of Schutzian phenomenology. In his concept of *alternation*, Berger also synthesized the work of American symbolic interactionism (as it relates to self-development) with Schutz's phenomenology.[178] By alternation Berger meant the change in identity that occurs when an individual changes his or her class position, reference group, or religious affiliation. Such an individual, according to Berger, will even reinterpret his or her past to conform to the new identity, which will be seen as the "real" self.[179]

Symbolic interactionism thus provided a major link between functionalism's conceptual categories (such as role sets) and the human subjective interaction that goes on during any social process. In fact, symbolic interactionism added a human content to functional theory, as Goffman claimed, while bridging the gap between positivism and phenomenology, as Berger claimed.

Sociological Theory in the 1970s

Revolutions often engender reactions that sometimes usher in eras of conservatism. This was the case in the United States in the 1970s. Whites thought that the blacks wanted "too much," men thought women had gone "too far," the older generation believed that the youth culture had become too sexual, too drug-oriented, too hippie, and too antibusiness.

Sociological theory, which had just incorporated the Marxist theory of history, social change, and class conflict, experienced a reaction against the Marxist overcritique of American capitalism and democracy and against the Marxist overidentification with such leftist revolutionary leaders as Fidel Castro, Mao Zedong, and Ho Chi Minh.

A growing segment of American sociologists wished to retain Marxist theoretical principles without any connection to Marxist politics. The Marxists themselves developed a new theoretical position, *neo-Marxism,* which incorporated new lines of thought connected to the emerging political and economic trends of the modern world. For instance, Ralph Miliband modified Marxism by making the power of the modern state an equal focus with the economic dimensions of Marxism.[180] This trend was rapidly duplicated in eastern Europe, where Milovan Djilas made the same emendations.[181]

In political science John Kautsky developed a neo-Marxist theory for the analysis of Third World development.[182] Immanuel Wallerstein extended this attempt beyond the Third World, analyzing the remarkable intertwining of the world's economic system (as dominated by the capitalist nations) in his *World Systems Theory.*[183]

Numerous other neo-Marxist approaches emerged during this period in both the United States and Europe. Along with the move to modify Marxism, there was a revival of interest in Weber's sociology. This, of course, was heralded by the work of Mills, as we have suggested. Some called Weber "the bourgeois Marx" because Weber's sociology was historical, focused on social change, and included an analysis of conflict. But it praised capitalism as more efficient than socialism, criticized state socialism as bureaucratically inefficient and politically authoritarian, and praised parliamentary democracy (though recognizing its weaknesses in providing dynamic leadership in a mass society).[184] Here was a theory that would allow sociology to incorporate what was missing in functionalism without rejecting the business-oriented, legal-democratic, middle-class values upon which America was founded.

Weberian sociology provided for the 1970s what Marxian sociology had provided for the 1960s—an analysis of the remarkable and unexpected trends that occurred, and a theoretical framework to support the analysis. Marxian theory, for instance, had explained the black revolution and the women's movement (at least in part), but it had no explanation for the disenchantment with world religions and the turn toward cults. Marxism could explain the rejection of religion, but it could not explain the anomic void left by its rejection (a concept of Durkheim) or the existential quest for new religious answers (a concern of Weber).

Weber had predicted that the rise of science would produce a rejection of magic, ritual, and prayer in a new rational-minded population, and that this would lead to a feeling of *disenchantment* rather than liberation.[185] This disenchantment might lead toward cultic religious revivals or—and here Weber had foretold a major trend that was right on target—a culture of narcissism.[186]

Weber had predicted that, since Puritan Christianity was the basic religious ideology, its decline would lead to the rise of sensualism. Modern, disenchanted, rational-minded individuals would pursue rational careers of a corporate or professional nature, but in their private worlds they would seek sensual pleasures. The *culture of narcissism* would emerge, wherein the private world of the individual (separated from the work world) would become a world of sexuality, drugs, and personal pleasures. When this occurred in the mid-1970s, this aspect of Weber's work suddenly became relevant.

Further, Weber had warned that the public world would become increasingly bureaucratized. Large-scale organizations in government, business, and the service sector would dominate our lives, leaving us helpless and politically alienated. Our role as democratic citizens would come into jeopardy as decisions were made by bureaucrats for whom we did not vote, and whom we could not remove from office. This alienation from the public world of bureaucracy would drive us further into sensualism in our private lives. The world would be run by "bureaucrats without soul," and inhabited by "sensualists without heart."[187]

Along with narcissism and bureaucracy, another development led to the sudden interest in Weberian sociology—the role of *charisma* in national politics. The death of JFK left our nation stunned. In a way American politics has never recovered from his assassination, the aftermath of which took us in a very different political direction from the one we had seemed to be moving in. That is, it took us away from the New Deal liberalism of the Kennedy-Johnson era to the neoconservatism of the Nixon-Reagan era. Kennedy's charisma was much discussed, especially because those who followed him in the presidency seemed to lack this characteristic. The rise of Martin Luther King, Jr., and Bobby Kennedy heightened interest in the charisma phenomenon.[188] Their assassinations in 1968 following upon President Kennedy's riveted American attention on charisma, because the void left by these leaders was more real than the space filled by their heirs.

Weber's sociology of charismatic leadership and its relationship to political legitimacy was incorporated into the American sociological theory of the 1970s. The sociology of charisma, bureaucracy, and narcissism thus catapulted Weberian sociology back into the mainstream, just as the sociology of conflict and social change had earlier rocketed Marxian theory back to center stage. The thrust of the Weberian inclusion into American sociology was at first substantive, but later theoretical, as the entire corpus of Weber's work became available in English. In fact, the revival of his sociology brought back into the sociological world a set of theoretical and epistemological debates that had lain dormant in the era of American functionalist "isolationism."

By the end of the 1970s, Weberian, Marxian, and functionalist sociology all existed side by side again—not quite interpenetrating, but not really separated.* The schools of thought still did not accept each other's work, but they were not unaware of it either. In fact, a reticent groping for areas of theoretical and substantive synthesis began slowly and cautiously to emerge.[189]

---

*See Essay 10 in this volume.

This was the American scene at the end of the 1970s. But the American scene was no longer the only stage on which sociological theory was developing in the seventies!

The European Revival of the 1970s

In Germany a young generation of sociologists also rediscovered the work of Weber. They resurrected his political reputation, for he was not a fascist sympathizer or a romantic communist, though two of his best friends, R. Michels and Georg Lukacs went dramatically to the right and the left of Weber's politics.[190] After clearing Weber's reputation, the young sociologists gathered, retranslated, and republished his entire opus—much of which was not well known either in Germany or the United States.[191] This effort produced a veritable Weber Renaissance in Germany, the United States, Britain, and Italy, and to a lesser degree, in France.[192] Much excellent Weber scholarship resulted, including the new translation of Weber's *Economy and Society* into English by Guenther Roth and Claus Wittich.[193]

Another important trend emanating from Germany was the revival of the Frankfurt school of sociology by Jürgen Habermas.[194] Since this school no longer emanated from Frankfurt, it was renamed *critical theory.* Habermas and others extended critical theory beyond its Marxian and Freudian origins to include a new version of systems theory, not unlike Parsons's original theory.[195] In fact, the works of Parsons became popular in Germany at the same time as they were becoming unpopular in the United States! (Partly perhaps this happened because Parsons presented a positive picture of modernity for which contemporary Germans were searching.)[196]

Unlike Parsonsian theory, critical theory was, as its title suggests, highly critical of modern capitalist society. The mass media, popular culture, and advertising techniques came under continuing scrutiny and condemnation by critical theorists in Germany and the United States.[197]

Further, critical theory not only began to synthesize Parsonsian systems theory, including his pattern variables, with the theories of Marx and Freud but also increasingly to synthesize Weber's theories of bureaucracy, legitimacy, and social action.[198] The inclusion of Weberian substantive, theoretical, and epistemological concepts into the theory proved quite fruitful, and represented—along with the incorporation of Parsonsian principles—another groping attempt at synthesis.* These attempts continued throughout the 1970s and 1980s. For instance, according to Habermas's *Legitimation Crisis,* the inability of *all* modern industrial systems to fulfill the needs of their people (that is, to provide affluence, order, equality, freedom, etc.) created a *legitimation crisis.*[199] According to Habermas, this was a *systems crisis*; in this concept he combined systems theory with Weberian legitimation theory.

Finally, during the rebirth of sociology in Germany, both empirically oriented bureaus of social research[200] and phenomenologically oriented method-

---

*See Essay 11 in this volume, "Critical Theory."

ological underpinnings (now called *hermeneutic analysis*) emerged without conflict. For in Germany the neo-Kantian epistemology has always been interpreted to include empirical observation within a framework that made central the role of the human mind and its conceptual categories. The German position is that the sophisticated synthesis of empiricism and idealism has already been achieved by the post-Kantians, and that only in the "Anglo-Saxon" world is this not recognized.[201] This convergence could lead to a new level of sociological synthesis. Stepping beyond the rigidities of the British and American positivist position, and beyond the philosophical ramifications of their own tradition, contemporary German sociologists have done much to lead sociology out of its epistemological war.

In France a whole series of fascinating revivals occurred, beginning with Marxism. Marxism was revived in France as part of the French intellectuals' critique of the United States and the multinational corporation. This trend also reflected support on the part of those intellectuals for the emergence of the Third World. The works of Marxists such as Lukacs[202] and Antonio Gramasci[203] became popular. This new Marxism culminated in the work of Nicos Poulantzas.[204] Poulantzas extended the Marxian analysis to include modern corporate capitalism and middle-class affluence. However, he still remained highly critical of the world of modernity produced by capitalism because he believed it was out of control in terms of the mad pursuit of "commodities" and the shallowness of the "culture" that was engendered by a single-minded pursuit of affluence.

Along with Marxism, there was a major revival of French functionalism. This postwar French functionalism leaned toward the late Durkheimian works, and tended to emphasize the symbolic (almost phenomenological) aspect of Durkheim's achievement.* But it also revived the kind of formalist functional analysis derived from Claude Lévi-Strauss, Marcel Mauss, and other Durkheim-influenced anthropologists and sociologists of the prewar French school. Modern French functionalism represents a new synthesis of Durkheim's functional analysis and symbolic analysis. It is very different from the German historical tradition, but yet incorporates the neo-Kantian epistemology in which ideas and empirical reality are inextricably linked.

A third trend in France was the revival of phenomenological and hermeneutic sociology, focusing on the subjective interactions of humans and de-emphasizing sociological categories such as roles, norms, and classes. Michel Foucault developed his own theoretical approach, utilizing a nonstructured subjectivist framework to analyze forms of power and control. His works on sexuality, knowledge, and prisons caused quite a stir in France and elsewhere.

There emerged in France yet a fourth school of thought, the structuralists, who insisted on the necessity of using structured categories in sociological analysis. If this premise was accepted, the question then became, Which categories should sociology use—classes, roles, or institutions? French structuralists answered this question in multiple ways. Louis Althusser produced a

---

*See Essay 12 in this volume.

synthesis of Marxian and functionalist categories. The integration of herme-neutic analysis with structured categories of social analysis has also developed, and this trend has produced some interesting studies.[*]

In short, a plethora of syntheses has emerged within French structural-ism, producing a bewildering array of approaches, ideologies, and epistemol-ogies that still have not been carefully sorted out. These syntheses may prove to be idiosyncratic, or they may lead the way to a higher order of analysis through the utilization of a wide range of theoretical and epistemological in-sights.

Next, we come to Britain, the country in which functionalism originated, but was never fully developed. Positivism was taken in Britain to its philo-sophical extreme by Alfred North Whitehead and Bertrand Russell, and by such logical-positivist philosophers as A. J. Ayer. However, positivism was never really applied to sociology by the British. Today, however, they are ex-periencing a sociological renascence of sorts. They are reexamining the works of Marx, Weber, and Durkheim, and reanalyzing the epistemological founda-tions of the profession.

Anthony Giddens[205] has led the way in this endeavor. Stephen Lukes[206] and Bryan Turner[207] as well as others have also contributed. The sociological revival in Britain—particularly the work of Giddens—may do much to clarify both the theoretical links between the great traditions and the limitations of possible syntheses. Giddens's latest work on structuration and time may clear up arguments generated by the French functionalists about using theoretical categories for analysis.[208] Giddens points out that a historical framework has to be employed in making such analyses.

A relativist, historical, so-called strong program has been propounded for the sociology of science. Historical studies have been undertaken from this perspective, challenging the Mertonian normative approach.[209] The sociology coming out of Britain today does not have the theoretical complexity of the best French and German work. Yet British sociologists have been very clear in their exposition, which has proved helpful in sorting out the conflicts and contradictions resulting from the recent outpouring of theory in Europe.

Sociological theory is also reviving in Italy and eastern Europe, renewing its roots and expanding on its traditions. Creative work has already come forth from these nations and will impact upon world sociology directly in the near future. Remarkably and ironically, the sociology of the Soviet Union has been, by and large, *positivist* in methodology, and has only recently focused on the deep social problems troubling Soviet society. This may all change with the coming of Gorbachev and *glasnost,* but the future remains to be seen.

To complicate the picture further, one more theoretical trend—*sociobiology*—has emerged out of Britain and gained some support in the United States. In a way this was the ultimate trend in an era rejecting the rad-ical, utopian ideas of the 1960s.

---

[*]For further information on these developments, see Essays 6 and 12 in this volume.

Sociobiology: The Ultimate Reaction

Sociobiology is the ultimate reaction against the "humanism" of the 1960s. This is a theory that derives all causality for human behavior from genetically determined factors.* Focusing on aggression, sexuality, and population-expansion factors, the theory of sociobiology—though provocatively fascinating—is also a throwback to social Darwinism.

Humans *are* primates, animals, and part of the world of nature. Therefore, insights gleaned from our animal realities should become part of the sociological enterprise. We do, for instance, kill each other in murderous and military actions. We would not marry each other if there were no sexual magnetism. The family would hardly be enduring if our offspring matured in six months. Population density and food production affect the structure of our settlements. In short, we have to eat, sleep, defecate, urinate, and copulate in order to live. And we do die.

Sociobiology might have become a mainstream trend in modern sociology except for the fact that some of its proponents became social Darwinists. Racism directed against blacks and Third World peoples emerged again. Blacks, the sociobiologists insisted, had lower IQs and *genetically* lower intelligence capacities.[210] Evolutionary and genetic explanations for black intellectual inferiority were propounded. Naked "savages" in Brazil were filmed to show the genetically inevitable aggressiveness of humans. The futility of a sociology based on humanism was confronted with the reality of our animal heritage. In this way social Darwinist nightmares, such as "blue-eyed" fantasies of racial superiority and the bestial-genetic causality of criminal violence, have returned to haunt American sociology, as they once haunted and nearly destroyed British sociology.

All the same, the animal side of human behavior needs to be analyzed along with the human side of that behavior. Theorists like Sigmund Freud,[211] Arnold Gehlen,[212] Herbert Marcuse,[213] Louis Leakey,[214] and Jane Goodall[215] have given us excellent direction in these matters.

Feminist Theory. Another trend that emerged in the 1950s was feminist theory, which was inspired by the women's movement.† This theory cuts across all epistemological and theoretical lines, holding that gender is as important a category of analysis as class.[216] Feminist theory brings the perspective of women into the analysis of social phenomena, which heretofore were reported from a purely masculine point of view. The emphasis on adjustment to the housewife-mother role, on power relationships, on historical trends involving war and military heroism are called male-oriented sociological perceptions. Feminist theories have pointed out that male sociologists rarely analyzed cooperative relationships, sexism, or women's achievements. Much broader than sociology in its influence, feminist theory has contributed to a rethinking of scholarly fields across the humanities and the sciences.[217]

---

*See Essay 14 in this volume, "Sociobiology: Theory and Controversy."
†See Essay 9 in this volume, "Feminist Theories."

THE END OF A CENTURY AND A NEW BEGINNING FOR SOCIOLOGY

The 1980s have been the era of the *neo* in sociology: neo-Marxism, neo-Weberianism, neofunctionalism, and dozens of variations on these basic themes. The reason for this neomania is that, for the first time, the *entire* sociological enterprise is *known* to sociologists all over the world. In Europe prior to World War I, there existed a growing knowledge of the varying traditions. But before the disagreeing factions could come to grips with each other's positions, the world wars intervened. In the United States, ideology—postwar and cold-war—prevented a full flowering of the two great traditions.

Today—because of the revival of European sociology and the rise of several alternative theoretical perspectives in the United States—the entire tradition stands before us. What has sociology learned about itself?

Neo-Marxism seeks to retain the strengths of the Marxian system, while adding elements that previously were weak or missing in that system. Thus the power of the state or the political dimension has been added to Marxian analysis. The mode of production or the economic dimension is no longer attributed to one cause in terms of the processes of social change and social organization.[218]

Neo-Weberian sociology, derived originally from Gerth and Mills, begins with the strengths of Weberian sociology in providing ideological, political, and social action analyses. Then it adds a more explicit class analysis to Weber's already detailed descriptions of comparative economic systems and their causal impact. Neo-Weberian analysis also blends the Durkheimian emphasis on religion (or the lack of it) with ideal-typical categories of a more historical nature. Thus this analysis adds ideological causalities to the material ones, while lifting the Durkheimian insights beyond their organicist base and into the realm of living history.[219]

Neofunctionalism attempts to retain the strengths of functional analysis dealing with the cohesion of society, role interrelationships, normative behavior, anomic or deviant behavior, and the social system as a cultural whole that is institutionally interlocked. Then neofunctionalism adds what was previously lacking: an analysis of conflict and change in a historical context.*

In fact, neofunctionalism has caused quite a sensation in the United States, with sociologists reacting both positively and negatively. If neofunctionalists can improve functional analysis by adding a genuine historical, political, and conflict-oriented framework, they will do a great service for the sociological enterprise by building upon the great work done by Merton, Smeltzer, and others.

Finally, neo-Durkheimian sociology has emerged in France, Britain, and the United States. Giddens[220] in England, Nisbet[221] in the United States, and many French sociologists have reanalyzed and extended Durkheim's work, emphasizing its comparative aspects and its symbolic orientation (along with

---

*See Essay 10 in this volume.

its functionalist approach). Giddens and Nisbet to a lesser extent have attempted to add to it the missing economic and political dimensions.

All of the *neos* represent a synthesis of one kind or another of the basic theoretical traditions of sociology. The neo phenomenon also represents a rejection of certain aspects of each of the traditions.

For instance, the organic analogy has been phased out of functional analysis and replaced with a more symbolic-interactionist form of analysis, in which institutional, role, and normative descriptions become "human" rather than abstract (reified). That is, human individuals in social interaction with each other come alive within the role analysis.[222] This advanced American-style blend of functional analysis and symbolic interactionism (generated by Blumer and perfected by Goffman), when synthesized with modern Durkheimian comparative functional analysis (as foreshadowed by Merton) produces a truly formidable style of functional analysis. Further, Alexander has suggested that this symbolic functional analysis should then be set in a historical and cultural context including an analysis of conflict.* Eisenstadt[223] and Coser[224] have been doing this for years.

Thus the biological analogy with its organic, homeostatic undergirding has generally been declining in functional analysis. This development has removed one of the major blocks to the synthesis of functional analysis with Marxian and Weberian analysis.

The program of neo-Marxism provides another example of the rejection of certain portions of sociological theories. Vulgarized Marxism is losing its appeal and is being replaced with a sophisticated neo-Marxism. The outright rejection of capitalism and parliamentary democracy, and the exaltation of romantic socialism, have been replaced with a more careful analysis of the strengths and weaknesses of capitalist and socialist systems. (Some of the Marxists are Immanuel Wallerstein and his circle,[225] Ralph Miliband,[226] and Eric Olin Wright.)

Furthermore, it is important to note that the literal-minded style of class analysis focusing on the proletariat and the bourgeoisie has given way to a very sophisticated style of class analysis linked to the complex alignment of classes in late-industrial societies.[227] Without abandoning the central causal influence of the mode of production (and the social relations engendered by it), neo-Marxists have added the causal consequences of political power and the institutional influence of the state as an independent fact of social relations.[228] The works of Barrington Moore, Jr.,[229] and Theda Skocpol[230] lie between Marx and Weber, exemplifying this approach. Neo-Marxism, which includes a full power analysis, is a formidable sociological tool, already fully equipped with a theory of history.

Both neo-Marxism and neofunctionalism have gone far in dropping what was problematical and adding what was lacking in their theories. In their neo versions these theories are less far apart than they once were, and the interpenetration between them is quite visible at certain points.

---

*See Essay 10 in this volume.

As another example, the limited type of Weberian analysis focused on bureaucracy, charisma, and the Protestant ethic has been dropped in favor of a fuller Weberian analysis. Modern Weberian analysis focuses on the rationalization of modern social life, comparative civilizations, political legitimations, and comparative economic analysis.[231]

Finally, the racist elements of sociobiology have been utterly rejected by world sociology, so much so that sociobiology has barely been absorbed into the sociological mainstream. We can hope that physical anthropologists will integrate sociobiology into their emerging theory. Once purified in this way, the insights of sociobiology may be incorporated into sociological theory. The works of Leakey and his students, the most popular of whom is Goodall, come to mind here.[232]

In terms of methodology, the two epistemological extremes have been increasingly rejected. So, for instance, positivism or empirical observation with no clearly intended analytical goal—what Mills called abstract empiricism—has been abandoned by a growing number of modern sociologists, including the neofunctionalists.* Empiricism for the sake of empiricism has, however, been championed by certain members of influential sociology departments, like the one at Harvard in the mid-1980s[233] and by avowed positivists, such as Stinchcombe.[234] Nonetheless, world sociology by and large has moved toward an empiricism framed in a sophisticated symbolic epistemology and connected to a set of neo theories which provide a proper contextual setting for the empirical research.

In a similar vein, phenomenology as a methodology, not as an epistemology, has been found wanting. The methodology called for by Garfinkel's ethnomethodology and European hermeneutic analysis asks us to suspend structural categories of analysis when observing social action patterns. But the further step of imposing structural categories on the empirically obtained observational data is absolutely necessary if sociological analysis is to proceed.

The use of structural categories in sociological analysis is a necessary part of the sociological enterprise, as both Marxists and functionalists have asserted. Neither abstract empiricists nor hermeneutic analysts should ignore this step. The sociological process is not, after all, complete at the epistemological or methodological levels, but necessitates further steps of analysis.

The reason for the rejection of *both* positivism and phenomenology—as extremes of epistemology and methodology—is the same. That is, the sociological analytical process is a multistep process, not a one- or two-step process. The phenomenologists and ethnomethodologists act as if the observation of society (through the suspension of standard conceptual categories) is the only necessary step, while the positivists act as if the collection of data through interviews or questionnaires and the statistical compilation of data are the only necessary steps.

---

*In this connection see Essay 10 in this volume.

Observed or collected data, however, must then be theoretically analyzed and thereby brought into a broad macroframework of structural and cultural contexts. Without this third step there is no meaningful sociology. We must also add a fourth step, which involves transhistorical and cross-cultural comparison and the amendment, expansion, or correction of the analysis based on this comparative process. Durkheim, Marx, and Weber all engaged in such macrocomparative analysis to test their theoretical conceptions. They modified their theories in line with the data gained from the comparative historical enterprise.

In light of the sociological renascence in which we now find ourselves, a fifth step could be added to the sociological process. A given set of observations (or data) should be analyzed differentially because differing theoretical categories lead us to differing macroanalyses. For example, a neo-Marxist analysis of a given phenomenon could be compared with a neofunctionalist analysis of that same phenomenon, or with a neo-Weberian analysis, etc. In this way a comparative theoretical analysis could be added as a step beyond the transhistorical and cross-cultural step.

Lastly, we must call for a sixth step of policy analysis and the application of theory to create a more humane society through inventing new social institutions and reforming old ones.[235] Though fraught with ideological problems, policy analysis has had an effect on socially difficult problem areas. The analysis of Headstart comes to mind here, wherein conservative and liberal sociologists disagreed as to what they found. In the long run, however, a good deal of agreement on preschool education and its effects has emerged. Were we to add in Weber's ethic of responsibility,[236] this sixth step could become an even more significant contribution to the sociological enterprise and of sociology to society.

If we have complicated the sociological enterprise by suggesting a six-step process, that is because the analysis of human beings in social relationships *is* a complicated enterprise. If it were not, sociology would not be so diverse in its theoretical outpouring, nor would it be at war with itself.

To conclude, a veritable renascence of sociological theory has taken place. This renascence includes the rediscovery of the complete sociological tradition, plus a remarkable set of extensions and syntheses of that tradition. As the extremes of epistemology and political ideology give way to sophistication in these areas, we can visualize a somewhat more unified discipline of sociology in the future. Though nothing like a single unified theoretical system is likely to develop, a growing interpenetration between theoretical systems has already occurred.

The Sociological Renascence. Much has happened in sociology since the 1950s. Theory, methodology, and epistemology have developed with new sophistication. Substantive analyses have reflected these changes, improving our view of the basic trends of modern society.

We know more about economic production and large-scale organizations than we knew before. We know more about marriage and divorce than we knew before. When women pursue a career and their husbands continue to expect them to fulfill the household role, we have theories and concepts that explain such behavior, and we can predict the possibility for changing attitudes. We can analyze mid-life crises, role overload, gender-role conflicts, and the causes of the new narcissism of yuppydom. The rising divorce rate, though extremely high, did not catch us unaware. When the teenage suicide rate went up, we came armed with theories that enabled us to understand this trend. When bureaucrats act in an officious or amoral fashion, we know why. When advertisers tease us into buying their products by using sexually suggestive ploys, we have theories to explain why they do this, and why it works. When the Russian economy sputters because of bureaucratic petrifaction, or the American economy fritters billions on corporate mergers while the homeless lie in the streets, we have theories to explain these peculiar events.

Sociology in its own fitful way has come of age. If our predictions have not always been on target, at least we have begun to address the major trends affecting modern society. The multiplicity of offshoots from the basic sociological traditions, though bewildering, has also been helpful. For each new theory has tended to focus on certain aspects of modern society—and given us insight into that area of social life.

Finally, if there is no unity in sociology, at least there are *convergences*. Sociology could be at the beginning of a great modern renascence or, embittered and embattled, it could drift into a new dark age of factionalism. In order for the renascence to occur, each of the warring factions must accept the terms of a new truce. These terms include the recognition and understanding of the other side's claims, and a recognition and understanding of the weaknesses and deficiencies in one's own position. From such a moderation in conflict among sociologists of different perspectives, cooperative sociological enterprises could be initiated. With the knowledge gained from such understanding we can move to the future, better educated about our own past.

NOTES

1. Alvin W. Gouldner, *The Coming Crisis in Western Sociology* (New York: Basic Books, 1970).

2. Henry Etzkowitz, "The Contradictions of Radical Sociology" in Rhonda Levine, Martin Murray, and Martin Oppenheimer, eds., *The Movement and the Academy* (Philadelphia: Temple University Press, 1990).

3. Thomas S. Kuhn, *The Structure of Scientific Revolutions* (Chicago: University of Chicago Press, 1962).

4. Barry Barnes, *T. S. Kuhn and Social Science* (New York: Columbia University Press, 1982).

5. David Hume, *A Treatise of Human Nature* (New York: World Publishing, 1962; first published in 1739).

6. Immanuel Kant, *Critique of Pure Reason,* trans. Norman Kent Smith (New York: St. Martin's Press, 1965; first published in 1781).

7. Karl Popper, *Objective Knowledge* (Oxford: Clarendon Press, 1972) and *The Critical Approach to Science and Philosophy* (New York: Free Press, 1964).

8. Alfred Schutz, *The Phenomenology of the Social World,* trans. George Walsh and Frederick Lehnert (Evanston, Ill.: Northwestern University Press, 1967).

9. Popper, *Objective Knowledge.*

10. Bureaus of social research now exist at the University of Frankfurt and other German universities.

11. Robert K. Merton, "Sociology as Multi-paradigmatic," in *On Theoretical Sociology* (New York: Free Press, 1967).

12. Robert K. Merton, *Social Theory and Social Structure* (New York: Columbia University Press, 1953). In "Social Structure and Anomie" Merton uses the category *rebellion.* In essence this is a Marxian category, and not really derivable from Durkheim, although Durkheim's last chapter in *The Division of Labor in Society* does hint in this direction.

13. G. William Domhoff, *Who Rules America?* (Berkeley, Calif.: University of California Press, 1976).

14. Auguste Comte, *Positivist Philosophy,* trans. Margaret Cleuke, ed. Stanislav Andreski (London: Croom Helm, New York: Barnes & Noble, 1974; first published in 1830-42).

15. Ibid.

16. John Locke, *An Essay concerning Human Understanding* (Oxford: Clarendon Press, 1924; first published in 1690).

17. See Sir Isaac Newton's discoveries on the laws of motion in *Principia Mathematica;* first published in 1687.

18. Charles Darwin, *The Origin of Species* (Cambridge, Mass.: Harvard University Press, 1964; first published in 1859).

19. Ibid.

20. Herbert Spencer, *The Principles of Sociology* (New York: Appleton, Crofts, 1897; first published in 1876–96).

21. A. R. Radcliffe-Brown, *Structural Functionalism in Primitive Society* (Glencoe, Ill.: Free Press, 1952).

22. Émile Durkheim, *The Rules of Sociological Method* (New York: Free Press, 1964; first published in 1895).

23. Émile Durkheim, *Suicide: A Study in Sociology,* trans. James Word and George Simpson, ed. George Simpson (New York: Free Press, 1965).

24. Émile Durkheim, *The Elementary Forms of Religious Life* (New York: Free Press, 1961; first published in 1912).

25. Émile Durkheim, *The Division of Labor in Society* (New York: Free Press, 1963; first published in 1893).

26. Ibid.

27. Robert Nisbet, *The Sociology of Émile Durkheim* (New York: Oxford University Press, 1974).

28. Ibid.

29. Ibid.

30. Ferdinand Tönnies, *Community and Society (Gemeinschaft und Gesellschaft)*, trans. Charles P. Loomis (East Lansing, Mich.: Michigan State University Press, 1957; first published in 1887).
31. See Durkheim's critique of Tönnies in Harry Liebersohn, *Fate and Utopia in German Sociology 1870–1923* (Cambridge, Mass.: MIT Press, 1988), Chap. 2.
32. Durkheim, *Division of Labor;* see especially the last chapter.
33. Durkheim, *Elementary Forms of Religious Life.*
34. Nisbet, *Sociology of Émile Durkheim.*
35. Ibid.
36. Marcel Mauss, *The Gift* (New York: W. W. Norton, 1967).
37. Maurice Halbwachs, *Morphologie Sociale* (Paris: Giraud, 1970) and *The Collective Memory* (New York: Harper & Row, 1988).
38. Bronislaw Malinowski, *Crime and Custom in Savage Society* (London: Routledge & Kegan Paul, 1961).
39. Claude Lévi-Strauss, *Les Structures de la parenté* (Paris: Presses Universitaires de France, 1949).
40. A. R. Radcliffe-Brown, *Structural Functionalism in Primitive Society.*
41. Ibid. See also Ruth Benedict, *Patterns of Culture* (New York: Harper & Row, 1952).
42. Charlemagne was known in Latin as *Carolus magnus*. His capital was at Aix-la-Chapelle (Aachen), a city on the border of present-day Belgium and West Germany.
43. See, in this connection, Theodor Mommsen's *History of Rome;* Georg F. W. Hegel's *Philosophy of History;* and Otto von Ranke's *World History.*
44. Among the German intellectuals who were distrustful of the democratic tradition were Johann Gottlieb Fichte, Georg F. W. Hegel, Heinrich von Treitschke, and Friedrich Nietzsche. The Germans liked the antidemocratic thought of Thomas Hobbes, but did not accept the views of such English liberal theorists as John Locke, Jeremy Bentham, and John Stuart Mill.
45. See especially in this connection Plato's *Republic,* 2nd ed, ed. James Adam (Cambridge: Cambridge University Press, 1963).
46. Immanuel Kant, *Critique of Pure Reason* (Oxford: Clarendon Press, 1958; first published in 1781).
47. *The Pre-Socratic Philosophers,* G. S. Kirk (New York: Cambridge University Press, 1983).
48. Plato, *The Republic.*
49. Kant, *Critique of Pure Reason.*
50. Locke, *An Essay concerning Human Understanding.*
51. Max Weber, *The Methodology of the Social Sciences* (New York: Free Press, 1949).
52. Alfred Schutz, *The Phenomenology of the Social World* (Evanston, Ill.: Northwestern University Press, 1967).
53. Max Weber, "Science as a Vocation" in Hans Gerth and C. Wright Mills, *From Max Weber* (New York: Free Press, 1962); see also Max Weber, *Methodology of the Social Sciences* (New York: Free Press, 1962).
54. Georg F. W. Hegel, *The Phenomenology of Mind* (New York: Harper & Row, 1967; first published in 1807).
55. Georg F. W. Hegel, *The Philosophy of History* (New York: Dover Books, 1973; first published in 1837).
56. Ibid.

57. Heraclitus, *The Cosmic Fragments,* ed. G. S. Kirk (Cambridge: Cambridge University Press, 1954; reprinted in 1970).

58. Ibid.

59. Hegel, *Philosophy of History.*

60. E. A. Burt, *The Metaphysical Foundations of Modern Science* (Garden City, N.Y.: Doubleday, Anchor Books, 1954).

61. See Karl Marx and Friedrich Engels, *The Communist Manifesto,* in *Selected Works* (Moscow: Foreign Languages Publishing House, 1951). *The Communist Manifesto* was first published in 1848.

62. Lewis Henry Morgan, *Ancient Society* (New York: Meridian Books, 1963).

63. See Karl Marx, *The Peasant Wars, The 18th Brumaire,* and *The Communist Manifesto* in *Selected Works,* vols. 1 and 2 (Moscow: Foreign Languages Publishing House, 1951).

64. Max Weber, *The Agrarian Sociology of Ancient Civilizations,* trans. R. I. Frank (Highlands, N.J.: Humanities Press International, 1976); see also Marx, *Selected Works.*

65. Karl Polanyi, "On Feudalism," in G. Dalton, ed., *Economic Development and Social Change* (New York: Museum of Natural History Source Books, 1971).

66. Karl Marx, *Das Kapital* (Moscow, Foreign Language Press, 1951).

67. The British Chartist movement of the 1830s and 1840s agitated for universal manhood suffrage and an end to property requirements for voters. These demands were repeatedly rejected and only gradually attained later in the nineteenth century.

68. Marx and Engels, *Communist Manifesto.*

69. Karl Marx, *The German Ideology* (New York: International Publishers, 1970).

70. V. Gordon Childe, *Man Makes Himself* (New York: Random House, 1956).

71. Durkheim, *Division of Labor.*

72. Marx and Engels, *Communist Manifesto,* and Karl Marx, *The Woman Question* (New York: International Publishers, 1970).

73. Ibid.

74. Karl Marx, *On Society and Social Change,* ed. Neil J. Smelser (Chicago: University of Chicago Press, 1973).

75. Although Edwin O. Reischauer, former U.S. ambassador to Japan, disagrees with this view, most historians recall the Japanese involvement with their "divine emperor," Hirohito.

76. The classic statement about the Protestant work ethic is contained in Max Weber, *The Protestant Ethic and the Spirit of Capitalism,* trans. Talcott Parsons (New York: Charles Scribner's Sons, 1958); for its application to American conditions, see Helen and Robert Lynd, *Middletown* and *Middletown in Transition* (New York: Harcourt Brace Jovanovich, 1929 and 1965); see also Henry Etzkowitz, "The Americanization of Marxism: *Middletown* and *Middletown in Transition,*" *Journal of the History of Sociology* 1 (1978).

77. Marx and Engels, *Communist Manifesto;* see also Karl Marx, *The Jewish Question,* in *Selected Works.*

78. For Marx evolution meant the historical development of humanity, not its genetic or organic evolution. Although he spoke of how humanity might achieve its *species potential* (species being) he did not mean this term in a genetic way but as self-development within a socialist structure of society.

79. See the last chapter of Durkheim's *Division of Labor.*

80. Robert K. Merton, "Social Structure and Anomie," in *Social Theory and Social Structure.*

81. R. H. Tawney, *The Agrarian Problem in the Sixteenth Century* (New York: Harper Torch Books, 1967).

82. Georges Lefebvre, *The Coming of the French Revolution* (New York: Vintage Books, 1947).

83. Ronald M. Glassman, *The New Middle Class and Democracy: Democracy and Equality* (New York, Praeger Publishers, 1987).

84. Karl Marx, "On Praxis," in *The Poverty of Philosophy (New York: International Publishers, 1967).*

85. Georg Simmel, "The Psyche in the City" and "The Stranger," in *A Collection of Essays,* trans. Kant Wolff (Columbus, Ohio: Ohio State University Press, 1959).

86. Tönnies, *Gemeinschaft und Gesellschaft.*

87. Weber, *Protestant Ethic and the Spirit of Capitalism.*

88. Max Weber, *Economy and Society,* ed. Guenther Roth and Claus Wittich (Berkeley, Calif.: University of California Press, 1979).

89. Max Weber, *The Religion of India* (New York: Free Press, 1973).

90. Max Weber, *The City* (New York: Harper Torch Books, 1974).

91. Ronald M. Glassman, William Swatos, and Paul Rosen, *Bureaucracy against Democracy and Socialism* (Westport, Conn.: Greenwood Press, 1986).

92. Max Weber, "On Bureaucracy," in *Economy and Society.*

93. Ronald M. Glassman and William Swatos, *Charisma, History, and Social Structure* (Westport, Conn.: Greenwood Press, 1985).

94. Weber, *Agrarian Sociology of Ancient Civilization* and *The City.*

95. Max Weber, "Class, Status, and Party," in *From Max Weber.*

96. Alfred North Whitehead and Bertrand Russell, *Principia Mathematica* (Cambridge: Cambridge University Press, 1925, 1957; New York: W. W. Norton, 1964).

97. Milton Friedman, *Capitalism and Freedom* (Chicago: University of Chicago Press, 1972); Fredrich Hayek, *The Road to Serfdom* (Chicago: University of Chicago Press, 1949); see also the work of Alexis de Tocqueville on the *ancien régime* in France.

98. Robert Michels, *Political Parties,* trans. C. C. Paul (Glencoe, Ill.: Free Press, 1915; reprinted in 1958).

99. Robert Park, *Introduction to the Science of Sociology* (Chicago: University of Chicago Press, 1929).

100. George Herbert Mead, *Mind, Self, and Society* (Chicago: University of Chicago Press, 1936).

101. Erving Goffman, *Presentation of Self in Everyday Life* (New York: Harper & Row, 1967).

102. Nietzsche's *Übermensch* or superman was perverted by Nietzsche's sister and other Nazi sympathizers into the ideal of the "blond beast."

103. Martin Heidegger, *Being and Time,* trans. John Macquerrie and Edward Robinson (New York: Harper Torch Books, 1983).

104. Wolfgang Mommsen, *The Age of Bureaucracy* (New York: Harper Torch Books, 1983).

105. Wolfgang Mommsen, "On Weber's Political Views," in Ronald M. Glassman and Vatro Murvar, *Max Weber's Political Sociology* (Westport, Conn.: Greenwood Press, 1983).

106. Glassman and Murvar, *Max Weber's Political Sociology;* see also Ira Cohen, "Marx, Weber, and Democracy," in Robert J. Antonio and Ronald M. Glassman, eds., *A Weber-Marx Dialogue* (Lawrence, Kans.: University Press of Kansas, 1985).

107. Robert K. Merton, "Social Structure and Anomie," in his *Social Theory and Social Structure* (New York: Columbia University Press, 1957); see also R. Nisbet, *The Social Bond* (New York: Free Press, 1961).

108. This was the case even though some of the works of Durkheim and Simmel were translated and published in the *American Journal of Sociology* as early as the 1920s.

109. Arthur Vidich and Stanford Lyman, *Protestantism and American Sociology* (New Haven, Conn.: Yale University Press, 1985).

110. Papers submitted to the *American Sociological Review* reflected the bias in favor of mathematical rather than sociological analysis.

111. Arthur Stinchcombe identified himself at the American Sociological Association's 1983 meeting in San Francisco as an "unreformed positivist" who does not believe in the use of theory. See also James Allen Davis, "The Chippendale Program," in *National Data for the Social Sciences* (Ann Arbor, Mich.: Interuniversity Consortium for Political Research, 1975).

112. Seymour M. Lipset, *Political Man* (Baltimore: Johns Hopkins University Press, 1985); James S. Coleman, *The Adolescent Society* (New York: Free Press, 1970).

113. Paul F. Lazarsfeld developed a method for obtaining latent functions through questionnaire studies.

114. Jeffrey C. Alexander, "The Use of Theory," in *Theoretical Logic in Sociology* (Berkeley, Calif.: University of California Press, 1988).

115. C. Wright Mills predicted a rebellion against the amorality and stultification of the white collar world. Herbert Marcuse predicted (or should we say "heralded") the sexual revolution of the 1960s.

116. Max Weber, "Theory of Social Action," in his *Economy and Society.*

117. Radcliffe-Brown, *Structural Functionalism in Primitive Society.*

118. For the homeostasis theory, see L. J. Henderson, *On the Social Systems,* ed. Bernard Barber (Chicago: University of Chicago Press, 1970); see also G. C. Homans, *Coming to My Senses* (New Brunswick, N.J.: Transaction Books, 1989).

119. Talcott Parsons, *The Social System* (Glencoe, Ill.: Free Press, 1951) and *Theory of Social Action* (Bloomington, Ind.: Indiana University Press, 1978).

120. Talcott Parsons, "On Suburbia," in *Family Socialization and Interaction* (New York: Basic Books, 1954 and 1960); also Talcott Parsons, *Institutions and Social Evolutions* (Chicago: University of Chicago Press, 1982); see also H. Becker, *Boys in White* (New Brunswick, N.J.: Transaction Books, 1976), and Morris Janowitz, *The Professional Soldier* (New York: Free Press, 1971).

121. Merton, *Social Theory and Social Structure.*

122. "Theories of the Middle Range," in ibid.

123. Ibid.

124. Robert K. Merton, "Role Sets," in Lewis A. Coser and Bernard Rosenberg, eds, *Sociological Theory* (New York: Macmillan, 1957).

125. Ralph Linton, "Status and Role," in ibid.

126. Merton, "Social Structure and Anomie," in *Social Theory and Social Structure.*

127. Lewis A. Coser, *The Functions of Social Conflict* (Glencoe, Ill.: Free Press, 1956).

128. S. N. Eisenstadt, *The Political Systems of Empires* (Glencoe, Ill.: Free Press, 1963).

129. Suzanne Keller, *Beyond the Ruling Class* (New York: Random House, 1963).

130. Gabriel Almond, *The Politics of Developing Areas* (Princeton, N.J.: Princeton University Press, 1960).
131. Merton, "Manifest and Latent Functions," in *Social Theory and Social Structure.*
132. Randall Collins, *Non-Obvious Sociology* (Berkeley, Calif.: Sage Publications, 1986).
133. On neo-Marxism, see Ralph Miliband, *Marxism and Politics* (London: Oxford University Press, 1977).
134. See Paul F. Lazarsfeld's latent functions mechanism.
135. Using Aristotle's theories of class, Lipset attempted to rebut some of Marx's theories. Lipset also made use of new theories of political action, including cross-pressures.
136. Robert K. Merton, "Theories of the Middle Range," in *Social Theory and Social Structure.*
137. Vidich and Lyman, *Protestantism and American Sociology.*
138. As indicated in Arthur Vidich and Maurice Stein, *Reflections on Community Studies* (New York: John Wiley & Sons, 1964), most studies of suburbia were quite positive. The exception that created quite a stir was John R. Seeley, *Crestwood Heights* (New York: John Wiley & Sons, 1967).
139. C. Wright Mills, *White Collar* (New York: Oxford University Press, 1959).
140. Hans Gerth, *Collected Papers,* ed. Arthur Vidich (Westport, Conn.: Greenwood Press, 1986).
141. Mills, *White Collar.*
142. C. Wright Mills, *The Power Elite* (New York: Oxford University Press, 1966).
143. Weber, "On Bureaucracy," in *Economy and Society.*
144. Arthur J. Vidich and Maurice Stein, *Sociology on Trial* (New York: Harper & Row, 1960).
145. Gouldner, *Coming Crisis in Western Sociology.*
146. C. Wright Mills, *The Sociological Imagination* (New York: Oxford University Press, 1959).
147. C. Wright Mills, *Listen Yankee* (Boston: Beacon Press, 1963).
148. See F. Sigmund Diamond, "Who Was Protected at Their Universities in the 1950s?" in *New York Review of Books,* April 28, 1977, p. 13.
149. Karl Marx also wrote articles for the *New York Herald-Tribune* about the American Civil War; see also Karl Marx, *The Woman Question* (New York: Monthly Review Press, 1971, 1972).
150. Feminist sociologists went far beyond Marx's criticism of the conditions of women; see Simone de Beauvoir, *The Second Sex,* trans. H. M. Parshley (New York: Alfred A. Knopf, 1954; first published in France in 1949–50).
151. Juliette Mitchell, *Women's Estate* (New York: Vintage Books, 1973).
152. See the journal *Studies on the Left,* which emerged in the 1960s; see also the works of Eric Olin Wright, Stanley Aronowitz, and G. William Domhoff for variations in Marxian-oriented American sociology.
153. At the American Sociological Association convention in New York in the 1970s. Lewis A. Coser spoke in favor of including Marxist analysis in sociology, but others vigorously opposed this suggestion.
154. Herbert Marcuse, *Eros and Civilization* (Boston: Beacon Press, 1966).
155. See, for example, Erich Fromm, *Escape from Freedom* (New York: Holt, Rinehart & Winston, 1941, 1960).

156. See Zoltan Tar, *The Frankfurt School* (New York: John Wiley & Sons, 1977); see also Andrew Arato, *The Frankfurt School Reader* (New York: Urizen Books, 1978).
157. Marcuse, *Eros and Civilization*.
158. Ibid.
159. Bennet Berger, *The Survival of the Counterculture* (Berkeley, Calif.: University of California Press, 1981).
160. Mills, *Sociological Imagination*.
161. Schutz, *Phenomenology of the Social World*.
162. Harold Garfinkel, *Studies in Ethnomethodology* (Englewood Cliffs, N.J.: Prentice-Hall, 1967).
163. Peter L. Berger, *Invitation to Sociology: A Humanistic Perspective* (Garden City, N.Y.: Doubleday, Anchor Books, 1963); and Peter L. Berger and Thomas Luckmann, *The Social Construction of Reality: A Treatise in the Sociology of Knowledge* (Garden City, N.Y.: Doubleday, Anchor Books, 1967).
164. Martin Heidegger, *Being and Time,* trans. David Ferrel Krell (New York: Harper & Row, 1977).
165. On this point see A. Giddens, *Positivism and Sociology* (London: Heinemann, 1974); see also Guy Oaks, *Introduction to Weber, Rocher, and Kneis* (New Brunswick, N.J.: Transaction Books, 1981); see also Max Weber, *Critique of Stammler* (New Brunswick, N.J.: Transaction Books, 1981) and Weber's concept *Verstehen,* which American positivists interpreted as "intuition."
166. For example, see Michael Lynch, *Art and Artifact in Laboratory Science: Shopwork and Shoptalk in a Research Laboratory* (London: Routledge & Kegan Paul, 1985).
167. Marvelous debates took place at the New School for Social Research and Columbia University between Aron Gurwitch and Sidney Morgenbesser as to whether or not phenomenology or positivism had the better epistemology.
168. George Herbert Mead, *Mind, Self, and Society* (Chicago: University of Chicago Press, 1934).
169. John Dewey, *Experience and Nature* (Chicago: University of Chicago Press, 1925).
170. Mead, *Mind, Self, and Society.*
171. Charles Horton Cooley, *Human Nature and the Social Order* (New York: Schocken Books, 1964; first published in 1909).
172. See Muzafer Sherif, "Reference Groups," in Coser and Rosenberg, *Sociological Theory.*
173. Ibid.
174. Erving Goffman, *The Presentation of Self in Everyday Life* (Garden City, N.Y.: Doubleday, 1959) and *Asylums* (New York: Anchor Books, 1961).
175. Janowitz, *Professional Soldier.*
176. Ibid. and Becker, *Boys in White.* One should compare the Janowitz and Becker books with Robert K. Merton, *The Student Physician: Introductory Studies in the Sociology of Medical Education* (Cambridge, Mass.: Harvard University Press, 1957).
177. Peter L. Berger and Thomas Luckmann, *The Social Construction of Reality* (New York: Harper & Row, 1968).
178. Peter L. Berger, *Invitation to Sociology.*
179. In this connection see Berger's treatment of alternation in *Invitation to Sociology.*

180. Miliband, *Marxism and Politics.*
181. Milovan Djilas, *The New Class,* trans. H. J. Johnson (New York: Praeger Publishers, 1961).
182. John Kautsky, *Political Change in Developing Nations* (New York: John Wiley & Sons, 1965).
183. Immanuel Wallerstein, *Africa: The Politics of Unity* (New York: Vintage Books, 1969).
184. For the revival of interest in Weber, see Guenther Roth and Claus Wittich's comments as editors of Weber's *Economy and Society*; Wolfgang Mommsen, *The Age of Bureaucracy*; Wolfgang Schluchter, *The Rise of Western Rationalism: Max Weber's Developmental History* (Berkeley, Calif.: University of California Press, 1987); Glassman and Murvar, Max Weber's *Political Sociology* (Westport, Conn.: Greenwood Press, 1978); Antonio and Glassman, *A Weber-Marx Dialogue;* Marianne Weber et al., *Max Weber: A Biography* (New Brunswick, N.J.: Transaction Books, 1987).
185. Max Weber, "On Disenchantment"; see also William Swatos, "Disenchantment and Charisma," in Glassman and Swatos, *Charisma, History, and Social Structure.*
186. Christopher Lasch, *The Culture of Narcissism* (New York: Warner Books, 1979).
187. Weber, *Protestant Ethic,* p. 181.
188. Glassman and Swatos, *Charisma, History, and Social Structure;* especially Arthur Schweitzer's essay on "Hitler's Charisma." Note that the term *charisma* was a popular buzzword in the media during the 1970s.
189. Antonio and Glassman, eds., *A Weber-Marx Dialogue.* Gouldner was concerned with a synthesis of functionalism and Marxist sociology.
190. Robert Michels became a follower of Mussolini, while G. Lukacs was for a time a Stalinist.
191. Benjamin Nelson, who knew Weber's work well, was an exception to this rule.
192. Ronald M. Glassman, "The Weber Renaissance," in Scott G. McNall, ed., *Current Perspectives in Social Theory* (Greenwich, Conn.: JAI Press, 1983).
193. Weber, *Economy and Society.*
194. Jürgen Habermas, *Knowledge and Human Interests*, trans. Thomas McCarthy (Boston: Beacon Press, 1971).
195. Richard Munch and Nikolas Lurmann are contemporary German systems theorists.
196. See Robert Holton and Bryan Turner, *On the Sociology of Talcott Parsons* (London: Routledge & Kegan Paul, 1988).
197. Arato, *Frankfurt School Reader;* Tar, *Frankfurt School.*
198. Jürgen Habermas, *Knowledge and Human Interests.*
199. Jürgen Habermas, *Legitimation Crisis* (Boston: Beacon Press, 1975).
200. For example, the Bureau of Social Research in Frankfurt am Main.
201. Giddens, *Positivism and Sociology.*
202. Georg Lukacs, *History and Class Consciousness* (Cambridge, Mass.: MIT Press, 1971).
203. Antonio Gramasci, *The Political Writings* (New York: Russell & Russell, 1950, 1965).
204. Nicos Poulantzas, *Political Power and Social Class* (London: New Left Books, 1973).

205. Anthony Giddens, *Capitalism and Sociological Theory* (New York: Oxford University Press, 1972).

206. Stephen Lukes, *The Sociology of Émile Durkheim* (London: Routledge & Kegan Paul, 1980).

207. Bryan Turner, *For Weber* (London: Routledge & Kegan Paul, 1979).

208. Anthony Giddens, *Structuration and Time* (New York: Free Press, 1986).

209. See, for example, Steve Woodgar, ed., *Knowledge and Reflexivity: New Frontiers in the Sociology of Knowledge* (London: Sage Publications, 1988); Karen D. Knorr Cetina and Michael Mulkay, eds., *Science Observed: Perspectives on the Sociology of Science* (London: Sage Publications, 1983).

210. Arthur R. Jensen et al., *Environment, Heredity, and Intelligence* (Cambridge, Mass.: Harvard Educational Review, 1969).

211. Sigmund Freud, *Civilization and Its Discontents,* trans. Joan Riviere (Garden City, N.Y.: Doubleday, Anchor Books; first published in 1930).

212. Arnold Gehlen, *The Theory of Social Institutions,* trans. Peter L. Berger (Garden City, N.Y.: Doubleday, 1976).

213. Herbert Marcuse, *Eros and Civilization.*

214. Louis Leakey, *Human Evolution* (Boston: Houghton Mifflin, 1964).

215. Jane Goodall, *In the Shadow of Man* (Boston: Houghton Mifflin, 1971).

216. See the journals *Gender and Society* and *Signs* for examples of feminist sociology and interdisciplinary feminist scholarship. Much recent feminist sociological theorizing has been rooted in the critique and revision of psychoanalysis. See, for example, Nancy Chodorow, *The Reproduction of Mothering: Psychoanalysis and the Sociology of Gender* (Berkeley, Calif.: University of California Press, 1978), and Jessica Benjamin, *The Bonds of Love: Psychoanalysis, Feminism, and the Problem of Domination* (New York: Pantheon Books, 1988). For a structured analysis integrating theory and data, see Kathleen Gerion, *Hard Choices: How Women Decide about Work, Career, and Motherhood* (Berkeley, Calif.: University of California Press, 1985).

217. See Evelyn Keller, *Reflections on Gender and Science* (New Haven, Conn.: Yale University Press, 1985) and "Feminist Perspectives on Science Studies," *Science, Technology, and Human Values* 14, nos. 3 and 4 (Summer and Autumn 1988), pp. 235–49.

218. Ralph Miliband and Milovan Djilas represent this neo-Marxist trend.

219. Stephen Kalberg, Lawrence Scaff, Ira Cohen, Robert J. Antonio, and Ronald M. Glassman are doing neo-Weberian work in the United States; see Antonio and Glassman, *A Weber-Marx Dialogue,* for the sources.

220. Giddens, *Émile Durkheim.*

221. Nisbet, *Sociology of Émile Durkheim.*

222. Erving Goffman's work is typical of this synthesis.

223. S. N. Eisenstadt, *From Generation to Generation* (New York: Free Press, 1973).

224. Coser, *Social Functions of Conflict.*

225. Immanuel Wallerstein, *The World System* (New York: Academic Press, 1972).

226. Ralph Miliband, *Marxism and Political Analysis* (New Haven, Conn.: Yale University Press, 1971).

227. Martin Oppenheimer does a complex class analysis in his work.

228. Djilas, *New Class.*

229. Barrington Moore, Jr., *The Social Origins of Dictatorship and Democracy* (Boston: Beacon Press, 1966).

230. Theda Skocpol, *States and Social Revolution* (New York: Cambridge University Press, 1979).

231. See the works of Friedrich Heinrich Tenbruck, Jürgen Kocka, Wolfgang Schluchter, and Wolfgang Mommsen. For sources, see Glassman and Murvar, *Political Sociology of Max Weber.*

232. Goodall, *In the Shadow of Man.*

233. Harvard's Department of Sociology is currently eclectic, partly as a result of Theda Skocpol's successful fight for tenure.

234. Stinchcombe still clings to positivism.

235. Henry Etzkowitz and Gerald M. Schaflander, "A Manifesto for Sociologists," *Social Problems* (April 1968), and *Ghetto Crisis* (Boston: Little, Brown, 1969); see also Henry Etzkowitz, "Solar vs. Nuclear Energy: Autonomous or Dependent Technology?," *Social Problems* (April 1984).

236. Henry Etzkowitz, "The Brief Rise and Early Decline of Radical Sociology at Washington University," *American Sociologist* 20, no. 4.

THE RENASCENCE OF SOCIOLOGICAL THEORY

FIFTEEN ESSAYS

ESSAYS

1. Émile Durkheim and the Sociological Enterprise

2. On Marxism

3. Max Weber, the Modern World, and Modern Sociology

PART ONE

CLASSICAL TRADITIONS

Émile Durkheim was the first theorist to explicitly attempt to establish sociology as a separate discipline in its own right. In his great works, *Suicide: A Study in Sociology* and *The Rules of Sociological Method,* he separated sociology from psychology and biology, and established the foundational principle of social causality.

In *Suicide, The Rules,* and his other classic works, Durkheim also provided us with many of the basic concepts for sociological analysis. Norms, roles, statuses, collective beliefs, anomie—can sociology be possible without these constructs?

Further, in *The Division of Labor in Society,* Durkheim attempted to come to grips with German sociology—not only through a critique of Ferdinand Tönnies's gloomy predictions about modern urban society but also through a dialogue with "the ghost of Marx" on the class structure of industrial society.

Finally, in *The Elementary Forms of Religious Life,* Durkheim not only produced one of the basic analyses of religion and its functions in society but also provided us with a link to both Max Weber's neo-Kantian sociology and modern phenomenological and symbolic interactionist sociology.

Durkheim's sociology is weak in its theory of social change, history, and power, but his functional analysis, comparative method, and empirical-statistical technique helped establish sociology as a social science, engendering causal insights of great significance for the understanding of human beings in groups.

Rosa Haritos and Ronald M. Glassman

ÉMILE DURKHEIM
AND THE SOCIOLOGICAL
ENTERPRISE

INTRODUCTION

Émile Durkheim (1858–1917) was, in a sense, the first sociologist. Karl Marx did not consider himself a sociologist; Max Weber did not begin as a sociologist; and Saint-Simon and Auguste Comte speculated about the possibility of this new science without actually establishing it. Durkheim, on the other hand, not only pursued the sociological enterprise with single-mindedness, but sought to establish sociology as a discipline in its own right—not reducible to biological or psychological determinants and separable from economic and political causalities.

Where Durkheim's work is at its best is in the establishment of the *realm of sociological analysis*—that is, the realm of social institutions, roles, norms, and collective beliefs. Where Durkheim's work is weak is in its single-minded pursuit of the *social* to the exclusion of historical, economic, and political causalities.

Before entering into an analysis of Durkheim's work, let us look at some of the intellectual influences on it.

French Influences

From Saint-Simon, Durkheim gained certain insights that would remain with him throughout his life. Saint-Simon, writing after the French Revolution, was perhaps the first social scientist to recognize the uniqueness of industrial society, with its urban individualism and secular intellectuality. Saint-Simon did not believe that industrial society could survive as it stood. He postulated the need for both socialism and a new humanistic religion to save industrial society from atomization and moral decline. He also believed that a new science of society was necessary in order properly to analyze the conditions engendered by industrialism and in order to derive from these analyses a proper set of social policies that could perfect it.[1]

69

Durkheim was fascinated by Saint-Simon's theories. He was skeptical about socialism, but he certainly was interested in the problem of *individual isolation* in urban society. The decline of religion and its anomic ramifications also became a source of life-long stimulations for Durkheim, though he himself was not religious. Finally, Saint-Simon's idea of the new science—an idea reiterated by Comte—influenced Durkheim to such an extent that he would spend his life attempting to establish it.

From Comte, Durkheim borrowed the idea of the utilization of the method of the natural sciences for the analysis of the social sphere.[2] This Durkheim would perfect in his *Rules for Sociological Method* and *Suicide.*

Ernest Renan, who had insisted on explaining social phenomena by social factors, not by psychological or biological ones, also influenced Durkheim in his desire to establish the new social science, sociology.[3]

Durkheim was also influenced by Fustel de Coulanges, who wrote on the religious bonds of the ancient Greek cities, thus reinforcing Saint-Simon's theories on religion and generating in Durkheim the desire to understand the origins and the functions of religions in society.[4] *The Elementary Forms of Religious Life* emerged from this quest.

In terms of French influences, Durkheim also recognized his debt to Montesquieu, Rousseau, and Tocqueville, especially in terms of their emphasis on law, democracy, and the dangers of the state. We shall discuss these influences in the section on Durkheim's political sociology.

German Influences

Durkheim spent a year in Germany studying sociology at a time of great intellectual fertility there. The work of Ferdinand Tönnies, Ernst Troeltsch, Georg Simmel, and others was causing quite a stir in Germany and had a profound influence on Durkheim.[5] It was not that he agreed with most of the German work—substantively or theoretically—but rather that he spent his life in negative dialogue with the German works, including those of Marx.

Durkheim, for instance, reviewed Tönnies's *Gemeinschaft und Gesellschaft*; from his review it became clear that Durkheim's first great work, *The Division of Labor,* was written to correct "The one-sidedness of his [Tönnies's] contrast between holistic Gemeinschaft and decadent Gesellschaft.[6]

The dichotomy between premodern and modern society drawn by Tönnies would obsess Durkheim's work to such a point that so many of his great ideas would emphasize the differences between primitive and modern society: mechanical versus organic solidarity, egoistic and anomic suicide versus altruistic suicide, a unified collective experience versus a fragmented collective conscience, and a rigid-static moral system versus a fluid anomic but creative moral system. Durkheim's debate with Tönnies has proven to be one of the most fruitful in the history of sociology.

Another influence from Germany was that of Albert Schäffle.[7] Schäffle had borrowed the *organic analogy* from English social Darwinism, but Durkheim found the German version of that organicism more acceptable than that found in, say, Herbert Spencer. We should not call this a German influence, because it was not at all mainstream German sociology. However, Schäffle's idea in the hands of Durkheim became one of the basic structural ideas in sociology. We shall have more to say on the organic analogy in our discussion of *The Division of Labor.*

And of course there was also the influence of Marx. Durkheim rarely confronted Marxism directly in his work. However, on occasion he made it clear that he was in dialogue with the work of Marx. For instance, in terms of primitive society, while focusing on religion, Durkheim launched into an analysis of property—affirming the communal nature of property under the conditions of mechanical solidarity.[8] Later, he described the problem of class conflict and the "forced" divisions of labor as disruptive of organic solidarity.[9] We shall discuss

Durkheim's dialogue with the ghost of Marx in a later section.

English Influences

Durkheim argued vociferously against the utilitarian philosophers, such as Jeremy Bentham[10] and James Mill,[11] who based their analysis of society on the competition of individuals. This may have been good economic theory (according to Adam Smith)[12] and interesting political theory (according to Thomas Hobbes[13] and John Locke[14]), but as sociological theory Durkheim thought it was terrible. After all, every individual was born into an existing social structure of institutions, roles, norms, customs, and beliefs which he or she could not ignore or simply step beyond. Thus Durkheim, in arguing against British utilitarianism, argued for the efficacy of *social structure* in the causal determination of human action. He did not mean by this that humans had no "will" or no ability to think rationally and creatively beyond social constraints, but that the reality of society and its web of order had to be accepted if true social science was going to occur. Who would deny this today?

If Durkheim was negatively influenced by the utilitarians, he was positively influenced by Spencer, though he does not acknowledge this debt.[15] Durkheim criticized Spencer's utilitarian bent and racist tendencies, which were morally controversial. However, Durkheim was heavily influenced by the organic analogy pushed by Spencer in his work. As mentioned above, Durkheim recognized Schäffle's work for this influence. Yet the German social scientists picked up this orientation from the social Darwinist current emanating from England. We can say, then, that Spencer indirectly influenced Durkheim's work, and influenced it profoundly.

Jewish Influences

Durkheim was a French Jew and the son of a rabbi. He was brought up in a small city, Épinal, and then went to Paris, where he spent his adult life. This was the period in Europe of the liberation of the Jews from their ghetto existence into the cultural life of the big urban centers. The Jews experienced this liberation—in Paris, Berlin, Vienna, Budapest, and other urban centers—as exhilarating. They loved the intellectual and cultural freedom of the new urban society, and remembered unpleasantly the days of the town ghettos.

The big cities were liberating, but frightening also, and the Jews did not fail to see the negative effects of modern life on the urban individual. But by and large they saw modernity in a positive light. In contrast, many French Catholic intellectuals, such as Joseph de Maistre, Louis de Bonald, and others,[16] and German Protestant intellectuals, such as Tönnies and Troeltsch (and even to some extent Weber), viewed modern urban society with alarm and negations, and longed for the good old days of "folk" society and small town life.

Jewish intellectuals like Durkheim and Simmel projected a much more positive view of modern life. Looking for the good side of modernity, Durkheim theorized his famous *organic solidarity* or *occupational-role interdependence*, which produced cohesion and order in the modern world. Simmel produced a similar idea in his work on the social interactions of modern society.[17]

Finally, in terms of the Jewish influence on his work, we could cite Durkheim's lifelong involvement with the function of religion in society. Did this emerge from his rabbinical background and his adult agnostic rejection of religion? We cannot really know, but we can point out that Jewish intellectuals such as Durkheim, Sigmund Freud, Marx, and Simmel seemed to analyze religion in a more detached fashion than their Protestant and Catholic counterparts. Freud, for instance, complained that Carl Jung's Protestant beliefs were clouding his scientific endeavors, while Troeltsch and Weber became obsessed with Protestantism. In France, acceptance or rejection of the Catholic church were acts of revolution or counterrevolution, hardly analyzed with detachment or objectivity. Thus it may be that Durkheim's Jewish background and agnosticism allowed him to discover the ideas contained in *The Elementary Forms of Religious Life.*[18]

DURKHEIM AND THE ESTABLISHMENT OF SOCIOLOGY

As founder of sociology, Durkheim deemed it necessary to prove to the scholarly world that *social causality* was, in truth, a central causality in human motivation. He sought to distinguish sociology from psychology, economics, and biology.

Some thinkers believed that human society was merely a sum total of individual psychological actions.[19] Others believed that human behavior was reducible to its biological roots—instincts and genetic evolution. Durkheim strongly disagreed with these points of view. He wished to develop a theory and method for the study of human behavior in society that would dispense with biological, geographical, and related monocausal explanations so prevalent in Durkheim's day—a theory that would also make unnecessary explorations of individual consciousness and feelings falling within the realm of psychology.

"The proper subject matter for the study of society," Durkheim wrote in *The Rules for Sociological Method,* "are the constituent elements of society: social roles, statuses, norms, and the distinctive mechanisms of interactions these generate...." Hence Durkheim's emphasis on *social* facts.[20]

In *Suicide: A Study in Sociology* Durkheim once and forever established that the social structure in which humans interact had a profound effect on their individual psyches. For the suicide rate fluctuated according to the degree of isolation from social groups which individuals experienced, and according to the strength or weakness of the collective beliefs and norms which guided human behavior.

If egoistic atomization and anomic confusion caused the suicide rate to go up, then social causality was a critical dimension for the analysis of human conduct. Thus in *Suicide,* Durkheim not only analyzed the causes for suicide as they never had been analyzed before but "proved" that sociology was a necessary social science.

"*Suicide* is a profound treatise in social psychology. I know of no other work in modern social science that precedes in time this book's analysis of the social nature of human personality and of the relation of personality to social structure."[21]

"It is in Durkheim's explanations of the nature of 'egoistic' and 'anomic' suicide—the two types to which he gave greatest attention, altruistic suicide being relatively rare [in modern societies][22]—that we find this brilliant exposition of the social roots of personality, of the dependence of personality on social structure and social value, and of the predictable pathological effects upon personality of substantial dislocations of structure and value in a population."[23]

Durkheim insisted that individuals were born into an existing social structure consisting of institutions, norms, rules, roles, customs, and ideals to which they conformed. These preexisting structures *constrain* the individual so that he or she cannot simply act. For Durkheim the social scientist had to study the social structure or remain a learned ignoramus when analyzing human social interaction. Thus Durkheim rejected the work of the British utilitarians and other theorists of individual psychological action.

Finally, though fascinated by the "organic analogy" generated by social Darwinism and exemplified in Spencer's work,[24] and carried into Germany by Schäffle[25] (whom, as mentioned, Durkheim read and liked), Durkheim rejected biological reductionism. That is, he would not participate in the attempt to reduce human behavior to motivations that were derived from instincts, animal drives, or genetically inherited characteristics.

Some thinkers believed that human behavior could only be understood by reference to our animal nature. (Modern sociobiology has regenerated this idea rejected by Durkheim.[26]) Durkheim answered such theorists indirectly by analyzing religious behavior and granting it great causal significance in its effect on both social structural and individual interaction. How could religious (or for that matter philosophical or scientific) behavior be understood in animal terms alone? Which chimpanzees have priests or debate the nature of their own death or their moral conduct toward other chimpanzees? Which elk could introduce monogamous mating to his herd?

It was not that Durkheim in any way denied our animal heritage, but rather that he believed that the central analysis for the understanding of humans in groups was the social analysis, which entails the study of our learned and changeable norms, roles, values, customs, institutions, and collective beliefs.

In separating sociological analysis from that of psychology, economics, and biology, Durkheim established that the realm of the social—social structure and social causality—was critical to the understanding of human behavior. Because of this we can say that Durkheim was truly the first sociologist. Marx had written on social problems before him; Tönnies, Simmel, and Weber had established sociology in Germany; but Durkheim established sociology for the world. The name Comte had coined and the dream of the new science Saint-Simon had envisioned became a reality through Durkheim's work. In *The Rules for Sociological Method* he set the guidelines for the analysis of *social facts,* which we now take for granted, but which at that time were barely understood.

Durkheim and the Scientific Method

The influence of Comte on Durkheim's work was profound. Comte epitomized French thinking in regard to the social sciences and their positive role in the perfectability of society.[27] He encouraged social analysts to go beyond religion and philosophy toward the creation of a science of society. The new science, sociology, would follow the method of physics in its analysis of the social world. Empirical observation, mathematization, and verification of findings would characterize sociology. Comte called *positivism* this emphasis on empiricism and mathematicism in the analysis of the social world.[28] For Comte and his followers positivism was the equivalent of the scientific method applied to the social sciences. And he believed that sociology, armed with the positivist methodology, would help create a better society for humans to live their lives in.

Comte's positivist sociology came under heavy criticism from both philosophers and natural scientists, and we shall explain these criticisms shortly. For now, let it be established that Comte's idea of a "scientific" sociology created great enthusiasm in France, where some years later Durkheim developed it into a viable school of sociological analysis.

The French school founded by Émile Durkheim fused the teachings of Comte with those of Spencer into a new scientifically oriented science of society. Although Comte had already named the new social science *sociology,* Durkheim was to generate its first great studies.

From Comte, Durkheim borrowed the idea that sociology should utilize the scientific method to study social facts and that, like the natural sciences, sociology should aim at constructing the fundamental *laws of social interaction* that would hold for all time—transhistorically and cross-culturally.

Durkheim adapted the scientific method to sociological analysis. Observation, mathematization, theory building, experimentation, and verification—the scientific method—became in Durkheim's hands: (1) the observation of society for the empirical determination of social facts; (2) the use of statistical analysis for the mathematical evaluation of empirically collected data; (3) the building of theoretical laws of social interaction through the sociological analysis of the statistically organized data; and (4) the transhistorical and cross-cultural comparison of such data in order to determine variations and regularities that might lead to the emendation and modification of the original theory.

Experimentation was never suggested by Durkheim, who founded sociology with the desire to study society as it exists (and existed), without altering it artificially by creating an experimental situation.

According to Robert A. Nisbet, "Durkheim, like his great contemporary Weber (who was somewhat more given, however, to political participation, and to more agonies of mind arising from this participation, than Durkheim), believed the vocation of science to be exemplary in its own right...." [29] He believed that science and its rigorous, objective method must be applied to the study of human societies. As he put it:

[The] pre-scientific stage is broken through by the introduction of *empirical method*, not by conceptual discussion alone. This is perhaps more important in social than in natural science, since here the subject matter relates to human activity itself, and consequently there is a strong tendency to treat social phenomena as either lacking in substantive reality, or on the contrary, as already wholly known: thus words such as "democracy," "communism," etc. are freely used as if they denoted precisely known facts, whereas the truth is that they awaken in us nothing but confused ideas, a tangle of vague impressions, prejudices, and emotions. [30]

"The maintenance of treating social facts as things, of *objectivity*, demands rigorous *detachment* on the part of the investigator of social reality." [31]

Durkheim, after asserting the necessity for scientific objectivity and empirical observations, then established that the social scientist must classify societies into types and find the laws through which they can be analyzed.

Science cannot describe individuals, but only types. If human societies cannot be classified, they must remain inaccessible to scientific description.... If societies are not subject to laws (or general principles), no social science is possible. [32]

And, Durkheim insisted, "We must possess a method appropriate to the nature of the things studied and to the requirements of science." [33]

In *The Rules for Sociological Method* Durkheim established the scientific orientation of his sociology by encouraging us to focus on social facts and the theoretically constructed social laws derived from them. [34] In *Suicide* Durkheim presented us with our first great cross-cultural study of a social phenomenon previously thought to be a phenomenon of individual psychology. [35] From the study of social causalities of suicide, Durkheim developed his now famous laws of interaction: *nomos* (social cohesion or order); *anomie* (the separation of the individual from community, family, and church); and *altruistic overintegration* (total enmeshment of the individual with community, family, and church).

Durkheim carefully compared the data on suicide cross-culturally—in one European society and another (within one religious group and another), and transhistorically—studying tribal data as well as data from modern urban-industrial societies. He expanded his theory of suicide through his comparative method. Thus Durkheim created the laws of suicide that would hold for all time, while at the same time taking historical, structural, and cultural variations as a given in the study of human societies.

Durkheim's avoidance of artificial experimental situations foreshadowed some of the problems involved in attempts to model sociology on a purely natural science basis. Nonetheless, Durkheim's empirical-statistical orientation and his theoretical mirroring of the natural sciences in the creation of universal laws of social interaction bore fruit. *Suicide, The Elementary Forms of Religious Life,* [36] and *The Division of Labor* [37]—

these works stand as monuments to his method and theory.

Whether a sociologist can take a purely objective view of social facts, and whether the empirical observation of society can truly uncover such facts, would become questions in a great debate over the years. The German sociologists called Durkheim's method naive, ahistorical, and not a true reflection of what natural scientists do. However, Durkheim's positivist scientific approach would go far to legitimate sociology to the world, and would become a veritable passion in the sociology of the United States during the 1950s.[38]

Functional Analysis

Perhaps even more important than his method, Durkheim's development of functional analysis had a monumental impact on sociology. For functional analysis, which is very different from historical analysis, sent sociology in a new direction, different from that of Marx and Weber, and unique in its approach to the analysis of social structure.

Two approaches may be used to explain social phenomena, the *functional* and the *historical*. The functional analysis of a social phenomenon involves establishing the "correspondence between the fact under consideration and the general needs of the *social organism,* and in what this correspondence consists."[39]

Notice Durkheim's usage of the term *social organism*—this is the key to the origin of the functional approach, as opposed to the historical approach, to social analysis.

The British school of thought was heavily influenced by the exciting work of Charles Darwin, and as a result it emphasized biological descriptions of reality. Although this mode of conceptualization also spread to Germany, it did *not* become a central trend of thought in that country. Durkheim, however, as mentioned, was familiar with the work of Schäffle[40] and also with the work of Lillienfeld.[41]

Schäffle made extensive use of organic analogies, comparing various parts of society to the organs and tissues of the body. (Spencer did this as well.[42]) Schäffle insisted that the use of biological concepts represented nothing more than a "metaphor" which can facilitate sociological analysis.[43]

Durkheim wrote approvingly of Schäffle's work. Enthralled with the organic analogy, Durkheim took it beyond Spencer and focused sociology on the institutions and norms which make up the organic whole of society and regulate its individual interactions. Durkheim's view—and here he gave sociology another of its major orientations—was that the basic institutions of each society must be studied, and the function of each institution identified as it relates to the whole society. Family and church, for instance, could be identified as basic social institutions; their functions in the organic whole could then be described and cross-culturally and transhistorically compared.

The functional analysis of social institutions became so basic for Durkheimian sociology that *functionalism* was its later title.

Durkheim, however, did not stop there. Taking the organic analogy further, he postulated that since humans, unlike bees or ants, have few instincts, humans create learned, shared norms for the regulation of social life. Society would be chaotic if it were made up of spontaneous individual human actions. Therefore, humans have evolved systems of shared, learned, normatively regulated patterns of social action.

The theory of norms and the normative regulation of social behavior is another great Durkheimian contribution to sociology. This theory of learned, shared norms, however, suggests a conception of humans in intersubjective interaction and of society as a collectivity of conscious human beings interacting in a learned, variable, changeable pattern of action. This pattern is not "organic" in Spencer's sense. But then Durkheim was a better sociologist than that, and his sociology transcended its own theoretical origins, providing an opening to the historical, cultural, and phenomenological schools of thought that would emerge to extend functionalism or to criticize it.

From Durkheim's organic analogy we thus get his functional sociology, and with it the great conceptual tools of the functional school: institutions, norms, roles, customs, etc. As Nisbet put it, "No idea has been more fruitful in modern sociology and social anthropology than the idea of *function*. It has had the effect of turning attention from the surface aspects of the relation of a given custom, tradition, structure, or habit to the larger social order." [44]

Nisbet suggests that Durkheim's functional analysis of religion is perhaps the best example of this kind of sociological paradigm. "It was Durkheim's demonstration of the function of religion in his *Elementary Forms*, a function that is, as he stressed, social, not philosophical or creedal, least of all cosmological, that, more than any other single part of his work, turned modern attention to the functional aspects of all social phenomena." [45]

Functional analysis—which focuses on the cultural unity of a society, its collective beliefs and its norms, roles, institutions, and values—would become not only the mainstream of sociological analysis in France, Britain, and the United States but also the major thrust of anthropological analysis. Functionalist theory would be further developed by sociologists and anthropologists in France, Britain, and the United States, but they would all be "Durkheim's children." For without Durkheim functional analysis would hardly have gained the widespread usage we now take for granted.

Of course, German sociology—Marxist, Weberian, or otherwise—would reject functional analysis outright and continue on its separate historically oriented course. Nonetheless, the mainstream of sociological development was generated by Durkheim. Functionalism and positivism would spawn a generation of social scientists whose productions have been formidable indeed. In

defense of science and his new sociology based on the scientific model, Durkheim wrote, "The future is already written for him who knows how to read it." [46]

The Comparative Method

Durkheim's use of the comparative method is quite crucial. For he believed that sociological analysis was not complete unless a comparative analysis was undertaken. In *Suicide,* for instance, he undertakes a wide-ranging comparative analysis which allowed him to test his hypothesis, and which forced him to create new concepts.

As Nisbet puts it:

The final point to be made about Durkheim's logic of explanation is his stress on the *comparative* nature of social science. He is not impressed by what experimentalism offers to causal analysis. The only way we are going to reach understanding of the causal process in any given relationship is through its comparison with like or unlike processes in other, cognate relationships. [47]

As Durkheim himself stated it:

Comparative sociology is not a particular branch of sociology; it is sociology itself, insofar as it ceases to be purely descriptive and aspires to account for facts. [48]

Durkheim was, however, critical of the evolutionary theorists of his day. He disagreed not only with Marx and Engels but also with Spencer, Edward Tylor, and James Frazer. For Durkheim believed that these theorists went too far in trying to compare institutions embedded in different types of societies, and which, therefore, held different functions within these different social types.

Here is how Durkheim puts it:

Social facts vary with the social system of which they form a part; they cannot be understood when detached from it. This is why two different societies cannot be profitably compared merely because they seem to resemble each other; *it is necessary that these societies themselves* resemble each other, that is to say that they be only varieties of the same species. The comparative method would be impossible, if *social types* did not exist, and it cannot be usefully applied except within a single type. What errors have not been committed for having neglected this precept?[49]

Durkheim then goes on to joust with the ghost of Marx:

It is thus that facts have been unduly connected with each other which, in spite of exterior resemblances, really have neither the same sense nor the same importance: *the primitive democracy and that of today, the collectivism of inferior societies and actual socialistic tendencies,* the monogamy which is frequent in Australian tribes and that is sanctioned by our laws, etc.[50]

Durkheim is warning the comparative social scientist that comparing institutions in types of societies that are so different is dangerous indeed. Yet he still encourages comparative work within sociologically dissimilar types, as with mechanical versus organic solidarity, or anomic versus altruistic suicide.

It is interesting to note that Marx himself was critical of the utopian-agrarian socialists, who, he insisted, were attempting to create socialism on a primitive economic base. In fact, Marx was vague on the specifics of industrial socialism, precisely for the reasons Durkheim makes central—that on this modern industrial base the primitive model of communal sharing could not be re-created.

Nonetheless, Durkheim's warning was well taken, as so many Marxists did fantasize romantically on the primitive model of communal sharing. In addition to the socialists, the evolutionary anthropological theorists also tended to create what Durkheim believed were illegitimate categories of comparison.

Again, some similarity with Weber's position emerged. Weber too was critical of those theorists who compared different types of societies indiscriminately. And if Durkheim referred to *cultural unities* as creating differing types of societies, Weber referred to *civilizational configurations* as exhibiting differing characteristics that

could not necessarily be fruitfully compared.[51]

Both Weber and Durkheim railed against the illegitimate comparisons of institutions produced by vulgar Marxists and teleological evolutionists, and both insisted that the comparative method—properly done—was absolutely essential for sociology.

Comparative sociology is not a particular branch of sociology; *it is sociology itself,* insofar as it ceases to be purely descriptive and aspires to account for facts.[52]

Weber, with his *ideal type* analysis, sought to place comparative sociology on an objective footing,[53] while Durkheim, with his analysis of "traits" within social types (and contrasted to differing social types) also attempted to establish a proper style of comparative analysis.

As we conclude this section, we need to note that whereas both Durkheim and Weber attempted to create a *proper comparative method* in dialogue with the evolutionary schools which they believed had erred, with a few notable exceptions, such as Robert K. Merton and Seymour M. Lipset, American functionalism attempted to flee from the comparative method. Durkheim would no more have approved of this than he did of the evolutionists.

To sum up:

The comparative method, properly understood, is the very framework of the science of society, but it must be comparative of structures and processes which are . . . legitimate "social types"; that is, modes of behavior in which function, contextual significance, and meaning, as well as mere overt form, are duly taken into consideration.[54]

THE COHESION OF MODERN SOCIETY: ORGANIC SOLIDARITY

During his year in Germany Durkheim became aware of Tönnies's work (which was not yet published), *Gemeinschaft und Gesellschaft.*[55] When it appeared in 1887, Durkheim reviewed it. He felt that Tönnies, like so many German intellectuals, was romanticizing premodern society and presenting a one-sided argument. The German intellectuals, Durkheim believed, were overly critical of and pessimistic about modern society. He believed they were creating a fantasy vision of their lost past, while bemoaning the ills of the emerging urban-industrial society. For the Germans, *Gemeinschaft* was almost a mystical phenomenon (as it was for Troeltsch[56]) or a glorified phenomenon full of *Volk* or German tribal images from the Teutonic past (as it was for Heinrich von Trietschke[57] and Friedrich Nietzsche[58]). Durkheim doubted that the small town, village, or tribal societies were so wonderful, and insisted that modern society, though problematic indeed (as he would show in his theories of egoistic isolation and anomie), held within it great liberating factors for individuals.

Here is Durkheim's negative description of *Gemeinschaft,* which he analyzed as static and stultifying:

The tribe as a whole forms a "society" because it is a *cultural unity*: because the members of the various clan groups all adhere to the same set of common beliefs and sentiments. Thus, any part of such a society can break away without much loss to the others—rather in the same way as simple biological organisms can split up. . . . Since in this condition [which Durkheim called *mechanical solidarity*] the society is dominated by the existence of a strongly formed set of sentiments and beliefs *shared by all members of the community,* it follows that there is *little* scope for *differentiation between individuals;* each individual is a microcosm of the whole.[59]

Having thus described the conformity and constraint of primitive society and the mechanical solidarity that characterized it, he then contrasted the primitive condition to the modern. In *The Division of Labor* Durkheim presented his theory of the social integration of modern society in contradistinction to Tönnies's negative description. Durkheim's conception, *organic solidarity,* has since become a classic concept in sociology, not because of its organicist basis, but

because of its establishment of the construct: *role interdependence,* which became the cement of modern society.[60] Durkheim brilliantly described the *differentiation and specialization* of occupational roles that accompanied modern industrial society. Few social scientists today can write about modern society without leaning on this Durkheimian analysis.

This second type of social cohesion [involving modern society] is *organic solidarity.* Here solidarity stems not from acceptance of a common set of beliefs and sentiments, but from *functional interdependence in the division of labor.* Where mechanical solidarity is the main basis of social cohesion, the "conscience collective" completely envelops the individual consciousness, and therefore assumes identity (sameness) between individuals. Organic solidarity, by contrast, presupposes not identity, but *difference* between individuals in their beliefs and actions. The growth of organic solidarity and the expansion of the division of labor are hence associated with increasing *individualism.*[61]

Durkheim's description of the increasing specialization of labor and the growing role interdependence this produces generated a theory of *social stratification* based on occupational analysis. His theory holds very nicely for the middle strata of society, but holds less neatly when applied to the rich or the poor. We shall discuss this and Durkheim's notions of the "forced" and "anomic" division of labor later on. For our discussion here we emphasize that Durkheim's analysis of occupational role differentiation, the specialization emanating from it, and the interdependence it generates is still undoubtedly one of the better theories for understanding the cohesion of modern society. Along with Marx's theory of the mode of production, class domination, and false consciousness, and Hobbes's theory of the power of the state and Weber's theory of rationalization, Durkheim's theory of organic solidarity stands as one of the key tools for the analysis of industrial society.

In *The Division of Labor,* Durkheim described the positive aspects of modern occupational life. Role interdependence and specialization created a whole sphere of middle-class professional and business occupations through which individual fulfillment and viability could be ensured. After all, was not Durkheim himself a case in point? His own success reflected the potentialities within modern society, and therefore he saw the liberating side of the modern world. Along with role integration came *individualism*. That is, though occupational role conformity produces cohesion in modern society, the remarkable specialization of occupational roles allows for a great deal of choice in personal careers. Such choice was much less available to tribal people.

Furthermore, the weakening of the collective conscience allowed for a wide range of individual variations in terms of values and ideals. Thus, with the cohesion and conformity of organic role interdependence, individualism and personal freedom become possible. This view of modernity is remarkably optimistic compared to the view expressed in Germany by Tönnies and Weber.

Durkheim, however, was an objective observer of modernity. If he saw its positive aspects, he also saw its faults. Therefore, he set out to describe what he saw as the major problems of the modern world—the isolation of the individual from family, church, and community, and the anomic conditions engendered by the weakening of the collective beliefs and normative structures of modern society.

Egoistic Isolation and Anomie

In *Suicide, The Rules of Sociological Method,* and *The Elementary Forms of Religious Life,* the picture of modern society that emerges alongside that of organic solidarity is one of the breakdown of communal ties, the shattering of the collective conscience, and the loss of the sacred quality of the norms.

The growing isolation of the individual in the modern world—while liberating in terms of artistic and intellectual creativity and political action (liberations not to be taken lightly)—left the individual too much alone in his or her confrontation with the vicissitudes of life.

Without family, church, and community, the individual might simply collapse in the face of life's challenges and toils, and drift toward a melancholy suicide—a phenomenon barely known to tribal humans. One wonders what Durkheim would have written today, since the problem of egoistic isolation has proceeded so much further than in his day (and the suicide rates are so much higher). Along with this growing isolation of the individual from personal ties, an increasingly anomic condition emerged in terms of social norms and collective beliefs. The modern world exhibited such a bewildering array of conflicting beliefs that the modern individual felt less constrained (more free), but morally confused. The norms that should guide our behavior were drastically weakened and perceived from a rational rather than a sacred perspective. Again, this allowed for a greater freedom of action than ever before, but created doubt about which action is "right" or "good."

The modern individual could leave a marriage, but for what—another marriage, a series of affairs, or aloneness? The modern individual could choose any career, but would it be the right career—which career was "the road not taken"? The modern individual could believe in any religion or no religion—we were and are all existentialists.[62] But where was our ethical guide? Were we forced to be sociopaths in our public behavior and psychopaths in our private lives?

Durkheim presented this view of what he saw as the anomic crisis of modern life and the isolatory nature of modern existence. From this he presented sociology with its basic theory of *deviance*. Expanding his analysis of suicide, Durkheim extended the theory of anomie and isolation into a general theory of deviance. For along with suicide, rates of crime, senseless violence, theft, rape, prostitution, alcoholism, and drug use increased in the modern urban world.

Years later Robert K. Merton would formalize Durkheim's general theory of deviance, but his theory was derivable from his corpus of work.[63] Durkheim's theory of deviance was one of the great monuments of sociological theory; it continues to be useful today, more so than ever. And in the sense that Durkheim's theory of deviance cut across class lines to explain, say, the drug use of middle-class youths or the stock fraud of wealthy brokers (insider trading), it transcended even the Marxian analysis of crime and violence which was linked to the rich and poor in Marx's schema.

Yet who would deny that the drug violence emanating from the lower class in America's cities today is resulting from the blocked upward mobility of our inner-city underclass? The Marxian analysis works well in this case, which Durkheim would have analyzed as part of the "forced" division of labor. Merton, in his essay "Social Structure and Anomie," to his credit attempted to combine this Marxian dynamic of blocked mobility with Durkheim's theory of anomically generated deviance.

Merton set the proper course, for Durkheim's theory of deviance was the architectonic theory of deviance. However, if the Marxian analysis of class-generated crime is combined with the overarching analysis of deviance presented by Durkheim, a rather comprehensive theory of pathological, criminal, and revolutionary behavior emerges.[64]

Collective Conscience: Durkheim's Sociology of Knowledge and Social Psychology

From Durkheim's *Elementary Forms of Religious Life* flowed one of his great contributions to sociology, his conception of the *conscience collective*, a term used in English as both the *collective conscience* and the *collective consciousness*. That is, in the first case the *moral* character of the beliefs is emphasized, whereas in the second case the collective nature of social beliefs is emphasized.

Searching for the origins and functions of religion, Durkheim not only established certain basic axioms concerning religion but also established a sociology of knowledge and social psychology. In this enterprise Durkheim left his organic analogy behind, and built his functional sociology on a cultural and humanistic base. His work thus leapt beyond organicists like Spencer and allowed for points of convergence with historical and symbolic interactionist principles. For at the same time as functional analysis was brought to its peak, symbolic representations emerging from the social structure became central.[65]

What is Durkheim's conception of religion? Religion is "a unified system of beliefs and practices relative to sacred things . . . *beliefs and practices which unite into a single moral community called a church, all those who adhere to them.*" He continued:

The special character of the *sacred* is manifest in the fact that it is surrounded by *ritual* prescriptions and prohibitions which enforce this radical separation from the *profane*. A religion is never simply a set of beliefs: it always also involves prescribed ritual practices and a definite institutional form.[66]

Durkheim then moved from the definition of religion to its function in society, which is to create a set of sacred collective beliefs and practices which, through their unification of individual actions and beliefs, created cohesion in society. *The more unified and ingrained the collective beliefs and practices, the more cohesive the society.*

What makes such a society a "society" at all is the fact that *its members adhere to common beliefs* and sentiments. The ideals which are expressed in religious beliefs are therefore the *moral ideals* upon which the unity of the society is founded. *When individuals gather together in religious ceremo-*

nies they are hence reaffirming their faith in the moral order upon which . . . solidarity depends. [67]

Of course Durkheim's obverse point was that where the religious collective conscience became weak, the cohesiveness of society declined, yielding to an anomic crisis and social disorganization.

The declining importance of religion in contemporary societies is a necessary consequence of the diminishing significance of mechanical solidarity: the importance we thus attribute to the sociology of religion does not in the least imply that religion must play the same role in present-day societies that it has played at other times. In a sense, the contrary conclusion would be more sound. . . .[68]

With the decline of religious belief in the modern world, as we have earlier suggested, came both intellectual freedom and moral malaise.

Sociology of Knowledge

Durkheim's notion of the collective conscience has significance beyond its substantive analysis of religion. In terms of its theoretical implications, Durkheim's "collective conscience" has much in common with Marx's sociology of knowledge.[69] Durkheim describes the collective beliefs of a society as embodying a reflection of the total institutional structure of society. By this he does not mean that the collective beliefs are an epiphenomenon, as Marx sometimes implies, but rather a projection derived from the institutional arrangements which, once generated, has an existence, function and causal impact all its own.

Certainly we consider it to be evident that social life depends upon its substratum and bears its mark, just as the mental life of the individual depends upon the nervous system and indeed the whole organism. But the "conscience collective" is something other than a mere epiphenomenon of its morphological basis, just as individual consciousness is something other than a simple efflorescence of the nervous system.[70]

Durkheim was debating the ghost of Marx here and insisting that the collective conscience was not *merely* a reflection of the social structure. Yet his position had much in common with Marx's view of ideology and with Weber's view of the relationship of ideas to their historical substratum.[71] Both Weber and Durkheim, however, emphasized the independence and causal significance of such ideological systems, while Marx emphasized the centrality and importance of the carrying classes, and made ideas secondary in causal significance.

It is interesting to contrast the similarities and differences in Durkheim's and Marx's theories of religion. Religion was for Marx the cement that held society together—but as the ideology of the ruling class. Religion for Marx was the false consciousness that kept the subject classes from revolting. Religion was the "opiate of the people," which lulled them into submission with dreams of an afterlife in which they would receive grace (while ignoring the real life in which they were deemed unworthy and unclean).

Yet though the major thrust of Marx's analysis was totally different from that of Durkheim, the result of powerful religious beliefs was the same—the production of stability in society. For Marx this stability was a stability of class domination, whereas for Durkheim this was not the case (though Durkheim recognized the constraining quality of sacred norms and beliefs).

Marx also believed that smashing the religious belief system would free the subject classes from domination and allow them to create a new society geared to their own needs. Marx saw no problem with the smashing of the collective conscience. Durkheim, on the other hand, warned that breaking the collective conscience would result in a twofold process—the one which Marx predicted, and another which he did not predict. That is, the smashing of the collective ideology would produce freedom and creativity, according to Durkheim, but would also engender a pathological anomic deviance, which Marx did not understand or which he viewed as part of the tumultuous period of revolutionary transition to an eventual socialist quiescence.

The work of Weber was very different from that of Durkheim; historical detail and transhistorical ideal types characterized Weber's approach, in opposition to Durkheim's functionalism in the analysis of religion. Still, there were some similarities. Both theorists disagreed with Marx as to the dispensability of religion. Both agreed that negative effects would accompany the decline of religion. Both saw the multiplicity of beliefs and the secularization of beliefs in the modern world.

Weber, however, focused on the specific historical quality of each religious system, focusing our attention most closely, of course, on the rise, significance, and decline of Puritan (Calvinist) Protestantism. Along the way he wrote monumental treatises not only on Protestantism but also on ancient Judaism, Confucianism, Hinduism, Islam, and more.[72]

For Weber, in analyzing modernity, the decline of ascetic Protestantism was the key fact of religious analysis, not the decline of religion in the abstract in Durkheim's terms.[73] For how else could one explain the outpouring of sexuality, sensualism, and narcissism that accompanied the modern religious decline? Anomie alone could not explain this trend.

Again, as with the works of Marx, the contrast and similarity between the work of Durkheim and Weber on religion proved to be enlightening and was well worth studying. If nothing like a unified theory of religion emerged, still the sociological analysis of religion became much richer and more sophisticated through that effort.

In fact, the sociology of knowledge in the broader sense became remarkably enriched through this comparative effort, for all three theorists emphasized the causal link between social structure and human collective ideas. Marx was the most extreme in his emphasis on the social structure (substratum), but Durkheim too placed heavy emphasis there. Weber and Durkheim emphasized the independent causal significance of collective ideas in acting back upon the social structure, while Weber focused on the historically specific nature of ideas, and Durkheim on their universal characteristics. While the three perspectives could not be blended, what a rich textural understanding emerged from their analyses of human collective beliefs and the social structure in which they were enmeshed!

Social Psychology

Along with the sociology of knowledge, Durkheim's work on the collective consciousness also lent itself as a foundation for social psychology.

Agnostic though Durkheim himself was throughout his life, he nevertheless declared religion the source of the fundamental categories of the human mind—space, time, cause, etc.—and the origin too of all the fundamental institutions, including kinship, property, law, which were linked to man's sense of the "sacred." For Durkheim indeed the sacred and the social bond are but two sides to the same coin.[74]

In the same sense we can consider *Suicide* "a profound treatise in social psychology." As Nisbet asserted, "I know of no other work in modern social science that precedes in time this book's analysis of the social nature of human personality and of the relation of personality to social structure."[75]

The opening of Durkheim's work to its own symbolic side took functionalist concepts such as roles and role sets,[76] and redefined them—that is, prevented them from appearing as abstract things and infused them with life. The human individual, with his or her identity and feelings, sprang forth from role and normative analysis if the symbolic side of the Durkheimian formulation was emphasized. Nisbet went so far as to say that the work of Mead and Cooley became synthesizable with that of Durkheim if this interpretation was followed.[77]

Just such an extension of Durkheim's functionalist categories occurred in the work of Erving Goffman, [78] Peter Berger,[79] and other contemporary symbolic interactionists and phenomenologists. The extension of Durkheim's functionalist categories to social psychological dimensionality has produced a higher order of sociological analysis and an important arena of convergence among sociological theories. Such a convergence can be extended both to macroanalyses and microanalyses.

DURKHEIM AND THE GHOST OF MARX

In a remarkable chapter at the end of *The Division of Labor* Durkheim lets go of his argument against Tönnies and begins a dialogue with Marx.

If one class of society is obliged, in order to live, to take any price for its services, while another can abstain from such action thanks to resources at its disposal which, however, are not necessarily due to any social superiority, the second has an unjust advantage over the first at law.[80]

If this is the case, that one class has an "unjust advantage" over the other, then instead of social cohesion, a situation of chronic class conflict may emerge. Instead of the unified moral regulations of relationships, coercive power may come into play.[81] Durkheim refers to this as the "forced division of labor."[82]

As Giddens puts it:

While the functioning of organic solidarity entails the existence of normative rules which regularize relationships between different occupations, this cannot be achieved if these rules are unilaterally imposed by one class upon another.[83]

Durkheim, however, believed that the situation of the forced division of labor was a *transitional* one. He believed that equality of opportunity would increase—that it was a definite historical tendency which accompanies the modern division of labor.[84] In this he foreshadowed contemporary neoconservative theorists who believe that equality of opportunity will create a long-term *meritocracy* in which class conflict will decline. Daniel Bell[85] has espoused this view. As Durkheim first stated it:

The division of labor produces solidarity only if . . . [there is] the absence of express and overt violence, [and] anything that might, even indirectly, shackle the free employment of the social force that each person carries in himself. This not only supposes that individuals are not relegated to particular functions by force, but also that *no sort of obstacle whatsoever* prevents them from occupying in the social framework *the position which accords with their capacities.*[86]

If, however, such obstacles exist to the degree that individuals cannot actualize their capacities and are coercively prevented from doing so, then "the division of labor does not everywhere produce cohesion because it is in an anomic state."[87]

Durkheim accepted Marx's analysis that the division of labor might be forced in the sense that the business class might exert undue control and inordinate political power over the working class. This forced division of labor did lead to what Durkheim described as an anomic condition. For working-class individuals would be prevented from actualizing their capacities and becoming absorbed into the middle strata of occupational role interdependence that produced the organic cohesion of society. Instead, the workers were left unintegrated, and therefore in a morally anomic condition.

Such anomie, which emanated from the forced division of labor, generated deviance, crime, and violence. And of course this for Durkheim was a terrible thing. Durkheim did not on the basis of this become a socialist. He did not because: (1) he did not believe that utilizing the state to accomplish the absorption of the workers into the organic solidarity was wise; state power would create something worse than that which it was supposed to remedy—a position he gained from Tocqueville[88]; and (2) he believed that the forced division of labor, and the anomic situation, were "transitional" [89] and would give way to a meritocratic occupational solidarity.

Though not a socialist, Durkheim was certainly a middle-class reformer who wished to alleviate the forced division of labor and integrate the working class into the occupational solidarity of modern society. If we follow his reasoning, we get an interesting picture from Durkheim. For the middle classes were linked together through occupational role interdependence, but the upper and lower classes are not quite included in the organic solidarity of modern society.

If we return all the way to Aristotle's *Politics*,[90] we will find this same observation. The middle class, said Aristotle centuries ago, produces stability in a democratic polity because of their nearly equal status and lawful behavior, whereas the rich and the poor—the former with too much power and wealth and the latter with too little—engage in political and criminal violence which rips apart the democratic fabric of politics.

Beyond Aristotle, Durkheim's belief that class conflict, the forced division of labor, and the anomic crisis of modernity would be ameliorated to some extent by the growing absorption of individuals—through their unimpeded self-actualization—into the occupational strata of the specialized world of differentiated careers typified the hopes of middle-class reformers like himself. And, in fact, Durkheim's prediction of the growing cohesion and occupational interdependence of the modern middle strata has been accurate. Lurking outside of this cohesive segment of society was the still real condition of the rich with their excessive wealth and power, and of the poor, who were left unintegrated and anomic. From Durkheim's conceptions of the forced and anomic division of labor, a Durkheim-Marx dialogue could emerge.

Another factor should be added before we become too optimistic about a Durkheim-Marx dialogue. We might well ask: From where does the process of differentiation and specialization of occupational roles emanate? What is its cause? If its cause is industrialization, then an analysis of the industrial system, its origins, and its structure should have been included in Durkheim's analysis. Such an analysis, however, was not included.

Durkheim worked so hard throughout his life to establish the uniqueness of sociology as distinct from psychology, biology, economics, and politics that he tended to deemphasize what he considered nonsociological facts. No analysis of political power or struggle emanated from Durkheim's work, and there was no analysis of the industrial economy. This was problematical. His *Division of Labor*, which was so brilliant in its description of the organic solidarity engendered by occupational role interdependence, was quite deficient in linking this role interdependence to the modern industrial system as it actually existed. Nor was there any analysis of the political processes involved in the forced division of labor.

Whereas Weber took on the ghost of Marx in a direct dialogue, Durkheim ran from the ghost and hid behind a philosophical organicism that even the most ardent of Durkheimians, like Nisbet, have dropped or deemphasized.[91] Further, today's disciples of Durkheim often hide behind new abstractions, such as cultural unity or cultural wholes that remain unlinked to the economic and political structures of society, and are equally unhelpful in attaching role integration to the industrial system.[92]

This is not to denigrate what Durkheim has given us in *The Division of Labor* and his other works. His analysis of the cohesion developed through role interdependence was indispensable for the understanding of the modern world. And his role, norm, custom, and collective conscience concepts formed the bedrock from which the functionalist approach to analysis of the human world of interaction emerged. In fact, we could go so far as to say that without

Durkheim there would be no sociology. What was missing from Durkheim's work, however, was important. For without an analysis of the economic and political structure of society, the division of labor had no roots.

Saint-Simon and Socialism

If Durkheim jousted with the ghost of Marx, he acknowledged directly his debt to Saint-Simon. Durkheim recognized the genius of Saint-Simon in analyzing industrial society. Saint-Simon's socialism, however, was another thing. Though basically sympathetic to the goal of socialism in terms of alleviating the wretched situation of the industrial workers and poorer classes in general, Durkheim was skeptical that this goal could be accomplished through centralization of the economy and the utilization of state power.

Like Tocqueville, Durkheim believed that the use of state power to institute socialist programs was dangerous and would produce more evil than it would alleviate.[93] In his lifetime Durkheim was an active Dreyfusard, that is, a part of the liberal reform movement demanding democratic and legal guarantees for all citizens, an end to discrimination against the Jews (especially against Alfred Dreyfus, a French army officer of Jewish origin falsely accused of treason), and a bettering of the condition of the lower classes.

Durkheim never suggested anything like an elaborate or detailed program for the accomplishment of these reforms, and he was especially vague on a program for upgrading the condition of the workers. His critique of socialism was simply a reiteration of Tocqueville's warnings on state power and the loss of democracy it would engender—a view he shared closely with Weber, even though they were not very familiar with each other's works. As we shall see in the next section, however, Durkheim's program for the preservation of democracy—his idea of *intermediary associations* between the state and the citizen—was very well developed and represented a great contribution to the theory of mass democracy. (This theory was further expanded by American pluralist theorists after World War II.)

Like most liberal reformers of his era, and very much like Weber, Durkheim tended to focus his political attention on the extension and preservation of democracy in mass society rather than on the establishment of economic equality.

Durkheim, like Weber, was sympathetic with the goals and values of the socialists, but suspicious of their program and perhaps not really deeply moved by the condition of the poor. Weber, for instance, hoped that the Social Democratic party could both help the workers and reinforce the democratic process to which they were committed. Weber was highly critical of the Bolshevik program in Russia, warning as Durkheim and Tocqueville had done that state power would create a new authoritarianism rather than a democratic-socialist Utopia.

In his later years Durkheim separated himself from the socialist movement, for he believed that academic sociologists should try to be objective in their scientific analyses of society. He felt that the socialists did not want such objectivity, but rather a commitment to "praxis" in service of their cause. The socialists made fun of bourgeois science, believing it to be an ideological tool of the capitalist ruling class. Durkheim disagreed, and worked his entire life to establish an objective sociology. In this project his views were similar to Weber's. For Weber too spent his life attempting to establish a value-neutral sociology—not one that was value-free, but objectively evaluative.[94]

Durkheim, then, though sympathetic to socialism, was not a follower of socialism. We have already described his discussion of the forced and anomic division of labor, which recognized the problem of class conflict and class domination. Durkheim, however, projected the vision that class domination and its resulting anomie could be partially overcome by the expanding phenomenon of differentiation and specialization in the organic role integration that would emerge to absorb the majority of the social strata in modern industrial society.

Durkheim's vision of an expanding, cohesive middle class was accurate enough; in point of fact, modern capitalist societies *have* held together. Therefore, liberal reformist thinkers today owe a debt to Durkheim in their analyses of modern society, and socialist theorists have had to deal with this reality as they grapple to adjust their theory to modern conditions. But the anomic conditions emergent from the classes in capitalist society have not disappeared and continue to plague society today, particularly in the United States and Britain, the most capitalist nations. Therefore, we cannot afford to forget Durkheim's analysis of anomie and pathological deviance.

Nor should we forget his warnings against state power. Like Weber, Durkheim, the liberal reformer, asked us to seek remedies within the democratic tradition—remedies that could upgrade the anomic condition of the lower classes. Like Weber, however, he was not explicit or passionate in this commitment. Part of the reason for this weakened commitment was the fear of both Weber and Durkheim that democracy might be sacrificed in the attempt to create greater equality. This is a problematic situation that still haunts us in the modern world.[95]

If Durkheim was not explicit on a program to produce equality, he was explicit on a program to increase democracy in mass society, while at the same time strengthening the cohesive potential within organic solidarity. Let us turn to Durkheim's political sociology for an analysis of this program.

Durkheim's Political Sociology

Durkheim's political sociology is less well known than his other theories because he tried quite consciously to separate his political views from his sociological endeavors. Durkheim, however, did have some strong political views, which he asserted quite directly and forcefully.

For instance, Durkheim rejected thinkers such as Georg W. F. Hegel and the French socialists, who placed their hopes for a better society in the actions of the state. Many German thinkers believed that the state could create order and cohesion and make *Gesellschaft* into *Gemeinschaft*, while the French socialists believed that the state could run a centralized economy for the benefit of all.[96]

Like Tocqueville before him, Durkheim warned that the power of the state could lead only to evil ends. He disagreed sharply with the socialists, who claimed that the state could create equality without repression. He also believed that the German conception of the state was a romantic illusion derived from a glorification of the German tribal past.[97]

If Durkheim rejected the state, however, he also rejected the ideal of pure individualist democracy in mass society. That is, he rejected the democratic idealism of Jean-Jacques Rousseau, which demanded a direct citizens' democracy like that of ancient Athens or Geneva, Rousseau's birthplace, which was a city-state at that time.[98] Durkheim believed that mass society was too large, its population too great, and its government too distant to allow for pure citizenship and direct democracy. Durkheim therefore proposed an intermediary set of institutions between the state and the individual citizen.[99] Sounding remarkably like a contemporary pluralist,[100] he suggested that the creation of occupational associations and voluntary organizations as organizational entities intermediate between citizens and the state would help preserve democracy by ''countervailing'' the power of the state.[101] Such an arrangement would help facilitate the democratic process by providing organized vehicles for citizens' action.

This was *interest group* and *pluralist theory* before it even had such a name. If in truth there was not enough mention by Durkheim of class domination, conflict, party politics, or political leadership, there certainly was an awareness of the way in which modern democracy actually functioned.

Thus if Durkheim's political sociology was wanting—and it was only barely developed—at least what he presented was not only interesting but perhaps it also pointed to the basic institutional process through which mass democracy has been able to function in the modern nation-state.

We need to make one last point concerning Durkheim's political sociology and the intermediary occupational associations. Durkheim believed that these intermediary occupational associations might help "promote organic solidarity" where that solidarity was marred by class conflict.[102]

Anomie is present in the occupational system in so far as moral integration is lacking at the "nodal points" of the division of labor—the points of conjunction and exchange between different occupational strata. *A primary function of the occupational associations would be to reinforce moral regulation at these points, and thereby promote organic solidarity.* This is a task which cannot be accomplished by the family in modern societies, since the family is becoming increasingly restricted in functions. The occupational group is the only one "which is close enough to the individual for him to be able to rely directly upon it, and durable enough to be able to give him a perspective."[103]

Durkheim concluded with a warning against the power of the state, asserting the necessity of secondary groups between the state and the individual citizen:

Where the state is the only environment in which men can live communal lives, they inevitably lose contact, become detached, and thus society disintegrates. A nation can be maintained only if, *between the state and the individual, there is intercalated a whole series of secondary groups* near enough to the individuals to attract them strongly in their sphere of action and drag them,

in this way, into the general torrent of social life. We have shown how occupational groups are suited to fill this role, and that is their destiny.[104]

Pluralist theorists in political science, who are working today almost exclusively with an analysis of these secondary groups, are also Durkheim's children, along with functionalist anthropologists and sociologists. What a remarkable influence Durkheim's work has had on the social sciences! And of course this influence has been good where Durkheim's work was strong, but where it was weak, his influence has left theoretical gaps. Let us conclude with a weakness—or why else would sociology, nay, the social sciences in general, need the work of Marx and Weber at all? Few texts do not acknowledge the threefold foundation of sociology. Why is this the case?

Durkheim's Theory of Social Change

How do we get from one cultural unity to another, and from one social type to another? Durkheim was clear that there were differing levels of societies, and he did not lean toward evolutionary theories or stage theories of history. Therefore he needed to provide a functionalist explanation of social change, which is what he did. He postulated his two-pronged theory of social change on the basis of population increase and the resulting increase in moral density.

Durkheim theorized that increases in population density forced the overlapping of differing collective beliefs, or a condition of moral density. From the moral density of population increase came conflict between competing collective consciousnesses, which resulted in anomie. From the anomic condition deviance emerged. Yet this deviance had a positive as well as a negative function.[105] That is, anomie allowed for new and creative ideas to emerge. From these "deviant" new ideas, new institutions, new norms, new collective beliefs developed that formed the bedrock of a new social structure, a new *social type*.

We should note that Durkheim's theory of social change contained a mixture of biological and symbolic aspects. Population increase was an organic analogue, while moral density, anomie, and creative, deviant ideas were purely symbolic. This was a peculiar mixture that was not without problems.

We might ask, for instance, What produces population increase? And here we might have to abandon Durkheim's biologism for some form of historical-structural analysis. For example, would a better economic or political-military organization produce a population increase? Or would the religious unification of a region also produce such an increase? A purely biological approach to population increase would not suffice, for the birth rate and death rate would be affected by some other causality.

If increased food supply was produced through an improved mode of production, or if a better military organization resulted in a larger political unification, then we were no longer analyzing population increase in the biological realm.[106] Obviously, the theories of Marx and Weber about social change and history were needed once we began to look for the causes of population density.

Durkheim, however, provided the opening to the more human side of social change with his idea of the *creative deviance* emanating from *anomic conditions*. For if new ideas became the motive force (following in the wake of increased population density), then such ideas might take on a specifically economic form (Marx), or a politico-military or religious form (Weber).

In any case, once we entered the realm of human ideas, we entered the realm of human history. This Durkheim sought to avoid. In avoiding it, he presented sociology with one of its great analytical systems—*functionalism*. However, in avoiding history he also left a gaping void in the base of sociology. For humans did not move from tribal society to industrial society in one great leap.

Obviously Durkheim neglected most of human history. Thus although he purposely set out to correct what he believed were flaws in evolutionary historicism and stage theories of history, by avoiding history entirely he avoided basic sets of causal principles that affect social life.

Therefore, though Durkheim was the first true sociologist, sociology cannot be based on Durkheim's work alone. The theory of social change, more than any other area of sociology, brings forth the necessity of a historically based sociology, along with its functional base. The works of Marx and Weber leapt forward at this juncture, and the economic, political, and military causalities Durkheim sought to avoid were forced back onto center stage.   □

CASE STUDY

The Positive and Negative Effects of Anomie in Science: The Case of the Discovery of the AIDS Virus

As we have seen, most sociologists credit Émile Durkheim as the first to introduce the concept of anomie into sociology in his book *The Division of Labor in Society* (1893).[107] He later developed the concept more fully into a theory in his masterwork, *Suicide: A Study in Sociology* (1897). In trying to explain human behavior, Durkheim emphasized the importance of the social structure in society as the causal factor in explaining other aspects of social life. Durkheim assigned a central role to the moral rules, social norms, and cultural values of society. These collective representations, or social facts as Durkheim called them, were the essence of religion and morality. They constrained individuals insofar as they brought them into conformity with society.

In the *Division of Labor* Durkheim sought to explain the moral sentiment of solidarity by explaining the evolution of society in terms of the continual increase in the division of labor. In simple societies individuals were tightly bound together by a common set of cultural beliefs and social norms. These societies were said to exhibit mechanical solidarity: social cohesion stemmed from the homogeneity and similarity of individuals. The structure of modern societies was characterized by a "system of different organs, each of which has a specialized role, and which are themselves formed of differentiated parts." [108] Mechanical solidarity was replaced by organic solidarity: social cohesion now stemmed from the increasing interdependence and specialization of individuals.

Durkheim foresaw the negative ramifications encompassed by the extreme weakening of the collective norms and sentiments of modern society. As individualism and personal freedom increased, the sentiment of obligation (duty) diminished. In admitting that there exists "a morality which rests in the independent creations of the individual, which no rule determines" [109] the stability of the normative system was disturbed. Durkheim defined this condition—*anomie*—as a state of normlessness—not in the sense that there were no relevant norms to govern behavior, but rather that the norms which formerly applied to individuals no longer held any meaning. Anomie therefore "is the contradiction of all morality." [110]

Many modern sociological theorists have built upon the concept of anomie. One such theorist, Robert K. Merton, sought to identify the sources of "differing degrees of anomie in different sectors of society . . . to examine the varying adaptations to anomie and the forces making for one rather than another type of adaptation." [111]

CULTURAL GOALS AND INSTITUTIONAL MEANS: ROBERT K. MERTON

In his paper "Social Structure and Anomie" (1938) Merton focused upon the social and cultural sources of deviant behavior. His aim was to "discover how some social structures exert a definite pressure upon certain persons in the society to engage in nonconforming rather than conforming conduct." [112] He observed that the imbalance between cultural goals and social norms was responsible for aberrant behavior: "It is, indeed, my central hypothesis that aberrant behavior may be regarded sociologically as a symptom of dissociation between culturally prescribed aspirations and socially structured avenues for realizing these aspirations." [113]

Merton's emphasis on the variable relation between goals and means led him to formulate a more precise definition of anomie. In instances where a goal is important and there is not a strong emphasis on the norms prescribing the means to be used in attaining the goal, individuals who cannot attain the goal by normatively prescribed means will use illegitimate means. Since his focus was not on individual or social value orientations, his theory of anomie did not address the question of desirability of ends, as did Durkheim's. Merton aptly demonstrated how the culturally induced pressure to be successful generated rulebreaking as a response. Here, then, we have an instance where unintended consequences flow from an otherwise desirable social value.

Applying his theory to American society, Merton argued that an imbalance existed between the prevalent emphasis on pecuniary success and the class system which created unequal opportunities for success.

It was the social structure which exerted definitive pressure upon variously situated individuals in society to be deviant. People who accept the goal of success but find the approved avenues blocked may fall into a state of anomie and seek success by disapproved methods. In the United States, for example, the poor and minorities have the least access to legitimate means. They are born into social circumstances that make it difficult to attain a good education; they are often the victims of discrimination; they are not able to become involved in relationships that will assist them in the pursuit of successful professional or business careers. It is, therefore, not surprising that one finds high rates of crime among these individuals: they have internalized the success goal but have used illegitimate means to attain that goal.[114]

AN APPLICATION OF ANOMIE THEORY: THE RACE FOR PRIORITY

In his paper "Priorities in Scientific Discovery" (1957) Merton turned his attention to deviant behavior in science. His analysis of the pathogenic elements in the culture and opportunity structure derives from his more general analysis in "Social Structure and Anomie." Deviant behavior in science is located in the disjunction between goals and normatively prescribed means, just as it is in society at large. The incidence of deviant behavior depends upon the structural opportunities available to scientists variously placed in the social system. The strong emphasis in science on making original contributions in order to extend knowledge has the same effect as the comparable strong emphasis on financial success. He notes, "Competition in the realm of science, intensified by the great emphasis on original and significant discoveries, may occasionally generate incentives for eclipsing rivals by illicit or dubious means."[115] In other words, failure to reach a goal—such as making an original discovery or advancing scientific knowledge—may cause a scientist to deviate from the norms of science in or-

der to get an advantage over the competition. In cases where there is a rush for priority—where the primary concern is to be the *first* to make a discovery—competition among scientists intensifies. This puts pressure on scientists to engage in any one of a number of deviant behaviors, ranging from the fudging of empirical data to the most extreme form of deviance—the fabrication of data.

This explanation of deviant behavior in science focuses upon the unintended, undesirable consequences which flow from the goal of originality in science: a negative notion of anomie. This is not unlike Durkheim's formulation, which emphasized the pathological consequences for society. However, implicit in both theories are glimpses of a positive notion of anomie.

Merton notes that the same anomic forces which contribute to aberrant behavior also underlie those of human accomplishment. "The free ranging intellect, exercising its muscles to the full, thrives in an atmosphere of relative autonomy."[116] As we have already seen, Durkheim did profess to positive consequences promulgated by anomie; augmenting the amount of personal freedom experienced by individuals cultivates a wide array of values and ideas. This multiplicity of beliefs and sentiments is not only inevitable but *necessary* for social change. In his *Division of Labor* Durkheim makes the following observation about the scientific enterprise:

"It is certain, however, that to gain an exact idea of science, one must practice it, and so to speak live with it...one must have been close to scientific life while it was still in a *free state*; that is to say *before it became fixed in the form of definitive propositions*. Otherwise, one will have the letter, but not the spirit [of science]."[117]

This evidently attests to an affinity between anomie and scientific advance. In this passage Durkheim alludes to the public and private components of science: "Alongside this actual, realized science, there is another, concrete and living;...beside acquired results, there are hopes, habits, instincts, needs, presentiments. All this is still science; it is even its best and largest part. . . ." [118] The essence of the discovery period is that of a free state, an anomic environment, where hunches and guesses are not strictly evaluated by the norms of science, for those norms apply only to the evaluation of results that have been made public. During this private phase scientists are permitted a great deal of normative variability, a freedom from the imperative uniformity of external norms. Such an environment contributes to both scientific advance and social change.

Keeping both the negative and positive concepts of anomie in mind, let us turn to our case study: the discovery of the AIDS virus.

A MODERN PLAGUE

It began with the 1981 appearance of a medical report in the *New England Journal of Medicine*.[119] A rare form of cancer was found in young white males, a group in which the disease had been extremely rare. Careful examination of the medical history of these men revealed a single common factor: they all had a previous history of homosexuality.

Shortly after the publication of that report, physicians noticed a dramatic increase in certain infections. It soon became clear that a new syndrome was involved—one that attacked white blood cells (T4 lymphocytes), leaving the patient's immune system susceptible to infections that would not ordinarily harm healthy individuals. This disease became known as Acquired Immune Deficiency Syndrome (AIDS).

A variety of hypotheses were advanced to explain the cause of AIDS, but as researchers collected more data, the observations supported those who argued in favor of a retrovirus. A retrovirus differs from a virus in that its genetic complement is RNA, not DNA. Retroviruses contain an enzyme, reverse transcriptase, which uses the RNA as a template for making DNA. This newly formed DNA integrates itself into the chromosomes of the host cell and serves as the

basis for viral replication. Scientists had been able to detect the presence of reverse transcriptase in AIDS patients, leading them to believe that a retrovirus was at work. This new virus was then compared with another known human retrovirus, human T-cell lymphotropic virus (HTLV-I), and similarities were detected: the virus was present in whole blood, plasma, and semen; it could be transmitted by sexual contact, blood, and congenital infection.[120] Scientists were beginning to get a handle on the characteristics of the disease, but they still needed to identify the exact retrovirus responsible for AIDS.

One scientist, Dr. Luc Montagnier, was hard at work on precisely this task. In January 1983 he and his colleagues at the Pasteur Institute in France were given a tissue sample taken from a homosexual man who suffered from lymphadenopathy, or swollen glands. Montagnier extracted cells from this sample in order to analyze the virus. While conducting a standard experiment, one of his colleagues observed an anomaly: the virus grew by killing the very cells in which it lived. This observation was surprising because the HTLV-I virus did not replicate in this fashion: it entered the T4 cells and caused them to multiply uncontrollably, like a cancer. This was one of several observations that led Montagnier and his team to suspect that they had isolated a virus that was different from HTLV-I.

In May 1983 Montagnier and his colleagues published their data in the journal *Science*. This was the *first* paper to describe the virus in such great detail. At this stage, however, Montagnier was not able to offer *conclusive proof* that this virus was the single cause of AIDS. Still, by the summer of 1983 Montagnier and his colleagues were convinced that the virus they had isolated was indeed the AIDS virus, and that it did not belong to the HTLV family. To indicate this, they named it Lymphadenopathy Associated Virus (LAV).

On the other side of the Atlantic, Dr. Robert C. Gallo and his associates at the National Cancer Institute were engaged in the same task as their trans-Atlantic counterparts. Gallo was also an advocate of the retrovirus theory. This was not surprising, for it was he who discovered HTLV-I, a retrovirus responsible for leukemia, and a variant of that virus, HTLV-II. The similarities between the AIDS retrovirus and HTLV-I,II reinforced Gallo's beliefs that this new virus was either a variant of, or at the very least belonged to, the HTLV family. He and his colleagues continued their efforts to prove this theory. The team had isolated a virus which they believed to be the cause of AIDS but, like their French counterparts, they were faced with an overwhelming obstacle: the methodology available at the time did not permit *unique identification*; it only showed that a retrovirus was present in a sample. To accomplish this task, large amounts of the virus were needed to produce a blood test. The test would accurately identify people who had the AIDS virus *and* provide the necessary chemical reagents to identify the virus. The new virus, however, resisted all attempts at laboratory culture. As was pointed out earlier, the virus killed the very cells in which it lived, thereby thwarting all efforts to produce the necessary chemical reagents. Whoever was able to overcome this obstacle would be accorded the honor of "the discoverer of the AIDS virus."

In September 1983 Gallo and Montagnier attended a conference at Cold Spring Harbor, where each presented his own research findings. Montagnier's experimental findings indicated that he had discovered a virus which was *clearly distinct* from Gallo's. Photographs of the LAV virus showed that it had a cone-shaped core and a new viral protein, P25, not present in either HTLV-I or HTLV-II. Montagnier was able to detect the LAV isolate in both lymphadenopathy and AIDS patients, and his preliminary blood test detected LAV antibodies in healthy homosexual males.

These results did not dissuade Gallo. His experimental findings indicated that his virus was, in fact, the cause of AIDS, and that

it did belong to the HTLV family of retroviruses. He provided photographs of a virus with a cylindrical core, similar to that of the HTLV-I virus, as well as the results of his preliminary blood tests.

In April 1984, at a press conference in Washington, D.C., Gallo announced that he had discovered the AIDS virus, which he named human T-cell lymphotropic virus type III (HTLV-III). This is where the story of the discovery of the AIDS virus would have ended were it not for one additional piece of information: Gallo turned out to be wrong. Evidence showing that the virus Gallo discovered was not closely related to HTLV-I or HTLV-II began to surface as early as 1985. In May 1986 a subcommittee of the International Committee on the Taxonomy of Viruses announced that the AIDS virus *was not* a member of the HTLV family, and renamed the virus Human Immunodeficiency Virus (HIV). It now appeared that Montagnier, whose work had been published a year before Gallo's but had largely been ignored by the scientific community, was correct.

Rights to the discovery of the AIDS virus now culminated in a heated priority dispute between Montagnier and Gallo. In December 1985 the Pasteur Institute filed a patent suit against Gallo with the U.S. Claims court, stating:

Montagnier and his colleagues were the *first* to discover the virus.

Empirical studies indicated that HTLV-III was, or was substantially identical to, LAV and therefore the samples supplied by the Pasteur Institute to the National Cancer Institute—under promises of confidentiality and noncommercialization—were used by Gallo to develop his blood test.

Therefore, the Pasteur Institute was entitled to some, if not all, of the royalties accrued by Gallo's test.

Translating these allegations into sociological terms, the French were saying that even though Gallo adhered to the institutionalized goal of science—the extension of knowledge—he had bypassed the normatively acceptable means. As we shall see, this imbalance between goals and means resulted in pathogenic consequences for science; once again, a negative notion of anomie. However, a closer examination of these allegations also reveals a desirable, positive concept of anomie.

THE NEGATIVE CONSEQUENCES OF ANOMIE

Sociologists have depicted the scientific community as being composed of a system of norms which define the expectations to which scientists are generally obliged to conform, because they are "procedurally efficient" and "they are believed to be right and good." [121] These norms are of two types: cognitive (technical) and social (moral). [122] Briefly stated, the cognitive norms are those which guide methodology and research procedures; they provide the relevant definition of knowledge. The social norms designate scientists' attitudes and behaviors in relation to their work and to one another; they provide a rationale for behavior. In trying to fulfill their roles, scientists often experience a certain amount of tension, or strain: they are expected to adhere to the cognitive and social norms, yet they are also expected to make original discoveries in an effort to extend the body of scientific knowledge. Both Montagnier and Gallo were aware of the other's attempt to discover the AIDS virus. As the competition between the two intensified, the emphasis gradually shifted *from* discovering the virus *to* being the first to make the discovery. This magnified the underlying strain of discovering the virus *within* the normative framework of science, since the accepted procedures (cognitive norms) for growing a retrovirus were of no use.

Several unintended, negative consequences resulted from this anomic environment. Gallo's insistence that the AIDS virus belonged to the HTLV group of human retroviruses deflected the work of others. His overcommitment to this hypothesis, indica-

ting a failure to abide by the norms of disinterestedness and emotional neutrality, was responsible for the delay in realizing the importance of Montagnier's work. Further, the blood test which was ultimately used to identify people with the virus was developed a year after Montagnier's discovery. This delay proved harmful to many patients who were transfused with infected blood from hospitals and blood banks.

One of the characteristics of the AIDS virus that scientists were able to uncover was its uncanny ability to transform itself—to change its genetic makeup. Several scientists who analyzed the genetic sequences of HTLV-III and LAV found that the two sequences were remarkably similar to one another. The findings of one report indicated that the differences between LAV and HTLV-III were *no greater* than the differences between the molecular clones of HTLV-III. [123] A great many scientists, including Montagnier, interpreted these findings in the following manner: Gallo did not take the necessary precautions in protecting against sample contamination. The LAV isolate, which was sent by the French to his laboratory, somehow contaminated his cultures. This contamination resulted in his growing the LAV virus and assuming it was HTLV-III.

In his 1984 landmark paper, the one in which HTLV-III was proclaimed to be the cause of AIDS, Gallo wanted to compare his virus with HTLV-I,II. He included a composite photograph of the three viruses at different stages of development. Two years later Gallo published a correction in the journal *Nature*, saying that the picture of HTLV-III was, in fact, a photograph of the LAV virus. [124] When questioned about this mistake, Gallo stated that the technicians who were responsible for photographing the viral samples had been careless, and that their carelessness had resulted in the wrong set of photographs being published in his paper. Yet one of the authors of that paper, Jörg Schüpbach, stated that it was purely Gallo's decision to include the composite set of photographs, and that his (Schüpbach's) draft did not originally include the photos.[125]

At the very least it can be said that Gallo did not properly supervise his research team. It can also be said that Gallo had been guilty of making "disreputable errors"—errors that are made when cognitive norms are abandoned.[126] As a result, a climate of distrust developed between the two research laboratories, and scientists lost a year in the quest for the AIDS virus.

SCIENTIFIC DISCOVERY AND THE POSITIVE ROLE OF ANOMIE

It can be said that science comprises both a private and a public phase. Once scientists make their research findings known, via publication or presentation at scientific meetings, this knowledge enters the public domain and is judged according to cognitive and social norms. During this public phase we have seen that failure to abide by these norms (anomie) results in pathogenic consequences for science. The precursor of this phase is the discovery period, which consists of hunches, instincts, guesses, and incomplete research. During this phase scientists are permitted a great deal of relative autonomy and personal freedom—freedom to replace strict universalistic norms with more flexible individualistic ones, making it possible for them to use their intuition and imagination freely.

Gallo and Montagnier each believed that a retrovirus was responsible for AIDS, but they could not specify the precise retrovirus, HTLV-III or LAV. To further complicate this task, the accepted procedures for growing retroviruses were of little use in this instance because this virus used a different mechanism for replication.

Aware that the solution to this problem could only be achieved through the use of specific chemical reagents, both scientists concentrated their efforts on growing the virus in large quantities. As a result, Gallo's colleague, Mikulas Popovic, elected to use an unorthodox procedure to grow the AIDS virus. Popovic was able to identify a cell line that could be infected with the AIDS virus and that resisted being killed. The next step was to inject this cell line with blood sera from people infected with AIDS. Popovic replaced the cognitive norm which called for the sera to be as pure as possible with a flexible, individualist norm; he pooled sera from ten different AIDS patients and inoculated the cell line with this pool. As a result, Gallo and his colleagues were the first to develop a cell line in which researchers could grow the AIDS virus. While it is true that Gallo did not correctly classify the AIDS virus, he did make a contribution to science: he provided new, useful techniques for growing retroviruses.

CONCLUSIONS

Using the discovery of the AIDS virus as our case study, we have attempted to identify both the positive and negative qualities of anomie. Although the two are inextricably linked, a vast majority of sociological studies have focused on the negative consequences, thus neglecting the "bright side of anomie."[127] Future research should focus upon the social structural conditions under which anomie promotes desirable social goals, such as the advancement of science, and abets social change.

NOTES

1. Claude-Henri de Rouvroy, Comte de Saint-Simon, *Selected Selections*, ed. Arthur Tilley (Cambridge, Cambridge University Press, 1920).

2. Auguste Comte, *The Positive Philosophy*, trans. Harriet Martineau (London, G. Bell, 1896).

3. Ernest Renan, *The Future of Science*, 1890; cited in Robert A. Nisbet, *The Sociology of Émile Durkheim* (New York: Oxford University Press, 1974), p. 28.

4. Numa Denis Fustel de Coulanges, *The Ancient City* (New York: Penguin Books, 1971).

5. Harry Liebersohn, *Fate and Utopia in German Sociology* (Cambridge, Mass.: MIT Press, 1988).

6. Ibid.

7. Émile Durkheim, "Review of Albert Schäffle: *Bau und Leben des Socialen Körpers*." For a discussion of this review, see Anthony Giddens, *Capitalism and Modern Social Theory* (Cambridge, Cambridge University Press, 1971), p. 67.

8. Émile Durkheim, *The Division of Labor in Society*, trans. George Simpson (New York: Free Press, 1964); comments in Giddens, *Capitalism and Modern Social Theory*, p. 76. (See also n. 49 on p. 76.)

9. For a discussion of Durkheim's concept, the *forced division of labor*, see Giddens, *Capitalism and Modern Social Theory*, p. 80.

10. Ibid.

11. Jeremy Bentham, *Utilitarianism* (New York: Harper Torch Classics, 1963).

12. James Mill, *Elements of Political Economy* (London, Henry Bohn, 1844).

13. Thomas Hobbes, *Leviathan* (New York: Penguin Classics, 1951).

14. John Locke, *On Civil Government* (New York: Penguin Classics, 1951).

15. Herbert Spencer, *On Social Evolution* (Chicago: University of Chicago Press, 1972).

16. For a discussion of Durkheim's relation to Maistre, Bonald, and other French conservative thinkers, see Nisbet, *Sociology of Émile Durkheim*.

17. For an analysis of Simmel's sociology of interaction, see Liebersohn, *Fate and Utopia in German Sociology*.

18. Ibid.

19. Bentham and Mill described utilitarianism in a way rejected by Durkheim.

20. Nisbet, *Sociology of Émile Durkheim*, pp. 32–33.

21. Ibid., p. 34.

22. Altruistic suicide does occur, however, even in modern societies, for example, in Japan during World War II and in the United States today, as manifested in certain teen suicides and in cult suicides.

23. Nisbet, *Sociology of Émile Durkheim*, p. 35.

24. Herbert Spencer, *On Social Evolution*.

25. Albert Schäffle, in Giddens, p. 67.

26. See Edward O. Wilson, *Sociology: The New Synthesis* (Cambridge, Mass.: Harvard University Press, 1975); "Human Decency Is Animal," *New York Times Magazine* section, October 12, 1975, pp. 36–37, 47–50; "Sociobiology: A New Approach to Understanding the Basis of Human Nature," *New Scientist*, May 13, 1976, pp. 342–44; *On Human Nature* (Cambridge, Mass.: Harvard University Press, 1978); and "What Is Sociobiology?" *Society* 15/6 (September/October 1978), pp. 10–14.

27. Comte, *Positive Philosophy*.

28. Ibid.

29. Nisbet, *Sociology of Émile Durkheim*, p. 47.

30. Giddens, *Capitalism and Modern Social Theory*, p. 89.

31. Ibid.

32. Nisbet, *Sociology of Émile Durkheim*, p. 48.

33. Ibid., p. 49.

34. Émile Durkheim, *The Rules of Sociological Method*.

35. Durkheim, *Suicide: A Study in Sociology*, trans. John A. Spaulding and George Simpson, ed. George Simpson (New York: Free Press, 1951).

36. Durkheim, *The Elementary Forms of Religious Life*, trans. Joseph Ward Swain (New York: Free Press, 1965).

37. Durkheim, *The Division of Labor*, trans. George Simpson (New York: Free Press, 1964).

38. See the Introduction to this volume.

39. Giddens, *Capitalism and Modern Social Theory*, p. 90.

40. For Schäffle, see ibid., pp. 67–68.

41. Ibid.

42. Herbert Spencer, *The Evolution of Society* (Chicago: University of Chicago Press, 1967).

43. Giddens, *Capitalism and Modern Social Theory*, p. 66.

44. Nisbet, *Sociology of Émile Durkheim*, p. 67.

45. Ibid., p. 68.

46. Giddens, *Capitalism and Modern Social Theory*, p. 93.

47. Nisbet, *Sociology of Émile Durkheim*, p. 70.

48. Ibid., p. 71.

49. Ibid.

50. Ibid.

51. For Weber's theory of civilizational uniqueness, see Essay 3 in this volume, "Max Weber, the Modern World, and Modern Sociology" by Ronald M. Glassman.

52. Nisbet, *Sociology of Émile Durkheim*, p. 7.

53. See Max Weber on the ideal type in *The*

Methodology of the Social Sciences (New York: Free Press, 1968).

54. Nisbet, *Sociology of Émile Durkheim*, p. 71.

55. See coverage of Tönnies, in Liebersohn, *Fate and Utopia*.

56. Ibid. See the chapters on Tönnies and Troeltsch.

57. Heinrich von Treitschke, *German Destiny*, trans. Adolph Hausrath (New York: Putnam & Sons, 1914).

58. Friedrich Wilhelm Nietszche, *The Complete Works*, trans. Oscar Levy (New York: Macmillan, 1911).

59. Giddens, *Capitalism and Modern Social Theory*, p. 76.

60. Nisbet discusses this problem throughout his analysis.

61. Giddens, *Capitalism and Modern Social Theory*, p. 77.

62. Jean Paul Sartre popularized the concept that "God is dead"—we are all alone, therefore, in the universe. See Sartre, *Being and Nothingness* (New York: Penguin Classics, 1953).

63. Robert K. Merton, "Social Structure and Anomie," in *Social Theory and Social Structure* (New York: Columbia University Press, 1951).

64. Ibid.

65. Giddens, *Capitalism and Modern Social Theory*, p. 107.

66. Ibid.

67. Ibid., pp. 111–12.

68. Ibid., p. 105.

69. Karl Marx, *The German Ideology* (New York: Foreign Language Press, 1953).

70. Giddens, *Capitalism and Modern Social Theory*, p. 114.

71. Steven Kalberg discussed strata as carriers of ideas (ideal interests), in Robert J. Antonio and Ronald M. Glassman, eds., *A Weber-Marx Dialogue* (Lawrence, Kans.: University Press of Kansas, 1986).

72. Max Weber, *The Sociology of Religion* (New York: Oxford University Press, 1972).

73. Max Weber, *The Protestant Ethic and Spirit of Capitalism*, trans. Talcott Parsons (New York: Harper & Row, 1951).

74. Nisbet, p. 36.

75. Nisbet, pp. 34–35.

76. Robert K. Merton analyzes role sets, in Lewis Coser and Bernard Rosenberg, *Sociological Theory* (New York: Free Press, 1960).

77. Nisbet, pp. 34–35.

78. Erving Goffman, *The Presentation of Self in Everyday Life* (Garden City, N.Y.: Doubleday, 1959) and *Asylums* (Chicago: Aldine Publishing, 1962).

79. Peter L. Berger, *Invitation to Sociology* (New York: Harper Torch Books, 1959). Berger discusses identity changes (alternations) and marriage as an antianomic institution.

80. Giddens, *Capitalism and Modern Social Theory*, p. 81.

81. Ibid.

82. Ibid., p. 80.

83. Ibid.

84. Ibid., p. 81.

85. Daniel Bell, *The Coming of Post Industrial Society* (New York: Basic Books, 1970).

86. Giddens, *Capitalism and Modern Social Theory*, p. 81.

87. Ibid., p. 80.

88. For an analysis of Tocqueville's antisocialist views, see Ronald M. Glassman, *Democracy and Equality* (New York: Praeger Publishers, 1989).

89. Giddens, *Capitalism and Modern Social Theory*, p. 80.

90. Aristotle, *Politics*, trans. Benjamin Jowett, in Richard McKeon, ed. *The Basic Works of Aristotle* (New York: Random House, 1941).

91. Nisbet rejects the organicism in Durkheim; see his chapter on the division of labor in Nisbet, *Sociology of Émile Durkheim*.

92. For example, Ruth Benedict, *Patterns of Culture* (Boston: Houghton Mifflin, 1934).

93. See the discussion of Tocqueville in Glassman, *Democracy and Equality*.

94. Max Weber, "Science as a Vocation," in *From Max Weber*, trans. Hans Gerth and C. Wright Mills (Glencoe, Ill.: Free Press, 1963).

95. Glassman, *Democracy and Equality*.

96. Among the German philosophers who discussed the state, see Hegel, *The Philosophy of Right*; Johann Gottlieb Fichte, *The Fatherland and the State*; and various works of von Treitszchke.

97. Liebersohn, *Fate and Utopia*.

98. Jean Jacques Rousseau, *The Social Contract* (New York: Penguin Books, 1949).

99. Nisbet, pp. 128–31.

100. See Robert Dahl, *Who Governs?* (New Haven, Conn.: Yale University Press, 1959).

101. John Kenneth Galbraith, *The Affluent Society* (Boston: Little, Brown, 1958). Galbraith popularized the concept of countervailing power.

102. Giddens, *Capitalism and Modern Social Theory*, p. 103.

103. Ibid.

104. Ibid., p. 104.

105. See Giddens, *Capitalism and Modern Social Theory*, p. 70, n. 26.

106. Ronald M. Glassman, *Democracy and Despotism in Primitive Societies* (Millwood, N.Y.: Associated Faculty Press, 1985).

107. In his book, *Anomie: History and Meaning* (London: Allen & Unwin, 1988), the sociologist Marco Orrú states that it was the French philosopher Marie Jean Guyau who first used the term *anomie* in his books, *Esquisse d'une morale sans obligation ni sanction* (Paris: Fayard, 1879) and *L'Irréligion de l'avenir: Étude sociologique* (Paris: Alcan, 1887).

108. Émile Durkheim, *The Division of Labor in Society* (New York: Free Press, 1933), p. 181.

109. Ibid., p. 431, n. 21.

110. Ibid.

111. Robert K. Merton, "Social Structure and Anomie: Continuities," in Merton, *Social Theory and Social Structure* (Glencoe, Ill.: Free Press, 1957), p. 176.

112. Robert K. Merton, "Social Structure and Anomie," in Merton, *Social Theory and Social Structure* (New York: Free Press, 1968), p. 186.

113. Ibid., p. 188.

114. According to Merton's typology of reactions to the discrepancy between the goals and the norms regulating means, individuals who accept the goal of success but reject the norms governing the means are innovators. See Merton, *Social Theory and Social Structure*, p. 194.

115. Robert K. Merton, "Priorities in Scientific Discoveries" (1957), reprinted in Robert K. Merton, *Sociology of Science*, ed. Norman W. Storer (Chicago: University of Chicago Press, 1973), Chap. 14.

116. Robert K. Merton, "Anomie, Anomia, and Social Interaction," in Marshall Clinard, ed., *Anomie and Deviant Behavior* (New York: Free Press, 1964), p. 224.

117. Durkheim, *Division of Labor in Society*, p. 362, emphasis added.

118. Ibid., emphasis added.

119. M. S. Gottlieb et al., "Pneumocystis Carinii Pneumonia and Mucosal Candidiasis in Previously Healthy Homosexual Men: Evidence of a New Acquired Immunodeficiency," *New England Journal of Medicine* 305, no. 24 (1981), p. 1425.

120. Robert C. Gallo, "The AIDS Virus," *Scientific American* 256, no. 1 (January 1987), pp. 48–49.

121. Robert K. Merton, "The Normative Structure of Science," in Merton, *Sociology of Science*, p. 270.

122. For a complete definition of these norms, see Merton, *Sociology of Science*, pp. 223–78; Bernard Barber, *Science and the Social Order* (New York: Collier Books, 1962).

123. A. B. Rabson and M. A. Martin, "Molecular Organization of the AIDS retrovirus," *Cell* 40 (March 1985), p. 479.

124. Steve Connor, "The Virus Reveals the Naked Truth," *New Scientist*, February 12, 1987, p. 57.

125. Jörg Schüpbach, *Nature* (scientific correspondence) 321, May 8, 1986, pp. 119–20.

126. Harriet Zuckerman, "Deviant Behavior and Social Control in Science," in E. Sagarin, ed., *Deviance and Social Change* (Beverly Hills, Calif.: Sage Publications, 1977), p. 112.

127. Marco Orrú, "The Bright Side of Anomie." (Paper presented at the 1988 American Sociological Association Meeting in Atlanta, Georgia.)

Marxian sociologists identify opportunities for the elimination of injustice and inequality through the analysis of class and class conflict. Four themes are present in all strands of contemporary Marxism: dialectics, historical materialism, capitalism, and communism. The dialectical nature of social reality can be seen in incompatible elements in social relationships. These contradictions continuously lead to social change, and even change in the processes of change itself. The goal of dialectics is the discovery of a law of motion through which a given society can be transformed.

Historical materialism views production as a necessary condition of human existence consisting of two elements: (1) the forces of production, including factors which affect technical efficiency; and (2) the social relations of production, or the ways in which people organize the use of tools and labor and take care of the disposition of goods. The mode of production of a society places limits upon the nature of other social relations, but does not directly specify their content.

Human history, then, is a complex sequence of evolution and revolution in which the forces of production outgrow existing social relations in an evolutionary pattern. This is followed by a revolutionary period in which social relations are transformed. A succession of such transformations take place until ultimately a social form will be achieved in which class divisions will disappear.

More than a method for critically analyzing society, Marxism contains a vision of a future society in which human needs will be met. The irrationalities of capitalism (insecurity, poverty, waste, etc.) will be eliminated through rational planning of the use of productive resources. A new form of personal freedom will be created based on the elimination of competitive individualism and the traditional division of labor. All persons will have the ability to engage in personal self-development, an activity heretofore restricted to a privileged elite.

The essay concludes with an analysis of the Russian Revolution critically based on Leon Trotsky's work. Revolutionary leadership and the class basis of the Russian Revolution, which left contradictions between the peasantry and the proletariat unresolved, demonstrate the possibilities and perils in moving from capitalism to communism.

Tom Mayer

ON MARXISM

AN INTERPRETATION OF MARXISM

What is Marxism? At first glance this does not appear to be an overly difficult question. Karl Marx and Friedrich Engels, after all, were usually lucid writers who left a large corpus of written work. Followers have extrapolated most, if not all, the themes found in the work of the founders, and a mountain of secondary literature exists. Nevertheless, this is a haunted question that remains alive.

Marxism, whatever else it may be, is a potent force in the modern world. An interpretation of Marxism is not merely an academic task. It is also a political action which can either strengthen or weaken Marxism as a social force; consequently interpretations of Marxism evoke the full range of feelings associated with any controversial political action. This irreducible partisanship does not vitiate the scientific value of Marxist thought or prove that Marxism is really a species of religion. On the contrary, it indicates the continuing capacity of Marxist analysis to address the central political and economic conflicts of our time. Interpretations of these conflicts inevitably reflect a person's location in social structure and historical time.

Having mentioned the irreducible partisanship of Marxism and interpretations of Marxism, let me now—in proper dialectical fashion—make the opposite (or almost the opposite) point. Intellectual discourse on Marxism need not bifurcate into worlds of pro and con. Some disagreement will be unavoidable in the sense just mentioned, but some will not. Some disagreement over the nature of Marxism will be what Herbert Marcuse called surplus conflict, that is, conflict not necessitated by the real structure of opposing interests. Intellectual discourse on Marxism may reasonably hope to reduce such surplus conflict and by so doing sharpen our understanding of which disagreements are fundamental and why. The reality of conflict, moreover, should not give license to unrestrained intellectual warfare provoking rhetorical excesses on all parts, and further obfuscating the question of what Marxism is.

The interpretations I find most congenial stress the dynamic unfolding nature of Marxism, portraying it as a process, a method, or a form of theoretical practice rather than as a fixed doctrine. Georg Lukacs, writing in the aftermath of World War I and the Russian Revolution, developed such an interpretation in his famous essay "What is Orthodox Marxism?":

Let us assume for the sake of argument that recent research had disproved once and for all every one of Marx's individual theses. Even if this were to be proved, every serious "orthodox" Marxist would still be able to accept all such modern findings without reservation and hence dismiss all of Marx's theses *in toto*—without having to renounce his orthodoxy for a single moment. Orthodox Marxism, therefore, does not imply the uncritical acceptance of the results of Marx's investigations. It is not the "belief" in this or that thesis, nor the exegesis of a "sacred" book. On the contrary, orthodoxy refers exclusively to the *method*. It is the scientific conviction that dialectical materialism is the road to truth and that its methods can be developed, expanded and deepened only along the lines laid down by its founders. It is the conviction, moreover, that all attempts to surpass or "improve" it have led and must lead to over-simplification, triviality and eclecticism[1] (author's italics).

Paul Baran expressed a somewhat similar understanding of Marxism in a 1958 article occasioned by the discouragement felt by many Marxists over the absence of a socialist-oriented labor movement in the United States:

Contrary to widespread opinion, Marxism is not and never was intended to be a "positive science," an assortment of statements about past and present facts, or a set of predictions about the shape and timing of future events. It was always an intellectual attitude, or a way of thought, a philosophical position and fundamental principle of which is continuous, systematic, and comprehensive *confrontation of reality with reason*...while uncompromisingly committed to the principle of confronting reality with reason, while convinced that this confrontation represents the indispensable basis of all humanist thought and the only valid guidepost for meaningful human activity, Marxism by no means implies a dogmatic finding as to what defines reason or what constitutes reality at any given time. To Marxism the meaning of reason and the nature of reality are closely interwoven, inseparable aspects of historical development. In terms of the *long run*, of the entire historical process, the content and the injunctions of reason are relative. They change with the changing forces of production, they enrich themselves with the expansion of our knowledge....Yet it is crucially important to realize that this relativity of the content of reason holds only in the longest run. In the *short run*, in any given historical period, what constitutes reason is *approximately* ascertainable. The determining factors are the level of social development, society's achieved fund of scientific insight, the accumulated wealth of practical human experience[2] (author's italics).

I interpret Marxism as an intellectual process which tries to unify scientific analysis and emancipatory social movements for the purpose of revolutionizing human society. The emancipatory component of Marxism is primary. It derives from recognition that societies are class-divided, and that overt or subterranean class conflicts account for the fundamental dynamics of the social order. Social life is inundated by systematic forms of injustice and inequality, but also by movements which in various ways struggle against oppression. Indignation at injustice as well as hopefulness about prospects of improving the human condition are both characteristic features of the Marxist intellectual process.

The scientific aspect of Marxism represents recognition that scientific procedures can produce reliable knowledge, that society itself can be the subject of scientific inquiry, and that reliable knowledge is mandatory for comprehending the realistic opportunities available for eliminating injustice and inequality.

Marxism is revolutionary because it regards culture and social structure as an integrated totality, rendering futile efforts at transforming specific institutions without reconstructing the social totality in which they lie embedded. Marxism is revolutionary because eliminating injustice and inequality means eliminating salient class privileges, something which simply will not transpire in the absence of intense social struggle. And Marxism is revolutionary because social classes can be emancipated only if they participate in their own emancipation. A liberation from above preserves the nexus of inequality, and thus would not be a real emancipation.

The intellectual process I call Marxism undergoes continual self-revision because its three components (i.e., emancipatory social movements, scientific analysis, and social revolution) and the relations among them continually change. The character of emancipatory social movements and the kinds of emancipation they seek shift as old movements are victorious, defeated, or neither; and new movements resisting different forms of oppression appear on the historical scene. Science, if it exists at all, is inherently dynamic, generating new empirical discoveries and new theoretical propositions. Relevant scientific advances must be appropriated by Marxism, and the appropriation advances the process of self-revision. Likewise the meaning and nature of revolution changes both in response to the experience of past revolutions and from mutations in the movements propelling revolutionary transformation.

But despite its continual self-revision, Marxism retains an essential identity as a process uniting science and social movements in the service of revolution. Specific conjectures made at specific stages of its social existence may be disproven, but while class oppressions continue to exist and while scientific methods can still produce reliable knowledge useful for revolutionary struggles, then Marxism, understood in this sense, will surely not be superseded or abandoned.

Part of the reluctance to accept this particular interpretation of Marxism springs from the name itself. Marxism is a rather poor name for the process we have been describing. It suggests an inalienable commitment to the ideas of Marx and Engels. The name *scientific socialism* better captures the jointly analytic and revolutionary spirit of the enterprise. Yet *Marxism* remains the designation generally used, and changing titles in midstream would probably sow more confusion than clarity.

This quibble about names does raise some important questions. The interpretation of Marxism offered above lacks substantive content. What is its relationship to the specific ideas put forward by Marx and Engels? To what positions does Marxism, at its present stage of development, actually subscribe?

Marx and Engels remain permanently established as the founders and first great practitioners of the intellectual process we have outlined. On an empirical and even on a theoretical level much of their work has been superseded, but on what we shall call a metatheoretical level, it still dominates Marxism. Robert Heilbroner identifies four premises which characterize all varieties of contemporary Marxism: a dialectical approach to knowledge, a materialist interpretation of history, a general view of capitalism which starts from the analysis of Marx, and a commitment to socialism.[3] It will be convenient to discuss the relationship between Marx and modern Marxism as well as the content of the latter using these general headings.

DIALECTICS

The mist and obscurity shrouding the entire subject of dialectics tempts one to repudiate the entire conception. The philosophy of dialectics, however, expresses certain critical assumptions with which Marxism approaches social reality, and is in fact one of its most durable aspects. Moreover, dialectics can be formulated in a way that eliminates or at least minimizes the mystical aura.

Reality is a process of change. This is the

simplest and most fundamental idea of dialectics. Society is in motion, and any satisfactory social theory must analyze its movement. Equilibrium theories, because they largely ignore the process of change, can only give superficial and highly transitory representations of social reality. To be sure, society sometimes gives the appearance of static immobility, but this is only an appearance. The task of scientific analysis is to penetrate the mask of immobility and reveal the social motion lying beneath. The process of change is itself changing, and therefore dialectics alerts its adherents to the notion of uneven development. Some Marxists regard uneven development as a universal law of human history.

A second and more subtle dialectical idea is an emphasis upon relationships rather than individuals. The identity of a social object is not determined by its individual properties, but by its relationships with other social entities. The husband is defined by the relationship to the wife; the ruler by the relationship to the subject; the capitalist by the relationship to the worker. Without wives, subjects, and workers there could be no husbands, rulers, and capitalists. Relationships constitute reality. Change relationships and you change not merely the external configurations of social objects, but also their fundamental identity and purpose.

An affinity exists between the dialectical concepts of change and relationship, and this affinity is expressed in a third major idea of dialectics, the notion of contradiction. The dialectical notion of contradiction is not logical contradiction. An insistence upon logical contradiction would eliminate the possibility of analytic reasoning, something Marxist dialecticians could not do without. Contradiction refers to the idea that social relationships contain opposing or incompatible forces. More exactly, it refers to a developmental process in which relationships spontaneously (that is, by virtue of their inner nature) generate forces incompatible with themselves, forces pushing toward the transformation of the very relationships by which they were constituted. This juxtaposition of spontaneous generation, incompatibility, and transformation is the heart of dialectical contradiction. For example, the relationship between slave and master might generate a tendency to use primitive but indestructible production tools—a tendency that hinders the efficiency of slave economies and ultimately eventuates in their disappearance. Or the relationship between the state and corporations under monopoly capitalism may result in a tendency toward military production that exhausts the resources of society, hinders technological advance in the civilian economy, and/or leads to war—all of which militates toward the transformation of monopoly capitalism.

"The truth is the whole." Hegel's famous dictum summarizes the viewpoint of totality, another essential part of dialectical philosophy. The viewpoint of totality arises as a natural consequence of the emphasis on relationships. Because relationships constitute social reality, segments of society remain incomprehensible when examined in isolation from the encompassing whole. A theory about the segment is not an approximation of the truth, but an essential distortion. What constitutes totality is not given in advance and cannot be determined on an a priori basis. An abstract universalism, imagining itself system-oriented merely because it deals with a multitude of factors each treated in a discrete, individualistic, essentially additive fashion, is of very little value. The concept of totality must be concrete. Its elements cannot be separable externally interacting units, but moments which achieve their meaning and identity from their participation in the totality. The concept of totality evolves continually as new relationships are comprehended. A scientific investigation must strive to attain the viewpoint of totality; otherwise it cannot be scientific. This does not mean that specialized investigations should not occur, but that the dialectical scientist must strive to locate the specialized topic within the totality and simultaneously search for traces of the latter within the former.

This leads directly to the final aspect of dialectics I shall touch upon. Dialectical philosophy understands science and scientific work in a special way. Social events are unique, being uniquely located in the process of historical time. Conventional hypothesis testing, a procedure which depends upon the aggregation of similar events, will therefore have limited value. The primary tasks of social science are to penetrate the veil of appearances (a veil reflecting commonsense—that is, ideological—understandings of events), to locate social events within the totality of social relationships, and to show how these events shape and are shaped by the fundamental movement of society.

The highest achievement of dialectical science is discovering the law of motion which underlies a particular social formation. A law of motion does not express itself mechanistically as an empirical regularity; the multiple determinations of social relations and the self-consciousness of social classes prevent any such direct correspondence. The law asserts itself as a structural tendency whose consequences can be temporarily averted by interventions of various kinds, but which continues exercising a tendentious force as long as the social relationship system from which it emanates remains intact.

The dialectical philosophy points toward history as the proper object of scientific concern. History is regarded as the concrete trace of social totality moving through time, embodying both the dialectical principle of motion and the practical resolution of the multiple determinations which affect society. By its seemingly endless wars, revolutions, famines, conquests, and discontinuities of every form, history provides ample testimony for the explanatory fruitfulness of the fundamental dialectical concept of contradiction.

Before we leave the subject of dialectics,

several questions require brief consideration. Why do we need a philosophy of dialectics? Why don't we discard the entire dialectical baggage as so much worthless rubbish? A major purpose of Marxism, as Paul Baran wrote in the passage quoted above, is to confront reality with reason. The constitution of a rational approach to reality requires a thoroughgoing consciousness regarding the procedures employed. The idea of approaching reality without prior assumptions may hold certain attractions, but it is fundamentally illusory, and actually imprisons the scholar within a passel of unrecognized and unchosen assumptions. Dialectics is simply the set of assumptions made by Marxists as a necessary ground for both their investigations of history and their subsequent efforts at confronting reality with reason. The dialectical assumptions seem to have considerable intuitive appeal. Their justification, however, must come not from intuition, but from a capacity to suggest productive historical investigations and illuminating confrontations between reason and reality.

HISTORICAL MATERIALISM

Dialectical philosophy is an epistemology. Historical materialism is a theory of history. Historical materialism uses dialectical concepts, but is surely not the only possible dialectical theory of history. To call historical materialism a theory of history may be misleading, because it is a highly general theory and not subject to verification in any simple way. It might better be described as a philosophy or a metatheory of history. Historical materialism provides an overarching framework for comprehending the whole of human history, plus suggestive guidelines for the construction of theories about specific social formations.

The process of material production is the foundation of all human societies. Here we have the central proposition of historical materialism. Note that the reference is to *production*—not to economics, not to exchange, not to consumption, not to markets, money, commerce, or any such thing. Note also that production figures as the *foundation* of all human societies, not as their origin, cause, or determining factor. These distinctions are important to an understanding of historical materialism. Production is the foundation of human society not from any inherent economic disposition of human nature, but because material production is a necessary condition of social existence.

The process of production has two general features: forces of production and relations of production. The forces of production include all those things which determine the technical efficiency of the production process, such as human skill, tools, knowledge, energy, land, etc. The relations of production refer to the social relations which govern the use of labor in production, and the disposition of the economic product. In the process of social development the forces of production may get out of whack with the relations of production, thereby generating a series of social crises. This happens, according to Marx and Engels, because the forces of production are inherently dynamic, forever thrusting (though at differential rates) in a forward direction, while the relations of production normally have a static character and can alter only with considerable difficulty. The static relations of production eventually slow down the development of the dynamic forces of production, and the resulting crisis can only be resolved by revolutionizing the relations of production. Modern Marxists tend to view this particular interpretation as overly schematic, but they still regard the contradiction between forces and relations of production as of signal importance.

What relationship exists between the activity of production and the remainder of social life? In the Marxist literature this issue is referred to as the base and superstructure problem—production being the base,

while law, politics, religion, family structure, etc., are the superstructure. To forestall a common misunderstanding, the relationship contemplated in this metaphor is not a simple one-way determination. The mode of production limits but does not uniquely determine the institutions of the superstructure. The superstructure, moreover, exerts influence on the production process because the latter is perpetuated over time, that is, reproduced through the activities of the superstructure. In order to analyze the complex relations between base and superstructure, some Marxists distinguish between *ultimate* and *determinant causation*. Determinant causation means capacity to determine the appropriation and use of social surplus, and in principle this can be exercised either by an institution of the base or by one of the superstructure. Under western European feudalism, for example, the political apparatus of society determined the appropriation and disposition of surplus, thus wielding determinant causation. Ultimate causation, on the other hand, means determination of how and by what social institution determinant causation shall be exercised; and ultimate causation is always situated within the base.

We cannot review the full range of Marxist thought on the relationship between base and superstructure. Some of the most interesting ideas on this topic have emerged in discussions on the Marxist theory of the state.[4] But our brief discussion should suffice to show that historical materialism is not intended as a species of economic determinism.

Social classes arise in the process of production. Actually this is just another way of saying that the production process creates definite social relations because relationships define classes. Much less obvious is the historical materialist contention that these structurally defined aggregates often acquire both a collective awareness and a political organization. Most surprising of all is the claim that the class struggle constitutes the underlying substance of history. This claim requires some explanation.

The cause of class conflict is not hard to find: differential wealth, power, status, and opportunity. While in the long run the relationship between classes may not be strictly zero-sum, over the short haul it very nearly is. The ubiquity of class conflict is more difficult to understand. Robert L. Heilbroner writes:

Occasionally the struggle is visible as a slave revolt or a peasant uprising. More often it is waged in mute contests over legal entitlements or economic prerogatives. It may indeed be almost completely disguised in the form of battles of ideas, or political or religious disputes, in which the immediate matters under debate conceal even from the protagonists themselves, the underlying theme of class opposition.[5]

But why should the class struggle be so general? The relationships constituted in the process of production have an enormous effect upon the lives of the people involved. To call these the fundamental social relationships is no rhetorical exaggeration. And for the reasons touched upon above, these relations are usually fraught with tension. It follows that the class relations, which are merely the collective expression of individual social relations, will wax tense and also be of fundamental significance in the determination of historical events. These primordial social strains (i.e., class conflicts) furnish the main agendas for law and politics, the issues that will concern writers and philosophers, the socialization tasks of educators and families, the practical impetus for priestly sermonizing, the control problems faced by the police and civil guard, the principal aims of foreign relations, not to mention the main managerial tasks within the productive enterprise. Class struggle is the substratum of history because production is the main business of humanity, and throughout history production has always been hierarchically organized and controlled.

The contradiction between forces and relations of production mentioned earlier is not enacted by disembodied social forces, but by antagonistic social classes whose conflict expresses the unresolved structural oppositions that exist within a given mode of production.

Historical materialism interprets history as a complex combination of evolution and revolution. The canonical pattern features a long evolutionary interval during which the forces of production outgrow the existing social relations and, as a corollary, class antagonism increases. There follows a revolutionary period when the relations of production are rapidly transformed. In the words of Marx:

At a certain stage of their development, the material productive forces of society come in conflict with the existing relations of production, or—what is but a legal expression for the same thing—with the property relations within which they have been at work hitherto. From forms of development of the productive forces these relations turn into their fetters. Then begins an epoch of social revolution. With the change of the economic foundation the entire immense superstructure is more or less rapidly transformed.[6]

Processes like this have generated a sequence of production modes which, by one reckoning, includes primitive communism, Asiatic despotism, slavery, feudalism, and capitalism. The culmination of this sequence, and in many respects the culmination of all previous human history, will be the emergence of a classless society. This will arrive in three stages: a brief dictatorship of the proletariat during which counterrevolutionary opposition to a classless society is defeated; a longer socialist stage featuring social ownership of the means of production, comprehensive economic planning, worker control of industry, and general extension of democratic rights; and finally a communist stage characterized by the disappearance (or radical transformation) of the division of labor, the elimination of market distribution in favor of direct appropriation, and the withering away of the state (whose existence is predicated upon the tensions arising in class-divided societies).

The historical materialist doctrines discussed in the last few paragraphs do not command general agreement from contemporary Marxists. Many see the interaction between forces and relations of production as more varied and complex than suggested by what we call the canonical pattern. The classical Marxist sequence of production modes is also disputed. Modern historical materialists view the sequence as multilinear rather than unilinear: not all societies pass through the same sequence of production modes. Moreover, there may be modes of production, in the past and in the future, not contemplated by the founders of Marxism. Quite a few Marxist scholars maintain that a new and previously unsuspected mode of production has arisen in the Soviet Union and other postrevolutionary societies.

Finally there is tremendous disagreement among Marxists about the emergence of a classless society. All Marxists remain committed to the general project of human emancipation, but many regard that part of historical materialism which postulates an inexorable thrust toward a classless society emerging directly from the contradictions of capitalism as a retreat into speculative philosophy. The notion that capitalism will be the last class-divided form of human society is no longer generally accepted by modern Marxists. Any further discussion on this important topic must be postponed until the section on socialism and communism.

CAPITALISM

The bulk of Marxist scholarship is concerned with the analysis of capitalism. Marxist analysis of capitalism has three general objectives: (a) to demonstrate that capitalism is an exploitative mode of production, (b) to discover the laws of capitalist development, and (c) to show how and why capitalism is a doomed system. We shall consider how Marxism tries to accomplish each of these objectives.

Capitalism has always had enemies who regarded it as an unjust and antihuman system. Marx differed from other enemies of capitalism by demonstrating, or trying to demonstrate, that capitalist exploitation was not a subjective value judgment but an objective fact which could be scientifically measured. His method of demonstration was both brilliant and audacious. Marx tried to show that the whole of capitalism—its inner tensions, its developmental tendencies, its pattern of exploitation—was implicit in the most elementary unit of capitalist production: the simple commodity. The analysis of any humble commodity would therefore unlock the secrets of capitalism, including its distinctive pattern of exploitation.

The key to understanding the Marxist theory of capitalist exploitation is the fetishism of commodities. Fetishism means the attribution of power to an object which that object does not really possess. Under capitalism all the powers of social labor are attributed to commodities. Human beings feel that their own existence is determined by the commodities which they themselves have created. The productivity of human beings working with physical equipment is treated as the productivity of capital. Commodities are thought to exchange because of their intrinsic attributes rather than because they are produced by human labor. Social relations in general take the form of relations between commodities.

One aspect of this fetishism of commodities is the treatment of human labor power as a mere commodity indistinguishable from any other, that is, obscuring and denying the unique capacity of labor to create new value, and assigning this capacity instead to capital. The difference between the value created by labor and the value of labor power—this difference being named surplus value—is one measure (but not the only measure) of capitalist exploitation.

The theory of surplus value as developed by Marx depends upon the labor theory of value, but Marx did not use the latter as a theory of relative prices. Instead, he used the labor theory of value as a theory of exploitation. He knew very well that commodities did not exchange in proportion to their embodied labor. This could not happen if capitalist social relations allowed every unit of capital to command an equal share of value. The creation of surplus value and the corresponding appropriation of value by capital both reveal the fetishism of commodities which flows from capitalist social relations.

Value, Marx maintained, emerged jointly from labor and nature. Nature's share in the production of value could be appropriated privately only through the intervention of some social relationship such as the private ownership of land. Produced means of production (e.g., physical equipment) were ultimately the result of this collaboration between nature and labor, and thus did not produce any value in addition to that engendered by labor and nature. Obviously Marx understood that laborers working with proper equipment could produce much more than laborers working without it. This difference merely reflected a change in the productivity of labor, namely, recognition that a sensible way of working involved first making the equipment and then using that equipment to produce the desired objects.

Capital is not physical equipment, or land, or minerals, or energy supplies, or anything of the sort. Capital is a social relationship which allows some people to possess means of production, to buy labor power, and then to own the commodities resulting from the production process (and along with them the new value created in production). Marx defined capital as a self-expanding value. This definition should not suggest that capital really produces value, only that the social relationship which puts capital into existence also allows it to appropriate surplus value disguised as value produced by capital.

Contemporary Marxists continue to regard capitalism as an exploitative mode of production, but some have chosen to abandon the labor theory of value (even as a theory of exploitation), and sidestep the seemingly unanswerable and irrelevant question of the production shares resulting from nature, labor, and capital. This tendency within Marxism has pursued the value analysis initiated by Piero Sraffa (with its concept of dated labor); it has frequently preferred the macroeconomic concept of surplus (roughly defined as difference between the value of the social product and the cost of producing it) to that of surplus value; and it has located capitalist exploitation in the relationship which gives possession of the results of production to the owners of capital, a relationship which creates and perpetuates enormous social inequality.[7]

The exploitivity of capitalism appears in many parts of the system which we have not yet mentioned. Consider the phenomenon of alienation, a fundamental aspect of wage labor under capitalism. Alienation exists because the wage laborer is compelled to give control over the laboring process to the capitalist, to give ownership of the product of his or her labor to this same capitalist, and to relate with other human beings mainly through the mediation of commodities. The wage worker is thus alienated from the labor process, alienated from the product of the labor, and alienated from fellow human beings. The social-psychological toll exacted by alienation upon the working class under capitalism remains to be determined.

Wage labor, bad as it may be, is preferable to unemployment. Yet unemployment under capitalism is utterly subordinated to the needs of capital. Work can be had only when it enables capital to earn a profit. This is but another example of the fetishism of commodities: the tyranny of human creations over human existence. Moreover, the capitalist mode of production is structurally constrained to maintain a substantial pool of unemployed people—the reserve army of labor—to prevent wage gains which might annihilate profits.

We turn now to the second major objective of Marxist analysis of capitalism—discovering the laws of capitalist development. The fundamental principle of capitalist development is the drive to accumulate capital. This drive arises from the competition of different capitals compelling each to expand on pain of extinction, and relatedly from the thirst for profits which pumps capital out of low-profit enterprises and into high-profit enterprises. The law of capital accumulation has a number of important consequences. It leads, for one thing, to a drastic expansion of commodity production as capital invades fields formerly given over to use-value production. This process continues down to the present as, for example, capital absorbs forms of economic activity previously carried on within the family.

Even more important, the law of capital accumulation propagates an unending series of technological revolutions through which the means of production are continually being transformed. Capitalism, claimed Marx, was by far the most dynamic mode of production the world had ever seen. Technological revolutions under capitalism are also stimulated by wage pressures which motivate the replacement of human labor by machines.

Yet another aspect of the accumulation process is the centralization of capital, by which the number of capitalist enterprises within a particular industry diminishes while the size of each surviving enterprise increases enormously. In the twentieth century centralization of capital occurs first and foremost as the emergence of giant corporations. Associated with the centraliza-

tion of capital is yet another expression of the capital accumulation principle, namely, the spread of capital over natural boundaries, which is sometimes called the internationalization of capital. The giant corporations just mentioned are multinational concerns, and the major financial institutions of advanced capitalism have long operated on an international basis.

The above conclusions which Marx drew from the law of capital accumulation—i.e., the expansion of commodity production, the technological revolution, the centralization of capital, and the spread of capital over national boundaries—have been brilliantly confirmed by the historical record. But these were not the only derivations made by Marx from the capital accumulation principle. Accumulation, he thought, would be accompanied by a fitful tendency for the rate of profit to fall because the volume of profit ultimately depended upon the amount of living labor used in the production process. But the main thrust of accumulation was to replace living labor by machines. The falling rate of profit, however, remained only a fitful tendency being partially negated by several important countertendencies which Marx dutifully pointed out.

Partly as a consequence of the falling rate of profit, capitalist accumulation could not proceed smoothly. It proceeded instead through an intermittent series of booms and crises, which together constituted the capitalist business cycle. In his treatise on *Marxist Economic Theory*, Ernest Mandel summarizes the capitalist business cycle in these words:

The cyclical movement of capital is...nothing but the mechanism through which the tendency of the average rate of profit to fall is realized. At the same time, it is the system's reaction to this fall, through the lowering of the value of capital during crises. Crises make possible the periodical adaptation of the amount of labor actually expended in the production of commodities to the amount of labor which is *socially necessary*, the individual value of commodities to their socially-determined value, the surplus-value contained in these commodities to the average rate of profit. Because capitalist production is not consciously planned and organized production, these adjustments take place not *a priori* but *a posteriori*. For this reason they necessitate violent shocks, the destruction of thousands of lives and enormous quantities of values and created wealth.[8]

Marx, it is fair to say, expected the capitalist economic cycle to become increasingly volatile, and this expectation has not come to pass. That capitalist accumulation proceeds in a cyclic rather than a monotonic manner, however, seems indisputable, and represents an enormously potent theoretical insight. We may take issue with the arguments by which Marx derived a falling rate of profit, but negative profit rates almost did in American capitalism during the Great Depression of the 1930s, and even enthusiasts for the capitalist system see insufficient profit rates as a continuing source of instability.

The weakest part of Marx's analysis of capitalist development lay in his treatment of labor income. Contrary to some claims, a theory of absolute impoverishment did not appear in the writings of Marx or Engels. They did predict, however, that labor would receive a declining share of the social product because of the encroachments of technology on the labor process, and because reductions in the relative share of labor helped combat the declining rate of profit. Long-term relative impoverishment of the working class has not been observed in any capitalist society for which adequate data are available. In fact, labor's share of the social product appears quite stable in almost all capitalist systems, a fact obviously germane to the absence of a revolutionary proletariat in advanced capitalist societies.

The nonexistence of a revolutionary proletariat is a major theoretical (not to say practical) problem for present-day Marxists, and has led to considerable rethinking of the Marx-Engels analysis of capitalist development. The rethinking has proceeded along three interrelated lines. One line investigates changes in the accumulation process occurring because capitalist markets are decreasingly competitive and increasingly monopolist.[9] A second line considers the relationship between the advanced center and the backward periphery of the capitalist system, analyzing accumulation as a world, not a national or even a continental, process.[10] A third line of inquiry examines the changes wrought by the increasing involvement of the state in the accumulation of capital.[11]

Before passing judgment on the classical Marxist theory of capital accumulation, we should remember its brilliant insights and recall that its main purpose was not predicting the future, but identifying the underlying laws of motion conceived as structural tendencies.

We may now consider the third and final objective of the Marxist analysis of capitalism: the demonstration of how and why capitalism is a doomed system. Much of the foregoing discussion bears upon this question simply because the doom of capitalism is a part—the terminating part—of capitalist development. The basic contradiction of the capitalist mode of production, from which all its major difficulties derive, is the contradiction between the intensely socialized cooperative form of the production process and the individualistic privatized way in which the results of production are appropriated. This is the capitalist form of the general contradiction between forces and relations of production postulated by historical materialism. The opposition between socialized production and privatized appropriation will eventually bring down the capitalist mode of production, provided, we must unfortunately add, it does not first eventuate in the common ruin of human civilization.

Upon this much most Marxists would agree. But regarding the specific manifestations of the production-appropriation contradiction, and the speed with which they will operate, great differences emerge. We have already discussed the falling rate of profit which may be seen as one manifestation of the basic contradiction. Another expression would be the anarchic conditions under which the totality of capitalist production and reproduction takes place. Under these conditions the various sectors of the capitalist economy will not generally produce in the proper proportions—some turning out too much, others not enough. Disproportionality can instigate a significant curtailment in capitalist production and thereby a major economic crisis.

The anarchy of capitalist production finds expression in many other forms of capitalist irrationality, such as the enormous resources wasted upon advertising and sales promotion or, far more ominously, in the cancerous expansion of weapons production for the military.

Still another manifestation of the socialized production-privatized appropriation contradiction is the underconsumption-overinvestment syndrome characteristic of mature capitalism. This arises essentially because capitalism expands the power of production far more rapidly than it expands the ability of the masses to consume. The consequence is the production of large quantities of unsalable goods and subsequent unemployment on a massive scale.

Whatever objective contradictions capitalism may have, whatever crisis they may induce, and whatever hardships they may visit upon the masses, still capitalism will not be overthrown unless there exists a class with the desire and capacity to overthrow it. Structural flaws alone cannot doom the capitalist system. Marx and Engels thought the process of capitalist development would create a revolutionary consciousness in the proletariat because wage labor brought workers together and established a cooperative organization among them, because the experience of production would demonstrate the power of the workers and the dispensability of capitalists and their henchmen, and because relative impoverishment plus alienated labor would impoverish the collective existence of the proletariat.

Yet aside from brief episodes under highly atypical circumstances, the proletariat in advanced capitalist countries has not acquired a revolutionary consciousness. Instead, the revolutionary initiative has devolved upon intellectuals and certain agrarian classes in countries of the capitalist periphery. Marxists have responded to these realities in various ways. Some anticipate that the next few waves of economic or political crisis will create a revolutionary consciousness and organization among the proletariat. Others think the revolutionary process in the Third World must be far advanced before serious revolutionary stirrings among the proletariat can be expected. Still others write off revolution in advanced capitalist countries as a romantic and ill-conceived fantasy. Capitalism they argue, will be transformed by methods other than armed revolution.

Modern Marxist scholarship continues to be preoccupied with the fate of capitalism, and continues to search for contradictions which will lead to its demise. James O'Connor proposes a fiscal crisis of the state, based upon the fiscal incapacity of the monopoly capitalist state to meet both its accumulation and its legitimation responsibilities.[12] Baran and Sweezy identify the incapacity to absorb a rising economic surplus as a major contradiction of late capitalism.[13] Arghiri Emmanuel hints that the termination of surplus transfers from periphery to center might put the proletariat of center capitalist social formations in a mood to revolt.[14] The logic of capitalism, suggests G. A. Cohen, automatically translates productivity gains into increased consumption rather than freedom from oppressive labor, thus making a balanced human existence impossible.[15]

The Marxist preoccupation with capitalism is not fortuitous. Marxism and modern industrial capitalism reached maturity at about the same time. They remain connected by an inner symbiosis, by a true unity of opposites.

As long as capitalism lasts, as long as men live under an irrational social order, Marxism can neither be discarded or refuted. For Marxism is nothing if not a powerful magnifying glass under which the irrationality of the capitalist system protrudes in all of its monstrous forms. Marxism will have outlived itself only when it has reached the end of its historical journey: when the confrontation of reality with reason has become redundant because reality will be governed by reason.[16]

COMMUNISM

In the first section of this paper, I interpreted Marxism as an intellectual process which tries to unify scientific analysis and emancipatory social movements for the purpose of revolutionizing human society. A major difference between Marxism and other perspectives on society lies in its vision of a higher, more rational form of social organization, and the concomitant effort of Marxism to constitute itself as a practical force for the attainment of this new society.

Why do Marxists regard communism—and here we speak of communism as a Marxist concept, not of existing Communist societies—as a superior form of social organization? The answer may be summarized under two headings: rationality and freedom. Capitalism developed enormously powerful forces of production, but was unable to establish rational control over its protean powers of production. Consequently the forces of production dominated humanity, and irrationalities of the worst kind proliferated under capitalism: enormous inequality, perpetual economic insecurity, poverty in the midst of plenty, unemployment, waste, harmful consumption, destruction of the environment, fascism, warfare, and preparation to annihilate the planet—the list could easily be extended. Communism will be the first form of human society in which the forces of production are sufficiently developed to satisfy human needs, and in which associated humanity can rationally control its productive powers so that they will easily and adequately fulfill human requirements. The tail of production will no longer wag—

and abuse by wagging—the body of humanity. As Marx wrote in a famous passage from his 1875 "Critique of the Gotha Program":

In a higher phase of communist society, after the tyrannical subordination of individuals according to the distribution of labor and thereby also the distinction between manual and intellectual work, have disappeared, after labor has become not merely a means to live but is in itself the first necessity of living, after the powers of production have also increased and all the springs of cooperative wealth are gushing more freely together with the all-round development of the individual, then and then only can the narrow bourgeois horizon of rights be left far behind and society will inscribe on its banner: "From each according to his capacity, to each according to his need." [17]

The main reason for the greater rationality of communist society lies in its capacity to plan production, but this source of rationality is supplemented by several others. The absence of class inequality will eliminate the need for domestic repression, and transcendence of the nation-state system will eliminate any stimulus toward international violence. Work, being creative self-expression rather than alienated labor, will not require coercion or special economic inducement. Individuals will feel a strong sense of identification with the community, and will eagerly fulfill their responsibilities toward it—as eagerly as they now pursue their private interests.

Rationality shades into freedom. Communism, as conceived by Marxists, entails a quantum leap forward in human freedom. The unfreedom of economic insecurity is totally abolished during the lower or socialist phase of collectivist society. Likewise the social and psychological barriers between people erected by competitive individualism will gradually disappear, and in their place will arise a new sense of community. Dismantled will be the tormenting prison of private ambition, which thrusts human beings into antagonistic and inwardly frustrating personal relations. At the same time communist society will witness a great flowering of personal development, which no longer becomes the province of a privileged minority, but the birthright of every person.

Nowhere is the quantitative extension of human freedom made possible by communist social relations more evident than in the realm of work. Work has always had a dual nature: on the one hand, it has been the curse of Adam, the daily renewed province of tedious burdensome necessity, the finite eternity painfully endured for the sake of survival and for the paltry compensation of unwork; on the other hand, it has also been the most exhilarating and exalting of human activities, the true means of self-realization. Throughout history most humans have experienced the former aspect of work, but a few in every age have known the latter, usually responding with a voracious enthusiasm for productive labor. By abolishing the traditional division of labor; by transforming the labor process so that its guiding principle is no longer efficiency in the fabrication of lifeless objects, but efficiency in the inducement of creative involvement by workers; by encouraging each person to develop manifold productive capabilities; and by rendering transparent the relationship between each unit of labor and the welfare of the human community, communism metamorphizes work from the bane of human existence into its highest fulfillment.

Visions of this sort explain why Marxists regard communist society as infinitely preferable to capitalist society. But the euphoric ruminations of the last few paragraphs may be misleading. Marxists are generally reluctant to speculate much about the nature of a future communist society. Such contemplation abandons the solid ground of science in favor of idle fantasy. It also effaces the distinction between Marxism as a science dedicated to the attainment of communism and any number of utopian philosophies, which compensate for their own practical impotence by erecting mythological realms in the future.

The next question is of a more practical bent. How will communism come about? The general answer to this question is through the class struggle, through the revolutionary struggles of the proletariat conceived as a universal class embodying the interests and potentialities of all oppressed classes. Earlier we mentioned some of the processes the founders of Marxism thought would create revolutionary consciousness within the proletariat. The proletariat, however, could not expropriate surplus and become a ruling class by dominating some other social class. The class struggle of the proletariat, if successful, could only engender a fully classless society.

What will be the nature of the proletarian revolution? This has been one of the sorest points of the controversy within the Marxist fold. The poles of the controversy—between which we find virtually every gradation of opinion—have been first the position that proletarian revolution is necessarily a process of armed insurrection which violently destroys the capitalist state. In full opposition is the claim that the proletariat, as an overwhelming majority, could use the institutions of bourgeois democracy to accomplish the transition from capitalism to socialism. Whatever their views on this controversy, most Marxists have recognized the importance of intensive political organization as an essential instrument of the proletarian class struggle.

Also of vital importance are alliances with other classes or class fragments. Two classes deserve special mention in this connection: the peasantry and the intelligentsia. Wherever revolutionary movements have prospered, the intellectuals of both middle- and upper-class extraction have been among the leaders. Why this should be so, and what kind of support can be garnered from the intelligentsia as a whole, poses an interesting question of class analysis. Peasants have been a major, if not the major, motive force in virtually every modern anticapitalist revolution, which naturally raises the issue of how a revolution can be proletarian in character if agrarian social classes furnish the overwhelming bulk of its foot soldiers and adherents.

The entire issue of the transition from capitalism to socialism and communism is one of the least satisfactory (though most important) parts of Marxist theory. In this highly sensitive area moral indignation and hopes for the future become easily confounded with science (or with a realistic analysis of any kind). We mentioned earlier the failure of the proletariat in advanced capitalist societies to develop revolutionary consciousness, but this is only the tip of the iceberg. Marxism can make a strong claim to having demonstrated that capitalism has fatal flaws which will eventually cause its demise. Its claim to proving that socialism or communism will be the successor to capitalism is far weaker. There seem to be other forms of social organization which can arise on the ashes of capitalism, and the possibilities are by no means all attractive ones. The methods of historical materialism can be successfully applied to the analysis of post-capitalist society, but this will require a thoroughgoing purge of the wishful thinking and powerful political loyalties presently contaminating the investigations.[18] Class struggle under capitalism is more complex, even asymptotically more complex, than suggested by a straightforward model of bourgeoisie-proletariat polarization. This unanticipated complexity creates the possibility of historical outcomes other than socialism or communism.

Indeed, how should we view existing communist societies? What is the attitude of contemporary Marxism toward these postrevolutionary social formations? We should make plain to begin with that none of these societies vaguely resemble what Marxists have in mind by even the lowest form of socialist society, and most of them do not seem to be moving in the socialist direction. Things like Stalin's purges, or the Gulag Archipelago, or the genocidal ruralization of Cambodia, or the Soviet invasions of Hungary and Czechoslovakia are broadly regarded as atrocities against the very concept of an emancipated society. That there exists among Marxists tremendous diversity of opinion about existing communist societies should also be understood.

Yet despite the many oppressive features of existing communist societies, most Marxists regard them as profoundly progressive moments in the overall sweep of human history. Virtually all of these societies came into existence under extraordinarily adverse conditions, and their development has been severely handicapped by the almost unremitting—though not unexpected—hostility of the capitalist world. Communist revolutions have occurred not in modernized industrial circumstances but in backward, benighted, impoverished, foreign-dominated, and often war-torn countries. To expect that these revolutions could usher in emancipated, rational, free, classless societies would be utopianism of the kind Marxism has always opposed.

The real tasks assigned to communist revolutions by their location within the historical process are to accomplish those modernizations which capitalism would not bring about; to end the domination of Asia, Africa, and Latin America by Europe and North America; and to demonstrate the viability of comprehensive economic planning. The historical justification of communist revolutions will depend upon whether they can fulfill these tasks. At some point—and that point may already be upon us in the case of eastern Europe—the social relations of production in existing communist societies will impede the further development of the forces of production, and we may expect the onset of an epoch of social revolution. Historical materialists expect such future revolutions to move these societies from aggressive communism to emancipating communism.

What responsibility must Marxism bear for the oppressions which mar existing communist societies? A Marxist is tempted to respond by asking what responsibility

Christianity must have for the crusades, the Inquisition, the Thirty Years' War, the destruction of the aboriginal population in much of the Third World, the centuries-long slaughter of supposed witches, European imperialism, and the many other catastrophes with which it has been associated. But this would be a defensive and not a very useful response. Certain commissions and omissions within Marxist theory could indeed be related to oppressive behavior by its adherents. Marxism, for example, depicts capitalism as so horrible and communism as so consummately desirable that any actions which might conceivably lead from one to the other would seem justifiable. Marxism locates the source of human oppression in the economic structure of society, and Marxists are sometimes insufficiently aware that political power concentrated in the state can be an independent source of oppression. The idea that totalitarian accumulations of state power could infringe upon human freedom finds scant support within Marxist theory.

Humanity is viewed by Marxism not as an atomistic collection of individuals, but as a complex constellation of social relations. This preoccupation with the social rather than the individual, when combined with a characteristic focus on the main thrust of the historical process, renders Marxism relatively unconcerned about individuals who might dissent from or oppose this main thrust. No doubt this contributes to the unconcern with civil liberties which deforms existing communist societies.

While there exist a few authoritarian potentialities within Marxism, these are very much in the minority. The oppressive features of communist societies spring overwhelmingly from sources other than Marxism, which remains—despite errors, lacunae, dogmatism, and ideological distortions—the most comprehensive and penetrating system of thought ever dedicated to the attainment of human freedom. Today, more than a century after its origi-

nal promulgation, Marxism remains the watchword of progressive people all over the globe, people who are attracted to it precisely by their hatred of oppression and their passion for human emancipation. The Marxist conception of communism is an effort to reconcile the dream of a liberated society with the real political and economic levers at the disposal of a unified humanity. Whether a communist society is attainable or not, the struggle for its attainment remains a stirring signal of the depth and sincerity of the Marxist commitment to freedom.

A MARXIST ANALYSIS OF THE RUSSIAN REVOLUTION

There is no generally agreed upon way of doing Marxist analysis, and in any case the Marxist method could not be reduced to something resembling a formal algorithm. In the best Marxist scholarship we can detect four levels of analysis ranging from the abstract to the concrete: the *mode of production analysis*, the *social formation analysis*, the *world system analysis*, and the *conjunctural analysis*. Marxist scholars differ in the attention they give to each of these analytic levels (and in their manner of analysis), but some trace of each level appears in virtually every Marxist work that aspires toward being scientific. The concepts of class and class struggle penetrate all four analytic levels, but function somewhat differently at each one.

The mode of production analysis is the most abstract level of Marxist historical thought. The objects of investigation here are coherent integrated systems of economic production and surplus appropriation such as feudalism, capitalism, or socialism. This is the level at which Marxists try to formulate broad laws of social motion. These laws are not empirical generalizations because the theoretical models from which they derive are highly schematized representations of real human societies. The laws of motion emerging from the mode of production analysis express tendencies emanating from society's underlying socioeconomic structure. But, as we know, human societies are in constant transition. Besides a presently dominant mode of production, they may include remnants of earlier production modes, prefigurations of possible future production modes, auxiliary modes of production, and the like. Real societies exist as complex changing combinations of different production modes, and this gives rise to a new level of Marxist analysis: the social formation analysis. This examines not only the combination of production modes interacting within a given society, but also the complex institutional superstructure arising upon such a conglomerate foundation. While attentive to laws of motion formulated at the mode of production level, the social formation analysis has a different objective. It offers a realistic depiction of the class structure and the fundamental dynamics of the class struggle. This means specifying which classes exist, identifying their inherent interests, establishing the relations prevailing between classes, giving special attention to class conflicts and class alliances, and analyzing how the processes asserted by the laws of motion impinge upon class existence.

Social formations are less abstract objects than modes of production, but they do not exist in isolation. Social formations are imbedded within an international context which shapes their history and internal class relations. World system analysis considers a social formation from the perspective of its relations with other social formations and in the context of the world division of labor. It shows how class relations and class struggles are reconstituted through their location in the world system. The state can have a role in the mode of production and in the social formation analysis, but it becomes of central importance at the world system level because states are the crucial

intermediaries between social formations or, to put it differently, between the social formation and the world system form of Marxist analysis.

One final step remains in moving from abstract to concrete analytic forms. The three levels of analysis discussed so far concern generalities—increasingly complex generalities to be sure, but nevertheless generalities. These analytic forms do not refer to a specific moment in history. They may be, indeed they should be, helpful in comprehending specific historical moments, but they are not indissolubly linked with any such instant. And yet real history is the unfolding of particular moments, the sequence of concrete conjunctures. The conjunctural analysis bases itself upon the other three levels, but moves beyond them in striving to comprehend specific historical moments in all their particularism. Here the precise condition of class consciousness, the detailed morphology of class organization, the competency of class leadership all become decisive considerations. The conjunctural analysis may be characterized as the highest and the most concrete form of Marxist explanation.

Scientifically oriented Marxist scholarship attends to all four levels of analysis, but as a rule does not schematically separate these levels. The insights gained at one explanatory level condition the analysis undertaken at other levels, even though the explanatory objectives, the analytic premises, and the modes of reasoning may be distinct. Sometimes the four levels interact as a seamless web requiring exegetical hindsight to determine when one analytic mode leaves off and another begins. Certainly this is so for Leon Trotsky's masterful *The History of the Russian Revolution* which, though published over fifty years ago, remains an outstanding example of Marxist social analysis as well as a literary masterpiece.[19]

Many students of history—and not only Marxists—regard the Russian Revolution of 1917 as the decisive event of modern times.

For this reason and also because the Russian Revolution has been the subject of intense Marxist scrutiny, I shall illustrate the general properties of Marxist analysis using it as an example. In so doing, I shall use Trotsky's work as a general guide, but will not hesitate to advance alternative explanations if this improves the clarity, the accuracy, or the incisiveness of Marxist analysis.

The laws of history have nothing in common with a pedantic schematism. Unevenness, the most general law of the historic process, reveals itself most sharply and complexly in the destiny of the backward countries. Under the whip of external necessity their backward culture is compelled to make leaps. From the universal law of unevenness thus derives another law which, for lack of a better name, we may call the law of *combined development*—by which we mean a drawing together of the different stages of the journey, a combining of separate steps, an amalgam of archaic with more contemporary forms.[20]

This passage in the very first chapter of *The History of the Russian Revolution* outlines the most general interpretive principles used by Trotsky, principles roughly corresponding to our mode of production level analysis. The primary feature of prerevolutionary Russian history was its slow pace of development and the consequent economic, social, and cultural backwardness. Lying geographically between Europe and Asia, Russia's social and political institutions acquired forms intermediate to and vacillating between their Western and Eastern prototypes. Of no institution was this more true than the tsarist state, approaching in form an Asiatic despotism yet inserted within the European state system. The pressures emanating from this contradictory reality brought about a hypertrophy of the Russian state whose bureaucratic structure absorbed an outlandish share of the economic surplus, and whose bloated power stunted the autonomous development of the landed nobility.

The politically impotent nobility had little part in the daily conduct of agriculture and, within the constraints set by the tsarist autocracy, the peasant community exercised significant local autonomy. Consequently, peasants viewed economic exactions by the nobility as entirely parasitic, while the latter became ever more dependent upon the state to protect its class privileges. Existing in so beholden a relationship to the autocracy, the nobility was ill equipped to compel a reform of the state structure.

The languid rate of development and the associated meagerness of urban growth meant that Russian commerce from its very beginnings evolved so as to swell the wealth and influence of foreign economic interests. By the dawn of the present century, British, French, and German magnates controlled a very large share of Russian industrial and bank capital. Caught between the powerful capitalists of the West and the archaic but still formidable autocracy, and haunted by the specter of social revolution, the Russian bourgeoisie was incapable of significant political initiative. At every point of crisis it bowed to the demands of the tsarist bureaucracy or of foreign capital.

Without a democratic revolution abolishing tsarism and solving the land question, Russian society was doomed to stagnate. But the only class able to lead a democratic revolution was the youthful urban proletariat, and it could do so only with energetic support from the peasantry, which constituted in 1917 over 80 percent of the Russian population. The processes of uneven and combined development were exceptionally obvious in the making of the Russian proletariat. The late-starting Russian industry did not blindly retrace the history of Western industrial development. Quite the contrary, it jumped right onto the highest technical and organizational plane attained by the latter. Thus the Russian working class was born in large and technically advanced capitalist enterprises, and quickly attained advanced forms of social consciousness commensurate with its economic location.

Other circumstances also facilitated the

precocious political development of the proletariat. The speed and extremity of the transition from the backward countryside to modern industry radically invalidated previous social conceptions. The absence of intermediate layers between the bourgeoisie and proletariat rendered the conflict of class interests unmistakable while diminishing petty bourgeois ideologies which might muddle working-class consciousness. The economic struggles of the Russian proletariat ran smack into the mailed fist of autocratic repression, and automatically acquired a political dimension. These realities made the Russian proletariat much more susceptible to the appeals of revolutionary Marxism than the older working classes in the more highly developed Western capitalist societies.

Military defeats exacerbated the class tensions in Russian society by visiting terrible hardships upon the proletariat and peasantry, and by exposing the decadence and utter incompetence of the autocracy. The defeats sustained by the tsarist regime in the war with Japan helped precipitate the revolution of 1905, described by Trotsky as the prologue to the revolutions of 1917. The 1905 revolution exhibited the main ingredients of the subsequent uprisings—including soviets (workers' councils)—but the political organization of the proletariat remained unconsolidated, the alliance between workers and peasants insufficiently secured, and the tsarist military intact enough to carry out domestic repression. At a critical point liberal sectors of the propertied classes recoiled from the revolutionary process.

The collapse of the 1905 uprising and the repression which followed on its heels temporarily deflated the working-class movement. Yet the basic problems of Russian society remained utterly unresolved: class relations in the countryside festered, the performance of industrial labor occurred under barely tolerable conditions or worse, state structure stayed backward and dictatorial, illiteracy and superstition benighted

the masses. A new wave of strikes began in 1912 and by the first half of 1914 seemed mounting toward a crescendo.

Meanwhile, the world capitalist system was preparing a conflagration destined to consume over 8 million lives on battlefields alone and to eradicate the Romanov autocracy in the bargain. The roots of World War I should be sought, argued Lenin, in the nature of monopoly capitalism and the imperialist international relations arising from it. Monopoly capitalism vanquished competition and yielded immense concentration of capital. The giant enterprises characteristic of monopoly capitalism accumulated huge stocks of surplus capital requiring investment in order to earn a profit. But the monopoly structure of industry restricted the opportunities for domestic investment, forcing surplus capital abroad in search of profitable deployment. The competition eliminated within advanced capitalist countries reappeared on the international scene as surplus capital frantically vied for investment opportunities in every corner of the world. Capitalist states intervened in support of their bourgeoisie. Before long the entire world was divided up between the capitalist powers, with redivision possible only through military combat. The very dynamism of the world capitalist system in which old capitalist countries declined and new ones arose made war almost inevitable. Thus Germany, as an ascending capitalist power, sought to wrest a share of the imperial spoils from Britain and France.

World War I was fought for global domination. The backwardness of Russia disqualified it as a serious contender for world power, but it became entangled in the conflict because of its historic insertion within the European state system and because of its dependent relationship to French and British capital. The tsarist regime certainly had its own imperial objectives, but these were local in nature and puny in comparison with the larger imperial matters at issue. World War I pushed class tensions in

Russian society to the breaking point. An initial wave of patriotism quelled the strike movement raging prior to the war's outset. But backward Russia, despite its geographic immensity and demographic advantage, was no match for industrialized Germany. As defeat followed disastrous defeat, as casualties reached ghastly heights, opposition to the bloodletting replaced patriotic militarism. The strike movement started up again as workers protested against starvation, the draconian factory discipline, and the accelerating self-indulgence of the ruling class.

The massive military mobilization increased the interaction between the peasantry and the proletariat. Workers and peasants mingled in the army and in the factories of Moscow and Petrograd, where recruits from the countryside replaced laborers sent to the front. Increased interaction meant opportunity to reconcile differences in class outlook, and exposed sectors of the peasantry to the more advanced political consciousness of the proletariat. And of course military mobilization placed modern weapons in the hands of the masses.

The February Revolution of 1917, which felled tsarism, began on International Woman's Day in Petrograd as a spontaneous demonstration demanding bread. Over the course of five days it grew in magnitude until virtually all workers in the capital city went on strike, chaotic but exuberant demonstrations filled the main streets, the tsarist police were disarmed, political prisoners were released, and the rebellious masses had seized all public buildings. In tactical terms the critical issue of the February Revolution was whether the soldiers sent to repress the turbulent demonstrations would fire upon the striking workers as commanded by their officers or whether, recognizing their class affinity with the demonstrators, they would join the insurrection. When on February 27, 1917 (old style calendar), the Petrograd garrison broke discipline by

swinging over to the popular movement, the triumph of the revolution was assured.

The political energies of Russian society had long been focused on its capital which, as Trotsky puts it, "concentrated in itself the will of the nation." [21] Moscow and other cities followed the lead of Petrograd. After some delay partly caused by a communications lag, villages and the countryside joined the revolutionary tide. So advanced was the degeneration of the 300-year-old Romanov dynasty, and so out-of-step was it with the developmental imperatives of Russian society, that in the hour of its supreme crisis the monarchy could muster almost no defenders. Tsarism exited from history more precipitously than anyone thought possible.

Peasants in the guise of soldiers and the proletariat of Russia's major cities made the February Revolution. To the question of who led this phase of the revolution, Trotsky answers, "Conscious and tempered workers educated for the most part by the party of Lenin." [22] The bourgeoisie and the liberal intelligentsia made no significant contribution to overthrowing the autocracy. Nevertheless, the February Revolution installed a Provisional Government drawn from and representing the class interests of the bourgeoisie and liberal intelligentsia. It did so for essentially two reasons. The most militant and politically conscious sectors of the proletariat and peasantry took part in the actual insurrection. Although these activist layers were a minority of their respective classes, they could count upon the support of a large majority and derived their strength from this. Still the majority remained decidedly more cautious and politically backward than the activist minority. In the election and organizational work directly following the victory of the February Revolution, the weight of the moderate majority exceeded that of the radical militants.

While the revolutionary masses possessed shrewd political instincts—they despised the bourgeoisie, assimilating it to the landed nobility and tsarist bureaucracy—they still lacked theoretical or organizational sophistication, and could not differentiate effectively between the various socialist parties competing for their support. Despising the bourgeoisie, in the first blush of revolutionary democracy the proletariat and the peasantry nonetheless chose as their political representatives moderate socialists—Mensheviks and Socialist Revolutionaries—who conceptualized the entire upheaval as a bourgeois revolution and insisted upon handing power to the bourgeoisie.

The Provisional Government was bourgeois in composition and orientation. Its ministers feared the revolution and yearned to halt it before the propertied classes sustained further damage. Parallel to and sometimes in opposition with the Provisional Government, councils of workers and soldiers sprang up all over Russia. By their actions the masses showed they wanted the February Revolution to take up where the revolution of 1905 had left off. It was the soviet network and this alone which had the confidence of soldiers, workers, and later of the peasants. Although not fully appreciated at the time, the Provisional Government existed only on the sufferance of the soviets. The Petrograd Soviet—leading element of the soviet network—functioned more or less as an alternative government, and Trotsky refers to the interval between the February and October revolutions of 1917 as a period of dual power. During this interval the unresolved class struggle between bourgeoisie and landlords on the one hand and workers and peasants on the other expressed itself politically through the interaction of the Provisional Government and the soviets. On the morrow of the February Revolution Mensheviks and Socialist Revolutionaries supportive of bourgeois rule comprised the soviet leadership. But the cauldron of revolution would soon throw up a new configuration of class forces and with it a new soviet leadership decisively altering the relationship between the Provisional Government and the soviets.

The war and the land question proved to be the undoing of the Provisional Government. The landholding class had only shallow roots in the countryside. It relied heavily upon the tsarist state to defend its possessions against peasant claims. With the Romanov gendarme eliminated, land seizures broke out all over Russia as peasants demanded the soil withheld from them in the grudging half-hearted tsarist emancipation from serfdom. Not only did the Provisional Government condemn the peasant land seizures, it tried insofar as it could to reverse them, and to postpone any decision about the land until the convening of a Constituent Assembly when the war was over, at which time (the bourgeois ministers hoped) revolutionary tumult would have waned and the propertied classes recuperated. This combination of disapproval and procrastination set the Provisional Government at loggerheads with the burgeoning peasant movement. It also accelerated the formation of a viable peasant-proletariat alliance.

The insistence of the Provisional Government upon continuing Russia's participation in World War I had even more disastrous consequences. Some of the ministers coveted the territorial booty promised Russia in the event of an Entente victory. A more significant factor prompting continued participation was the long-term relationship between the Russian bourgeoisie and Western capital. The former needed the latter to finance the economic development of Russia—a dependent form of economic development to be sure—and to stiffen it against revolutionary assaults upon bourgeois property and power. The Provisional Government feared the political consequences of demobilizing millions of peasant soldiers trained in the use of arms, disillusioned by their subjection to a corrupt incompetent military apparatus, politically educated through their contacts with advanced workers in uniform, and vastly emboldened by the experience of the February Revolution. Unleashing an avalanche of politically volatile ex-soldiers upon the countryside would hugely increase the number of land seizures and visit general chaos upon rural Russia.

The bourgeoisie feared peace. It was therefore condemned to suffer the consequences of a hated, sanguinary, economically paralyzing war, which Russia could not hope to win. Instead of peace the Provisional Government under Alexandr Kerensky ordered another offensive, hoping thereby to bolster its declining prestige and distract the insurgent classes from the work of revolution. After some initial successes the June-July offensive suffered an overwhelming defeat weakening the already tenuous position of the Kerensky government, while strengthening the credibility of those political parties, particularly the Bolsheviks, who resolutely opposed the war.

A Marxist class analysis considers social classes and their interaction on three levels: the level of objective class location, the level of subjective class consciousness, and the level of class leadership. The first level—that of objective class location—refers to the analysis of objective class interests and relations to other classes. The level of subjective class consciousness refers to the present understandings of class members about their collective interests and possibilities for action. The level of leadership—the third component of Marxist class analysis—designates the capacity for class mobilization in a specific historical conjuncture, and the forms this mobilization will take. Subjective class consciousness is based upon objective class location but is not reducible to it. Similarly class leadership, while ultimately deriving from class consciousness, is not identical to the latter.

Leadership was an extremely important consideration in the Russian Revolution, but no leader—not Lenin, not Trotsky, not Stalin—"made" the Russian Revolution. Effective leadership must understand the possibilities inherent within a concrete situation, and the mood of the class or classes being mobilized. If the objective possibility of revolution exists, and the temper of the masses is insurrectionary, still revolution may be thwarted because of inadequate leadership. But without the objective possibility or an insurrectionary temper of the masses, even the most brilliant leadership cannot produce revolution.

Moreover, the emergence of leadership does not occur independently of the revolutionary process. Leadership is forged in the same historical matrix by the same class struggles which bring forth the objective possibility of revolution and the insurrectionary temper of the masses. In a nutshell, the class struggle *tends* to produce leadership adequate to its nature.

Prior to the arrival of Lenin in April 1917, the Bolshevik leadership in Russia did not support an immediate proletarian revolution. The bourgeois revolution had not yet exhausted itself, and therefore the Bolsheviks felt Marxists should give critical support to the Provisional Government. The local Bolshevik leadership also believed that the February Revolution had transformed the imperialist war into a war in defense of the revolution. Lenin opposed both these positions. The Russian bourgeoisie was far too moribund to carry through a democratic revolution. Given the opportunity, it would certainly betray the revolutionary movement. In the era of imperialism, capitalist social relations could no longer play a progressive role in developing a country's forces of production. They would lead only to perpetual wars for redividing the imperialist loot. Therefore Lenin argued the slogan of the Bolsheviks should be "All Power to the Soviets." World War I was still a bloody imperialist enterprise. The February Revolution had not changed the objectives of Russian foes or allies. It had not changed the burning desire of soldiers, workers, and peasants to be done with the grisly madness. The Bolsheviks should spurn all arguments for continuing the conflict.

According to Trotsky, Lenin was able to swing the entire Bolshevik party behind his position not because of personal genius and not from any hypnotic powers of persuasion, but because his revolutionary conceptions conformed to the actual practice of the Bolshevik rank and file, and because events soon vindicated his analysis.[23] Reoriented in this way, the Bolshevik party experienced enormous growth in membership.

The function of revolutionary leadership is not always to prod the masses toward revolutionary action. It can also be to resist premature impulses toward insurrection. Between July 3 and 5, 1917, masses of workers and soldiers in Petrograd staged tumultuous demonstrations amounting to a semi-insurrection. The demonstrations wanted to overthrow the Provisional Government and urged the Bolsheviks to seize power. The party leaders, however, determined that the time was not yet ripe. The Bolsheviks did not have a majority in the Petrograd Soviet, the armed forces were not firmly in favor of insurrection, and the provinces lagged behind Petrograd in political consciousness. In the aftermath of these violent demonstrations—subsequently called the *July Days*—the Provisional Government initiated repressive measures against the Bolsheviks, forcing Lenin into hiding and arresting Trotsky.

The event decisively tipping the class balance in favor of the Bolsheviks and setting the stage for the October Revolution was the attempted counterrevolution by General Lavr Kornilov, commander-in-chief of the army. This was critical because it demonstrated that some elements in the Provisional Government were sympathetic to counterrevolution, and that others not sharing these sympathies nevertheless were ineffectual in preventing its occurrence largely because a smashing defeat of the counterrevolutionaries would render the Provisional Government more vulnerable than ever in confronting the left. Hence

the revolution would remain in danger as long as the Provisional Government retained power. All this seemed to validate the Bolshevik slogan of "All Power to the Soviets."

As it happened, the Kornilov counterrevolution came to naught because railroad workers under Bolshevik instigation sidetracked the troop trains. Interaction between Bolshevik organizers and soldiers in the stalled trains prompted desertion by many of the latter, rendering Kornilov's military forces useless, or more precisely, nonexistent. The entire incident convinced workers and soldiers all over Russia that the Bolsheviks were the most dedicated and effective defenders of the revolution.

Kornilov's attempted coup collapsed at the end of August. In September the Bolsheviks gained a majority in the Petrograd Soviet, and Bolshevik resolutions began to carry in the Moscow Soviet as well as others. The pace of the revolutionary activity was accelerating as the proletariat finally grasped that the soviets already possessed the lion's share of power. Early in October Lenin insisted that the situation was ripe for the overthrow of the Provisional Government, and that preparations for an armed insurrection should begin immediately. With much debate and some dissension the Bolshevik Central Committee adopted Lenin's proposal. In the weeks before the October Revolution, soviets in Petrograd, Kiev, Minsk, the Ural region, and elsewhere declared in favor of soviet power.

The operational preparations for the October Revolution were carried out by the Military Revolutionary Committee of the Petrograd Soviet under the leadership of Trotsky. Prior to the start of the insurrection on October 25, all major military installations in the Petrograd region had come over to the soviet side. So preponderant were the forces at the disposal of the revolutionaries, that the insurrection in Petrograd required only twenty-four hours to overthrow the Provisional Government. In Moscow the fighting lasted longer but the outcome was the same. By the end of October political power in most parts of Russia clearly belonged to the soviets, and to the Bolsheviks as the dominant party within the soviets.

The October Revolution provides a logical termination for this illustration of Marxist analysis. The regime which came to power in October 1917 had the backing of workers, soldiers, and a majority of the politically conscious peasants. Its class base, however, contained formidable contradictions, the relationship between proletariat and peasantry being largely unresolved. Also problematic was the relationship between the revolutionary state and the classes which carried it to power. The October insurrection was accomplished with little bloodshed, but the sternest trials of the Bolshevik Revolution lay in the future.

The previous section considers the relationship between existing communist societies and the Marxist concept of communism. It is unnecessary to repeat that discussion here. Marxists continue to study the Russian Revolution both as a problem for scientific analysis and as a clue to the perils and possibilities of moving from capitalism to Marxist communism.[24]

NOTES

1. Georg Lukacs, *History and Class Consciousness: Studies in Marxist Dialectics*, trans. Rodney Livingstone (Cambridge, Mass.: MIT Press, 1971), p. 1.
2. Paul A. Baran, *The Longer View: Essays Toward a Critique of Political Economy*, ed. John O'Neill (New York: Monthly Review Press, 1969), pp. 32–34.
3. Robert L. Heilbroner, *Marxism: For and Against* (New York: W. W. Norton, 1980), pp. 20–22.
4. See James O'Connor, *The Fiscal Crisis of the State* (New York: St. Martin's Press, 1973); Nicos Poulantzas, *Political Power and Social Class* (London: New Left Books, 1973); Eric Olin Wright, *Class, Crisis and the State* (London: New Left Books, 1978).
5. Heilbroner, *Marxism*, p. 68.
6. Karl Marx, *A Contribution to the Critique of Political Economy* (New York: International Publishers, 1970), p. 21.
7. See, for example, Paul A. Baran and Paul M. Sweezy, *Monopoly Capital: An Essay on the American Economic and Social Order* (New York: Monthly Review, 1966); Ian Steedman, *Marx after Sraffa* (London: New Left Books, 1977); G. Abraham-Frois and E. Berrebi, *Theory of Value, Prices and Accumulation: A Mathematical Integration of Marx, von Neumann and Sraffa* (London: Cambridge University Press, 1979); and J. Schwartz, ed., *The Subtle Anatomy of Capitalism* (Santa Monica, Calif.: Goodyear Publishing, 1977).
8. Ernest Mandel, *Marxist Economic Theory*, 2 vols. (New York: Monthly Review Press, 1968), p. 349.
9. Baran and Sweezy, *Monopoly Capital*.
10. Samir Amin, *Accumulation on a World Scale: A Critique of the Theory of Underdevelopment*, 2 vols. (New York: Monthly Review Press, 1974).
11. O'Connor, *Fiscal Crisis of the State*; Poulantzas, *Political Power and Social Class*.
12. O'Connor, *Fiscal Crisis of the State*.
13. Baran and Sweezy, *Monopoly Capital*.
14. Arghiri Emmanuel, *Unequal Exchange: A Study of the Imperialism of Trade* (New York: Monthly Review Press, 1972).
15. G. A. Cohen, *Karl Marx's Theory of History: A Defence* (Princeton, N.J.: Princeton University Press, 1978), pp. 302–7.
16. Baran, *The Longer View*, p. 41.
17. H. Selsam and H. Martel, eds., *Reader in Marxist Philosophy* (New York: International Publishers, 1963), pp. 262–63.
18. See, for example, Charles Bettelheim, *Class Struggles in the USSR: vol. 1, 1917–1923; vol. 2, 1923–1930* (New York: Monthly Review Press, 1976, 1978); or P. Corrigan, H. Ramsay, and D. Sayer, *Socialist Construction and Marxist Theory: Bolshevism and Its Critique* (New York: Monthly Review Press, 1978); or Rudolf Bahro, *The Alternative in Eastern Europe* (London: New Left Books, 1978).
19. Leon Trotsky, *The History of the Russian Revolution*, trans. Max Eastman, 3 vols. (New York: Simon & Schuster, 1932).

20. Trotsky, *History of the Russian Revolution*, vol. 1, pp. 5–6.
21. Ibid., p. 140.
22. Ibid., p. 152.
23. Ibid., pp. 323–26.
24. In addition to Trotsky's *History*, Marxist scholarship on the Russian Revolution includes the works by Bettelheim and Corrigan et al. mentioned in note 18, the biographies of Stalin and Trotsky by Isaac Deutscher, Lieberman's *Leninism under Lenin*, and Neil Harding's study of Lenin's political thought. E. H. Carr's multivolume work, *A History of Soviet Russia*, though not written from an explicitly Marxist perspective, uses analytic methods and articulates positions many Marxists will find congenial.

There is currently a major revival of Weber scholarship in Germany, Britain, and the United States. The upsurge of interest in his work is due to the fact that it is uniquely relevant for the analysis of contemporary social events, both substantively and theoretically.

Substantively, Weber's sociology focused upon precisely those processes which have become problematical in the modern world. Such processes include the growing power of the state, bureaucratization, legitimation, charismatic leadership, religious disenchantment, and rapid social change. Theoretically, Weber's sociology represented a dynamic synthesis of theories of political power with theories of social structure and social change. Further, his conceptualization of charisma allows us to combine the study of history with an analysis of the lives of great leaders.

Recently, there have been new interpretations of Weber's work emanating from the more complete availability of his entire corpus of writings. From these new interpretations the concept that has emerged as the unifying theme in Weber's total opus is *rationalization*, which we will consider in this essay.

Ronald M. Glassman

MAX WEBER,
THE MODERN WORLD,
AND MODERN SOCIOLOGY

RATIONALIZATION AND CONCEPTION OF THE MODERN WORLD

The process of rationalization gives us the key to the understanding of modernity. Two related processes constitute the foci of Weber's analysis: (1) the decline of the "enchanted" religious worldview and the rise of the rational scientific worldview—with the dramatic alteration in personal lifestyles that has resulted; and (2) the decline of traditional authority and the rise of legal-rational authority with bureaucratic administration—resulting in an enormous growth of bureaucratization in government, the economy, and the service sector.

This conception of modern society, which is based on the rationalization of thought and large-scale organization, clearly transcends earlier conceptions, based primarily upon categories such as urbanization, industrialization, and the division of labor. This is not to say that the latter are not central characteristics of the modern world. Without denigrating the work of

Ferdinand Tönnies, Georg Simmel, Émile Durkheim, and Karl Marx, contemporary Weber scholars believe that Weber's vision of the *rationalized world* is crucial to our understanding of modernity.

Rationalization of Thought: Science, Sensualism, and Narcissism

When we focus on the rationalization of thought which has emerged as part of the scientific worldview, a Durkheim-Weber dialogue becomes possible. For in this regard both Weber and Durkheim emphasized the positive and negative aspects of the rise of science and the decline of religion.

The Enlightenment thinkers and, of course, Marx had focused on the negative effects of religion—the superstition and subjugation it engendered. Rationality and science were viewed as liberating thought processes that would have a positive effect on society. Weber shared Marx's optimistic views of science and reason.[1] As is well known, Weber believed that scientific ob-

125

jectivity was possible and that, in fact, science could help us find practical and responsible solutions to social ills.[2] The control over nature which the rational scientific worldview promised was just as exciting for Weber as it was for the Enlightenment intellectuals.

However, just as Durkheim warned of the anomie that could result from the breakdown of a system of unified meaning (religion),[3] so Weber warned of the disenchantment[4] and narcissism[5] that would follow in the wake of the decline of religious belief.

According to Weber, the decline of religion and the rise of scientific rationality would cause a decline of Puritan asceticism and a disbelief in magic, rituals, prayer, and miracles.[6] The decline of Puritan asceticism would result in pleasure seeking and a self-indulgent, self-centered ethic of everyday life—"me first"; "if it feels good, do it." Further, the modern individual, because of his or her rational orientation to the world, cannot believe in magic. Therefore, ritual and prayer cannot be seen as meaningful acts, nor can the miraculous intervention by God in the affairs of everyday life appear conceivable. Since scientific rationality, however, cannot remove the facts of death and injustice in the world, nor provide us with an absolute means for controlling nature, society, or our own personal fate, a kind of withdrawn cynicism will emerge in the modern populace.[7]

The narcissistic withdrawal into a privatized world of pleasure was presented by Weber and Durkheim as another problem of modernity.[8] Weber never rejected science or reason, though these were part of the problem, but exhorted us, as social scientists and public servants, to attempt to find viable solutions within the context of modern conditions.

Rationalization of Social Structure: Bureaucracy against Democracy

Along with the rationalization of thought, Max Weber produced the pioneering work on the rationalization of large-scale organizations, or bureaucratization. Weber was not formulating a theory of large-scale organizations as such, but rather was attempting to focus our attention on the political, economic, and social consequences of bureaucracy.

Weber was convinced that the bureaucratization of the state and economy would occur, since the administrative needs of modern society were increasing at a dramatic rate. Weber was also convinced that the structure of domination emanating from bureaucracies would be authoritarian.

Bureaucracies exhibit a hierarchical structure of authority, a chain of command not unlike that of a modern military organization. The bureaucratic hierarchy is controlled by an elite of top managers who make decisions with the technical advice, but without the consent, of those below them in the hierarchy. Furthermore, the bureaucratic rules and regulations that govern the official actions of giant modern organizations are not laws. They do not guarantee the rights of those who work within bureaucracies; they do not limit the power of bureaucratic leaders, nor are they open to discussion.[9]

Weber saw in bureaucracy a new form of despotic domination. This form of domination was subtle in that it controlled decision making and negated civil liberties without a secret police or conquering army. The hallmarks of democratic government—citizens' participation, limitation of the power of tenure of leaders, and lawful procedures—were replaced by an administrative megamachine controlled from the top down and insensitive to individual needs.[10]

The authoritarian tendencies Weber saw as emanating from modern bureaucracies—governmental, economic, and service—produced in him a profound pessimism concerning the future of the world. He believed that parliamentary democracy, which he spent his life fighting to establish in Germany, would be overwhelmed by the superior bureaucratic organizations of technical specialists and administrative experts. In the end Weber envisioned the world turning away from parliamentary democracy and toward a new land of serflike bondage similar to that of the ancient empires.[11]

Not even Marx's vision could save us from the new "iron cage."[12] For socialism, like democracy, was doomed in the face of a growing bureaucratization. Ownership of the means of production would become control by government bureaucrats in the rationalized world of modernity. And a planned economy would become an inefficient economy, no more geared to the needs of consumers than capitalism had been. Socialism, instead of producing Utopia, would increase the amount of bureaucracy and, therefore, increase the authoritarian, antidemocratic tendencies within modern society.

This nightmare vision of the future produced in Weber what Wolfgang Mommsen[13] has called a *heroic pessimism*—heroic because Weber exhorted social scientists to attempt to find responsible, workable solutions to the pressing problem of bureaucratic authoritarianism.[14]

Rationalization of the Economy

Part of the Weber renaissance involves a renewed interest in his economic writings. *The General Economic History,* for instance, has been republished in English.[15] In the economic writings of Weber one finds the possibility for a meaningful Marx-Weber dialogue.[16] It is not that the two thinkers agree in either their descriptions or analyses of economic systems or action, but both of them focus their attention on: (1) the uniqueness of industrial capitalism; and (2) a general comparative analysis of other economic systems.

From Marx and Weber we gain critical insights into capitalism in both its preindustrial commercial form and its industrial form. We also gain the foundation for a genuine comparative analysis of economic systems from their descriptions of agrarian economies.

In this latter regard, Weber, in *The Agrarian Sociology of Ancient Civilizations*, though differing from Marx substantially in his analysis, focused on the very same problem, i.e., the contrast between the slave-capitalist latifundia (private estate) agrarianism of Rome and the peasant-bureaucratic, kingly-aristocratic agrarianism of the Oriental empires.[17]

Of course, Marx and Weber disagreed in their orientations toward industrial capitalism. But both were obsessed with the attempt to describe its inner functioning and place it within a comparative-historical context. We know that Weber viewed capitalism favorably and tended to focus upon its positive contributions to economic production, such as rational capitalist accounting methods and efficient market production orientation. We know that, by contrast, Marx viewed capitalism negatively and focused on the surplus value extorted from the laborers. Yet taken together, even with their value orientations intruding into their analyses, they gave us a more complete understanding of industrial capitalism.

Marx accepted industrial capitalism as an improvement over agrarian economies. He wished to retain the industrial portion of the economy while replacing the capitalist portion with a system owned and run by the people. However, Weber's vision of the ongoing bureaucratization of the economy and state could not allow him to accept Marx's optimism in this regard. The historical reality of this mushrooming bureaucratization has forced all contemporary thinkers to reevaluate their predictions about future economic systems. Though Weber favored free-market capitalism over a bureaucratically planned economy, he knew that a free-market economy was more likely to survive in a bureaucratized world than a people's socialist economy.

Therefore, as part of Weber's renaissance, the question of the best practical economy, given the rationalized conditions of modernity, arises in the same way that Aristotle's question of the best practical polity arose in contradistinction to Plato's utopianizing.

IRRATIONAL ELEMENTS IN SOCIETY: CHARISMA AND LEGITIMACY

Though riveting our attention on the rational processes that have emerged in the modern world, Weber was also very much aware of its many irrational elements. Modern populations, though rational in their orientation to the world, also remain haunted by existential anxieties about death and the meaning and morality of life. A quest for pure mysticism, along with a descent into cultism, characterize today's population, along with the ultrarational, secular-scientific approach to daily life.

Similarly, in our approach to political leadership we desire a technocratically trained, managerially effective individual, while at the same time longing—in desperate, irrational, infantile fashion—for a god-like leader who will, at once, lead us to the promised land and take care of all our needs. Weber captured this irrational longing in his concept of *charisma*.

Search for Charisma

Charismatic leadership is perhaps the most creatively compelling ideal-typical tool in Max Weber's very extensive conceptual arsenal. In formulating this construct, Weber drew on historical examples of known leaders (persons acknowledged both in their own time and recognized as such by later generations), and then selected a core of definitive characteristics that appeared to explain the type of authority relationship between them and their followers that enabled them to rule. Weber writes:

The term charisma will be applied to a certain quality of an individual personality by virtue of which he is considered extraordinary and treated as endowed with supernatural, superhuman, or at least specifically exceptional powers or qualities. These are such as are not accessible to the ordinary person, but are regarded as of divine origin or as exemplary, and on the basis of them the individual concerned is treated as a "leader." [18]

Weber also distinguished among the differing spheres of society from which charismatic leadership might emerge. For instance, the charismatic might emerge as a religious prophet, war leader, or great orator. In each of these spheres, human anxiety levels could run high, while signs from "the Beyond" attained increasing significance.

Our existential awareness of our own impending death or that of others, and our search for the meaning of life in an infinite, hostile universe, opened us to charismatization by religious leaders, who seemed to create meaning and hope out of meaninglessness and hopelessness. Likewise, the dangers and horrors of war opened us to the hero worship of the successful war leader who could bring us through the holocaust safely and triumphantly—"like a god." In times of crisis, in societies in which decision making was open to public debate, the great orator could mesmerize us and sway us to his banner, speaking "like a god," lending us a feeling of confidence, cohesion, and moral superiority that had heretofore been lacking. Weber emphasized but never focused on leadership divorced from the political, structural, and cultural context in which it functioned. History, biography, and social structure became causally interrelated in a complex Weberian synthesis. [19]

Routinization of Charisma

Weber was concerned not only with the period of charismatic domination but also with the routinization of charisma that followed the decline of charismatic authority. Two dimensions of Weber's analysis are of interest to us in this regard.

First, Weber made it clear that the routinization of charisma might move in a traditional or a modern direction. This was especially important to theories of social change because it meant that a society in transition did not necessarily move "onward" toward a progressive stage of development. Charismatic leadership might not always lead the way to the future; it might lead to a contemporized version of the past, or even "backward" to a past unknown within a particular civilizational context. On a theoretical level this was important because it voided all unilinear theories of social change. Practically, it served to remind us that change was not always change for the better. To concretize this point, think of Hitler's Third Reich and Ayatollah Khomeini's regime.

Second, charisma might be routinized in a democratic or despotic direction. Weber was especially interested in the structural and cultural processes that led a nation toward a democratic or despotic form of routinization.

Humanistic and Evil Charismatic Leaders

Weber on one hand presented us with examples of berserk warrior leaders, linked obviously with the blood lust, slaughter, rape, and pillage of conquest. On the other hand, there were religious prophets linked with the extension of ethical codes and the inculcation of social justice.

Given the emergence of the murderous, yet genuinely charismatic, Hitler just after Weber's death, we believe that the distinction between the heinous and the humanistic charismatic leader is worth emphasizing and investigating. Even among warrior leaders we can find the demonic Attila or the relatively humanistic Alexander. Religious charismatics, too, can run the gamut from Jesus' pacifism to Khomeini's repression. Among great orators Pericles and Alcibiades come to mind—the one enchanting the Athenians with the spirit of freedom and democracy, the other degrading them to acts of civil violence and foreign domination.[20] In the modern context, both Hitler and Roosevelt enmeshed entire nations in their oratorical spells, but how can one ignore the differences in the character of the charismatic message? Apparently charismatic leaders may be possessed of the gift of the devil as well as the gift of grace.

Fate of Charisma in the Modern World

As we enter the world of modernity, we see a world in which charisma can be falsified and denigrated—falsified by its artificial manufacture, denigrated by the cynicism and disenchantment that permeate the rational approach to social life in our time. Modern societies are increasingly run by faceless managers, impressed by media celebrities known only as faces, and inhabited by individuals who retreat into private spheres of narcissistic self-development.

Yet moderns still long for charisma. The world of modernity is one in which the individual is increasingly isolated from the mediating structures of family, community, religion, and even friendship.[21] In this "lonely-crowd" existence of "familiar strangers," we feel a great need for connectedness to a leader who in some sense unifies us with an imaged society at large. Instead of finding genuine charisma, however, the isolated individual of modernity becomes a bystander to the media campaigns of superstars attempting to sell ideology in the guise of camera-projected personalism.

The manufacture of charisma through the mass media creates a whole new category of leadership; charismatic leaders seek the enhancing devices of the mass media to broaden their charismatic effect into a mass phenomenon of an all-encompassing kind. But leaders lacking genuine charisma have to turn to the mass media in order to attempt to manufacture pseudocharisma in its place. Though this manufactured charisma does not create the same intense bonding that genuine charisma generates in the charismatized followers, it does create an aura of ever-present recognition and "star" status. The pseudocharismatic leader enters the world of media celebrities that appears to exist beyond the world of ordinary individuals and in this sense gains partial legitimacy.

The phenomenon of electoral leadership in legal-democratic nation-states in this era of mass media becomes one of the central foci of contemporary political analysis. Amplified by the mass media, electoral charisma—in both its genuine and manufactured forms—represents a new dimension in political leadership.

In communist societies, too, after the era of genuine revolutionary charisma, there comes the time of stultifying bureaucratic administration. To counteract this development, attempts at the manufacture of pseudocharisma have often taken place. The style in communist nations has been more heavy-handed than in legal-democratic nations. Nonetheless, there is no doubt that the manufactured charisma created for such communist leaders has produced a partial legitimation, especially within their own societies.

Political Legitimacy in the Modern World: Consent and Crisis

Legitimation is the social-psychological process through which leaders and the led (that is, government and the population) relate to one another. At the heart of the legitimation process is the concept of consent. Consent giving by the people and consent getting by the leadership are central to the process of legitimacy.

Now the process of consent may be controlled either by the leadership or by the led. If this process is controlled by the people, then rational procedures of legitimation may emerge. That is, rational legitimacy will be based upon participation, limitation, and law. The people will institutionally participate (directly or indirectly) in decision making, limit the power and tenure of its leadership, institute rational rules for succession to and access to leadership positions, operate with debatable, amendable rules for political action, and institutionalize participatory procedures for the punishment of rule breaking.[22]

Weber refers to such a system as *legal-rational authority*.[23] Legal-rational authority is predicated upon the rational consent of the population. But legitimate domination may also be controlled by the leadership, in which case nonrational or emotional processes may characterize the process. The leadership or leadership stratum may break the bonds of the limitations and constraints of power implicit in the process of rational consent giving. They may do this because (a) they are culturally directed to do so by their inherited tradition[24]; (b) they are motivated to do so by their own charisma, megalomania, or venality[25]; and (c) they are impelled to do so by what they perceive as anarchic circumstances engendered by a rapid social change, revolution, or political crisis.

Under such circumstances the reciprocal relationship between leaders and led may yield to a usurpation of power and privilege by the leadership.[26] In order to maintain this usurpation of power and privilege the leadership may attempt to manipulate the population into granting a kind of irrational consent, or it may even become coercive in order to pressure the people into granting a kind of forced acquiescence.[27]

The irrational, emotional, and traditional processes utilized by leaders include: (1) charisma; (2) manufactured or depersonalized charisma[28]; (3) ideological manipulation (including childhood socialization); (4) co-optation (the buying of subservient cooperation through office giving and wealth giving); and (5) displays of force and terror.

Weber's famous categories of legitimate domination—traditional, charismatic, and legal-rational (with bureaucratic administration)—were among his monumental contributions to the study of political power.[29] The problems of consent and force were at the core of his analysis. Attempting to maintain his objectivity, Weber nonetheless enunciated a value preference for legal-rational authority and rejected traditional authority. He also, quixotically perhaps, hoped that charismatic leadership of the electoral-democratic kind would be able to cut through the stultification of bureaucracy.[30]

Legitimation Crisis in the Modern World

In the contemporary world the legitimation of political systems has become problematical for many reasons. Among them, rapid social change presents itself as an endemic crisis-level problem and systems inadequacies are another.[31]

Rapid social change may have become a permanent social fact within our technocratic, scientific, industrial society. If it has become permanently institutionalized, then anarchic and anomic trends, which are the general by-products of rapid social change, may also become permanent features of such societies. In such a situation political legitimacy becomes increasingly difficult to establish.

Along with rapid social change, the rational evaluation of political and economic leaders has also become a typical feature of modern societies. In Weber's terms modern, highly educated populations will make the following demands: (1) political order combined with freedom and participation; and (2) economic stability combined with abundance and equity. Since contemporary political and economic systems—capitalist as well as communist, democratic as well as despotic—cannot satisfy all these demands, a deepening legitimation crisis is emerging.

In the United States, 50 percent of the electorate finds the government and political leadership unresponsive to its needs and alienated from its influence. In the Soviet Union and China the people have grown impatient with the inefficiencies of bureaucratically planned economic systems and disillusioned over the lack of legal protection and democratic participation. (Such protection and participation were promised by Marxism, put off by Leninism, crushed by Stalinism, and inhibited by Maoism. They have been promised again and put off again by the current leadership of the Soviet Union and China.)

Legitimation crises exist under both the capitalist and communist systems, and are not likely to disappear unless enormous progress is made in the political and economic spheres. Such progress, however, may be beyond the reaches of modern governments.

WEBER'S THEORY OF HISTORY, SOCIAL CHANGE, AND SOCIAL STRUCTURE

Marx provided social science with its first well-developed theory of social change, which was derived from a dramatic alteration of Hegel's theory of history.[32] But Marxian theory—and this is accepted by most contemporary Marxian scholars—focused too one-sidedly on the material conditions of change, that is, on the mode of production and the classes and class conflicts engendered by it.

Of course, Marx was reacting against Hegel's overemphasis on the spiritual and ideational causes of social change. Also, Marx was reacting against the chroniclers, who presented history as a series of battles, dates, and deeds of great men. Nevertheless, he did overemphasize the material forces of change and the structural conflicts linked with them. In spite of this, sociology will remain ever grateful to Marx for creating the first truly useful theory of the stages of history and the causes of revolution. Weber acknowledged that *The Communist Manifesto* was a remarkable sociological work to which he owed a great analytical debt.[33]

Against the backdrop of the debate between Marxists and Hegelians on the material versus ideal causes of social change, Weber attempted to present a balanced view of social change and history. Weber's theory included not only material causalities but also ideological and political causalities, which he regarded as fundamental causalities in their own right. Furthermore, while not altogether rejecting Marx's stage theory of history, Weber also presented a theory that provided for civilizational uniqueness and atypical lines of historical development.

If the Marxian theory presented us with a set of unilinear evolutionary stages of history based on the mode of production, the Weberian theory of social change explains: (1) how specific societies actually evolve from one stage to another; (2) why societies do not evolve in the same way, even while developing somewhat similar modes of production; and (3) why some societies do not create, or adopt, the new mode of production at all, but instead remain the same, move in a different direction of social organization, or regress to a simpler, less effective mode of production.

As Milovan Djilas[34] and Stanislaw Ossowski[35] have shown, in their analyses of the process of social change in eastern Europe, the Marxian theory of social change has given us a monumental beginning, but without the Weberian theory of social change most of history could not be understood. That is, the process of social change in eastern Europe included ideological diffusion, political organization, and charismatic leadership as prior causal processes to the establishment of the new mode of production. Once the new mode was established, the specific form of that mode of production and the ownership and control of it were, in part, determined by ideological, political, and charismatic processes that existed before its establishment.

Let us now look further at this Weberian extension and critique of the Marxian theory of history and social change.

The Independent Action of Ideology

Weber began his critique of Marx's theory of social change by standing Hegel on his feet once again. While acknowledging that the economy led, Weber made central the independent effect of ideology on social action and social change.[36]

Ideas, of course, were in part a product of social structure, but once created, they had a life of their own. They were not only absorbed, developed, and altered by intellectuals grappling with their nuances but also altered and developed by nonintellectual segments of the population whose vulgarized renditions of these ideas often had an impact equal to that of the intellectuals.[37]

Furthermore, societies often had organized strata and institutions for the control and dissemination of ideas which might or might not be synonymous with the power and intentions of the ruling class. Further still, the diffusion of ideas might have profound effects on a given society, creating contradictions, conflicts, and changes not necessarily inherent in the society, and directing that society toward a kind of dramatic change that would not have been consistent with the society's evolutionary, teleological stages or internal contradictions. For example, the introduction of modern political and economic ideas into Third World countries has created processes of change, wrenching societies in some cases from a tribal state directly into the processes of industrialization, urbanization, and rational state administration. This pattern hardly fits the Marxian model of change.

Weber's most famous example of the independent effect of the ideology of social change was his theory of the causal link between Puritan Protestantism and the emergence of industrial capitalism in the Low Countries and Britain. It isn't just that Puritan asceticism and work-ethic, individualistic Protestantism were not engendered by the merchant capitalism of the free market cities of northwestern Europe. Weber pointed out that the vulgarized doctrines produced as a result acted upon the social structure of mercantilism and became a causal link in the turn of human creativity toward machine production, factory organization, the so-called free wage labor, and the capital reinvestment process. This reinvestment process, Weber affirmed, was an "unnatural attitude," foreign not only to the conquistadors but also to the merchants of "ancient" or "trade" capitalism.[38]

Ideology as a Revolutionary Force

Weber did not doubt for a moment that Marx's conception of ideology as a legitimating factor for the ruling classes was accurate—hence, Marx's condemnation of religion as the opiate of the people. However, Weber added that a closer look at political history would show us that ideology—religious or secular—could also become a revolutionary force, uniting the lower classes against the upper classes. Recent events in Iran, wherein a Moslem leader, the Ayatollah Ruholla Khomeini, united the population and overthrew the shah of Iran despite U.S. economic and military support for the shah was a remarkable example of Weber's thesis. Gandhi's overthrow of the British power in India was another example.

Thus, according to Weber, religion or any ideology might act as an opiate or might become revolutionary. Because Marx shared this view, he stressed in his statements on praxis—that is, the spreading of revolutionary ideas among the proletariat—that mere "philosophizing" without political action and a political organization would be fruitless in producing social change.[39]

Military Conquest and Social Change

Marx was fully aware of the military history of the world. But in emphasizing his own causality for change, he deemphasized military causality. Weber brought military causality back to center stage. For he believed that conquests themselves produced new fusions between conquerers and conquered through which monumental, even epochal, changes might occur. The conquests of the divine-kingly empires by nomadic herdsmen were a prime example of Weber's point. After undergoing waves of conquests at the hands of wild herders, the divine-kingly empires of Egypt, China, and Mesopotamia developed very different political, economic, and social structures than they had previously exhibited.[40]

Next, feudalism, a form of social organization studied by Marx, certainly developed its structure from a military organization rather than an economic organization. Although Marx was fully aware of this fact, he concentrated on the property relations rather than the political relations of feudal society. These factors, of course, were interrelated, but the military dimension was the causal factor of change.

None of this means that after such events the mode of production and the social relations engendered by it might not still become the central organizing factor of the emerging societies. This might very well occur. The Weberian approach attempted to integrate the Marxian approach more fully with these other dimensions of change.

Political Action and Social Change

It was not only true that ideological currents might, through diffusion or the internal creativity of the intelligentsia, precede economic change but also that concerted political action along demarcated ideological lines might bring about economic change rather than vice versa. This, of course, as mentioned above, was the case with Russia, where Lenin, Trotsky, and the other Bolsheviks created an industrial and class structure as a self-conscious politically directed act. The events in the entire Third World must be seen, in neo-Weberian perspective, as combining a concerted political, ideological, and military activity in order to create a new economic and political structure after the fact.

Once this structure has been created, it will, in turn, "produce" the societies that have produced it. But even then intervention by outside military, political, and ideological forces (for example, actions by the superpowers or events in the cold war) or the rise of peculiar, internal trends (such as the nativist movements within Islam) might fuse with trends caused by the mode of production or the class structure to produce great variations in the emergent Third World societies along with their growing structural similarities.

Charismatic Leadership and Social Change: The "Great Man" and History

Charismatic leaders, as Weber has so brilliantly described them, usually did not produce change, but rose to power during periods of rapid change or crisis.[41] However, even though they did not produce the change, they were often able to put their stamp on the emerging change because of their ability to ease the transition to a new order. Whether their personal influence was to be long-lasting or temporary was decided by other circumstances—structural or historical—in each case. Yet in some cases their effect may be long-term. For if they were able successfully to routinize their charisma, the routinization itself might have some permanent impact on the emerging society.[42]

Civilizational Peculiarities

Another key contribution to Weber's theory of social change was his concept of social peculiarities or uniqueness. As was quite obvious to Weber, the absorption of change into a society did not occur on a blank slate. The particular social, economic, political, and ideological compositions of any given society, along with the particular cultural-historical nexus in which that society existed, necessarily produced civilizational differences in the emerging societies—even where the long-term trend of change was similar enough so that it seemed to be creating a stage of history.

Weber compared China and India in this way—the differences perhaps outweighing the similarities in his comparison of social change and social organization. Certainly

India's caste integration was so unique as to make comparisons to China's social structure almost impossible. On the other hand, China and Egypt showed so many similarities in the ancient world that comparison in that case was quite fruitful.

Weber was one of the first to point to the unique structural developments in Japan, and to suggest a unique line of development there, compared to that of the other Asian nations. Finally, Weber's most famous case of civilizational uniqueness was ancient Greece, which, because of the peculiarities in its military organization and its dependence on imperialistic trade capitalism, developed an unusual economic structure. Ancient Greece did not have a centrally directed river-flood system of culture, and its religious system lacked a mystical, monotheistic, moral basis. All of this resulted in the Greeks' experimentation with democracy, rational law, nonlegitimate dictatorship, trade capitalism and a money-oriented market system, a secular philosophy, science, and mathematics—in short, a unique and most peculiar civilization that became the basis for all of Western civilization, which Weber considered unique in itself.

Thus Weber emphasized long-term civilizational peculiarities in contradistinction to the Marxian stages of development. Along with the Marxian stages the Weberian theory allowed for the analysis of great similarities among societies attaining similar stages of production as well as for differences produced by the unique cultural and historical nexus into which the productive stages blended.

Unintended Effects

Weber added a further dimension to the theory of social change: the concept of *unintended effects*. Social change and history did not evolve as rationally ordained by the perfectly planned actions of human beings. Both the rationally planned actions of humans and their irrational, emotional, or spontaneous actions often produced results totally unintended by people involved in the process. The future was never fully predictable, not only because humans would continue to collectively create new ideas, new institutions, and new things but also because human actions and ideas often confounded their origins and produced wholly unpredictable results. Sociology could predict long-term, near-future trends, but it had to constantly amend and alter its predictions as more information from unintended and newly created social phenomena emerged.

Weber's theory of unintended effects could perhaps be synthesized with Hegel's and Marx's theories of the dialectic of change. For in the dialectic the creative interactions of humans, directed toward spiritual survival, according to Hegel, or material survival, according to Marx, always produced new phenomena. Human creative, intersubjective consciousness produced new ideas, institutions, and values, which negated the old. This negation of the past, fusing with the past itself, produced something new, which was not foreseeable in the old perspective.

Furthermore, was this not what Durkheim intended when he theorized about the moral density of a breakdown among the population of the unity of the collective consciousness to such a degree that new ideas, new norms, and new moral values would emerge and compete with the old, thus engendering social disorganization, anomie, and social change?

The theories of Weber, Hegel, Marx, and Durkheim on social change were not the same, but the dialogue with their ghosts and the ghost of Heraclitus—the father of the theory of change—could go far in producing the kind of synthesis modern sociology continues to lack.

Weberian Conception of Social Structure

Weber's conception of social structure flowed from his theory of social change. Again, he attempted to present a balanced view, in contrast to Marx's overemphasis on material causalities. Weber provided us with a multidimensional description of the various processes of social action that created the social organization of society. This description included the basic structuring spheres of society, such as:

1. *The Mode of Production*. Perhaps no one except Marx has written more on the structure of ancient, precapitalist, and capitalist economic systems than Weber.[43]

2. *The State and the Mode of Administration*. This is an institutional sphere much neglected by Marx (a factor which modern Marxists have tried to remedy[44]) and ignored by Durkheim (a factor which contemporary functionalists have failed to remedy).

3. *The Church and Other Institutional Sources of Ideology*.

Weber's descriptions of social structure then turned to the strata engendered by the following structuring institutions:

1. *Classes*. The classes, according to Weber, were based on the mode of production (the Marxian dimension).

2. *Status Groups*. The basis of these groups might be political, military, religious, or administrative. (Such aspects were neglected by Marx or interpreted by him in an economically derivative manner.)

3. *Ethnic Groups*. Whether cultural, religious, or racial groups, they were analyzed by Weber as groups in their own right, independent of their economic enmeshment. (Such groups, according to Weber, had an independent causal impact on the social structure.)

Taken together, economic classes, status groups, and ethnic groups formed a stratification system. This complex strata analysis was the hallmark of Weberian structural analysis.

Two theoretical points must be made here. First, Weber's strata analysis was different from functionalist stratification theory. And second, Weber's strata analysis incorporated the Marxian theory of class analysis.

In contrast to the functionalist stratification theory, Weber's strata were wealth, power, and status groups linked to economic, political, or religious institutions and generating competition and conflict. They were not analyzed as occupational groups linked together in a Durkheimian interdependence pattern and generating social cohesion.

Social structure held together for Weber because political domination and the state existed in the Hobbesian and Hegelian sense, and because the economic system absorbed the various strata in unequal interaction (according to Marx). Finally, the religious system (or secular ideological institutions) created enough cultural unification to bind the various strata in a civilizational value nexus. But such a system might generate ideological conflict or disruptive social alterations as well.

Thus there was social cohesion, but not in a biological or organic sense. This cohesion was always tenuous, and the competition and conflict among the various strata often stressed the social structure to the breaking point.

In terms of Marxian theory, Weber incorporated class analysis, but added to it the independent causal action of noneconomic status strata, such as knights, priests, bureaucrats, and ethnic groups like the Italians and Irish in America, the Moslems and Hindus in India, the blacks and whites in Kenya, or the Albanians and Montenegrins in Yugoslavia.

To sum up, for Weber the conception of social structure flowed not only from the control of the means of production but also from the control of the means of violence (by the state), the mode of administration (by the bureaucracy), and the control of ideas (by the church or secular organs concerned with the production of ideology).

The power and influence flowing from the strata engendered by these structuring institutions would depend on particular institutional arrangements in the society under question. They were not predetermined in Marxian terms, nor was Durkheimian cohesion the necessary outcome of the interaction of such strata.

EPISTEMOLOGY, METHODOLOGY, AND SCIENTIFIC OBJECTIVITY

In approaching the epistemology and methodology of the social sciences, Weber offered us something unique. For Weber's sociology combined the perfect blend of subjective and objective analysis. Now that Weber's total opus has become available, it should be clear that the subjective elements of the human being in history were always central for Weber, while at the same time objective categories of analysis derived from human sociohistorical contexts were constructed and utilized in order to make possible a scientific analysis.

Ideal categories such as bureaucracy, capitalism, and the state were developed from varying sociohistorical contexts and then applied as objective devices for the analysis of other sociohistorical situations. Classes, status, strata, ethnic groups, civilizational nexuses were all utilized as objective categories of analysis, but always as derived from the subjective context of human beings interacting with one another.

These objectified categories were never reified or made into things that act beyond the dynamics of human beings in human social situations. Human social action in a cultural and historical context was the starting point for Weber's work, while the objective categories of analysis derived from the subjective contexts made the work scientifically manageable.

Contemporary critical theorists have been influenced by Weber in this regard. They see an affinity between Georg Lukacs's Marxism and Weber's neo-Kantianism. Lukacs was a member of Weber's intellectual circle for many years, as Zoltan Tar has clearly documented.[45] Of course, Weber rejected Lukacs's Dostoyevskian religious romanticism and Eastern Marxism, just as Weber would have also rejected Lukacs's later communist political activities.

This is not to suggest that the Frankfurt

school and its contemporary adherents are Weberian, or that Western Marxism is substantively similar to Weber's work. There is, however, an attempt to blend subjective and objective elements in both contemporary schools of thought.[46]

Ideal Typification

While looking upon history and world society as a totality, neo-Kantian epistemology allows us to separate out portions of that totality into categories. Since they are ideal typifications, they have no existence in any actual sociohistorical situations. To make the difficult simple, simply think of the category *table*. This category goes beyond any particular table you might imagine or perceive. It allows you to imagine and recognize white tables, red tables, long tables, circular tables, square tables, etc. Thus, insofar as you have created an ideal category, *table*, this category transcends any particular table. While it does not exist in perceptual reality, it still does clearly exist in the reality of the conscious mind as an idea.

If we extend this notion to the study of society and history, we have the Weberian methodology. We create ideal-typical categories, such as church, sect, bureaucracy, capitalism, world religion, etc. We do this the same way we have created the category *table*. We perceive certain sociohistorical events that begin to suggest themselves as a category. We continue to search out other transhistorical and cross-cultural examples until the broad characteristics of a particular category emerge. Once the essential characteristics have been identified, the ideal-typical category becomes a viable *idea* from which particular examples may be compared in terms of their similarities and differences.

Weber's study of bureaucracy exemplified this process. First, Weber identified the general characteristics of bureaucracy, which he arrived at through his preliminary studies.[47] Then he systematically studied sociohistorical bureaucracies until he was able to identify the general characteristics of bu-

reaucracy in a more detailed fashion. Next he used the ideal-typical category, *bureaucracy*, which, like the idea of *table*, existed nowhere in its ideal-typical form, to compare historical examples of specific bureaucracies with other historical examples.[48]

The ideal-type category was never presented as something static, but rather as something always changing under the impact of the social and historical processes with which it is intimately interrelated. Such change took place because the ideal-type category was not a thing in itself, but was made up of the action patterns of human individuals, who, though affected by it, could also affect it in turn.

Understanding (*Verstehen*): Synthesis of Phenomenological Subjectivity and Scientific Objectivity

In criticizing positivism, Weber emphasized the differences between the natural and social sciences. He insisted on conceptions of human beings that included consciousness and intersubjectivity, will or ego-rational actions, and historical and cultural change.

According to Weber, the observer, or scientist, did not stand outside his or her subject matter like an impartial observer describing and analyzing events to which he or she was not a party. As a social scientist, the observer was a part of an ongoing society—someone active in society's institutions and participating in its collective consciousness. In this sense the social scientist could not step outside society and history. When the social scientist attempted to observe society and history, he or she was interreacting with it in a particular way—a way that might change society slightly or even significantly.

Furthermore, according to Weber, society was always changing, that is, not only was our scientific conception of society changing but society itself was always in sociohistorical flux. This was also the case with the natural sciences, whose conceptions of the universe, matter, and life were always changing. Theoretically, at least, the physical universe was not supposed to be changing in the same sense. Of course, the universe and nature did change—new stars appeared while others disappeared; movement occurred; some species died off, while new breeds, if not new species, did appear; and weather patterns might change. But society changed even more completely, and this problem was more central for the social sciences.

Since society was always changing, according to Weber, we should not expect to find laws that hold for all time; instead we should be content to formulate generalizations that might hold only for certain historical and cultural epochs, and be prepared to alter these generalizations when changed social conditions necessitated such an alteration. This critique of the positivists' attempts to create ahistorical laws of behavior that would hold for all time should not be misconstrued. For Weber definitely believed that it was possible to predict social actions, but he held that such laws would be historically and culturally circumscribed and would need constant amendment.

But did all this mean that the social sciences could not be scientific, precise, or predictive? On the contrary, Weber believed that the social scientist possessed an advantage that was not available to the natural scientist.

This advantage of the social scientist was the very process that differentiated the social sciences from the natural sciences in the first place, that is, the process of conscious intersubjective interreactions of the social scientist with the subject of study itself.

Why was this seeming disadvantage actually an advantage? It was an advantage, according to Weber, because the social scientist had the ability to intersubjectively interreact with his or her subject—to talk to people and read the words of history and thereby gains a kind of understanding completely impossible for the physicist or biologist. Precisely because humans were humans and not electrons or amoebas the

social scientist had an advantage over the natural scientist.

Thus Weber turned an apparent disadvantage into an advantage, and insisted that the methodology of the social sciences must utilize this advantage. Positivism did utilize this advantage inadvertently, but then squandered it by obscuring it with ahistorical laws, reified descriptions, and attempts at mathematical logic.[49]

But did this advantage then produce a great disadvantage, namely, that the social sciences could never really be sciences because objectivity was not possible in the phenomenological schema? On the contrary, Weber believed strongly that scientific objectivity *was* possible, and that social scientists could get beyond their sociohistorical enmeshment and beyond their values as well.[50]

Weber arrived at the following affirmations:

1. The continuing interchange of ideas between social scientists as members of an ongoing, worldwide, intercontinental community of scholars, scientists, and intellectuals could raise the generalizations of social science above their social and historical enmeshment, and could produce an objective body of social science knowledge.

2. If the social scientists stated their values in advance, making their readers and the social scientists themselves aware of them, then perhaps the values could be transcended.

For example, even though Plato and Aristotle thoroughly disagreed on the merits or demerits of the Spartan polity (Plato idolized it, while Aristotle vilified it), yet from their combined writings we obtain a clear picture of the structure of the Spartan polity.

Weber never suggested a value-free sociology as such, but rather a sociology aware of its value enmeshments. He hoped that this awareness could help produce a body of objective social science knowledge. It was Weber's hope, then, that the social sciences could proceed, even given their major drawback. Whether Weber was right can be argued, but that we must proceed as if he were right cannot be argued.

A WEBERIAN ANALYSIS OF CHINA IN TRANSITION

The events occurring in China today are remarkable in and of themselves. Whether one applies Weberian categories or not, China's transition to a more liberal polity and a mass consumption economy is exciting indeed. However, Weber's theories are especially useful in understanding nations in transition to modernity. His concepts—rationalization, the bureaucratic middle strata, the greater degree of efficiency of capitalism over socialism, the independent power of the state, and charismatic leadership—are remarkably useful tools for the analysis of the transition to modernity.

Rationalization

Rationalization, as earlier defined, has to do with the transition to scientific thinking and away from a magical-ritualistic world orientation. It also has to do with the bureaucratization of large-scale organizations, inculcation of a legal system, and movement toward capitalist accounting, banking, and profit orientation.

In China the rational-scientific worldview has swept up the university-educated strata, and the urban classes in general. As always, the peasant countryside makes this transition more slowly. In cities and at universities, however, the scientific world orientation has catapulted the urban strata, including many younger workers, into the modern world of rational disenchanted ideas and discourse.

These rationally oriented strata are demanding that the world of modernity be allowed full sway in China—that is, high consumption levels, electoral participation, and freedom of speech. The romantic so-

cialism of Mao Zedong has little appeal to these rationally oriented classes.

Bureaucratization was accomplished early by the Chinese Communist party. Following the Russian model, they created a rational government bureaucracy capable of establishing political order and unification, and capable of founding the infrastructure for a modern industrial economy. One should not denigrate these two remarkable achievements of the Communist party in China. Mao inherited a nation ripped asunder by civil war. China was then feudal and completely disunified in its political structure, and chaotically backward in its productive techniques. Though Chinese agriculture, for instance, was good by traditional standards, it was backward by modern standards, and, of course, no machine industry whatsoever existed outside of that established by European colonialists in coastal cities.

Thus the establishment of a unified rational-bureaucratic state made China into a modern nation, and the establishment of a centralized, planned, bureaucratic economy—though it now seems inefficient—created the first stages of industrial development in China. This was not an easy task if we consider China's history from the 1880s to the Japanese invasion in 1938.

With the establishment of China's bureaucratic state and economy, Weber's sociology becomes all the more prescient. For Weber was one of the first theorists to grapple with the socialist dream and reject it as a nightmare. Like Alexis de Tocqueville, Weber warned that a centralized, socialized, bureaucratized economy would be both *inefficient* and *authoritarian*. Bureaucracy, predicted Weber, would put the "little dictators" of the bureaucratic hierarchy into control of everyday life. Given the inherently authoritarian structure of bureaucracy, legal democracy would be overridden and overwhelmed. This authoritarianism, of course, occurred wherever Communist parties took power. Yet the Communists themselves promised a "people's democracy"—the Paris Commune writ large.

Weber and Tocqueville were correct about the authoritarian nature of a state emerging from bureaucratic socialism. According to Weber's thesis, in order to ensure the establishment and continuance of legal democracy, the bureaucratic state and economy must be contained and partially dismantled.

The main feature of the dismantling, in Weber's theory, revolved around the establishment of capitalism rather than a centralized, state-run, bureaucratic socialism. Weber believed that: (1) the separation of the state from the capitalist economy was one of the cornerstone principles for the safeguarding of legal democracy, and (2) that capitalism was more efficient and almost as equitable (in the long run) as bureaucratic socialism.

In China this separation of state bureaucratic power from the economic sphere is occurring. Managers of giant industrial units are being trained in business and management techniques drawn from noncommunist ranks. Stocks are being sold and industries privatized to a degree. Market principles of coordination and pricing are slowly being introduced (not without great difficulty). For if capitalism brings efficiency and productivity, it also brings inflation and greed.

Further, small business has been encouraged, and the Chinese are legendary at small-business techniques. The explosion of small businesses among rural peasants has brought not only increased prosperity and disparity in income but also it has brought the rural population headlong into the rational modern nation-state. The growth of small businesses has brought to the marketplace every kind of new consumer goods, from vegetables in abundance to porno VCR cassettes from Hong Kong. The sudden growth of independent small business (and big business) has created a twofold demand in the general populace: high levels of consumption and political freedom.

Thus Weber was right that the separation of the economy from the socialist state and the establishment of a more independent capitalist economy—in big and small businesses—does create the basis for legal democracy, whether in Prussia or China. The power of the state—and Weber was very much aware of this as he observed Prussia in the early part of the twentieth century—could, of course, subdue the fragile legal-democratic yearnings of the capitalist-oriented populace. But at least the conditions for the possibility of legal democracy would have been established. Whether the Chinese state will yield to, be overthrown by, or crush its legal-democratic proponents is yet to be determined. However, the impulse toward capitalism, high consumption levels, and a legal-democratic polity has begun.

In terms of economic efficiency, Weber was adamant that his socialist friends, like Lukacs, had things all wrong. Weber insisted that a centralized bureaucratic economics would be inefficient—inherently inefficient and inherently inequitable because the economy would follow the dictates of a bureaucratic hierarchy that would make economic decisions on political or administrative grounds, and would take to itself the lion's share of production.

This, of course, has occurred in Communist-dominated states. The modern Chinese see this with great clarity. They understand the inefficiency and graft built into their economic system, and are demanding a change to a capitalism modeled after that of Hong Kong, Korea, or Japan. (I'll have more to say about this later on when I discuss the "four tigers.") It should also be mentioned that older members of the Chinese Communist party, like Deng Chao Ping, see the great riches accumulated by Chinese capitalists and are appalled by this lack of socialist sharing. This is a real problem in capitalism which Weber was not unaware of. In asserting the superior efficiency of capitalism over socialism and its link with legal democracy, he also supported the Social-Democratic party in the hope that the condition of the poorer classes would be improved. In time this will become a real issue, given the disparity between rich and poor that could very well develop. Whether this issue will be handled through electoral parties or not depends, of course, on whether the Communist state will wither away or continue to assert its military dominance.

Will the Communist party state wither away? It might. Let us look at the conditions for such a change through the theory of the white-collar middle classes—as established by Weber, developed by C. Wright Mills, and originated by Aristotle.

The New Middle Classes and Democracy

Aristotle was the first to establish the principle that a large and prosperous middle class was the key to the establishment of democracy. Marx was aware of Aristotle's theory, but believed that under capitalism the insatiable greed of rich business owners would inevitably split the society into rich and poor. According to Marx, the middle class of small shopkeepers and farmers would be destroyed by big business. Marx, when he wrote (approximately 1850–1883), was not incorrect. Small business and the middle classes were being overridden by the upsurge of big capitalists.

However, Weber, writing later (approximately 1900–1918), saw that the rationalized world of big capitalism, the nation-state, and modern services would engender a new middle class composed of corporate managers, government bureaucrats, accountants, lawyers, professionals, scientists, teachers, professors, and an army of white-collar clerical workers. This new white-collar middle class would provide the Aristotelian (middle-class majority) foundation for a modern legal democracy. C. Wright Mills, writing in the 1950s, took up the Weberian proposition and warned that the new middle class, unlike the old small-business middle class, was not economically

independent, and therefore might not provide the base for legal democracy, but rather for some new form of affluent subservience. Both Weber and Mills warned of this problem. However, at this point in history—and this could change—the white-collar middle classes, though locked into large-scale bureaucratic organizations from nine to five o'clock, seem to behave politically independently afterhours.

In China the new middle class is growing in numbers and in rationality. They are demanding law, democracy, and consumer goods, as Weber said they would. The growth of the new middle strata in China will continue at a rapid pace. The government, though it fears these strata, cannot run a modern society without them. Therefore, though it may clamp down on university students, it will continue to churn them out. As the numbers of the new middle class increase, and are added to the remarkable increase in the numbers of the small business leaders (rural and urban), the middle strata will become the "carrying class" for the rational, high-consumption, legal-democratic society that China may become. The emerging middle strata do not have to become an absolute numerical majority in order for their worldview to predominate. For within the cities they will become a majority, and in the countryside the emerging entrepreneurs will back them. Finally, the working class in the cities, through its leaders, has already shown an inclination to back the demands for abundant consumer goods and legal democracy.

Thus, as the new middle classes and petite bourgeoisie emerge in China in ever larger numbers, the transition away from a state-run, bureaucratic socialism will heighten. But will the Chinese state dominated by the Communist party allow such a transition to occur? One of the highlights of Weberian theory, as opposed to Marxian and Durkheimian theory, is its analysis of the centrality and independent causal importance of the state in social life.

The Power of the State

Both Marx and Durkheim for differing reasons ignored the analysis of the role of the state in society. One of the great strengths of Weber's sociology is his focus on the power of the governmental institution. Recent events in China, wherein student, labor, and even military leaders were crushed by the Communist party–dominated state, show how important the analysis of the state can be. How can we analyze the transition in China without focusing on the role of the state? If the Communist party continues to oppose electoral democracy or free speech, and if it continues to appoint and control the military and police leadership, then it can continue to dominate China in an authoritarian manner.

However, the Weberian analysis of the power of the state is not a static one. That is, the state—though powerful—can itself change. Weber spent his lifetime attempting to alter the Prussian military state toward the legal-democratic model of the United States and Britain. In China the alteration of the state could occur in this manner.

First, the economic system probably will slowly move out of Communist party control. Already the party leadership has agreed that corporate managers must be properly trained in modern managerial and business techniques. Further, engineering and scientific middle managers have been trained successfully and encouraged to establish their input. The days of the "command economy" when Communist party bureaucrats ran the economy are over—at least in part.

The party still has the last word, and can reassert itself if it wishes. Inflation and high profit levels to individuals still bother the Communist leaders. Yet economic productive efficiency and the high-tech economy of the Western world and Japan are drawing the economy of China away from Communist party control. The growth of a stock market and the dramatic upsurge in small- to medium-size businesses will also swing the economy outside the immediate control of the Communist party.

Second, a civil service for government officials, modeled after those of the United States and Japan, is due to be instituted in China. This will mean that indoctrination into, and loyalty to, the Communist party will no longer be a prerequisite for government office holding. In the long run this will depoliticize the officialdom of the state and weaken the Communist party's hold on power.

Third, competitive elections are slowly being allowed for representation in the local and national parliaments. In the long run this could lead to opposition candidates being run against the Communist party slates. As in Poland (and soon Hungary) non-Communist candidates could become the majority party. Of course, the Communist party—if it still controls the military—could nullify such elections, or simply ignore them and overrule them through politburo decision making. However, if an overwhelming popular majority supports the opposition, as in Poland, the Communist party might yield. China will go through such a struggle in the near future, but the long-term results are not yet clear.

Fourth, the establishment of rational law, in the form of contract law, criminal law, and constitutional law, could permanently alter the Chinese state, pressuring it toward the liberal-democratic model.

The introduction of contract law has become necessitated by the influx of foreign capital, technology, and business firms. American, European, Japanese, and Chinese (Hong Kong, Taiwan, etc.) business firms will not do business in China without certain legal guarantees. Since the Chinese desire the technology, capital, and trade goods, they have begun to institute *contract* law. Contract law, in the past and present, engenders an interest also in rational *criminal* law. Right now, the Chinese are actually studying American criminal law in order to rationalize their court system. And, in non-political cases especially, a system of rational criminal law will probably be established in China.

The study of criminal law seems always to stir interest in constitutional law—and so it has in China. American professors of political science and law are amazed at the zealous interest Chinese students have shown in constitutional law. The Chinese have studied, line and verse, the American Constitution, and there is no doubt that the intelligentsia will increasingly, in the near future, demand constitutional safeguards against the state, and liberties for the Chinese citizenry. Of course, again the Communist party state could ignore or override such constitutional guarantees. However, an increasingly rationalized citizenry will come to accept such constitutional principles.

Fifth, the desire for modern consumer goods such as television sets, VCRs, cars, home appliances, and designer clothing has begun to overwhelm the younger members of the Communist party (as well as their new middle-class counterparts outside the party). An older member of the Communist party told me in confidence, and with a kind of resigned regret, that young Communist party officials will encourage business, stocks, elections, free speech, etc., because they can't resist the lure of owning a Mercedes, a television set, and dressing in style. He could be correct. The transition to legal democracy and a modified capitalist economy may occur, not because of student idealism but because of petty status seeking.

Sixth, the new middle strata and small business class may become a psychological majority, in that their impact on the economy and worldview of society will spill over into the political sphere. As these new middle strata become more numerous and prosperous, the pressure for legal democracy will increase. As the older members of the Communist party are replaced by younger ones, these younger party members will reflect the world orientation of the newly dominant social strata.

Seventh, the existance of the four tigers as a Chinese role model may have shifted Chinese cultural orientations away from traditional Chinese ideas and from Mao's communist principles. Let me expand on this latter point.

The Impact of the Four Tigers (Plus One) on the Civilization Nexus of China

One of Weber's great concepts—a level of analysis not emphasized by Marx or Durkheim—is his notion of civilizational differences, uniquenesses, peculiarities. He did not mean by this only the conception of culture, but that of a cultural nexus, wherein a group of societies were intertwined historically through years of ideological and institutional interchange. Thus, for instance, China and India were not only differentiated from each other as civilizationally distinct but also from Western civilization by Weber. Notice that the Hegelian category *Oriental* was not at all precise enough for Weber, whose penchant for historical detail showed him that China and India were not really alike, whereas certain structural similarities between China and Egypt certainly did exist (in the Marxian sense, beyond the civilizational differences).

In any case, if we follow out this Weberian notion of civilizational uniqueness we see immediately that traditional China was totally resistant to Western civilizational institutions and ideas. Only when China was in ruins did the Chinese begin studying the institutions that had overwhelmed them. Even then, the Western model of economy, polity, and social life simply seemed unsuited to China in the eyes of most Chinese.

The communist revolution didn't change this cultural prejudice as much as Mao would have liked. A suspicion of all things Western continued, and the world of modernity was not viewed as the world of the Chinese. The communist model that was adopted, as borrowed from Russia, included, after all, a centralized all-powerful state run by hallowed officials, with a near-deified leader at its center. This model was highly consistent with China's traditional economic-political model and not at all consistent with the Western model the Chinese still rejected.

But then the deified leader faltered, and the four tigers (plus one) emerged.

I shall have more to say about Mao Zedong's mistakes in the next and final section of this essay. For now let us simply emphasize that the Great Leap Forward ended up as a great leap backward and set the Chinese economy back who knows how many years. The Cultural Revolution disrupted the political stability of China and disillusioned an entire generation of Chinese.

Taken together, the Great Leap Forward and Cultural Revolution may have delegitimated communism in China forever. Without a doubt it destroyed the *charisma* of Mao, changing him from a god to a devil in the minds of this disenchanted generation.

At the same time that Mao and his romantic communism were faltering in China, Hong Kong, Taiwan, Singapore, and South Korea (the four tigers)—plus Japan—were emerging as world-important, even world centers, of capitalist economic success and power. Here at last was a non-Western model of Chinese modernity. Hong Kong, Taiwan, and Singapore *were* Chinese; South Korea was nearly Chinese in culture; and Japan was certainly non-Western.

The incredible success of these societies with capitalist business firms and legal-democratic politics (Korea, of course, is in transition in this process, but nonetheless is making tremendous progress) has led a new generation of Chinese to accept these models for China's future. As role models for the future of Chinese civilization, they are remarkable. For whatever good or bad emanates from these societies, they are actually Chinese (or almost Chinese).

The success of Chinese business leaders and intellectuals in the four tigers and the emergence of Japan as a world economic power have had a profound civilizational influence on China. Young Chinese look to the four tigers and Japan as models of their own future, and can now look to the West, not as an alien world, but as a world in which the Chinese can excel, and even extend their cultural horizons.

This is a remarkable change in cultural orientation in China. The civilizational nexus of China is definitely evolving, and the rationalized world culture Weber envisioned will undoubtedly envelop China.

One last Weberian conception—perhaps his most famous—must be discussed in terms of China. For Mao's charisma—real and later manufactured—had a profound effect upon China's modern development.

Mao: From God to Demon

Charismatic leaders do not produce social change. However, they rise to the fore during periods of transition or crisis, and they often put their stamp on a nation in some permanent way. Mao, of course, has left an indelible imprint on modern China. Before detracting from him by discussing his mistakes, look at what he helped China accomplish. He helped unify China politically and create governmental order and authority throughout the land. He helped create an economic infrastructure and heavy industry, along with a well-organized army with a high morale. (This latter had been a terrible problem for earlier Chinese leaders.) He stood up to the United States in the Korean War—something most Chinese leaders believed could not be done. Truly, Mao helped forge China into a modern nation-state—a nation that could provide food, military defense, political order, and the beginnings of a modern productive system.

If Mao had died younger, his legend would be deified. However, Mao lived on, and in his old age he began having dreams of a romantic socialism that he wished to see in his lifetime. Although the Great Leap Forward and Cultural Revolution failed utterly, they were Mao's attempts to speed up the historical process in order to create a great socialist-industrial paradise—now! His great leap was based on ancient Chinese principles, such as mass corvée labor teams. But the Great Wall and a modern machine economy demand different social organization. The Great Wall was built by corvée, but corvée failed to increase modern industrial and agricultural production.

Mao's Cultural Revolution was supposed to obliterate traditional Chinese ways of thinking and acting, and at the same time obliterate capitalist Western world orientations. The result was the creation of an anomic vacuum, in which the young, set upon the old by Mao himself, simply attacked authority figures, attacked the older generation in general, and finally attacked each other in rival factions.

Mao saw the anarchy and chaos, and stopped it militarily as he had stopped the Great Leap Forward. But in so doing, he alienated an entire generation of Chinese not only from his charismatic authority but from the authority of the Communist party as well.

Ironically, after Mao had established and helped legitimate communism in China, he was responsible for its delegitimation.

Delegitimated from communism and the party leadership that purveyed it, the new generation of Chinese sought alternatives. The four tigers plus Japan emerged as the alternative. With the lessening of tensions with the United States, America itself was viewed as a role model. For not only were the four tigers and Japan modeling the United States, but Chinese, Korean, and Japanese Americans (as well as Chinese exchange students) were doing exceptionally well in the United States itself. Mobility into the American middle class by Oriental business leaders and college students was (and is) phenomenal. Furthermore, the general acceptance of Oriental Americans by the American middle class was carefully noted by the Chinese and has spread throughout Chinese intellectual circles.

Thus Mao's charisma both legitimated

and delegitimated communism in China—a remarkable and unusual phenomenon. The ghost of Mao serves to both conservatize the older generation and radicalize the younger one in today's China. If China completes a transition to legal democracy with a modified capitalist economy and a relatively successful welfare state, then historians can say that love of Mao led China in transition from traditional to modern society, and that hatred of Mao led China to complete the transition.

Conclusions

In today's fluid sociological world there is a desire for a new theoretical synthesis. Weber's work, standing as it does between Durkheim and Marx, can provide a bridge between them—at least at certain junctures. While nothing like a unified foundation for sociology is ever likely to emerge because the varying epistemological, theoretical, and methodological models simply conflict on too many points, still we all desire some kind of a "ragged synthesis."

Anthony Giddens, for instance, has attempted such a synthesis, but warns us that it is incomplete.[51] French sociologists like Michel Foucault, Louis Althusser, and others, have attempted syntheses, and the great variation we find among them reminds us of the difficulty of the task. Contemporary critical theorists have also attempted to borrow from differing schools of thought and have produced a variant synthesis of their own.

The gulf among the Durkheimian, Marxian, and Weberian schools of thought is very great, and the ideological debates among functionalists, conflict theorists, positivists, and phenomenologists are as vociferous and obstructionalist as ever. Yet all of them in their own ways are attempting to achieve the ragged synthesis. If the Weber revival is helpful in this regard, it will have proved useful indeed.

In a different vein, and undoubtedly a more important one, we note that the conditions of modernity themselves have turned our attention to Weber's work. These conditions seem to be wearing out some of the pessimistic forecasts that haunted Weber's visions. Will we be dominated by technically trained bureaucrats "without soul," while we ourselves become narcissistic "sensualists without heart?" [52] Will we withdraw into our private world of sensual pleasures, while waiting for a "charismatic god-leader" to take us to the promised land? Or will we act "responsibly," in our own behalf, in a "rational" [53] orientation to the world?

We can only hope that Weber's heroic pessimism can lead us to a better understanding of the modern world and to a more hopeful reconstruction of it.

NOTES

1. Reinhard Bendix, *Embattled Reason* (New York: Oxford University Press, 1970).
2. Max Weber, "Objectivity in Social Science," in Max Weber, *The Methodology of the Social Sciences*, trans. Edward Shils and Henry Finch (New York: Free Press, 1949).
3. Émile Durkheim, *Suicide: A Study in Sociology* (New York, Free Press, 1951); *Elementary Forms of Religious Life* (New York: Free Press, 1965).
4. William Swatos, "The Disenchantment of Charisma," in Ronald M. Glassman and William Swatos, *Charisma, History, and Social Structure* (Westport, Conn.: Greenwood Press, 1983).
5. Christopher Lasch, *The Culture of Narcissism* (New York: Warner Books, 1979).
6. Max Weber, *The Protestant Ethic and the Spirit of Capitalism*, trans. Talcott Parsons (New York: Harper & Row, 1951); see especially the Introduction.
7. Max Weber, *Economy and Society*, trans. Guenther Roth and Claus Wittich (Berkeley, Calif.: University of California Press, 1979).
8. Lasch, *Culture of Narcissism*; Herbert Marcuse, *Eros and Civilization* (Boston: Beacon Press, 1955).
9. See in Weber, *Economy and Society*, the section on bureaucracy.
10. Lewis Mumford, *The Myth of the Machine* (New York: Harcourt Brace Jovanovich, 1968).
11. Weber, *Economy and Society*, p. 1123.
12. Weber, *The Protestant Ethic*, p. 181.
13. Wolfgang Mommsen, *The Age of Bureaucracy* (New York: Harper & Row, 1958).
14. Max Weber, "Politics as a Vocation," in *From Max Weber*, trans. Hans Gerth and C. Wright Mills (New York: Free Press, 1958).
15. Max Weber, *The General Economic History* (New Brunswick, N.J.: Transaction Books, 1981).
16. Robert J. Antonio and Ronald M. Glassman, *A Weber-Marx Dialogue* (Lawrence, Kans.: University Press of Kansas, 1985).
17. Max Weber, *The Agrarian Sociology of Ancient Civilizations* (Highland, N.J.: Humanities Press, 1981).
18. Weber, *Economy and Society*; see the section on charisma.
19. C. Wright Mills, *The Power Elite* (New York: Oxford University Press, 1967).
20. Thucydides, *The Peloponnesian War* (New York: Penguin Classics, 1952).
21. David Riesman, *The Lonely Crowd* (New York: Random House, 1951).
22. Ronald M. Glassman, *The New Middle Class and Democracy*.
23. Weber, *Economy and Society*; see the section on legal authority and the types of legitimate domination.
24. Weber, ibid.
25. Ibid.; see the section on charismatic authority.
26. Gerhard E. Lenski, *Power and Privilege: A Theory of Social Stratification* (Chapel Hill, N.C.: University of North Carolina Press, 1984).
27. Ronald M. Glassman, "Rational and Irrational Legitimacy," in Arthur J. Vidich and Ronald M. Glassman, *Conflict and Control: The Challenge to Legitimacy in the Twentieth Century* (Beverly Hills, Calif.: Sage Publications, 1979).
28. See the section on charisma and social structure in Ronald M. Glassman and William Swatos, *Charisma, History, and Social Structure* (Westport, Conn.: Greenwood Press, 1986).
29. Weber, *Economy and Society*; see the section on the types of legitimate domination.

30. Mommsen, *Age of Bureaucracy*.

31. Jürgen Habermas, *Legitimate Crisis* (New York: Harper Torch Books, 1980).

32. Georg W. F. Hegel, *The Philosophy of History* (New York: Penguin Classics, 1951).

33. Franco Ferrorratti, "Weber and Marx," in Robert J. Antonio and Ronald M. Glassman, eds., *A Weber-Marx Dialogue* (Lawrence, Kans.: University Press of Kansas, 1985).

34. Milovan Djilas, *The New Class: An Analysis of the Communist System* (New York: Harcourt Brace Jovanovich, 1982).

35. Stanislaw Ossowski, *Class Structure in the Social Consciousness*, trans. Sheila Patterson (London: Routledge & Kegan Paul, 1963).

36. Weber, *Protestant Ethic and the Spirit of Capitalism*.

37. Ibid.

38. Ibid.

39. Karl Marx, *The Poverty of Philosophy* (New York: International Publishers, 1948).

40. Ronald M. Glassman, *Democracy and Despotism in Primitive Societies* (Millwood, N.Y.: Associated Faculty Press, 1986).

41. Weber, *Economy and Society*; see the section on charisma.

42. Glassman and Swatos, *Charisma, History, and Social Structure*.

43. Weber, *The General Economic History; The Agrarian Sociology of Ancient Civilizations*.

44. George Miliband, *The State and Marxian Theory* (New Haven, Conn.: Yale University Press, 1977).

45. Zoltan Tar, "The Weber-Lukacs Dialogue," in Glassman and Murvar, *Max Weber's Political Sociology* (Westport, Conn.: Greenwood Press, 1983).

46. Douglas Kellner, "Critical Theory and Weberian Sociology," in Robert J. Antonio and Ronald M. Glassman, eds., *A Weber-Marx Dialogue*.

47. Weber, *Economy and Society*; see the section on bureaucracy.

48. Ibid.

49. Max Weber, *The Methodology of the Social Sciences* (New York: Free Press, 1972).

50. Ibid.

51. Anthony Giddens, *Capitalism and Modern Social Theory* (Cambridge: Cambridge University Press, 1971).

52. Weber, *Protestant Ethic and the Spirit of Capitalism*, p. 181.

53. Ronald M. Glassman, "Rational and Irrational Legitimacy" in Arthur J. Vidich and Ronald M. Glassman, *Conflict and Control: The Challenge to Legitimacy in the Modern World* (Beverly Hills, Calif.: Sage Publications, 1976).

ESSAYS

4. Symbolic Interaction

5. Phenomenological Sociology

6. Hermeneutics and Sociology

7. Surrender-and-Catch and Sociology

8. Cultural Resistance to Rationalization: A Study
   of an Art Avant-Garde

PART TWO

NEW DIRECTIONS IN SYMBOLIC THEORY

Symbolic interactionist sociologists focus on questions of how personal life takes on meaning and how meanings are lost, transformed, or renewed.

Symbolic interaction rests on three premises:

1. Human beings act on the basis of the meanings things have for them.
2. Meanings grow out of social interaction.
3. Meanings are modified through an interpretive process in which people choose among alternative meanings.

From the perspective of symbolic interaction, the self is both a process and an object. For in developing a self, an individual becomes an object to herself, something which is socially defined and redefined through further interaction. As a process the self is both an *I*, the individual's subjective experience of the world in the present, and a *me*, the individual's reaction based on past experience.

Society constantly undergoes change as order is negotiated and renegotiated. Shared symbols and meanings make joint action possible. Stability arises through the persistence of shared meanings and the acts of like-minded people interacting with each other. Socialization as the creation of the self takes place through interaction with significant others. The child takes the role of others in playing, and games present a model of society to the child. Through play the child develops the ability to understand how others view her from their points of view. The child develops a *generalized other*, which serves as the basis of social control. Adult socialization takes place through reference groups which give rise to new perceptions of the self.

Interactionist research is inductive, with theory and analysis arising from the data. The goal of the researcher is to see how people maintain social reality in the face of anomalies and how they reinterpreted it to increase their personal autonomy. Learning the special languages used by people in different arenas of society is the key to entering their social worlds.

Barbara Katz Rothman

SYMBOLIC INTERACTION *

WHAT IS SYMBOLIC INTERACTION?†

The ideas of symbolic interaction were first crystalized in the work of George Herbert Mead, and most clearly shown in his posthumously published book, *Mind, Self, and Society*.[1] Mead was a philosopher concerned with the relation between the individual and society. Others whose work was especially important in shaping the perspective include W. I. Thomas and Charles Horton Cooley. It is Herbert Blumer, however, who coined the term *symbolic interaction*, and is the foremost exponent of the per-

---

*Portions of this chapter appeared in *In Labor: Women and Power in the Birthplace*, by Barbara Katz Rothman (New York: W. W. Norton, 1981).

†A note on language: The language of symbolic interaction can be confusing: discussions of self and other make the use of pronouns rather complicated. Many of the usual corrections for the sexist bias of the generic *he* serve to confuse matters further. I have therefore sometimes referred to self as *he*, sometimes as *she*.

spective as it emerged in the work of Mead and the sociologists at the University of Chicago.

Symbolic interaction is a loosely structured cluster of fundamental ideas, assumptions, or propositions about human beings in society. It is a perspective, a point of view, which guides the way one sees the social world. It is frequently called a *perspective in social psychology*, and more than half of the books on symbolic interaction include *social psychology* in the title. Other symbolic interactionists, myself included, object to limiting the perspective to social psychology. Symbolic interaction is a perspective on the social world which focuses on interaction as the unit of study, and can and should be used to study and to understand the larger social structure as well as the nature of individual interactions.

What unites the ideas and shapes the perspective or the tradition, what has provided the historical thread tying together the work of philosophers, sociologists, and social psychologists in symbolic interaction, has been the dual emphasis on *symbol* and on *interaction*.

Symbol refers to *meanings*. For symbolic interactionists, things (objects, ideas, beliefs, people, values, states of being) do not simply exist: they exist in the meanings they have. What is meaning, how personal life takes on meaning, how meaning persists, is transformed, lost, and regained—these are core questions for symbolic interactionists.[2] Meanings are established in communication: hence the importance of interaction. Our world exists in the meanings it has for us, and our meanings come from our interactions. People, like meanings, exist in a social context.

THE BASIC PREMISES

According to Herbert Blumer, symbolic interaction rests on three basic premises:

1. Human beings act toward things on the basis of the meanings the things have for them.

2. The meanings of such things are derived from, or grow out of, social interaction.

3. These meanings are handled in and modified through an interpretive process used by the person in dealing with the things he encounters.[3]

The first premise has to do with meanings. It states that the nature of a thing lies in its meanings. What, after all, is this thing before you right this moment, this "book"? It is, at various times, a "purchase," for which you paid, which you then had to carry home with your other purchases which may have included other books, but might also have been groceries, clothes, or baseball bats. These things, taken together, are "possessions," for which you may feel the need of more closet space, or may have to pay by weight to move to another apartment. The book also has meaning as a book, as something to read, something to study, something for which you may be "responsible" on a test. And, if you use

your imagination, you can think of circumstances under which the book would have yet other meanings: something to prop up the bed; the murder weapon ("Yes, detective, sir, when he came at me I bopped him with my sociology book"); and lots of other things. What you do with this book, the way you act toward it, is going to be based on the meaning(s) it has for you, and these meanings are not fixed once and for all. Meaning is rather an emergent property of objects. Things come to have meaning, and meanings are never absolutely fixed or established.[4]

Where meanings come from is the subject of Blumer's second major premise. Meanings come from social interaction: meanings are the products of people in interaction. As an example, a child who picks up a bug from off the ground learns the meaning of that bug from the people around her. In one family someone slaps the child's hand and then washes it: the bug is a bad, dirty thing. In another setting someone brings a piece of paper to hold the bug and a magnifying glass with which to view it: the bug is interesting, something to study. In another setting someone ties a string around the bug and teaches the child how to play with it: the bug is a toy. And in some other setting the child is thanked and the bug put aside to be cooked: the bug is food. The meaning of the object lies not in the thing itself, but in the way people define it, and these meanings are shared between people in interaction. As a child learns meanings, she is becoming *socialized* into her society. As she goes through life, meeting new people and new situations, she continues to learn new meanings.

The third premise, that the meanings are handled in and modified through an interpretive process, is the most far-reaching of the three. In order to understand human behavior, not only must the meanings of things be understood but also the ways in which these meanings are handled, that is, the process of interpretation. The first part of the process of interpretation is the actor indicating to himself those things toward which he is acting: he notices, takes note of, indicates to himself, the object. Noticing something, or indicating it to oneself, involves an interaction within the individual, a kind of talking to oneself. The interactionists postulate that this ongoing internal conversation is always there, and it is that which allows people to choose between many meanings for the same object and to interpret meanings in the light of situations.

The idea is that people can and do choose between meanings, choose how to respond to things. Of great importance in the symbolic interactionist perspective is the belief that the individual is both active and rational. Historically the perspective, as it developed in the Chicago school, was antideterminist. This was in contrast to the behaviorism of the 20s and 30s, Freudianism and neo-Freudianism, biological determinism and Marxism. These perspectives saw all human action as the result of some preceding cause. Since the cause inevitably led to the result, behavior was determined and free will not possible. Mead's work provided some philosophical justification for the general antideterminist thrust of sociology as it was then being developed.[5] The symbolic interactionist perspective emphasizes the individual as an actor, and as a thinking being, making choices and controlling his or her own behavior. Thinking, or minded behavior as it is called, involves, as stated above, interaction with oneself. This means that individuals are active in shaping their own behavior.

Action and interaction are thoroughly entwined with the idea of meaning: meanings are learned in interaction, and the interpretation and manipulation of meanings (thinking) precedes all action, enters into all social interaction. Hence symbolic interaction: interaction based on symbols. Symbols, or to use Mead's term, significant symbols, are the fundamental elements of which language is composed. The meaning of a significant symbol cannot be determined by examining the symbol itself. Words are the best example, but not the

only kind of significant symbol: bodily movements such as the curtsy or objects such as a white flag or a burning cross are also significant symbols. There is nothing about the symbol which conveys its meaning other than our agreement. A white flag *stands for* surrender because we say it does. The word *dog* means dog because we say it does.

Compare the communication of people in language with the communication of, for example, bees. A bee which finds a source of pollen will, on its return to the hive, engage in a particular dance. Watching that dance, other bees can then find the pollen. We might say that the bee "told" the others where to go. The bee, however, will do that same dance no matter which, if any, bees are there to see it. The dance is not done in order to tell: there is no intentionality in the act. The same is true of, for example, the bird who "warns" the others of impending danger by chattering as it flies away. The chatter is not done in order to warn. This is communication by natural sign.

A more sophisticated communication can occur with the use of gestures. Gestures are abbreviated acts: a bully raises his arm and another child flinches. Even among animals we can see what Mead calls a *conversation of gestures*. The snarling and growling of two dogs, for example, as they circle each other, are gestures substituting for a full struggle. The one moves toward the attack position; the other responds by backing off or repositioning for a better defense. They respond to each other's gestures.

The significant symbol emerges from the gesture when intentionality is added, when the symbols are used for the purpose of communication, and are understood that way. Thus an arbitrary sound comes to mean something, and is used to convey its meaning. The response to a symbol is a response to its understood or interpreted intention. If someone burns a cross on your lawn, your response is to what cross burning is intended and understood to mean, and not simply to the fire. To respond to the meaning or intention of the symbol requires the interpretive process: people respond to the imagined meanings of others. For communication to be possible, there must therefore be consensus as to the meaning of symbols. Shared and common meanings make language, and so make society possible.

To respond to a symbol is to first acknowledge it, and then to decide what it means. What it means is what the other is understood to have meant by its use. How one knows what the other meant, is by imagining oneself to be the other. We know what it means when one uses a symbol because we ourselves use these symbols. The individual in interaction takes the role of the other. As I write a sentence, I read it to see if it makes sense, that is, I put myself in the role of the other, in this case the reader. I can then see my communication just as you, the reader, see it. That is the interesting thing about language: we can provide the same stimulus to ourselves as to others. When I speak, I hear myself. I can respond to myself as I think others respond to me. I can take the role of others and thus communicate with them.

This then is the basic problem for symbolic interaction: to develop theory and method for studying human interaction which views people as capable of active and self-reflexive behavior, taking their own and others' points of view in constructing their interactions and dealings with the world. The interaction is to be the unit of analysis, and interaction is understood to include the covert process of taking the role of the other. Societies are made up of interacting, role-taking individuals: studies of social life must, for the symbolic interactionist, look at the processes of which human life and human society are constructed.

MIND

Consciousness, thinking, minded behavior—all of this involves interaction with oneself. Mind is a process, not a thing, a process through which people carry on transactions with their environment, and deal with their world. Mind is not the same thing as the brain; the brain *is* a thing, a lump of gray matter. Nor is the mind, in the symbolic interactionist view, the structure implied by personality factors or IQ or attitudes. Think instead of the mind as a process, an ongoing activity.

Mind works by making indications to itself, that is, by noting things in the world. In others words, we talk to ourselves. *Mind* is the symbolic interaction the individual engages in with herself. People interact within themselves all the time. Sometimes we are very aware of doing it, even talking aloud to ourselves; and at other times it is very vague, almost like the mind mumbling. But the things we come across as we move about in the world are noted by us, or indicated by ourselves to ourselves.

This process, which Blumer calls *self-indication*, he defines as "a moving communicative process in which the individual notes things, assesses them, gives them a meaning and decides to act on the basis of the meaning."[6] "To indicate something is to extricate it from its setting, to hold it apart, to give it a meaning, or in Mead's language, to make it into an object."[7] Minded behavior thus makes objects, constructs the world for us and by us.

Because people have minds which engage in self-indication, people do not exist in a world of preexisting objects which call forth always predictable responses. We are not like Pavlov's dogs, salivating to a bell. People construct objects on the basis of ongoing activity, and respond to their constructions. If, for example, you see an apple on a table, you do not necessarily eat it, not even if you are hungry and like apples. You think about the apple, notice it, decide what it *means*, what if anything to do about it. If you see the apple in an artist's studio, sitting near a candle and a wine bottle, with a canvas and brushes and paints nearby, you may see it as part of a still life and not as food. The same apple in a bowl on your kitchen table has a different meaning. The meaning is something one gives the object in the process of self-indication. The apple is not just a stimulus calling forth a response, because between the stimulus and the response there is a *mind*, making *self-indications*. The behavior of the individual is therefore not simply a response being released, as it is with the salivating dog, but an action which is constructed. Mind is always there in action: "Whatever the action in which he is engaged, the human individual proceeds by pointing out to himself the divergent things which have to be taken into account in the course of his action.[8]

In this way people construct the world in which they live. That is not to say that there is no "real" world out there, but that the world can only be grasped by us in the form that we know it. And the only form in which human beings can know the world is in terms of making indications to themselves about that world.[9]

Related to the process of self-indication is the idea of conceptualizing. For the symbolic interactionist, a *concept* is how we know an object. It is formed as the end product of this process of making indications to ourselves and conceptualizing reality. The concept serves three functions:

1. It introduces a new orientation or point of view.
2. It serves as a tool or as a means of transacting business with one's environment.
3. It makes possible deductive reasoning and so the anticipation of new experience.[10]

All knowing involves the process of conceptualizing, even the taken-for-granted reality. Consider again the example of the apple. At an even more basic level than what to do with the apple on the table, how does one know that there is an apple, and that it is on a table? How does one see the apple as an object separate from the table? How does one, seeing it, know it is round, know how big it is? The individual imposes meaning on the chaos of sense data, on the patterns of light which stimulate retinal nerves so that one "sees" an apple. As one moves toward the apple, the shape changes: seeing it at different angles it presents different degrees of roundness. Yet one perceives it as round and unchanging. Perception is an interpretation of signs that our senses provide, a hypothesis that the mind evokes to explain its perceptions to itself.[11] The act of perception (mind in process) creates meaning out of the sensory stimulation, by making explanations to itself. Perception is a judgment. Thus we see what we know to be there. One sees only the top of the apple, but seeing the top and realizing that one sees an apple, one can make anticipatory statements about the bottom—constructing it.[12]

The judgments, the constructed perceptions, come from experience, and experience is limited by environment. Environment is a social as well as a physical construction. The society in which we live provides us with certain sensory experiences and ways of conceptualizing those experiences. People living in dense forests must see space differently than people living on flat plains. And babies whose world is bounded by ceilings must learn to see spaces differently than babies whose world is open to the sky.

In learning concepts, one learns to which objects to attend, and how to see them. Blumer says that "through conception, objects may be perceived in new relations, which is tantamount to saying that the perceptual world becomes reorganized."[13] Concepts sensitize perception, and thus impose meaning on the chaos of sense data. We use concepts to organize the world, while at the same time we are limited, or at least directed, by the concepts we use. Concepts fashion perception: the world in which we live is constructed by us and the process of construction is minded behavior.

SELF

The self is a product of minded behavior. As a product it is both a process and an object, or more accurately, a process experienced as an object.

Selfhood is distinguished by the capacity

to be an object to one's self, to respond to one's self in the same way one responds to other objects and individuals. For Mead, it is the ability to experience one's self as an object that is the hallmark of selfhood.

In developing a self, the individual becomes an object to himself, and like all objects, something which is socially defined and redefined in interaction. One of the implications of this is that the self, like other objects, can have many meanings or definitions arising out of different interactions and coming from different perspectives. The sources of these different perspectives which give meaning to the self have been called *reference groups*.[14] William James, one of Mead's teachers, said that "a man has as many social selves as there are individuals who recognize him and carry an image of him in their mind." These individuals, William James pointed out, tend to fall into classes or groups: family, coworkers, friends, teachers, and so on.[15] In interaction with her children, for example, a woman sees herself one way; in interaction with her colleagues, another self emerges.

Each of these reference groups provides the individual with a perspective which shapes the way the person sees the world, including the self. What we look like to ourselves is shaped by what we think we look like to selected others. The idea of a self then includes the imagination of how the self appears to others, and how they judge that appearance: what Charles Horton Cooley called the *looking glass self*. When we think of ourselves, "we always imagine, and in imagining share, the judgements of the other mind."[16]

But the self is more than an object, it is also a process. As a social process within the individual, the self, according to Mead, involves two phases: the *I* and the *me*. The distinction between the I and the me, at the simplest level, can be clarified by thinking about how memory works. The I is constantly present in experience as that which remembers, while the self it remem-

bers is always a me.[17] The I is the subjective and the me the objective aspects of the self.

The I and the me are phases of the self, part of a process, and not hypothesized structures such as Freud's ego, superego, and id. Also unlike Freud's constructs, the I and the me interact in a complementary way, working with and not against each other. These two phases, the I and the me, operate together to constitute the self.

Every act in which the self engages begins in the form of an I and then usually goes on to the me. The I, as the subjective component of the self, provides the impulsive and spontaneous aspect of behavior. The me provides the direction needed by the otherwise undirected impulses constituting the I. The me is the incorporated set of definitions, understandings, and expectations, the meanings common to the social group. It is the I which gives propulsion, while the me gives direction to behavior.[18]

The me represents the social situation of the self, consisting of internalized attitudes of others, of others' conceptions of one's self. The I is responsive to the me, and to that extent is independent of the social situation. Mead stated: The "I" is the response of the organism to the attitudes of others which one himself assumes. The attitudes of the others constitute the organized "me" and then one reacts toward that as an "I."[19]

In sum, the self is an interactive process within the individual. The I and the me are analytic distinctions made between phases of the ongoing process.

SOCIETY

"Human society," according to Blumer, "is seen as consisting of acting people, and the life of the society is to be seen as consisting of their actions."[20] Rather than focusing on structure, here too, as with mind and self, the symbolic interactionist perspective shifts our attention to the process. "Human society," Tomatsu Shibutani said, "might best be regarded as an on-going process, a becoming rather than a being." [21] Social change is thus inherent in the definition of society, because society is seen as constantly undergoing organization and reorganization. "The arrangements that make up society are constantly being 'worked at' by those who live within them; they are constantly being arranged, modified, rearranged, sustained, defended and undermined." [22]

The idea of society as eternally in flux is exemplified in the work of Anselm Strauss.[23] He sees society as "negotiated order." Negotiation is an ongoing process in the life of groups and societies. Sometimes negotiations occur in a formal and structured way (as is the case with treaties between countries, the resolution of labor-management disputes, and business contracts between individuals); sometimes negotiations occur in such a loose, unstructured way that we are unaware of what is going on (as is often the case when lovers "negotiate" a relationship in the way they treat each other, or when parent and child interact); and in many in-between situations (as when a student and teacher "figure out" what the requirements will be for a term paper, or when two children in a family decide which television show to watch). In their negotiations people order the social world, that is, through interaction, they create the social order.

Structuralists, who view society as an established organization, or set of organizations, find social change difficult to explain. But from the interactionist perspective, as stated above, social change is very easy to understand—negotiations and thus the creation and re-creation of the social order occur constantly. What gets harder to explain within the interactionist perspective is the stability or persistence of the social order, the very thing the structuralists do explain. Social order may be a constructed reality, but there are patterns and order which we observe, and which influence us, and which appear to maintain themselves. Our very ability to negotiate

depends on these patterns; we can negotiate with others because of shared language, shared meanings, and often some shared sense of the distribution of power. Thus a three-year-old knows "how far" she can go in how-much-dinner-before-dessert negotiations with a parent, but there is no negotiating with a hungry (or not hungry) infant.

Given shared symbols and meanings which make interaction possible, people can act together. This *joint action,* Blumer's term for individuals or groups in alignment and meeting each others' goals, is the basis for society. Society, and its stability and persistence, then comes to rest on the shared meanings facilitating joint action. But meanings are the products of interactions. This circle, from society to meaning to society, is the flow, the sharing of meanings, the negotiations, the interactions that produce and reproduce the society, but it is hard to get a bearing on the society itself, existing in the thinglike way we experience it. It is somewhat like the problem of observing the electron: one can either know how fast it is going or know where it is, but not both at once.

Cooley explained the other, society-as-thing experience by saying that society exists in the minds of individuals constituting a social unit. It, society, *exists*—we certainly experience it as existing—and where it exists is in our minds. Society as an *object* exists in our interactions and in our belief that it exists and as what it exists. And it is in our acting on those beliefs that we construct, reconstruct, and maintain the social order.

Let us take the example of a particular social institution, a college. How does that institution exist? It exists in interactions: the interactions of students with faculty, of faculty with administration, of administration with students, and so on and on. For example, a particular set of interactions between students and faculty (earning a grade) leads to a particular set of interactions between faculty and administration (turning in grades), which in turn leads to a particular interaction between student and administration (graduating). Then there are the interactions outside of the institution, which also create and sustain it, those interactions, for example, between employers who acknowledge the existence of a college and employees who claim to have graduated from that college. If no one, anywhere at all, thought that colllege existed, if no student, faculty, administrator, janitor, employer—simply nobody—believed in that college, would it exist? The buildings would not disappear in a puff of smoke, certainly, but would the college continue to exist *as a college* without any social acknowledgment? The college, as any social institution and the thing we call society itself, exists in our acknowledgments of it, in our interactions in and concerning it, in our minds, which declare it to exist. All institutions, all the social patterns that we observe, rest on the acts of minded individuals interacting with one another.[24]

That is why the interactionists so frequently lose sight of the larger picture, the macrostructure of society. Blumer said that "it's not macro or micro; it is rather a case of human beings contained within a small fold, and that contained within a wider fold, and beyond that within a wider fold, and so forth."[25] The tendency in symbolic interactionism has been to look at the interactions occurring in the smaller folds, and use that as a basis for understanding the larger folds. Thus social change, negotiations, interactions, and the processes of social life are understood, but one loses sight of the social structure created by those processes.

SOCIALIZATION

There is no *self,* as interactionists define it, at birth. Instead, selfhood is developed and acquired in a social context. Since the key aspect of defining self in the symbolic interactionist perspective is the ability to experience one's self as an object, acquiring a self means acquiring the capacity for self-reference. At root then, the acquisition of self is tied into the development of language, because only then can the self be an object that one can symbolically designate. Things are picked out from the world and named; learning names, the things become objects which the mind can indicate to itself. Learning name(s) for self, self too becomes an object.

The development of self is of course more complicated than simply learning one's name. It also involves the development of the I and the me, the phases of self in action, and coming to know the self as perceived by others. In learning symbols, such as names for oneself, one learns also the meanings and values attached to those symbols. A child learns that she is a "girl," and all that means; that she is "naughty," "sweet," "sleepy," "dirty," and all the other things the others in the world see her as. She learns to see herself as she is seen by her significant others. *Significant others* is Mead's term for those people in our lives who provide the perspective from which we learn to view ourselves.

We learn to see ourselves by taking the role of these others. A little child, for example, approaching a stove can sometimes be heard to say, "Hot! hot! don't touch!" The child here takes on the role of the parent, and tells himself the same things the parent tells him. Similarly, a toddler who is still being breastfed will, in doll play, lift up his shirt and hold the doll to the breast. The child (boy or girl) doing this is acting out the role of the mother. In so doing, he can see himself as a nursing baby. By taking the role of the other, the child sees himself as he is seen by others: someone likely to touch hot stoves, someone who nurses, and so on. Thus Mead sees the child's play as serving the fundamental purpose of constructing the social self. Play is more than anticipatory socialization—preparing the child for adult roles. It is a basic step in the development of self.

The child in taking the role of others learns to view herself from their perspective, seeing herself as an object in the world.

This *play* was seen by Mead as the first phase of the child's socialization, or development of self. The child plays at being parent, Wonderwoman, or big sister, taking the role of the other, and thus learning to see self as an object.

There is another way in which play supports the development of self. The child may play at being someone or something. For example, when pretending to be a puppy, a child crawls around underfoot, barking and growling. In doing this, the child is learning the difference between puppy's behavior and self's behavior. As a puppy, the child is on the ground. When she stands up, then standing up is itself seen as an attribute of herself as not-puppy, as child. Or to take another example, a child playing "dress up" tries on different costumes—mommy's shoes, a ballet dancer's shoes, daddy's shoes. When he then puts on his *own* shoes, he can see them as the costume appropriate for himself. If some behavior or piece of clothing is appropriate for the other role, then behavior one engages in and clothing one wears oneself can be seen as appropriate to a role also. Thus mes are established: me as a "kindergarten boy," or me as a "big boy who doesn't wear diapers."

At the play stage the child is limited to taking on one other role at a time, and using that perspective to view the self. The child at the play stage is not yet capable of integrating roles into any sort of pattern. But as the child matures and as expectations for her grow more complex, the child grows to the stage of *games*. The game is an organized social activity. It involves several people interacting in accordance with a set of rules. The demands of the game thus epitomize what the child will have to do in the society as a whole. The child has to put herself into the context of the game, so that her actions are coordinated with those of other players. The game serves as a model of the organized social activities in which the individual functions by taking on not a single other role, but the generalized view of the others. The *generalized other* is the term Mead uses for the expectations of the society at large. In the earlier, play stage, the child sees herself from many discrete points of view. But people do not continue to see themselves in this fragmented way: they see themselves as wholes, or units. It is the ability to take the role of the generalized other which gives the self unity, which unites and organizes the self.[26]

The generalized other also serves as the basis for social control, as the child moves from the expectations of a single other to those of the society as a whole. The generalized other is society's representative within the individual. Here too, as with the I and the me, it may be useful to distinguish Mead's ideas from those of Freud. Freud also postulated an internalized basis for social control—the superego. The superego, however, is a childhood conscience, the internalization of a single authority, the parent. In the interactionist perspective the adult is not stuck with the childhood conscience. Being able to take the role of others means that the individual's conscience, along with values, goals, and all else which serves to regulate our behavior, is eternally in flux, growing, changing, adapting, and being redefined.

The development of the ability to take on the role of the generalized other makes continued socialization possible. People are not passively created, formed by outside forces, but active participants in the continuing construction of self. Socialization, within the symbolic interactionist perspective, is (in what should by now be a familiar refrain) an ongoing process. People go through life seeing themselves as seen by others, and do sometimes take on new others, or new *reference groups*, as Shibutani has said.[27] These new reference groups give rise to new views of self.

Adult socialization is a ubiquitous process, something made especially clear in complex societies. Socialization into a new job, college, marriage, medical school, hospitals, and old age homes, all these and many more situations, involves the reformulation of the self. In some circumstances, especially within the context of the *total institution*, such as the army, jail, or a mental hospital, this socialization can be so dramatic as to lead to basic changes in individual conceptions of self.

Even in these drastic situations, the individual is not merely buffeted about by outside forces. In the symbolic interactionist perspective the individual is, above all, an actor. Socialization is not the manipulation or modification of the person, but the ongoing creation of the person, a creation in which the individual is an active participant. The individual learns from her society but at the same time modifies that society. Minded behavior allows the person to construct the society for herself. Creating constructs and defining situations are also a way she can construct society for others. We turn now to a discussion of how situations are defined.

THE DEFINITION OF THE SITUATION

''If men define situations as real, they are real in their consequences.'' This idea, presented by W. I. and Dorothy Swaine Thomas, has been the basis for much of the thinking and research done by symbolic interactionists.[28] The statement represents a dual focus in symbolic interaction: first, what goes into the definition of a situation, that is, what are the processes involved in defining situations; and second, what are the consequences of that socially defined situation. The work of Erving Goffman represents the first focus; that of the labeling theorists, the second.

Events, occurrences, and happenings present themselves to the individual, and are perceived as situations. As situations they are objects which can be indicated, named, identified, and thus processed by mind. In this way situations organize the world into meaningful constellations: situations are the contexts for the creation of social reality. The otherwise random events, happenings, or occurrences are, when conceptualized as situations, invested with meaning by participants and by observers, and then treated in terms of that meaning. That is how they become real in their consequences. An example may help to clarify the point: a variety of bodily sensations, experiences, and changes will suddenly come to be seen as *symptoms* if cancer is diagnosed. The diagnosis will give meaning to these otherwise random physical happenings. Once the cancer is diagnosed, the person becomes a cancer patient. And one is equally in the role of cancer patient whether the diagnosis is accurate or wrong. The treatments, hospitalization, pity, and grief are all real: they are consequences of the definition (diagnosis) of the situation.

Situations clarify or organize reality by providing people with categories of meaning for the things, people, and behavior to be found in the situation. Let us consider some further examples. First, what is a situation, and how does it order reality? If you suddenly woke up to find yourself lying on a high bed in a pale green and white room with only a metal chest of drawers with a plastic pitcher and drinking glass on top, where would you be? And if a door opened and a woman in a white dress holding a clipboard under one arm walked in, who might she be? You are almost certainly going to figure yourself to be in a hospital, which means you must be sick, hurt, or damaged in some way. Even if you felt no pain, you would probably begin exploring your body to find the problem which must, you assume, have brought you here. You ''recognize'' the situation: you take cues, put them together, and construct what ''must'' be going on. And the person walking in? Knowing the situation, you know the probabilities: a doctor, nurse, maybe a lab technician, or some other hospital staff member. If the same woman, same costume, showed up somewhere else, say a dentist's office, you would think she is a dental hygienist, dentist, dental assistant perhaps. If she showed up entering a mayonnaise factory production area, you might think she is a supervisor.

Thus the situation provides people with a way of ordering the social world and the other people in it: "If this is a hospital, you must be a nurse." Situations also provide expectations for self: "If this is a hospital, I must be sick." In such a situation as that described above, you would probably begin the interaction based on those assumptions, acting like a patient (not jumping out of bed, for example) and expecting the woman in white to act like a medical practitioner (not being offended if she lifts the covers and pokes your abdomen).

Some situations are very clear, very conventional, or standard, as is the one I have described. Yes, even in that situation things could be other than they seem, but other explanations are farfetched, surprising, more appropriate to drama than real life. Other situations may be far less standardized, and the definitional processes more idiosyncratic. Two students from the same sociology class, for example, may be sitting together discussing what will be on the next exam. The situation is *studying together*. Then one student puts an arm around the other. The situation may have changed. It may now appear as a sexual advance. Either of the two students, let us say that they are both women in this example, may understand the arm as a sexual overture. That is, the woman who put her arm around the other may have intended it that way, and the other woman may have understood it that way. Or either may see it as a simple, friendly gesture. Their definitions of the situation may match, and then again they may not. The situation will be negotiated in their interaction. Thus two (minded) individuals will take each other into account as they seek a single definition of the situation.

Thomas, when he originally introduced the phrase, said, "Preliminary to any self determined act of behavior there is always a stage of examination and deliberation which we may call the 'definition of the situation.'" [29] With each act, each individual defines the situation for himself or herself, and attempts to do so for others. Successfully defining the situation, that is, having one's definition become the definition accepted by all participants, means controlling the situation.

To control a situation means controlling the behavior of others. Since roles are reciprocal, the role one takes on in a situation serves to constrain and to limit what others can do. This process of limiting the behavioral possibilities for the other has been called *altercasting*, [30] casting the alter (other) in a role. Picking a fight, for example, involves casting the other into the role of protagonist. An actor also attempts to define situations by manipulating the presentation of self and the environment. Dressing formally and sitting behind a large desk, for example, sets up a different situation for meeting someone than dressing informally and walking up to him or her. Consider meeting a distant relative for the first time, under each of these circumstances. What are the possibilities for you in the interaction?

Situations are staged, their elements "assembled, arranged, manipulated, and controlled." [31] But people do not have to accept situations as defined. Redefining situations is a creative human endeavor. That is the basis for much of our humor, intelligence, and delight in life. Consider the following, perhaps apocryphal, story. A group of pacifists were organizing voter registration in a black community in the deep South. Word was out that the Klan would be riding that night. When white-hooded Klan members arrived, they were greeted with "Welcome Ku Klux Klan" banners and lanterns strung across the street, lemonade and cookies, and children singing. A creative, intelligent, and thoroughly human response.

RESEARCH IMPLICATIONS

How can we study people, how can we possibly make an object of study out of the processes of mind, self, and society, the becoming, maintaining, and constant changing that is human life?

There is no one research method that can do all that in all times and all places. The specific question being asked must shape the research technique employed. Thus familiar questions of *hard* versus *soft*, or *quantitative* versus *qualitative*, do not get at the real issue, which is to construct a methodology that will do justice to the data. The datum, or the real subject matter of sociology for the symbolic interactionists, is the meaningful (to the actors involved) social process.[32] Researchers working within the symbolic interactionist framework have used laboratory settings, experiments, and surveys in an attempt to get at the experience of participants in the social process.[33]

The most usual research techniques, however, are participant observation and in-depth interviewing. These research techniques are used most often by symbolic interactionists because they allow the researcher to enter into the social world being researched. The researcher who participates in the situation being studied, who interacts with the people being studied, can learn to see the world through their eyes. Taking the role of the other, the basis for all interaction, including interaction with the self, is also the basis for research. By taking the role of the other, the researcher can gain an understanding of covert as well as overt reality, of underlying meanings, of how situations are defined, and what the consequences are of those meanings and situational definitions. As an actor in the social world, the researcher can come to know that world as it is known to those who construct it. And as a sociologist, the researcher can come to an understanding of the processes involved in its construction, the making and remaking of reality.

USING THE INTERACTIONIST PERSPECTIVE IN RESEARCH

My own work on the management of childbirth provides one example of the many ways the interactionist perspective is used for research. This project was an attempt to make some of the connections between interaction (the microlevel) and social structure (the macrolevel), using the substantive area of the management of childbirth as an example. It is equally true to say that my work was an attempt to understand the ways childbirth is managed in America, using symbolic interactionism as a perspective which provides useful insight. I began with both parts: an interest in the management of birth, and the perspective of the symbolic interactionist.

I interviewed medically trained nurse-midwives who had begun to attend home births. These nurse-midwives were trained in one setting—hospitals—and were now working in another—homes. The same physiological event, the birth of a baby, can occur in either place: women labor and babies are born in a variety of settings. But the social definitions are vastly different in different settings, and these differences create new social realities. In turn, these new social realities, or definitions of the situation, create new physiological reality, as the birth process itself is shaped by the socially constructed setting in which it occurs.

As a symbolic interactionist looking at childbirth, I focused on the ways the event is socially constructed. I looked at the meanings attached to the things—objects, events, and people—related to childbirth, and how these meanings emerge and are maintained or transformed. I found that there were two different models, or constellations of meanings related to childbirth, one developed by the medical specialty of obstetrics, and the other being developed by home birth advocates and lay or empirical midwives (birth attendants who are not medically trained). By examining some of the interactions which occur in childbirth, the existence and implications of these alternative models will become clear.

Situation 1

A woman comes to the maternity floor of a large hospital. She is upset, almost crying, holding her huge belly and leaning against her husband, who seems nearly as upset as she is. "My wife is in labor," he states, and hands over a scrap of paper with times marked off—the seven- to eight-minute intervals they have timed between contractions. The woman is ushered into a cubicle and examined. "No," the doctor tells her, "you're not in labor yet. You have not yet begun to dilate. This is just a false alarm, false labor. You can go home and come back when you really are in labor."

Here we have a physiological event—the painful contractions of the uterus—defined two different ways, as labor and as not-labor. The woman and her husband are basing their definitions on her feelings, the sensations she is experiencing as she has been taught to measure them—in minutes, for example. The doctor is basing his or her definition on what the doctor feels as an examiner, the degree of dilatation—how much the cervix (the opening of the uterus into the vagina) has dilated. Each definition of the situation carries with it a way of acting, a set of behavioral expectations, for the actors involved. As not-labor, the doctor is finished with the woman and can turn his or her attention elsewhere. The woman is to go home and stay simply pregnant a while longer. Defined as labor, however, the situation is very different. The woman changes from her status of pregnant woman to the new status of laboring woman. She will put on the appropriate costume (change from maternity clothes to a hospital gown) and become a patient. The doctor will be expected to provide examination and treatment, to begin managing her condition. Only in labor will she become the doctor's responsibility.

Situation 2

Cara (an empirical midwife): I got a call that Roberta was having heavy rushes but wasn't dilating and was having a hard time. I wanted to go see her and help. When I got there, Roberta was writhing with each rush and shaking. She just didn't have any idea how to handle the energy. Joel was sitting beside her looking worried. The whole scene was a bit grim for a baby-having. I got them kissing, hugging, and had Roberta re-

ally grab on to Joel and squeeze him. Joel is a big, strong, heavy-duty man. He and I rubbed Roberta continuously and steered in the direction of relaxed. I let her know that she was having good, strong rushes, and that if she'd relax and experience it and let it happen, her rushes would accomplish a lot and open her up. She gradually accepted the fact that there was no getting out of this, except to let it happen and quit fighting it.[34]

Here we have the same physiological event, two women experiencing the same sensations and the same lack of dilation, defined along yet other lines. First notice the difference in the language used. The empirical midwife describing this situation is not talking about *contractions*, the medical word for what the uterine muscle is doing, but *rushes*. This midwife lives and works on The Farm, a Tennessee commune which has published a book on *Spiritual Midwifery*. The midwives explain their language:

On the farm we've come to call these contractions of the uterine muscle "rushes" because the main sensation that happens when these muscles contract is exactly the same as the sensation of rushing while coming on to a heavy psychedelic, which feels like a whole lot of energy flowing up your back and into your head. It leaves you feeling expansive and stoned if you don't fight it.[35]

This language relies on internal or subjective cues, on sensations the woman herself experiences. The medical language, in contrast, relies on external or objective cues, on information available to the examiner—how much the woman has dilated. Thus when the subjective and objective cues are at variance, in the medical situation the subjective cues are discounted. The woman's sensations of labor are "false," and the doctor's definition is "true." In the midwifery situation, the woman's experienced reality of the rushes is acknowledged. The "problem," the variance between subjective and objective measures, is here defined as the woman's inability to cope effectively, to "let it happen." This definition of course also carries with it consequences for the people involved: the midwife and the husband are expected to help her cope, relax, let it happen. For the woman, one of the negative consequences of this definition of the situation is that it tells her that it is in some way her own fault that she is having a hard time. In that way the midwives are doing the same thing as the doctors: imposing their definition of the situation on the laboring woman. Whereas the doctor's responsibility is very narrowly defined, however, only to manage "real" labor, the midwives responsibility is defined to include "helping" or "managing"—controlling the emotional as well as the physical situation.

Thus each of these alternate definitions carries with it quite different consequences, consequences which will shape the experience of all those involved, but most dramatically that of the pregnant woman. It is one thing to be a pregnant woman, and quite another to be in labor. And it is one thing to be told that the labor which you are experiencing is false, not real, and yet again another to be told that the rushes are real and you have to learn how to relax and stop fighting them. The meaning given the particular uterine contractions of any particular woman becomes the basis for the way the event, and thus the woman, is treated.

For the symbolic interactionist, an event such as this one raises some of the core questions of the discipline: Where does meaning come from? How does one come to know the meaning of this thing, the contraction, the rush? How do these meanings come to be shared? How, in the interaction, does one meaning become *the* meaning, one definition of the situation become *the* definition of the situation?

These questions raise still other questions. Meanings exist in a social context—what is involved in the social context underlying any one meaning? The same thing has different meaning in different groups. Why? How? And there is a social structural component here. What in the social structure allows, within the interaction, one person's meanings (those of the doctor or midwife) to dominate over the other person's (those of the laboring woman)? And what in the social structure generally allows one *group*'s meanings (those of the doctors) to dominate over another group's (those of the midwives)? For the symbolic interactionist, the larger structure, the thing we call society, consists of interactions. A major concern of the sociologist is to make the connections between the micro- and macrolevels of analysis. The symbolic interactionist perspective claims that in the analysis of interactions and meanings we uncover both culture and social structure.

NOTES

1. George Herbert Mead, *Mind, Self, and Society* (Chicago: University of Chicago Press, 1934).
2. Gregory P. Stone and Harvey A. Farberman, *Social Psychology through Symbolic Interaction* (Waltham, Mass.: Xerox College Publishers, 1970), p. 1.
3. Herbert Blumer, *Symbolic Interaction* (Englewood Cliffs, N.J.: Prentice-Hall, 1969), p. 2.
4. John P. Hewitt, *Self and Society: A Symbolic Interactionist Social Psychology*, 2nd ed. (Boston: Allyn & Bacon, 1979), p. 122.
5. Bernice Fisher and Anselm Strauss, "George Herbert Mead and the Chicago School of Sociology," *Symbolic Interaction* 2, no. 2, pp. 9–20.
6. Blumer, *Symbolic Interaction*, p. 81.
7. Ibid., p. 80.
8. Ibid., p. 81.
9. Herbert Blumer, Thomas J. Marrione, and Harvey A. Farberman, "Conversations with Herbert Blumer: I," *Symbolic Interaction* 4, no. 1, p. 127.
10. Blumer, *Symbolic Interaction*.
11. M. Merleau-Ponty, *Phenomenology of Perception* (London: Routledge & Kegan Paul, 1965), p. 33.
12. Hans Neiser, *On the Sociology of Knowledge* (New York: James H. Heineman, 1965), p. 27.
13. Blumer, *Symbolic Interaction*, pp. 164–65.

14. Tomatsu Shibutani, "Reference Groups as Perspectives," *American Journal of Sociology* 60, pp. 562–69.

15. William James, *Psychology* (New York: Henry Holt, 1915), pp. 179–80.

16. Charles Horton Cooley, *Human Nature and the Social Order* (New York: Schocken Books, 1970), p. 184.

17. Andrew W. Reck, in George Herbert Mead, *Selected Writings*, edited and with an Introduction by Andrew W. Reck (Indianapolis: Bobbs Merrill, 1964), p. xxxii.

18. Bernard Meltzer, "Mead's Social Psychology," in Jerome G. Manis and Bernard N. Meltzer, *Symbolic Interaction: A Reader in Social Psychology* (Boston: Allyn & Bacon, 1978), p. 19.

19. Mead, *Selected Writings*, p. xxxii.

20. Blumer, *Symbolic Interaction*, p. 85.

21. Tomatsu Shibutani, *Society and Personality: An Interactionist Approach to Social Psychology* (Englewood Cliffs, N.J.: Prentice-Hall, 1961), p. 20.

22. E. C. Cuff and G. C. Payne, eds., *Perspectives in Sociology* (London: George Allen & Unwin, 1979), p. 109.

23. Anselm L. Strauss, *Negotiations: Varieties, Contexts, Processes, and Social Order* (San Francisco: Jossey-Bass, 1978).

24. Hewitt, *Self and Society*, p. 206.

25. Blumer et al., "Conversations with Herbert Blumer," p. 128.

26. George Herbert Mead, quoted in Gregory P. Stone and Harvey A. Farberman, *Social Psychology through Symbolic Interaction*, p. 540.

27. Shibutani, "Reference Groups as Perspectives."

28. W. I. Thomas and Dorothy Swaine Thomas, *The Child in America* (New York: Alfred A. Knopf, 1928).

29. W. I. Thomas, quoted in Manis and Meltzer, *Symbolic Interaction*, p. 331.

30. Joel M. Charon, *Symbolic Interactionism: An Introduction, an Interpretation, an Interioration* (Englewood Cliffs, N.J.: Prentice-Hall, 1979), p. 141.

31. Stone and Farberman, *Social Psychology through Symbolic Interaction*, p. 151.

32. Leon H. Warshay, "Letter," *Symbolic Interaction* 3, no. 1, pp. 5–6.

33. Clark McPhail, "Experimental Research Is Convergent with Symbolic Interaction," *Symbolic Interaction* 2, no. 1, pp. 89–94.

34. Ina May Gaskin and the Farm Midwives, *Spiritual Midwifery* (Summertown, Tenn.: Book Publishing Company, 1976), p. 126.

35. Ibid., p. 364.

Phenomenological sociologists examine the ways in which we experience the world through our minds. Phenomenological sociology is based on the premise that the social world is created by attributing meanings to specific objects and experiences. Freedom begins with our becoming aware that all human societies operate to produce compliance by obscuring the fact that humans make their own worlds through cognitive processes. Phenomenological sociology emphasizes the creative potential of individuals to counter socialization and social coercion.

Myron Orleans offers a comparison between the Durkheimian social fact perspective and the phenomenological perspective of radical doubt. Phenomenologists view sociological concepts such as roles, norms, and institutions as the results of intentional processes rather than as facts inherent in the social world. *Typification* is the process through which social abstractions are created. Language contains all typifications, but is also a means of modifying them.

The phenomenological method consists of a bracketing procedure of *reduction* that encourages the revelation of the constituent elements of a social phenomenon. We cast ourselves into our own consciousness in order to examine the processes that give rise to our experience of the social world. For example, the phenomenologist sociologist asks: What is essential to a social relationship such as marriage? In a series of mental experiments the sociologist selectively sets aside features of the commonsense world in order to uncover the assumptions on which that world is based.

PHENOMENOLOGICAL SOCIOLOGY

INTRODUCTION

My purpose in writing this essay is to present a basic and provocative introduction to phenomenological sociology for the uninitiated yet available reader. I do not wish to claim that the entire approach, along with its wealth of research, is represented here. While an exhaustive bibliography is not attempted, the interested reader will find references to the principal sources. In order to maintain narrative pace, I have not used quotations and footnotes. Controversies within the field have been avoided, and the technical vocabulary has been kept to a minimum. The exposition has been designed to highlight the thematic consistency which unifies the diverse branches of phenomenology. The first section offers a very general discussion of the framework of phenomenology as related to the social world. The second section offers a more specific description of the elements

and methods of phenomenological sociology, while the third section explores some applications of phenomenological sociology.

THE FOUNDERS OF PHENOMENOLOGICAL THEORY

Phenomenological sociology is derived from a school of philosophical thought pioneered by Edmund Husserl, a German thinker active in the early twentieth century.[1] As is generally the case for many intellectual ground breakers, Husserl displayed great courage and boldness in putting forth his notions. Unfortunately, his writing was particularly dense, providing great difficulty for most readers. Moreover, since his thinking was essentially antithetical to conventional scientific approaches, Husserl's work did not receive a great deal of attention initially. However, his thoughts eventually provoked a rich and growing body of literature in the humanities and social sciences. For our purposes Husserl's most important follower was Alfred Schutz.[2] Schutz was a student of sociology in pre-Nazi Germany. His study of Max Weber's analysis of social action revealed serious deficiencies. He felt that Weber's sociology needed to be more solidly founded on a theory of everyday social life. Schutz was able to draw such a theory of the life world from Husserl's writings. Had Nazism not intervened, Schutz would have worked personally with Husserl.

However, Schutz emigrated to the United States, where he reestablished himself and proceeded to develop his sociological phenomenology at The New School for Social Research in New York. Here he worked with other phenomenologically inclined social scientists, writing papers which by the 1970s came to have a significant impact on sociology. His colleagues and students, particularly Peter L. Berger and Thomas Luckmann, integrated some of his thought into the classical themes of sociology.[3] This body of work has been termed *macrophenomenology* because much of it has focused on the broad-scale process of reality constructionism.

In the early 1950s a Harvard graduate student in sociology, Harold Garfinkel, came upon Schutz's work and saw how phenomenology might enable him to solve some of the problems contained in Talcott Parsons's analysis of social action.[4] (Parsons had used Weber's ideas to develop his own approach.) Ironically, phenomenology came to be used in very different eras to solve essentially similar conceptual problems. Garfinkel developed the obscure but fascinating term, *ethnomethodology*, to label his approach. The term refers to those methods ordinary people use in order to get through everyday life. Garfinkel developed a strong following at the University of California campuses at Los Angeles, Santa Barbara, and San Diego. With the additional influence of dramaturgical and symbolic interaction models, microphenomenology has emerged as an analytic approach to the study of ordinary life.

Currently, phenomenology is fairly widely espoused. Research and instruction in this area are rather widespread, with possibly one or two members of most larger departments of sociology expressing serious interest in this approach. Sessions on phenomenological sociology are held regularly at national and regional meetings of sociologists. Scholarly journals are becoming increasingly receptive to phenomenological analyses and publishers are recognizing the growing market for this kind of writing.

Many adherents of conventional sociological approaches find phenomenology distasteful, and the term, *phenomenologophobia* has been offered to describe the hostility expressed toward this approach.[5] Phenomenology presents a complexity and level of abstraction which put off the kind of student who is seeking to master specific formulas and techniques. There is no data-processing hardware to be used; little opportunity exists to form research organizations; and phenomenology has only limited appeal to agencies which fund research. The phenomenological approach cannot claim the legitimating mantle of conventional science, nor does it offer magic keys to manipulate behavior in desired directions. However, phenomenology holds much promise as a way of understanding and even affecting social life.

Phenomenology rewards the persevering student with a new and exciting perspective. Although it may not provide concrete answers, it does afford a way of understanding the limitations and dangers of all ''answers'' to human questions. At the same time it provides conceptual foundations for educative and liberative modes of counseling and therapy. Phenomenology, as is the case with most paradigms in the social sciences, is neither correct nor incorrect. It is either adequate or not, interesting or not, useful or not. The only measure of its benefit is whether the reader feels that the exposure provided by this introduction provokes further thought and inquiry.

THE PHENOMENOLOGICAL APPROACH TO SOCIAL ANALYSIS

Of all social scientific approaches, the phenomenological approach is perhaps the most radical. It is certainly the most unconventional. Its radical quality lies not in its political implications, as does Marxian radicalism. Phenomenology is radical in that it compels us to take a look at the basic way in which we experience the world. It promotes a personally significant radicalism of inner examination and doubt. Phenomenology asks us to come to know in a new way those aspects of life with which we have become so familiar that we have ceased to have a conscious awareness of their dimensions. This unique approach requires that we probe into the very assumptions that make both ordinary social action and intellectual inquiry possible.

Phenomenology, a philosophical approach developed in the twentieth century, emphasizes the primacy of the human mind as the creator which produces all that human beings experience as real. This approach can be used not only in philosophy but also in the social scientific study of the human condition. The integration of phenomenology into the social sciences, which has occurred over the last fifty years, suggests that we can soon expect to see a branch of the social sciences which focuses on the social creativity of human consciousness.

Phenomenology, as generally defined in sociology, refers to the study of how the social world is constructed. We might think of how an architect blueprints a project and then oversees its realization. Phenomenology suggests that we are all, in a sense, collective architects of our identities, actions, communities, and social realities. Patterns of social life appear to exist independently of ourselves, but phenomenology seeks to reveal how people produce an apparently independent world in the course of their own daily lives.

Phenomenology proposes that we study our immediate involvements and perceptions of reality as the products of our own creative minds. Within the framework of this conceptual perspective, human beings continuously construct their world, but are usually not aware of doing so. It is only by pulling away from the constructive process that one can become aware of it. Most often we tend to accept the world as given and as external to us; however, phenomenology provides the means through which to understand the ways in which we experience the world. The key procedure of phenomenological analysis is to strive to view dispassionately our own perceptual processes and, more specifically, how we ourselves construct a world that we come to perceive as an object existing independently of us.

As a phenomenological sociologist, this approach asks me to look at the ways in which my own consciousness constitutes my fantasies, emotional life, attitudes, and my stance toward the things I take to be of the outer world. Phenomenology gives me distance from what is closest to me. As an ordinary person, I interpret the external world and act. Then, as a phenomenologist, I remove myself mentally from these involvements and examine my own perceptions and subsequent actions. Thus I am afforded another view of ordinary life. This approach enables me to understand the relationship between my inner being and external "reality" and convinces me that these externalities are molded by my own interpretive processes and actions.

This is not to deny physical reality. When I come into contact with physical objects or other human beings, I know that they do not exist solely in my mind. Sudden contact between the corner of a coffee table and my shin brings instant recognition that the object exists. Phenomenology does not deny the obvious. It focuses instead on the individual experience of a given object or situation. In my experience with the coffee table, cultural and personal factors interact with the physical event in my perceptual process. I know, because I have bumped into it, that the object is a physical reality. However, previous experience with similarly shaped objects tells me that this is a table. Placement in the room tells me that this is what is known in my culture as a coffee table. I therefore construct the event in my mind as "bumping into the coffee table."

In order to put the phenomenological approach into more concrete terms, one might approach the situation as though one were from another culture, or even another world.[6] How would such a person interpret the object we have called a coffee table? Perhaps the table would be viewed as a receptacle for items which lack all apparent use. Perhaps, after bumping into it, it would be viewed as an object dangerous to life and limb, particularly limb.

Many authors have emphasized that the meanings attributed to physical and social items vary cross-culturally.[7] Let us consider, for example, those items which might be considered trash in cultures which are at differing stages of economic development. Empty frozen orange juice containers are definitely trash for people in economically developed societies. However, for people in less developed economies, these containers might prove useful as drinking "glasses." In fact, people in less developed economies might find many useful items in the "trash" of a developed economy.

Phenomenologically speaking, trash is made through the attribution of meaning to a specific object. Certain items are considered according to certain definitions. These items are then treated in a certain way, indicating that they are trash. A change in one's perception of an object therefore changes the object. As in the case of the orange juice container, viewing it as

an object to be used as a drinking glass makes it, in fact, a drinking glass for the person using it.

In dealing with more abstract human constructs, we find much of the same variation in meaning. Lack of awareness may convince us that all people experience certain universal constructs in a similar fashion. However, close scrutiny allows us to see that there is some degree of variation. We have become increasingly aware that the experience of pain, for example, varies among individuals as well as among groups. The individual's construction of the inner sensation of pain depends to a large extent on how he or she has been taught to feel that sensation. The variation among ethnic groups in modes of experiencing pain has been understood for quite some time. Let us return to the example of the coffee table. The stoic Yankee, who does not admit pain, would more than likely not show any outward sign of pain. And, according to recent research, this denial of pain in itself serves to reduce the pain felt. In contrast we have the Mediterranean who seeks immediate relief from the sensation. His response might be to grab the injured shin, dance around a bit, and declare vociferously that the experience was extremely painful to him. And, for him, it would be much more painful than it was for the stoic Yankee. The question remains, of course, whether or not the pain itself is changed by the individual's perception and experience of it or whether the individual's perception of the pain simply creates for him an alternative means of experiencing it. While the ultimate answer to this is not accessible, it is known that therapy which changes the individual's way of interpreting chronic pain can enable him or her to live a more comfortable existence.[8]

In a similar manner even an experience as apparently absolute as death itself is subject to a variety of constructions. In recent years there has been some controversy in medical circles about the definition of death. Does one measure death by the absence of brain wave activity? Is a person in a comatose state as a result of severe brain damage alive? Could that same person be considered dead when the brain ceased to function even though the body could be maintained through the use of a life-support system? Under these circumstances the definition of death becomes qualitative. Each society must therefore attribute meaning to specific physical signs, compare the quality of life indicated by those signs to the quality of life desired within their society, and thereby arrive at a definition of death.

Even more closely related to phenomenology is the much documented recognition that members of different cultures face and react to death with very different attitudes.[9] In some cultures death is viewed as a transition, while in other cultures it is viewed as an absolute end. However, perceptions of death are not static. In our Western culture new modes of death awareness are emerging, affecting how people are constructing death.[10]

Some contemporary writers have reported that through the experience of recovering from temporary death, they have discovered that the moment of death is not terrifying, as typically envisioned. These writers have suggested that dying can be seen as an experience of personal fulfillment. Thus it seems that our cultural construction of death is moving in a more cosmological, even mystical, direction. And further, even though death is a universal reality, the way in which it is perceived, and therefore the way it is experienced, varies significantly.

As the reader will note, phenomenology is not a technique of pure research and analysis, a way of processing data in the usual scientific ways. It offers a reformulation of the conventional sociological way of knowing. Moreover, it is not limited to academic pursuits; it provides an intellectual life pattern. The ultimate objective of phenomenology is to enable us to become aware of and learn to control what we are doing in and to the world. In Western culture the world beyond ourselves is experienced as separate. Common life obscures the linkage between self and external physical and social objects. Phenomenology provides an approach which helps to bring about a reintegration of the human being and his or her externalities.[11]

Certainly, there are philosophical and ethical overtones to this presentation which appear to go well beyond the traditional domain of social science or of sociological theory. However, sociologists have become increasingly aware of the inevitable ideological and metaphysical dimensions of theorizing.[12]

In phenomenology one is asked to penetrate the belief that society is an objective entity, existing independently of its constructors. Fundamentally, one is posed the challenge of understanding how it is that we are commonly taken in by appearances and assumptions of the social world.

The gullibility of the members of a society is directly related to their personal need to find order and attribute meaning to their own existences.

Phenomenology does not ask one to reject the common world, nor does it urge one to seek out alternatives. It does not directly promote political, economic, or social change. One is merely asked to recognize the cognitive processes that are an inevitable dimension of social order.[13] Freedom, from the phenomenological viewpoint, begins with the awareness that all societies operate to produce compliance by obscuring the fact that humans organize their own world. If we understand the practical expediencies which underlie the images of awe that are propagated in society, and if we recognize the necessity for the maintenance of order, decisions to participate in ongoing social organization can be based more on reason than on blind faith in the social order.

As an illustration of the phenomenological analysis of social action, let us briefly consider how it is that a society is able to conscript an individual into the armed services and eventually locate him in situations which will endanger his life. Why would anyone be willing to risk his life for something so nebulous as "country"? Country has, however, come to be symbolized in various ways as a real and personally significant social unit. Members of society are then members of a large family and are willing to risk their lives in order to maintain the security of that family.

The wizardry of society creates the impression that one is compelled to undertake certain actions. One "has to" do this or that because one is "forced" to do so. Parents, peers, circumstances, pressures, etc., seem to shape or to limit options and even to channel actions. The social sciences have, unfortunately, added some new terminology to this rhetoric. In order to explain human behavior, social scientists propose that humans are conditioned by their environment, shaped by significant others, socialized into compliance, commanded by legitimate authority, and guided by their own role expectations. Looking at this phenomenologically, one can see that ultimately it is the individual who interprets these "forces" and who undertakes an action. And further, that individuals have the capacity to do other than what they are led to do by any and/or all external "realities." The phenomenological view suggests that although human beings do not have complete control over every circumstance of their lives, that is, the sociocultural objects of their world, they ultimately can choose their life projects. They are neither determined nor caused by anything outside themselves.

When people explain or excuse their actions by reference to external causes or determinations, according to phenomenologists, they are acting in bad faith.[14] For them to claim that "I have always been this or that way" or "my personality is such that. . ." is to make a statement of their bad faith.[15]

Phenomenological sociology does not demean its subject by viewing him or her as a puppetlike being, programmed through childhood to act in preset ways. This approach respects the autonomous and creative potential of human actors and their capacity to counter socialization, habit, circumstances, and pressures. Phenomenological sociology places primacy on the individual, his or her dilemmas and projects.

An individual's stock of knowledge is the basis for orienting that person to the world.[16] Phenomenology accepts the biographically based distinctiveness of each individual's knowledge and therefore is concerned with the variable and uneven distribution of common knowledge throughout a culture. Members of the same culture will know, and thus experience, slightly different modes and aspects of that culture. Each knower is somewhat unique; that is, each person exists in his or her own life world. However, our social organization obscures this for most people. We believe that we share common mental outlooks and we "know" that we have a common language. We feel we communicate with one another and, evidently, we need to feel this way. Otherwise, the burden of fear and anxiety, the overwhelming loneliness, might be too much to bear and our commitment to society would be weakened. Indeed, our perceived "common" experience of the world leads us to conclude that there is communication, an approach to a consensus, and a common life world. The phenomenologist must then seek to account for how it is possible for unique individuals to collectively construct an apparently cohesive social world. The way in which individuals apply their stock of knowledge, negotiate, and maneuver with each other in order to create the appearance of a common world is a central theme of phenomenological sociology.

In order for phenomenological sociologists to systematically examine the very immediate and all too familiar world, it is necessary for them to suspend their commonsense knowledge of the world.[17] A loose interpretation of the fairy tale of the emperor's new clothes permits us to understand how ignorance, whether real or assumed, of a common social construct can advance one's ability to analyze phenomenologically. The only way to know that the emperor is not wearing clothes is to be an unknowing child.... In a sense one must become a child, filled with wonder at the extraordinary accomplishments of ordinary life.

A word of caution must be given, however. The purpose of phenomenological analysis is not to reveal that the emperor is "in fact" nude.[18] The emperor's true sartorial state or the "true nature of things" in the world is not and cannot be the focus of phenomenology. This approach is concerned with explaining the process by which the emperor becomes "dressed." That is to say, phenomenology studies the creation of what is taken to be real. It is not the task of the phenomenological sociologist to tell people that their perceptions are wrong, but merely to reveal how those perceptions and actions come to be what they are.

The phenomenological approach asks one to selectively unknow features of the commonsense world. Thus, putting aside certain of our a priori concepts enables us to step back from or outside of the assumptions unconsciously made about the world. For the phenomenologist reality is the process of making real or *realization*.[19]

Up to this point, we have focused primarily on *microphenomenology*, a discussion of how everyday life situations are the products of our collective actions. This approach can be extremely useful in analyzing our world on a larger scale. *Macrophenomenology* points out that the organizations and institutions of society are constructed in a similar manner although on a more complex scale.

The modern corporation is legally defined as a *fictional individual* and is certainly treated as a being independent in its own right. Indeed, corporations take on a life of their own, commanding the abstract loyalty of their employees. Macrophenomenology seeks to examine the processes whereby the larger social structures, even society itself, come to be commonly experienced as an objective entity.

Both the micro and macro branches of phenomenology are essentially concerned with the way in which human beings tend to *reify* their categories of thought and their actions, that is, to make static *things* out of abstractions and processes. A major task of phenomenology then becomes to dereify or to reveal the roots of apparent personal, sociocultural, political, and economic facticities. The microphenomenological concern relates to the level of individuals and their immediate surroundings, implicitly promoting awareness of domination of the person by false objects. Macrophenomenology suggests the same liberative potential for the larger sphere.

Phenomenology is not a technique of pure research and analysis. There are, however, specific methods which are used in doing phenomenological research. According to one method, we are asked to cast ourselves into our own consciousness in a disciplined and systematic manner. We thus probe introspectively in order to examine the roots and processes whereby our own consciousness gives rise to our own experience of the world. Another method asks the phenomenologist to endeavor to sense the way in which the consciousness of others operates to produce their particular modes of life experience.[20] This approach is an empathic, inferential one based on thorough observation of actors and their actions as well as immersion in the contexts which are to be studied. The analyst delves into the consciousness of the actors in order to understand the meanings of the subject under investigation.[21]

Since the phenomenological approach assumes a unique experience for each actor, the introspective and empathic methods of analysis are inextricably bound together. In order to infer the consciousness of another, one must first examine one's own consciousness with regard to an action or situation. One asks oneself how the action could come about, substituting one's own knowledge and experience of the situation for the consciousness of the actor under analysis. Then, after an objective analysis of the action on a personal level, one seeks to analyze the ways in which other actors attribute meaning to the action. For example, should one wish to study some aspect of the drug addiction process phenomenologically, one would observe intensively a group of people who use drugs. An effort would be made to understand their meaning systems by analyzing the ways in which they attributed meaning to specific acts and situations. In order to accomplish this end, one would examine, as objectively as possible, one's own experience as well as one's own process of attributing meaning to drugs and drug-related activities. Striving to remain attuned to their "reality" and avoiding as much as possible the imposition of one's own categories, personal experiences, and meaning system can then be related to the experiences and meaning systems of others.

At this point in our discussion, we have arrived at what can be a major problem in phenomenological research. Care must be taken to remain objective and yet become involved in a phenomenon on a very basic level.

It is at this level that the traditional methods of an empirical science fail. The usual survey method of sociological research adds a new and confounding dimension to the process which is being studied. Unfortunately, direct questioning of the actor as to the meanings of his or her actions may very likely produce distortions. In answering a questionnaire, respondents will, in effect, produce a new construction in order to account for themselves. All that can be obtained, even in an intense, lengthy interview, is an actor's constructed account of his or her own actions and orientations.[22]

Phenomenology warns us against accepting the individual's account as being a true depiction of the causes of his or her actions. Not only may individuals be lying, but they are using culturally derived categories of thought in order to do their accounting.[23] Because we ordinarily make sense of ourselves, our actions, and our thoughts in terms of the stock of knowledge we have accumulated through our personal biography, not only may individuals' accounts of themselves serve as after-the-fact justification for actions but their accounts of the past serve to justify current, and even projected, behaviors.[24]

As an investigator of the social world, when listening to people, one must be aware of the functions which self-accounting serves. The phenomenological inquirer seeks to understand the mental outlook of people, but at the same time must reveal how the subject's thought patterns are rooted in the commonsense world. The investigator must reveal how these patterns function within the individual's own mind in order to sustain his or her personality, the community with which that person identifies, and the commonsense world from which his or her interpretive tools were drawn. The phenomenological approach presented here does not merely report the stream of consciousness of actors, but rather seeks to process and analyze the actors' reports.

The phenomenologist must begin work as a stranger to the phenomenon under investigation. This involves the developing of an *objective consciousness,* the ability to step outside of even the most familiar situations. The phenomenological analyst realizes he or she cannot know the phenomenon immediately, but must slowly come to know it through its most intricate and complex details.

In order to become the phenomenon, to convert to it, one need not actually be a member of it. For example, one need not be a lesbian in order to do a phenomenological analysis of the world of the lesbian.[25] But one must immerse oneself as far as possible into this world and imaginatively introject oneself into lesbianness in order to feel what it is to be a part of the phenomenon. As a phenomenological analyst one must, whether male or heterosexual female, arrive at an empathic understanding of the phenomenon. By "sharing" the experience, the phenomenological sociologist becomes the phenomenon and is able to communicate his or her sense of it to other individuals.

THE PHENOMENOLOGICAL METHOD OF SOCIAL ANALYSIS

Phenomenological sociology stands in rather sharp contrast to conventional sociology. The essential distinction between the two is that what conventional sociology assumes as its foundation, phenomenological sociology takes as its topic of investigation. Thus, conventional sociology assumes that structure, along with norms, roles, attitudes, and groups, exists in a real social world. Conventional sociology seeks to study the appearances of these facticities using objective methods and enumerative measures similar to those used in the natural sciences. Phenomenological sociology questions how these facticities came to be viewed as real. That is, why people act as if they were playing roles or how people talk as if they had attitudes. Phenomenological sociology studies the ways in which the very foundations of society are made to appear real.

In its most general sense phenomenology seeks to provide a detailed description and examination of human experience. It covers the entire range of human experience—science, technology, the arts, and culture—revealing how these phenomena are essentially human constructs, derived ultimately from the world of common sense.

The starting point is found in an understanding of how ordinary people experience the world, how they perceive, interpret, and plan their actions. The phenomenologist calls the way in which the ordinary person is oriented to the world in his daily life the *natural attitude*.

The natural attitude is guided by certain presuppositions or basic assumptions made in the course of everyday living. Ordinary persons assume that they are human beings and that other beings exist. They assume that they, along with others of their kind, think. These assumptions of thought, within the framework of phenomenology, are called *subjective experiences*. Thus ordinary people assume that there is subjectivity, that people have minds and a consciousness which has relevance to the world. It is for this reason that one relates to other humans using different sets of assumptions than one would use in relating to plants, for example. Rarely, however, does one become aware that one assumes existence or thought.

Ordinary people assume the constancy of an outer world which exists independently of themselves. It preceded them and will continue to exist after they are gone. It is an object, a reality, that cannot be wished away. Even when individuals turn away from some specific sphere of that world, they do not assume that it ceases to exist. Their office exists for them even though they are at home.

The assumed world provides an order for existence that comforts and protects. If perceptions contradict what is "known" to be true about the world, one generally seeks to explain the event as an aberration which fits some reasonable explanation. When no reasonable explanation appears to fit the event, it is considered a misperception, perhaps even a practical joke. Thus, the normalcy of the world is maintained. The struggle to maintain a meaningful organization of the world protects one from the potential terror of the unknowable and nonsensical. Therefore, one does not generally want to hold this normal world in question.

Historians have documented the struggles of many peoples to preserve their assumptions of their world in the face of competing worlds. In order to protect their world from disintegration, people often seek to use their own categories in order to explain new phenomena. For example, if one were an Aztec living in the Yucatan in the sixteenth century, how would a conquistador be perceived and interpreted?[26] With no prior knowledge of or experience with a horse, let alone an armored man on an armored horse, no categories for interpreting the phenomenon would be immediately available. Since the components of the perception would not be distinguishable, one might not see the man, the horse, and the armor as separate items. Rather one might see a composite, an armored-man-horse being. This entity would not be understandable as a normal being, and a struggle would ensue to define it in an acceptable way. It could be defined as a god, since this category would be culturally available. But a constant struggle for definition takes its toll. Eventually, the Aztec world view was substantially annihilated because it could not adequately cope with the European cognitive intrusion. The drastic Aztec population decline had as much to do with the nihilation of their intersubjective world as with the diseases, corruption, and malnutrition experienced by them.

Every culture produces essentially the same basic assumptions regarding the existence of human subjectivity, and the independence and fundamental constancy of the world. Each culture does, however, shape its world in particular ways. And each people, of course, believes that other versions of reality are, at worst, inferior to theirs or, at least, quaint. Historically crusades have often been undertaken in order to demonstrate the validity and superiority of one worldview over another.

In the West today our general sense is that scientific rationality is the final and supreme version of the world. Through the application of certain techniques to the control of nature, a generally high standard of living has been achieved in the West. But other ways of defining reality are extant which emphasize, for example, spiritual dimensions providing achievements unavailable through rational scientific modes of conceptualization. However, the complexity and permeability of the contemporary Western reality construct permits the absorption of alternative elements without forcing abandonment of what Schutz has called the *paramount reality*.

Whatever particular worldview one assumes, one trusts that it is a correct depiction of reality. And as long as one is able to hold a belief in one's own worldview, life within that view is comfortable. In this natural attitude disbelief is suspended, and the objective existence of the world is not doubted. Children are quickly brought into the natural attitude. They are encouraged to ask questions, to probe and inquire. In this interchange, not only is specifically useful information conveyed but the existence of the world is also confirmed and the child's doubt is canceled. The natural attitude is thereby not essentially natural to human beings; rather it is the commonsensical way in which people generally think and act within a culture. The natural attitude ensures that doubt is held in check, for if doubt were to prevail, a potential for chaos would be ever present. The chance that people's actions would be shaped in a patterned, predictable manner would diminish. Objects, situations, and events would be sources of concern rather than easily interpreted aspects of a taken-for-granted world.

Science and, of course, social science usually proceed under the same assumptions of the world as contained in the natural attitude. Social science assumes that individuals are thinking selves. If one asks people a question during a survey, it is assumed that they think about the response and reveal their attitudes. It is also assumed that they possessed this attitude and that the question posed merely discovered it. Social scientists assume that social phenomena exist as independent entities. Institutions, rules, values, norms, etc., are thought to be social facts following Durkheim's conceptualization.[27] Social facts are said to exist in the same manner as do physical facts. That is to say, a marriage is said to exist in the same sense that a table is commonly experienced as existing.[28] It has been claimed that social facts exist independently of human volition and are not subject to human control. For example, social roles are said to exist and people play these roles by following norms set for them by society.[29] The conventional paradigm of social science assumes the social world to be objectlike.[30] Phenomena are processed within this paradigm, and members of the disciplines become committed to it. Rather than abandon the paradigm when inconvenient phenomena are uncovered, the paradigm is adjusted. Thus functionalism, a major paradigm of sociology, has accommodated the process of conflict, which it ignored during its development.[31] Social scientists assume the constancy of the world and the adequacy of their interpretive tools to process the world. These are, of course, the assumptions of the ordinary individual. The more sophisticated analysts suggest that no paradigm is valid, that no one scheme can adequately encompass all phenomena in a discipline's domain. A multiparadigm approach is viewed as necessary. These analysts accept the variability of the world and alternate paradigms according to the subject matter and purposes of their research. This mode of inquiry has been called *instrumentalist* because paradigms are conceived as relatively useful tools which serve limited ad hoc purposes and which afford only a partial and variable view of the world.

The phenomenological attitude, in comparison to the natural attitude, is founded on doubt. But such doubt is neither a negation nor a denial of reality. To doubt the phenomenon under investigation, one puts it within brackets, i.e., one performs an epoche.[32] According to the classic phenomenological mode, the phenomenon is first isolated, and then the whole phenomenon is called into question—one no longer believes it as it is presented within the framework of the natural attitude.

In order for phenomenologists to analyze social life, they must use their own experiences of the world to form a basis for their bracketing approach. In analyzing social action, phenomenologists must be able to resort to their repertory of experiences and then use these experiences as a basis for empathic understanding of others.

In classical phenomenology, the bracketing procedure leads us into the meditative stance called the *reduction*.[33] A reduction occurs while one is within the phenomenological brackets. One disengages, puts aside the assumptions of the natural attitude, and seeks to uncover the constitutive elements of the phenomenon in question. In the eidetic reduction the philosopher searches for the *eidos* or the essences of the phenomenon in consciousness. Essences are those elements which are required for the phenomenon to be what it is. Without the essences, the phenomenon would not be what it is typically taken to be. By descending through the layers of meaning in the eidetic reduction to the essences, one discards the confusing layers which are not essential to the phenomenon. An inner ray of consciousness is shot out to scan our conception of the phenomenon. Its various aspects and presentations are reviewed. Mental experiments are performed to determine what is crucial to the phenomenon. The essential and inessential features of it are distinguished as one considers whether the phenomenon remains.

In an eidetic reduction we might ask, for example, what constitutes the essence of marriage? Can a common dwelling place be eliminated and the marriage remain? Is it possible for people of the same sex to be married? If one removes the sexual relationship, does the marriage remain? In doing the eidetic reduction of marriage, one seeks to define the commonly held typification of the phenomenon. The concern is not to derive the dictionary definition or the sociological conception of marriage, but to understand the commonsense essentials of the phenomenon. The eidetic reduction is the study of the process by which the ordinary person using the natural attitude arrives at the essence of the phenomenon, aside from any of its particular manifestations.

In a similar way phenomenologists do not accept the notion that history makes us do what we do. The only way history has an effect on behavior is by affecting the actors' intentional processes. History is not a force independent of people and their ideas. People experience history as a part of their reality. It is only insofar as knowledge is transmitted between generations and then guides action that history is relevant to the present and to the future. Of course, as George Orwell points out in *1984,* the past may be consciously reconstructed in order to shape the present.[34] Thus, history and any other deterministic causes are subjectively experienced constructs, not independent entities which enter into consciousness and intentionality.

Roles, situations, norms, and institutions are intentional processes in phenomenology, not facts inherent to the social world. In the natural attitude one normally assumes that social facts preceded us and will survive us. A phenomenologist would suggest that people, on some level of awareness, must know these facts, know the practices appropriate to them, and then must implement these practices in order for these facts to have an effect. For example, it is clear that people do not simply obey the social norms of elevator behavior. Indeed, there are no such norms, except insofar as people know the proprieties of eye avoidance and body positioning and generally act properly in terms of the situation. The frequent variations of behavior observable on elevators suggest that individuals very flexibly adapt to the fluid qualities of the situation. On some occasions the rules are directly contradicted without difficulties arising. The range of norms and permissible exceptions, even in a supposedly simple situation, reveals that a rather complex interpretive process is at the heart of everyday interaction.

For the phenomenologist, people are nei-

ther products of history nor of society. People are not programmed to fill established roles or perform established duties. Environments do not directly create or even shape individuals. Nothing exists independently of human consciousness, specifically the intentional process. Phenomenology suggests that humans are complex, sensitive, subtle beings with minds, the crucial feature of human life. Each mind is unique, interpreting its world in a somewhat different way because of its different knowledge. Very importantly, humans may be aware of the possibility of refusal to conform to circumstances. People, however, generally do seem to function as if they were products of their environments. In the natural attitude, they are not aware of their intentional construction of the world. Since they are not aware, they act *as if* they are the products rather than the constructors, but they are, nonetheless, processing and creating their world.

Throughout the individual's life or biography, knowledge is accumulated from all sorts of sources.[35] Knowledge is communicated directly by significant others as well as indirectly through mediations such as television. As our stock of knowledge grows, we learn about family life, community life, street life, work life—in short, how to think about the world.

In doing any sort of phenomenological analysis of the life world, one might begin by asking what sorts of knowledge do people have that are relevant to the occasion. The phenomenological investigator focuses on the members' knowledge of the situation, questioning the reasons for the selection of elements entering into the stock of knowledge at hand. This knowledge serves as a frame or scheme with which to interpret an individual's experience in the world. The occasion activates the individual's sedimented knowledge, calling forth appropriate *typifications* and producing actions which in turn constitute the occasion itself. Humans perceive and make sense of particular instances by applying typifications. I only know that the item on which I am seated is a couch because I have a typification in my mind of *couch*. Since we have a common sense, members of a culture "know" a fairly similar type and are thus able to communicate regarding couches, etc. But *couch*, or any typification, may have idiosyncratic or peripheral meanings for individuals based on their particular learning experiences. When a substantial number of people share a set of idiosyncratic typifications with patterned peripheral meanings, they are called a *sect*. A sect constructs its own reality in a manner that is relatively different from the most popular version.[36]

Language is the totality of typifications and ways of relating or modifying these typifications. The names for typified items and processes are the nouns and verbs of language. In order to understand the world of another, access may be provided by investigation of the nature of his or her language. One would study the nomenclature, the kinds of distinctions made, and the relational categories used. In this way one is able to ascertain what is important to the group and the ways that it perceives the world. If a people or sect lacks a vocabulary or has a less developed one for a particular type of experience, this suggests that the members lack the capacity to identify the experience, think about it, make sense of it, or communicate regarding it in very sophisticated ways.[37] Any kind of human group develops its own vocabulary or language embedded in its context. This jargon permits the members of the group to make subtle distinctions relevant to their needs and to make precise analyses of their problems. The group develops a language that is derived from the members' common stock of knowledge.[38]

Translated words often do not have precisely the same meanings in different cultures. Since language provides the tools used to perceive and organize the world, and since there is significant variation in the concrete-occasioned application of language, one must logically conclude that there is significant perceptual and cognitive variation in the meanings of items for different individuals and peoples.[39] This, of course, leads back to the problem of achieving accuracy in intercultural translation and the possibility of intersubjective communication.

One of the glaring features of contemporary life is the proliferation of professional groupings with their sectlike qualities.[40] Each grouping establishes its own jargon, agencies of socialization, and overseers to promote its version of the world. Lawyers, doctors, computer specialists, academicians, etc., by emphasizing their portion of the world, their perspectives, and their techniques, constitute special realities which many members may take to be the world as a whole. Others not of this grouping may be perceived as inferior strangers, perhaps barbarous, or at least as people who do not understand "reality." This process of exclusion can provoke rifts, for example, within families, where members are affiliated with groupings which provide different and compelling versions of the world.

With the intense elaboration of occupational, recreational, and spiritual sects, the question of whether a *paramount reality,* the unifying perspective of a people, persists in the contemporary world is an important one to raise.[41] Without such a paramount reality, even the facade of accurate communication and an intersubjective world might dissolve. In order to sustain a common perspective and facilitate communication, it might be necessary for us to develop translation capacities which could include translation specialists. These translators would be capable of communicating realities. For example, they would facilitate the communication between doctors and lawyers. This trend has certainly commenced already, as can be noted by the increase of multidegreed professionals, the extensive use of consultants, liaison personnel, and public relations experts as well as the inclusion of generalists on authoritative boards.

Ethnomethodology is particularly concerned with how people account for themselves, their actions, and the circumstances of their lives. The motivations that people refer to as the foundations of their actions depend on the context in which they are expressed. Indeed, organized discussion of motivation is the way that people make sense of these contexts as well as the constituent features of these contexts. Thus the focus of ethnomethodology is on talk as the stuff of interaction, with much detailed attention devoted to the organization of conversation, the rights of speakers, sequencing of words, etc.[42]

Ethnomethodology emphasizes that social structure is accomplished in the course of interaction. Members flexibly interpret each other's meanings, evolve a feel for the situation, and selectively apply relevant social rules. If situations appear orderly, it is not because a structure exists which elicits standardized conduct, but rather that members use their background knowledge to gain some sense of what it is that is happening and what courses of conduct they might undertake.[43] Members invoke a sense of structure when they produce a situation.

Phenomenological sociology thus offers a way of thinking about the social world that is fundamentally distinct from that of conventional sociology. This does not mean that they cannot coexist. Indeed, the current status of research reveals that both phenomenologist and conventional sociologists are making advances within their respective frameworks. The challenge of each to the other has proved invigorating. In the 1960s and 1970s, a substantial body of sociological research using the phenomenological approach emerged. More is certainly to be expected in the future. In macrophenomenology much work has been done in such areas as religion,[44] communication,[45] crime,[46] family,[47] science,[48] education,[49] and work.[50] This research emphasizes the theme of social construction, revealing how the institutions under investigation come to be experienced as objectlike. Microphenomenology has developed even more programmatically, with its practitioners remaining in close contact. The areas of ethnomethodological research are diverse: crime,[51] deviance,[52] language,[53] education,[54] etc. However, the themes of how people make sense of their situations, how their practices create their interactions, and how ordinary reality is constructed provide cohesion for ethnomethodology. Thus sociological phenomenology is producing a significant body of research, and it holds out great promise as an alternative approach in sociology.

APPLYING PHENOMENOLOGY TO SOCIAL LIFE

Phenomenological sociology offers a whole set of new possibilities for dealing with social and personal troubles. It poses new challenges to the ways in which concerned individuals as well as professional helpers might relate to people in difficulty. Phenomenological sociology implies a particular kind of approach to counseling and therapy. Since phenomenology has already begun to influence some thinkers and practitioners, a few programs have already been instituted which utilize phenomenological features.

Phenomenology can most appropriately be used to analyze the strategies of other modes of therapy and social work intervention.[55] The roots of a variety of therapies in commonsense can be uncovered. By studying the shared assumptions and linguistic structure which make it possible for the therapeutic enterprise to proceed, the phenomenologist can examine how the reality of the therapeutic interview is created and maintained.[56]

Some practitioners, finding phenomenology consistent with existential models, have sought to synthesize the two.[57] Thus these philosophies have become ideological bulwarks of certain contemporary orientations, such as Gestalt therapy. A kind of pretension is apparent in the use of philosophies of world construction in conveying essentially commonsense notions of personal adjustment.[58] If there is some human gain to be made in detaching oneself from the commonsense orientation and in critically describing one's experience of the world, it would be best to do phenomenology in an authentic manner.

Such an authentic application of phenomenology would accept the constituted and meaningful nature of the social world. Emotions or acts are not inherently deviant or troublesome, but only become so through a process of reality bargaining. In this process individuals apply their typifications to the experience and so will others apply their own typifications. Thus family members, counselors, teachers, law enforcement personnel, etc., participate by negotiating the trouble into an understandable pattern for which particular treatments, therapies, or punishments are deemed appropriate.[59] The central question is how will the trouble be conceptualized? It might be viewed as a personal problem requiring individual adjustment of a psychological/moral nature, or it might be defined as something requiring changes in the social contexts which constitute the experience.

Certainly the phenomenological approach recognizes the political nature of resulting constructions. For example, the apparently bizarre expression of a young black man who advocates the annihilation of all white people may be taken as a sign of internal derangement or as an indicator of intense frustration with what he experiences as a totally oppressive existence. The young man himself would claim the validity of his remarks and might admit his frustration, but he would deny any accusation of insanity. A radical-militant analyst would emphasize the roots of the expression in the unequal distribution of opportunities and wealth in society, while an analyst who takes for granted the fundamental validity of the given social order would seek to locate the roots of the trouble within the deranged mind of the individual.

Phenomenology, as a practical discipline, can reveal how people organize their self-interpretations, feel their emotions, create their fantasies, use reason and logic, and generate their actions. Phenomenology unifies these dimensions of the human experience, emphasizing how all identity, feeling, imagining, thought, and behavior are rooted in consciousness.

Alternation is one therapeutic strategy of phenomenological practice.[60] Alternation is achieved by exposing people to new possibilities. It is designed to promote the awareness that other perceptions, experiences, definitions, and realities are entirely possible. The individual's stock of knowledge is mutable. New typification can be added to the stock thus expanding the individual's potential for alternative experiencing. Transactional analysis, Gestalt, client-centered therapy, and other orientations are in some ways implicitly phenomenological in the sense that they may encourage the client to reduce the burden of his or her background and engage in new ways of thinking, feeling, and living. Phenomenological practice goes further by focusing on the taken-for-granted routines of life, thus raising the possibility of breaking out of these modes. By selectively and carefully utilizing the phenomenological attitude in the course of therapy, by applying the reduction in a modest way, the client might gain distance from his or her problem. The problem might become relativized, that is, seen as a personal construct in relation to other personal and collective constructs. In some cases this might lead the individual to question the power over himself or herself of such assumptions as "I must do this" or "It will always be the same for me."

A purpose of phenomenological practice is to promote consciousness of self-construction, not to trap individuals in a solipsistic universe. That is, phenomenological practice does not take a solely individualistic view of subjectivity. It is concerned with the collective constructive process in which the interaction of subjectivities provides the knowledge individuals may use for personal transformation.

The recent decades offer many examples of how significant individual change was accomplished through collective effort. One such instance is the women's movement. Feminists have claimed that many women suffered from nameable and unnameable personal ailments related to their isolation in the household and their dependency on mates.[61] However diverse the movement, the importance of raising consciousness was central to the varied tasks of producing changes in individuals and society. Women formed themselves into groups, sharing their experiences, fears, and aspirations. Many realized that they had experienced much in common.[62] Through this collective effort, new ways of conceiving of themselves emerged among the participants. Awareness of exploitation has led to awareness of alternatives, and it is clear that many participants in consciousness-raising groups have changed their construction of the world and migrated from the presuppositions of their background. By enhancing their awareness of the foundations of their actions, and by recognizing the possibility of alternatives, these women, along with others who have gone through similar consciousness-raising activities, become more authentically self-constructive. After greater individual authenticity is achieved, collective action for social reconstruction becomes possible. The process may move from the group to the individual, and up to the level of broad political, social, and cultural change both within persons and within collectivities.

The full promise of phenomenological practice has only been outlined in this section. The insight engendered by phenomenology might well serve to help us humanize social institutions, promote authenticity in organizations, and imbue role-playing with responsibility. We might improve our capacity to communicate and produce a more liberated mode of ordering social life. Specifically, phenomenology could well be applied to the reconceptualization of the use of rules in bureaucratic organizations, so that these rules would not be taken to be determining facts. We might be able to improve the quality of interviewing and intercultural translation.[63] In sum, phenomenology as a form of philosophy, psychology, and sociology can constitute its own practice and contribute to the enhancement of life. At this point in its development, phenomenology has been applied only in limited ways by practitioners and activists who in many cases lack a firm grounding in this approach. The praxis of phenomenologically influenced practitioners could benefit from a deeper knowledge of their foundations and from a greater awareness of application.[64]

This essay has presented a proposal for phenomenological practice. Such a practice would derive from Husserl's and Schutz's writings and include the reality construction and ethnomethodological approaches of recent years. It would be directed toward humanistic social goals and challenge the pretension of personally and collectively generated objectivities. The foremost concern would be the integration of the person and the dissolution of emotional objects within his or her being. Ultimately, its ethic would be liberationist in the sense that persons under phenomenological practice would be more aware of their intentional processes on the individual and collective levels. Thus, choice-making possibilities would be realized, and individuals could construct their lives and their social order in accord with their will.

NOTES

1. Maurice A. Natanson, *Edmund Husserl: Philosopher of Infinite Tasks* (Evanston, Ill.: Northwestern University Press, 1973).
2. Maurice A. Natanson, "Alfred Schutz," in David Sills, ed., *International Encyclopedia of the Social Sciences,* vol. 14 (New York: Macmillan and Free Press, 1968), pp. 72–74.

3. Peter L. Berger and Thomas Luckmann, *The Social Construction of Reality: A Treatise in the Sociology of Knowledge* (Garden City, N.Y.: Doubleday, 1966).

4. Kurt H. Wolff, "Phenomenology and Sociology," in Tom B. Bottomore and Robert Nisbet, eds., *A History of Sociological Analysis* (New York: Basic Books, 1978), pp. 521–40.

5. Edward G. Armstrong, "Phenomenogophobia" (Paper delivered at the Seventy-second Meeting of the American Sociological Association, Chicago, September 1977).

6. Fred Davis, "The Martian and the Convert: Ontological Polarities in Social Research," in Jeffrey E. Nash and James P. Spradley, eds., *Sociology: A Descriptive Approach* (Chicago: Rand McNally, 1976).

7. Mark Zborowski, "Cultural Components in Responses to Pain," in Howard Robboy et al., eds., *Social Interaction: Introductory Readings in Sociology* (New York: St. Martin's Press, 1979).

8. Michael R. Bond, *Pain: Its Nature, Analysis, and Treatment* (New York: Longman, 1979). Also see David E. Bressler, *Free Yourself from Pain* (New York: Simon & Schuster, 1979).

9. Richard Kalish and David K. Reynolds, *Death and Ethnicity* (Los Angeles: University of Southern California Press, 1976).

10. Herman Feifel, ed., *New Meanings of Death,* (New York: McGraw-Hill, 1977).

11. Karl Marx, *The Economics and Philosophic Manuscripts of 1844,* ed. Dirk J. Struik (New York: International Publishers, 1964), pp. 142–46. Also see Hugh Mehan and Houston Wood, *The Reality of Ethnomethodology* (New York: John Wiley & Sons, 1975), pp. 221–22.

12. Alvin Gouldner, *The Coming Crisis of Western Sociology* (New York: Basic Books, 1970), pp. 40–45.

13. Peter L. Berger, *Invitation to Sociology: A Humanistic Perspective* (Garden City, N.Y.: Doubleday, 1963), pp. 142–45.

14. Gresham Sykes and David Matza, "Techniques of Neutralization: A Theory of Delinquency," *American Sociological Review* 22, no. 6 (December 1957), pp. 667–70.

15. Berger, *Invitation to Sociology.*

16. Alfred Schutz, *On Phenomenology and Social Relations*, ed. Helmut R. Wagner (Chicago: University of Chicago Press, 1970); *Collected Papers I: The Problem of Social Reality,* ed. Maurice Natanson (The Hague: Martinus Nijhoff, 1962); *Collected Papers II: Studies in Social Theory,* ed. Arvid Brodersen (The Hague: Martinus Nijhoff, 1964); *Collected Papers III: Studies in Phenomenological Philosophy,* ed. I. Schutz (The Hague: Martinus Nijhoff, 1966); *The Phenomenology of the Social World,* trans. George Walsh and Frederick Lennert (Evanston, Ill.: Northwestern University Press, 1967); and *Reflections on the Problem of Relevance,* ed. Richard M. Zaner (New Haven, Conn.: Yale University Press, 1970). Also see Robert A. Gorman, *The Dual Vision: Alfred Schutz and the Myth of Phenomenological Social Science* (London: Routledge & Kegan Paul, 1977).

17. Edmund Husserl, *Ideas: General Introduction to Pure Phenomenology,* trans. W. R. Boyce Gibson (New York: Humanities Press, 1931); *The Paris Lectures,* trans. Peter Koestenbaum (The Hague: Martinus Nijhoff, 1964); *The Idea of Phenomenology,* trans. William P. Alston and George Nakhnikian (The Hague: Martinus Nijhoff, 1964); Phenomenology and the Crisis of Philosophy, trans. Quentin Lauer (New York: Harper & Row, 1965); *Formal and Transcendental Logic,* ed. Dorion Cairns (The Hague: Martinus Nijhoff, 1969); *The Crisis of European Sciences and Transcendental Phenomenology,* trans. David Carr (Evanston, Ill.: Northwestern University Press, 1970); *Logical Investigations,* trans. J. N. Findlay, (London: Routledge & Kegan Paul, 1970).

18. Melvin Pollner, "Mundane Reasoning," in *Philosophy of Social Sciences* 4, no. 1, pp. 35–54.

19. Husserl. *Ideas,* pp. 56–62.

20. Robert Bogdan and Steven J. Taylor, *Introduction to Qualitative Research Methods: A Phenomenological Approach to the Social Sciences* (New York: John Wiley & Sons, 1975). Also see Severn T. Bruyn, *The Human Perspective in Sociology: The Methodology of Participant Observation,* (Englewood Cliffs, N.J.: Prentice-Hall, 1966); George Psathas, ed., *Phenomenological Sociology: Issues and Applications* (New York: John Wiley & Sons, 1973).

21. Marcello Truzzi, *Verstehen: Subjective Understanding in the Social Sciences* (Reading, Mass.: Addison-Wesley, 1974).

22. Aaron N. Cicourel, *Method and Measurement in Sociology* (New York: Free Press, 1964).

23. Standord M. Lyman and Marvin B. Scott, *A Sociology of the Absurd* (New York: Appleton-Century-Crofts, 1970), pp. 111–43.

24. Kenneth Leiter, *A Primer on Ethnomethodology* (New York: Oxford University Press, 1980), pp. 175–76.

25. Barbara Ponse, *Identities in the Lesbian World: The Social Construction of Self* (Westport, Conn.: Greenwood Press, 1978).

26. Jamake Highwater, *The Sun, He Dies* (New York: Lippincott and Crowell, 1980).

27. Émile Durkheim, *The Rules of Sociological Method* (1895), trans. Sarah A. Solovay and John H. Meuller (Chicago: University of Chicago Press, 1938).

28. Jack Douglas, ed., *Understanding Everyday Life: Toward the Reconstruction of Sociological Knowledge* (Chicago: Aldine Publishing, 1970).

29. T. P. Wilson, "Normative and Interpretive Paradigms in Sociology," in ibid.

30. Thomas S. Kuhn, *The Structure of Scientific Revolutions* (Chicago: University of Chicago Press, 1962); Thomas Luckmann, "Philosophy, Social Sciences, and Everyday Life," in *Phenomenology and Sociology,* ed. Luckmann (Baltimore: Penguin Books, 1978).

31. Lewis A. Coser, *The Functions of Social Conflict* (New York: Free Press, 1956).

32. Alfred Schutz, *Collected Papers I: The Problem of Social Reality* (The Hague: Martinus Nijhoff, 1962), pp. 104–6.

33. Kurt H. Wolff, "Phenomenology and Sociology," in Tom Bottomore and Robert Nisbet, eds., *A History of Sociological Analysis* (New York: Basic Books, 1978), pp. 500–6.

34. George Orwell, *1984* (New York: Harcourt Brace Jovanovich, 1949), pp. 34–37.

35. Schutz. *Papers I,* pp. 7–10.

36. Berger and Luckmann, *Social Construction of Reality,* pp. 116–17.

37. Matthew Speier, *How to Observe Face-to-Face Communication: A Sociological Introduction* (Pacific Palisades, Calif.: Goodyear Publishing, 1973).

38. Benjamin Lee Whorf, *Language, Thought, and Reality: Selected Writings,* ed. John B. Caroll (Cambridge, Mass.: MIT Press, 1956).

39. Beryl L. Bellman and Bennetta Jules-Rossette, *A Paradigm for Looking: Cross-Cultural Research Using Visual Methods* (Norwood, N.J.: Ablex Publishing, 1977).

40. Joseph Bensman and Robert Lilienfeld, *Craft and Consciousness: Occupational Technique and the Development of World Images* (New York: John Wiley & Sons, 1973).

41. Schutz, *Papers I,* pp. 226–28.

42. Hugh Mehan and Houston Wood, *The Reality of Ethnomethodology* (New York: John Wiley & Sons, 1975), pp. 125–36.

43. Kenneth Leitner, *A Primer on Ethnomethodology* (New York: Oxford University Press, 1980), pp. 85–118.

44. Peter L. Berger, *A Rumor of Angels: Modern Society and the Rediscovery of the Supernatural* (Garden City, N.Y.: Doubleday, 1969); Berger, *The Sacred Canopy: Elements of a Sociological Theory of Religion* (Garden City, N.Y.: Doubleday, 1967).

45. Gary Gumpert and Robert Cathcart, *Inter/Media: Interpersonal Communication in a Media World* (New York: Oxford University Press, 1970), pp. 283–412.

46. Richard Quinney, *The Social Reality of Crime* (Boston: Little, Brown, 1970).

47. Peter L. Berger and Hansfried Kellner, "Marriage and the Construction of Reality," *Diogenes* 5, no. 46 (Summer 1964), pp. 1–23; Diane Vaughn, "Uncoupling: The Social Construction of Divorce," Department of Sociology, Ohio State University (Presented at the Seventy-second American Sociological Association meeting, Chicago, September 1977); Anthony Blasi et al., *Toward an Interpretive Sociology* (Washington, D.C.: Catholic University of America Press, 1978), pp. 287–322.

48. Bruno Latour and Steve Woolgar, *Laboratory Life: The Social Construction of Scientific Facts* (Beverly Hills, Calif.: Sage Publications, 1979).

49. Alan Peshkin, *Growing Up American: Schooling and the Survival of Community* (Chicago: University of Chicago Press, 1978).

50. Barry A. Turner, *Exploring the Industrial Subculture* (New York: Herder and Herder, 1971).

51. Robert Emerson, *Judging Delinquents* (Chicago: Aldine Publishing, 1969); Aaron V. Cicourel, *The Social Organization of Juvenile Justice* (New York: John Wiley & Sons, 1968).

52. David Sudnow, "Normal Crimes: Sociolog-

ical Features of the Penal Code in a Public Defender Office," *Social Problems* 12 (Winter 1965), pp. 255–75.

53. Aaron V. Cicourel et al., *Language Use and School Performance* (New York: Academic Press, 1976); Courtney Cazden et al., eds., *Functions of Language in the Classroom* (New York: Teachers College Press, 1972).

54. Aaron V. Cicourel and John Kitsuse, *Educational Decision-Makers* (Indianapolis, Ind.: Bobbs-Merrill, 1963).

55. Stuart Rees, *Social Work Face to Face: Clients' and Social Workers' Perceptions of the Content and Outcomes of Their Meetings* (New York: Columbia University Press, 1979).

56. Constance T. Fischer and Stanley Brodsky, *Client Participation in Human Services: The Prometheus Principle* (New Brunswick, N.J.: Transaction Books, 1978).

57. Nicholas M. Ragg, *People Not Cases: A Philosophical Approach to Social Work* (London: Routledge & Kegan Paul, 1977).

58. T. E. Greening, *Existential-Humanistic Psychology* (Monterey, Calif.: Brooks/Cole, 1971). Also see Richard Rosen, *Psychobabble: Easy and Quick Cure in the Era of Feeling* (New York: Atheneum Publishers, 1977).

59. Robert M. Emerson and Seldon L. Messinger, "The Micropolitics of Trouble," *Social Problems* 25 (December 1977), pp. 121–34.

60. Berger and Luckmann, *Social Construction of Reality,* pp. 144–48.

61. Sheila Rowbotham, *Woman's Consciousness, Man's World* (Baltimore: Penguin Books, 1973).

62. Sandra Lee Bartky, "Toward a Phenomenology of Feminist Consciousness," in Sharon Bishop and Marjorie Weinzweig, eds., *Philosophy and Women* (Belmont, Calif.: Wadsworth Publishing, 1979).

63. Molefik Asante et al., *Handbook of Intercultural Communication* (Beverly Hills, Calif.: Sage Publications, 1979).

64. Elizabeth Crawford and Rokkan Stein, *Sociological Praxis: Current Roles and Settings* (Beverly Hills, Calif.: Sage Publications, 1976).

Hermeneutical sociologists work through a circular process of projection and anticipation of meaning in which a revision of preconceptions allows a text to speak for itself.

Hermeneutics differs from other sociologies that deal with meanings in two ways:

1. It locates the investigator and subject matter in their historical context.
2. It is able to present a macroanalysis of cultural and social structures.

Hermeneutics as a methodology from which a single objective interpretation can be obtained is contrasted to hermeneutics as a philosophy in which interpretations necessarily vary from one vantage point to another. The major tenets of hermaneutics are exemplified in Hans-Georg Gadamer's work. For Gadamer, knowledge is perspectival, and understanding can only take place from our own point of view in the historical present.

Janet Wolff discusses the problem of relativism and the possibility of a nonrelativist interpretation. Objectivist hermeneutics, the recovery of original meaning, is presented through the work of E. D. Hirsch, Jr., and Emilio Betti. Hermeneutical autonomy distinguishes original meaning from later interpretations. The structuralist hermeneutics of Paul Ricoeur attempts to combine objectivist and subjectivist approaches by analyzing the multiple meanings of symbols and the codes that are embedded in structures of social phenomena. The critical hermeneutics of Karl-Otto Apel and Jürgen Habermas emphasizes the necessity of subjecting language, the means of hermeneutical interpretation, to the methodology of hermeneutics. The critique of ideology makes possible the emancipation of knowledge from unrecognized dependencies. Through the analysis of the ways in which understanding takes place, hermeneutics contributes to a sociological theory of knowledge.

Janet Wolff

HERMENEUTICS
AND SOCIOLOGY[1]

Hermeneutic sociology is, among other things, an attempt to deal with the problem of meaning. It is not, of course, the only sociological approach that does so. Weberianism, phenomenology, symbolic interactionism, ethnomethodology, and all the varieties of *verstehende* sociology also focus on the essential meaningfulness of human behavior, and reject positivistic accounts of social action.[2] Hermeneutics differs from all of these sociologies in two ways: first, it operates with a historical perspective, locating both investigator and subject matter in their historical context; and second, it is able to present a macro-analysis of cultural and social structures (for example, a religious movement or a literary genre) rather than remaining restricted to the microanalysis of individuals and small groups. The understanding of meaning in the hermeneutic perspective may be of the meaning of an individual (as the frequent use of psychoanalysis as a model of hermeneutic activity indicates), of a text, of a social group, or of a historical period. Both of these distinctive characteristics give it certain advantages over other approaches, though it is possible that phenomenology, for example, has a peculiar sensitivity to individual meanings, a sensitivity that is unavailable to hermeneutics. Certainly the hermeneutic approach in sociology has its own limitations.

In this essay I shall give an account of some main variants of this approach; I shall also outline some difficulties it gives rise to, particularly the problem of the apparently inevitable relativity of any account; and I shall review one or two of the most important critical revisions of hermeneutics by other sociologists. I shall conclude, with some of these writers, that the hermeneutic approach is essential, but not sufficient, for sociological analysis, and that it must be complemented by an analysis that locates and explains meanings, as well as interpreting them.

HERMENEUTIC THEORY

The origins of hermeneutics in fact lie outside the social sciences, and in the disciplines concerned with the study and exegesis of texts, particularly in theology, philology, and jurisprudence. I do not intend to go into the history of hermeneutics here.[3] In the work of Wilhelm Dilthey (1833-1911), the concept of *Verstehen* led to a dual, and parallel, development of theory: one, through Max Weber, into the social theory of action, and the other, through historians and philosophers rather than sociologists, into the hermeneutic tradition.[4] In recent years developments in hermeneutics have taken place in theology, in literary criticism, and in the social and cultural sciences. In all cases the questions raised are the same: How can we understand/interpret meanings of other people/other periods? Can we ever attain a final or valid interpretation, or is interpretation always provisional? Does interpretation provide an adequate account of a phenomenon, or must it be supplemented by another kind of analysis?

Hermeneutics is usually defined as "the study of understanding"[5] or "the theory or philosophy of the interpretation of meaning."[6] That is, it is a theory or philosophy, and not a methodology. In general, it is concerned with the investigation of what actually happens when people try to interpret meanings or texts, and with the consequent evaluation of the adequacy of that interpretation. It is not, in its main variants, a set of rules for how to go about the task of interpretation. Nevertheless, within the hermeneutic tradition there has been a division between those concerned with the basic philosophical questions of hermeneutics (Martin Heidegger, Hans-Georg Gadamer) and those for whom theory involves lessons for methodology (Emilio Betti,

E.D. Hirsch, Jr.).[7] Josef Bleicher makes the useful distinction between *hermeneutical theory* and *hermeneutic philosophy* to distinguish theory as method from theory as explication.[8] The former, through an analysis of the interpretative process, suggests ways in which such interpretation may best avoid distortion and aim at correctness. The latter is content to describe the human phenomenon of interpretation itself. As Hans-Georg Gadamer has written in a debate with one of his critics, "I am *not proposing a method*, but I am describing *what is the case*."[9] However, as I shall show, even hermeneutic philosophy allows for better or worse interpretations.

The concern with the methodological aspects of interpretation has usually been connected with a belief in the possibility of *objective interpretation*—that is, the view that we can somehow attain a "correct" understanding of our subject matter. What this correctness consists in varies from one author to another. They share an objection to what they see as the radical relativism, or skepticism, of hermeneutic philosophy (in Bleicher's sense),[10] which appears resigned to the conclusion that as interpretations necessarily vary from one vantage point to another, there is no way of adjudicating between accounts, and therefore one interpretation is as good as another. This critique will be examined in a moment.

The rest of this section will be devoted to an exposition of the major tenets of hermeneutics, as presented in the work of Gadamer. I take his work as my starting point and as central to the tradition for a number of reasons. In the first place, his work over the last twenty years is unparalleled for its careful and exhaustive discussion of the origins and development of hermeneutics and of its present status.[11] Second, there is a real centrality to his contribution to the field, in that every other author I shall be discussing is either in direct dialogue and debate with Gadamer, or at least (in the case of Paul Ricoeur) aware of similarities in and divergences between their work. For this reason, the distinction between hermeneutics seen as a methodology and hermeneutics as a philosophy can be overstated, for writers in both camps engage in controversy with Gadamer, and the issues they have raised have appeared to him to merit his response.[12] In any case a discussion of Gadamer's hermeneutics and its critics will raise all the most important issues for sociological theory.

For Gadamer interpretation is always a circular process. We can only understand (the past, a text, another person) from our own point of view and from our own historical present. In this he disagrees with earlier writers, who argued that the interpretation of the past somehow involved *re-living* the past. In Gadamer's view (and in this I think he is undoubtedly correct), there is no question of totally eliminating our own identity in the act of interpretation. Nor is it possible to experience the past, or another society, just as those who lived in that world would have experienced it. Interpretation is always *re*-interpretation. It is the mediation of past and present. Or, as he puts it, it consists in the *fusion of horizons* of the past and the present.[13] (What Gadamer says about historical understanding is equally applicable to the understanding of other groups or people in the present, when we interpret their meanings too from within our own perspective.) More specifically, the hermeneutic operation involves an approach to our material with certain questions we wish to pose of it. Clearly, we cannot begin our investigation with a totally blank mind, and even if we could, we would not get anywhere faced with the infinite number of aspects of the material. This much is, of course, accepted by most philosophers of science, whether in terms of our formulating hypotheses before beginning research, or in more general terms of orientation to the project in the first place. In this regard, Gadamer resuscitates the notion of *prejudice*, which he maintains is crucial to historical and cultural understanding. Against the

scientistic heritage of the Enlightenment, he argues that prejudices are both ineliminable and essential for any such understanding. That is not to say, however, that we decide in advance what we shall find, and remain blind to any alien features which do not fit into our preconception. A proper interpretation (and here we do have the suggestion that some interpretations may be better than others[14]) retains an *openness* to the text or other subject matter, allowing its prejudices or preconceptions to be modified and corrected on confrontation with the material. Thus, in a circular process of *projection* or *anticipation* of meaning, and the *revision* of these preconceptions as we allow the text or the past to speak for itself (in what Gadamer calls "the logic of question and answer"[15]), we arrive at an interpretative account of our object.

From a totally different starting point, and with quite other interests, Gadamer here concurs with the sociologists of knowledge in the recognition that all knowledge (for he extends his argument from the interpretation of meanings in the cultural sciences to any kind of human understanding[16]) is perspectival. He argues that the very possibility of interpretation arises from our coexistence in a common tradition, linking past and present and one culture with another. Moreover, the medium of hermeneutic experience and of interpretation is language, and language is at the same time the guarantee of our understanding. This is because we formulate both our meanings and our interpretations linguistically, and also, and more important, because our only experience of the world *is* through language and concepts, with which from our earliest years the world is constructed for us. Although this emphasis on the linguistic nature of experience and of hermeneutics will not be central to the rest of the discussion in this essay, it is important to recognize the philosophical tradition within which Gadamer, following Heidegger's later work, locates his hermeneutic philosophy. For the moment, though, all we need take into account is the hermeneutic principle expounded by Gadamer and, as far as I know, never successfully contested, that interpretation of text, past or other, is always and necessarily from the historical situation and perspective of the interpreter, but that the intervention of prejudices in the process need not mean the distortion or *mis*-understanding of the material. This raises the important question of the subjectivity or relativism of interpretations.

THE PROBLEM OF RELATIVISM

As we in the present can never re-create the past as it was, or relive an event or period as if we were contemporaries of that period, how can we evaluate one account of the past as compared with another? Is a twentieth-century interpretation of the Middle Ages better than a nineteenth-century one? If so, and apart from the question of availability of more information in the later period, on what grounds can we maintain this? Of course, we have the advantage of knowing and judging the nineteenth century itself, and we may say that its perspective was narrow, or distorted, or partial, or whatever. But we only say this from our own perspective. This problem is particularly apparent in the evaluation of works of art, where we clearly see throughout the history of the arts changes in taste and the rise and fall of certain schools and genres. (The recent revival of interest in Victorian paintings, after decades of disdain and banishment to the basements of museums, is one example of this.) It is also a more general problem. We may ask whether we understand the phenomenon of witch burning or the religious beliefs and practices of an earlier age "better" than our predecessors of twenty or fifty years ago. In one way, given the apparently radical relativism of hermeneutics, this question cannot even be asked. Our understanding is seen to be determined and limited by our own horizons; other

perspectives are similarly determined and limited, though through different preconceptions and ideas. Perhaps the most we can conclude is that some horizons fuse more easily than others with another age or culture.

For on the one hand, we may argue that the accumulation of knowledge over the centuries ensures that the most recent account is the best; on the other hand, it may be objected that the present is even further removed from the fourteenth century (for example) than the nineteenth century was, and therefore more likely to be wrong in any interpretations it produces. In any case the nearest we can get to an "objective" interpretation, according to Gadamer's hermeneutics, is an interpretation which properly conducts the dialogue of question and answer to its limit. It will not get the past wrong, but neither will it nor could it produce a comprehensive understanding. Our attention is only directed to those elements which relate to our own contemporary interests.

However, there are other versions of the hermeneutic approach which defend an objectivist hermeneutic, and here I shall discuss two contemporary writers: E. D. Hirsch, Jr., and Emilio Betti. The primary interest of the former is in the interpretation of literary texts, and that of the latter is the interpretation of law, but in both cases they deal with the problem of nonrelativist interpretation in a way which may be of more general relevance. Both explicitly take issue with Gadamer on this question, and propose their own solutions to the problem.

Hirsch argues that we can attain a valid interpretation of a text, and that it is the task of literary interpretation to do so. According to him, this would be an account of *what the author meant*.[17] (In this he includes unconscious meaning, as well as conscious intention:

For example, poets may not be able to explain or even articulate (apart from in their poetry) the meanings of their work, which the analyst and literary critic identifies. Nevertheless, those meanings, implicit and unconscious though they may be, originate with the poet.

This meaning, though not always necessarily recoverable, is determinate. So although Hirsch agrees with Gadamer that all interpretation is perspectival, the original and unchanging meaning of the text (that is, its author's intention) represents an objective fact, to be grasped by the hermeneutic approach. He explains the ways in which we can best approximate to the original meaning (for example, by using extrinsic evidence, or by comparing the text with other similar texts, by the same author or by others of the period).[18] In thus postulating an ultimate, and potentially recoverable, meaning, Hirsch believes the problem of relativism has been avoided.

But his theory of interpretation raises its own problems. In the first place he admits that the recovery of original meaning is an ideal, and may not be possible in practice, though it is possible in principle. Second, he also admits that even when we have recovered this meaning, we have no way of knowing that we have done so. (However, neither of these points is itself an objection to the project he outlines; they simply make it appear rather an odd one.) Third, a text has other meanings besides its author's intention. Hirsch recognizes that a text may have new meanings, or significances, for new readers, which go beyond its original meaning.[19] However, he wants to separate this issue clearly from the question of the valid interpretation of the text (that is, the recovery of the author's meaning, which remains for him primary in this regard). But his insistence on this distinction blurs certain important features about the text (which is the product in its own time of a multitude of inputs and determinants, including nonauthorial ones like prevailing artistic codes), and also about the nature of reading and interpretation. And lastly, it is difficult to see how this particular guarantee of objectivity can be applied more widely in interpretative studies. What

would be the equivalent of the author's meaning in, for example, a particular wedding ceremony, or a harvest festival, where there is no "author" or single intending actor? Both within its own terms, and for a general hermeneutics, this notion of objective interpretation does not take us very far in solving the problems raised by Gadamer's analysis.[20]

Betti argues for an objective hermeneutics on similar grounds, though from a more sophisticated philosophical base.[21] Like Hirsch, he wants to reinstate the priority of the object of study—what he calls its *hermeneutical autonomy*.[22] He also, again like Hirsch, insists on an important distinction between the (objective) meaning of an historical phenomenon and its present significance, the former being the only legitimate goal of hermeneutic study.[23] Although Betti is rather more prepared than Hirsch to see the implications of Gadamer's recognition of the constructive role of the interpreter in the hermeneutic exercise, he does not allow this as an argument against the objectivity of understanding, and argues that Gadamer wrongly grants the interpreter a monopoly of truth.[24] So his position regarding the attainment of a valid interpretation is similar to Hirsch's; Betti agrees that the task of interpretation can never be regarded as completed, but refuses the radically relativist corollary to this, that the interpreter is at least as important as the subject matter in the recovery and production of meaning. He says:

The fact that the hermeneutical task can never be completed entails that the meaning contained within texts, monuments and fragments is constantly reborn through life and is for ever transformed in a chain of rebirths; but this does not exclude the fact that the objectivated meaning-content still remains an objectivation of the creative force of an Other, to which the interpreter should seek access, not in arbitrary way, but with the help of controllable guidelines.[25]

As the reference to "controllable guidelines" suggests, he believes that an adequate hermeneutics will follow certain rules or canons of interpretation, which guarantee, as far as is possible, the autonomy of the object as an objectivation of mind, and the consequent objective (or relatively objective) interpretation of it by a differently located investigator.

The attempt by these two writers to secure objectivity by transforming hermeneutics into methodology does not negate its essentially intersubjective and interpretative character. As they both have to admit, final interpretative accounts are impossible, either in practice (Hirsch) or in principle (Betti), which means that to all intents and purposes the present will necessarily direct and inform the interpretation. Moreover, Gadamer's own insistence on the openness of interpretation is not so far removed from Betti's canon of hermeneutic autonomy as the latter believes, for the circular process of anticipation and modification of hermeneutics is a long way from the extreme relativist position which grants infinite license to the reader/investigator. But it is difficult to avoid the conclusion which the hermeneutic perspective has illuminated, that sociological and historical understanding is always provisional and context-bound. I shall go on to consider another, very different, attempt to secure some kind of objectivity for hermeneutic sociology, in the work of the critical theorists, Karl-Otto Apel and Jürgen Habermas, but before doing so I will consider briefly the structuralist hermeneutics of Paul Ricoeur.

STRUCTURALIST HERMENEUTICS

Paul Ricoeur's hermeneutic studies have covered such diverse fields as psychoanalysis, linguistics, religion, and textual interpretation. Moreover, over the years he has modified his views, turning to new concerns, and incorporating in an entirely productive eclecticism the work of other writers and disciplines.[26] In this discussion I concentrate on one or two central concerns in his writings on problems of interpretation, and in particular his very individual discussion of the problem of subjectivity in hermeneutics.

Ricoeur has argued that both in the case of a text and in the case of meaningful action, meaning is fixed or objectified.[27] However, this meaning is *not* equivalent to the meaning of the author or the agent; here he differs sharply from Hirsch. Moreover, the text or the action is open and has a universal range of addressees. It is plurivocal: that is, it is open to several readings. However, he maintains, not all readings are equal, and there are criteria of judgment between competing readings. He distinguishes between *explanation* and *understanding*, which he presents as conjointly involved in interpretation rather than mutually opposed.[28] In his view understanding is necessarily completed by explanation, which deals with the objective structures of the text rather than its subjective meanings. In his criticisms of structuralist accounts of myth and culture, his main objection is their blindness to the hermeneutic task of understanding and self-understanding. However, hermeneutics is equally inadequate so long as it ignores the structures and codes of writing and of action.[29]

To the extent to which the aim of structuralism is to put at a distance, to objectify, to separate out from the personal equation of the investigator, the structure of an institution, a myth, a rite, to the same extent hermeneutics buries itself in what could be called "the hermeneutic circle" of understanding and of believing, which disqualifies it as science and qualifies it as meditating thought.[30]

Explanation—the analysis of the structures of social phenomena, their objective features—does not destroy intersubjective understanding, "that is, the recovery of meaning by an interpreter," but rather is its essential counterpart.

Understanding precedes, accompanies, closes, and thus *envelops* explanation. In return, explanation *develops* understanding analytically.[31]

The symbols and meanings discovered in hermeneutic inquiry, potentially available for multiple readings, are anchored in their objectified meaning systems with the aid of structural analysis. For example, Ricoeur argues that we can only comprehend Hebrew and biblical myths by a *combination* of structural analysis (similar to that proposed by Lévi-Strauss in his analysis of totemism and of North American Indian myths) and historical interpretation, which recovers their meaning.

Ricoeur thus emphasizes the mutual interdependence of hermeneutics and structuralism in the interpretative sciences. In this way both the familiar aspect of hermeneutics, which consists of the appropriation of meaning by the present (the reader, the historian, the sociologist), and a certain autonomy of the subject matter are retained. We might object to this that even the analysis of the logic of symbols, evident in our subject matter, is conducted from the point of view of the present, and indeed there is a tendency for Ricoeur's discussion of structuralism to overstate its objectivity. But what is interesting in this approach is, as Bleicher has pointed out, that it "forms a necessary mediating link between naive understanding, that accepts symbols in their surface-meaning, and hermeneutic understanding proper."[32] Interpretation is thereby appropriation without distortion or violence to the original. Nevertheless, as I think is apparent, it is at the same time still perspectival and relative, though with a limited guarantee of structural objectivity.

In the essay entitled "Explanation and Understanding," Ricoeur makes it clear that structural analysis is still an *intrinsic* study of texts.[33] That is, it restricts itself to the symbols and codes—the *signs of narration*—and does not locate these in their wider sociohistorical setting. In the final version of hermeneutic theory which I shall consider, we find a different argument for supplementing understanding with explanation, which relies on a reference to the *non*-textual and *non*-symbolic.

CRITICAL HERMENEUTICS

Apel and Habermas have both acknowledged the importance of the hermeneutic approach in the social and cultural sciences. Habermas reasserts the need for an interpretative approach in those areas which by their nature involve meanings and signs, and commends Gadamer's contribution in recognizing the essential historicity of hermeneutics, as against the more static and individualistic approaches of other *meaning-sociologies*.[34] However, he insists that hermeneutics is unable to fulfill the crucial sociological task of *explaining* meanings— their origin and genesis, and their function. In Gadamer's hermeneutics, interpretation is presented as an unproblematic mediation of subjectivities, united by their existence in a common tradition. Habermas argues that this tradition itself must be subjected to critical analysis; we need, as sociologists, to know what lies behind consensus and, moreover, how *dis*-continuities in meaning, or *mis*-understandings may be explained. Against Gadamer's elevation of language as the primary ground of communication and, indeed, of existence and experience, Habermas objects that language is also a medium of domination and power in society.[35] Language itself must be subjected to scrutiny, and the structures of communication related to other, underlying social features. Habermas proposes as centrally determinant the structures of *work* and of *power*.[36]

The way in which we perceive the world is determined not only by communicated and learned meanings, but also both by the practical and material constraints of an external world and our activities in (and on) it (work) and by the systems of power and coercion operative in society. An example of this might be the analysis of working-class consciousness, *both* in relation to alienated work conditions and industrial relations, *and* in relation to the dominant formulation of these issues in the media.

When we understand that meanings themselves arise in the context of these structures, it becomes possible to perceive communication as unequal or distorted. Critical sociology supplements interpretation, not in the way that for Ricoeur intrinsic structural explanation supplements subjective understanding, but by leaving the terrain of the text/action/meaning system altogether.

On much the same lines, Apel gives as an example the case of non-European cultures forced to break with the past and adapt to technical-industrial ways of life. In such a case, hermeneutic understanding is inadequate to the task of accounting for the break in tradition.

What they seek above all is a philosophical and scientific orientation that mediates the hermeneutic understanding of their own and foreign traditions of meaning by sociological analyses of those economic and social orders to which they belong.[37]

This is, of course, an extreme example. But even in the case of nondisrupted everyday life in contemporary society, there exist objective structural forces which determine and sustain (inter)subjective meanings. Sociology must distance itself from hermeneutics, in order to "go beyond" the author's or actor's understanding of the world and of himself or herself. As Apel puts it, the sociologist must desist from "taking the other seriously hermeneutically," and by partially suspending communication, regard the subject as a quasi-natural entity, as happens, he claims, in ordinary conversation. In this distancing, the listener (or sociologist):

. . . no longer attempts to create the unity of language in communication, but rather seeks to evaluate what the other person says as the symptom of an objective situation which he [sic] seeks to explain from outside in a language in which his partner does not participate.[38]

Human beings and their lives are not transparent to themselves, and they are, in the normal course of events, unable to perceive the material and social forces which underlie the language, ideas, and culture which they inhabit. To that extent, hermeneutics is not equipped to expose these

forces, since it operates only at the level of the given linguistic and ideological codes and meanings. Critical social science, in the form of the *critique of ideology*, is therefore a vital corrective to interpretation.

Habermas and Apel both make it clear that in arguing the need for an objectivist social science, which goes beyond or behind the subjective, they by no means support a return to positivistic or scientistic research. They consider the latter to have been well discredited in its philosophical and methodological naïveté (not least by Gadamer himself). Critical social science is self-reflexive in a way in which the behavioral (and natural) sciences are not; it assumes the origins of all thought and knowledge in certain human interests, and whereas the interest behind the natural and behavioral sciences lies in technical control (and that of the interpretative sciences in intersubjective communication), the knowledge-interests of critical theory lie in *emancipation* from "unrecognized dependencies."[39] In other words, as well as revealing the determining interests of technical and hermeneutic knowledge, critical theory simultaneously takes account of its own conditions and constituting interests. This is not the place to develop the main arguments of critical social science and the theory of knowledge-interests and their social-political base. With regard to the critique of hermeneutics, the important point is the location of objective understanding *outside* the sphere of meaning and communication. For the sociologist, the standard of adequacy of interpretation is now judged according to extrinsic factors, and it concerns the identification of social relations and processes which produce, distort, and maintain meanings. The hermeneutic moment is thus a crucial one, but only as a step toward a social-scientific understanding.[40]

HERMENEUTICS AND SOCIOLOGY

The fundamental insight of the hermeneutic approach, that human actions and cultural products are comprehended by other human beings (including sociologists) in an interpretative and dialogic act, based on a shared existence in tradition (or what Apel calls a "communication-community"[41]), is essential to social science. Moreover, hermeneutic sociology has important advantages over other *verstehenden* sociologies, in particular the following: (1) it is equally relevant to both micro- and macroanalysis, for example, the single text or the cultural institution; (2) unlike some approaches, hermeneutics recognizes the historical and dynamic nature of social and cultural life; (3) at the same time, it does not pretend to a false objectivism, but incorporates an understanding of the historicity of its own vantage point and the consequent dual historicity of interpretation. It should be remembered that hermeneutics is not a methodology, although hermeneutic theory may differentiate proper (open) interpretation from distorted interpretation (which remains within its initial prejudices). Hermeneutics is a philosophy or a theory of knowledge which analyzes the ways in which understanding actually *does* occur. With regard to sociological inquiry, then, its importance lies in formulating the actual nature of the interpretative moment in the human sciences.

However, as the critical theorists have argued, interpretation of meaning alone is less than a complete sociological understanding of phenomena. It is idealist, insofar as it does not go any further than the comprehension and description of ideas and meanings. But sociology, at least since the time of Marx, has clearly demonstrated that we may penetrate behind the facade of ideas in order to explain their genesis and nature, and to relate them to real, formative influences in society. For this reason hermeneutics must be supplemented by the critique of ideology, for a more comprehensive sociological understanding of cultural phenomena. For example, having interpreted a particular text (a novel or a letter), we may go on to look at the social relations in which such a text was produced (censorship, literacy, methods and relations of production and distribution of literature, and so on). There is always more to say about meaningful phenomena than precritical hermeneutics can tell us.

To illustrate the possibility of such a hermeneutic-critical sociology, I turn briefly to work I was recently involved in on the social history of British art, and, specifically, the visual arts in the first half of the nineteenth century.[42] A noninterpretative, or positivistic, sociology would be likely to give an account of this phenomenon in terms of the following kinds of information: the social class of artists; the social organization of the art market; statistics and data concerning sales and prices of certain works; the numbers and types of works bought and sold through dealers; and so on. (A traditional art-historical account, on the other hand, would ignore all these factors, and present Victorian art in its historical relationship, in terms of style, theme, technique, etc., to earlier genres and schools.) A hermeneutically oriented social history of art, however, would take as its primary concern the *meaning* of the paintings, attempting as far as possible to re-create their original contemporary sense for artist and viewer. The common themes of domesticity and morality, nationalism and heroism, and the idealization of nature and landscape would thus be grasped in the light of what we know about nineteenth-century British attitudes and experiences (the effects of the Industrial Revolution and of urbanization, the privatization of the family, the newly leisured, nonproductive role of middle-class women, the celebration of Western civilization in its superiority to recently discovered "primitive" peoples, and so on). These beliefs and attitudes are, of course, independently accessible through fiction, diaries, letters, the press, and so on. A sensitive interpretation would avoid imposing twentieth-century values and ideas by simply reading back into the past our own meanings. Nevertheless, even the most careful and open interpretation is a twentieth-century reconstruction, in its identification of certain themes *as* worthy of study, and in many other ways. For example, the women's movement in Britain and the United States and recent feminist work in sociology and art history have been the essential prerequisite to my own sensitization to issues of sexuality, gender characterization, and domestic roles.

The value of the hermeneutic study of art is that, unlike positivist sociology, it enables us to discuss questions of meaning and signification in paintings. Quantitative or non-*verstehende* approaches are bound to ignore these, and to treat paintings as so many data or facts. But, as I have been arguing throughout this essay, a simple hermeneutic sociology of art is a one-sided and partial analysis. From this we need to go on to investigate the origins and determinants of those meaning systems and ideologies we have identified, and to ascertain why and how such ideas predominated in early and mid-nineteenth-century Britain. In this particular case, this critique of ideology has a dual aspect. In the first place, it is a question of the analysis of ideology in general in that period: the relationship of certain values and ideas to material factors, political power, and so on. But it also involves a close study of the production of art, for it is by no means clear that generally pervasive or dominant ideas *will* be expressed in painting. This depends on the relations of artistic production, the specific integration of the aesthetic sphere into wider social and political structures, and the actual involvement of representatives or members of dominant groups in the production and distribution of art. To this end our research involved a close attention to forms of patronage, to the role of the new middle class of merchants, manufacturers, and industrialists, and to their support and encouragement of the arts (focusing particularly on the North of England—Manchester and the West Riding of Yorkshire—where industrial, economic, and social developments were more advanced than elsewhere). To put it simply, identifying bourgeois themes in painting must involve an explanation of *how* the bourgeoisie or its ideology could, in practical terms, invade the aesthetic domain, and also an objectivist account *of* those themes, in art and elsewhere. Thus, an adequate hermeneutic sociology of nineteenth-century British art provides both an understanding *of* that art, as far as possible in its contemporary context, and a structural, *non*-interpretative, explanation of its determinants and sustaining interests.

THE LIMITS OF OBJECTIVITY

I have argued that sociology must be both hermeneutic and critical. The final point I shall raise in this essay concerns the limits of objective thought in even a critical hermeneutics. Here I think Gadamer's comments on Habermas's critique are difficult to refute. Basically, his point is that it is *impossible* to "get outside" meaning, and hence to supersede hermeneutic reflection. The task of critical theory, to look at real factors underlying ideas and meanings, and thus to produce, in some sense, an objective account of subjective phenomena, is a misguided one. As he says, "The critique of ideology overestimates the competence of reflection and reason."[43] Our *only* access to reality is through language and communication. This is what Gadamer means when he talks of the "universality of the hermeneutical problem," for *all* knowledge, including scientific and technical knowledge, is ultimately hermeneutic—that is, both linguistic and perspectival.[44] Indeed, Apel also wishes to stress the similarities in this respect between the cultural sciences and the natural sciences, both of which presuppose what he refers to as an "*a priori* of language-communication."[45] So even critical sociology is bound within the confines of language and meaning. As Gadamer says:

Habermas sees the critique of ideology as the means of unmasking the "deceptions of language." But this critique, of course, is in itself a linguistic act of reflection.[46]

The problem is not just one of language. Even in a critical perspective, it is still the case that knowledge and understanding are produced from particular perspectives, and with particular prejudices. Critical sociology forces us to reflect on our own prejudices. But this in itself does not amount to their removal. There is, indeed, no standpoint outside history, and I think Gadamer is right to insist that Habermas has failed to acknowledge the force and implications of this truth. In other words, even the real and material forces detected by critical analysis are sought and perceived by a situated investigator. (It is quite clear, too, that there is plenty of room for dispute among sociologists as to *which* particular interests and forces are in fact the crucial underlying ones, but that is another matter.) In short, critical theory's claim to truth is at least a problematic one, which requires a careful and sophisticated defense.[47] As hermeneutic theory has demonstrated, if we are to use the notion of objectivity in knowledge, then at the very least our existing, naive concept must be redefined.

NOTES

1. This essay was written in August 1980.
2. Zygmunt Bauman, *Hermeneutics and Social Science* (London: Hutchinson, 1978), uses the term *hermeneutics* generally to cover various of these approaches. In the present article the narrower definition will be retained.
3. For such accounts see the following: Richard E. Palmer, *Hermeneutics: Interpretation Theory in Schleiermacher, Dilthey, Heidegger, and Gadamer* (Evanston, Ill.: Northwestern University Press, 1969); Josef Bleicher, *Contemporary Hermeneutics: Hermeneutics as Method, Philosophy, and Critique* (London: Routledge & Kegan Paul, 1980); and Janet Wolff, *Hermeneutic Philosophy and the Sociology of Art* (London: Routledge & Kegan Paul, 1975).
4. See William Outhwaite, *Understanding Social Life: The Method Called "Verstehen"* (London: George Allen & Unwin, 1975).
5. Palmer, *Hermeneutics*, p. 8.
6. Bleicher, *Contemporary Hermeneutics*, p. 1.
7. See David Couzens Hoy, *The Critical Circle: Literature, History, and Philosophical Hermeneu-*

tics (Berkeley, Calif.: University of California Press, 1978), pp. 43 ff. However, Hoy maintains that Gadamer, while not promoting any particular *method*, is promoting a methodology (p. 105).
8. Bleicher, *Contemporary Hermeneutics*, pp. 1-3.
9. Hans-Georg Gadamer, *Truth and Method* (London: Sheed & Ward, 1975), p. 465; italics in original text; first German edition in 1960.
10. See, for example, E. D. Hirsch, Jr., *Validity in Interpretation* (New Haven, Conn.: Yale University Press, 1967), pp. viii-ix.
11. His major work is *Truth and Method*. I refer also to the essays collected in translation in Hans-Georg Gadamer, *Philosophical Hermeneutics* (Berkeley, Calif.: University of California Press, 1976) (essays originally published in German between 1960 and 1972); and also Gadamer, "Hermeneutics and Social Science," *Cultural Hermeneutics* 2 (1974/5).
12. He takes up the criticisms made by Betti in *Truth and Method*, pp. 464 ff., and by Habermas in *Philosophical Hermeneutics*, pp. 26 ff., and in "Hermeneutics and Social Science." Ricoeur and Hirsch in their turn address Gadamer's work in Paul Ricoeur, *The Philosophy of Paul Ricoeur*, ed. Charles E. Reagan and David Steward (Boston: Beacon Press, 1978), pp. 144 and 154; and in Hirsch, *Validity in Interpretation*, pp. 245 ff., and E. D. Hirsch, Jr., *The Aims of Interpretation* (Chicago: University of Chicago Press, 1976), pp. 39 ff.
13. Gadamer, *Truth and Method*, p. 273.
14. In this respect Hoy contrasts Gadamer with Roland Barthes, who rejects the notion of truth in any interpretation, and for whom, at least in some of his work, all accounts are subjective; see Hoy, *Critical Circle*, pp. 141-46. For Gadamer, truth is an expectation of interpretation guaranteed by processes of criticism.
15. Gadamer, *Truth and Method*, p. 333.
16. See his essay "The Universality of the Hermeneutical Problem," which is reprinted in both Gadamer, *Philosophical Hermeneutics*, and Bleicher, *Contemporary Hermeneutics*.
17. Hirsch, *Validity in Interpretation* and *Aims of Interpretation*.
18. See Hoy, *Critical Circle*, and Janet Wolff, "The Interpretation of Literature in Society: The Hermeneutic Approach," in Jane Routh and Janet Wolff, eds., *The Sociology of*

Literature: Theoretical Approaches (Keele; 1977).

19. Hirsch, *Aims of Interpretation*, pp. 1–13 and 78–81.

20. More detailed and complex criticisms of Hirsch's project can be found in Hoy, *Critical Circle*, Chap. 1.

21. Emilio Betti, "Hermeneutics as the General Methodology of the *Geisteswissenschaften*," in Bleicher, *Contemporary Hermeneutics*. [1962] (For Betti's work see also Bleicher, *C.H.* Hoy, *T.C.C.* and Palmer, *Hermeneutic*.)

22. Ibid., p. 58.

23. Ibid., pp. 68-69.

24. Ibid., p. 80.

25. Ibid., pp. 68-69.

26. See, for example, the autobiographical comments on his intellectual progress in the essay "From Existentialism to the Philosophy of Language" (in Ricoeur, *Philosophy of Paul Ricoeur*).

27. Paul Ricoeur, "The Model of the Text: Meaningful Action Considered as a Text," *Social Research* 38; reprinted in Fred R. Dallmayr and Thomas A. McCarthy, eds., *Understanding and Social Inquiry* (Notre Dame, Ind.: University of Notre Dame Press, 1977). [1971]

28. Ricoeur, *The Model of the Text*, p. 556. Also the essays "Explanation and Understanding," in Ricoeur, and "Structure and Hermeneutics,"in Paul Ricoeur, *The Conflict of Interpretations: Essays in Hermeneutics* (Evanston, Ill.: Northwestern University Press, 1974).

29. Ricoeur, *Philosophy of Paul Ricoeur*, p. 153.

30. Ricoeur, *Conflict of Interpretations*, p. 30.

31. Ricoeur, *Philosophy of Paul Ricoeur*, p. 165; italics in original.

32. Bleicher, *Contemporary Hermeneutics*, p. 227.

33. Ricoeur, *Philosophy of Paul Ricoeur*, p. 154.

34. Jürgen Habermas, *Theory and Practice* (London: Heineman, 1974), p. 11. See also Jürgen Habermas, *Zur Logik der Sozialwissenschaften* (Frankfurt: Suhrkamp Verlag, 1970); Janet Wolff, "Hermeneutics and the Critique of Ideology," *Sociological Review* 23, no. 4 (1975); Anthony Giddens, "Habermas's Critique of Hermeneutics," in *Studies in Social and Political Theory* (London: Hutchinson, 1977).

35. Jürgen Habermas, "A Review of Gadamer's *Truth and Method*," in Dallmayr and McCarthy, *Understanding and Social Inquiry*, p. 360.

36. Jürgen Habermas, "Knowledge and Interest," *Inquiry* 9. Also in Dorothy Emmet and Alasdair MacIntyre, eds., *Sociological Theory and Philosophical Analysis* (London: Macmillan, 1970).

37. Karl-Otto Apel, *Towards a Transformation of Philosophy* (London: Routledge & Kegan Paul, 1980), p. 66; German edition published in 1972/1973.

38. Ibid., p. 68.

39. Habermas, *Theory and Practice*, pp. 8-9.

40. It will be clear by now that often the terminology of interpretation studies can get rather confusing. For example, where critical theory maintains that for an adequate (total) understanding, we must supplement interpretation with explanation, Ricoeur reverses the terms *understanding* and *interpretation*, the former now meaning the subjective grasp of meanings, and the latter a more overall, or total, grasp of the material combining understanding with explanation. Ricoeur's usage appears to me to be rather more eccentric than Habermas's.

41. Karl-Otto Apel, "Communication and the Foundations of the Humanities," *Acta Sociologica* 15/16 (1972–73), p. 21.

42. Janet Wolff and John Seed, eds: *The Culture of Capital: Art, Power and the Nineteenth-Century Middle Class* (Manchester: MUP 1988)

43. Gadamer, "Hermeneutics and Social Science," p. 315. See also Gadamer, *Philosophical Hermeneutics*, pp. 26–36.

44. *Ibid.*, pp. 3–17 and 38–42.

45. Apel, "Communication and the Foundations of the Humanities."

46. Gadamer, *Philosophical Hermeneutics*, p. 30.

47. See Jürgen Habermas, "The Hermeneutic Claim to Universality," in Bleicher, *Contemporary Hermeneutics*. For critical theory the concept of truth is closely linked with that of *consensus* and with the "ideal speech situation." See Bleicher, ibid., p. 163.

To *surrender and catch* is to suspend received notions and risk being hurt in order to gain an extraordinary awareness.

Contemporary human existence is in a state of crisis because of several new and old conditions. These include the shrinkage of resources to meet physical needs, the inequitable distribution of those resources across humanity, the shrinkage of distance, and the capacity for annihilation. This crisis has elicited a number of responses, including religious and cult movements, drug use, nationalist movements, and cynicism. Surrender-and-catch is an alternative response which grew out of the author's experience of learning a new culture as a fieldworker. To surrender is to be in a state of cognitive love in which everything becomes pertinent in an area of experience to the exclusion of all else. The drawing of the line between these two areas is the *catch* from which a new concept or clarification arises.

The use of surrender-and-catch as a community study methodology encourages students to become aware of the human features of the society rather than of received approaches or generalizable propositions. The capacity to surrender is both maturational and situational. On the one hand, surrendering received notions presupposes that such notions already exist, while, on the other hand, the body must not intrude to interfere with the taking in of new experience. Surrender-and-catch is a radical methodology in that it provides a means for apprehending the coincidence of the unique and the universal in human experience. It also provides a means for rebelling against the inadequacies of the human condition.

Surrender-and-catch connects to critical theory, structuralism, hermeneutics, and phenomenology. Kurt H. Wolff suggests a research proposal to study aspects of surrender-and-catch, including mental concentration, alternative physical states of the body, perceptions of physical relief, and psychic circumstances of first experiences. Finally, the relationship of surrender-and-catch to traditional scientific sociology is explored.

Kurt H. Wolff

"SURRENDER-AND-CATCH"
AND SOCIOLOGY

1. THE PLACE AND TIME OF SURRENDER-AND-CATCH

The place to which the idea of *surrender-and-catch* is meant to speak is here, and the time out of which it comes and which it seeks to address is now. In a first approximation *here* is this Earth, the home of all human beings, and *now* is this time in human history. At this time in human history, the place in which all of us human beings live has shrunk as never before, and in more than one sense. Two senses at least are most pressing.

One is the shrinkage of the means to satisfy physical human needs for all sorts of raw materials. *What* the shortages are in a given spot depends on the particular needs of the society and the individuals who live there. The most basic need is for food, which is so scarce in many societies and for so many human beings that we, who read this essay and are far less likely to feel hunger, cannot even imagine it. Of course,

there are many other needs. The point is, however, that they exist in the face of the extraordinary technology available to meet them. In fact, it is probable that enough human beings know what it takes to meet them actually—but there are at least two reasons why these needs aren't met. One is the fantastically uneven distribution of resources; the other is the ever increasing population, that is, the number of human beings whose needs must be met. Of these two reasons, the former—maldistribution—is almost certainly more important. For what is missing above all is the knowledge of how to overcome the existing maldistribution of the Earth's wealth—that is, of its raw materials and the products of human skill—in the most just manner: many studies have shown that a better standard of living quickly has a negative effect on the birth rate, and thus decreases population growth.

The shrinkage of the means to satisfy physical human needs, then, is one mean-

201

ing of the statement that the Earth has shrunk as never before. Its second huge meaning is inseparable from it; that is the shrinkage of distances. And the extent to which this has occurred, and is continuing to occur, is for most of us as unimaginable as it is unimaginable for us not to know for the rest of our lives how to secure enough food so as not to starve. The shrinkage of distance means not only that an individual can get from any place on Earth to any other within hours, and not only that a missile can move from any place on Earth to any other within minutes or even seconds but it also means that communication from any place to any other place is practically instantaneous. And while for economic and other reasons only a tiny number of people actually do go vast distances despite the enormous growth of travel, an incomparably larger number can and do hear by radio and see by television what goes on anywhere on Earth, and even beyond the Earth. We often see such things ''live''— even though most of us have no control, or at least think we have no control, over all that is going on and shown to us on the seven o'clock news. Nevertheless, because of the telephone, radio, television, and satellite broadcasting as well as other technological achievements, it is more difficult than ever before in human history for something to occur anywhere without its being known everywhere—at least everywhere there is a news-gathering apparatus.

The shrinkage of the globe in these two senses has enormous ramifications. To mention only one: the sheer possibility of our knowing what is going on anywhere is bound to have changed already today, and it will change even further in the future, the meaning of what is relevant for us to know—politically, economically, socially— of all the infinite number of happenings in the world. But those who are aware of the global shrinkage are still a small minority among the members of humanity because most of them are concentrated in the industrial countries, that is, the very coun-

tries that have caused this shrinkage. And the foremost meaning for us who live in the industrial nations has not been mentioned yet—it is that the human species now has the knowledge and capacity to virtually instantaneously annihilate itself (along with many other living things, animal and plant). Indeed, sometimes it feels as if we are rushing to our own suicide.

This is the time and place of surrender-and-catch. Its idea is a response to the crisis in which we find ourselves—in which, more or less directly, *all* of us human beings find ourselves. It is *a* response: evidently, it is unthinkable and would be foolish to believe that it could be *the* only response. For the crisis has elicited a very large number of responses of many different kinds. Some of them, notably totalitarianism, have deepened the crisis instead of alleviating it. Totalitarianism—whether we think of nazism or Russian communism or Italian or Spanish fascism, or any other variety—has been obviously a response to a crisis, whatever that crisis was in the particular country in which that particular form of totalitarianism arose. But it is clear that that form of totalitarianism only intensified the general crisis or at the very least made the situation of humanity more complex.

There also exists a myriad of other responses. Among them we can mention nationalist and irredentist movements; all kinds of religious movements and cults; drug taking; mental disturbances, including apathy, cynicism, despair, and a tendency to suicide; problems within families and between generations. Closer to the spirit of surrender-and-catch than these social, political, or emotional responses are responses of an intellectual nature in the arts, humanities, and social sciences. They range from the various ''isms'' of painting, the twelve-tone or serial schools of music, and the stream-of-consciousness style of writing to such movements in philosophy and sociology as phenomenology, existentialism, structuralism, hermeneutics, and critical theory. The last-named schools of sociology have the greatest affinity perhaps to surrender-and-catch. While we cannot describe this affinity in detail in the present essay, we'll make some suggestions about it in the last section.

At this point, however, we need to describe how the surrender-and-catch idea began.

2. THE CONCRETE ORIGIN OF SURRENDER-AND-CATCH

When I speak of the concrete origin of this concept, I am referring to the way in which the idea of it arose. Since its rise was an unforgettable experience, I will now describe how it happened.[1] My experience of surrender (although not as yet its conceptualization) occurred in field work. At the time my task was to test the concept of *culture patterns* by finding a method that would provide anyone familiar with the concept a procedure for checking the claims any student might make about it.[2]

In 1944 my field work took me to "Loma," a small, largely Spanish-speaking, and somewhat isolated community in northern New Mexico. (This was not my first visit to Loma.) I was so taken by the landscape and people of Loma that I felt the kind of study I was supposed to engage in to be an arbitrary intrusion. Instead, I fell in love with Loma. I became passionately curious about all things there—whatever I heard, saw, smelled, or tasted. I recorded sayings, songs, prayers, people, houses, meals, roads, fields, the smell of Loma's flowers, especially the smell of sagebrush. I recorded the look of adobe walls, the feel of old blankets, the hands and cheeks of an old woman, weathered wood. I collected recipes, herbs, stories about witchcraft, hundreds of kin relations. I was absorbed—voraciously and omnivorously taking in as much as I could and was able to stand, wondering and thinking about all these experiences.

Only years later did the expression surrender-and-catch occur to me. I had surrendered to Loma (or so I thought) and my "catch"—as when we speak of the catch in a fishnet—was not all the data I had gathered but rather the very concept of surrender-and-catch itself. In fact, much of what I have written, including this very essay, is a part of that catch. For I have presented in this essay a more comprehensive and more forthright statement of the connection between surrender-and-catch and the crisis that now threatens human existence than I have done before.[3]

The main point I wish to make at the moment is that we are dealing here with two quite different matters: (1) the concrete circumstances during which I came upon the idea of surrender-and-catch, and (2) surrender-and-catch as a response to our crisis. The idea originated at a specific time and place, perhaps as the result of a crisis in the social sciences, including sociology. It originated in an individual (myself) who has since thought a great deal about the way in which this concept dawned upon him. I am still not done thinking about this experience. But at the same time I am able to abstract from myself and look at the place of surrender-and-catch—not just in my own life but also in our own time and society.

3. WHAT, THEN, IS SURRENDER-AND-CATCH?

a. Surrendering means to be in a state of cognitive love, such as the love I felt during my stay in Loma. In surrender generally, *everything is pertinent. Everything* means everything in the surrenderer's awareness, just as for lovers everything they are aware of in the beloved as well as in their love is pertinent and important. This means that all *outside* the surrenderer's (or the lover's) awareness is irrelevant; not only doesn't it count, it doesn't even exist. Compared to it, surrender is far too extraordinary. (What could possibly compare with the beloved or the love?) In this experience or in its memory, the division between the *everything* that defines the area of the experience and *everything else* may challenge the surrenderer to draw the line of this division as accurately as possible. If so, the task of drawing this line is a task of the "catch," and the line drawn is a part of the catch or the catch itself.

Reflecting on what is pertinent and what turns out not to be pertinent can lead one to gain fresh insight into the boundaries of oneself, of what is and is not pertinent to oneself. We can also describe surrender as an experience of *identification*—but not in the sense of identifying oneself, because *this* identification, as has just been implied, results from reflecting on the experience of surrender; it is not the experience itself, but its catch, or part of the catch. What identification does take place *in* surrender is not a finding of one's identity but a process or a state of identity with the experience itself, with its occasion, its object, oneself—none of which are experienced differentially. (What was I identical with in Loma? With Loma or the Lomans? With all that I so eagerly collected, recorded, experienced, and thought about? With myself? To repeat, these and incalculably many other things were not differentiated in the experience.)

The identification described must not be aimed at, that is, it must not be the aim of the catch. For if it were the aim of the catch, surrender would not be *cognitive* love, the surrenderer would not want to know but, by definition, would want only to identify (an important aim in many religions and cults), and thus—in a far broader sense than the customary anthropological sense—would want to "go native." That is to say, the experience of surrender would be exhaustively understood by the surrenderer as just that, however extraordinary an experience, and, in a later retrospect, as an episode, no matter how weighty. The surrenderer, instead, wants to *know*, catch, understand, conceive, so that others can be told—none of which would be possible if identification itself were the catch. Here again, there is a similarity with

lovers, who must lose themselves to find themselves (and each other): they must not lose themselves for their own sake, for this would be self-destructive and destructive of their beloved.

Thus far, we have talked about surrender in two ways: by characterizing it as a state or experience whose essential feature is the *pertinence of everything* and as *identification*. A third way of talking about it is to stress what has come up already in the remarks about identification, namely, *total involvement*. In surrender I am undifferentiatedly and indistinguishably involved in its occasion, in myself, in my experience or state, in my object (e.g., Loma) or my partner (e.g., a Loman). Once more, the parallel with physical love is obvious: lovers do not know where each of them "ends" and the other "begins"—in various senses, from the physical to the mental and moral. Here we also see that even the very important, taken-for-granted distinctions we ordinarily make—in this case, the distinction between me and you, subject and object, self and other, subject and act or experience—do not figure, are irrelevant or inapplicable, disappear.

This observation leads to a further characteristic of surrender—the *suspension of received notions*. This is the characteristic that connects surrender most clearly with some of the contemporary movements in the humanities, especially philosophy: phenomenology, existentialism, and hermeneutics. In surrender I suspend, to the extent and in the way made possible by my very being, all that I feel has anything to do with what I am so eager to find out, to know, to learn, or at least to explore. Note the word *suspend*, which means not to affirm or deny, but to call into question. To use the phenomenological term, to *bracket*. Among the matters suspended are my very convictions about what is real and unreal, about the credibility of theories and hypotheses, the accuracy or inaccuracy of concepts, the dignity of ideas, the validity of assumptions and postulates, even of such fundamental notions (categories)—we have just seen it—as subject and object, self and other. All that I feel has anything to do with what I am so eager to find out, to know, to learn, or at least to explore, is all that I am aware of or know of.

There is a last aspect of surrender we must consider before we come to a more direct analysis of the phenomenon itself: the *risk of being hurt*. This characterizes not only surrender but also the catch and acting on the catch—and, of course, an infinite number of other activities and circumstances as well. But surrender itself brings with it two kinds of risks of hurt; they lie in its very nature. Both of them are the risks of false surrender; in both there is the promise of surrender, but surrender does not occur. Aside from this, however, the two are the opposites of each other. In one of them, an idea—a received notion—has too much sway over the would-be surrenderer to allow itself to be suspended; cognitive love cannot embrace it. The would-be surrenderer is left with what there was before but what he or she feels ought to have been suspended, yet could not be suspended. A further degree of surrender, a fresh insight, a new recognition, is frustrated. This is *surrender aborted*.

The other kind of false surrender is its opposite: here a person suspends too much, namely, that which alone makes surrender possible and thus can *not* be taken as a received notion to be suspended. This—that which must not be suspended—is the faith that surrender is possible. But that means the person's very self, for one's self is at this time in our history all that one truly has to make a beginning with. This second kind of false surrender may thus properly be called *surrender betrayed* or *self-betrayal*. Here would-be surrenderers resemble lovers who lose themselves in order to lose themselves. In other words, the risk of surrender betrayed is the risk of insanity. The dangers of surrender aborted and surrender betrayed may be avoided if we are aware of them. If this is too weak, these dangers may be avoided by a new surrender or an attempt to surrender (of which we shall say more when we come to discuss *surrender-to*). Still, they *are* risks.

b. What, then, is surrender, and what is catch? To surrender is to take as fully as possible, to meet as immediately as possible the situation, occasion, experience, state, object, self, or partner. This (very incomplete) list must do for the one word that would point to these and indefinitely more things which experientially are not differentiated, as we said before. To surrender—to put it negatively—is *not* to select, *not* to choose or pick or decide, *not* to believe that one can easily or quickly know what one's experience of surrender means, and thus what is to be understood and acted on. It means *not* to suppose that we can do right by the experience through our received notions, including our received feeling and thinking, even the structure of that feeling and thinking. Or, to put it again positively, to surrender means to meet or receive the experience (with all its elements and aspects) in its originariness, its *itselfness*, as best we can—as best we *are* at our very best.

Surrender, however, this extraordinary experience, cannot be brought about by an effort of the will. It happens or occurs like grace (to use a religious term). There can be no list, therefore, of its occasions, which are endless in number and variety. On the other hand, I *can* make an effort to *surrender-to* something or somebody, that is, I can try to turn my utmost attention to that thing or person. If this concentrated attention is analyzed, it is seen to have the same characteristics surrender has: *pertinence of everything*, that is, identification, total involvement, the suspension of received notions, and the risk of being hurt, and more particularly, the two risks of surrender aborted and surrender betrayed.[4] The difference between surrender and surrender-to is that these characteristics are inborn in surrender (they were here analyzed, of course, *post factum*), whereas in surrender-to, they are consciously striven for. Since the occasions of surrender cannot be predicted, surrender-to itself may be one, that is, it may change into surrender. This possibility merely illustrates the unforeseeability of surrender and the indeterminability of its occasions. But it does nothing to diminish the difference, which is both analytical and experiential, between surrender and surrender-to.

And what is *catch*? It is the result, outcome, harvest, yield, *Fang* (catch), the emerging *Begriff* (concept, from *con-cipio,* literally, "to catch-together") of surrender, the beginning (*Anfang*), that is, the new conceiving or conceptualizing attendant on surrender (and surrender-to). *What* this is cannot be anticipated, for the catch is as unforeseeable as surrender itself. Indeed, the catch may not be a concept in the ordinary or the scientific sense of the word at all. But—to mention only a few among the more easily formulable outcomes—it may be a resolution, wish, work of art, an essay, or the clarification of a personal problem. Still, whatever it may be, it is a new conceiving, a new seeing, a new understanding, and thus a new being-in-the-world or a new beginning. The catch, however, cannot exhaust the experience of surrender (as no analysis, recollection, or description can exhaust any experience). It is as if the experience recedes from the experiencer like water from a net, and the experience challenges the surrenderer to explore, to come into (literally, to *invent*) what is left in the net, the catch.

c. But *why* this peculiar word *surrender*? It sounds like capitulation; it has both a military and a passive ring. After all, in ordinary parlance surrendering is to give up or give in. But no other word will do as well in conveying what surrender is meant to convey. *Abandonment*, for instance, suggests a dissoluteness wholly alien to surrender. *Exposure* alludes to exhibitionism. *Devotion* or *dedication* points to an attitude and introduces a moral tone. *Penetration* lacks the element of dedication and, moreover, misleads by its masculinity. *Laying oneself open* or *laying one's cards on the table* conveys no more than the unconditionality and honesty of surrender.

Surrender is more comprehensive than any of these terms. In addition, it is polemical, the word itself announcing militancy against the predominant Western and potentially earthwide consciousness in which our relation to both human beings and nature instead of surrender is mastery, control, exploitation, efficiency, handling, manipulation, calculation. Here we see the first relation since the beginning of this chapter of surrender-and-catch with our time and our society. The sexual connotation of this expression also speaks to this connotation of the word: in the predominant consciousness of control, which is virile, the woman surrenders and gives, while the male who does so might be suspected of losing his manliness and being considered effeminate. In recent decades, of course, this consciousness has been shaken: in regard to nature, natural resources have become problematic or at least thematic, and some of them have become scarce. In regard to virility, we have seen the women's movement and more recently the gay movement. Nevertheless, surrender clearly has a political and a sexual implication, and the two reinforce each other. Surrender is a revolutionary idea; part of its irony, which is turned even toward the individual to whom this idea occurred, is its bland, perhaps titillatingly subversive appearance.

A synonym of surrender is *total experience*. Parallel to the polemic of the word *surrender* itself is that of *total*. *Total* is against totalitarianism, which is so intimately a concomitant of the consciousness against which surrender polemicizes. Furthermore, unlike other adjectives we might think of as characterizing the experience of surrender—perhaps important, critical, seminal, germinal, or crucial—*total* also connotes its undifferentiatedness, its suspension of received distinctions.

Just as a synonym of "surrender" is *total experience*, a synonym of "catch" is *invention* (hinted at in the presentation of "catch" itself). *Invention* derives from *invenire*, literally "to come into," "to come upon." "Surrender," we saw, has a feminine connotation; "invention" (like "penetration"), a masculine one. Still, "to come into," most obviously in the tabooed "come," which refers to the orgasm of both men and women, should be read, like "surrender" itself, as bisexual.

Finally, related to *invention* is *breakthrough* (at this time, an unbearably misused word): it is the triumph over whatever would obstruct surrender.

d. Part of the extraordinary nature of the experience of surrender as well as of surrender-to is the change which takes place in the individual who has these experiences. In surrendering, the individual is transformed from the particular, everyday, ordinary person he or she is commonly identified with into quite another being. The individual no longer is such and such—this son or daughter, husband, bachelor, member of this church, holder of such a degree, a person of such an age, sex, or looks. All these characteristics by which people are ordinarily identified become irrelevant and vanish, for they are among the received notions that get suspended. But what is left? What is the individual transformed in surrender? What is left is who the person then feels he or she really is: someone thrown back on one's self. But since this occurs to whomever experiences surrender, that which each is thrown back on is what each shares with humankind. In surrender the individual becomes a human being. (In traditional philosophical terminology: in surrender, the empirical subject becomes the transcendental subject.) In surrender, I *am*, I am as a human being, thus as a representative of humankind, rather than as the empirical human being which I am, too.

In surrender, I try to know as a human being, suspending as best I can my received notions—for most of these are unexamined accretions gathered in the course of my life, and in suspending them I test them, thus testing my biography and the various traditions sedimented in it. This means—as is entailed already by the idea of "received notions" itself—that I am historical, and that I cannot shed my historicity even in surrender. In surrender, I *assay* my historicity, that is, I pit humanness against historicity. What I am thrown back on in surrender—which is what I share with mankind, namely, the *human being I am*—is the representative of mankind in its ineluctable (inescapable, real, essential, true) historicity, thus showing forth that continuity of man which is true, man's absoluteness within the ineluctable boundaries of his historicity.[5]

The ground of surrender was interpreted earlier as the desire to respond to our crisis. We may now add that every case of surrender is, or is preceded by, a crisis—of which the experiencer may be conscious or which may be recognized only afterward. It should be clear that to say this does not contradict the unpredictability of surrender. In analytic, not necessarily experiential, terms, every surrender is or results from a crisis, but (evidently) not every crisis is or results in surrender. To claim this would contradict not only the unpredictability of surrender but also the possibility of the many responses to our crisis mentioned above. In fact, I pointed out that surrender is and is bound to be *a* response, submitted for inspection by whoever would care to inspect it. The prerequisite of such inspection is surrender to this response. (The proponent and the examiner of the response are forming a *good* human society, although a tiny one. But miniaturization can be far-reaching, as we see in its technological application!) Both proponent and inspector, that is, the two surrenderers, proceed, by definition, on the *un*suspendable basis of surrender (which is betrayed in *surrender betrayed* or *self-betrayal*), namely, faith in its possibility. It is the faith that (1) the suspension of received notions is a liberating act—an *emancipatory act*, to use a term characteristic of the vocabulary of critical theory; (2) its experience or exercise deepens this faith in liberation ("knowledge makes free"); and (3) the maximally bearable suspension of one's culture—the sum total of one's received notions—need not drive one insane, but, on the contrary, *at this time in human history is the utmost exercise of one's reason, of human reason,* that is to say, of the capacity to find out what is *for,* rather than against, human beings.

By throwing me back on what I really am, which is what I share with humankind, surrender lets my very uniqueness appear as distinctly as it can appear at all: this very uniqueness is my very humanness or humanity.[6] My reason, that is, my human capacity, allows me and enables me, by suspending and thus testing my received notions, to find out what I can and must believe, not because my parents, teachers, friends, or books have told me so, but because it has stood the test of my most unconditional experience, because it is the catch of my surrender. It is what I can *rationally* believe.

Insofar as I have been led by surrender or reason exclusively, I must believe what *all* human beings so led must believe. *What* I investigate when I do, what the occasion of my surrender or the object of my surrender-to is, results from my biography, which is my particularity. This particularity—the setting and product of which is the individual that can be described by social and personal characteristics—is transformed into a human uniqueness when it allows reason to guide the investigation I as an individual venture on. In such an investigation I make appear and show what a human being can be, but this is possible only because the universal in me avails itself of my potentially unique particularity by actualizing it. Once more, the humanly unique and the humanly universal become identical in surrender. The universal can be perceived only in the unique; what a human being can be can appear only in how a unique human being is.[7] But of course the inverse proposition also holds: the unique is perceptible only in the universal, for what a human being can be appears only through that human being's utmost exercise of reason—and

through the utmost exercise of the reason of those who help the surrenderer. Just as in the human being what is unique is universal, that which is particular is general:

Particularities such as sex, age, social characteristics are found among many people, diffused, general in given places and times. But particulars, even universal particulars, such as age and sex, remain general, namely, *predicates of objects* (of discourse, investigation, manipulation) as long as they are not candidates of uniqueness-universality; and this they become only on being explored by the utmost exercise of reason, that is, when their received (traditional, habitual, customary) conceptions are suspended: in surrender. Its catch, that which stands the test of surrender, is the emergent, the new structure of the unique-universal.[8]

4. MAN AS A MIXED PHENOMENON

Clearly, the idea of surrender-and-catch bears on the understanding of an indefinite number of phenomena. There are first analyses of how it might bear on our crisis (see above and *SC,* Chap. 6); religion (*SC,* Chap. 2); rebellion (*SC,* Chap. 11); community study (*SC,* Chap. 13; cf. references to Loma above); aesthetic experience (*SC,* Chap. 15); radicalism[9]; teaching (*SC,* Part 2); the nature of beginning (*SC,* Chap. 18); Hegel's "cunning of reason" today (*SC,* Chap. 20); one's body (*SC,* Chap. 24); sociology and phenomenology (*SC,* Chap. 22). The last four essays, however, do not deal with their topics as one would be led to expect. Instead, they exemplify instances of surrender-to changing to surrender, something mentioned in the discussion of surrender-to above. But they do contain statements pertinent to a discussion of their topics. Even the inspection of these topics suggests that the essays on surrender and community study and on sociology and phenomenology are the most explicitly relevant to sociology. Some readers might also expect a certain pertinence of the relation between surrender and teaching and of the papers on rebellion, radicalism, and surrender and the body. Elements of these pertinences will be suggested in the present essay.

We need at this point to discuss the connection between surrender and sociology, especially the notion of the human being as a *mixed phenomenon*. The conception or definition of the human being derived from the idea of surrender is that of a being who can surrender and catch. But evidently this is not an exhaustive definition since human beings are and do many other things as well. We eat, drink, sleep, satisfy or sublimate our sexual urges, work, make things, and do much more. For we are not only endowed with reason but also with bodies. But we share many *more* characteristics with other animals, with other organisms, and with inanimate objects—from our birth and death to our metabolism, weight, and volume. It follows that an adequate "study of man" must do justice to all these characteristics, that is, those exclusive of human beings and those shared by us with other members of the cosmos. The study of humanity comprises the sum total of the investigations of all these characteristics. This means the natural sciences, which deal with nonhuman or not exclusively human features alone. It includes the social sciences, which deal with features common only to humanity and features shared with other creatures, that is, with *mixed phenomena*. Finally, it includes the humanities, which deal only with exclusively human features. These three branches of learning are quite properly named: human beings are a part of nature, which is what the natural sciences explore. While we are social animals, we are not the only animals that are social. We use symbols, such as verbal language; we philosophize; and we create works of art. All of these activities are the concern of the humanities.

Of special poignancy for the social sciences in general and for sociology in particular is our realization that human beings *are* mixed phenomena rather than surrendering spirits. They must come to terms with their habitat, the external world, as must

also its nonhuman inhabitants. Human beings transmit their successes and failures in meeting this inexorable condition to each other and from generation to generation. These transmitted, common, received experiences—our culture, habits, and routines—are what makes living together, that is, society, possible. Nobody could do anything but surrender if surrender or surrender-to were the prerequisite for doing everything. I could never meet you so that we could open ourselves up to the possibility of surrender, together or to one another, if I did not first type you (more or less roughly, correctly, falsely, or subtly), and if you did not type me (by sex, language, age, looks, and so forth). First there must be something to suspend before I can suspend it. The idea of the human being as a mixed phenomenon is thus essential to the idea of all of the social sciences, including sociology.

Let us now consider in more concrete and specific terms the implications of what we've just discussed.

5. SURRENDER-AND-CATCH AND SOCIOLOGY

a. Surrender and Community Study

We will try to show the bearing of the idea of surrender on sociology by analyzing it in regard to community study. Here we are helped by the Loma experience and thoughts attendant on it. The social sciences, we just said, deal with mixed phenomena. Among the elements studied by the social sciences, especially sociology, are institutions, groups, individuals, customs, traditions, and communities.

In studying a community as a sociologist, I often focus on features not exclusive of human beings and not essentially human, for instance, on demography, mobility, power distribution, conflict, transportation, or hygiene. That is to say, I focus on *objects*. I am not surrendering to these elements, and thus whatever exclusively or essentially human dimension they might show me remains hidden; I continue to stay in the world of everyday life or of science. This means that I *intend* to suspend received notions selectively insofar as this serves my momentary curiosity or my research project. I don't find pertinent everything but only what relates to the problem I want to explore. The problem is likely to derive from the outside (e.g., the state of my scientific discipline or a particular theory or my research contract), rather than from the occasion of the study. I am not totally but only conditionally involved. I do not "identify" with humanness in its essence in all its dimensions but rather with my subject matter or theory. I risk being hurt, not in my human essence but as an empirical individual in my scientific accomplishments, my reputation, or my career. If physical danger is present, I may even risk my life. In short, I am not fully a studying human being and I am not studying fully a human being or human beings.

To say that only through surrender-and-catch can we do justice to human beings in their essence, and to what is characteristic of them, implies that we can do justice to what human beings share with other phenomena only by scientific procedure, that is, by systematized everyday ("mundane") description and analysis. For this reason those studying a community must do justice to both the community's features that are essentially human and those that are shared with nonhuman phenomena. Only in this way do students concern themselves with the community as a mixed phenomenon. Let's say that someone interested in a particular community decides to write a novel, poem, or short story; compose a work of music; or do a painting. His or her focus would be primarily on the community's essentially human features. On the other hand, if a student focuses only on the community's street grid plan, population distribution, or other not exclusively human features, he or she would have a differ-

ent point of view. But in neither case would the subject of the study be the whole community.

To sum up, I have to avoid two approaches if I wish to do justice to the study of a community: (1) I must not treat the community as a specific example of a generalization, for this would mean treating it as an object only and thus failing to explore its essentially human features, which would include also my own human features; (2) I must not lose control over my objectivity as I investigate and report on the community. For the danger then would be that my analysis would be incomplete as a result of distortion or misrepresentation. I might, for instance, neglect features not exclusively human. Such features might include relations between the community under study and other communities; the community's economy; its political and historical situation—and such features also in their impact on me and my study.

Given such a viewpoint, we believe that the majority of extant community studies focus on features that are not exclusively human, inasmuch as they concentrate on generalizable propositions or do not question the author's approaches. If this is the case, it probably reflects the concept of sociology as a generalizing, detached, and "value-free" enterprise, and this, in turn, is related to the "official" consciousness of control against which the idea of surrender and the word itself polemicize.

In contrast, a comparatively small number of studies have been more focused on essentially human features rather than on shared features. They are dramatized by attention to the authors' experiences in the setting and their efforts to present as intimately as possible the individuals met in the communities studied. Examples (almost all by anthropologists rather than by sociologists) are *Winter* by Cornelius Osgood; *The Forest People* by Colin M. Turnbull; *Return to Laughter* by Elenore Smith Bowen (Laura Bohannan); *World on the Wane (Tristes Tropiques)* by Claude Lévi-Strauss; *Haven* by

Gregory Bateson; *Five Families* and *The Children of Sánchez* by Oscar Lewis; and *Let Us Now Praise Famous Men* by James Agee and Walker Evans.[10]

Whatever the merits of these works, unfortunately none of them meets the requirements of surrender-and-catch as applied to community study. In other words the surrender-and-catch idea has yet to be tried out here. Thus we have no results that can serve as an example at this time.[11]

b. Surrender Is No Panacea

We need to do away at this point with a possible misunderstanding. Surrender is no panacea, and it would be a grievous misunderstanding to assume that we should handle all situations by surrendering to them. Quite to the contrary, *not* all situations or studies call for surrendering to them; in fact, very few do. We have to limit the discussion to surrender-to since, as we said previously, surrender itself cannot be brought about and thus cannot be prevented either. Furthermore, we couch the discussion in terms of interest to the sociologist. Actually, only an extreme situation calls for surrender. But for the scholar, what is an extreme situation? It is one with which the scholar's received notions (his or her general and specific culture) cannot cope. Thus a crisis may arise, and if it is severe enough, it may lead to a suspension of received notions, a letting go, a readiness for the unexpected—for the catch.

There even are certain situations where surrender-to is not only not called for but should be condemned. For example, suppose that before we condemn the murder of innocent people, we must test this received notion by surrendering to it, thus exercising our reason, that is, our capacity to find out what is for rather than against human beings—whether this received prohibition against killing innocent people stands the test of surrender, is its catch. If we were so to proceed, we would be hypo-

crites. Why? Because the faculty—both cognitive *and* affective—of distinguishing between good and evil as well as between true and false and beautiful and ugly, cannot be the catch of surrender because it is a *prerequisite,* the "constitutional" prerequisite of the capacity to experience surrender-to. Unless an individual is endowed with this discriminating faculty, there is no possibility of surrender. But everybody within the furthest range of "normalcy" is so endowed, even though, obviously, there is extraordinary variation among individuals, just as there is in regard to the capacity to surrender, including the capacity to surrender on the occasion of, or to surrender to, a *problem* or a *crisis* of right or wrong, true or false, beautiful or ugly.

A widely discussed example of such a crisis was—and still is—the Eichmann case. Individuals who thought most seriously about it, perhaps surrendered to it, came to sharply different assessments.[12] Here, the incompatibility of the phenomenon with any image of the human being which an individual who thinks about it (in contrast to a typical Nazi, totalitarian of another ideology, fanatic, possibly "professional" murderer) can seriously entertain throws its student into a cognitive and affective (undifferentiated) crisis, to which surrender can easily be imagined as a response, provided that the student has suffered no impairment or loss of the capacity to make moral distinctions—but this, to repeat, is very unlikely.

What is equally unlikely, however, is that there should not be circumstances external to surrender (and surrender-to) which are more favorable or more unfavorable to these experiences. It would appear that these circumstances are of two kinds, personal and social. (We are talking, of course, of statistical probabilities, not of causation.) On the one hand, there are personality types—perhaps the stranger, the outsider, the marginal individual—and personality features, such as a feeling of security rather than insecurity, self-acceptance rather than self-distrust or self-rejection, maturity rather than immaturity, ego strength rather than ego weakness, which favor surrender and surrender-to instead of being inimical to them. On the other hand, there are types of social structures or cultural settings similarly conducive to these experiences or, on the contrary, ignoring their possibility. (There will be something more on this in the discussion of surrender and rebellion in the next subsection.) As has been implied in 3c above, contemporary industrial societies on the whole are hostile to surrender and surrender-to. We need to recall that the very word *surrender* is meant to polemicize against their official consciousness.

But now we must present a more systematic statement on the prerequisites of surrender-to.

c. Prerequisites of the Possibility of Surrender-to

The faculty of discriminating between good and evil, true and false, beautiful and ugly, in short, reason (whose utmost exercise at this time in our history is surrender), may be called the *constitutional* prerequisite of the capacity or possibility of experiencing surrender and surrender-to because it lies in the very constitution of human beings. But there are other prerequisites, of which one is *maturational;* another, *situational.* It should be stressed that these apply to surrender-to only, for (as was suggested before) aside from its constitutional prerequisite, surrender itself has no specifiable conditions.

The maturational prerequisite of surrender-to arises from the fact that surrendering to something entails suspending received notions, which means that such notions must exist. Typically speaking, therefore, the child cannot surrender to anything. Instead, again typically speaking, the child is *receiving* notions.[13] In this view the child's play, which might look so much like surrender (the child is fully absorbed,

entirely identified with the play, etc.), is more correctly understood as learning about the world or, as we just put it, as receiving or acquiring an orientation toward the world, knowledge about it, *notions*. Georg Simmel makes the general point that there must be something to suspend before I can suspend it:

That we ourselves know our knowing and not-knowing and again also know this more comprehensive knowing; and so on into the potentially endless—this is the real infinity of the movement of life on the level of the spirit. With this every barrier is transcended, *but of course only because it is set, that is, there is something to be transcended.*[14]

The situational prerequisite of surrender-to arises from the fact that I have or am a body, which can interfere with anything I may do or with any state I am in, thus also with surrender and surrender-to. In surrender-to (as well as in surrender) I am fully absorbed, "gathered," "one"—as I am in any activity that can be thus characterized. For instance:

A woman who types as an informal activity knows that if she starts thinking in detail technically about what she is doing with her fingers and where the letters are located she will have trouble. Beginners who are studying shorthand are told that they "have to get it in their fingers" or they will not pick up any speed. A friend of mine, a neuropsychiatrist, once pointed out that it was often enough to draw attention to one level of activity while a person was operating on another to stop all coherent thought. He used the example of a mother who is mad at her son and is berating him. The boy looks up and says sweetly, "Gee, Mommy, your mouth moves funny when you're mad." The mother is apt to become speechless.[15]

Anybody who practices a sport or *any* skill knows that coordination or what was called above absorption or gatheredness is a prerequisite, something that must be learned with great effort.

"The body must not interfere" does not mean that I must feel well or happy; in fact, I may feel in pain (and perhaps just then discover that there is something to suspend). What it does mean is that I must feel at one, that my body must not intrude so as to make this impossible—and I may feel so while feeling good or bad, happy or desperate, as long as my state is self-contained, self-fulfilled, self-consummatory, un-self-conscious, gathered. And I can also surrender *to* my body or any part or activity of it or feeling in it (as is the tradition in several Eastern practices), but not if my body interferes because then I do not wish to surrender ("Why? I am so happy! I feel so good!") or cannot wish to surrender ("How could I with this headache!").

Why call this prerequisite of the body's noninterference *situational?* Consider what else than my body can interfere with my surrendering to something: weather, too much or too little light, the temperature, too much or even too little noise, a knock at the door, somebody screaming, singing, talking, something I have to do, such as keep an appointment or meet a deadline. Every one of these or other interferences reaches me through my body or senses, or I must move bodily to postpone my appointment or deadline (I must phone or write a letter). My body mediates interferences by the situation or elements of the situation in which I find myself. Without my body, interferences (and everything else of my concern) would be unimaginable. Hence, the situational prerequisite of surrendering to something.[16]

d. The Radicalness of Surrender-and-Catch

A further characteristic of surrender is potentially important for sociology: its radicalness.

Radical is an adjective derived from the noun *radix,* which means "root." "The root," Marx said, "is man." The root of what? Of our orientation toward the world, our understanding of it, our bearing or being in it. That is, if we would understand who and how we are and must and ought to be in the world, we must understand our-

selves and each other. It is clear that such understanding changes both historically and in the course of individuals' lives. It is never definitive or complete; at most it is at any given time the best an individual can achieve, but tomorrow the achievement may be better yet. It is never absolute but, at best, relatively absolute, that is, absolute relative to the individual's best effort: it is the catch of the individual's surrender.

Radical thus means "the root found in one's (relatively) absolute conviction, as one's catch." Reflection on the idea of surrender-and-catch has led to several points where digging for such a root seems promising. That is to say, the radicalness of the idea has several meanings. One is the very radicalness of the surrenderer's being in the world—the being of the individual in surrender or surrender-to is the world. This meaning is the individual's maximum directedness, immediacy, and freedom from the crutches that received notions amount to—independence from traditions (which is not to be confused with ignorance, acceptance, or rejection of traditions).

A second meaning results from the human coincidence of the unique and the universal that comes to the fore in surrender—but also in the catch. That it does so, the fact that it also characterizes the catch, is perhaps most plausible if we consider the great works of art (literature, painting, music, sculpture, architecture, philosophy, science, and religion). For here the creator's uniqueness and creation's uniqueness are typically (though not empirically) universal. This is the reason that the adequate approach to the work of art, philosophy, science, or religion is surrendering to it.[17] In surrendering to another human being's catch, I prove, by reenacting it, intersubjectivity in its most radical meaning. It may well be that without this basis, less radical relations among human beings—everyday, casual, instrumental, fragmentary, "secondary" relations—would be impossible and could not be accounted for. Surrender to another human being thus appears to be the root of sociality, and thus the basis of the study of sociality—of sociology. Yet this concept of radical intersubjectivity can be no more than an *element* in a theory of society since human beings are not exhaustively defined as beings capable of surrender-and-catch but are mixed phenomena.

A third meaning of the radical character of the idea of surrender has already been presented, though not in these terms. This is the radicalness of the student's surrendering to a topic, which was suggested as resulting from an "extreme" situation, one in which the student's whole outlook is at stake. We said that in surrender the human being is thrown back on what *the* human being really is, in other words, on the human being's roots ("the root is man").[18]

The fourth meaning of the radicalness of surrender is surrender as the most radical rebellion against the human condition, against the fact that for us human beings "all reality...is incomplete"...."except for vivid moments of fulfillment,"[19] that is, except in surrender. Surrender thus is rebellion against the incompleteness of reality, which is the human being's experience of reality, the human condition. This is what Albert Camus calls *metaphysical rebellion*; he contrasts it with historical rebellion, rebellion against a *particular* human condition—an injustice or otherwise intolerable situation. But because metaphysical rebellion is surrender, I cannot *will* it:

because even if I *will* to suspend myself as part of my condition and as part of creation, I am nevertheless powerless to do so. Such suspension, instead, can only occur irrespective of my willing it; it can only befall me. This is, of course, a characteristic of surrender (as against "surrender to"), and...metaphysical rebellion *is* surrender. On the other hand, however, not every instance of surrender is metaphysical rebellion: that depends on its catch. Emerging from surrender, I may recognize its catch as metaphysical rebellion—or as an indefinite number of other things.[20]

Both the historical rebel and the advocate of surrender-and-catch strive for a better society. More particularly:

being interested in envisaging a social setting in which man would have an ever better chance of coming closer to who he potentially is (a setting which would be more inviting to recall surrender), the person whose image of man is the being who can surrender and catch may come to outline such a setting; being interested in envisaging a social setting in which man would have an ever better chance of affirming, that is, *in which he would have an ever better chance of rebelling for ever more essentially human concerns,* the person whose image of man is the being who can rebel may come to do likewise—and the outlines sketched by the former and by the latter will reflect the affinity and the similarity between surrender and rebellion.[21]

More accurately, they will reflect the similarity between surrender-to and historical rebellion.[22]

One of the most gifted students in a tutorial on surrender thus formulated its radical or critical thrust in his term paper:

The outcome of surrender might very well be a terrible pronouncement on the nature of our everydayness, namely, that it is *false*....It should be clear...that by "false" we...mean existential falseness....This existential falseness can be "translated" into practical terms, namely, by presenting the world as capable of being changed....We are, more than ever, participants, and our naïveté, if genuine, has to go through quite an elaborate process which includes surrender as the negation...[in the sense of the] suspension of received notions, of the very stuff of the everydayness of our participation....[23]

The idea that our everydayness is false may remind some readers of critical theory, especially of Herbert Marcuse. Compare the following thought (from Marcuse's preface to the 1960 edition of his *Reason and Revolution*):

No method can claim the monopoly of cognition, but no method seems authentic which does not recognize that these two propositions are meaningful descriptions of our situation:

"The whole is the truth," and the whole is false.[24]

There emerges, then, a connection between the idea of surrender-and-catch and critical theory. This connection was mentioned in the first section of this essay, in the discussion of responses to our crisis. But like the other connections then indicated—the connections with phenomenology, existentialism, hermeneutics, etc.—it cannot be developed here, although a few remarks on this topic will be ventured at the end of this essay. First, however, we need to present one more aspect of the relation between surrender and sociology and then we need to sum up what we have found concerning this relation.

e. Study Tasks That Have Arisen in Reflecting on Surrender

This aspect of the relation between the idea of surrender and sociology arises because in the course of thinking about surrender in a number of contexts, questions have come up that invite research. We will now list some of them; a few require a word of introduction. These tasks are mentioned in the order in which they arose.

1. In introducing the suspension of received notions (Section 3a above), we incidentally mentioned a synonym used by the phenomenologist: *bracketing*. We *bracket* received notions. Instead of assuming, as we usually do, that the world of everyday life is the way it is, the way we have been socialized to understand it, we call it into question. In doing so, we enter another world; we abandon the world of everyday, the mundane world, the world of the "natural attitude," and enter the world of philosophy (Socrates, the archphilosophizer, questioned everything). Or, as phenomenologists also call it, we enter the *reduced sphere*. With these hints, let us, nevertheless, use *world* and *worlds* in the ordinary sense as we do when we speak of the world of the theater, the world of religion, science, and dreams. The point—as emphasized especially by Alfred Schutz—is that each world has its own "cognitive style" and "system of relevances." [25] One of the characteristics of a world is that within it certain doubts are suspended. In the world of everyday life, for instance, we do not doubt that this table is "really" this table, that unless interfered with by circumstances whose nature we do not doubt either, the airplane will depart on schedule, and so on. In the phenomenologically reduced sphere or world of philosophy, on the other hand, we do not doubt that the reality of the table or airplane (and anything about them) can be questioned. The study task arising from these considerations concerns the identification of the doubts that are suspended, the matters that are taken for granted, in a sample of worlds, to start with.[26]

2. The idea of this research proposal arose as a result of thinking about the state of absorption or "gatheredness." It suggests the need to investigate the circumstances (of personality and social structure) that are correlated with various degrees of concentration on a task, in the hope of ascertaining elements (of personality and social structure) favorable and unfavorable to high degrees of concentration.

3. This proposal and the next four proposals originated by reflecting on various aspects of the relation between surrender and the body. The first resulted from observations of the physical conditions certain writers and composers have claimed to need in order to do their work. They were of three kinds: body posture (e.g., walking, sitting, lying, standing, driving); the artist's immediate physical environment (e.g., indoors or outdoors, a certain scent, certain colors or upholstery materials); and ingestion or injection of external materials (e.g., alcohol, drugs). The study concerns the conditions of creativity with regard to these three circumstances. A promising way to start might be the vast literature on human creativity.[27]

4. The perception of relief or liberation or "feeling good" while engaged in acts of bodily voiding (cleaning one's nails, blowing one's nose, urinating, defecating, having an orgasm) suggests reference to them as *little surrenders*. Not, evidently, because they are instances of cognitive love, but (except for the orgasm, to which we shall turn in a moment) because they are accompanied by the feeling that things are again put in order or are again what they ought to be. In surrender proper, such a feeling is replaced by (or intensified into) extraordinary concentration or gatheredness. The greatest differences between the orgasm and all other voidings is that in all the others what is expelled is waste, while in the orgasm it is potential life. But what are the differences between the solitary (masturbatory) orgasm and the coital orgasm? What types are there of coital orgasm with respect to the kinds of partners and the relations between them? Thus we have two problem areas: the first is concerned with the psychic accompaniments, antecedents, and sequels of the different kinds of voidings other than the orgasmic.

5. The second problem area involves the study of human male and female orgasms and their social and individual correlates. Extant relevant literature is likely to go far toward accomplishing this investigation.

6. What are the psychic circumstances of first experiences of anything like surrender? We might begin by inspecting Marghanita Laski's collection of ecstasies, checking to see whether there are "first instances" among them.[28]

7. We have pointed out that no particular occasion or type of occasion can be assigned to surrender, that it "befalls" one, that *anything* can be its occasion, just as nothing can assure it, no matter how propitious the setting in all imaginable relevant respects according to some theory or other. To test this claim, as well as to understand it better, we need to analyze responses to extreme situations which have as vast a range of meanings as possible. The study proposed thus calls for an examination of experiences of surrender in the lives of saints, in memoirs and memories of former inmates of concentration and slave-labor camps, and in other records of individuals who have experienced extreme situations.

8. Let me quote one such experience:

This happens (happens?) to be summer. How difficult to define "this." It means, of course, "this time in which I am writing this paper." But what is "time," and "time in which"? As if it were a space or a room, containing me engaged in the activity of writing. Is "during which I am writing" any better? "During which" indicates passing—but where am I while the time is passing? On its bank, watching it flow by? Can I be watching and writing "at the same time"? What is *this* time of "at the same time," and what is its relation to the time "during which"? We are back to our spontaneously spatial imagery: the time of my simultaneously watching-time-and-writing sits inside the time-which-flows-by-or-passes. The first two (my watching time and the time while I am writing) *together* are like, or are, Simmel's "immanent time" (of a battle, a war, a reign) within "historical time" (the 16th century, the Middle Ages),[29] these two again with their spatialization, one within the other; and indeed, for Simmel "history as a whole . . . is atemporal."[30] But I must leave these questions standing there as questions without bending them by attempting answers, for they point to another landscape [than the one within which they arose: surrender and the body] . . . : surrender and time.[31]

9. The first study task had to do with several unspecified worlds; it here followed the introduction of the concept of world, briefly illustrated by some characteristics of two worlds, that of everyday life and the world in which the former is bracketed. A look at some non-Western worlds and a preliminary comparison of surrender and Zen—largely on the basis of Eugen Herrigel[32]—suggests the task of ascertaining the parameters of the world (more likely worlds) of shamanism, Taoism, and Zen Buddhism with particular attention to their relations (differences and similarities) to the world of surrender, which, too, needs to be identified.

10. Another gifted student wrote a paper in which he compared the *heroic cycle* and surrender and catch; his major sources were Mircea Eliade's *Myth of the Eternal Return* and Joseph Campbell's analysis of the hero.[33] The writer claimed:

Recognition of the necessity for "gentle sympathy" in the highly masculine hero is a recognition of a certain degree of androgyny. Tiresias, the blind seer of the Oedipus myth, is both male and female; and it is he who, according to the myth, "sees" more of what will be than any other person. This suggests that to be all of one or all of the other is to be blind to half of the world, while to be both is to have sight.[34]

The project resulting from this comment is the analysis of the relations between the sexuality of the mythical hero and his heroism and of the surrenderer and surrender.

But here is the place to remove another possible misunderstanding of surrender, although it has probably been laid to rest by what has been said about the irony of the word and the radical, critical nature of the idea, especially in the comparison with rebellion. This is the misunderstanding that surrender essentially is an Eastern notion. On the contrary, it is an essentially Western notion. It is not otherworldly but this-worldly; it is, as we said, the highest exercise of reason; it finds its fulfillment in the catch, which—not surrender—is the new beginning: Eastern views tend toward the opposites of all three propositions, which are related to one another.[35]

11. Finally, from the same paper on the heroic cycle in its relation to surrender there arose another question. This is the particular passage which stimulated it:

There is no human being who could have been all that is meant by an Achilles, a Moses, a Christ, or a Buddha. The hero is a composite of all that the society deems important, in order that he may properly represent the importance of the societal achievement which is being celebrated—the synthesis of the old forms into new.[36]

This suggests a study of the hero as exemplary, the surrenderer as transcendental subject, and a comparison between the two.

f. Relations between Surrender and Sociology

The purpose of what now follows is to present a synopsis of claims concerning this relation; let us begin by recalling them.

The first claim was that since sociology deals with mixed phenomena, it must as a whole be both a surrendering to them and a dealing with them in traditional scientific fashion; this was argued and illustrated in regard to the community study previously described. Immediately we emphasized (in 5b), however, not only that surrender-to is not to be understood as *the* method of sociology but, on the contrary, that it is called for only in rare instances, in the extreme situations in which the student's received notions (theories, concepts, hypotheses, even paradigms) are to the best of his or her consciousness and conscience not commensurate with the task at hand. We may now add that sensitivity in identifying such an extreme situation is presumably heightened for the student whose assessment of our present crisis as an extreme situation resembles the assessment presented in Section 1 above ("The Place and Time of Surrender-and-Catch").

The question asked next concerned the prerequisites of surrender-to. (See 5c.) What has this question to do with sociology? Three types of prerequisites were distinguished: constitutional (the faculty of discriminating between good and evil, true and false, beautiful and ugly); maturational (having received notions to suspend); and situational (noninterference of the body, whether the locus of the interference is within the body or originates outside it). The constitutional prerequisite implies a *normative* conception of the human being, as that being which can surrender and catch, or which exercises the human faculty of reason. The maturational prerequisite implies a *normative* conception of socialization or acculturation, whose aim is adulthood. For in contrast to the child, the adult can suspend received notions. Furthermore, the maturational prerequisite implies a normative injunction to make maximal or optimal use of this faculty of reason. Finally, the situational prerequisite implies a *normative* conception, not only of the individual (whose body itself must not interfere with the possibility of concentration, including surrender-to) but also of the society (which must be so arranged as to avoid what might be called surplus interference with the individual's life, occupation, and privacy). The sociology on which these prerequisites bear thus is seen to be itself *normative;* it is one which, by implication, has a normative view of society by which it assesses existing and past societies.

Hence, there is an intimate connection between these prerequisites of surrender-to and the radicalness of the idea (as well as the experience or state) of surrender. (See 5d.) This radicalness was seen to have four meanings: (1) the surrenderer's being in the world; (2) the human coincidence of the unique and the universal as radical intersubjectivity,[37] hence as founding society and thus sociology; (3) surrender-to as the radical approach to study; and (4) surrender as rebellion against the human condition and surrender-to as (the radical mode of) historical rebellion.

The connection between the prerequisites of surrender-to and the radicalness of surrender is not only that both are normative but also, in particular, that both are inspired by the conception of a good society. As indicated, hints of this fact are given in the constitutional, maturational, and situational prerequisites, in the conception of the root of intersubjectivity, and in the realization of the close affinity between surrender and metaphysical rebellion and surrender-to and historical rebellion. We also showed in 5d above that both surrender and critical theory take a radically critical view of contemporary society—indeed of all societies that have ever existed or are now in existence. For all of them, no matter how good they were or have been, could have been and should be better.

Finally, we had (in 5e above) a glimpse of a very different relation between surrender and sociology, which derives from the circumstance that in the course of writing and talking about various aspects of surrender, a number of study tasks or research projects emerged (some of which may seem to be rather far from surrender itself). They were, to recapitulate, inquiries into (1) doubts suspended in several worlds; (2) elements in personality and social structure favorable and unfavorable to the individual's concentration; (3) the influence on creativity of body posture, elements of the physical environment, and the ingestion or injection of foreign materials; (4) the psychic accompaniments (antecedents and subsequences) of bodily voidings (except the orgasm); (5) human male and female orgasms and their social and individual correlates; (6) first experiences of surrender; (7) surrender in saints, former inmates of concentration and slave-labor camps, and others who have experienced extreme situations; (8) surrender and time; (9) characteristics of the worlds of shamanism, Taoism, Zen Buddhism, and surrender; (10) the relation between the sexuality of the mythical hero and his heroism and of the surrenderer and surrender; and (11) the hero as exemplary, the surrenderer as transcendental subject, and a comparison between the two.

All these study tasks have to do with surrender—some more directly than others. To illustrate: both the first and ninth study tasks deal with worlds; both of them show a close connection between the approaches taken by surrender-and-catch and by phenomenology. The second study task (on concentration) and the third study task (on creativity) can be seen to be in the service of the normative view of the individual mentioned above. Thus they are in the service of the society favorable to it and of the sociology that espouses it.

This set of proposed study tasks reveals a number of things. First, the exploration of surrender in its various contexts has resulted in some unexpected research problems. Second, no matter how unexpected, these problems do indicate aspects of surrender. Third, while hardly any of them is sociological in the mainstream sense of contemporary sociology, we have shown their pertinence to other currents in sociology— for example, to phenomenology, on the one hand, and to the normative sociology sketched out on the other hand. Fourth, the absence or scarcity of traditional sociological investigations of the other suggested study tasks may be due to the present stage in the development of the surrender-and-catch concept. Comparatively speaking, surrender and catch is still in its beginning stage; still preoccupied with clarifying its many aspects, origins, and bearings.

To sum up, we have here the outlines of a sociology whose ideals are the human being who can exercise exclusively human capacities, and the society which maximally favors this human being. It is a sociology which is critical of extant societies as falling short of this ideal. But—and this is perhaps the most important meaning of the study tasks—it is a sociology which is reflexive[38] or, more accurately, self-corrective. Among its research problems are those which require surrender-to; and here this means above all the suspension of received notions, including its own definition and its own tenets concerning humanity and society.

Centrally, the normativity of this sociology calls for ever new surrender to it, just because it calls on the human being's utmost responsibility: its relative absoluteness must be tested lest it degenerate into absolute absoluteness, which by definition would be false and harmful.

We should point out that the present section on surrender and sociology is—a surprise to myself!—an instance of surrender to the topic. The last subsection, which you are now reading, is the catch. As the catch always is, this catch is subject to being surrendered to again and again. With the catch and its efforts to glean lessons that can be stated in everyday language, we return to the everyday world.[39] We will not depart

from that world in the next section, which takes up the relations between surrender and other contemporary intellectual concerns.

6. SURRENDER-AND-CATCH AND SOME RELATED CONTEMPORARY CONCERNS

These concerns, which we anticipated in the beginning of this essay, are phenomenology, critical theory, existentialism, structuralism, hermeneutics, and certain linguistic theories. Meanwhile, we have seen relations between surrender and phenomenology (*bracketing*, mentioned in connection with the suspension of received notions (3a) and the idea of worlds (5e) and *critical theory* (which is critical of all extant societies for the sake of a good society, just as surrender is). (See 5d and 5f above.) Let us first say something more about these two connections before we take a look at the others.

Phenomenology. There are at least two further parallels. First, in surrender the empirical subject changes into the transcendental subject (cf. 3d above). This distinction, which stems from German idealism, lives on in phenomenology, in which the empirical individual becomes the transcendental subject in the "reduced sphere," that is, on bracketing the empirical world. Second, we have already mentioned the other affinity when we listed phenomenology among the responses to our present crisis (see the first section of this essay). At this point we may make a more particular reference to Edmund Husserl's *Crisis*, a book in which he comes closer to history than anywhere else in his work.[40]

Critical Theory. The difference within the similarity just mentioned (both surrender and critical theory are critical of the extant society for the sake of a good society) is that most representatives of critical theory base their views on a predominantly Marxian conception of history. This is not true of the approach to our crisis to which surrender responds, although surrender is not in conflict with such a conception.[41] Furthermore, there is a close similarity between surrender and Jürgen Habermas's view of the human being as developed above all in the notion of emancipatory interests.[42]

Before we take up the other currents mentioned, we should say a word about mainline or traditional empirical sociology.[43] Like all the social sciences, mainline sociology speaks the language of the everyday world (except for technical terminologies). But the social sciences do not examine the constitution of this world, how it came into being, since the goal of the social sciences is to examine this world as they find it. Both surrender and phenomenology, by contrast, do call it into question, as we have seen. We have also seen that such suspending characteristically occurs in a crisis. It may be a general crisis, our global crisis, or it may be a crisis occurring within science, as Husserl was inclined to think. Thomas S. Kuhn has analyzed the crisis that occurs when "normal science" is replaced by "revolutionary science," to use Kuhn's terms.[44] Here arises the question of whether it makes sense to think of surrender as a case of revolutionary science or what the relation between them is. Finally, this may be a personal crisis. In any case we have seen in effect that surrender also questions empirical sociology. What of it stands its test?

Existentialism. A widely accepted definition of existentialism is that it is the philosophy for which "existence comes before essence." But as Marjorie Grene points out, existence is "the unique, inexpressible *that* of any one conscious being's particular existence."[45] It follows that there is a parallel between existence/essence and unique/universal. The task is to work out the variations and ramifications of this theme of

"existence before essence" in the existentialist thinkers described by Marjorie Grene: Søren Kierkegaard, Jean Paul Sartre, Martin Heidegger, Karl Jaspers, and Gabriel Marcel. Then we need to analyze again the bearing of the idea of surrender, enriched by such comparisons, on sociology.

Structuralism. A plausible way of presenting structuralism is to call it:

the systematic attempt to uncover deep universal mental structures as these manifest themselves in kinship and larger social structures, in literature, philosophy and mathematics, and in the unconscious psychological patterns that motivate human behavior.[46]

How do the conceptions of structure analyzed by the thinkers Edith Kurzweil discusses (Claude Lévi-Strauss, Louis Althusser, Henri Lefebvre, Paul Ricoeur, Alain Touraine, Jacques Lacan, Roland Barthes, and Michel Foucault[47]) bear on the conception of the structure of the human being envisaged by surrender?

Hermeneutics. Hermeneutics is not only the intimate study of texts but concerns the whole problem and the whole area of understanding in its broadest sense. As a self-conscious effort, it arose in Germany in the early nineteenth century; it has influenced, and indeed transformed, all the humanities and social sciences, first in Germany and then elsewhere, by explicating the problems of understanding between individuals and between individuals of different cultures and times (problems of translation, understanding texts, philosophical and scientific paradigms, works of art, and nature). Systematically, as one of its most authoritative contemporary representatives, Hans-Georg Gadamer, argues, hermeneutics is based on:

the essential linguisticality of all human experience of the world, which has as its own way of fulfillment a constantly self-renewing contemporaneousness.[48]

One of the common denominators of hermeneutics and surrender clearly is the aim of maximum understanding, of understanding as far as possible in terms of who or what is to be understood, rather than in terms of the individual who seeks understanding.[49] This commonality as well as the differences between surrender and hermeneutics needs explication.

Certain Linguistic Theories. Two of these theories have been mentioned already: Noam Chomsky's deep structures[50] and Gadamer's claim that "all human experience of the world" is essentially linguistic. The immediately evident pertinence of a juxtaposition of language analysis and surrender is the attention both pay to the spoken and written word. Both instruct us to examine what we mean; both can be argued to distinguish social and perhaps historical situations in which we must say what we mean from those in which we must not; both explore the relations between words and things, language and meaning, language and truth, indeed between linguistics and ontology. In addition to the linguistic theories, historical semantics and etymology are of direct importance to this juxtaposition.[51]

There seems little doubt that the examination of such connections, including the determination of their specific nature—a problem which has been glossed over here by such vague terms as *connections, relations, parallels, affinities,* and more—will also benefit sociology, making it deeper and larger, less parochial, more relevant to our contemporary crisis.[52]

NOTES

1. Kurt H. Wolff, *Surrender and Catch: Experience and Inquiry Today* (Boston Studies in the Philosophy of Science, vol. 51; Synthese Library, vol. 105) (Dordrecht/Boston, Reidel, 1976), pp. 71–74, 18–19 (in this order) henceforth referred to as *SC*.
   In "The Disciplining of Reason's Cunning: Kurt Wolff's *Surrender and Catch*," *Human Studies* (1981), pp. 365–89, esp. 377–78, Richard M. Zaner has argued why "surrender and catch" should be hyphenated, and I have spelled it "surrender-and-catch" ever since.

2. Kurt H. Wolff, "A Methodological Note on the Empirical Establishment of Culture Patterns" (1945), in Kurt H. Wolff, *Trying Sociology* (New York: John Wiley & Sons, 1974), pp. 356–78.

3. *SC*, pp. 30–35, 159–60.

4. The first sketch of these characteristics dates back to 1951 when they were articulated by David Baken in "Some Elaborations of the Meaning of the Concept of Surrender" (unpublished manuscript, August 1951).

5. *SC*, p. 24.

6. The closest formulation to this concept I have found is in Herbert Fingarette, *The Self in Transformation: Psychoanalysis, Philosophy, and the Life of the Spirit* (New York: Harper & Row, Harper Torchbooks, 1965), p. 289: "The therapist sees, ideally, what is at once universal and unique in all men."

7. That the universal can be perceived only in the unique is expressed in the idea that history can teach us something. See R. G. Collingwood's poignant formulation of this idea. Collingwood, *The Idea of History* (1946) (New York: Oxford University Press, 1957), p. 10: "Knowing yourself means knowing what you can do; and since nobody knows what he can do until he tries, the only clue to what man can do is what men have done. The value of history, then, is that it teaches us what man has done and thus what man is."

8. *SC*, p. 25 (slightly revised).

9. Kurt H. Wolff, "Toward Understanding the Radicalness of Surrender," *Sociological Analysis* 38 (1977), pp. 397–401; Peter Ludes, "The Radicalness of Surrender: Reflections on a Significant Concept," ibid., pp. 402–8.

10. Cornelius Osgood, *Winter* (New York: W. W. Norton, 1953); Colin H. Turnbull, *The Forest People* (London: Methuen, 1961); Elenore Smith Bowen, *Return to Laughter* (1954) (Garden City, N.Y.: Doubleday, Anchor Press, 1964); Claude Lévi-Strauss,

World on the Wane (Tristes Tropiques) (1955), trans. John Russell (London: Hutchinson, 1961); Gregory Bateson, *Haven* (1936) (Stanford, Calif.: Stanford University Press, 1958); Oscar Lewis, *Five Families* (1959) (New York: Science Editions, 1962) and *The Children of Sánchez* (New York: Basic Books, 1961); James Agee and Walker Evans, *Let Us Now Praise Famous Men* (1941) (Boston: Houghton Mifflin, 1960). A few other candidates for illuminating analysis are Ronald Blythe, *Akenfield* (New York: Pantheon Books, 1969); Robert R. Jay, *Javanese Village* (Cambridge, Mass.: MIT Press, 1969); Jean Briggs, *Never in Anger* (Cambridge, Mass.: Harvard University Press, 1970).

11. For a fuller treatment of the relation between surrender and community, and of the studies mentioned, see *SC*, Chap. 13.

12. Cf. Hannah Arendt, *Eichmann in Jerusalem: A Report on the Banality of Evil* (New York: Viking Press, 1963). To mention two of the most serious responses out of the vast discussion of this work, see Bruno Bettelheim, "Eichmann; The System; the Victims," *New Republic* 143, no. 24, June 15, 1963, pp. 23–33; Gershom Scholem, "On Eichmann," trans. Miriam Bernstein-Benschlomo, in Scholem, *On Jews and Judaism in Crisis: Selected Essays* (New York: Schocken Books, 1976), pp. 298–300, and "Letter to Hannah Arendt," trans. John Mander, ibid., pp. 300–6.

13. Cf. *SC*, pp. 339–40.

14. Georg Simmel, *Lebensanschauung: Vier metaphysische Kapitel* (Munich and Leipzig: Duncker and Humblot, 1918, p. 7, italics added. Cf. Georg Simmel, *On Individuality and Social Forms*, ed. and intro. Donal N. Levine (Chicago: University of Chicago Press, 1971), p. 358. For a slightly different translation, see *SC*, p. 208, n. 21.

15. Edward T. Hall, *The Silent Language* (1959) (New York: Fawcett Premier Books, n.d.), p. 68, quoted in *SC*, p. 186.

16. For a fuller treatment of surrender and the body, see *SC*, Chap. 24.

17. Ibid., Chap. 15, "Surrender and the Aesthetic Experience," pp. 96–108.

18. Cf. Wolff, "Toward Understanding the Radicalness of Surrender."

19. Albert Camus, *The Rebel: An Essay on Man in Revolt* (1951), trans. Anthony Bower (New York: Vintage Books, 1958), p. 260.

20. *SC*, p. 64. This precedes a comparison between surrender-to and historical rebellion regarding total involvement, suspension of received notions, pertinence of everything, identification, and the risk of being hurt. Ibid., pp. 64–67.

21. Ibid., pp. 62–63.

22. See previous treatment of the word *surrender* in this essay; it does *not* refer to capitulation or passivity! For a fuller discussion of surrender and rebellion, see *SC*, Chap. 11.

23. Quoted in ibid., p. 267.

24. Herbert Marcuse, "Preface: A Note on Dialectic," in Marcuse, *Reason and Revolution: Hegel and the Rise of Social Theory* (1941) (Boston: Beacon Press, 1960), p. xiv.

25. Alfred Schutz, "On Multiple Realities" (1945), in Schutz, *Collected Papers I, The Problem of Reality*, ed. and intro. Maurice Natanson (The Hague: Nijhoff, 1962), pp. 207–59, esp. p. 230; ibid., *Reflections on the Problem of Relevance*, ed. and intro., Richard M. Zaner (New Haven, Conn.: Yale University Press, 1970); also cf. Brenda Venable Powell, "The What and Why of Experience: The Contrapuntal Relationship between Cognitive Style and Systems of Relevance," *Annals of Phenomenological Sociology*, vol. 2 (Dayton, Ohio: Wright State University Press, 1977), pp. 107–33; Kurt H. Wolff, "Phenomenology and Sociology," in Tom Bottomore and Robert Nisbet, eds., *A History of Sociological Analysis* (New York: Basic Books, 1978), pp. 500–6, 515–20.

26. Cf. *SC*, pp. 163–65.

27. Cf. Ibid., pp. 179–80.

28. Marghanita Laski, *Ecstasy: A Study of Some Secular and Religious Experiences* (London: Cresset Press, 1961). This collection is based both on responses to a questionnaire and on literary and religious writings. Also see Laski, *Everyday Ecstasy* (London: Thames & Hudson, 1980).

29. Georg Simmel, "The Problem of Historical Time" (1916) in Simmel, *Essays on Interpretation in Social Science*, trans. and ed. Guy Oakes (Totowa, N.J.: Rowman and Littlefield, 1980), pp. 127–44.

30. Ibid., p. 131.

31. *SC*, p. 188.

32. Eugen Herrigel, *Zen in the Art of Archery*, trans. R. F. C. Hull, intro. D. T. Suzuki (New York: Pantheon Books, 1953).

33. Mircea Eliade, *The Myth of the Eternal Return* (1948), trans. Willard R. Trask (New York: Pantheon Books, 1959); Joseph Campbell,

The Hero with a Thousand Faces (New York: Pantheon Books, 1949).

34. Quoted in *SC*, p. 292.

35. Cf. ibid., pp. 28, 35, 44, 51, 89, 94, 193–99.

36. Ibid., p. 293.

37. For an earlier but more detailed treatment of this radical intersubjectivity, see *SC*, Chap. 18, "Beginning: In Hegel and To-day." V, 3, "The Possibility of Intersubjective Existential Truth," pp. 128–132.

38. Cf. Alvin W. Gouldner, *The Coming Crisis of Western Sociology* (New York: Basic Books, 1970).

39. *SC*, Chap. 22, esp. p. 172.

40. Edmund Husserl, *The Crisis of European Sciences and Transcendental Phenomenology*, trans. and intro. David Carr (Evanston, Ill.: Northwestern University Press, 1970). For readers acquainted with Husserl, the suggestion that if Husserl radicalized Descartes, surrender radicalizes Husserl may make sense. Also see Kurt H. Wolff, "Surrender-and-Catch and Phenomenology," *Human Studies* 7 (1984), pp. 191–210.

41. Cf. Peter Ludes, "Radicalness of Surrender."

42. Specifically see Jürgen Habermas, "Knowledge and Human Interests: A General Perspective" (1965) in Habermas, *Knowledge and Human Interests*, trans. Jeremy J. Shapiro (Boston: Beacon Press, 1971), pp. 301–17, 346–49. On critical theory in general, see Essay 11 in this volume, "Critical Theory" by Zygmunt Bauman. Also cf. Kurt H. Wolff, "Surrender-and-Catch and Critical Theory," *Praxis International* 3 (1983), pp. 147–60.

43. Literature on the philosophy of science generally and of sociology in particular is vast. A most lucid and concise treatment of the field with its focus on sociology, especially on recent revisions of fundamental understandings of science and other aspects still in need of revision, is Michael Mulkay, *Science and the Sociology of Knowledge* (London: Allen & Unwin, 1979). Most directly of interest is Chap. 2, "Revisions of the Standard View," pp. 27–62. The book contains a very good bibliography.

44. Thomas S. Kuhn, *The Structure of Scientific Revolutions*, enlarged ed. (Chicago: University of Chicago Press, 1970).

45. Marjorie Grene, *Introduction to Existentialism* (first published in 1948 as *Dreadful Freedom*)

(Chicago: University of Chicago Press, 1959), p. 4; see also as of specific interest to sociologists, Gila Hayim, *The Existential Sociology of Jean-Paul Sartre* (Amherst, Mass.: University of Massachusetts Press, 1980).

46. Edith Kurzweil, *The Age of Structuralism: Lévi-Strauss to Foucault* (New York: Columbia University Press, 1980), p. 1. Also see her Essay 12, "Structuralism in France," in this volume.

47. We might add to this list Noam Chomsky and Jean Piaget as well as Roman Jakobson and Ferdinand de Saussure.

48. Hans-Georg Gadamer, "On the Scope and Function of Hermeneutical Reflection" (1967), trans. G. B. Hess and R . E. Palmer, in Gadamer, *Philosophical Hermeneutics*, trans. and ed. David E. Linge (Berkeley, Calif.: University of California Press, 1976), p. 19. See also Richard E. Palmer, *Hermeneutics: Interpretation Theory in Schleiermacher, Dilthey, Heidegger, and Gadamer* (Evanston, Ill.: Northwestern University Press, 1969). Of special interest to sociologists is Zygmunt Bauman, *Hermeneutics and Social Science* (London: Hutchinson, 1978) and Janet Wolff, *Hermeneutic Philosophy and the Sociology of Art* (London: Routledge & Kegan Paul, 1975) as well as her Essay 6, "Hermeneutics and Sociology," in this volume. Cf. Kurt H. Wolff, "Surrender-and-catch and Hermeneutics," *Philosophy and Social Criticism* 10 (1984), pp. 1–15.

49. In Alfred Schutz's terms both hermeneutics and surrender seek "subjective meaning" instead of being contented with "objective meaning." See Schutz, *The Phenomenology of the Social World* (1932), trans. George Walsh and Frederick Lehnert, with an introduction by George Walsh (Evanston, Ill.: Northwestern University Press, 1967), *passim* and esp. Sect. 27, pp. 132–36.

50. See, for example, Noam Chomsky, *Language and Responsibility* (New York: Pantheon Books, 1979).

51. In undertaking these comparisons, it is most useful to consider Richard J. Bernstein's analyses of empirical theory; language, analysis and theory; the phenomenological alternative; and the critical theory of society in his *The Restructuring of Social and Political Theory* (Philadelphia: University of Pennsylvania Press, 1976).

52. There is one sense in which only the author of this essay knows how incipient, clumsy,

awkward, or ignorant it is in many ways. There also are many ways that are known only to others. To them, his fellow students, he would be genuinely grateful for critical comments. Readers interested in this essay may also be interested in related ones (in chronological order): "Surrender to Morality as the Morality of Surrender," *Analecta Husserliana* 15 (1983), pp. 495–99; "The Sociology of Knowledge and Surrender-and-Catch," *Canadian Journal of Sociology/Cahiers canadiens de sociologie* 8 (1983), pp. 421–32; "Exploring Relations between Surrender-and-Catch and Poetry, Sociology, Evil," *Human Studies* 9 (1986), pp. 347–64; "Sociology?" in William Outhwaite and Michael Mulkay, eds., *Social Theory and Social Criticism: Essays for Tom Bottomore* (Oxford: Basil Blackwell, 1987), pp. 10–16; "The Idea of Surrender-and-Catch Applied to the Phenomenon Karl Mannheim," *Theory, Culture & Society* 5 (1988), pp. 715–34; "Anomie and the Sociology of Knowledge, in Durkheim and Today," *Philosophy and Social Criticism* 14 (1988), pp. 51–67; "From Nothing to Sociology," *Philosophy of the Social Sciences* 19 (1989), pp. 321–39.

Art is capable of influencing the future direction of society through cultural resistance, even though art itself is influenced by its social origins.

Georg Lukacs's thesis of the connection between rationalization and a capitalistically imposed domination pointed the way to a critique of Max Weber's thesis, which was seen as related to a particular social form of capitalism and therefore not as something inevitable. The Frankfurt school developed Lukacs's formulation of a reification through its analysis of the historical, ideological, and dialectical nature of rationalization. The Frankfurt school divided on the future, with Max Horkheimer and Theodor W. Adorno taking a pessimistic view of the possibilities of countering rationalization, while Herbert Marcuse and Jürgen Habermas took an optimistic view of emancipatory potential. Moreover, Marcuse and Habermas pointed to the domain of art as having a special potential for resistance to rationalization.

Jeffrey A. Halley presents a model of delegitimation and reenchantment in the context of modernism. Its features, in contrast to those of legitimation, are particularization, disruption of linear time, randomization, and subjectivity. The features of delegitimation are then traced in the Dada movement, and an extended example is offered of the practice of Dada art as a counterideology developed by World War I war resisters in order to attack the rationalization of the modern world. The cultural politics of Dada as an egalitarian movement questioned the order of reason as domination, but Dada represented only an incomplete rebellion.

Jeffrey A. Halley

CULTURAL RESISTANCE TO RATIONALIZATION: A STUDY OF AN ART AVANT-GARDE*

INTRODUCTION TO THE PROBLEM

The sociology of art typically examines the particular social institutions of the art world, and the process of socialization of the artist. In doing so, it limits the analysis to specific institutions, and confines itself to the effects of these institutions. While this is important, it leaves out an examination of the larger social significance of artistic production. For example, what are the effects, beyond the particular cultural and social institutions, of the more global ideological, political, and economic forces that influence culture? And further, what are the relationships between modernism, the avant-garde art movements that have arisen since the Industrial Revolution, and mod-

*Thanks to several anonymous referees, and to Bennett Berger, Michael Brown, Lindsey Churchill, Henry Etzkowitz, George Fischer, Loren Shumway, and Jerold Starr for their valuable suggestions at various stages of this manuscript. They, of course, are not responsible for any remaining errors.

ernization, the development within capitalism of a rationalizing drive to raise productivity? Are they perhaps reciprocal?

This approach demands that we look at art and culture as part of a society's total development. One recent theorist who has attempted to understand the contradiction between modernism and society treats culture as dysfunctional to capitalist modernization. Modernization means for him the tremendous emphasis on production and efficiency, supported by structures of bureaucracy and hierarchy that are not concerned with persons, but with the management of functions and roles. Daniel Bell attacks modernist culture as antisocial because it works against the very processes of modernization. Yet he separates the two as having radically different histories.[1] In so doing, we are left with an inability to understand the relationship between them.

On the other hand, there is a critical tradition, from Georg Lukacs and the theorists of the Frankfurt school, that conceives of cultural production as both an ideological response to our social situation and constitutive of the social totality. At issue here are the complex relations among cultural products and processes, consciousness, and the economic and social organization of society.

Thus, in contrast to much work in the sociology of art, and in contrast to Bell, this tradition defines the effectivity of cultural activities as not simply determined by their specific individual and institutional origins. For not only is cultural practice influenced by broader historical processes, it can also react against them as a form of cultural resistance.

One of the clearest examples of this resistance is the Dada art avant-garde, which arose during World War I in Zurich. Dada, like other art practices of modernism, reacts against and refuses the world as it is. This essay describes how the Dadaist activities were a form of cultural resistance, a critique of the social totality.

I will formulate this as the problem of rationalization and the forms of resistance which develop to it in the domains of art and culture. *Rationalization* can be briefly defined as the trend, within the process of industrialization, in which the division of labor and social relationships become subordinate to the market in the search for profit.

In the next section I will develop the argument that rationalization breeds a response of resistance, generated by needs and interests not fulfilled by the process of rationalization. One important sphere in which these needs are expressed is that of art and culture. Here I will also clarify the terms necessary for our argument: rationalization, *cultural resistance, ideology, counterideology*, etc.; and I will develop a model of cultural resistance to rationalization. In the final section I will analyze concrete examples of Dadaist artworks and activities.

In sum, this article examines how cultural resistance to rationalization is possible, what the specific forms of cultural resistance are within modernism and how they

are structured, and how these forms are exemplified by the Dadaist artworks and practices. In conclusion, I show that these cultural practices, while part of the totality of social relations, have a specificity that is different from political forms of resistance.

CONCEPTS

Rationalization and Resistance

Central to our problem is the line of critical analysis from Max Weber, through Georg Lukacs, to the theorists of the Frankfurt school. All these social critics are concerned with the problem of rationalization as, ultimately, a form of domination in our time. This section will discuss this problem of rationalization and the resistance that arises to it.

Weber's concern with rationalization is bound up with the problem of how human values are chosen. He characterized as the fate of the Western world a movement toward formal rationality. Weber distinguished between formal and substantive rationality. Formal rationality orients action to explicitly formulated rules, and ensures numerical calculation and control. Substantive rationality is concerned, on the other hand, with absolute values, needs, and ultimate ends of human action. The major expressions of formal rationality—bureaucracy, science, and technology—stress means, not ends.

Weber was concerned with rationalization because he believed that formal rationality would pervade everyday life as a form of domination. For Weber bureaucracy and technology cannot give meaning to the world. The problem with formal rationality is that it drives out any consideration of final ends and values of action, and instead models action in terms of impersonal functions and roles. Only the imperatives of the bureaucratic organization are deemed important, and the individual becomes a simple cog in a vast machine.

In this sense bureaucracy is rationalized

domination. Formal rationality presupposes the establishment of values. But for Weber bureaucratic social organization does away with a discussion of what our values and needs should be. Social organizations, with their stress on means, become fixed, and develop their own logic. Weber pessimistically sees bureaucracy doing away with any value determination as it grows and engulfs society. Instead of establishing values, then, bureaucracy merely administers them.

At the conclusion of *The Protestant Ethic and the Spirit of Capitalism*, Weber summarized a trend of routinization and the denial of substantive rationality, the loss of community, the mysterious, and the sacred, which he called the disenchantment of the world. I quote more fully Weber's crucial complaint:

The puritan wanted to work in a calling; we are forced to do so. For when asceticism was carried out of monastic cells into everyday life, and began to dominate worldly mentality, it did its part in building the tremendous cosmos of the modern order. This order is now bound to the technical and economic conditions of machine production which today determine the lives of all individuals who are born into this mechanism, not only those directly concerned with economic acquisition, with irresistible force. Perhaps it will so determine them until the last ton of fossilized coal is burnt. In Baxter's view the care for external goods should only be on the shoulders of the "saint like a light cloak, which can be thrown aside at any moment." But fate decreed that the cloak should become an iron cage....

No one knows who will live in this cage in the future, or whether at the end of this tremendous development entirely new prophets will arise, or whether there will be a great rebirth of old ideas and ideals, or if neither, mechanized petrification, embellished with a sort of convulsive self-importance. For of the last stage of this cultural development, it might well be truly said: "Specialists without spirit, sensualists without heart; this nullity imagines that it has attained a level of civilization never before achieved." [2]

Note here that disenchantment articulates a cultural dimension. Weber finds that rationalization pervades the production and reproduction of all spheres of life.

And further, Weber is clearly critical of disenchantment, yet he was fatalistic about the ultimate outcome: the end result of formal rationality is the iron cage.

But the searching for a way of expressing and justifying values is left out of this "iron cage," for values within the rationalized world are no longer fit for discourse. They cry out to be heard, but under the conditions of rationalization can't achieve expression. Sensitive to this process, Weber also stressed the unintended consequences of disenchantment, emphasizing the fact that rationalization produced problems and resistance. Thus substantive rationality, expressed as the desire to satisfy subjectively felt needs, keeps recurring in opposition to formal rationality.[3] Most notably, he discussed the possibility of a reenchantment, locating some of these counterforces in the esthetic[4] and the erotic. For example, of the latter he writes:

The erotic relation seems to offer the unsurpassable peak of the fulfillment of the request of love in the direct fusion of the souls of one another. The boundless giving of oneself is as radical as possible in its opposition to all functionality, rationality, and generality.[5]

He also notes the importance of spontaneous play and intense interpersonal communal efforts to give radical opposition to the trend of disenchantment.[6] This intervention of a reenchantment is important in that it is a return to a world in which the value issue is restored.

Yet elsewhere he is skeptical of these countertrends.[7] However suggestive his speculations may be, this resistance is clearly a marginal concern for Weber. He remains unshaken in his pessimistic belief about the outcome of rationalization, viewing it as the fate of the Western world.

One reason for his pessimism about rationalization stems from Weber's method of constructing ideal types. Weber's ideal-type method selects the common traits and typical elements of a phenomenon. It is an analytical construct that, in an attempt to be coherent, scientific, and objective, excludes all the ambiguity and contradictions of the real world, and becomes a standard by which to judge the world. But in so doing, his ideal-type method separates facts from values, and the concepts appear as value-free. His ideal-type method thus reduces the contradictoriness and value-laden dimension of reason to the iron cage of formal rationality. Weber does concede that in everyday life, ''formal and substantive rationality are always in principle in conflict,''[8] but he cannot follow up this insight. For within the restrictions of his ideal-type method, they clash only within the rationalized world of domination. Hence, by typifying reality, and excluding values and contradictions, Weber takes for granted the very rationality that he lays bare,[9] and allows no real place for an analysis of subjective interests, needs, or values that can resist rationalization.

Weber's seminal development of the problem of rationalization as domination was filled out and adumbrated by the cultural Marxism of Georg Lukacs and the Frankfurt school. Georg Lukacs wrestles with the problem of domination in the form of alienation and reification.[10] In line with Marx's analysis of the commodity, Lukacs sees that in a capitalist system all human relationships are reduced to the function of the exchange of commodities.[11] This fetish character of commodities means that they take on a life of their own, over and against their producers; they become thinglike, or, in his terms, reified. Thus reification implies in Marx's terms that people become reduced to their market relations, as their labor power is bought and sold as a thing. Exchange value dominates use value. And in Weber's terms reification is the domination of formal rationality over substantive rationality. Thus for Lukacs reification signifies the increased calculability of formal rationality that Weber felt led to the disenchantment of the world.

But Lukacs criticizes Weber here for depicting the growth of formal rationality as neutral, fated, and part of the development of a broad process of rationalization in the West. Rather, Lukacs's concept of reification calls attention to the fact that rationalization is not autonomous, but in fact is a form of capitalism. For example, the development of bureaucracy and the increased division of labor allows for the growth of the capitalist economy. Therefore, rationalization is not an independent force, but is an extension of capitalist rationality. The distinction between the two might be sharpened in this manner: for Weber capitalism is an example of the unfolding process of rationalization. But for Lukacs rationalization is an imposition that flows from the form of capitalism.

The theorists of the Frankfurt school extend and deepen Lukacs's formulation of reification by stressing the historical, ideological, and dialectical nature of rationalization. Max Horkheimer, Theodor W. Adorno, Herbert Marcuse, and Jürgen Habermas all stress that rationalization is not simply development, but the legitimation of domination in our time.

For example, Horkheimer and Adorno, in *The Dialectic of Enlightenment*, argue that instrumental reason, in the sense of knowledge in the technical control of nature, has eclipsed a practical reason that could guide people's emancipatory interests.[12] The technical domination of nature includes the domination of humanity. In Adorno's terms, the growth of instrumental means-ends rationality ends in the ''totally administered'' society.

And Marcuse criticizes Weber on the same grounds, for Weber's notion of rationalization forgets that instrumental rationalization is capitalist rationalization:

. . . the very concept of technical reason is perhaps ideological. Not only the application of technology but technology itself is domination (of nature and men)—methodological, scientific, calculated, calculating control. Specific purposes and interests of domination are not foisted upon technology ''subsequently'' and from the outside; they enter into the very construction of the technical apparatus. Technology is always a historical-social project: in it is projected what a society and its ruling interests intend to do with men and things. Such a "purpose" of domination is "substantive" and to this extent belongs to the very form of technical reason.[13]

Marcuse's concept of a "one-dimensional society" expresses the alarming degree to which instrumental rationality has developed as a form of domination, becoming "totalitarian to the extent to which it determines not only the socially needed occupations, skills, and attitudes, but also individual needs and aspirations."[14] Thus as technology institutes more and more effective modes of social control, it attempts to block the dialectic between instrumental and substantive rationalization.

But there is a crucial difference between the positions of Horkheimer and Adorno, on the one hand, and Marcuse and Habermas, on the other. That difference is in the degree to which they keep the tension between instrumental rationalization and substantive rationalization.

Horkheimer and Adorno's position loses this tension in characterizing instrumental rationalization as a total system of domination. They could not shake the pessimism of Weber, possibly because of the trauma of fascism. Therefore, they do not develop the notion of a substantive resistance to rationalization.

In contrast, Marcuse and Habermas make an important contribution in that they leave the pessimism of Weber behind. They suggest that resistance to rationalization is neither irrational, primitive, or deviant behavior nor totally eclipsed by instrumental rationalization, but is a pervasive and recurrent feature of late capitalism. They thus restore the tension between instrumental and substantive reason by stressing that social groups are involved in an ongoing critique of instrumental rationalization itself.

Marcuse's suggestive work, *An Essay on Liberation*, sees new emancipatory needs arising in late capitalism that resist technical rationality.[15] He discusses the development of a new sensibility, esthetic, language, and imagination, which have begun to contest the growing forms of domination.

And, most notably, Habermas speaks of the development of a critical interest. He counterposes *work*, or instrumental action, which is interested in the domination of nature and humanity, to *interaction*, or communicative action, which is concerned with communication without the desire for domination. Habermas believes that there is a human interest in emancipation, and that undistorted communication and reflection can be a force toward overcoming instrumental domination.[16]

Regardless of the details of these two positions, they are important in that each of them posits a recovery of human needs, desires, and interests. They are a theoretical advance in that they revive the possibility of a practical or substantive reason that can oppose instrumental reason. In a world dominated by instrumental rationality, then, this new formulation of the problem suggests that human freedom can be recovered through activities which resist rationalization.

Marcuse and Habermas suggest that the domain of art, among others, has a special role in this process of resisting rationalization. As Habermas puts it:

Only bourgeois art . . . has taken up positions on behalf of the victims of bourgeois rationalization. . . . I refer here to the desire for a mimetic relation with nature; the need for living together in solidarity outside the group egoism of the immediate family; the longing for the happiness of a communicative experience exempt from the imperatives of purposive rationality; and giving scope to imagination as well as spontaneity. Bourgeois art . . . collected residual needs that could find no satisfaction within the "system of needs." Thus . . . art and aesthetics (from Schiller to Marcuse) are explosive ingredients built into the bourgeois ideology.[17]

But how does this actually come about? So far sociological literature has focused little on the forms of resistance to rationalization. The major theoretical problem of this article is to show how a set of activities, programmatic statements, and products in modernism in general, and as exemplified by Dada in particular, can be understood as an attempt to resist the increasingly rationalized and reified world that Weber and the Frankfurt school spoke about.

Ideology

Central to the conceptualization of rationalization and resistance is the notion of ideology. When Marx uses the term *ideology,* in most cases he is speaking of bourgeois ideology. That is, he recognizes that the term is polemical and implies a position within a conflict. Thus when we speak of ideology, we recognize that there is a struggle between the dominant ideology and the ideology of resistance, that they come in pairs.

This view of ideology allows us to contrast control with resistance to control. Toward that end throughout this section I have contrasted notions of instrumental rationalization as an ideology of control, with practical or substantive rationalization. This means that we can reflect on our constraints and resist control. For an ideology that resists control, I will use the term *counterideology.*

But ideology does not only refer to beliefs, ideas, or what people say. The problem with that use of the term is that it is incomplete. Are we referring to what people say or to what they do? The term must be taken as an evidence of a commitment, i.e., a practice. The analysis of ideology is thus an analysis of the forms of commitment to specific class-related practices.

Marx intended to draw attention to the notion that ideology is rooted in practice. In fact, Marx characterized as ideological the very abstraction of ideas from practice in the dominant ideology, which gives these ideas an autonomous appearance.[18] Ideology, whether dominant or counterideology, cannot be separated from the practices of which it is part.

A number of recent theorists have treated ideology in this manner, as rooted in practice.[19] For example, in terms of the dominant ideology, Pierre Bourdieu and Renée Balibar respectively link artistic consumption and literary practices to the educational institutions and the state.[20] But these practices, reinforcing the power of the dominant groups in society, are recognized as such by subordinate groups. Thus any control-oriented practice breeds resistance, and our analysis of forms of domination must also show resistance. As I have noted earlier, for Habermas the practices of avant-garde art are counterideological in that they resist rationalization.

Turning to this counterideology of the avant-garde, their critical practice attacks the apparent rationality of modern social life. Further, counterideology has both a negative and a positive side: on one hand, it attacks the legitimacy of instrumental rationalization; on the other, it puts forward a vision of social change.[21] The negative side I see as one of delegitimation of instrumental rationality, and the positive one as a reintegration or reenchantment of the world.

Summing up, we have a unitary ideology of delegitimation and reenchantment. This counterideology has two sides, the negative one of delegitimation and the positive one of reenchantment.

I have suggested that art is a domain that has a special role in resisting rationalization. If we look at the history of avant-garde art as an example of a critical ideology, we find that delegitimation of rationality takes a variety of forms, such as radical refusal, disaffiliation, deconstitution of authority, and negation of meaning, rationality, and standard language use.

And within the same avant-garde cultural practice, there is much emphasis on the positive side of this ideology of resistance to rationalization, that which I call the reenchantment of the world. I stress reenchantment in the sense of rediscovering and rebuilding some vision of unity and integration. Within the avant-garde and counter-cultures we find an emphasis on ecstatic or special states, a denial of utilitarian interest, a search for unity.

A Model of Delegitimation and Reenchantment

As I have suggested, avant-garde art is one important domain that resists the pervasive rationalization of modern life. These practices of resistance can be shown to form a structured totality. In order to understand this totality I would like to develop a formal model of the features of delegitimation and reenchantment. The purpose of this model is to help us understand the cultural practices of resistance to rationalization carried out by Dada artists.

First, I would like to develop an idea of what any legitimation of an order of instrumental rationality requires. Then, I shall examine what is required to delegitimate that rationality. Lastly, I shall propose that each delegitimating phase is linked to a consequent reenchantment since, basically, this is a unitary ideology with two poles.

Features of Legitimation

Ideologies which legitimate a social order, such as that of the universalizing rationality of industrial capitalism, must accomplish the following:

1. They must create a new hierarchy of goals, which by its very inclusiveness disciplines particular interests, and establishes for practice a consensus that attempts to deny conflict.

2. These goals must be ordered in time as accomplishments or failures. This order imposes a dimension of growth or regression, a universalistic scale for evaluating action.

3. They must define human conduct in terms of these concrete goals and goal directions, that is, in terms of a rationality of means and ends.

4. They must produce a discourse in which these criteria are objectified and universalized so that no thinking is possible outside the categories of this discourse. This ideological discourse becomes reified; it appears to be an objective and reliable language which is independent of particular speakers.

These are the four features necessary for the legitimation of any social order.

In passing, we note that the rising bourgeoisie in the age of modernization not only had to produce new forms of legitimation, as I have discussed above, but also had to attack the legitimacy of feudal ideology and social practices.

1. Thus, in order to establish a new social hierarchy, the new capitalist order attacks "tradition" or "archaic social practices" in order to legitimate a rational order for production and "progress."

2. Within the dimension of temporality, it attacks the cyclical time of agriculture and the Church, and establishes a strictly linear time (e.g., the clock; time-motion studies in the factory).

3. In terms of means-ends relations, it delegitimates practices of "magic," and establishes a scientific and mechanistic concept of cause and effect.

4. In terms of subject-object relations, it attacks the subject's place in the feudal hierarchy (as stated by St. Thomas Aquinas) and introduces a scientific notion of objectivity, and the change in subjectivity that comes from selling one's labor power as a commodity (the transition from peasant to worker). (See Table 8.1.)

While delegitimation of an ideological discourse can take different forms, I will focus on the forms within modernism. As noted earlier, Max Weber sets the stage for us in his characterization of radical resistance to the disenchantment of the world as "opposition to all functionality, rationality, and generality."[22] Thus he points to the essential element of delegitimation as resisting the trend toward instrumental rationalization.

Certain artists of the European avant-garde have developed self-conscious

TABLE 8.1

Model of Features of Delegitimation of Feudal Practices
and Legitimation of Rationalization

Features	Delegitimating Phase	Legitimating Phase
1. Social hierarchy	Attacks "traditional," "archaic" social practices	Establishment of a rational order for production and "progress."
		A new hierarchy of goals is established.
2. Temporality	Attacks cyclical time of agriculture and the Church.	Establishment of strict linear time (the clock in the factory).
		Goals are ordered in time.
3. Means/ends relations	Attacks practices of "magic."	Establishment of scientific and mechanistic concept of cause and effect.
		Concrete goals and goal directions are organized in terms of rationality of means and ends.
4. Subject/object relations	Attacks the subject's place in the feudal hierarchy.	Establishment of scientific objectivity and of the change in subjectivity resulting from the commodification of labor.
		Production of a discourse of objectivity.

stances, programs, and positions that are ideological in the sense that they justify their position, and attack the generalized rationality that Weber describes. But how is this delegitimation actually accomplished? How do the Dada artists, whose privileged domains are language and the visual arts, accomplish a delegitimation of rationality? It is interesting to recall the art critics who, in the form of a distinctly negative epithet, labeled the new artists of their time *impressionists, fauves* (wild men), and *cubists*. These critics immediately perceived the threat of delegitimation in the concrete violation of established norms, and the artists eagerly embraced these negative epithets in recognition of their delegitimating function.

The question can be raised: How do these violations differ from merely "bad art"? It's not "bad art" because of the deliberateness and intentionality of the viola-

tions. It is clear, then, that these avant-garde artists are taking a critical position in their art because the concrete violations of the structure of rationality are perceived and available to audiences.

To delegitimate the ideology of rationality, then, is to deny the fundamental opposition within that ideology: the distinction and the subordination of the particular to the universal. Thus the attack on rationality is to particularize, and the dialectic of the attack is to turn the tables. Particularizing is the negation of rationality.

More specifically, in terms of the above four features of legitimation, to delegitimate is to break with each of these. (In Table 8.2, see Features and Delegitimating Phase.)

Particularization. The negation of hierarchy is accomplished by a segregation of elements. Language, thought, and action are broken down into discrete elements. In this way they cannot be reconstructed into an overall design. Particularization is accomplished through a separation of words or images out of their rational context, which distorts or undermines taken-for-granted meaning.

Disruption of Linear Time. Delegitimation of directionality in time is accomplished by practices which disrupt linear time.

Randomization. Delegitimation of means/ends rationality is accomplished by the selection of material or events at random. These chance practices go far to separate activities from set goals.

Subjectivity. Objectivity is negated by an intense emphasis on the subjective relativity of all values.

Features of Delegitimation and Reenchantment

The above techniques of delegitimation also provide a reenchantment: delegitimation and reenchantment are thus two moments of a unitary ideological practice. Along with the radically destructive moment of delegitimation, there is a reenchanting moment which emphasizes reconstruction and restoration of a new unity.

Tracing these linkages in the Dada movement, I have found the following four features of delegitimation and reenchantment:

1. Particularization, through separation of words and "meaning," accomplishes the state of synesthesia, becoming a "seer," and mystical silence—in short, a state of mystical reintegration.
2. Annihilation of time leads to presentness and simultaneity.
3. Randomization accomplishes a perceived "synchronicity" and liberation from "causality."
4. The cumulative and interpenetrating effect of the above features points to an intense subjectivity, expressed in the relativity of all values, which unleashes the imagination and allows "everything to be possible." (See Table 8.2 below.)

Dada, therefore, can be profitably studied as an ideological transformation in which the disenchanted, rationalized world is confronted with an ideology that attacks its legitimacy, and attempts to reenchant it. Having developed a model of features of delegitimation and reenchantment, we can now turn our attention to their articulation in Dada.

TABLE 8.2

Model of Features of Ideology of Delegitimation and Reenchantment

Features	Delegitimating Phase	Reenchanting Phase
1. Social hierarchy	Particularization through separation of words and meaning.	→ Synesthesia, becoming "seer," silence.
2. Temporality	Disruption of linear time.	→ Presentness, simultaneity.
3. Means/ends relationships	Randomization, separation of activity from goal.	→ Infinite, acausal synchronicity.
4. Subject/object relations	Relativity of all values.	→ Imagination, open possibilities.

THE EXAMPLE OF THE DADA ART AVANT-GARDE

This section will develop an extended example of the model we have developed above, to illustrate the practice of Dada as a counterideology that attacks the rationalization of the modern world.

To make a dadaist poem
Take a newspaper.
Take a pair of scissors.
Choose an article as long as you are planning
to make your poem. Cut out the article. Then
cut out each of the words that make up this
article and put
    them in a bag.
Then take out the scraps one after another in
the order in which
    they left the bag.
Copy conscientiously.
The poem will be like you.
And here you are a writer, infinitely original
and endowed with a
    sensibility that is charming though beyond
    the understanding of the vulgar—[23]
                                    Tristan Tzara

Dada emerged in 1916 in Zurich, Switzerland, which was then a refuge for European draft resisters. From all over Europe came Tristan Tzara, Hans Richter, Hans Arp, Sophie Tauber, Hugo Ball, Marcel Janco, Richard Huelsenbeck, and others. As Marcel Janco has put it, they completely rejected the culture that produced the butchery of World War I:

We had lost confidence in our "culture." Everything had to be demolished. We would begin again after the tabula rasa. At the Cabaret Voltaire we began by shocking the bourgeois, demolishing his idea of art, attacking common sense, public opinion, education, institutions, museums, good taste, in short, the whole prevailing order.[24]

Evenings at the Cabaret Voltaire included a collage of sounds, images, and music: Ball's noise music, Tzara's simultaneous poems, Huelsenbeck's tom-tom rhythms, Janco's purposely ugly costumes. Dada activities were also centered in Berlin, Cologne, Hanover, New York, and Paris. After World War I, the major Dada centers were Paris and Berlin, where the radical climate brought it closer to leftist political activities. John Heartfeld, who developed the technique of photomontage, and George Grosz, the caricaturist, were both active Dadaists and communists. In Paris, after Tzara's arrival Dada continued in a more provocative and anarchic literary direction, until disputes between Tzara and André Breton led to the codification of its principles in the name of surrealism.

The Dadaists have left us with a bewildering array of art objects, biographies, and autobiographies. They have also attacked the possibility of historical reconstruction. Marcel Janco writes: "No dadaist will ever write his memoirs. Do not trust anything that calls itself 'dada history.'..." And Max Ernst states: "...a dada exhibition. Another one! What's the matter with everyone, wanting to make a museum piece out of dada? Dada was a bomb...can you imagine anyone, around a half a century after a bomb explodes, wanting to collect the pieces, sticking it together and displaying it?"[25]

How then can one make sense of Tzara's "paper bag" poem, Marcel Duchamp's "ready-mades" such as his *Fountain,* a urinal on a pedestal, Léger's movie, *Ballet Méchanique,* or the fracturing of any normal discourse in Dada poetry? As one writer put it:

How is one to define, let alone confine, a movement which cannot be identified with any one personality or place, viewpoint or subject, which affects all the arts, which has a continually shifting focus, and is moreover intentionally negative, ephemeral, illogical, and inconclusive?[26]

What does all of this work amount to? What is its sociopolitical accomplishment? In what sense is Max Ernst right that the Dadaist cultural products and practices are "bombs"? It is clear from the works, from the social circumstances surrounding their display, and from the reception of critics and audience, that Data constituted a radical practice of subverting the dominant ideology. The Dada artifact is difficult precisely in its strangeness, in its inability to be thought of within the given system; its concrete violations lay bare the limits of that system.

The following discussion will draw upon the model of features of delegitimation and reenchantment developed in the previous section, and will focus on Dada's practice of breaking down the rational unities into particulars, and on chance or random practices.

Negating Meaning through Practices of Particularization

Let's consider the Dada practice of fragmenting the system of meaning into particulars. This practice attempted to negate language as an instrument of rationalized meaning. As the Dadaist Hans Richter states:

This dissolution was the ultimate in everything that Dada represented, philosophically and morally; everything must be pulled apart, not a screw left in its customary place, the screwholes wrenched out of shape, the screw, like man himself, set on its way towards new functions which could not only be known after the total negation of everything that had existed before. Until then: riot, destruction, defiance, confusion. The role of chance, not as an extension of the scope of art, but as a principle of dissolution and anarchy. In art, anti-art....[27]

Similarly, Hugo Ball spoke of "spitting words." Tzara states that "words must be ploughed up," and that "thought is produced in the mouth."[28] Thus we see that speech, in its radical particularization, becomes disassociated from language itself. In this manner the concept of *chatter* becomes important for the Dadaists. Chatter for Dada is a form of particularized speech that is immediate and without meaning. The delegitimating nature of chatter is placed in opposition to the legitimating, universalizing nature of discourse.

Chatter is liberating because it is inherently useless, and by its feature of uselessness negates what Marcuse has called the *performance principle.*[29] Chatter, then, is the Dadaist concept of what will become for the surrealists the principle of stream of consciousness thought expressed in automatic writing. For the Dadaists, in particularizing language, it becomes emptied of its reified implications of cultural domination, and rediscovers its raw intensity and immediateness. In this manner of total negation through dissociation, the Dadaists believed that a "truer," less alienated language would be recovered.

In the same sense, speaking of Dada as a literary movement, Tristan Tzara advocated: "Destroying the taste for literature ...even while writing," that is, to attack literature, "by its own means, and in its own formulas...." He continues in an invocation "to disorder meaning..." and indicates that in its attack on art Dada is perfectly willing to also "wither away." Dada does not look for any permanence as another reified "art movement."[30]

The progressive autonomization of a language which no longer refers to the world is extended to the limits in Dada. As the external world is rejected, images hermetically turn inward. In the words of Tzara: "All that one looks at is false," or in the words of Louis Aragon: "I have thrown away my eyes to put in new ones."[31]

Thus the Dada metaphor, in its resistance to any instrumentalizing function of language, refuses to explain or even refer to a reality other than itself. The image is victorious over meaning, and is liberated from instrumental content. The end result of this process of complete separation of signifier and signified in Dada is the expression of total incommunicability. There are no explanations given, but only immediate expression. As Tzara declared: "There are people who explain because there are others who learn. Remove them, and you're left with dada."[32] They reduced expression to incommunicability or senselessness, not by saying the opposite but rather by juxtaposing a thing and its opposite, its negation, in the same line, or, as Tzara puts it, "in a single fresh breath,"[33] pushing to the limit the noninterpretable. It is "a way of blowing up 'their' language and therefore of destroying the main bridges between 'them' and 'us,' by incommunicability."[34]

These extreme expressions of language particularization gave great joy to the artists in the Dada movement. Their radical activities of delegitimation of meaning in language led to a reintegrated state of reenchantment. Richter, for example, takes pains to emphasize that the Dadaist subversion was one of affirmation and fun. He notes that, after the destruction, they were "known, to laymen and expert alike, more by our roars of laughter than by the things we were really doing."[35] Freed from the need to justify their actions, the Dadaists "reached that vital level where joy, movement, spontaneity, and metamorphosis have their being; language is no longer a poor means, but a game, a celebration."[36]

Negating Means-Ends Relations through Chance Practices

An ideology of rationality prescribes that there be concrete goals and goal direction, or, in other words, a coordination of means and ends. To negate this, the Dadaists have developed the practice of randomization, or chance. Delegitimation of means-ends rationality is accomplished by the selection of materials or events at random. This method goes far to separate activities from set goals.

A notable example is the montage of the woman climbing and reclimbing the stairs in Léger's *Ballet Méchanique*. The scene, with intercut smiles, is repeated five times. The audience finally perceives that the narrative will never be complete, in that the woman will never arrive at the top. By disassociating the activity from the goal of completing the sequence of action, Léger brings our attention to the particularity of the movement itself.[37] By this process Léger in effect is denying the fact that actions can

be known by their consequences. In this sense he challenges one of the tenets of the bourgeois order—the logic of means-end relations.

Hans Richter relates for us two further examples of chance practices in his autobiography:

Dissatisfied with a drawing he had been working on for some time, Arp finally tore it up, and let the pieces flutter to the floor of his studio on the Zeitweg. Some time later he happened to notice these same scraps of paper as they lay on the floor, and was struck by the pattern they formed. It had all the expressive power that he had tried in vain to achieve, namely expression. He accepted this challenge from chance as a decision of fate and carefully pasted the scraps down in the pattern which chance had determined.[38]

And further, of Tristan Tzara's paper-bag poem:

It was left to Tzara to follow the principle of chance to its logical conclusion in literature. Sounds are relatively easy to put together rhythmically and melodically in chance combinations; words are more difficult. Words bear a burden of meaning designed for practical use, and do not readily submit to a process of random arrangement. It was, however, exactly this that Tzara wanted. He cut newspaper articles up into tiny pieces, none of them longer than a word, put the words in a bag, shook them well, and allowed them to flutter on to a table. The arrangement (or lack of it) in which they fell constituted a "poem," a Tzara poem.[39]

Randomization both held back the rational mind from acting as a censor over the material and created more leeway, that is to say, language and image were unfrozen from their straitjacket of rationality. In this way a liberation is effected, and the mind produces striking images from the discordant material.

Marcel Duchamp has spoken of his readymades in this manner. Chance helps the artist forget his "hand," and thus acts to negate perceptual habits. His *Fountain* places a standard urinal on a pedestal. In this manner Duchamp wrenches a mass-produced object out of its utilitarian context.

Similarly, Max Ernst articulates the practice of chance as the random juxtapositioning of dissimilar elements to produce the "marvelous" out of the resultant shock to our lived experience of rationality. Randomization meant the cultivation of the systematic putting out of place of objects and their frame of reference. As he writes in discussing the mechanism of collage:

I think I would say that it amounts to the exploitation of the chance meeting on a non-suitable plane of two mutually distant realities (a paraphrase and generalization of the well-known quotation from Lautréamont, "Beautiful as the chance meeting upon a dissecting table of a sewing machine and an umbrella")....

A complete, real thing, with a simple function apparently fixed once and for all (an umbrella), coming suddenly into the presence of another real thing, very different and no less incongruous (a sewing machine) in surroundings where both must feel out of place (on a dissection table), escapes by this very fact from its simple function and its own identity; through a new relationship its false absolute will be transformed into a different absolute, at once true and poetic: the umbrella and the sewing machine will make love. The mechanism of the process seems to me to be laid bare by this very simple example. Complete transmutation followed by a pure act such as the act of love must necessarily occur every time the given facts make conditions favorable: the pairing of two realities which apparently cannot be paired on a plane apparently not suited to them.[40]

Randomization, then, is a systematic practice that produces a delegitimation of the rationality of means-ends relationships by totally putting things out of place, or dislocating the given system of reference. This randomization is both a fundamental negation of the wider rationality that Max Weber refers to by *disenchantment* and the narrower sense of bourgeois reality kept within the confines of the commodity system.[41] The work disturbs the order of accomplishment and the order of exchange, of ends installed by the market system but taken for granted.

An even stronger attempt at reenchantment is articulated by the following artists as contact with the infinite and the magical. For example, in the early Aragon

chance encounters are the means of reaching the infinite.[42] And as Richter notes, chance restores the magical, numinous, incantory aspect of art:

The adoption of chance had yet another purpose, a secret one. This was to restore to the work of art its primeval magic power, and to find the way back to the immediacy it had lost....By appealing directly to the unconscious, which is part and parcel of chance, we sought to restore to the work of art something of the numinous quality of which art has been the vehicle since time immemorial, the incantory power that we seek in this age of general unbelief, more than ever before.[43]

Chance for the Dadaists was a form of opposition to nineteenth-century mechanistic and deterministic principles. What was being affirmed was a transcendent principle beyond bourgeois rationalization. The practice of chance could accomplish a perceived freedom from causal relationships, coupled with a feeling of synchronicity with each other and with "higher laws of the universe." Richter, first speaking here of Carl Gustav Jung, discusses in his autobiography this Dadaist belief in freedom from causality:

He includes chance in his concept of synchronicity, which he described as "acausal orderedness." This order independent of causality is...the momentary pattern formed by a continually changing order....Chance appeared to us as a magical procedure by which one could transcend the barriers of causality and of conscious volition....The official belief in the infallibility of reason, logic, and causality seemed to us senseless....We had adopted chance, the voice of the unconscious—the soul, if you like as a protest against the rigidity of straight-line thinking.[44]

Thus, through randomization, one reaches a higher order not linked to the linear thinking of means-end logic, and is thereby free from causality. For Richter, the reenchanting nature of this randomization is apparent, for what follows is a call for man to synchronize with the cosmos:

The duty of man...would thus be to be conscious of this order, to become aware of this continuous act of creation, and to achieve, through

tion, intuition, and concentration, complete identity with the orderedness which has no cause.[45]

A final expression of this noncausal synchronicity is Ernst's and Duchamp's descriptions of themselves as indifferent spectators to their works:

The author is present at the birth of his work as an indifferent or passionate spectator and observes the phases of its development. Just as the role of the poet, ever since the celebrated "Letter of a Clairvoyant," consists of taking down, as though under direction, all that is articulated within him, so the painter's role is to outline and project what is visible within him. By devoting myself more and more to this activity (passivity) . . . and by increasingly trying to restrain my own active participation in the development of the painting so as to enlarge the active part of the mind's hallucinatory faculties, I succeed in simply attending as a spectator the birth of all my works. . . . Being a man of "ordinary constitution" (to use Rimbaud's term), I have done everything to make my soul monstrous. Blind swimmer, I have made myself a seer.[46]

This citation is drawn from a discussion by Ernst of his process of frottage, or random rubbings, in which the rational self is "decentered" by reducing to a minimum the authorship of the work. Similarly, Duchamp, in his ready-mades, rejects personal expression, and goes out of his way to minimize his intervention in the selection of materials. Thus, in both frottage and ready-mades, the artists accomplish a minimalization of their role, and thereby perceive synchronicity with some universal principle beyond the rationality of causality.

Randomization is a further systematization of the process of particularization. Through randomization, or separating the activity from the goal, these artists have effected the delegitimation of a rationality of means and ends. The reenchanting result is the restoration of the domain of the infinite and the magical in art, and the accomplishment of a perceived liberation from causality and synchronicity with the cosmos.

Negative Objectivity: All Things Are Possible

The cumulative effect of these practices of negating the rationalized ideology leads to an opening up of the possibilities of imagination. As Richter writes:

Even without going to extremes, the use of chance had opened up an important new dimension in art: the techniques of free association, fragmentary trains of thought, unexpected juxtapositions of words and sounds. In the field of visual art this new freedom has consequences that were possibly even more far-reaching.[47]

And further, he speaks of the liberation of the imagination effected by the breakdown of boundaries between the arts. Painters turned to poetry, and poets to painting.[48]

If all things can be related, then all things are possible. The Dadaist belief that all things are possible is a reversal of the order of objects and people. "All things are possible" restores to the community of people power over objects. It is a dereifying principle that restores human creativity, but not by reestablishing the individual author or fixed text. The Dadaist artistic practice is to take fragments of the rationalized world and collide them against one another. The audience, in the process, become active participants in the deconstructive practices.

CONCLUSION

The Critical Accomplishment of the Dada Art Avant-Garde

The critical contribution of Dada is in its practice as a counterideology that attacks the pervasive rationalization of modern life. One must look within the work of art itself to see how it accomplishes an attack on the legitimacy of the bourgeois social order, and presents the possibility of a reenchanted future existence. This is the critical accomplishment of the work of art—the subversive and deconstructing practices within the artwork, and its active effect on audiences. It is in this sense that Dada was a "bomb," and the specific site of its radical power is to be found here.

It is certainly not found in its absorption as a commodity in the marketplace. Dada is now enshrined in the museum as a holy relic, and safely detonated by the art critics as an art movement, part of the triumphant history of modernism which leads, with barely a break, right to the present.

Further, we need to be sensitive to the specificity of Dada practices in relation to the political movements of the time. Cultural explosions like Dada often precede and set the stage for more instrumental, that is, goal-oriented movements. These movements can be called expressive (versus instrumental) in that they tend to develop their opposition in totalistic ways. As a result, they develop a practice and a total critique of society. These kinds of total cultural movements play a role in social change precisely because they bring attention to the details of domination.

In this sense Dada was not a movement, but a *moment*; its politics were not narrowly instrumental, but expressive and totalistic; it was not a contestation of power, but a provocation; it did not see power as a resource but as a constraint.

In contrast, cultural politics, in the case of Dada, deliberately avoided organizational leadership and hierarchy, believing that the means defined them every bit as much as the ends they sought. Their slogan was: "Everyone is the director of the Dada movement."[49]

Moreover, institutional political movements seek to persuade their audience in order to enlarge its constituency. As Alfred Willener points out, Dada practiced provocation, not contestation. It had no desire to convince or persuade an audience to any point of view, but only to shock people out of their apathy, in order to overcome passivity in its audience.[50]

Dada's political specificity was in its cultural provocation, which, in the sense of Bertolt Brecht and the Russian formalists, "lay bare the device," by unmasking social contradictions. For if what is ideological in art and literature is the presentation of imaginary solutions to ideological contradictions,[51] then Dada consistently refuses to do this. Dada had "no wish to resolve contradictions, but to experience them and to act them out together; no wish to define, but to create confusion."[52] This is the site of its specific power as cultural politics.

It was a moment rather than a movement because it never existed as a movement, or organization, or tendency in art. It had no fixed purpose, end, or program to achieve. It had no sense of origin; it had nothing to accomplish. It never stopped evolving and transforming itself. Thus it cannot be studied as something fixed, but only understood in its radical position of tension and opposition, transformation and evolution.

Cultural politics, like Dada, is different in both form and object from institutional politics. Institutional politics is instrumental or goal-oriented. An organization is needed in order to maintain a consistent ideological viewpoint, and present itself as an organizationally viable alternative to the dominant structure. Each kind of politics accomplishes a different kind of critique. The strength of cultural politics is that it can widen the discourse of social criticism. But this is also its limit, in that it is antithetical to any organization.

Thus we can say that the Dadaists perceive power as a constraint, rather than the instrumental view of power as a resource to seize for class control. Perceiving power as a constraint means that they do not want to use state power to better their lives or the lives of others. In this sense they do not address the class issue of power as a resource used by the hegemonic class over the subordinate one.

Another way of saying this is that Dada is rebellious, but it is an incomplete rebellion. It is the first moment of rebellion, one that raises the problem and vitiates the order of reason as domination. This is its political significance. If we follow the biographies of the Dadaists, there seem to be two outcomes: a further political radicalization, or a movement toward mysticism. The liberatory potential of Dada lies in this first but incomplete moment.

When cultural and political radicalism join, it is at a time when political movements are more open and less concerned with ideological control. And when they succeed politically, they often begin to exclude cultural radicals. The response of the political radicals is to tighten up their constituency and demand conformity. This demand for conformity, as much as the diminished possibilities of cultural change, is what drives the cultural radicals out.

But if cultural radicalism is politics by other means, and if political authorities repress leftist political organization, then too close an identification between art and politics would destroy all resistance. And cultural radicals may be so sensitive to the deep structure of domination that they feel that the kinds of concessions to bourgeois reality necessary to achieve political power in themselves undermine the most radical thrust of the movement. The structure of bourgeois politics itself, then, can corrupt the intentions of cultural activists.

I am not suggesting that art movements by themselves constitute radical politics. But there is an autonomous critical aim that cannot have the same force if appropriated by instrumental movements.

If cultural resistance is to make a political contribution, its autonomy must be respected. Cultural resistance is all too often dismissed as not being "really" political. This usually implies that cultural politics should be reduced to political-instrumental struggles. We need, rather, to pay attention to and respect the specificity, mutual influence, and differential sites of each form of critical practice. Or, as has been said of another period, Gustave Courbet's realism is not less radical a contribution than his participation during the revolutionary uprising of the Paris Commune in 1871, in the destruction of the Vendome Column, a symbol of the domination of the Second Empire.

Perspectives for Further Research in the Sociology of Art and Culture

What is the contribution of this analysis of an instance of cultural resistance to rationalization for future research in the general sociology of art and culture?

A critical analysis of modern culture needs to recognize not only that modernism emerges from within the social process of rationalization but also that art has a role in unveiling these alienated relations. It is in this double sense, of rationalization and cultural resistance, that art and culture are involved in the totality of capitalist social relations.

Further, we need to pay more attention in cultural analysis to the specific effectivity of art products; these effects are not limited by their institutional origins. For this reason I have stressed the notion that artistic practices are structured in a manner which opposes the dominant ideology. The critique of the social world that these practices accomplish is congealed in the art products, and is available to new audiences beyond the time of its original production, and beyond the intentions of both the artist and his or her immediate audience.

NOTES

1. Daniel Bell, *The Cultural Contradictions of Capitalism* (New York: Basic Books, 1976).
2. Max Weber, *The Protestant Ethic and the Spirit of Capitalism,* trans. Talcott Parsons (New York: Charles Scribner's Sons, 1930), pp. 181–82.
3. Max Weber, *The Theory of Social and Economic Organizations,* trans. A. H. Henderson and T. Parsons, ed. T. Parsons (New York: Free Press, 1947), p. 185.
4. Max Weber, *From Max Weber: Essays in Soci-*

ology, ed. Hans Gerth and C. Wright Mills (New York: Oxford University Press, 1958), p. 342.

5. Ibid., p. 347.

6. Ibid., pp. 155, 341.

7. Ibid., p. 154.

8. Weber, *Theory of Social and Economic Organizations*, p. 212.

9. Karl Loewith, "Rationalization and Freedom," in Dennis Wrong, ed., *Max Weber* (Englewood Cliffs, N.J.: Prentice-Hall, 1970), p. 107.

10. Georg Lukacs, *History and Class Consciousness: Studies in Marxist Dialectics*, trans. Rodney Livingstone (Cambridge, Mass.: MIT Press, 1971).

11. Karl Marx, *Capital: A Critique of Political Economy*, vol. 1 (Moscow: Progress Publishers, 1961).

12. Max Horkheimer and Theodor W. Adorno, *Dialectic of Enlightenment*, trans. John Cumming (New York: Seabury Press, 1972).

13. Herbert Marcuse, "Industrialization and Capitalism in the Work of Max Weber," in H. Marcuse, *Negations: Essays in Critical Theory*, trans. Jeremy J. Shapiro (Boston: Beacon Press, 1968), p. 223.

14. Herbert Marcuse, *One Dimensional Man* (Boston: Beacon Press, 1964), p. 15.

15. Herbert Marcuse, *An Essay on Liberation* (Boston: Beacon Press, 1969).

16. Jürgen Habermas, "Technology and Science as Ideology," in J. Habermas, *Toward a Rational Society*, trans. Jeremy J. Shapiro (Boston: Beacon Press, 1970); Jürgen Habermas, *Knowledge and Human Interest*, trans. Jeremy J. Shapiro (Boston: Beacon Press, 1971); Jürgen Habermas, "Toward a Theory of Communicative Competence," in H. Dreitzel, ed., *Recent Sociology #2* (New York: Macmillan, 1970), pp. 115–48.

17. Jürgen Habermas, *Legitimation Crisis* (Boston: Beacon Press, 1975), p. 78.

18. Karl Marx, "Introduction to the Critique of Hegel's Philosophy or Right," p. 49, and Karl Marx, "Theses on Feuerbach," in Marx and Engels, *Selected Works*, vol. 2 (Moscow: Progress Publishers, 1962); Marx, *Capital*, vol. 1, pp. 372–73.

19. Jean Baudrillard, "Toward a Critique of the Political Economy of the Sign," *Substance* 15 (1976): pp. 111–16; Louis Althusser, "Ideology and Ideological State Apparatuses,"

L. Althusser, *Lenin and Philosophy*, trans. Ben Brewster (New York and London: Monthly Review Press, 1971), pp. 127–86; Nicos Poulantzas, *Political Power and Social Classes* (London: New Left Books, 1973); Pierre Macherey, *A Theory of Literary Production* (London: Routledge & Kegan Paul, 1978).

20. Pierre Bourdieu and Jean Claude Passerson, *Reproduction in Education, Society, and Culture*, trans. Richard Nice (London and Beverly Hills, Calif.: Sage Publications, 1977); Renée Balibar, *Les Français fictifs* (Paris: Hachette, 1974).

21. Henri Lefebvre, *The Sociology of Marx*, trans. Norbert Guterman (New York: Vintage Books, 1967), p. 87; Max Weber, *Economy and Society*, ed. G. Roth and C. Wittich (New York: Bedminster, 1968), p. 946; Karl Mannheim, *Ideology and Utopia*, trans. Louis Wirth and Edward Shils (New York: Harcourt Brace Jovanovich, 1936), p. 192.

22. Weber, *From Max Weber: Essays In Sociology*, p. 347.

23. Tristan Tzara, "Seven Dada Manifestos," in R. Motherwell, ed., *The Dada Painters and Poets* (New York: Wittenborn, 1951), p. 86.

24. Marcel Janco, "Dada at Two Speeds," in Lucy R. Lippard, ed., *Dadas on Art* (Englewood Cliffs, N.J.: Prentice-Hall, 1971), p. 36.

25. Marcel Janco and Max Ernst, cited in C. W. E. Bigsby, *Dada and Surrealism* (London: Methuen, 1974), p. 4.

26. "The Dada Movement," *The Times Literary Supplement*, no. 2699, London, October 23, 1953, p. 669.

27. Hans Richter, *Dada: Art and Anti-Art* (New York and Toronto: McGraw-Hill, 1965), p. 48.

28. Hugo Ball, cited in Alfred Willener, *The Action Image of Society: On Cultural Politicization*, trans. A. M. Sheridan Smith (New York: Pantheon Books, 1970), p. 203; Tristan Tzara, cited in Willener, *Action Image of Society*, pp. 204–25.

29. See Herbert Marcuse, *Eros and Civilization* (New York: Random House, 1955), p. 32.

30. Tzara, cited in Willener, *Action Image of Society*, p. 204.

31. Renato Poggioli, *The Theory of the Avant Garde* (New York: Harper & Row, 1971), p. 196.

32. Tzara, cited in Willener, *Action Image of Society,* p. 207.
33. Ibid., p. 206.
34. Ibid. The above argument draws from Willener's important work.
35. Richter, *Dada,* p. 64.
36. Willener, *Action Image of Society,* p. 207.
37. Annette Michelson, "Bodies in Space: Film as 'Carnal Knowledge,'" in *The Discontinuous Universe: Selected Writings in Contemporary Consciousness,* ed. Sallie Sears and Georgianna W. Lord (New York and London: Basic Books, 1972), p. 324.
38. Richter, *Dada,* p. 51.
39. Ibid., p. 54.
40. Max Ernst, "Inspiration to Order," in *The Creative Process: A Symposium,* ed. Brewster Ghiselin (New York: Mentor Books), pp. 66–67.
41. Fredric Jameson, *Marxism and Form: Twentieth-Century Dialectical Theories of Literature* (Princeton, N.J.: Princeton University Press, 1974), pp. 96–97.
42. Anna Balakian, *Surrealism: The Road to the Absolute* (New York: E. P. Dutton, 1970), p. 136.
43. Richter, *Dada,* pp. 59–60.
44. Ibid., pp. 57–58.
45. Ibid., p.57.
46. Max Ernst, "Beyond Painting," in Patrick Waldberg, *Surrealism* (New York: McGraw-Hill, 1965), p. 98.
47. Richter, *Dada,* p. 55.
48. Ibid., p. 57.
49. Willener, *Action Image of Society,* p. 200.
50. Ibid., p. 200.
51. Macherey, *A Theory of Literary Production.*
52. Willener, *Action Image of Society,* p. 200.

ESSAYS

9. Feminist Theories

10. Neofunctionalism and Modern Sociology

11. Critical Theory

12. Structuralism in France

13. New Directions in Neo-Marxism: A Marxist
Social Psychology

14. Sociobiology: Theory and Controversy

15. Technology and Social Change: Alternative Paths

PART THREE

NEW DIRECTIONS IN STRUCTURAL THEORY

Feminist sociologists exemplify Simone de Beauvoir's classic injunction that "the personal is the political" in their work on gender issues. Three major approaches to feminist theory are identified: socialist/Marxist, radical, and liberal. Liberal and radical feminists agree that theory should be based on substantive issues such as rape and motherhood, but they differ on the degree to which society must be changed to attain feminist goals. Socialist feminists are more self-consciously theoretical and divide into those who place their feminism ahead of their Marxism and vice versa. Socialist/ Marxist feminists agree that classical Marxist theory does not account for such women's experience as housework, rape, and incest. Nevertheless, Marxian frameworks can be utilized to analyze the oppression of women under capitalism. Cross-cultural research demonstrates, with one possible exception, that there is no society in which women have complete equality with men. A table delineates the structural factors affecting the position of women in societies with different modes of production.

Radical feminist theories emphasize the importance of gender, but not to the exclusion of such factors as race and class. The centrality of sexuality and consciousness-raising, dealing with feelings and attitudes and power, is the key to such feminist issues as abortion, birth control, sterilization abuse, rape, incest, lesbianism, and pornography. The guiding criteria is that to feminism, equality means the eradication not of gender differentiation but of gender hierarchy. Catharine A. MacKinnon's theory of the interconnection and social nature of sexuality and gender is discussed through her analysis of rape and the relationship of women to the state. A comprehensive table outlines radical, socialist-Marxist, and liberal feminist perspectives on such issues as reproductive rights, rape, pornography, relations to men, and the family.

Pauline B. Bart

FEMINIST THEORIES

> Liberal feminism is liberalism applied to women.
> Socialist feminism is socialism applied to women.
> Radical feminism is feminism applied to women.
> —Catharine A. MacKinnon
> (*Personal communication, May 22, 1982.*)[1]

In order to do feminist work—and feminist theory is feminist work—we must always ask Adrienne Rich's question, "But what was it like for the women?" Feminist theorists search for the origin of oppression, suppression, and repression. They examine women's worth, women's world, and women's legal being.

It was Simone de Beauvoir who said that the personal is the political, and set the stage for feminist theory.[2] Such theory is arrived at inductively and from our everyday lives. Some theorists oppose Beauvoir's belief in the universal subordination of women. Historians and anthropologists have written countertheories. Beauvoir joins in affirming human brotherhood, while feminist theorists such as Arlie Russell Hochschild reject male values, notably in Hochschild's 1975 essay, "Inside the Clockwork of Male Careers."[3] Sociologists like Elise Boulding[4] and Jessie Bernard[5] transvalued the women's world, as did the historians Estelle Freedman[6] and Amy Swerdlow.[7]

The legitimization of feminist theory, if not of feminism, in sociology was demonstrated in a seminar at the 1982 American Sociological Association meetings on that topic given by Catharine Stimpson, the first editor of *Signs*, the prestigious journal of women in culture and society. She noted that the first feminist theories were more "blasphemous" than those set forth now, and suggests that we may be too sober. Because of the power of conservatives in the United States, she believes we have had to adopt a siegelike posture. Feminist theory seeks to advocate change in the condition of women and thus describes our condition in order to change our subjugation. Such theory can blur into ideology or into academics. (We might add that it can do both.) Feminist art and literature constitute the source for such theory as the poetry of Audre Lorde and Adrienne Rich as well as an articulation of theory. Feminist theory has an oppositional quality, rejecting, refuting, and transvaluing how it is in the real world. Thus lesbian feminist philosopher Marilyn Frye says that the only posture for a feminist in a university is adversarial,[8] and Marcia Freedman, founder of the women's movement in Israel and former member of the Israeli Knesset, says that female values have transformative ability.[9] For a good society men must be transformed by such values.

In this essay I will present the differences among socialist/Marxist, radical, and liberal approaches to feminist theory. I have charted these differences, although I am aware that a table, by its nature, cannot deal with the subtleties of the approaches. I have, however, shown the table to socialist and radical feminists, and they agree with the labels. (See Table 9.1, "Views of Feminists Compared and Contrasted," on pages 252–53.)

SOCIALIST/MARXIST FEMINISM

Socialist/Marxist feminists argue that classical Marxist theory is insensitive to the *woman question* as well as to sexuality. It cannot and does not account for women's experience—from housework through rape, woman abuse, and incest.

Dorothy Smith

Dorothy Smith says of the feminists:

1. They take the standpoint of women.
2. They oppose women's oppression.
3. They recognize sisterhood.

Like Catharine A. MacKinnon, Smith recognizes the centrality of consciousness-raising (CR) groups to women. It is in these groups that women have their experiences validated, many for the first time. She notes the importance of sisterhood "because it is in sisterhood that we discovered the objectivity of our oppression . . . in relation to other women, in discussion with

other women, in exploring with other women the dimensions of the oppression."[10] To use C. Wright Mills's terminology, we would say that it was in CR groups that we learned that what we were suffering from was not private problems but public issues. In fact, Smith says that her Marxism developed "in large part" from her discovery of feminism. Indeed, for her, becoming a Marxist "was an enterprise in trying to discover and trying to understand the objective . . . relations which shape and determine women's oppression in this kind of society." Marx and Engels, she adds, have given us the intellectual tools that enable us to understand our particular situation. She states that understanding our relationship to women is prior to our taking a position. We discover that women's experience matters to us, as does our knowing that we are on the side of women historically and cross-culturally. "Sisterhood is a relocation. You take up a different place in the world." Her way of approaching phenomenologically the early feminist axiom that the personal is the political is to note that we begin from "the personal inner understanding . . . which is distinctive to women's experience of oppression." This oppression is not only externally constraining but part of our interpersonal relations, including our sexuality. She, unlike some radical feminists, rejects calling on "the magic of a distant matriarchy as a source of power," since that is "a mythology rather than an analysis of actual relations—what is going on now and why it is happening to us." Note that she uses *we* rather than *they* when speaking of women.

Smith addresses the problem of battered wives, an area in which Marxist theory is weakest and radical feminist theory strongest (see Table 9.1). She speaks of "this tacit alliance among men which unites them across class lines. . . ."[11] Women are trapped and powerless in the family relationship because of capitalism. Women do not make enough money to support themselves and their children outside of marriage. Moreover, when they try to leave, the institutions of the society conspire to keep them in—the church, social welfare groups, the state through its lack of legal protection for women, the reigning ideology, women's socialization, which makes a woman feel useless without a man, etc. Occupational segregation keeps women in low-paying work; their training is training for incompetence, and their work at home is not recognized. She notes that Marxist ideology traditionally calls women "backwards," that "unions have not traditionally organized women, that women have been forced out of the labor force. While women are not backward except perhaps from a male perspective, women behave rationally given their choices."

The family relationship is organized by capitalism. It is one in which "women serve men in the home in exchange for their security and their children's security...." When we examine women's condition from a feminist viewpoint, what emerges is "a built-in complicity" within Marxist thinking both with the working classes and with the institutions by which the ruling class dominates the society. "It is an alliance across class and among men against women...it is not represented as the product of an extra-historical patriarchal relation of male dominance over women. It is represented as the outcome of a definite historical process, which has established the forms under which women are oppressed now.... It is a division which in fact aligns men in this respect on the other side in the class struggle, that is, on the side of the ruling class."[12]

Men of the ruling class and men in general have maintained their domination over women by using the state and the institutions of domination. Yet "women's oppression is an integral part of capitalism."[13] Thus, "there must be some more fundamental change in the economic and social relations of the society, if there is to be a change in the position of women—a real change."[14] Capitalism, through its development, brings changes which "appear as relations between things, commodities and money exchanged in the market," but these developments come from the work of people and occur through social relations.

We, however, would add that while women's oppression is an integral part of capitalism, it was also an integral part of feudalism, manifested in the *droit du seigneur* (the feudal lord had first access to women in his domain), and also of pastoral societies (remember the Old Testament).

Smith's work draws from ethnomethodology as well as from feminism and Marxism. She summarizes her more recent thinking in her syllabus to the course "Women's Standpoint in the Sociological Organization of Knowledge" (Northwestern University, Department of Sociology, 1983). She writes:

The logic of this enterprise [a sociology for women] comes from the women's movement and its disclosure of a male-occupied ruling apparatus...which women have confronted as subordinates and outsiders. Sociology is one part of this apparatus. Its objectified forms of knowledge conceal and presuppose a position within it.

Making a sociology for women thus involves more and other than requiring sociology to address women's issues and concern itself with women (important as that is). It calls for a sociology analysing and investigating society from the standpoint of women, and hence from a position outside forms of discourse lodged in and conforming to the logic of the ruling apparatus.

From the standpoint of women, sociological discourse appears as a constituent of relations of ruling. Its objectifying methods of thinking and research are concordant with this function. Hence, the problem for a sociology for women goes beyond that of content to that of remaking modes of thinking and inquiry in ways which reconstruct the discursive relations between sociological inquirer and other sociological knowers, and create novel constraints on how discourse might relate us to one another and the societies of which we are part.[15]

Smith in another paper states that "the problem of a relation of sociological inquirers and other knowers is explored as a problem both of method and relation. Very tentatively a macrosociology and a method

TABLE 9.1

Views of Feminists Compared and Contrasted

Issue	Radical Feminists	Socialist/Marxist Feminists	Liberal Feminists
Reproductive rights, especially abortion and sterilization	Women should have total control over their bodies. The model is self-help and Jane, the feminist illegal abortion collective, is the example.	They primarily focus on showing the connection between reproductive rights and the "New Right." Are concerned over the involuntary sterilization of women of color.	Tend to view birth control, sterilization, and abortion as private issues between woman and physician as stated in *Roe v. Wade*. Support reform in medical profession; for example, they consult more female physicians.
Violence against women	Regarded as the bottom line in the social control of women and a salient, if not the most important, issue.	They regard bad economic conditions, e.g., unemployment, as factors leading to violence against women by males. This issue is frequently overlooked in their analysis of women's condition, especially by U. S. feminists.	Seek remedies in new laws and enforcement of old laws. Regard individual violent men as sick or suffering from communications problems.
Rape	All men benefit from rape. Normal men rape as a result of typical male socialization, misogyny, and male sense of entitlement. Women should cope with rape by learning self-defense, preferably from other women. Relationship between pornography and rape is emphasized.	Rape is not a central issue for this group. Rape by men of color is played down, even when the victims or survivors are women of color because of racism in the criminal justice system.	Rape is seen as a crime against women; rapists are sick individuals; most men don't rape. Professionals, such as social workers, police officers, court officials, and hospital employees, should be specially trained to deal sympathetically but not politically with the victims of rape.
Pornography	For most radical feminists, this is a salient issue. Pornography is seen as an outgrowth of institutionalized misogyny. Most support the MacKinnon Dworkin civil rights ordinance rather than obscenity law, so that people harmed by pornography can civilly sue for damages.	Among Socialist/Marxist feminists there is disagreement on the harm of pornography. Concerned about empowering the state with new laws and about having a position similar to that of the Right Wing. Some see pornography as liberating for women because it separates sexuality from motherhood and gives some women the freedom men have.	Many liberal feminists are basically opposed to pornography, but they draw a distinction between erotica and pornography. Many are concerned with the First Amendment rights of pornographers and consumers of porn because of the alleged slippery slope.
Language	They agree with the other feminists on language, but are also more likely to take non-patriarchal names, such as Sarasdaughter or Star.	According to this group, sexism in language and nonverbal communication is a micropolitical method of exercising social control over women.	This group opposes the generic use of *he*, *him*, and *his*; it is also concerned about sex-role stereotyping.

Sexuality and lesbianism	One's identification with women logically leads to lesbianism. Lesbianism is seen as a form of resistance to patriarchy.	Marxist theory has no way of dealing with this issue in its own terms. Socialist feminists, considering patriarchy as well as capitalism oppressive, support lesbian and gay male issues, e.g., AIDS, but from the perspective of people with AIDS. Some Marxist feminists are profamily and anti-lesbian in order to increase their outreach to the working class.	Since one's sexual orientation is a civil liberties issue, there should be no discrimination against lesbians.
Sexual harassment	This is an important issue; it occurs because of the male sense of entitlement to goods and services from women as a class, especially our sexuality.	Concerned over sexual harassment of working women and students.	Remedies against sexual harassment should be sought through laws, the courts, codes in the workplace, and education in the schools.
Motherhood	Radical feminists have two positions on motherhood. The first group considers motherhood as an experience, viewing the mother-child relationship as the ideal; the second group believes this ideal relationship cannot exist under patriarchy and thinks women should forgo motherhood. Belief in demedicalization of childbirth, such as home birth with midwives.	These feminists consider it critical to involve men in child rearing. Marxist/Socialist feminists believe in socialized child care.	Liberal feminists have the same position on male participation in child rearing as the Marxist feminists. Men should be educated in the art of nurturing children. Men are hurt by being left out of child rearing. See the need for a more enlightened birthing process, especially the need for birthing rooms.
Relationship to men	Various degrees of separatism are favored. Women must control the women's movement; men who want to help should work with other men.	Socialist/Marxist feminists see the need for women to join with men of color and gay men, i.e., oppressed men, to build a society free of oppression.	According to this group, women's liberation will also liberate men. Men are welcome as members of the organization. For the most part heterosexuality is assumed. An important concern for this group is shared housework; another is androgyny.
Social change	Some expect the feminist revolution to bring back the golden age of matriarchy. Some hope for substantive, not just legal, equality.	These feminists expect that the socialist revolution will come about through the dialectic process and the class struggle. There has to be an autonomous women's movement for women's status to improve; this group admits that women are not equal to men in any socialist country.	Liberal feminists believe that social reform will come about through the attainment of political power by more women and by profeminist men. Change will come about as a result of nonsexist education. The National Women's Political Caucus and N.OW. is important to these feminists, who expect these groups to bring about better laws and passage of the ERA.

of investigation in which the subject is not dissolved into a function of a system and in which the historical co-location of knower and inquirer is preserved, is put forward. She does so in "The Experienced World as a Problematic: A Feminist Method," and suggests "an institutionalized ethnography as a feminist method of research." [16] But she also wants to "develop a macrosociology as an essential complement of a problematic located in the everyday world."

Rae Lesser Blumberg

In "Sexual Stratification: A Paradigm of Female Productivity, Power, and Position" Rae Lesser Blumberg uses the Human Relations Area Files to delineate the basis for women's power historically and cross-culturally. [17] First, she notes that with the possible exception of the Tasaday, there is no society in which women have complete equality with men. Blumberg looks at female power relative to the men of their class or group (or tribe if a preclass society) and "the extent to which females approach equal treatment and opportunities with males of their class or group." [18] While the amount of female power varies with respect to property, men monopolize the power of position and the power of force (although "where female economic control is high, male resort to wife beating tends to be low"). She defines economic power as "women's degree of control...of the means of production and allocation of surplus." Noting that "slaves work, too," she points out that simply being economically productive without controlling the fruits of production does not necessarily lead to power.

Two principal factors are involved in the variation in women's participation in their societies' main productive activities. They are: (1) "the extent to which the economic activity in question is compatible with women's child-care responsibilities, especially breast-feeding"; and (2) "the state of

available male labor supply relative to demand." [19] Thus they consist of tasks that can be done close to home such as horticulture, tasks that are not dangerous to small children, and tasks that can be interrupted. Women must have gained control over their production and, for that to be true, female producers should be strategically important and indispensable. In addition, women's power increases when maternal kin are emphasized, when the residence is *matrilocal*, and when the social relations of production are such that women as well as men control the means of production and allocate its surplus.

When women have economic clout, they can use it to restrict male use of political and physical force. In order to measure women's power in a society, Blumberg examines a woman's options relative to men in her class and group: (1) marriage—if, when, and to whom; (2) terminating marriage; (3) premarital sex; (4) extramarital sex; (5) control of reproduction—abortion and contraception; (6) geographic mobility; (7) exercise of household authority; and (8) taking advantage of educational opportunities. Economic power was "overwhelmingly the most important predictor of women's life options." Force was the only one of the remaining factors that had a substantial "impact on women's life options over and above that produced by women's economic power."

Mary O'Brien

It has been said that Max Weber engaged in a struggle with the ghost of Karl Marx. Socialist/Marxist feminists also engage in the same struggle with the ghost of Karl Marx. Both Dorothy Smith and Mary O'Brien point out that women's lives do not fall neatly into class categories. The war between the sexes, which O'Brien calls the *generic struggle*, "was not considered an integral part of class struggle." [20] For starters, they both note that it is not only the bourgeoisie who beat their wives. O'Brien maintains that "male supremacist praxis is transhistorical." The triumph of working-class men does not result in an end to the subordination of women.

The social structure of male oppression "is the structure in which the social relations of reproduction have been developed historically. It is no accident then that this is the structure by which private life and the personal have been separated from public life and the political. The opposition of public and private is to the social relations of reproduction what the opposition of economic classes is to the social relations of production." [21] While Marxists have admitted that domestic labor benefits capitalism, there is a reluctance to admit that women's unpaid labor benefits men of all classes or, as I would put it, men as a class. Thus while men and women may be united by class consciousness, they are divided by reproductive consciousness common to women (as a class) whether or not they are biological mothers. Men are alienated from reproduction, but have appropriated its fruits. (Note the custody fights and the surrogate mother litigation as striking examples of such male appropriation.)

We should note men's blindness or at least myopia to the reality that "paternity is essentially an idea while maternity is experienced fact." [22] Sometimes even the existence of children and of pregnancy, a labor-intensive activity, is erased, as in the Marxist utopia in which men fished in the morning, farmed in the afternoon, and had critical discussions in the evening. To all this O'Brien trenchantly notes, "Who was minding the kids?" [23] Male brotherhood is a means to transcend "the alienation of their seed." [24] For women, the family is not a haven in a heartless world but a breeding ground of violence as well as of children. Men believe this violence to be the triumph of power over nature and history.

Feminist socialists try to transform Marxist theory and praxis to include the "actual historical experience of women." [25] Socialist men need to understand that capitalism and patriarchy must go down together or not at all. Piecemeal efforts, such as maintaining women's right to have an abortion and day-care centers without working for the "absorption of men into domestic labour," will have little effect. [26] Until men give up male privilege (including male sexual privilege) and see its relationship to the exploitation of their own labor in the marketplace, then the "class struggle will soldier on with all the fizzle of day-old beer." [27]

Lorenne M. G. Clarke

Clarke states that one can test the strength of an ideology by its apparent obviousness, its taken-for-grantedness. The ideology of male supremacy is paradigmatic in this respect. It is "the conceptual meta- or super-structure which is assumed at the foundations of political and legal theory." [28] It follows that "virtually all male theorists have been sexists." Her focus, like O'Brien's, is on reproduction rather than production. She notes that reproduction is denigrated in traditional political theory, a theory in which women and children were relegated to the private sphere, perpetually in a state of nature. "Politics and its derivative structures is [sic] the formalized attempt by men to retain exclusive control of the means and products of both production and reproduction." [29] Traditional political theory has four central features: the need for the state and the corporation, with the interests of the individual reconciled with the interests of the state; private property and the justification of inequality; illegitimacy and primogeniture, which justify inheritance; and the legitimization and justification of authority. "Thus, political theory provides the justification of sexual and class inequality, and legal theory provides the articulated structures by means of which these inequalities are enforced and perpetuated through the state authority, private ownership, and inheritance." [30] Our inequality as women is socially constructed.

RADICAL FEMINIST THEORISTS

In this section, we will discuss the *ovular* works of Marilyn Frye, Catharine A. MacKinnon, and Adrienne Rich. This is not a complete list. Radical feminism emphasizes the importance of gender. But contrary to its critics, it does not for the most part ignore race and class. An informal content analysis of two key radical feminist publications, *Off Our Backs* and *Sinister Wisdom*, shows substantial space devoted to women of color and issues of poor women, e.g., women in prison. And indeed, gender is an extremely powerful variable. It's the best variable for predicting income, occupation, and even doctor-patient interaction patterns,[31] to say nothing of rape, incest, and sexual harassing.

Catharine A. MacKinnon

The work of Catharine A. MacKinnon, this most ovular feminist theorist, is the cutting edge of feminist theory. Her work is to feminism what *The German Ideology* is to Marxism. Key sentences in her article, "Feminism, Marxism, Method, and the State: An Agenda for Theory," are her first two sentences: (1) "Sexuality is to feminism what work is to Marxism: That which is most one's own, yet most taken away"; and (2) "Man fucks woman: Subject, verb, object." [32]

Unlike other feminist theorists, she argues for the centrality of sexuality and for objectification as the keystone of female oppression. "Sexuality is that social process which creates, organizes, expresses, and directs desire (a term parallel to 'value' in Marxism)." She continues, "Marxism and feminism are theories of power and its distribution: Inequality. They provide accounts of how social arrangements of patterned disparity can be internally ra-

tional yet unjust." Deprivation of our work or our sexuality renders us powerless. Each theory argues "respectively that the relations in which many work and few gain, in which some fuck and others get fucked, are the prime moment of politics." [33]

MacKinnon states in "Women as Women in Law: On Exceptionality," "To know you are equal, you have to be equal to somebody who sets the standards you compare yourself with." [34] According to this, gender differences are the evil of women's situation because they enforce the nonsameness of women to men. Feminism draws from socialist feminism lessons about work and privilege, from lesbian feminism lessons about sexuality, and from the feminism of women of color lessons about racism and communities of resistance. As a result, feminism defines equality very differently from Marxism. To feminism, equality means the eradication of *gender hierarchy*, not of gender differentiation. She adds that "for the purposes of sex discrimination law, to be a woman means to be like a man or to be like a lady. We have to meet either the male standard for males or the male standard for females." [35]

She develops this point in her germinal "Toward Feminist Jurisprudence," [36] a review and elaboration of Ann Jones's book, *Women Who Kill*.[37] Addressing the issue of women who kill men, and noting that the *Wanrow* decision implies that women's weakness relative to men should be taken into account when judging women, MacKinnon notes that the question of "how the exceptional woman is a member of her gender" is crucial to both equal protection doctrine and to feminist theory.

In that decision, the doctrine was put forth by feminist attorneys that Wanrow's use of a gun, while her leg was in a cast, in defending a child from a known child molester was, in fact, the use of "equivalent force." They observed that the doctrine of equivalent force, i.e., a gun versus a gun, though applicable in the case of males, was not appropriate when the man was unarmed but the woman had a gun.[38] While on the face of it, this perception appears to be good for women, MacKinnon states that "the price of this special consideration seems to be that woman's right to protect herself requires that the state protect her," and the price of this "special consideration seems to be that women not only be perceived as weak, or as rationally perceiving themselves as such, but that we actually remain so."[39]

This is because in equal protection two doctrinal constructions are equally consistent with *Wanrow*. In one, the history of sexual inequality renders the sexes "not similarly situated" with regard to the ability to resort to less than deadly force in self-defense. Thus, one rule for women and one rule for men is not only discriminatory, it violates a woman's right to equal protection, to assess her situation on male terms. In the other construction, the sexes are similarly situated with regard to the statutory requirement that persons acting in self-defense have their perceptions subjectively measured. The standard itself is unitary. Constitutionally, it produces two different outcomes when applied to men's and women's subjectivity, because their experiences have differed historically. The first approach embraces duality as a necessary response to social inequality. The second denies that; it erects a dual standard even when it emerges with a different rule for each sex.[40]

MacKinnon's critique of *Roe* v. *Wade* rests in large part on the detrimental effects for women of a doctrine based on privacy.[41] Since women's sphere traditionally has been the private rather than the public sphere, the sanctification of privacy leaves women vulnerable to what men may do to them in private. That doctrine "reaffirms what the feminist critique of sexuality criticizes: the public/private split." The private sphere is political, where battery, marital rape, and unpaid household labor take place. Since the abortion decision was based on privacy, the Supreme Court could then find restrictions on abortion constitutional, such as those preventing public funds from being used to pay for abortion, since they were not relevant to the question of privacy. (For a further statement about abortion, see MacKinnon's introduction to Dworkin's paper, 1983.[42]) Additionally, she notes that abortion is inextricable from heterosexuality, and that abortion's proponents and opponents tacitly assume that sex is consensual, although in fact control is not "coequally determined." The exemptions for rape and incest in most versions of bills outlawing abortion are based on this assumption since they would allow exemptions in those cases where force is recognized. Women get pregnant "as a consequence of intercourse under conditions of gender inequality . . . ."

> In feminist terms, I am arguing that the logic of Roe, consummated in Harris [the decision making it allowable to deny Medicaid for abortions] translates the ideology of the private sphere into the individual woman's legal right to privacy as a means of subordinating women's collective needs to the imperatives of male supremacy. . . . Reproduction is sexual; men control sexuality; and the state supports the interest of men as a group.[43]

There are two major ways in which MacKinnon disagrees with the official feminist canon. First, she refuses to accept the fashionable distinction between sex and gender. It is no accident that in sociology the section called The Sociology of Sex Roles was changed to The Sociology of Sex and Gender Roles, and Women's Studies is disappearing only to reappear as Gender Studies, omitting what MacKinnon in another context called "that truly obscene word *women*" and bowing to the liberal ideology of gender neutrality.

MacKinnon believes:

> Sexuality is fundamental to gender and fundamentally social, and that biology is its social meaning in the system of sex in equality, thus, the sex/gender distinction resembles a nature/culture distinction.[44]

Second, she refuses to make the politically convenient distinction between sex and power when discussing rape (and pornography). Rape is not just about violence, "Rape is a sexual crime and...much sexuality is very violent, which is why courts, etc., have had such trouble distinguishing them. It is to see the rape in intercourse, rather than the intercourse in rape—the latter is what has gotten men off the hook." [45] MacKinnon criticizes Susan Brownmiller for not describing rape "in normal circumstances, in everyday life, in ordinary relationships, by men as men." [46] As examples of this, she cites date rape and marital rape:

The more feminist view to me, one which derives from victims' experiences, sees sexuality as a social sphere of male power of which forced sex is paradigmatic. Rape is not less sexual for being violent; to the extent that coercion has become integral to male sexuality, rape may be sexual to the degree that, and because, it is violent.

The point of defining rape as "violence not sex" or "violence against women" has been to separate sexuality from gender in order to affirm sex (heterosexuality) while rejecting violence (rape). The problem remains what it has always been: Telling the difference. The convergence of sexuality with violence, long used at law to deny the reality of women's violation, is recognized by rape survivors, with a difference: Where the legal system has seen the intercourse in rape, victims see the rape in intercourse. The uncoerced context for sexual expression becomes as elusive as the physical acts come to feel indistinguishable. [47]

Nor does MacKinnon analyze rape "as men treating women as property in the manner of many socialist-feminist adaptations of Marxian categories to women's situation. That analysis short-circuits the analysis of rape as male sexuality and presumes rather than develops links between sex and class. We need to rethink sexual dimensions of property as well as property dimensions of sexuality." [48] Her point is well taken. Until a reform rape statute was passed in 1983, Illinois law stated that if you enter a woman's hallway without her permission, that is termed home invasion, a Class X felony, the most serious category of offenses. But if you enter her vagina with an object or your fingers, it is only a misdemeanor—battery. We would be better off were we treated as property. In this society property is valued, and damage to property is taken seriously and punished.

Continuing her critique of liberal thinking, MacKinnon questions whether the concept of woman's consent itself can be meaningful under conditions of gender inequality. Moreover, the law assumes that consent once given may never be retrieved. [49] Rape law, like other crimes and torts, requires that the accused have a criminal mind for the act to be understood under those conditions. But the problem is that the injury of rape rests in the meaning of the act, in "what really happened," thus presuming "a single underlying reality." Men usually consider "their experience of the real" as constituting reality. "When the reality is split...the law tends to conclude that a rape did not happen." (Let me cite as examples of this viewpoint the police and cab drivers who told me [PB] that a prostitute could not be raped). I (Bart) sometimes say that it is only considered a "real" rather than a "bullshit" rape by the police when the accused broke into the home and the victim was a fourteen-year-old virgin, babysitting her siblings, and watching "The Waltons" while crocheting the flag. Thus, when MacKinnon says that from a woman's point of view rape "is not prohibited; it is regulated," she is right. [50]

MacKinnon notes the schizoid nature of feminist attitudes toward the state on issues central to our survival. Liberal strategies which work for legal change assume that rape and battery are deviant, and such strategies "entrust women to the state. Left theory abandons us to the rapists and batterers." [51] She calls for a feminist theory of our relation to the state. Currently, "The state is male in the feminist sense. The law sees and treats women the way men see and treat women, ensuring male control over our sexuality while de jure prohibiting its excesses." [52] It is male formally "in that objectivity is its norm" and "objectivity is liberal legalism's conception of itself." [53]

MacKinnon turns to the law of rape to demonstrate her point, and everything she states is mirrored by my experience as a rape researcher.[54] The law divides women into categories according to how much consent women are presumed to have over sexual access to them. Statutory rape says little girls may not consent, and the marital rape exemption and the laws on "voluntary social companions" state that wives and dates must. At that point the law's problem is to distinguish rape from sex, in each case adjudicating the level of acceptable force to the "rational rapist."

MacKinnon carries the sociology of knowledge to its logical conclusion in her post-Marxist methodology, stating that feminism does not claim that it is unpremised, abstract, or universal, and it knows that there is no unpremised audience. "Its project is to uncover and claim as valid the experience of women, the major content of which is the devalidation of women's experience." Such a task is not easy because "male dominance is perhaps the most pervasive and tenacious system of power in history" and nearly perfect metaphysically:

Its point of view is the standard for point-of-viewlessness, its particularity the meaning of universality. Its force is exercised as consent, its authority as participation, its supremacy as the paradigm of order, its control as the definition of legitimacy. Feminism claims the voice of women's silence, the sexuality of our eroticized desexualization, the fullness of "lack," the centrality of our marginality and exclusion, the public nature of privacy, the presence of our absence. This approach is more complex than transgression, more transformative than transvaluation, deeper than mirror-imaged resistance, more affirmative than the negation of our negativity. It is neither materialist nor idealist; it is feminist.[55]

Women do not fare well in socialist countries—they are seen simply as productive workers, and their labor is used by the regime. (These are women in male roles, not men in female roles, it should be noted.) "Sexuality, if noticed at all, is like 'everyday life,' analyzed in gender-neutral terms, as if its social meaning can be presumed the same, or coequal, or complementary, for women and men."

MacKinnon does not argue for the centrality of sexuality either from Freudian or Lacanian roots, but rather "from feminist practice on diverse issues, including abortion, birth control, sterilization abuse, domestic battery, rape, incest, lesbianism, sexual harassment, prostitution, female sexual slavery, and pornography. In all these areas, feminist efforts confront and change women's lives concretely and experientially." The feminist political theory which emerges from these areas centers upon sexuality, "its social determination, daily construction, birth to death expression, and ultimately male control."

Gender socialization is the process through which women come to identify themselves as sexual beings, as beings that exist for men. It is that process through which women internalize . . . a male image of their sexuality as their identity as women. . . . Sex as gender and sex as sexuality are thus defined in terms of each other, but it is sexuality that determines gender, not the other way around. She concludes, "Feminism stands in relation to Marxism as Marxism does to classical political economy; its final conclusion and ultimate critique."

Adrienne Rich

The author of "Compulsory Heterosexuality and Lesbian Existence," Adrienne Rich, reminds us, as the article's title implies, that heterosexuality is neither natural nor voluntary.[56] If indeed it were, then women who did not bond with men—independent women, women who loved women—would not have been persecuted. Rich's article is divided into two sections—the first on *lesbian existence*, and the second on the *lesbian continuum*. In the first section Rich addresses the silencing or peripheralization of the lesbian existence. Rich documents this silencing even in women's movement literature, such as Barbara Ehrenreich and Deidre English's *For Her Own Good*.[57] Although Rich picks three publications which have this flaw, she states that it can be seen in other widely read and respected publications. Her point is more eloquently made when she notes that the peripheralization is as damaging to the lesbian existence as is the silencing. The view of the lesbian as *the other* in the women's movement has made many women unable to become aware of and analyze the lesbian continuum.

It is Rich's definition and analysis of the lesbian continuum that provoke criticism. She maintains that the institution of heterosexuality is the primary social force perpetuating male domination. She further suggests that there exists, cross-culturally and transhistorically, a lesbian continuum, that is, a resistance to compulsory heterosexuality through female bonding and the withdrawal of energy from men. Rich's article was so important, albeit controversial, that in a later issue *Signs* printed several critiques of the work. Ann Ferguson and her coauthors take issue with Rich's position.[58]

Two of Rich's premises—heterosexuality is compulsory, and it is the primary source of women's oppression—are attacked by Ferguson and her co-authors. They attack the first premise by pointing to voluntary heterosexual relationships that exist among "single mothers, black women, and women who are economically independent."[59] In so saying, they discount the very real psychological as well as economic pressure upon women to tie themselves to a man even if that tie is for social reasons only. The second premise—heterosexuality is the primary source of women's oppression—is fallacious, according to both Ann Ferguson and Martha Thompson, because it does not make connections between racism, sexism, capitalism, and classism.[60] Both claim that Rich is shortsighted in setting forth this one factor as primary to all women's oppression.

LIBERAL FEMINISM

Liberal feminism speaks a language to which most people in this country can relate, according to Sandra Harding.[61] Such feminists speak about fairness and equality, though by equality they mean that women should be treated the same as men. Their legal strategy is *gender neutrality*, a strategy which has resulted in a father's obtaining child custody or using the threat of such custody as a bargaining chip in divorce negotiations. This contrasts with MacKinnon's view that equality means an end to hierarchy. Liberal feminist organizations focus on electoral politics, including lobbying, as a means to achieve equality for women, a method well within the American tradition. The National Organization for Women (NOW), which is sometimes confused with the entire women's movement, the National Women's Political Caucus, and the National Abortion Rights Action League (NAROL) represent this perspective. Until recently NOW focused completely on the ratification of the Equal Rights Amendment (ERA).

Geraldine Ferraro's nomination for the vice presidency in 1984 was a triumph for liberal feminism. I wondered, as I and my friends wept with joy, if I had been wrong in my view of the obduracy of *phallocracy*. But the response to her campaign, the misogyny her candidacy elicited, the intensity of the opposition to her position on abortion (a response which did not appear in Ted Kennedy's or Mario Cuomo's campaigns, even though they held similar positions) demonstrated the power of the radical feminist analysis.

Betty Friedan is the best-known liberal feminist, and her pronouncements appear in *The New York Times* rather than *Off Our Backs*, a radical feminist monthly newspaper. In 1985 Friedan's article, "How to Get the Women's Movement Moving Again," was featured in *The New York Times* Sunday magazine section.[62] It suggests a new round of consciousness-raising for young professionals having problems "having it all." Friedan favors mobilizing the new professional networks and established volunteer organizations "to save women's rights." By this she means passing laws and issuing executive orders against sex discrimination. Friedan also proposes that women should get off "the pornography kick" and deal instead with "the real obscenity of poverty." She further confronts the illusion of equality in divorce, which leads to the feminization of poverty. Next, she supports women's choice to have an abortion, while eschewing an attack on the Catholic church. She affirms "the difference between men and women" so that women will not be penalized for giving birth to children.[63] In addition, Friedan advocates focusing on the problems of older men; bringing in men and continuing the fight for real political power for women; moving beyond women's issues to work against fundamentalism and for humanism, liberalism, pluralism, and environmentalism.

Friedan does not discuss working to end violence against women. While she focuses most on professional women—unlike both socialist and radical feminists—her program differs most from that of the radical feminists in her desire to bring men in and her silence on the issues of violence against women. Yet she joined with radical feminists and some other liberal and socialist feminists in opposing the judicial erasure of Marybeth Whitehead, who was the biological mother in the so-called surrogate mother case, which awarded the child to the sperm donor, Dr. Stern, who was also known as the biological father.

One way to compare and contrast radical feminist theory with socialist feminist theory is by examining their treatment of a particular issue. I have chosen motherhood since so many feminists are addressing this issue. Feminists are now facing decisions about whether or not to have children; whether to adopt them or bear them; whether to be inseminated or impregnated through heterosexual intercourse; whether

to marry, have children as single mothers, or have them in a relationship with another woman; and what if any reproductive technology should be avoided (other than artificial insemination). These decisions could be avoided when feminists were in their twenties.

At the beginning of the women's movement, some feminists considered the ability to bear children a source or even *the* source of our oppression. That tradition still exists. More recently the mother-child relationship has been considered the paradigm of what relationships should be— nurturing, caring, growth-inducing. It has also been noted that formerly some apparently equalitarian marriages drastically changed as mothers became primary caretakers and lost much of the freedom they once had. Moreover, feminists as daughters realized that their mothers were also women, and if they, as feminists, were concerned with women as a class, their mothers were also members of that class.

To highlight the differing approaches to motherhood, I will compare the concept of motherhood held by radical feminists Judith Arcana[64] and Adrienne Rich[65] with the concept held by socialist feminists Nancy Chodorow[66] and Dorothy Dinnerstein.[67]

1. Arcana and Rich believe that role theory and *patricentric* institutions, respectively, can account for gender behavior. Chodorow and Dinnerstein consider that explanation insufficient. They believe one must invoke psychodynamic constructs to account for such behavior.

2. Rich and Arcana distinguish between the institution of motherhood and the experience of motherhood. Dinnerstein and Chodorow do not.

3. Both Rich and Arcana have an intimate knowledge of feminist scholarship and use it in their work. Chodorow and Dinnerstein not only do not cite such scholarship but are unaware of or unwilling to use the literature on female friendship. Thus they speak of hostility between women,

which they believe stems from socialization by one's mother.

4. Your mother can read Rich and Arcana. But most nonacademic women cannot read Dinnerstein, and certainly cannot read the middle part of Chodorow unless they are familiar with object relations theory. For those who believe that one purpose of feminist theory is to demystify the world for women, accessibility is an important criterion by which to evaluate the feminism of a work.

5. Their solutions are different. Rich and Arcana state that the solution lies with women. Chodorow and Dinnerstein say the solution lies with men, specifically the participation of men in infant care and child care.

6. Mother-blaming is absent from Arcana and Rich and present in Dinnerstein and Chodorow.

7. The criterion for what is evidence is different for the two groups. Arcana and Rich use their own experience; in Arcana's case, she uses a systematic interview with over a hundred women of different classes and ethnicities. Chodorow and Dinnerstein write abstractly, never mentioning their own experience. One of the tenets of feminism is that the personal is political. That is, our lives are our data, and thus women's experience is a valid source of information about women. It is considered more valid than the psychoanalysts' accounts of what their female patients said, which Chodorow considers to be data.

8. Dinnerstein and Chodorow have been widely praised and rewarded by the liberal establishment. Rich and Arcana have not.

9. Dinnerstein and Chodorow recognize men's lack of training for nurturance, but Rich and Arcana go one step further. They note that women reinforce each other in a mothering attitude toward men by using language more appropriately directed toward and about children.

10. Chodorow and Dinnerstein are much less clear about the endemic misogyny in our society. Rich describes misogyny in the history of gynecology, and Arcana does so in her discussion of incest. Rich criticizes Dinnerstein for the ahistoricism exemplified by her use of the term *sexual arrangements*, a term implying voluntarism on the part of men and women. Such a term erases the persecution and systematic violence against women. It also erases those women who lived without men and thus did not "collaborate" with men in making sexual arrangements. Similarly she criticizes Chodorow for ignoring the "practical reasons like witch burnings, male control of law, theology, science, or economic nonviability within the sexual division of labor." Such factors are "glossed over" in accounting for our current subordinated life.

CONCLUSION

If there were more time and space, we would include many other representative works of feminist theory. Surely the socialist feminist literature on housework (e.g., Glazer, 1981; Hartman, 1981) should not be overlooked. Most certainly, we would have used more of Marlene Dixon's work on the triple oppression of women and on professionalism and repression (1976, 1983). In the original version of this paper, I used Nancy C. Hartsock's critique of Marxism in *Quest,* a feminist journal she helped start, but I was told that article was not recent enough. Had I time I would have included her more recent, ovular *Money, Sex, and Power: Toward a Feminist Historical Materialism* (1983). Nor should we omit, at least, mention of Alice Rossi's more recent work integrating biological variables into sociological accounts of mothering and life-cycle stages. These writings are controversial because, in part, they seem to contradict her earlier feminist work, "Equality between the Sexes: A Modest Proposal," which called for androgyny (1964). Undoubtedly, we would have summarized Marcia Freedman's unpublished lectures on feminist morality. And all the other women who have inspired me, such as Mary Daly (1979), Susan Griffin (1981), and Diana E. Russell (1983), should have been included.

However, this paper will have fulfilled its function if it encourages you to read further in this area. I have focused on the work of sociologists, particularly in the section on socialist/Marxist feminists, not only because I am a sociologist but because I truly believe that the sociological variables are most powerful in explaining how and why things happen the way they do in general, and our subordinated condition as women in particular. That too many sociologists do not use this conceptual scheme for this purpose saddens me. It could be said that sometimes sociology appears to suffer from reverse Rumpelstiltskinism, turning the gold of our way of our accounting for and perceiving the world into the straw of academic triviality.

We did not use the work of women of color, but certainly we could have included Audre Lorde's "The Uses of the Erotic: The Erotic as Power" (1978) had we dealt extensively with sexuality or her brilliant *The Cancer Journals* (1980) had we dealt with health issues. In concluding this paper, I realize that I did not include the statement from the Combahee River Collective (1977), a black feminist group named from the conceptualization and guerrilla action of Harriet Tubman. I urge you to read *This Bridge Called My Back: Writing by Radical Women of Color* (1981), and Gloria T. Hull, Barbara Smith, and Patricia B. Scott's *All the Women Are White, All the Blacks Are Men, but Some of Us Are Brave: Black Women's Studies*. While I agree with Audre Lorde (1981) that "it is a particular academic arrogance to assume any discussion of feminist theory in this time and in this place without examining our many differences, and without a significant input from poor women, Black and third-world women and lesbians" (lesbians are included in this paper), perhaps it is because what is called *theory* derives from the aca-

deme, and women of color are predominantly artists, writers, and poets working outside "the groves of academe." I completely agree with Lorde that "The Master's Tools Will Never Dismantle the Master's House" (1979); thus, I tried to make this paper *feminist* theory rather than feminist *theory*. I think the radical feminists are more successful in this enterprise. To the extent that women teaching in Women's Studies departments must be nominated by and tenured in departments representing traditional disciplines, they would be *more* likely to use the master's tools (traditional methodologies) and not to have dismantled the master's house, just patched it up here and there. Thus, the outlook for *feminist* theories emerging from the universities is bleak, although it can be done.

Penelope Seator, a feminist attorney, pointed out at the 1983 Women and the Law Conference that the difference between radical feminist analysts such as MacKinnon and Bart and socialist and liberal feminist theorists such as Chodorow (1978) and Snitow (1983) is that the former describe the world as it is and draw inferences from that analysis. The latter, having the goal of a humanistic, classless, nonracist, nonsexist society, focus their analysis on how to obtain that goal. In so doing, they soft-pedal the horrors of life for women now and in the past, notably the endemic misogyny and violence against women by *men*. When socialist/Marxist feminists confront the issue of the pain of women's existence, that pain is frequently attributed to factors other than or in addition to gender, to class, and to race (but rarely to age). But "seeing women's victimization as *not* socially exceptional marks the feminist argument" (MacKinnon, 1982, 205).

Would that the radical feminist analysis were wrong! Would that gang rape were not a spectator sport! Would that incest and child sexual assault were exceptional, as we once thought! Would that battered women were able to obtain justice in the courts! Would that poverty were not being feminized! Would that all we needed were a piece of the pie, and that the pie were not ptomaine! Would that the liberals were right and more legislation were the answer! Would that the socialists were right and the socialist revolution were the answer! Would that the feminist spiritualists were right, and that feminist ritual and goddess worship would solve our material problems!

Yet, as MacKinnon states, "Feminism relies upon the ultimate possibility of resistance, even though the feminist analysis of the crushing totality of subordination has difficulty accounting for it."[68]

NOTES

1. In 1983 Catharine A. MacKinnon rephrased her definition of feminist theories in the following way: "Feminism has been widely thought to contain tendencies of liberal feminism, radical feminism, and socialist feminism. But just as socialist feminism has often amounted to Marxism applied to women, liberal feminism has often amounted to liberalism applied to women. Radical feminism *is* feminism. Radical feminism—after this, feminism unmodified—is methodologically post-Marxist." Thus MacKinnon considers the divisions of feminism shown in Table 9.1 on pages 252–53 to be "interesting but misleading" because it is divided into those three categories. In her view radical feminism—feminism unmodified—has redrawn the dimensions.

2. Simone de Beauvoir, *The Second Sex*, trans. H. M. Parshbey (New York: Alfred A. Knopf, 1953).

3. Arlie Russell Hochschild, "Inside the Clockwork of Male Careers," in Florence Howe, ed., *Women and the Power to Change* (New York: McGraw-Hill, 1978).

4. Elise Boulding, *Women in the Twentieth Century World* (Beverly Hills, Calif.: Sage Publications, 1977).

5. Jessie Bernard, *The Female World* (New York: Macmillan, 1981), and Bernard, *Sex Roles*

and Social Policy: A Complex Social Science Equation (Beverly Hills, Calif.: Sage Publications, 1979).

6. Estelle Freedman, "Separatism as Strategy: Women's Institution Building and American Feminism 1870–1930," *Feminist Studies* (1979), pp. 512–29.

7. Amy Swerdlow, "Ladies' Day at the Capitol: Women Strike for Peace Versus HUAC," *Feminist Studies* 8, no. 5 (1982), pp. 493–520.

8. Marilyn Frye, "Who Wants a Piece of the Pie?" in Charlotte Bunch, ed., *Quest: Building Feminist Theory* (White Plains, N.Y.: Longman, 1981), pp. 94–100. See also Marilyn Frye, *The Politics of Reality: Essays in Feminist Theory* (Trumansburg, N.Y.: Crossing Press, 1983).

9. Marcia Freedman, "Four Essays on Morality" (Unpublished lectures translated from Hebrew; originally presented at Women's Voice meeting at Haifa, 1980).

10. Dorothy Smith, *Feminism and Marxism: A Place to Be in, a Way to Go* (Vancouver, Brit. Col.: New Star Books, 1977), p. 3.

11. Ibid., p. 30.

12. Ibid., pp. 51, 52.

13. Ibid., p. 26.

14. Ibid.

15. Dorothy Smith, "Women's Standpoint in the Sociological Organization of Knowledge" (Syllabus for a seminar presented at Northwestern University, Evanston, Ill., 1983).

16. Dorothy Smith, "The Experienced World as a Problematic: A Feminist Method" (Paper presented at the Twelfth Annual Sorokin Lecture, University of Saskatchewan at Saskatoon, 1981).

17. Rae Lesser Blumberg, "Gender and Stratification," in Randall Collins, ed., *Social Theory* (San Francisco: Jossey-Bass, 1983). See also Blumberg, *Stratification: Socioeconomic and Sexual Inequality* (Dubuque, Iowa: Wm. C. Brown, 1978).

18. Ibid., p. 23.

19. Ibid., pp. 25–26.

20. Mary O'Brien, "Feminist Theory and Feminist Practice," in Geraldine Finn and Angela Miles, eds., *Feminism in Canada* (Montreal: Black Rose Books, 1982), pp. 251–68. For a more detailed analysis, see also O'Brien, *The Politics of Reproduction* (London: Routledge & Kegan Paul, 1981).

21. Ibid., p. 254.
22. Ibid., p. 257.
23. Ibid., p. 258.
24. Ibid.
25. Ibid., p. 260.
26. Ibid., p. 265.
27. Ibid.
28. Lorenne M. G. Clarke and Lydia Lange, *The Sexism of Social and Political Theory* (Toronto: University of Toronto Press, 1979), p. 36.
29. Ibid., p. 51.
30. Ibid., p. 52.
31. Candace West, "When the Doctor Is a 'Lady,'" in Ann Stromberg, ed., *Women, Health, and Medicine* (Palo Alto, Calif.: Mayfield Publishing, 1981).
32. Catharine A. MacKinnon, "Feminism, Marxism, Method, and the State: An Agenda for Theory," *Signs* (Summer 1983), pp. 635–58.
33. Ibid., p. 517.
34. Catharine A. MacKinnon, "Women as Women in Law: On Exceptionality" in *Feminism Unmodified* (Cambridge, Mass.: Harvard University Press, 1987).
35. Ibid.
36. Catharine A. MacKinnon, "Toward Feminist Jurisprudence," *Stanford Law Review* 34, no. 2 (1982), pp. 703–37.
37. Ann Jones, *Women Who Kill* (New York: Holt, Rinehart & Winston, 1980).
38. Elizabeth Schneider and Susan Jordan, "Representation of Women Who Defend Themselves in Response to Physical or Sexual Assault," *Women's Rights Law Reporter* (1978), p. 149; this article also appeared in *Heresies* 6 (1978), pp. 100–14.
39. MacKinnon, "Toward Feminist Jurisprudence," p. 732.
40. Ibid., p. 730.
41. Catharine A. MacKinnon, "Roe *v.* Wade: A Study in Male Ideology," in J. Garfield and P. Hennessey, *Abortion: Moral and Legal Perspectives* (Amherst, Mass.: University of Massachusetts Press, 1984).
42. See Catharine A. MacKinnon's introduction to Andrea Dworkin, *Right Wing Women* (New York: Perigee, 1983).
43. Ibid.
44. Ibid.
45. Personal communication to the author, 1982.
46. Catharine A. MacKinnon, "Feminism, Marxism, Method, and the State: An Agenda for Theory," *Signs* (Summer 1983), pp. 635–58.
47. Ibid.
48. Ibid.
49. Pauline B. Bart, "A Study of Women Who Were Both Raped and Avoided Rape," *Journal of Social Issues* 37, no. 4 (1981), pp. 123–37.
50. MacKinnon, "Roe *v.* Wade."
51. Ibid.
52. Ibid.
53. Ibid.
54. Pauline B. Bart and Patricia O'Brien, *Stopping Rape: Successful Survival Strategies* (New York: Pergamon Press, 1985).
55. MacKinnon, "Feminism, Marxism, Method, and the State."
56. Adrienne Rich, "Compulsory Heterosexuality and Lesbian Existence," *Signs* 5 (1980), pp. 631–60.
57. Barbara Ehrenreich and Deidre English, *For Her Own Good* (Garden City, N.Y.: Doubleday, Anchor Books, 1979), p. 19.
58. Ann Ferguson, J. Zita, and K. Addelson, "On Compulsory Heterosexuality and Lesbian Existence: Defining the Issues," *Signs* 7 (1981), pp. 158–98.
59. Ibid., p. 171.
60. Martha Thompson, "Comment on Rich's Compulsory Heterosexuality and Lesbian Existence," *Signs* 6 (1980), pp. 790–94.
61. Sandra Harding (Personal communication to the author, 1984).
62. Betty Friedan, "How to Get the Women's Movement Moving Again," *New York Times Magazine*, Section 6, November 3, 1985, pp. 26–28, 66–67, 84–85, 89, 98, 106, 108.
63. Ibid.
64. Judith Arcana, *Our Mothers' Daughters* (Berkeley, Calif.: Shameless Hussey Press, 1979).
65. Adrienne Rich, *Of Woman Born* (New York: W. W. Norton, 1976).
66. Nancy Chodorow, *The Reproduction of Mothering* (Berkeley, Calif.: University of California Press, 1978).
67. Dorothy Dinnerstein, *The Mermaid and the Minotaur* (New York: Harper & Row, 1976).
68. MacKinnon, "Toward Feminist Jurisprudence," p. 720.

In the course of the turbulent period of the 1960s, an older generation of functionalists initiated subtle but often far-reaching changes in "orthodox" theory. Suggesting new twists on traditional ideas incorporating what had usually been taken to be antagonistic theories, these sociologists drew upon Alexis de Tocqueville, Max Weber, Karl Marx, and Jürgen Habermas in their efforts to attain new levels of empirical specificity, a fuller appreciation of *power* and *conflict,* and more probing kinds of *ideological critiques.*

Following in their wake, theorists in the younger generation have taken up a variety of neofunctionalist paths in the United States and Germany. All of them argue for a form of functionalism that is epistemologically multidimensional.

Neofunctionalism responds sharply to the attacks that were leveled at the orthodox tradition, especially from the conflict and interactionist approaches. The lessons of twenty years of debate have now been articulated in a functionalist way. That is as follows: the idea of a system with interrelated parts, the distinction between personality, culture, and society, the sensitivity to differentiation as a master trend—all of these features are the basic fundamentals of functionalist thinking to which the conflict orientation, the interactionist tradition, and the neo-Kantian epistemology have been accommodated.

Within a neofunctionalist framework, materialist reference is never separated from culture or personality; thinking about conflict is intertwined with themes of cohesion; and criticism of society occurs within a multifaceted understanding of social differentiation.

Jeffrey C. Alexander

NEOFUNCTIONALISM
AND MODERN SOCIOLOGY

Sociological theory is at a turning point. The once youthful challengers to functionalist theory are becoming middle-aged. Their polemical lessons have been well learned; as established traditions, however, their theoretical limitations have become increasingly apparent. Despair about the crisis of sociology marked the birth of the postfunctionalist epoch. Now, when this postfunctionalist phase is itself coming to an end, one senses not a crisis but a crossroads, a turning point eagerly anticipated.

Parsonsian sociology, which is also known as *functionalism*, was radically questioned in the 1960s. For a long time it appeared as if its demise was certain, but it has now become clear that this is not the case. The Parsonsian legacy—if not Talcott Parsons's original theory—has begun to be reconstructed. We are witnessing today the emergence of neofunctionalism, not functionalism exactly, but a family relation.

Functionalism was never a particularly good word for Parsons's sociological theory. Its use was more the upshot of intuition and tradition than of theoretical logic. The term evidently emerged from a study group that L. J. Henderson conducted at Harvard in the 1930s. A physiologist deeply affected by biological functionalism and by Vilfredo Pareto, Henderson introduced Parsons, G. C. Homans, R. K. Merton, and other fledgling theorists at Harvard to Walter Canon's powerful use of homeostasis in *The Wisdom of the Body*. Henderson also evangelized for Pareto's general theory, in which systems and equilibrium concepts played prominent roles.[1] Homans moved from here to the functionalist anthropology of A. R. Radcliffe-Brown. Parsons went on to Durkheim and Weber. He began using the term in the late 1930s, implying by it a vague notion of system and interdependent parts, and he made it a central and elaborate feature of his Presidential Address to the American Sociological Association in 1945.[2] Yet if we look at references to functionalism among the younger group of

Harvard-trained theorists in the 1930s and 1940s—George Homans, Talcott Parsons, Robert K. Merton, Bernard Barber, and James Floyd Davis among others—we see quite a bewildering variety of epistemological, ideological, empirical, and theoretical connotations.

Even as functionalism emerged as a major theoretical movement in the late 1940s, Merton set out to strip the term of its ideological implications, its status as an abstract model, and its substantive empirical commitments.[3] He sought to reduce it, via the anthropology of Radcliffe-Brown, to a kind of supermethod. To be functionalist, Merton held, was quite simply to explain causes by effects. But although this response to critics was enormously successful in a diplomatic sense, it was not, it seems to me, particularly helpful theoretically. It had much more to do with the anthropologists' critique of nineteenth-century evolutionary theory than with the actual practice of sociological functionalism in the twentieth century. It did not, in fact, actually describe what the foremost practitioners of functionalism, Merton himself very much included, actually did.

Merton's students, themselves key figures in the first functionalist heyday, provide further evidence for the ambiguity of the term. Lewis A. Coser,[4] Alvin W. Gouldner,[5] and William J. Goode[6] developed a distinctively *left-functionalism*, to use Gouldner's term. They stressed the theory's accessibility to critical and materialist thought and claimed that functionalism was a crucial element for explaining disintegration and social conflict. By the mid-1960s Parsons—the arch integrationist of the tradition—himself denied the functionalist designation, suggesting that his cybernetic emphasis and interchange model made such a static label obsolete. Henceforth, his collaborators and students would refer to their work as *action theory*.

Despite such contradictory usage and internal dissent, *functionalism* seems to be a name that has stuck. I want to take the bull by the horns and suggest that the term indicates nothing so precise as a set of concepts, a method, a model, or an ideology. It indicates rather a tradition qua tradition. Certain distinctive characteristics can, indeed, be adduced fairly by the efforts that have been conducted and criticized in their names. Traditions, of course, are accessible only through interpretation. What follows indicates my own sense of the future direction of this tradition as much as a discovery of its past:

1. Although functionalism does not provide a model in an explanatory sense, it does provide a general picture of the interrelation of social parts, a model in a more descriptive sense. Functionalism models society as an intelligible system. It views society as composed of elements whose interaction forms a pattern that can be clearly differentiated from some surrounding environment. These parts are symbiotically connected to one another and interact without a priori direction from a governing force. This understanding of system and/or "totality" must, as Louis Althusser has forcefully argued, be sharply distinguished from the Hegelian, Marxist one.[7] The Hegelian system resembles the functionalist, but it posits an "expressive totality" in which all of a society's or culture's parts are seen as representing variations on some "really" determining, fundamental system. Functionalism suggests, by contrast, open-ended and pluralistic rather than monocausal determinism.

2. Functionalism concentrates on action as much as on structure. Its conception of action, moreover, focuses as much on expressive activity and the ends of action as on practicality and means. In particular, functionalism is concerned with the degree to which ends succeed in regulating and stipulating means. It seems quite mistaken, in this regard, to equate functionalism with the sociologism of Durkheim or the quasi utilitarianism of Radcliffe-Brown.

3. Functionalism is concerned with inte-

gration as a possiblity and with deviance and processes of social control as facts. Equilibrium is taken as a reference point for functionalist systems analysis, though not for participants in actual social systems as such. It is used in several different ways—as a homeostatic, self-correcting equilibrium, as a moving equilibrium to describe developmental structures of growth and change, and as a partial equilibrium model of the type that John Maynard Keynes used to describe the systemic strains in a capitalist economy.

4. Functionalism posits the distinctions among personality, culture, and society as vital to social structure, and the tensions produced by their interpenetration as a continuous source of change and control. In addition to social or institutional analysis, then, functionalism focuses on a relatively autonomous culture and on the centrality of socialization.

5. Functionalism implies a recognition of differentiation as a major mode of social change—whether cultural, social, or psychological—and of the individuation and institutional strains that this historical process creates.

6. Functionalism implies the commitment to the independence of conceptualization and theorizing from other levels of sociological analysis. Each of these six theses can certainly be identified with other lines of work in the social sciences. No other tradition, however, can be identified with all of them.

It is true, of course, that these are not the only, or even the principal, characteristics of functionalism that are lodged in the mind of social science. Functionalism has been burdened with anti-individualism, with antagonism to change, with conservatism, with idealism, and with an antiempirical bias. Parsons's defenders have usually dismissed this baggage as ideological illusion. In my own work, by contrast, I have found Parsons's functionalist theory to be highly ambivalent and often contradictory.[8]

Every element critics have polemicized against is there, though these elements by no means exhaust the meanings of his work. Parsons's functionalism gave sociologists a lot to choose from. Depending on their intellectual and historical circumstances, they took their choice.

Beginning in the early 1960s, historical and intellectual developments allowed the negative elements in this complex picture increasingly to dominate the collective consciousness of the discipline. By the mid-1970s they had crystallized into a conventional wisdom that froze the functionalist image in time. This was doubly unfortunate, for it was precisely at this time that the most sophisticated interpretations of Parsons's theorizing had begun to change dramatically.

This changing understanding has unfolded over recent years. It has taken place for several reasons. One must look first, ironically, to the very success of the "vulgate." The critical vulgarization of Parsons succeeded in undermining his overwhelming authority. Once this hegemony had been destroyed, parts of his theoretical system could much more easily be appropriated in creative ways. One was no longer viewed as a Parsonsian if one incorporated significant insights from Parsons's work, despite the best efforts of recalcitrant "anti-Parsonsian warriors" to make the anachronistic and polemical label stick. Second, the ideological climate had noticeably cooled. A younger generation of theorists emerged who did not experience the political need to attack the liberalism for which Parsons stood. In the present neoconservative climate, indeed, it is hard to remember how Parsons's social-democratic reformism could have inspired such political hatred and venom. Third, European social theory has begun to grow once again. Without the earlier, exaggerated American attachment to Parsons, the Europeans, especially the Germans, have been able to appropriate Parsons in surprisingly positive ways. Fourth, functionalist theory was, quite simply, a very sophisticated theoretical scheme. Parsons had a genial intelligence matched by few of his peers, or ours. That is the necessary, if not the sufficient, reason why the functionalist tradition still had the makings of a successful sociological theory.

What has been emerging from this reconsideration is less a theory than a broad intellectual tendency.[9] I call it *neofunctionalism* in conscious similitude to neo-Marxism. First, like neo-Marxism, this development has involved a determined critique of some of the basic tenets of the original theory. Second, like neo-Marxism, it has sought to incorporate elements of purportedly antagonistic theoretical traditions. Third, like neo-Marxism, this neofunctionalist tendency is manifest in a variety of often competing developments rather than in a single coherent form. Let me consider each of these parallels in turn.

Neo-Marxism began in the 1950s as a movement of critical reflection on what came to be called orthodox Marxism; it began, that is, as an interpretive genre. What happened was that a series of self-consciously revisionist interpretations "discovered"—in reality, produced—a different Marx. Neo-Marxist interpretation emphasized a radically different periodization of Marx's work, highlighting the significance of the early over the later writings. It found in Marx a very different epistemological framework, emphasizing idealism rather than materialism or Kantianism. It located new, significant intellectual precursors like Hegel, rather than thinkers like Saint-Simon and David Ricardo. It claimed for Marx strikingly different ideological affinities, arguing for a democratic and humanistic Marx rather than a Leninist, authoritarian one.

Over the last decade a similar process of reinterpretation has ensued within, or on behalf of, the functionalist tradition. The ideological rereading has perhaps been the most dramatic. The argument for a nonconservative functionalism, a more conflict-oriented and critical reading, was begun by

leftist theorists like D. Atkinson in the early 1970s, who claimed that Parsons's theory was not fundamentally different from Marx's or even from that of Marcuse, which embodied the theory of the New Left.[10] Other critical theorists, like J. G. Taylor[11] and H. Gintis,[12] who identified even more closely with Marxism, began also to stress the parallels between Parsons and Marx and the critical side of the functionalist approach. The latest development of this influential movement within critical theory is the interpretation that Jürgen Habermas has developed in the *theory of communicative action*,[13] which finds significant liberating elements in Parsons's thought even while it scores his conservatism. Liberal theorists have also contributed to this ideological reevaluation. G. Rocher's early interpretation, for example, stressed that Parsons's theory could rise above its American bias despite Parsons's own personal commitment to it.[14] K. Menzies documented some socialist implications in Parsons's stratification theory.[15] In an extraordinarily revealing reversal of his earlier postion, Gouldner described Parsonsian sociology as contributing to a liberal theory of civil society that could provide a democratic and humanistic alternative to orthodox Marxism.[16]

The most ambitious effort to transform disciplinary understandings of the functionalist *Weltanschauung* can be found in Robert Holton and Bryan Turner's work.[17] As the only major theorist rooted in a society that did not experience the damaging transition from feudalism to capitalism, Parsons has been the only theorist to conceptualize the possibilities of a positive and stable modernity. Compared to Marx, Weber, and Durkheim, Parsons escapes from nostalgia because he sees the moral and communal possibilities of *Gemeinschaft*.

An alternative option is to consider the possibility that *Gesellschaft* permits authentic expressions of values, rather than the "false," or "fetishistic," forms of consciousness diagnosed by exponents of the Frankfurt school. In addition, value pluralism under *Gesellschaft* need be considered neither as a series of narcissistic worlds, in retreat from the public domain, nor as an irreducible battle of Nietzschean wills. Rather it can be conceived as generating a normative basis for the orderly resolution of pluralism and diversity.[18]

My own work on Parsons's ideology has tried to bring out its critical potential, though I have pointed to the much more quiescent view of modern life that develops in his later work.[19]

Most of these theorists have revised the epistemological understanding of Parsons as well, viewing him as much less idealistic than the earlier, established position had claimed. Taylor sees functionalism as giving significant weight to economic and political, not just cultural, factors; and Habermas goes to the extent of criticizing Parsons for an antinormative explanation of political and economic spheres. Menzies, too, sees the later Parsons as all too naturalistic. More recent works, like those of F. Bourricaud[20] and H. P. M. Adriaansens,[21] provide detailed evidence for an anti-idealist epistemology. S. Savage's Althusserian interpretation dismisses the idealist interpretation.[22] Although I have found Parsons's idealism to be, on the contrary, quite debilitating, I have also found that there is a significant multidimensional theme as well.[23] The most ambitious reconstruction of Parsons's epistemology, that conducted by R. Munch, argues that Parsons's Kantian framework allowed material factors free reign while preserving the freedom that comes with a normative bent.[24]

These new epistemological and ideological interpretations clearly call for different precursors, though the construction of a new, intellectual lineage for Parsons has not yet proceeded so far.[25] Whereas Mills linked Parsons to the conservative Hegel, and Gouldner to the English and French antirevolutionary reaction, H.J. Bershady[26] and Munch place him squarely in the democratic and humanistic tradition of Kant. I have linked Parsons to the social-democratic, welfare state tradition of T. H. Marshall and have suggested, in addition, that the more critical strain in his work has roots in the reformist social control tradition of American pragmatism.[27]

Finally, most of these new interpretations of the meanings of Parsons's work have generated a new periodization. The thrust has been to argue against the orthodox position that Parsons's work necessarily improved with age. Habermas and Menzies, for example, praise his earlier writings, but see in the later work a systems bias that involves serious reification. Adriaansens attacks the middle-period work, especially *The Social System*, as a fundamental deviation from the synthetic thrust of the early and later work.[28] I have also suggested that Parsons's essays of the late 1930s and 1940s, because they are more group-oriented and more critical, provide a significant corrective to his later work on social change.[29]

Neo-Marxist interpretation gradually paved the way for social scientific explanation that moved in the same direction. New substantive theory and new empirical work were produced by the older generation of scholars like Eric Hobsbawn and Eugene Genovese, who sought to salvage the Marxian legacy, and eventually by a younger generation attracted to neo-Marxism for intellectual and political reasons. Once again, within functionalism the situation has been much the same. In the course of the turbulent period of the 1960s, an older generation of functionalists initiated subtle but often far-reaching changes in orthodox theory. Suggesting new twists on traditional ideas and incorporating what had usually been taken to be antagonistic theories, these sociologists drew upon Tocqueville, Weber, Marx, and Habermas in their efforts to attain new levels of empirical specificity, a fuller appreciation for power and conflict, and more probing kinds of ideological critiques. Following in their wake, theorists in the younger generation have taken up a variety of neofunctionalist paths. This recent movement, moreover, has not been confined to the United States. The extraordinary revival of Parsonsianism in Germany has, in fact, been a reconstruction of Parsons's legacy in a neofunctionalist vein,[30] providing new substantive theories and empirical explorations (e.g., the work of B. Miebach) of diverse scope and outstanding quality.[31]

All of them, for example, argue for a form of functionalism that is epistemologically multidimensional. A few are overtly critical of idealist tendencies in Parsons's original work, as when Barber argues against the Parsonsians'—i.e., the orthodox—tendency to credit professional groups with purely normative, altruistic interest. Turning Parsons's professional theory against itself, Barber outlines a more synthetic functionalist approach to social control that can incorporate the insights of materialist critics like Eliot Friedson and Jeffrey L. Berlant. Other theorists eschew the critical mode. Whatever Parsons's own inclinations, they themselves start from the assumption that a materialist, or conditional, reference must always be there. Thus Paul Colomy writes about the cultural and political-economic bases of party formation; S. N. Eisenstadt and Neil Smelser argue for the recognition of group self-interest and coalitions explaining social change.

There is also the unmistakable strain of ideological critique. Virtually every theorist pushes functionalism to the left. Several theorists warn against Parsons's optimism about modernization. Norbert Lechner turns Parsons's change theory on its head by converting his focus on the problem of order into a theory of disorder. In this way he can use categories of Parsons's later change theory to investigate fundamentalist reactions to modernization rather than progressive realizations of it. In a similar vein Colomy formulates an approach to differentiation that is as prepared to explain its failure as its success. But this leftward push also takes a specifically Marxian form. Alvin Gouldner argues that functionalist theory must be developmental as well. He uses

Hegel, Marx, and Jean Piaget to develop—within the functionalist vocabulary of Parsonsian theory—an explanatory framework for the transitions between feudalism, capitalism, and socialism. D. Sciulli also elaborates a functionalist-Marxist integration. On the one hand, he suggests that Parsons's empirical generalization about growing collegiality is the necessary complement to Habermas's proposal for consensual and voluntary communication. On the other hand, he insists that functionalist theory is lacking just the kind of normative and critical dimension that a theory like Habermas's can provide.

We can also find in these theorists an argument for an explicit democratic thrust within functionalist analysis. Barber's demand for a commitment to informed consent in the theory of professions is one example; Sciulli's emphasis on the necessity for antiauthoritarian collegiality is another. The most detailed elaboration of the democratic framework that is implied by Parsons's theory can be found in Jeffrey Prager's theory of the public. A differentiated societal community, Prager shows, involves the commitment to a vigorous and democratic public life.

Neofunctionalism, then, responds sharply to the ideological and epistemological attacks leveled at the orthodox tradition. In fact, neofunctionalism can be distinguished from functionalism by its reconstructionist attempt to alter the core of the Parsonsian tradition. Elaborate and revisionist efforts remain; indeed, the emergence of reconstructionist efforts have relegitimized these more moderate, internalist lines of development. It is reconstruction, however, that has established the framework for a neofunctionalism in the contemporary phase. Among those loosely associated with this movement, there is virtually no effort to return to the research program or discourse of the earlier period. A surprisingly large portion of earlier peripheral criticism has been accepted, just as the core itself is being reshaped in a responsive way. From this perspective, neofunctionalism is post-Parsonsian.

Two other major substantive challenges to functionalism have emerged from conflict and interactionist approaches. If anything, neofunctionalist theorists have been even more concerned with responding to these. For instance, where Parsons not only neglected but in effect tried to repress Marx, Alexander makes Marx paradigmatic of the material and instrumental theorizing that he criticizes Parsons for trying to ignore.[32] He sets Weber against Parsons in much the same way, arguing that Parsons underplayed the objectification that for Weber was the necessary dark underside of individuation. In a similar vein Alexander has stressed the symbolic and culturalist elements in Durkheim, playing them off against the culturally reductionist tendencies in the orthodox functionalist concentration on value.[33] Gouldner has treated Marx, Hegel, Keynes, and Piaget in much the same way, stressing their distance from Parsons in the first instance, the need to incorporate their antifunctionalism in the second. His theory of revolution and radical collective behavior has emerged from the reconstructed mix. There has also emerged from within neofunctionalist interpretation significant dialogue with the central texts of the microsociological tradition.

Alexander has emphasized, for example, a collective thrust in George Herbert Mead, Charles Sanders Peirce, and Erving Goffman, and also in the phenomenological theory of Edmund Husserl, Alfred Schutz, and the early Harold Garfinkel, arguing, indeed, that these theoretical resources have been largely ignored by these traditions' contemporary interpreters.[34] These theoretical appropriations are openly present as remedies to the acknowledged shortcomings of orthodoxy, and defend Parsonsianism as a means by which the original, creative, and synthesizing project of neofunctionalism can be advanced.

It is a remarkable fact, which Munch in his commentary has quite rightly underlined, that almost every contribution to neofunctionalism is a conflict theory of one sort or another. Gouldner argues for a third, structuralist dimension to sociological theory because he wants general functionalist reasoning to be specified by historically concrete predictions of strain and contradiction. Eisenstadt argues against the reified approach to system boundaries because he sees them as constructed through conflict and maneuver. Smelser rejects the notion of differentiation being decided by adaptive efficiency in favor of a criterion that resembles hegemonic group interest, defined in ideal and material ways. Colomy makes group conflict the central object of his analysis, insisting that differentiation and conflict are two sides of the same coin. Prager conceptualizes the public as an arena for democratic conflict; Barber inserts a conflict dimension into the professional/client relationship.

These references to conflict, moreover, are often accompanied by an emphasis on contingency and interactional creativity. Peter H. Rossi finds a convergence between the indeterminacy of subsystem exchange and the dialectical tension between subjectivity and constraint that he himself stressed in his own revisions of structuralist theory. Eisenstadt insists on the openness of systemic tendencies to individual choice and group process. Colomy draws upon Eisenstadt's work on symbolic entrepreneurs to elaborate a systematic theory of how voluntary *strategic groups* modify and direct the more structual elements of social change.

What is truly important about these contributions, however, is not that they have taken account of contemporary theoretical developments. It is that they have done so from the point of view of a common tradition; it is this common tradition that allows the whole of each contribution to be more than the mere sum of its parts. *The lessons of twenty years of theoretical debate become articulated in a functionalist way.* The idea of a system with interrelated and relatively autonomous parts, the tension between ends and means, the reference to equilibrium, the distinction among personality, culture, and society, the sensitivity to differentiation as a master trend, and a commitment to independent theorizing—all of these basic fundamentals of functional thinking permeate neofunctionalist theory. Ideological critique, materialist reference, conflict orientation, and interactional thrust can in this way emerge as relatively coherent variations on a theme rather than as a collection of eclectic, completely diverse essays in sociological theory. In the quest for scientific accumulation, the coherence that this kind of coordinated revision provides is a definite advantage. But there are more substantive advantages as well. *Within a neofunctionalist framework, materialist reference is never separated from culture or personality systems; contingency is related to systemic process; ideological criticism of society occurs within a multifaceted understanding of social differentiation; thinking about conflict is interwined with theories of integration and societal solidarity.*

No one knows where such developments will lead, whether a neofunctionalist school actually will emerge or whether, instead, neofunctionalism will shape contemporary sociology in less conspicuous ways. In the past Parsons's controversial reputation meant that even some of the participants in this revival were loath to acknowledge his influence. The movement to reappropriate Parsons in a neofunctionalist way is gaining momentum. Whether it is simply old wine in new bottles or a new brew is something history will decide.

NOTES

1. G. C. Homans, *Coming to My Senses* (New Brunswick, N.J.: Transaction Books, 1984).
2. Talcott Parsons, "The Present Position and Prospects of Systematic Theory in Sociology," in Talcott Parsons, ed., *Essays in Sociological Theory* (New York: Free Press, 1945).
3. Robert K. Merton, ed., *Manifest and Latent Functions: Merton on Theoretical Sociology* (New York: Free Press, 1967).
4. Lewis A. Coser, *The Functions of Social Conflict* (New York: Free Press, 1956).
5. Alvin W. Gouldner, "The Norm of Reciprocity," *American Sociological Review* 25 (1960), pp. 161–78.
6. William J. Goode, "A Theory of Role Strain," *American Sociological Review* 25 (1960), pp. 483–96.
7. Louis Althusser, "Marxism Is Not a Historicism," in Louis Althusser and E. Balibar, eds., *Reading Capital* (London: New Left Review Books, 1970).
8. Jeffrey C. Alexander, "The Modern Reconstruction of Classical Thought: Talcott Parsons," in *Theoretical Logic in Sociology*, vol. 4 (Berkeley, Calif.: University of California Press, 1982), pp. 151–276.
9. D. Sciulli and D. R. Gerstein have documented this dramatic revival of functionalist interpretations, theory, and empirical work in their article, "Social Theory and Talcott Parsons in the 1980's," *Annual Review of Sociology* 11 (1985).
10. D. Atkinson, *Orthodox Consensus and Radical Alternation* (New York: Basic Books, 1972).
11. J. G. Taylor, *From Modernization to Modes of Production* (London: Humanities Press, 1979).
12. H. Gintis, "Alienation and Power: Towards a Radical Critique of Welfare Economics" (Ph.D. diss., Harvard University, 1969).
13. Jürgen Habermas, *Theory of Communicative Action*, vol. 1 (Boston: Beacon Press, 1984).
14. G. Rocher, *Talcott Parsons and American Sociology* (New York: Barnes & Noble, 1975).
15. K. Menzies, *Talcott Parsons and the Social Image of Man* (London: Routledge & Kegan Paul, 1976).
16. A. W. Gouldner, *The Two Marxisms* (New York: Seabury Press, 1980).
17. Robert Houlton and Bryan Turner, *Parsons and Modernity* (London: Routledge & Kegan Paul, 1986).
18. Ibid., pp. 215–16.
19. Jeffrey C. Alexander, "Formal and Substantive Voluntarism in the Work of Talcott Parsons: A Theoretical and Ideological Reinterpretation," *American Sociological Review* 43, pp. 177–98; and Alexander, "Modern Reconstruction of Classical Thought," pp. 128–50.

20. F. Bourricaud, *L'Individualism institutionel* (Paris: Presses Universitaires de France, 1977).

21. H. P. M. Adriaansens, *Talcott Parsons and the Conceptual Dilemma* (London: Routledge & Kegan Paul, 1980).

22. S. Savage, *The Theories of Talcott Parsons* (New York: St. Martin's Press, 1981).

23. Alexander, "Modern Reconstruction of Classical Thought," pp. 8–150.

24. R. Munch, "Talcott Parsons and the Theory of Action," Parts 1 and 2, *American Journal of Sociology* 86, pp. 771–826.

25. Michael A. Faia has written an interesting and revealing echo of that response to functionalist theorizing and its critique. His book—*The Strategy and Tactics of Dynamic Functionalism* (New York: Cambridge University Press, 1986)—responds to critics by defining functionalism as a logic of empirical analysis that studies causes through effects. He suggests that this is much more widely practiced than is usually thought, and argues that it should be taken as the best way to approach structural and dynamic explanations. Faia's impressive book very much reflects the revived interest in functionalism, but its "methodological" definition places it outside of what I call neofunctionalism.

26. H. J. Bershady, *Ideology and Social Conflict* (New York: John Wiley & Sons, 1973).

27. Alexander, "Modern Reconstruction of Classical Thought," pp. 385–87.

28. Ibid., pp. 61–73, 194–211, 259–72.

29. See K. Bailey's efforts to differentiate the ways in which Parsons used equilibrium and to develop a more precise way of talking about systems integration. K. Bailey, "Beyond Functionalism: Toward a Non-Equilibrium Analysis of Complex Systems," *British Journal of Sociology* 35 (1984), pp. 1–18.

30. Jeffrey C. Alexander, "The Parsons Revival in German Sociology," *Sociological Theory* 2 (1984).

31. See B. Miebach, *Strukturalistische Handlungstheorien: Zum Verhältnis zwischen soziologischer Theorie und empirischer Forschung im Werk Talcott Parsons'* (Opladen, West Germany: Westdeutscher Verlag, 1984). This German work brings out clearly what is also a pronounced tendency in the American material. Neofunctionalism sets up "hyphenated" relationships with other traditions, including critical Marxist theory, Weberian thought, Durkheimianism, Freudianism, and so forth. In its orthodox Parsonian phase, functionalism tried to coopt these other classical theories; in the post-Parsonian phase their differences with Parsons's thought seem, to the contrary, positive and fruitful, and functionalist theorists have taken them up once again. This, of course, has also been a striking characteristic of the neo-Marxist movement, which has produced psychoanalytic Marxism, structural Marxism, and existential Marxism, to name the best-known cases.

32. Alexander, "Modern Reconstruction of Classical Thought."

33. Jeffrey C. Alexander, *Twelve Lectures in Sociology* (New York: Columbia University Press, 1988).

34. Ibid.

Sigmund Freud's theory of civilized personality and Karl Marx's theory of capitalist society are examples of emancipatory theories. The aim of critical sociological analysis is to discover in a given structure of domination the contradictions and conflicts which make repression ultimately untenable. It is exemplified in Jürgen Habermas's concept of a crisis of legitimation brought about by the inability of a state-dominated capitalist economy to deliver promised rewards and his vision of a rational society.

Critical theorists hold that reality and alternative utopias are both conditional on practices susceptible to modification. Critical theory as a theory of the foundation and validation of theory is an ongoing activity rather than a set body of knowledge. Critical theorists reject the notion of facts as irreducible entities imprinted on the mind and subsequently grasped and organized by theory. Instead, they shift the epistemological emphasis from the cognitive act to the social production of the cognized world.

Many sociologists have mistakenly adopted the language of natural science and made unwarranted assumptions about lawful regularities. This explains their acceptance of the solidity and relative unchangeability of social structures. The goal of critical theory is to release this grip of constraints through a two-step strategy of taking utopian hopes seriously and testing whether the failure to overcome such constraints derives from invariant features of human action or from persisting relations of power and dominance. This cultural mode of analysis based on the freedom and autonomous activity of humans contrasts with the natural science mode of necessity and constraint.

Critical theory is distinguished from phenomenology and existentialism in its combination of self-reflection with a socially based emancipatory effort. Horkheimer's distinction between traditional and critical theories is important to this definition. Zygmunt Bauman elucidates the link between critical theory and critical practice through a discussion of the relationship between knowledge and human interests. A continuity between everyday knowledge and science is posited, and the concept of emancipatory knowledge is defined.

Zygmunt Bauman

CRITICAL THEORY

THE PROJECT

Critical theory is not, strictly speaking, an alternative sociological theory. It is, rather, a mode of theorizing. Critical theory is not constituted by its opposition to some other body of theoretical assertions, which for the sake of brevity can be given a collective name of *traditional*, *normal*, or simply *non-critical* theory. It is constituted, rather, by bringing theory into the focus of analysis, by refusing to accept its authority without proof, by demanding that the grounds on which this authority is claimed be revealed, and, eventually, by questioning these grounds. Critical theory, in other words, is not a theory in the ordinary sense, but a theory of the foundation and validation of theory. Critical theory is a name of the activity through which the building site is cleared, not the name of any particular building. It may (and should) be considered as relevant to the search of alternative sociological theories only insofar as, once its task

has been accomplished, a substantive sociological theory may be constructed, conscious of its foundations and resting its self-confidence on its constant readiness to examine them.

The term *critical theory* stands, therefore, for an activity rather than a body of knowledge. For this reason the name is potentially misleading, as it may suggest that critical theory is something it is not, and cannot strive to be without violating its own identity and betraying its own principles: a model of the world negating other models, and by the same token sharing their substantive concerns. Critical theory is not in opposition to any theory of the world in particular; it is in opposition to the refusal by any substantive theory to examine its grounds. For this reason it opposes, indirectly, all theory which renders its own validity claim dependent on the concealment of its grounds.

There are several tacit assumptions of knowledge which critical theory forces into the open and articulates as topics of analysis, suspending the acceptance of any theory based on them until these assumptions are discursively redeemed.

First and foremost, it is a set of assumptions related to the status of theory in general, and its relation to its object in particular. More precisely, the beams of critique are first cast upon the very separation of theory and its object. It is assumed that knowledge is knowledge *of* facts; that, in other words, there is a sphere of tough, irreducible facts which the theory tries to penetrate in order to grasp them, capture them, handle them, learn their shape, color, and smell, and reconstitute them later in a verbal account. "Let us first get the facts straight." Theory is a stranger, a visitor in the world of facts—an observer whose wisdom consists in respecting local habits, dissolving his own distinctiveness, trimming whatever is out of place in his behavior. Theory will fulfill its calling only if it respects the facts. It has, after all, little choice: in the encounter between theorizing reason and the facts, only the first is impressionable, vulnerable, and also flexible. As to the facts, they are hardly affected at all by the visit of the stranger; even less likely are they to be impressed by the judgment the visitor might wish to pronounce. In this view, the building of knowledge occurs in the encounter between inquisitive reason and facts oblivious to its presence. Facts go about their daily business unaware of Peeping Tom's curiosity. Wary of disturbing their natural conduct, reason expends its energy on keeping its active impetus in check. The activity specific to reason consists in its achieved passivity; the measure of its success is the faithfulness with which it records the facts *as they are* in order later to reflect, emulate, and reproduce them in theory.

The naïveté of this image of mind as a surface covered with a pliable stuff in which objects leave their exact imprint so that their verbal replicas may be later cast, was first exposed two centuries ago. Immanuel Kant, a German philosopher of the late eighteenth century often described as the first critical theorist, represented cognition as a creative work of reason. In the encounter between reason and reality, facts are not found or discovered, but produced. More precisely, what is produced are facts of knowledge, as distinct from the facts of reality. The latter can be only guessed. For all practical intents and purposes, their presence is merely postulated; we will never approach them directly, and so never satisfy ourselves fully of their existence. What we can be sure of is what we know; but what we know is our knowledge. What is evident to us with a high degree of certainty is what has been already processed by the activity of cognition: that is, facts of knowledge. It follows that in the emergence of knowledge the role of the mind is far from passive. It is, on the contrary, active and crucial. Whatever the reality may be in itself, as an object of theory it is constituted by the work of reason. Our knowledge is therefore a combined product of the object and the subject, of the world and the reason, of things out there and the organizing, ordering, interpreting activity of mind.

Kant's critique of the naive model of passive reason, of which we have presented above only its essential imagery, originated a long chain of philosophical research in the role of reason in the production of knowledge. Kant's imagery determined the theme and set the boundary of the research. It has been directed at the exact nature and degree of the influence exerted by reason upon the process and the results of cognition. It has been accepted that the facts do not exist by themselves; if they do, or insofar as they do, they are not accessible to knowledge; the facts which are so accessible are not given at the outset of the inquiry, preformed in advance; they are products, not the raw materials of theory. In the post-Kantian model of knowledge, the facts have been shifted from input to the output of cognition. The attention of philosophical research has been accordingly focused on the *through-put*, on what is done to the part of the world, subject to the process of cognition, by the cognizing mind. Epistemology—the theory of cognition—has been set apart from ontology—the theory of the world. It has become now mainly an exploration of the activity of the subject. Various aspects of this activity have been singled out as decisive for the shape of knowledge. It has been pointed out that the subject's cognitive interests are selective, that any cognitive effort consists in a differential allocation of relevance to various elements of studied reality, in sharpening the perception of some elements while blinding the observer to some others. It has been pointed out that the previous training of the subject results in a cognitive framework which prearranges the data of experience; their arrangement, therefore, is not derivable from the data themselves, but without a framework no arrangement whatsoever (and, therefore, no cognition resulting in knowledge) would be possible. It has been pointed out, more generally, that unless related by theory to other data, and tied with them into an orderly totality, experience has no meaning—an alternative way of saying that no order can be perceived in the givens of experience unless supplied by theory.

Even when, in loyalty to Kant, the intervening role of the subject was conceived as indispensable and irremovable, it was, more implicitly than overtly, felt as an irritant. The persistent uneasiness found its most spectacular expression in these variants of the sociology of knowledge which thematized the cognitive framework as the pernicious, distorting impact of prejudice, bias, or ideology, and set about exploring the conditions of their elimination. In philosophy proper the dream of finding the way back *to the things themselves* survived all successive refinements of Kantian critique. As a return to pre-Kantian naive sensualism was no more a realistic option; the hope, as in Edmund Husserl's phenomenology, was now attached to the *other side of critique*: perhaps the things themselves may be retrieved from the inside of the subject, if only one suspends all worry about the world outside consciousness and takes the things for what they realistically are: intentional meanings generated by the activity of the *trascendental subject*. The unconvinced rightly indicated that Husserl dodged the issue instead of solving it.

Whether the role of theory is seen as neutral, technical, or partisan and substantive, the post-Kantian critique shares with the naive image of the world embossed in the soft tissue of mind the essential imagery of cognition as a process in which the subject *captures* its object; and the view that the problem of perfecting the cognition is confined to a strategy of making the *grasp* sure, and what is grasped trustworthy. In this sense critical theory steps beyond the Kantian critique of reason.

Critical theory is not, essentially, in quarrel with what the post-Kantian critique of cognition says; its reservations are aimed at what the critique of cognition does *not* say, what it fails to notice or what it voluntarily declares as being out of its concern. The post-Kantian critique was concerned exclusively with such distortion, or formative action, as may be, or must be, accomplished inside the act of cognition by the cognizing subject, moved solely by his or her urge to grasp the object which he or she conceives as complete in itself, as something which has acquired its identity *before* it comes into the focus of his or her cognition. But the post-Kantian critique has by and large assumed that epistemology, the theory of cognition, should not concern itself with this before. That whatever might have happened during this before bears no relevance to whatever epistemology wishes to propose; that, in other words, the problem of the relationship between reason and the world may be translated into the problem of the subject-object relation in the act of cognition. Accordingly, the degree of adequacy, rationality, truth, etc., of knowledge may be fully measured by the analysis of the cognitive act. It is to this self-limitation, to the reduction of the idea of knowledge-production to the cognitive process, that critical theory objects.

In a crude approximation we could say that if critical theory sides with the post-Kantian critique in underlining the active role of the cognizing subject in producing the facts of knowledge in the course of its encounter with the world, it insists also that the world itself, assumed complete at the outset of cognition, has come into being with the active participation of reason. Therefore, the analysis of theory-object relation should go beyond the act in which the theory tries to recapture the world in whose production it took part. Adequacy, rationality, truth, etc., of the theory would depend not just on the success of recapturing effort; it will depend also, and perhaps to a yet higher degree, on the way in which the recaptured objects have been first constructed. A theory which adequately grasps or reflects a poorly constructed world will be still a poor theory. Whatever happened *before* the act of cognition is not, therefore, another matter as far as epistemology is concerned. On the contrary, it must be its part and parcel. It organically and irretrievably belongs with any analysis aiming at the conditions and productive rules of adequate knowledge.

The problem of the relation between reason and the world is, in consequence, translated by critical theory not as a question of subject and object cognition, but as the question of *theory* and *practice*. Theory and practice meet in the act of cognition, when theory strives to explain and to interpret practice, to make sense of it; but they meet as well in the process of labor, when the practice as it comes later within the sight of cognizing subject is brought into being and made into a potential object of cognition. In other words theory both produces and (intellectually) reproduces practices. Before theory can err in the act of reproduction, it might have already been charged with a still more serious weakness: with producing

wrong practice. No set of exquisite cognitive tools will then repair the results.

Critical theory shifts the epistemological emphasis from the cognitive act to the social production of the cognized world. It allows for the possibility that the world itself, not only its reflection in theory, may be untrue. This may happen when a wrong theory is applied to its construction. A theory which insists that its test should be confined to the framework of cognition may therefore, contrary to its intention, perpetuate and aggravate the error. It may do so simply by elevating the world as it is to the status of ultimate authority to which all knowledge should submit, and which theory has no tools to evaluate. The world, like nature, would be then neither true nor false, neither right nor wrong, neither good nor evil.

If the world which theory strives to recapture is recognized, however, as practice, untenability of the latter stance becomes easy to expose, and the way to the theoretical critique of the world is reopened. It can be seen then that any form the world-practice takes on in its history bears a cumulative imprint of previous practices guided by past theories. These practices and theories, like all practices and theories, were selective; they actualized some possibilities while leaving behind, and often repressing, others. They produced in the result a one-sided, mutilated world in which alternative options are not easily visible. It is a world which hides as much as it reveals. It is a living memorial to a limited historical practice, inheriting in full all its wrongs. It has already forged human potential. To take it as the ultimate criterion of truth would be like accepting counterfeit coins as the currency standard.

Unlike other theories, critical theory will not be, therefore, satisfied with the optimally faithful reproduction of the world "as it is." It will insist on asking, "How has this world come about?" It will demand that its history be studied, and that in the course of this historical study the forgotten hopes and lost chances of the past be retrieved. It will wish to explore how come that the hopes have been forgotten and the chances lost. It will also refuse to accept that whatever is, is of necessity; it will suggest instead that the structures be explored which perpetuate what is and by the same token render the alternatives unrealistic. It will assume, in other words, that until the contrary is proved, reality of some attributes of the world and utopianism of their alternatives are both conditional on the continuation of some practices which, in principle, can be modified or altered. For critical theory the universally accepted inconclusiveness of our knowledge derives not only from the notorious, but removable, imperfections of our cognitive efforts but also from the yet unused potential of human historical practice, and from the resulting inconclusiveness of the world itself, from the fact that its stubborn solidarity is always a reality "until further notice."

Surely the reader for some time now must have wished to object: we cannot say things like this about the world! The world is subject to laws and regularities which are tough and permanent not just from the perspective of a single cognitive act but also from the vantage point of the total human history. Possibly you meant only the world of human beings? So-called man-made institutions, like political forms, habits, beliefs? But even if only this part of the world was meant, should we not assume that a lot in it is very much like nature, that is, beyond human control and practicably unchangeable? Something which ought to be treated with respect, obeyed rather than tinkered with?

This objection is by no means unwarranted. On the contrary, it draws its justification from thinking habits firmly entrenched in the wake of the triumphant ascent of modern science. This science was, after all, born of the assumption that the world is not a haphazard product of whimsical and unpredictable divine will, but a precision clockwork with repetitive, regular, and calculable movements; that however important might have been the role of the Great Designer who conjured up the world clock and set it in motion, it has no bearing on its further rotation; the mechanism of the world is now ruled by its own irresistible and immutable laws, and its movements, unlike godly intentions, can be unmistakably computed and predicted. The assumption allowed Nature (*natura*, the created) to be fully described without any but ritualistic and otherwise inconsequential reference to the will of its Creator. The completeness, the self-sufficiency of nature guaranteed the realism of the ultimate end of cognitive efforts: the attainment of absolute (to wit, full and unassailable) truth. Nature came to mean reality that can be intellectually reproduced in a language that does not contain words like *intention, motive, will*, and similar terms referring to the admittedly irregular domain of subjective choice.

This language of natural science discourse developed in the course of the seventeenth century. By the eighteenth century, the time of the Enlightenment, it was firmly established as the dominant, authoritative, and intellectually attractive mode of world perception. This language was well geared to the suddenly changing fortunes of western Europe—a relatively obscure corner of the world fast becoming an economically and militarily potent territory reaching for world domination. First encounters with distant lands and peoples revealed the unsuspected superiority of Western armor and know-how; indeed, that superiority seemed so decisive that the rest of the world appeared to the Western explorers as a vast, empty expanse ready for mastery, control, and exploitation. The cramped, overcrowded world of the late Middle Ages rapidly turned into a universe of limitless opportunity in which only human knowledge and skill set the (temporary) boundaries to improvement. The practice of expansion dethroned the overpowering Divine Will playing the world as an instrument of punishment and source of calamity. Instead, the world appeared as a mechanism which with sufficient knowledge can be used for right and profitable purposes. The image of the world as a law-governed nature reflected the new European bid for mastery and control. Respect for the objective necessities of Nature was a corollary of the growing self-confidence of an expansive society aspiring to the control of the world.

It was said above that in the new image of nature the willing, benevolent, or vindictive God had been reduced to a ritualistic incantation. From Newton to Kant the pioneers of the modern view interpreted the study of natural laws as the revelation of God's rational plan and purpose. But this interpretation had little bearing on the substance of the argument. And yet there remained a vast field of experience which ill fitted the image of a morally indifferent, monotonous, and inexorably lawful nature—an experience which could not be easily articulated in a language devoid of concepts referring to subjective will, erraticism, and choice. This was the field of human behavior. Observed at close distance, human actions appeared wayward and obstreperous, lacking the majestic regularity of nature; the difficulty in establishing over this behavior a control as strict and reliable as that gradually extended over nonhuman nature was perceived as the *free will* of individuals; as the presence of an extra factor of a kind different from the laws of nature for its ineradicable contingency and unpredictability. A practical obstacle to the thrust for control and mastery, this factor was a major irritant for the unified vision of a law-abiding world.

The difficulty was never solved in either a practical or a theoretical sense. Instead, it turned into a lasting source of tension and controversy in the Western imagery of the world. On the one hand, there was a continuous effort to develop an argument proving that, in spite of the self-guided conduct of individuals, the development of society as a whole is ruled by necessary laws which cannot be changed by humans, singly or severally. French economist Claude-Frédéric Bastiat spoke of the *digitus Dei* (God's finger) which guides human action without the actors being aware of it. Montesquieu sought in a stubborn and immutable natural environment the determinant of ostensibly free human choices. Adam Smith wrote of the "invisible hand," which causes the confused bustle of selfish individuals to promote an end which was no part of anybody's intention. Kant, and Georg F. W. Hegel after him, located the rational and inexorable design of the universe in nature or in universal history. The *should* was redefined as the work of the world rather than moral duty. Marx presented the apparently free domain of human thought and communication as an epiphenomenon of economic activity, which is intrinsically the kingdom of necessity. Engels elaborated the difference between individual actions, which are, in principle, conscious and willed, and their ultimate consequences, which are as a rule unintended. On the other hand, doubts never ceased to be voiced as to the suitability of the *natural mode* to the understanding of human reality. It has been stressed over and over again that since human action is guided by purposes, motivated, geared to ends which humans set for themselves, it cannot be, after all, described in a desubjectivized language. Subjectivity is neither an epiphenomenon nor a factor visible only at close distance but receding into insignificance once our vision extends to embrace wider tracts of space or time. It is an irreducible attribute which defies the natural mode and demands a distinct cognitive attitude.

For the sake of brevity, and not without a risk of oversimplification, we can describe the postulated alternative to a natural mode as a cultural mode. Unlike the first, the latter emphasizes in human action the element of freedom rather than constraint and necessity; motive rather than cause; and individualized meaning rather than generalizable regularity. The cultural mode unites the practice of autonomous activity with the vision of a purposeful, choosing character of the human life process. It underlines the creative rather than the merely reproductive role of learning, interaction, and communication. It posits the human condition as flexible and potentially open to change even in its seemingly most resilient and persistent aspect. Insofar as motive and intention are irremovable constituents of phenomena perceived as cultural, such phenomena may be influenced and modified in the way motives and intentions normally are—in the course of discussion and argument. Cultural phenomena are products of human choices; they have a history with an appearance of determinatedness arising merely from the irreversibility of past choices, and an uncertain future as a result of the essentially argumentative mechanism of motivational change.

To avoid confusion, it is better to repeat that the two modes contrasted above are analytical types and not descriptive categories; and that what they typify are cognitive attitudes, not parts of objective reality. Once elements of reality have been classified into sections distinguished by the application of one or another of the two cognitive modes, they can be later approached by a mode different from the one which served as the basis of their classification. Indeed, repeated efforts have been made to articulate phenomena, already classified as cultural, in a way typical of the natural mode. Thus sociology as well as anthropology has been for many years dominated by the effort to reveal the elemental, supraindividual character of culture; to discover culture's inner, objective logic; to lay emphasis on the self-perpetuating inertia of cultural systems; to describe the cultural process in a way which excludes intention and argument as a significant factor of reproduction or change. The confusion of the analytical with the descriptive, of the attitudes of cognition with the attributes of its object, has rendered the original theoretical and practical problems underlying the nature/culture distinction hardly redeemable, and has forced them to seek alternative articulations. (We can understand, for example, phenomenology or existentialism as alternative accommodations for the problems evicted from their original abode.) None of the alternatives, though each for its own reason, appeared satisfactory. This is why, in spite of the long and yet unfinished record of confusion, it is preferable to reclaim the original ground rather than follow the central dilemma of human existence into the obscurity of philosophical exile.

The original objection which prompted the above considerations stemmed from the commonsensical observation that some parts of human experience are somehow better fit for interpretation in the natural mode, while other parts equally obviously call for the application of the cultural mode. There are many elements of experience where we normally do not hesitate in selecting, almost automatically, one cognitive mode rather than its alternative. Thus when trying to capture or understand what happens to acids or alkali in a testtube, to compute the carrying capacity of a bridge span, or to account for the hereditary transfer of family traits, we employ a language which does not contain reference to intentions, motives, or purposes. Such a language does not allow for the possibility that a decision made by genes, steel beams, or chemicals was a factor among determinants of what has happened to them. That language is productive only of such accounts as render the accounted-for observations independent of the internal view the objects in question might or might not have of the events they have been a part of. (This feature of natural mode language makes it difficult for us to articulate, much more to comprehend, the most recent discovery of the unqualified indeterminacy on the subatomic level of physical reality.) On the other hand, when attempting to understand the demotion of a public person, the

failure of a friend to turn up at an appointed time, or the endurance of a long-
distance runner, we infallibly and
unhesitatingly use the language of the cultural mode—a language in which terms like
purpose, *will*, and *passion* loom large. The accounts this language generates are never
complete unless they articulate a hypothesis concerning the internal view of the person whose conduct we try to make sense of.
To give an account of an event in the language of the cultural mode is to spell out its
meaning; such an account always tacitly assumes that the event in question could not
happen if not for the application of will—
that is, it allows for the possibility that the
will could not be applied. In the language
of the cultural mode, we constitute the human object, whose behavior we wish to interpret, as an autonomous, self-conscious
source of determination.

This distinction is, again, best grasped in
its ideal-typical form; accordingly, it is least
controversial when projected upon radical
extremes of experience. But a considerable
part of experience does not fall into one of
the extremes. The greater the distance from
the analytical poles, the wider the field for
ambiguity and controversy. We can only recall the ongoing and inconclusive debate
between the so-called Whig version of history, which sees the development of societies as the march of reason and rational
argument, and the Tory version, which interprets history as the work of invisible and
inscrutable forces with historical actors as
their unsuspecting agents. Close to the extreme ranges, the injudicious choice of the
cognitive mood is easy to expose and hard
to defend—like, on the one hand, theologi-
cal interpretation of the laws of physical
universe and, on the other hand, the be-
havioristic explanation of the individual
act. But in the wide middle stretch between
the extremes, the freedom of choice between the two modes is considerable, and
an argument raised against one or the other
mode is most likely to remain inconclusive.
In other words, if nature and culture as an-

alytical types can be sharply and ever more
precisely defined, the borderline between
them, when applied as empirical, descriptive categories, is bound to remain vague
and contentious.

BASIC CONCEPTS

Critical theory is prominent for its tendency to culturalize the interpretation of
the human world. It makes a point of not
taking nature's hold for granted. To paraphrase the famous legal principle, for critical theory an aspect of human existence is
cultural unless proved natural. Cultural
theory accepts as its constant working hypothesis that even most obstinate necessities may well be artifacts of historically
made cultural choices that can be challenged. If the hypothesis is true, then the
exposure of the cultural essence of ostensibly natural facets of the human predicament is an important and urgent task, as
the imposition of the natural mode may be
itself a crucial factor in concealing and suppressing possibilities of a better society.

Indeed, between the natural mode of
cognition and the naturelike social situation, there is a looplike, dialectical interaction. Application of the natural mode is
painless and uncontroversial as long as its
object's conduct manifests repetitiveness
and regularity. In the case of human objects, such a regularity can be only achieved
by an effective repression of a great number
of alternatives. This, in turn, more often
than not includes the application of
coercion—physical or mental. It takes a lot
of pain to smother the intrinsically refrac-
tory propensity of human activity. As Barrington Moore put it with remarkable
cogency:

[T]he assumption of inertia, that cultural and social continuity do not require explanation, oblit-
erates the fact that both have to be recreated
anew in each generation, often with great pain
and suffering. To maintain and transmit a value
system, human beings are punched, bullied, sent
to jail, thrown into concentration camps, ca-

joled, bribed, made into heroes, encouraged to read newspapers, stood up against a wall and shot, and sometimes even taught sociology.

As a rule of thumb, we can say that with the growth in the volume or efficiency of coercion the plausibility of the natural mode also grows. Routine monotony of behavior is always enforced. It requires a forceful and continuous repression of alternative responses to repetitive situational settings. As long as the repression remains effective, the conduct of its objects is indeed amazingly regular and as such can be calculated and predicted with a negligible margin of error. It is strikingly like the conduct of nonhuman nature. Its interpretation *modo naturae* retains, therefore, its credibility. We have few reasons to doubt, for instance, that effectively tamed slaves are more animal than human, driven as they are by outside pressures and reacting to them in a boringly predictable manner. We easily believe that the indigent confined to poorhouses are moved solely by laws of nature, and thus could—and should—be goaded into the right demeanor by the sheer manipulation of external conditions. We can believe, at least for a time, that the frightened, disoriented migrant workers clinging convulsively to their fragile chance of survival are fully creatures of nature, reacting in a dull, machinelike fashion to the visual and acoustic stimuli cleverly arranged by their supervisors. We can believe, as long as women docilely consent to their confinement to the cozy little world of kitchen and bedroom, that they are somehow closer to nature and less artificial, that their animal self is closer to the surface and harder to domesticate or conceal.

 The credibility of nature-mode interpretations is, therefore, an outcome of successful oppression. But once established and gotten hold of human imagination, these interpretations turn into powerful factors of reproducing and perpetuating the oppression which made them credible. More precisely, they become a major obstacle standing in the way of exposing the empirically observed regularity as oppression. As long as these interpretations remain in force, the sheer repetitiveness of the oppressed objects' conduct effectively hides the oppressive determinants of reality instead of indicating their presence. The validity of nature-mode interpretations must, therefore, be challenged and called to prove its case against the humanity of its objects *before* the oppression which is simultaneously its cause and effect can be sapped. It must be challenged, in consequence, *before* the empirical sources of its legitimation dry out.

The successful challenge of the nature-mode interpretation is a necessary condition of success in fighting the oppression which lies at its foundation. The practical opening up of repressed human potential depends, therefore, on the intellectual redemption of the cultural roots of the human condition. Theory, therefore, is a serious matter. It reveals just how serious it is once it refuses to follow slavishly the petrified product of its own past activity. That is to say, when it reclaims its own priority over practice—its ability to dissolve the ostensibly tough and indomitable bone structure which consigned the limits of practical freedom. Theory becomes such a powerful solvent of naturelike constraints once it builds its strategy on the assumption that, unless proved false, the hypothesis that human condition is culturally made and can be culturally unmade must be believed to be true.

The validity of such a cultural mode of interpretation can be confirmed only if it is demonstrated that the part of human reality which is its object owes its *materiality*, its apparently necessary character, to the forceful suppression of discursive challenge. Practically, this can be confirmed only negatively; i.e., if the discourse of the normative foundations of reality is initiated and if it eventually succeeds in changing the shape of reality. All reality, whatever its foundations, is perceived as *reality* insofar as it is experienced as constraint. People call reality whatever is revealed as an obstacle to their will. Discovery of reality is unthinkable unless people first set purposes for their action and then act to attain them, as the German philosopher Arthur Schopenhauer pointed out a century and a half ago: by defining themselves as *I wish*, human beings discover the *objective world*—a term they coin to denote resistance to their will. Without first wishing, the constraining impact of the world can well pass unnoticed and successfully evade challenge. If wishing is suppressed, reality becomes invisible. The call to realism—the call to set human sights low, not to fight difficult or uncertain battles, not to dream of never-never (thus far) lands—is in its practical consequences, even if not in its intentions, a defense of the current constraints by *deproblematizing* them and preventing them from turning into topics of discussion. The hold of reality is inversely related to its visibility. The less visible these constraints are, the more potent, lasting, immutable, and real do they become.

To release the grip of constraints requires, therefore, a two-step strategy. First, the hopes once discredited by defeat and subsequently cast into disdain as utopias must be redeemed and awarded at least a provisional credit. When fed into human practices, they bring the actors into a confrontation with the resistance of the world and expose the exact nature of the world as constraint. Second, once this happens, the continuing resistance of the world must not be interpreted as a clinching proof that its present state cannot be transformed. The task still remains of testing whether the failure to overcome constraints derives from invariant features of human action that are not given to discursive renegotiation, or whether it has been temporarily effected by the persisting relations of power and dominance, hiding behind the yet unproblematized forms of oppression. The failure is, therefore, an invitation to further testing and the extension of analysis into the regions heretofore glossed over.

This is, in rough outlines, the stance taken by critical theory. Its strategy is often condensed into the postulate of *self-reflection*. Indeed, self-reflection is an indispensable and crucial factor in the revelation of structures owing their power to the concealment of their presence, and in the ensuing *pulverization* of allegedly solid realities. When reduced to self-reflection, critical theory is, however, insufficiently articulated. It is then indistinguishable from a host of mostly philosophical theories which also put their stake on self-reflection as a powerful solvent of alleged realities.

In particular, critical theory must be distinguished from phenomenological and existentialist currents in modern philosophy, with which it shares a number of propositions and strategies and for this reason is frequently confused. Phenomenology sees in self-reflection the royal road to the purification of truth from sedimentations of mystifying practices. It advocates a chain of *transcendental reductions*, consisting in *bracketing* or *suspending* commonsensical assumptions about the existence of things, of historically and culturally contingent *oughts*, and of all other extrinsic bodies contaminating the subjective world of a real, empirical person. Phenomenology hopes that by so doing the empirical person can dig through into the usually hidden realm of *transcendental subjectivity*—subjectivity which is nobody's in particular subjectivity, which is truly universal and immune to the vagaries of history or cultural whims. The phenomenological version of self-reflection is, therefore, a program of self-transcendence attainable through philosophical analysis. In the last account, it is a recipe for individual rumination. It does not include stipulation of any other activity except for the activity of cogitation. On the contrary, it calls for a decisive disengagement from the world. The emancipation it offers is a liberation *from* the world, rather than *of* it. Critical theory doubts whether the two tasks can be separated; whether one can be accomplished in disregard of the other. However deeply humans may descend in their effort to reach the pure essences suspended in the aseptic void of transcendental subjectivity, they will find always in the end their *socially* produced selves. Beyond the social, there is only nothingness; with the social *thought away*, there is no thought. The emancipatory effort must, therefore, engage the social essence of human existence, and this means coming to grips with the network of human interaction in which truth or untruth are communicatively produced and reproduced. Recovery of truth means undermining the social grounds of the repression of human potential—and this requires theory as well as practice, the work directed to restructuring the condition of interhuman communication. The road to truth leads not through further suppression, but through untying people's active interest in their life-world.

The emancipatory project offered by existentialist philosophy goes perhaps further still toward articulating freedom as the matter of individual self-redemption. It boils down, by and large, to the transformation of *in itself* (an objectified existence, defined for me from outside, an existence into which I have been cast, in which I am acted upon, looked at, told what to do, and judged) into the *for itself* (the subjectivity restored, my life is again controlled by me, subordinated to the project I have pondered and chosen). In the writings of the most prominent representatives of the existentialist current in philosophy, Martin Heidegger and Jean Paul Sartre, this transformation is presented as a single-handed job. In fact, it can be only performed single-handedly or not at all. One can hardly think of external, social conditions which would be particularly propitious to the task. Indeed, the success of self-redemption is measured by the degree to which any external, social conditions have been rendered irrelevant. Because success does not depend on the structure of the external world, it does not matter what the content of the emanci-

pating project is. Any project will do, providing it is freely chosen and uncompromisingly adhered to. The critical edge of existentialism is turned inward; its moral message is reduced to the intense preoccupation with its own autonomy combined with disbelief in the chance of designing a world that offers more congenial conditions for autonomous persons. Existentialism, in the last resort, cedes the world *out there* to the natural mode, confining the cultural mode to an intellectual operation which, in the middle of an essentially strange world, the ego should commit upon itself. Again, critical theory doubts the viability of the existentialist program and rejects its defeatist withdrawal into the self. Critical theory points out that it is the matter of socioculturally produced conditions whether individual autonomy is identified as the emancipatory topic; it is the matter of such conditions whether the emancipation, however defined, is easier or more difficult to achieve. We would expect that the image of the *good life* providing a blueprint for improvement rarely takes account of the totality of human possibilities. More often than not this image is imposed as, simultaneously, the result and a factor of domination and repression. The model of improvement can outgrow its normally maimed, truncated form only if the repressive situation is transcended. This, in turn, as we remember, depends on the progress made by the discursive redemption of the repressed aspect of human potentiality—a social, interactive process by definition. The social character of the process assures the substantive character of the emancipatory model which will eventually emerge. It is the very disregard for the validating power of interaction which left existentialism with no choice but a purely formal moral injunction.

The self-reflection of critical theory differs, therefore, from similar concepts developed by phenomenology and existentialism in that it designates a collective, interactive, and communicative practice. It grounds its hope in the effectivity of self-reflection, not on the intellectual prowess of the individual, but on the reality-producing ability of a self-conscious collective practice. This ability turns into a moral force once this practice reaches the degree of self-awareness which gives it complete mastery over the situation, the possibilities it contains, and the decisions taken on the basis of their examination. Critical theory sees itself as an important constituent of such self-awareness of emancipatory practice. As one of the founders of critical theory, Max Horkheimer, declared in his famous comparison of traditional and critical theories, "The object with which the scientific specialist deals is not affected at all by his own theory. Subject and object are kept strictly apart.... A consciously critical attitude, however, is part of the development of society." Critical attitude is such a part since it penetrates areas normally guarded by the protective fence of silence. It questions the grounds of habitual recognition of necessities and impossibilities and, by transforming usually tacit and uncontrolled assumptions into the topic of discourse, it opens new, previously unconsidered, alternatives. This multiplying of possibilities has emancipatory significance. Its effect is the enhancement of freedom. The fuller clarification of the genuine meaning of tradition, the resurrection of its hopes, and keeping its promises alive, all these make the future perhaps less certain, but more hospitable for freedom. The exposure of the relations of dominance which hide behind the *naturalness* of social reality and praise for adjustment to the necessary are in themselves a powerful step toward the realization of a self-conscious history.

Critical theory is not just another moral indictment of an oppressive reality. After all, the remarkable resilience of any social reality does not rest on moral self-glorification. People submit to domination because primarily they believe in the uncontrollable and unassailable power of *facts* and because they strive to be *rational* and

aim at *realistic* targets—not because they necessarily accept the superiority and higher intellectual or moral virtues of their superiors. This has been particularly true during the long period of market capitalism, in which the outcomes of human labor solidified into a network of seemingly *natural* economic necessities, able to impose the needed pattern of behavior without recourse to ideological legitimation, by the sheer pressure of a reality which offered survival only in exchange for submission to the rules of the game. Under these conditions emancipation is not a matter of a moral battle or of a struggle between ideologies. It is, rather, a matter of the thorough study of the process normally exempt from examination: the process through which the respect-claiming reality is produced and reproduced. By the same token, the otherwise unconscious process becomes a potential object of conscious control. Critical theory, to quote Horkheimer again, "considers the overall framework which is conditioned by the blind interaction of individual activities...to be a fiction which originates in human action and therefore is a possible object of planful decision and rational determination of goals." Critical theory is not an ethical system, an ideology, a philosophy of human nature, or a platform for political action. Instead, it is a program of serious study of society. It does not intend to offer advice as to the substance of decisions the actors of history ought to take—apart from its belief that unhampered depth study of the grounds of the situation in which historical action takes place may render all historical decisions more conscious than before.

Clarification of the intellectual and situational grounds of historical action, making these grounds a topic of study and debate rather than taking them for granted or repressing them into silence, is a necessary condition of self-conscious history.

It is not, however, its sufficient condition. Can we reasonably expect that the sheer availability of such a clarification will increase people's control over their own history? Set them on the road to what they decide is akin to their idea of the good life? Can we hope, following the eighteenth-century philosophers of the Enlightenment, that the power of reason and argument will prove stronger than the entrenched powers resting on the control of the means of survival and life fulfillment? Once asked, these questions immediately expose the vulnerable points of the critical theory project. Questions of this kind can be addressed to any theory which offers an interpretation of the human condition, but while other theories may disregard them and continue with their business unperturbed, critical theory must take them seriously, since it knows of no criterion of its own validity except the practical transformation of historical process.

Most writers within the orbit of critical theory sensed, and made this explicit, that physical and economic oppression are not the only powerful forces standing in the way of emancipation. Perhaps still more vexing is the likelihood that people who are to gain most from the advance of critical theory will be reluctant to accept its findings. Critical theory, as it were, relativizes what seems to be absolute, pulverizes the solid contours of reality, transforms certainties into a mere game of chance, strips external pressures of their authority and brings them into the reach of human control. This has three consequences, each likely to cause resentment and none experienced as psychologically pleasant and satisfying. First, as Theodor W. Adorno and Max Horkheimer indicated in their study of the *Dialectic of Enlightenment*, the western European cultural tradition which gained dominance in the eighteenth century instilled in the psychic makeup of Western people a constant fear of the unknown: Adorno and Horkheimer described the Enlightenment as "mythic fear turned radical," this fear emanating from "the mere idea of outsidedness." Just as pre-

Enlightenment myths tended to compound the inanimate with the animate, the Enlightenment attempted, with success, the reverse. The result was a culture of the *universal taboo*, in which everything which resists *naturalization*, which cannot be easily routinized, schematized, and modeled as a mechanism, is repressed in practice and banned in theory. Its possibility is not admitted. The obstinate manifestations of its presence, as always in the case of tabooed phenomena, have a terrifying effect. *Horror vacui* is the psychological defense of the Enlightenment project. Fear and panic having been the learned reactions to the project's failure, most people would experience the mechanized world as a protective shield as much as an oppression. Far from resenting it, people will run to its defense. Its defeat they will perceive as a personal disaster. Second, the life process in the world we know consists of an incessant, always difficult, and sometimes heroic effort of adaptation—of designing a bearable, possibly gratifying *modus vivendi*. Most people like what they have won in a hard, uphill struggle. They come to cherish it and they would not be happy for its loss. What they would resent more than anything else is the devaluation of their life achievement of which they are proud and from which they draw their self-dignity. To learn that the task as they set it for themselves, the task to which they dedicated their life and by which they measured their life's success, was a result of self-deception and, therefore, misdirected, would be indeed a high price to pay for the offer of liberation. We would therefore expect the would-be beneficiaries of critical theory to develop vested interests in perpetuating the fiction of a mechanized, naturelike, extrinsic world composed of unchallengeable necessities and irrefutable facts. Third, the exposure of an essentially pliable, artificial nature of the world and the widening of the perceived range of human choice makes life a moral responsibility. It is less easy then to lay the blame for our action on indomitable external necessities. The self-absolving excuse, "I had to do it," is not available, and if resorted to, sounds hollow. Life history is redefined as a series of personal choices, and the only allegedly indestructible constraints limiting the next choice are consequences of previous choices. This vision of life puts the responsibility fairly and squarely on the actor's shoulders. It calls for an unfading vigilance, a continuous self-scrutiny, a never relenting effort of self-correction, a constant urge to transcend the horizons already reached and to challenge the ever new ultimate frontiers of yesterday. Intense ethicality, unabated by the tranquilizing drug of divine will, natural law, or historical inevitability, makes life a heroic task. Again it is unlikely that the demand for this kind of life will be massive and enthusiastic.

Unlike the eighteenth-century philosophers, critical theorists do not believe, therefore, that the insights of reason will be embraced and followed automatically. They do not believe, either, that history by its own relentless logic will conquer the world for the rule of reason. They are skeptical about Marx's hope that the unique position of the proletariat, the class of the deprived, the universal sufferer most painfully experiencing the incongruities of an oppressive world, will make it keen to absorb the truth and defy the falsified reality. They doubt the wisdom of Max Weber's expectation of an increasingly rational world, warning against the confusion of the rationalization of mastery and domination with the rational self-designing of life. With economic and political domination safely entrenched behind the protective walls of physical inertia, the prospects of emancipation are bleak. The call to liberty may fall on deaf ears. The chance of emancipation may be seen as a threat. Critics may be cast at best as troublemakers, at worst as insane.

Reflecting on radical critics of the past, Adorno and Horkheimer noted that they might have spoken the truth, but that they were "not in step with the course of social life," and because of this they were forced

into the role of madmen. This was partly for the original intention to keep their ideas pure and uncompromising, partly because of the banishment from the orderly society they wished, or had to wish, for in order to break all links with normal life. The most radical among them, like St. John the Baptist, or the Cynics among the Greek philosophers, refused to marry, bear children, and own property, as all this required involvement in the world and, therefore, entailed a seed of future compromise and surrender. This made their ideas indeed pure, but also powerless. Their successors (St. Paul, the founder of the Church, and the Stoic philosophers, the founders of the Academy) set about winning for the ideas a worldly success. They knew that "the price of survival is practical involvement, the transformation of ideas into domination." But then, are the ideas that have conquered the world and attained the dreamed-of domination the same ideas that once challenged the old reality? The odds are that they were compromised and truncated in the process. While criticism turned into administrative action, critique turned into religion, doctrine, or dogma. From a weapon of liberating change, the ideas became instruments of an oppressive stability.

This reflection made some among the most prominent representatives of critical theory wary of any apostolic, proselytizing activity. Any attempt to turn critical analysis into communal practice will necessarily impoverish the message, blunt its cutting edge, be, in other words, self-defeating. Such a conclusion had two significant consequences. On the one hand, compassion for the deplorable plight of the oppressed has been now mixed with disdain for their cowardly diffidence to part with the piteous comforts of the oppressed life. People unwilling to lift their eyes above the level of perhaps ungratifying, but known and secure, existence, are referred to as the *herd*; they are victims of *cultural barbarity*, but they have come to enjoy their incarceration and are willing actually to defend it. On the other hand, some theorists criticized all classes and their particular forms of selfishness and longing, and hoped for the preservation of critical thought with groups "in which an established psychic make-up does not play the decisive role and in which knowledge itself has become a vital force." (This was the view of Max Horkheimer in *Authority and the Family*.) The work of criticism came to be seen, in other words, as a task inescapably confined to a highly selective intellectual elite. This elite should never relent in its effort to reduce the tension between its critical insights and the oppressed humanity these insights are supposed to serve, but should be conscious at the same time that the tension will never vanish completely. Critical theory is, so to speak, the only practice it can hope for. Critical practice, so to speak, has been collapsed into theory. It has been fully confined to reflection, detached analysis, and the critical spirit.

Such a conclusion has, in turn, two truly devastating consequences for critical theory. First, it defeats the original legitimation of the project. If the *denaturalization* of the world is reduced to an operation accomplished on the intellect of the thinkers endowed with a critical spirit, if it does not change a thing in the state of the world, if it leaves the world counterfeit as it was before, then the claim of critical theory that there is nothing necessary about the *naturalness* of the world and that it can be restored to its cultural character, is belied.

If, for example, one confines oneself to the discovery that the inequality of human life chances and individuals' shares in socially available goods depends on man-made legal and economic institutions, rather than on inviolable features of social existence, these institutions will continue unperturbed to act with the indomitable power of natural forces and the hypothesis of their artificial nature remains in doubt.

There is nothing left to distinguish critical ruminations from self-centered projects of personal salvation offered by, say, existentialism, and ostensibly opposed by criti-

cal theory. There is nothing critical theory could offer sociology. It becomes instead a variant of personal philosophy. Second, and still more important, the above conclusion makes the insights of critical theory untestable. With its anchor in historical activity severed, critical theory is reduced to a set of more or less ingenuous, inventive, or appealing ideas which can be, however, neither proved nor refuted. Their claim to verity must remain forever inconclusive; their authority, a never attainable horizon. This, of course, makes critical theory a body of ideas which science (which, in critical theory view, rests on the very assumptions this theory is set to undermine) has neither duty nor compulsion to treat seriously. A sociology which would wish to follow critical theory inspiration would limit itself to the generation of, in principle, untestable hypotheses and, therefore, would have to satisfy itself with the status of art or philosophy.

Because of these two consequences, the conclusion offering intellectual self-contentment as the only reason to accept critical theory must be seen by many an attentive reader of its analyses as unsatisfactory. It is likely to be rejected not just because of its lack of coherence with the rejectors' particular ambitions or purposes, but because it is intrinsically unfit to provide a basis for any communal practice. Whatever its own merits, it does not belong with the historically established tradition of scholarship, distinguished by its standing invitation to communal participation and its determination to make its propositions, at least in principle, open to test.

The second generation of critical theorists (among which the names of Jürgen Habermas and Otto Appel are the most prominent) has been preoccupied with the task of rebuilding the bridge linking critical theory with this tradition—a bridge which the disenchanted older generation all too carelessly discarded. The twin pillars on which the bridge can be erected are, first, a reason why the emancipatory propositions could and should find their way from intellectual ruminations to historical practice, and second, a method of testing the truth of such propositions.

To start with the first pillar, the link between critical theory and critical practice can be elucidated through exploring the general relationship between knowledge and human interests. This topic has been neglected by ordinary science. Science is an attempt to prove something about its object; it neither intends nor is able to prove anything about itself. It is a commonplace that science, which purports to be a codification of rational thought and rational action, cannot rationally prove why it should be selected as a commendable approach to the world in preference to other attitudes. The choice of science over other types of knowledge is ultimately a value judgment, and as such it escapes the strict criteria of choice that science developed for its own propositions. Assertions about the virtues of science are not themselves scientific assertions. This circumstance detracts nothing from the coherence and consistency of science, as the theoretical cohesion and practical usefulness of its propositions can be established without reference to the reason which justifies concerns leading to their pursuit. The set of scientific propositions is complete and self-supporting without the propositions articulating the reasons of their generation. This lack of concern of science with its own pragmatic grounds derives, as it were, from the nature of its rules, which cannot be applied to questions of preference among ultimate ends. This lack of concern is, however, a minor irritant, or not an irritant at all, since in spite of the suspicious and vigilant stance science takes toward commonsensical beliefs, the normative structure of science is not divorced from the tacit but ubiquitous concerns of common sense. To the contrary, there is remarkable continuity between the two, with science pursuing in a systematic and self-conscious way the inter-

ests which on the commonsensical level are already followed, though in a somewhat diffuse and usually unself-conscious fashion. Science may afford the neglect of its own normative groundings precisely because it is so permanently and securely rooted in ordinary life. As Horkheimer states:

After all, it helps to perform better, more efficiently, at a lesser cost what people in their daily life must do anyway. It supplies instrumental knowledge of how to make people's shelters warmer, how to get to wherever they need quicker, how to construct more reliable bridges spanning the shores of a river; and a more general knowledge which helps to solve such tasks. Through telling us why things happen the way they do (this function makes it explanatory), it tells us as well how to anticipate, or even correlate their appearance (this makes it predictive). On the other hand, science offers us means to facilitate our mutual communication and agreement, by clarifying for us the meaning of linguistic and other signs providing the right orientation of behaviour, and making plain the message contained in strange cultural lores or our own historical tradition.

It is in everyday life that we first encounter the two practical tasks which require knowledge already embedded in daily routine action, but later raised to a higher level of sophistication and exactitude by organized science. The two tasks are mastery and cooperation. Mastery applies to the elements of experience which are constituted as movable objects; bodies which, by application of right action, can be set in motion required or moved into desirable places. What we need to know about such bodies is ''what makes them move''; once we know it, we can manipulate them, or at least know what sort of force we should muster in order to do so. The kind of knowledge which serves mastery consists, therefore, of explanatory/predictive propositions— propositions which simultaneously tell us about the external forces responsible for the movements which occurred and the movements which a given external force would without fail evoke. Cooperation, on the other hand, applies to these elements of experience which in all circumstances cannot be grasped as, simply, movable objects: objects which cannot be seen as set in motion by just application of external force; objects which, in other words, are constituted as self-activating entities—as sources rather than objects of action. These elements of experience are acting and speaking individuals. They are "acting," not "moving," since in order to make sense of their behavior, we need to visualize the motives they set for themselves, rather than pressures exerted upon them by other agents. The information about these motives, and therefore the indispensable link in our "making sense" activity, is contained in the utterances they generate, and cannot be drawn simply from the nonverbalized observations. Accommodation to their presence in our experience calls for cooperation, a mutual adjustment of motives, achievable in the course of communication, consisting in the exchange of utterances. Knowledge required for this purpose is not, as in the case of mastery, explanatory/predictive. It is instead interpretive knowledge, consisting of the "hermeneutical" (concerned with understanding) rules of the passage from symbols to meanings, from collectively available utterances to the autonomous world of motives.

To sum up, the interest in mastery calls for instrumental action served by explanatory/predictive knowledge; the interest in cooperation demands interaction, made possible by hermeneutical (interpretive) knowledge. Without these two types of knowledge, no daily life is possible. For this reason Jürgen Habermas described the interests which underlie the two categories of knowledge as *species-transcendental*. They are transcendental, as no social life is possible without them; they are, so to speak, universal preconditions of all forms of human existence. They are, however, *species*-transcendental, as their ubiquity may be traced to the characteristic form which the

human species attained in the course of evolution; hand and tongue, labor and language—all have evolved as the principal instruments of this species survival and perfectibility.

Being ubiquitously present in the specifically human way of life, interests in mastery (technical interest) and in cooperation (practical interest) determine the way in which human experience is collectively perceived, categorized, and typified. The aspects of experience are selected according to their relevance to the two fundamental interests. This is what we all, singly and communally, do all the time. Recent ethnomethodological studies have shown how elaborate and sophisticated are the commonsensical rules which guide this activity. In spite of all its revisionist attitude toward common sense, science is indeed an extension of this activity. It rests ultimately on the same silently accepted assumptions as common sense. It derives its legitimation from the same interests which sustain everyday life activity. This is why its wisdom might be questioned, but its purpose never is. Science has to prove that it goes rightly about reaching its end. It need not legitimate the end itself. Having been excused from this onerous requirement, it can concentrate fully on the instrumental task of sharpening its cognitive tools. It can, therefore, legitimately claim rationality without being unduly worried about the ultimate grounds of its action.

The status of emancipatory knowledge is a different matter. Emancipatory interests are not a transcendental condition of human survival. Human life is inconceivable without the pursuit of technical and practical interests, but it is fully imaginable and logically noncontradictory without any interest in emancipation. Experience of subjects capable of speech and action cannot be "objectified," reacted to, coped with, unless appropriate instrumental and hermeneutical skills have been developed. But it can, in principle, be adequately handled, up to the standards required by the continuation of species life without emancipatory knowledge. At least it may be the case for long stretches of human history. We can conclude that if technical and practical interests are suprahistorical (they explain history, rather than requiring a historical explanation), emancipatory interest has its historical origins. If at any time a claim is made that it is as compellingly necessary as the other two interests are, it must be justified by reference to specific historical circumstances. The necessity of emancipation can be only historical; it appears under particular, not species-universal, conditions.

Being deprived of prescientific, indeed precognitive, roots, cognitive knowledge cannot leave its activating/legitimizing interest outside its focus of attention. Hence, it cannot limit itself to the realm of fact leaving value behind. No knowledge, as we have seen, is truly disinterested; but emancipatory knowledge is the only one which cannot pretend being such. It must consciously and overtly articulate not only its instrumental procedure but its ends as well; and it must bear responsibility for the legitimation of both, without right to appeal for commonsensical support.

The general strategy of historical legitimation consists in demonstrating that, under specific conditions, emancipatory knowledge and corresponding practice do become prerequisites of survival; that emancipatory interest becomes a compelling necessity (i.e., if it is not followed, no continuation of social life is feasible). Necessity of emancipation is, as we have seen, an outcome of a historically specific situation. The acquisition by the emancipatory interest of pressure power sufficient for its satisfaction is not, therefore, precognitively assured. The necessity of emancipatory action must be argumentatively vindicated. Thus this interest must be consciously incorporated into the main body of emancipatory theory. Without such an incorporation this theory is incomplete and inconclusive. To try to construct a case for the desirability of technical or practical interests would be equivalent to the attempt to force open a gate permanently ajar; it is, however, a matter of theoretical argument, and a difficult one, that survival may require going beyond the horizons drawn by technical and practical interests together.

Emancipatory knowledge is in effect distinguished by a double function in relation to the practice it serves. Like other types of knowledge, it is capable of *instrumentalizing*, *rationalizing*, smoothing, and facilitating the ensuing action. But in addition, it also creates conditions for the action to be willingly undertaken. Without it, the action not only would be less effective; it would be hardly attempted. Technical and practical interests may be well met without people being conscious of their imperatives. This does not apply to emancipatory interest. It may exist only in the conscious form; it becomes reality once it has been identified, recognized, and admitted. In this sense it may be said that emancipatory knowledge generates not only assertions about reality but the very reality of which assertions are made; emancipatory theory is itself an element of emancipation, as it relativizes reality which the other two interests could only further solidify in its objectivity.

Habermas has chosen Marx's theory of capitalist society and Freud's theory of the civilized personality as examples of emancipatory theories. Marx showed that social reality as determined by capitalist practices creates a necessity of its own transcendence; that emancipation from the apparently compelling realities objectified by capitalist practices has become an indispensable condition of the continuation of social life able to pass the criteria established by civilizing history. The alternative to emancipation, as Rosa Luxemburg later summarized, would be (by the same criteria) barbarism. It is the recognition of this alternative which, according to Marx, was needed for the emancipatory interest to be realized in practice. The reality of interest was, therefore, mediated by theory. Historical situation preceded theoretical reflection; but theoretical reflection, in turn, was prior to the reality of interest and to the historical action which such an interest, having become a historical reality, was likely to trigger off. A similar strategy was followed by Freud in substantiating the claims of his metapsychological theory. The reality of civilized existence, unless elucidated by emancipatory interest, often leads to psychological disturbance. Ill health is caused by the repression of needs, by barring important constituents of personality from becoming conscious. Almost by definition, without the intervention of a theory armed with a knowingly postulated ideal of healthy existence, ill health can be only vaguely experienced as discomfort, but it cannot be identified as a case of normative distortion. Definitions generated within already distorted reality serve to conceal, not to articulate, the trouble. Hence the hidden needs must first be drawn to the surface of consciousness to regain their action-motivating potency. Not only liberated conduct but the very recognition of the emancipatory interest depends, therefore, on the availability of theory which saps the seemingly overwhelming power of distorted reality.

To sum up, the peculiar difficulty encountered by critical theory in establishing its link with practical action is traceable back to the historical, rather than transcendental, character of emancipatory interest. The practical consequence of this historicalness is the need of critical theory to perform tasks which other theories are ill prepared to fulfill but can legitimately dispense with. In addition to the normal tasks routinely performed by other sciences, critical theory must first accomplish the job which for other sciences is normally done by common sense: it must justify its own validity, prove that its undertaking is significant and its possible consequences are relevant to social survival. Critical theory is the one discourse which openly topicalizes its own grounds.

This brings us to the second of the two pillars: can critical theory subject itself to a test of truth? If so, in what way? Obviously, not in a way legitimized by the long practice of other sciences. Other sciences confront phenomena already objectified, congested into "things," by the incessant, tacit work of commonsensical practices. They, therefore, can, in principle, measure their own assertions against objects *out there*. They can accept without further discussion that the objects are independent from, and unaffected by, statements made about them. This is not the situation of critical theory, however. As we have already seen, critical theory constitutes its own object and neither can nor intends to hide its active role in reality production. In the case of critical theory, this production is an organic element of the theory itself. It has to account for its own development as a process of interaction between the subject and the object of knowledge.

Emphatically rejecting the authority of a commonsensically established social reality, critical theory shifts its testing ground into the yet unaccomplished future—this territory of, simultaneously, freedom and uncertainty. Moreover, critical theory is itself a factor in bringing this hypothesized future to pass. The unique position of critical theory does not consist merely in the delay of a test. It is not related just to the impossibility of testing its hypotheses here and now, by measuring them against an already available existence. If this were so, the distinction of critical theory from traditional theories would be only the question of a time lag. Unlike traditional theories, critical theory would have to wait and see whether its hypotheses come true, much like, say, daily weather forecasts. But this is not the case. The gist of critical theory is, as we have seen, the *culturization of nature*, the discovery of historical contingency and choice behind the ostensibly natural necessities. In critical theory's view, the illusion of necessity has been achieved above all by the repression of cultural alternatives. The illusionary character of natural necessities can be proved only if the repression is over-

come, and repressed alternatives are redeemed. This would not happen if
alternatives were not first theoretically postulated and efforts were made to implement them practically. Critical theory,
therefore, not only generates theory to be
tested. It participates in producing conditions of the test.

SOCIOLOGICAL APPLICATIONS

It has been said that the truth of critical
theory is a "truth in the making." The articulation of hypotheses is a crucial part in
the production of social reality which corresponds to the hypothetical anticipation.
We can express this differently: hypotheses
of critical theory are not truth-tested, but
actualized. They can find their confirmation only in the changed social conditions
they themselves help to bring about. The
question of truth testing in the case of critical theory turns, therefore, into the problem of bringing about the conditions of its
actualization. This problem, in turn, splits
into two. First, we must ask what features a
condition must possess which can be seen
as offering the adequate testing ground for
social theory. Second, we have to explore
the mechanism by which such a testing
ground may, and is likely to, be created.

To start with the first question, we must
recall that the authority of truth is in all
cases related to the rationality of discourse
in which the truth was argued and vindicated. A rational discourse is, of course, an
ideal rarely reached in practical circumstances. Most discussions depart from the
ideal. But thanks to an agreement on what
the ideal conditions would be like, participants in empirical discussions can criticize
the achieved results as inconclusive (because attained in imperfect conditions),
and strive to improve them. In Jürgen Habermas's precise description, a genuinely
rational discussion would mean that:

validity claims of assertions, recommendations,
or warnings are the exclusive object of discus-

sion; that participants, themes and contributions are not restricted except with reference to
the goal of testing the validity claims in question;
that no force except that of the better argument
is exercised; and that, as a result, all motives except that of the cooperative search for truth are
excluded.

The idea of rational discourse as the only
acceptable ground of credible and trustworthy opinion has been long established in
the European tradition. In *On Liberty* John
Stuart Mill was already appealing to general
agreement when he concluded that "the
beliefs which we have most warrant for,
have no safeguard to rest on, but a standing
invitation to the whole world to prove
them unfounded." The ideal of rational
discourse, or the authority granted to it, is
not an invention of critical theory. What
critical theory has contributed to the time-
honored intellectual tradition is a sharpened understanding of socially produced
conditions under which the ideal of rational discourse cannot be actualized—
under which, moreover, it tends to be
systematically and continually distorted.
Critical theory shows that a "standing invitation to the whole world" is not a sufficient guarantee that the whole world will
indeed try to prove the established beliefs
unfounded. It is enough to spell out the requirements which must be met in order to
enable the whole world to make such an effort, to see how far the real society departs
from the ideal:

Since all those affected have, in principle, at least
the chance to participate in the practical deliberation, the "rationality" of the discursively
formed will consists in the fact that the reciprocal
behavioural expectations raised to normative status accord validity to a *common* interest ascertained *without* deception. The interest is
common because the constraint-free consensus
permits only what *all* can want; it is free of deception because even the interpretations of
needs in which *each individual* must be able to re-
cognise what he wants become the object of discursive will-formation. The discursively formed
will may be called "rational" because the formal
properties of discourse and of the deliberative
situation sufficiently guarantee that a consensus

can arise only through appropriately interpreted, *generalisable* interests, by which I mean needs that can be *communicatively shared*.

In these words of Jürgen Habermas, universality, equality of participants, no prohibitions or other restrictions imposed on the selection of topics of discourse, and lack of deception are all named as conditions under which a discourse can be described as rational. None of these conditions are met in the real world. Hence, the consensus reached in this imperfect condition cannot be awarded authority, which can be granted only by rational discourse. A commonsensical verdict of the utopianism or irrealism of alternative situations cannot be accepted as conclusive for the same reason. But critical theory does not only refuse to comply with the verdict. It also explains why the authority of the verdict cannot be admitted. It does so by developing a sociology of communication. In particular, it studies the social structures of domination which are responsible for systematic distortion of public communication. The study shows that a large part of society is in practice excluded from the public discourse in which decisions concerning their fate are formed; that vital elements of the decisions themselves, and of their true reasons, are systematically excluded from public discourse; that the concealment of vital information, the structure of secrecy, and the formalization of procedures generate a systematic deception; and that the summary result of all these departures from the ideal of rational discourse is the situation in which the stipulation of the equality of participants cannot be met.

It is hoped that by bringing these facts into relief while invoking the tradition-rooted, universal commitment to the principles of rational discourse, critical theory can both invalidate the allegedly empirically confirmed reality of public authority institutions and expose the repression involved. Critical theory hopefully can show that forces capable of exploding the existing net-

work of repressions are organically present and perpetuated within the structure of dominance itself; that, in other words, this structure breeds conditions of its own supercession and, so to speak, cannot help it.

We can now return to the point from which our analysis of critical theory started. We said at the beginning that critical theory is not, strictly speaking, an alternative sociology; that it is, rather, a mode of theorizing. Now we can summarize the conclusions to which the analysis starting from these assumptions has brought us. The consequence of the mode of theorizing which critical theory practices is the demand to extend the realm of sociology to include areas normally ceded to philosophical study. The mode of theorizing practiced by critical theory leads us to conclude that the question of truth grounding, of the validity of beliefs, is not a matter for epistemology—a philosophical theory of cognition—to decide for the empirical sciences in general, and for sociology in particular. Epistemology should be *resociologized*, as the problem of truth is ultimately the sociological question of the historically shaped conditions under which normative beliefs are founded. Critical theory is not, therefore, an alternative sociology. But it may be internally coherent only if it substantiates a drastic expansion of the sociological project. It calls for a sociology which, on the one hand, makes social practice an organic constituent of itself and, on the other, includes its own grounds in the field of its professional concerns. Wishing to be of service to the civilization whose foremost value is the attainment of rational consensus (an agreement grounded in truth), sociology cannot confine its interests to comprehending and elaborating upon the currently attained consensus, an agreement reached in conditions unsuitable for rational discourse. Neither can it regard its own activity as unconstrained by mundane consensus, and hence overconfidently accept its own activity as a sufficient foundation on which true knowledge of the human condition could be built. Sociology can serve the central values of civilization, the search for a truth-based agreement, only if it does not neglect the task of constructing an evolutionary theory, showing the way which society could follow toward conditions progressively emancipated from obstacles to rational discourse.

The central point around which such a sociological project rotates is a notion of rational society fundamentally distinct from one produced as a simple extrapolation of the control-and-mastery-oriented model of instrumental science. The latter stems from the belief that there is a continuous way leading from technical mastery over nature-like, objective processes to the conscious practical control over historical processes. The second will be attained only if the first sufficiently develops; there is only a quantitative, not qualitative, difference between the two. Instrumental science entails all the rationality one needs to achieve a rational society. But, as Habermas reminds us:

[T]he root of the irrationality of history is that we "make" it, without, however, having been able until now to make it consciously. A rationalisation of history cannot therefore be furthered by an extended power of control on the part of manipulative human beings, but only by a higher stage of reflection, a consciousness of acting human beings moving forward in the direction of emancipation.

A simple extension of control-and-mastery technology without a parallel progress toward emancipation may result only in "the splitting of human beings into two classes—the social engineers and the inmates of closed institutions," as Habermas states in *Theory and Practice*. Such a splitting can be avoided only through the process of rational discourse, through making sure that the willingness to comply, to accept the legitimation of societal decisions, derives from "good reasons," and not from overt coercion or tacit repression.

In *Communication and the Evolution of Society* Habermas comments:

But whether reasons are "good reasons" can be ascertained only in the performative attitude of a *participant* in argumentation, and not through the neutral *observation* of what this or that participant in a discourse holds to be good reasons...

The truly rational society entails, therefore, the notion of critical practice. It needs critical theory; it needs a sociology informed by this theory. It needs a sociology actively engaged in seeking the extension of rational discourse—a sociology examining the roots of current consensus, exposing the element of distortion incurred by the extant forms of coercion and repression, and pressing toward the condition of undistorted communication in which good reasons can be argumentatively established.

Jürgen Habermas sketched an outline of such a sociology in his famous and seminal *Legitimation Crisis*. It is impossible to reconstruct the complex argument of this densely reasoned book in a short article, and every reader wishing to know how penetrating and important the insight is that critical theory has to offer must study the book in its totality. Here we can follow only the crucial steps of the reasoning, and even this in an unduly simplified form.

In *Legitimation Crisis* Habermas traced the increasing complexity of the present capitalist system, which is prompted by the incapacity of the market, and of the market economy in general, to secure conditions of the reproduction of capital and labor. Since the economy is incapable of surviving on its own, the responsibility for the continuation of the capitalist relations has been taken over by the state. The state "skims off" the economy fiscally while attempting to steer its performance. To the general public it offers welfare services in exchange for their moral and political acquiescence. With its new central position within the social system, the state may counteract, with a degree of success, economic crises in their old form of productive disturbances generated by blindly operating market forces. Instead, the state becomes a focus of a new type of crisis. The new type is political; it stems from the state's inability to deliver on its pledge. Its cause is the imperfect rationality of political decisions, which are not a reflection of generalizable norms, but of conflicting self-preferential interests. It is manifested in the progressive weakening of the state's legitimation to rule, and consequently in the weakening grip of *civic privatism*—the political indifference of the public that was the condition of the state retaining its autonomy from generalizable norms, its ability to repress public discourse of the grounds of its decision, and its tendency to translate substantive issues of social life into the ostensibly technical problems of administration.

The legitimation heretofore used by the state to justify its claim to obedience has been purely formal; it referred to the procedure through which vital decisions affecting society had been allegedly reached. These procedures included delegation of authority to duly elected or appointed representatives. In opposition to the facts of life, it claimed an institutional guarantee of popular control over the content of decisions the delegated authority may impose. At the same time it rendered such a substantive control implausible in case meticulously observed formal rules of delegation failed to yield desirable policies. The conflict between claim and delivery could remain a minor irritant (it could, indeed, remain unnoticed) as long as the state continued to pay handsomely for the universality of civic privatism: as long as the economy continued to grow, the standard of living to rise, and the reassuring effect of welfare provisions to allay uncertainty as to the stability of gratifying conditions. As long as all this remained the case, the continuous flow of welfare cast the question of meaning into insignificance. Satisfactory results were taken as a clinching proof that the formal rules are sufficient—that in the legal-rational procedure a key had been found to the secret of the constant turnout of values everybody desired and was interested in acquiring. Formality of legitimation did not

seem to bother people as long as the generally approved substance continued to be supplied by the substantively uncontrolled system. But a "legitimation crisis arises as soon as the demands for...rewards rise faster than the available quantity of value, or when expectations arise that cannot be satisfied with such rewards."

Formal legitimation is a sufficient condition of the maintenance of capitalist society when the institutionalized patterns of behavior used to reproduce the capitalist network of relations yield individually gratifying results. The present legitimation crisis is the outcome of the latter requirement not being met any more. The *work ethic* which sustained capitalism in its boisterously expansive phase was first undermined by the routinized, uncreative character of factory work and by the invisibility of the connection between individual effort and the final product. Lack of intrinsic gratification had been soon redressed by a hierarchical scale of money inducements. But the impact of this makeshift gratification was also fast eroded because of the eradication (under political pressure) of extreme poverty, the provision (under similar pressure) of the security cushion of welfare, and the general tendency to reduce the differentials of income. As a result, the automatic connection between compliance with the work-ethic requirements and increasing rewards has been consistently belied by experience. The *achievement principle*, which used to justify discrepancies of income in terms of difference of talents, dedication, and skills, also finds less and less corroboration in life experience. On the one hand, it becomes increasingly evident that group privileges reflect more the collective ability to disturb smooth functioning of the economic or political process, rather than an objectively measurable level of contribution to productive activity. On the other, with the growing bureaucratization of economic enterprises and public institutions, individual progress is regulated by an appointing procedure over which individuals exert little, if any, control. Performance or achievement appears more as an ex-post-facto justification of status and income differentials, rather than as a meaningful explanation of their distribution. *Familial-occupational privatism* (an essentially self-centered orientation to the solution of life problems and satisfaction of needs), which fueled the growth of the capitalist market, becomes ever less meaningful as the rapidly expanding proportion of life conditions depends on factors that cannot be influenced by the growing purchasing power of the individual. Elements so vital as freedom from air, water, and noise pollution, housing and transport conditions, educational opportunities, etc., respond but little to the traditionally economic titles of access, and require instead an essentially political action. The proved means of keeping life business away from politics do not, therefore, work any more. Belief in the intrinsic wisdom of an only formally regulated social system is fast losing its credibility. Demands of substantive legitimation will inevitably grow in force. But substantive legitimation must refer to ethical choices; unlike formal legitimation, it cannot be reduced to the issue of technical efficiency in implementing goals already backed by universal consensus.

If technical decisions are sufficiently grounded in the wisdom of instrumental science, ethical choices evidently cannot hope for a similar support. Instrumental science can rationalize the execution of purposes it has neither will nor tools to evaluate. The necessity to bring the ethical problems of the social system into focus requires an alternative grounding of authority. As its institutional basis, it calls for a rational society rather than a rational administration. The foundation of ethical authority may be only a process described before as *rational discourse*. Rational discourse turns, therefore, from the moral postulate of a better society into a necessary prerequisite of societal survival.

This assigns a new role to critical theory, and to a sociology that implements its pro-gram. Critical sociology performs a function toward rational society equivalent to the function performed by instrumental science in relation to rational administration. It supplies discursive models of possible decisions. It simulates in advance of practice the course of action which would take place if the conditions of (administrative or societal) rationality were fully observed. It thereby facilitates the search for a solution geared to the rational assessment of generalized interest.

The critical edge of this sociology is turned against ideological mystification embodied in the current state of distorted communication. The mystification, which is safe as long as it is allowed to remain inconspicuous, is exposed by being forcibly confronted with a hypothetical state of normative order—one that demonstrates, as Habermas puts it in *Legitimation Crisis*, "how would the members of a social system, at a given stage in the development of productive forces, have collectively and bindingly interpreted their needs (and which norms would they have accepted as justified) if they could and would have decided on organisation of social intercourse through discursive will-formation, with adequate knowledge of the limiting conditions and functional imperatives of their society." In other words, critical sociology simulates a truly democratic, undistorted discourse which under the current conditions of repressed interests cannot take place in real life. It attempts, so to speak, to fill the gap between an argumentatively attainable good society and the practice of distorted communication, thereby losing somewhat the grip of the latter over collective will formation. This task puts sociological analysis ahead of actual progress toward rational discourse. Hence, the inevitably hypothetical character of its propositions. They may remain hypothetical for a long time; their confirmation could occur only if the propositions in question became the subject of practical discourse by members of society, which is not an immediate possibility. Rather, the legitimation crisis is likely to lead in the first instance to intensification of conflict between self-interested partisan groups, which will not consciously seek generalizable foundations for agreement (as distinct from mere compromise). Critical sociology would have, therefore, to assume an "advocacy role," which, according to Habermas in *Legitimation Crisis*, "would consist in ascertaining generalisable, though nevertheless suppressed, interests in a representatively simulated discourse between groups that are differentiated (or could be nonarbitrarily differentiated) from one another by articulated, or at least virtual, opposition of interests."

In its hermeneutical role, focused on human communication as it stands or stood at the moment of investigation, sociology interprets for people what they have already done or what they are doing. In an informed, systematic fashion it represents the meanings, intentions, and motives which knowingly or unknowingly must have guided their actions—meanings which made these actions sensible. In its instrumental role, focused on the struggle to order and control the world, sociology generates propositions about individual or group behavior which tend to be generated in response to the given structure of coercions and repressions, provided the coercions retain their force and the repressions keep their hold. The latter assumption (if sociology is to remain in its instrumental role) is made matter-of-factly, normally hiding behind the uncommittal phrase of *caeteris paribus* ("other things being equal") or detopicalized by the suggestion of a naturelike mode of described regularities. Critical sociology consciously rejects the latter assumption. It interprets what people have done in overt reference to the circumstances under which they have done it. By the same token, it discloses the coercive and repressive aspects of the circumstances to which the content of what has been done could be meaningfully related. And then it hypothesizes circumstances free of

these aspects, and asks the vital question: What would people have done under such circumstances? Critical sociology brings back into focus the possibilities of history making which have not found their way into real history and which real history suppressed and either obliterated or declared irrealistic. It is this activity of critical sociology which warrants the metaphor of *advocacy*. The presence of the advocate turns the tables on the prosecutor. It forces the prosecutor to take upon himself or herself the burden of proof; to demonstrate by summoning sufficient evidence (none of which can hope to be accepted uncontested, without its alternative interpretations being explored by the defense) that the suggested necessary link between known events must be accepted as *beyond reasonable doubt*. The case of the prosecutor, at least ideally, remains unproven if an alternative interpretation of events, suggested by the advocate, retains plausibility. The task of the prosecutor is to show what has been the case; the task of the advocate, to demonstrate what could be the case.

Here the validity of the metaphor ends. Prosecutor and advocate quarrel ostensibly about facts, not about the grounds on which this or that meaning of events is accepted (though the latter in fact constitutes the subject matter of their debate). Critical sociologists' argument with their colleagues is overtly about the grounds on which it may be assumed that something which has taken place has taken place with necessity. So the form in which the topic of debate is topicalized is in each case different. But the division of roles is similar.

The advocacy of critical sociology prevents the debate from being closed. Unlike in the courtroom, there is no specific moment when the verdict is pronounced and the argument stopped. Unlike in the courtroom, there is no impartial judge with the power to make one interpretation binding and final. The debate in which critical sociology performs the advocate's role is the perpetual work of history. Critical sociology guards its possibilities against being prematurely closed; and it strives to reopen such past chances that failed to be noticed or properly worked upon.

BIBLIOGRAPHICAL NOTE

Like most other currents and tendencies in modern sociology, critical sociology is an area of lively discussion and sometimes fierce controversy, rather than a closed system of beliefs and methodological rules. It is very much an area of development resisting codification which everybody would recognize as representative. In attempting to sum up the most fundamental and general marks of critical sociology, I strove to elucidate the premises on which any version of this sociology must be necessarily based. The result, however, is another personal version of critical sociology, as any presentation of a living current will have to be. There is, therefore, no substitute for studying the tradition at the source. Any reader interested in the project will have ultimately to inquire into the historical development of ideas which led to the present concerns and methods of critical sociology. Only within this context will the present concerns be truly understandable.

Critical theory, of which critical sociology is an offspring and an application, is associated with the work of the Frankfurt School—a group of scholars, mostly philosophers, gathered in the 1930s around the Institute of Social Research in Frankfurt. (By far the most comprehensive history of the institute to date is Martin Jay's *The Dialectical Imagination*, New York, 1973). The School could legitimately claim to be a rightful heir of the most seminal traditions in German philosophy and social science, but one relatively less known author deserves to be specifically mentioned as an influential forerunner: Ernst Bloch. His major works are not yet available in English, but one could form a fairly reliable view of his original contribution (mostly by retrieving the neglected *active dimension* in the Marxist tradition) from the collection of his essays *On Marx* (New York, 1971).

As to the Frankfurt School itself, three writers—Adorno, Horkheimer, and Marcuse—though by no means seeing eye to eye on often crucial issues, can be seen as jointly forming the mainstream. Perhaps most lucid and straightforward, and therefore particularly suitable as a starting point, are Max Horkheimer's essays collected in *Critical Theory* (New York, 1972) and *Critique of Instrumental Reason* (New York, 1974). Horkheimer and Adorno jointly wrote *Dialectic of Enlightenment* (New York, 1972), a difficult and rather opaque book, still widely considered the fullest and most consequential statement of the school's views. Adorno's *Negative Dialectics* (London, 1974) also defies an easy interpretation and also contains ideas of great importance to the spirit of critical theory. An exquisite attempt to systematize the notoriously obfuscatory ideas of Theodor W. Adorno can be found in Gillian Rose's *Melancholy Science* (London, 1978); also a useful critical introduction to the works of Adorno and other members of the Frankfurt Institute is contained in Richard Kilminster's *Praxis and Method* (London, 1979). Herbert Marcuse's works are relatively popular and well known. To the assessment of the foundations of critical sociology, his *Negations* (London, 1968) and *Counterrevolution and Revolt* (Boston, 1972) are perhaps the most relevant. *The Critical Spirit*, a book of essays collected by Kurt H. Wolff and Barrington Moore, Jr. (Boston, 1967), contains a most useful collective assessment of Marcuse's work.

The present stage in the development of critical sociology is dominated by the powerful mind of Jürgen Habermas. English translations of his works are numerous, but several deserve special attention: *Toward a Rational Society* (London, 1971), *Theory and Practice* (London, 1974), *Legitimation Crisis* (London, 1976), and *Communication and the Evolution of Society* (London, 1979). Habermas's books are, as a rule, written in technical language and densely argued. Reliable comprehensive interpretations of Habermas's work are not, however, available at the time of writing. The reader may obtain some indirect help from Albrecht Wellmer's *Critical Theory of Society* (New York, 1971), Trent Schroyer's *The Critique of Domination* (New York, 1973), and perhaps from my own *Towards a Critical Sociology* (London, 1975). The American quarterly journal *Telos* offers a highly informed, continuing commentary on developments in the critical theory of society.

Structuralists attempt to uncover unconscious universal mental structures which manifest themselves in social structures.

There are a variety of structuralist theories such as Claude Lévi-Strauss's theory of kinship structures, Noam Chomsky's grammatical theory, and Louis Althusser's theory of revolutionary situations. These theories use the methodology of structural linguistics to analyze societies. The Saussurean model of language in which a linguistic signifier only has meaning within a specific system of significations is the key to understanding all of these structuralisms.

Lévi-Strauss believed that language itself could be conceptualized as the production of society. From the laws of spoken language one could understand the hidden structures that lay within customs, rites, habits, gestures, and other cultural phenomena. He hypothesized that the resemblance of languages and myths from different cultures meant that the societies were similar. Lévi-Strauss used his understanding of mythology and his reading of Sigmund Freud to explain the transition from nature to culture. He also tried to show how the unconscious emerges into consciousness through the common unifying structures of mythology. His goal was to decipher the symbolic systems of myth in order to reconstruct cultural history. Lévi-Strauss also developed an interpretation of Marxism, showing the dialectic between people as social beings and as unconscious bearers of a universal order.

Althusser presented a new reading of Karl Marx which repudiated the early work of Marx and refuted humanist and reformist Marxisms. Althusser argued that Marxian dialectics should be understood in terms of an identity of opposites rather than a Hegelian unity of opposites. This methodology allowed for an explanation of unevenness of development, rather than capitalist development, as leading to revolution—a thesis attractive to Third World Marxists faced with the former situation.

Michel Foucault placed the history of psychology and psychopathology in relation to social conditions and beliefs about deviance. His goal was to set forth the unconscious codes of knowledge that underpinned illness, madness, and crime. He arrived at a methodology of *enunciative units,* comparable to Lévi-Strauss's *constituent unit* in myth, which enabled him to expose hidden systems of power in medicine and law. Foucault's maverick relationship to American sociology is discussed, as are his challenges to Marx and Durkheim.

Jacques Lacan applied Saussurean linguistic oppositions and transformations to Freud's clinical writings, focusing on the signifier or the word within a sentence which designates the meaning of what follows. Through this methodology Lacan hoped to improve our understanding of Freud and thus of the practice of psychoanalysis.

In the United States, structuralism as a search for answers about existence has been more influential in the humanities than in the social sciences.

Edith Kurzweil

STRUCTURALISM IN FRANCE

Structuralism's approach to social science is complex and confused: its radical quality lies in its attempt to introduce an explanatory order among the most diverse and incoherent phenomena, while its political impact, except in its Althusserian cast, ultimately tends to be conservative. But structuralism has a number of incarnations and its methodology is not unified. Each of the various structuralist theories depends upon previous research in a specific field, and upon the characteristics of the objects of study. Claude Lévi-Strauss's theory of kinship structures or Noam Chomsky's grammatical theory, for instance, can be more exact than their Althusserian counterpart: they allow for *neoexperiments*, insofar as kinship arrangements or rules of grammar can be more easily compared to specific social customs and needs than revolutionary situations in capitalist countries. Nevertheless, all structuralisms, as we will note, claim to be scientific.

In this essay I will limit myself to the most important French structuralisms (they peaked around 1967) which aimed to uncover deep universal, unconscious mental structures that were said to manifest themselves in kinship and larger social structures. The inclusiveness of the phenomena examined as well as the assumption of hidden structures led some social scientists to think of structuralism as a catchall category for all the theories dealing with structures—social, psychological, mathematical, etc.—while others identified it with the work of a specific thinker. Even now, anthropologists tend to know Claude Lévi-Strauss; Marxists are familiar with Louis Althusser; intellectual historians with Michel Foucault; and literary critics with Roland Barthes.[1] They all incorporate some aspects of the methodology of structural linguistics—a methodology which Lévi-Strauss, for the first time, applied to social phenomena directly. Thus all structuralist theories rely on some aspects of linguistic theory to analyze societies, and many of the polemics themselves are about interpretations and applications of linguistic parallels. (Some commentators include Marx and Freud among the structuralists because they too rely on the emergence of unconscious structures.)

In any event structuralism—in its different forms—promised to uncover the roots of nature and culture. In the process the term *structure* itself was used in different contexts—operatively and/or intentionally. In its operational context it would relate to other concepts (i.e., *structure* and *function*, *structure* and *organization*), and when used intentionally, it would apply to an environment (i.e., structure of an organism, of a system, or of a personality). And because the development of structuralism has gone through many transformations, even structuralists could never agree on a definition. In 1964, for example, Roland Barthes stated:

Structuralism is neither a school, a movement, nor a vocabulary, but an activity that reaches beyond philosophy, that consists of a succession of mental operations which attempt to reconstruct an object in order to manifest the rules of its functioning.[2]

Such a vague definition, in turn, allowed Jacques Derrida to state that "structuralism lives within and on the difference between its promise and its practice."[3] It allowed Barthes later on to refute various aspects of structuralism when the structures did not emerge.

In fact, Barthes himself has become one of the poststructuralists who are now quite popular in some American departments of literature and philosophy. But I will not discuss poststructuralism. Nor will I develop the political implications of structuralist thought which, ultimately, are conservative. Instead, I will begin by showing what some structuralists took from Saussurean linguistics and will go on to exemplify how these structuralists applied linguistic dichotomous constructions to social phenomena.

INFLUENCE OF SAUSSUREAN LINGUISTICS

Variations on the Saussurean model of language, which postulates that a linguistic *signifier* only has meaning within a specific system of *significations*, served as the basic reference point for the different structuralist theories.[4] They all extrapolated from the rules and/or relations of grammar and of speech to explore social phenomena in terms of linguistic oppositions and transformations. This practice was justified because speech and language are central to every individual within every culture, even before he or she could ever have formally learned the words and usages of his or her particular language. The centrality of language to culture, and culture to language, and their presence in all discourse (including scientific discourse) were taken as proof of a specific underlying human universality. Lévi-Strauss expected this universality to become apparent with the help of his new methodology, so that modern intellectual and social fragmentation would prove to be no more than a superficial phenomenon which hides deeply rooted common origins. Since French structuralists claimed that unconscious motivations and underlying sources of language and/or behavior are shared by all of humanity, the search for these deep-rooted structures—as part of both the methodology and the promised results—has engendered much confusion.

What then were some of the central theoretical premises? To what extent did Lévi-Strauss's original understanding of Freud and Marx invite criticism from Freudians and Marxists? Or why, for example, did he inspire Lacan, Foucault, and Barthes? What were the political and philosophical implications which inadvertently supported and/or disputed every political and intellectual position?

Inevitably the polemics revolved around Ferdinand de Saussure, the first linguist to go beyond the study of grammar, philosophy, and comparative philology, and around Roman Jakobson,[5] the Czechoslovak formalist linguist who had postulated binary paths between *phonemes*—the small units of sound—and *morphemes*—the smallest units of meaning. Because both Saussure and Jakobson had examined the formation of language in relation to its social base and studied it as a system of signs, Lévi-Strauss believed that language itself could be conceptualized as the production of its society. He went beyond Saussure: from the laws and rules that underlie spoken language he tried to get to the origins of customs, rites, habits, gestures, and all other cultural phenomena—phenomena which were themselves said to be intrinsic to the creation of language. This was to lead him to the hidden structures which he believed to exist in some sort of archetypal fashion, in a so far undetected universal programming of every human brain. Like Saussure, he focused on *la langue* (language) rather than *la parole* (the word), that is, on the system of signs rather than on the spoken word. Saussure, however, had studied these signs in both their static interrelations and permutations, that is, *synchronically*, as well as *diachronically*. But Lévi-Strauss emphasized the *diachronic* dimensions. Saussure had developed the traits of synchrony, when, in contrast to previous language theory which had for the most part conceived language as an expression of thought, he conceived it as a system of signs. Within this system he postulated a dialectical relation between *signifiers* (acoustical impressions) and *signifieds* (mental images). But Saussure's primary concern had been the *signifiers*, which he analyzed formally, within their total system: i.e., the meaning of the word *hot* cannot be understood without its opposite *cold*, or without the relationship between the two. Hence, language was perceived as a structure, whose meaning could not be located in the thoughts of a speaker, but only in the context of its system of signs. Such binary oppositions allowed Lévi-Strauss to mediate between opposing elements—*hot* and *cold*, *earth* and *water*, *old*

and *new*, *male* and *female*, etc. And opposition between *phonemes* and *morphemes*, though alleged to be meaningless in terms of the formalization of language, were found to be useful in explaining the evolution of language in its society: these mediations theoretically legitimated structuralism's third dimension, the relational dimension of time, which is constantly being brought up to date. This theoretical possibility, as we will see, was Lévi-Strauss's most original—as well as his most controversial—contribution.

CLAUDE LÉVI-STRAUSS

Because Lévi-Strauss had been intrigued by the way languages as well as myths in different cultures resemble each other and seem to be structured in similar fashion, he postulated that they are constituted in the same way.[6] This notion was an extension of his work on *The Elementary Structures of Kinship* (1949) and on *The Structural Study of Myth* (1955). For he had been struck by the similarities of tribal myths in cultures that could not have had contact with each other, and he had found similar structural elements in very diverse tribes. He also had found that natives who recount the myths of their tribes tell and retell events that took place long ago as if they were still true in the present. And he observed that in these tales dimensions of time would become irrelevant, and that mythic events themselves seemed to move back and forth in time. This was where he found yet another parallel to language.

He decided to break down each myth into short sentences and to catalogue it; each of these short sentences (*constituent units*) could not produce a functional meaning unless it was combined with other such units into *bundles of relations* that would account for the two-dimensional, time-referrent, revertible and nonrevertible time, and that would constitute the primary element of most myths.

In order to record the many versions of

every myth, Lévi-Strauss proposed to organize two-dimensional charts in three-dimensional order, so that it would be possible to read diagonally (see illustration).

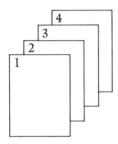

He thought that after all known myths were charted in this fashion, a structural law of myth would emerge and an orderly analysis would ensue from the existing chaos.

As long as Lévi-Strauss discussed only straight inversions, transformations, and oppositions, everything seemed relatively simple. But he set out to show how the transition from nature to culture was paralleled by changing customs: i.e., food was no longer eaten raw but cooked, and eating utensils replaced fingers. However, this was only the beginning. The theory began to seem hopelessly abstruse when, for instance, Lévi-Strauss gave the following explanation:

Carrion eating animals are like prey animals (they eat animal food) but are also like foodplant producers (they do not kill what they eat). Ravens are to gardens as beasts of prey are to herbivorous animals. But it is also clear that herbivorous animals may be called first to act as mediators on the assumption that they are like collectors and gatherers (plant-food eaters), while they can be used as animal food though they are not themselves hunters.[7]

Such transformations and oppositions, though part of the method, seemed to obfuscate the fact that the unconscious structures remained hidden. All the examples that opposed the raw and the cooked, fire and ashes, honey and table manners (they were to explain changes in tribal life) only pretended to explain the common ingredi-

ents in myth, or to reveal their constituent units. It is difficult to agree, for instance, that because two Bororo myths reveal the advent of culture as dependent on the massacre of a community, the transition from "nature" to "culture" always corresponds, in native thought, to the transition from the "continuous" to the "discontinuous."

Lévi-Strauss always stressed that analysis of myth goes beyond the analysis of its terminology or contents; he focused on discovering the relations which unite all mythologies. These relations became the ultimate objects of his structural analysis. According to Lévi-Strauss, the meaningful and unifying structures of mythology surface through the analysis of myths in the way that unconscious thought emerges into consciousness through psychoanalysis. Hence the unveiling of structures became a kind of cultural psychoanalysis.

Lévi-Strauss's reading of Freud, however, leaned toward the philosophical rather than the clinical. The Oedipus complex, which as we know has acquired a special importance in Freudian theory, appeared to be one of Lévi-Strauss's universal structures; it seemed to supply at least partial credence to the argument for structuralism. Lévi-Strauss also adapted Freud's idea of defense mechanisms, repression, reaction formation, substitution, and blocking in order to explain transformations of structures from logical to irrational and from conscious to unconscious thought. But whereas Freud asked his patients to free-associate in order to remember traumatic events, Lévi-Strauss listened to natives retell the traumatic memories of their tribe in myths. The myths, for instance, tell of a boy who fell in love with his sister. The sister, in order to escape the advances of her brother, took refuge in the sky and became the moon; he, in turn, became the sun so that he could pursue her but—alas—catch her only briefly during an eclipse.

In that this myth of the origin of the sun and moon—or other native myths—exchanges one type of reality for another, it resembles dreams. Yet where Freud used the symbolic systems of dreams to reconstruct an individual's history, Lévi-Strauss tried to decipher the symbolic systems of myth in order to reconstruct cultural history. Thus, for example, he incorporated this myth about the transformation of the sister and brother into the moon and the sun in order to show the dialectic process of transformation between the two in relation to the incest taboo.

Lévi-Strauss was also influenced by his contemporary, Jacques Lacan, who, in his linguistically inspired psychoanalysis, used notions of structural anthropology. Their common concern with unconscious structures—of tribal myth or individual thought—led a few of their followers to cooperate for a brief period. They attempted to use computers to establish the connection between the constituent units of myth and the constituent units of analysands' dreams. Inevitably, the task failed. Had it succeeded, the emergence of Lévi-Strauss's structures would have proven the scientific claims of structuralism; and the use of computer technology would have furnished it with scientific credentials. As it turned out, Lévi-Strauss's interpretation of Freud seemed more like inspired fantasy than science.

But Lévi-Strauss's application of Marx was even more controversial: it undercut most of the political aims of practicing Marxists. Jean Paul Sartre, for instance, who himself had denied the existence of an unconscious, considered Lévi-Strauss's complex method of free association as a methodological tautology which demonstrates the truth of an idea simply by showing its connection to other ideas. He dismissed Lévi-Strauss's interpretation of Marx and of history as simplistic, and as contradicting his own very carefully reasoned view of the functioning of history on several levels:

[that] "the forces of production" were progressively developed with the inner contradiction of

private ownership and socialization; [that] the "relations of production" engendered the contradictions of the class struggle; [and that] underlying the whole drama of human history was the increasing alienation of human powers that dialectically prepared the ground for emancipation, for a humanization of man, in which nature was to be transfigured in a higher symbiosis of man and nature.[8]

Lévi-Strauss's special brand of Marxism appeared to be related to fundamental notions of exchange and production, and to the way in which culture emerges from nature.[9] But this application of the dialectic ignored some of Marx's central concepts. Like Marx, Lévi-Strauss assumed economic production to arise from human needs; yet whereas Marx argued that production is conditioned by the economic structure of society, Lévi-Strauss added the notion that culture emerges from universal unconscious structures.

This is why Lévi-Strauss seemed to be more concerned with Marx's ideas of cultural transformation than with questions of causality:

Dialectical materialism should always be able to proceed by transformation, from economic or social structure to the structure of law, art or religion... [and] these transformations were dialectic, and in some cases Marx went to great lengths to discover the crucial transformations which at first sight seemed to defy analysis.[10]

Although Lévi-Strauss's dialectic "springs directly from the customs and philosophy of the group, from whom the individual learns his lessons...[from] his belief in guardian spirits...", and from the fact that "society as a whole teaches its members that their only hope of salvation within the established social order lies in an absurd and despairing attempt to get free from that order,"[11] he never touched on Marx's conclusions about the polarization of the classes, the inevitability of revolution, or the withering away of the state. Of course, some of these omissions resulted from the difficulty of applying Marxism to primitive cultures that are preindustrial and therefore preclass in our sense. Lévi-Strauss later attempted to surmount this problem when he began to differentiate between primitive ("cold"), and industrial ("hot") societies. Nevertheless, his neo-Durkheimian vision of personal freedom—based on tribal organizations in which the means of production are communally owned—sidestepped Marx's idea of false consciousness as well as class consciousness.

The disagreement between Lévi-Strauss and Sartre, however, was centered not only on ideology, on fundamental epistemological differences, and on their approach to history. Were Lévi-Strauss's structures to emerge, Sartre's whole theory of human existence and its fundamental condition of freedom would be disproven. So Sartre considered the structuralist approach to be guilty of transforming humans into static, timeless objects related to things in the world and to other humans in purely formal, objective, and timeless ways. He himself located consciousness of self and things in praxis, so that "it is no more than an apprehension of reality" [12]—which implies, of course, outer reality, not inner structure. Sartre's dialectic was between humans and their surroundings. Lévi-Strauss's dialectic was between humans as social beings and humans as the unconscious bearers of a universal order (derived from as yet undiscovered structures).

LOUIS ALTHUSSER

Lévi-Strauss's disagreements with other structuralists appeared to be as fundamental as those with Sartre. Inevitably his interpretation of Marx was equally unacceptable to Althusser, for theoretical, political, and ideological reasons—even though Althusser shared the concern for unconscious structures. For Althusser's structuralist Marxism aimed at a rereading of Marx which was to help construct a nonrepressive communist state. To this end Althusser used two new theoretical concepts. He derived the first concept from Bachelard, a historian of science who maintained that in the course of the development of a science, epistemological acts and thresholds suspend the continuous accumulation of knowledge, interrupt its slow development, force it to enter a new time, cut it off from its empirical origin and original motivations, cleanse it of its imaginary complicities, and direct historical analysis away from the search for silent beginning toward the search for a new type of rationality and its various effects. [13] In other words Bachelard postulated scientific epochs that ostensibly could create epistemological breaks of a kind Althusser then could locate in Marx's works.

The second concept derived more directly from structural linguistics—from the notion that a system of lexical relationships is part of our linguistic competence. Since readers' competence comes from experience and knowledge, some structural linguists allow for a "superreader" as a tool of analysis, as a technique to "reread" a text. For a superreader is able to "work through and to sniff out places which can be shown as particularly significant in relation to the specified knowledge which he [the superreader] possesses." [14] Althusser's intimate acquaintance with Marx's texts allowed him to function as a superreader—to liberate Marxism from its customary reading. He could immerse himself in the texts and reinterpret them in relation to specific events in Marx's life so as to understand the problems of scientific Marxism through the theory itself.

It is in this context that Althusser was sympathetic to psychoanalytic notions of the unconscious. He was interested in Lévi-Strauss's and Lacan's elaborations on "the discourse of the unconscious," because these might have helped his rereading of Marx. He explained, for instance, how Marx's informed gaze, when analyzing David Ricardo's or Adam Smith's economics could, on second reading, articulate what, at first, had been left out. Or he looked, in *The Piccolo Teatro: Bertolazzi and Brecht*, for Marxist themes, emphasizing the existence of the "visible" and the "invisible" of his "symptomatic reading."[15]

Reminding the reader that Marx, in *The German Ideology*, had dismissed philosophy as having neither a history nor a subject and that Lenin too had found philosophy useless—it lives on politics, and politics are usually fatal to philosophy,[16]—Althusser began to reread the different meanings of alienation in *The Manuscripts of 1844* and in *Capital*. In the course of this rereading, according to Norman Geras, Althusser distinguished in Marx the theoretical deficiencies, the terminological ambiguities, and the ideological "survivals" of the early works from the later "scientific concepts."[17] Thus Althusser perceived an epistemological break in Marx's texts that denoted the new problematic which had cut all links to bourgeois ideology; he then returned to events in Marx's life and works. This epistemological break, he argued, had occurred when Marx wrote *The German Ideology*, although it could already be detected in the *Theses of Feuerbach*. Althusser considered everything prior to *The Manuscripts of 1844* immature, including *The Holy Family*; the early works or Marx's writings from 1845 to 1857; and the transitional works (first notes for *Capital*, the *Manifesto*, *Poverty of Philosophy*, *Wages*, *Price and Profit*). Only after 1857, beginning with the *Grundrisse*, had Marx fully matured and dealt with his science—that is, with political economy.

By locating a major shift in Marx about 1845, and arguing that from then on Marx was solely committed to the proletarian revolution, Althusser could repudiate the early Marx along with all reformist and humanist Marxists.[18] And this refutation itself, by discrediting the basic assumptions of figures like Sartre, Henri Lefèbvre, or Roger Garaudy,[19] might have had far-reaching consequences. In the process, however, he did not escape accusations that explaining Marx through Marx's life and works might be circular. But as he showed how Marx and Engels had "settled ac-

counts with . . . [their] former political conscience" through the epistemological break, Althusser established himself through his method.[20] Its structuralist cast, of course, was attuned to the discourse around him as well as to his rereading of Marx. Sometimes Althusser sounded like a psychohistorian, when, for example, he discussed Marx's Hegelianism as an "adolescent phase" that inspired only the 1844 *Manuscripts*, which deliberately attempted to invert Hegelian idealism into Feuerbachian pseudomaterialism, or when he "proved" two stages of development (thresholds) before the total rupture in the *Early Marx*. From 1840 to 1842, according to Althusser, Marx was a rationalist-humanist, close to Kant and Fichte, and conceived the essence of humanity as liberty and reason, whereas between 1842 and 1845 Feuerbach's humanism became predominant. At that point Marx is said to have reacted to the reality of the state, which had not transformed itself. Disillusioned, he dropped his former humanism and no longer saw philosophy and the proletariat as allies in the communist revolution. By 1845 he had given up every shred of idealism.[21] Cleansed of a Hegelianism that he "had only used once," on the eve of his rupture with his "erstwhile philosophical conscience," Marx "liquidated this disordered consciousness" in an "abreaction" that was corollary to his maturing and to the true beginning of Marxism.[22]

By accepting this new interpretation—that is, the destruction of Marxist humanism—Marx's economic theories (i.e., the labor theory of value and surplus value) could be rethought and Marxists were asked to concentrate on "scientific Marxism." Althusser's works were praised for their serious intent by those who thought that only a revolution could save us, and that such a revolution needed planning. He was attacked by the "idealist" Marxists and by anticommunists who questioned his underlying political assumptions and the viability of his increasingly Leninist stance. His use of structural textual analysis, however, enlarged his potential readership and its accompanying interest in Marx. Now Althusser instructed everyone not only to read *Capital* but to read it in proper sequence, that is, in relation to the knowledge that existed at the moment this knowledge was produced.

Although I have shown the political ideas and the roots of Althusser's structuralist Marxism, I have ignored the many polemics with humanist Marxists—inside and outside the Communist party. Predictably, the attacks on humanism and anthropologism got Althusser into conflict with Sartre, who all along had minimized the importance of *Capital* and of Marx's political economy to refine the concepts of *praxis*. Hence, their antagonism was built into their work. Raymond Aron, eager to discredit Marxism in any form, found that their actual opposition was "less radical than would seem, for Althusser did not know *Capital*, capitalist economy, or Soviet economy any better than Sartre." [23] Reading *Capital* was too abstract, said Aron. And while Sartre, in *Critique de la raison dialectique* had wanted to base Marxism on the "comprehension of the *historical totality* . . .Althusser had wanted to detach theory [or the practice of theory]. . .in order to show the scientism of *Capital*—an impossible task for a philosopher unfamiliar with economics." [24] Aron, among others, concluded that Althusser and his friends were rethinking Marxism-Leninism to remain in the party; that "engagement" in reflections could not be censored by the "guardians of the faith"; and that the theory was sufficiently abstract that, even when condemned as revisionism, it would offend neither Moscow nor Peking. [25]

Althusser's Marxism not only served as an antidote to the idealist hopes of existentialism but, more generally, against the structuralist search for total history in which all the differences of a society are reduced to one form, one world view, or one value system. Michel Foucault, who also argued against this "sovereignty of the subject and the twin figures of anthropology and humanism," [26] and who could, therefore, be seen as aligned with Althusser, nevertheless was a strong and outspoken opponent of repression in Soviet Russia. Foucault, like Althusser, postulated Bachelardian-type breaks in historical epochs (his epochs were said to be dominated by codes of knowledge corresponding to dominant structures), and thus was perceived as a structuralist Marxist by some. I believe, however, that Foucault has always been eclectic, and that his Marxism was implicit insofar as he denounced structures of power, and nonexistent insofar as he never predicted a revolutionary struggle. In any event, we will note below how he differed from Althusser.

MICHEL FOUCAULT

Foucault addressed structuralist linguistics much more directly than Althusser ever did. From the very beginning, in *Madness and Civilization* (1961), Foucault extrapolated from linguistic methods by focusing on oppositions and transformations to study the history of psychology and psychopathology in relation to social conditions and beliefs about deviance. Second, Foucault's theory derived from empirical observation: it was deductive rather than inductive. And third, the unconscious structures were general codes of knowledge rather than Marxist ones.

We can trace Foucault's evolution through his books which initially concentrated on methodology and the establishment of his epistemological epochs of knowledge, then on the theoretical linguistics he used throughout, and most recently, on power. But this type of schematization is the sort of oversimplification that led at least one reviewer to accuse Foucault of having written the same book over and over again. True, he became repetitious, but each book dealt with a different central topic and, theoretically, refined the previous works.

In *Madness and Civilization* (1961) he painstakingly documented how the elite's definition of madness depended on the composition of this elite itself, upon society's need for outcasts, and upon the examination of madness as a phenomenon only when leprosy disappeared. All societies need deviants, argued Foucault, because their exclusion and the act of their exclusion makes for everyone else's feeling of inclusion—for social solidarity.

Furthermore, Foucault found that everyone had been fascinated by madness; its very ambiguity and its existence at the edge of experience helped people deal with their anxieties about death. In literature and art the fool seemed to know both more and less than the sane. But rather than asking the customary questions that connect madness to the creative mind, Foucault looked at the fool in relation to the sane. Because the fool seemed to be able to look into the future, he or she was frequently cast in the role of prophet, or placed at the "midpoint of man's origin, between life and death."

Confinement, Foucault concluded, marked the beginning of a new age, when madness still preserved its ambivalences and appearances, but was also tied to the rise of scientism and to the loss of religious values. Now the mad were available for discussion and treatment, for legal regulation and scientific diagnosis, even though it was not until the nineteenth century that they were separated from thieves and criminals, squanderers and beggars, vagabonds and unemployed. Their separation from other deviants was said to have become a scientific question that occupied doctors, lawyers, and the police.

Examining medical archives, Foucault discovered that doctors began to form a new language of signs and symbols; he perceived "language as the first and last structure of madness, its constituent form." [27] He medi-

ated between insanity and sanity the way Lévi-Strauss did between myth and reality. And like Freud, he linked the language of delirium to dreams, and to a "blindness of words that abandon reality." [28] He began to connect the structure of language to the structure of madness, and increasingly employed Saussurean dichotomies, which he located within Bachelardian epochs of knowledge. The placing of the mad inside asylums, which, as he argued in his book *The Birth of the Clinic*, paralleled the placing of the sick in hospitals, led to a system of organization that allowed the mad and the sick to be supervised, and to be clearly distinguished from the sane and the healthy.

After the dissection of corpses, for instance, was legalized at the doctors' instigation, doctors could begin to "gaze" at death. For Foucault, this was the basis of more new knowledge. Foucault maintained that there then evolved an unconscious code of knowledge, of new moral methods which responded to the social conditions and needs the French Revolution had created, and that a "science of the individual" was born.

In order to get at this unconscious code, Foucault developed his linguistic methodology, first in *The Order of Things* (1965) and later in *The Archeology of Knowledge* (1970). Essentially, he tried to get at the underside of discourse and at structures of knowledge by unveiling the strategies that sanction their "conceptualizing rituals".

Extrapolating from structural linguistics, Foucault maintained that until then, madness, illness, and crime had been dealt with in a very similar fashion. But as scientific discourse evolved, signs began to be arranged in binary fashion as the connection of a *significant* and a *signifier*. [29] Chains of resemblances led to signatures (recognitions and similitudes, or signs that tie resemblances) as "intermediate forms of the same resemblances," or as "marks of sympathy" to delimit the world and "to form one vast single text for those who could read." [30]

Foucault's entire effort was a search for the ultimate explanation of our universe. But the conclusion, which postulated three faces of knowledge—mathematics and physics, the sciences (language, life, the production and distribution of wealth), and philosophical reflection—left many questions unanswered. The human sciences were said to exist at the interstices of these knowledges, because they lend relevance to the others (their constituent models are said to be based on biology, economics, and language) and operate in interlocking pairs: function and norm, conflict and rule, signification and system. History, Foucault's own discipline, was perceived as the oldest of the human sciences that existed long before humanity, who appeared only at the beginning of the nineteenth century. Hence Foucault could perceive history as the environment for the human sciences—a history delimited by epochs of knowledge. This "bracketing" of epochs, in part, was also to counteract the ahistorical thrust of Lévi-Strauss's ethnology—"a study of societies without history." For Foucault's own structuralism was meant to address questions of humanity itself, and of knowledge that "spans the sciences and dissolves man."

Foucault's subsequent works, *I Pierre Rivière, Having Slaughtered My Mother, My Sister, and My Brother . . .* (1972) and *Discipline and Punish* (1975), again were more empirical, although "archaeological analyses" explained the development of crime and prisons, and the symbiotic relationship that arose between the medical and the legal professions. In both books Foucault demonstrated how current legal language (i.e., particulars, circumstances, explanations, and occurrence) became popular then to explain the grotesque, the gruesome, or the despicable; how new words helped make the transitions from the familiar to the remarkable, from the everyday to the historical; and how, suddenly, the act of writing turned gossip into history. Since then, histories of street brawls and murders were said to have "joined" the histories of power as the symbiotic collusion between medicine and law became the norm.

Combining data from various fields to provide new insights, Foucault included both Marxist and capitalist as he constructed his horizon of crime. New rituals were compared to previous ones, arbitrary sovereigns were contrasted to the new egalitarian legality, and old-style executioners to modern and anonymous electric chairs. He even juxtaposed the people's solidarity against real criminals to their near-identification with the new postrevolutionary delinquencies—delinquencies that are investigated by the rising class of inspectors and police.

Where can we go from a police state, whose police do not even know whom they are policing, from a repressive society whose citizens think they are free, and who, for the most part, do not even have the capacity to recognize their own delusion? Foucault located the reasons for this false consciousness in the production and the perpetuation of surveillance by the legal-medical powers. Social workers and therapists, for instance, by helping individuals to "adapt" were cast as unwitting accomplices of this power. But socialist theory—itself a failure and a victim of the police state in a more conscious form—never presented a solution for Foucault. The only salvation, if any, could be through knowledge, knowledge that he expects to grow on the ruins of our own epoch. Although he does not predict just how this will happen, he seems to imply that his own method will be instrumental, as he searches for the locus of power even Marx and Freud did not find—power that is both visible and invisible, both present and hidden, and invested everywhere.[31]

American sociologists have "applied" Foucault to various theories of deviance. In this context his criticisms are used radically, even though his lack of political affiliation places him among French conservatives. Actually, his trenchant exposure of justice and medicine in relation to modern power and belief systems could, conceivably, influence policy—especially in America, where radicalism is practiced by idealistic attacks on those in power. In France such action would be located in the Communist party or in the various anarchist and Marxist groups, and there, history is related to the class struggle.

Yet Foucault not only challenged Marx, but also Durkheim's notion that social solidarity increases with an increase in written laws. Instead, however indirectly, he showed that the myriads of laws—laws engendered with the help of medicine—made doctors and lawyers our new "priests," who have legalized and medicalized us into increasing anomie, and who perpetuate their own mystification. Their high remuneration "expresses their worth"—a worth achieved through strong professional organizations that prohibit access to many and indoctrinate the elected few—in a society whose values, as Georg Simmel said long ago, are all eventually expressed through money. The Patty Hearst trial, for instance, with its show of celebrity-type psychiatrists—to prove guilt or innocence—exemplified Foucault's themes. The very prominence of professional expertise to establish innocence or guilt serves to legitimate authority and to further social solidarity.

Foucault foresees the end of our age, because the therapeutization which linked up with legalization in the interest of social order has created chaos, and chaos has become the norm. Crime has become everybody's business, and business crime is as normal as the therapy that eases its accompanying guilt and helps adaptation. Thus more therapy and more police are needed and produced, as manipulation has taken over, as every action requires legal advice, and as the honest person has, gradually, taken the place of the fool. Analogous

to Foucault's fool of the Renaissance, he or she is uninfluential, poor, and marginal; the fool might appear as the prophet, predicting the doom of our scientific era. Foucault himself seems to be one of the prophets. Whether we gaze at his fools, his criminals, or his geniuses, at Don Quixote or at Velasquez, his dialectic of language does not leave a loophole: Foucault's millenarian predictions, it appears, were solidly grounded. If he is correct, and the era of humanity is ended, his structuralist analysis already carries the seeds of the next epoch.

CONCLUSIONS

The structuralisms of Lévi-Strauss, Althusser, and Foucault, as we have noted, have different disciplinary bases, political practices, and concerns. Although they all aimed to get to the rock bottom of social customs and knowledge, and to unconscious structures, and although they all shared a general Marxist perspective, they differed in their interpretations of Marx—interpretations whose political overtones, though implicit, were not always spelled out.

Lévi-Strauss assumed that the "savage mind" and the "modern mind" still share underlying structures of thought. This concern with human existence did, of course, approximate the problems addressed by the young idealist Marx—problems both Sartre and Lefèbvre (among others) also had tried to solve. Lévi-Strauss, however, ignored their work when he began his anthropological exegeses. His treatment of myth in ahistorical fashion not only clashed with Sartre and Lefèbvre but also with portions of Marx.

Althusser was bound to attack Lévi-Strauss, since for him the young Marx was *persona non grata*; and only the mature Marx of *Capital*, who focused on political economy, on the labor theory of value, and who had abandoned his youthful idealism, was valid. So he insisted on rejecting the "anthropological given" that was subsumed in the Sartre/Lévi-Strauss controversy in order to follow up Marx's economic concepts, and separated the social phenomena that meet the eye from the underlying laws of class struggle which operate behind the scenes. This made him a structuralist insofar as he emphasized economic structures, class situations, and polarization.

The French, as Raymond Aron so aptly put it, have been fed Marxism along with their mother's milk, so that they have incorporated it in their thought. Thus, Althusser, as well as Sartre, Lefèbvre, Garaudy, and Lévi-Strauss, all claimed to practice the proper Marxist dialectic. For Sartre the dialectic concerned the relations between subject and object; for Lefèbvre it was located between formal logic and humanistic philosophy; for Garaudy it was between human beings; for Lévi-Strauss the dialectic occurred primarily between nature and culture; for Althusser it was internal to Marx's texts and explicitly rejected every Hegelian influence. Foucault's history of knowledge, in its mediation within Bachelardian scientific epochs that examined deviants in relation to power, lacked specific Marxist formulations.

Structuralist assumptions of the unconscious, as well, differed from Freud's. For the most part they derived from Jacques Lacan's specific rereading of Freud's texts. Undoubtedly Lévi-Strauss's success helped French psychoanalysis, even though Lacan's takeoff from structural linguistics was very different from Lévi-Strauss's. Because both became fashionable around the same time, it is difficult to say whether French psychoanalysis bolstered structuralism or whether Lacan's recourse to language popularized Freud. In the late 1950s some of Lévi-Strauss's and Lacan's disciples, together, hoped to uncover unconscious common roots in individuals' dreams and in social myths—myths that had been around since the time of the totemic father of *Totem and Taboo*. Both Lévi-Strauss and Lacan stressed social influences and the early Freud who had studied hysteria, and focused on Freud's language rather than on symptomatology. Lacan's pronouncements, especially about the unconscious, which is allegedly "structured like a language," engendered a specific psychoanalytic ideology.

Essentially, Lacan applied Saussurean linguistic oppositions and transformations to the psychoanalytic relationship as well as to Freud's texts. He argued that by examining Freud's clinical writings from this new perspective, from an emphasis on Freud's use of language, we can find out more about what Freud *really* meant.

Althusser's attempt to convert the language of the Oedipus complex which would facilitate socialization of infants into a new social order (by changing family ideology) appealed to Marxists. This in turn inspired Lacan to look into the social and/or psychological meaning and origin of religious and political family practices by investigating, for example, the meaning of *Le nom du père* (the father's name and family heritage) as a conservative ideology.

Foucault, when addressing these issues from a more sociological perspective by linking madness, psychiatry, and medicine to the emerging power structure, focused on structures of family, medicine, law, etc., which, however, by reinforcing control of individuals by guilt rather than through physical punishment allegedly "prepared the ground for Freud."

Clearly the original aims of the structuralists were unattainable, though they did introduce some intriguing and suggestive modes of analysis. The poststructuralisms, of course, have their own rationales. If they have for the most part replaced structuralism, this may be because in France, as well as in America, we continue to look for answers about existence in the humanities; and because partial answers may be preferable to no answers. But all the structuralist enterprises demonstrate once again the fantastic intellectual virtuosity of French thinkers.

NOTES

1. For a more comprehensive treatment of this argument, see Edith Kurzweil, *The Age of Structuralism: Lévi-Strauss to Foucault* (New York: Columbia University Press, 1980); Raymond Boudon, *The Uses of Structuralism* (London: Heinemann, 1971); Jean Piaget, *Structuralism* (New York: Basic Books, 1970).

2. Roland Barthes, "L'activité structuraliste," *Essais critiques* (Paris: Editions du Seuil, 1964), p. 214.

3. Jacques Derrida, *Dissertations*, trans. Barbara Johnson (Chicago: University of Chicago Press, 1981), p. 123.

4. Although in this essay I deal only with the most prominent structuralists, it is important to remember that structural linguistics is a separate discipline, and that the post-structuralists also extrapolate from structural linguistics (in various ways).

5. Roman Jakobson, in studying aphasics, had found two major types of disorders (similarity disorder and contiguity disorder), and had found them to be strikingly similar to the two rhetorical figures of metaphor and metonymy. And he had connected the polarities between "horizontal" and "vertical" aspects of language to the twofold process of *selection* and *combination* of constituent elements in language.

6. This point is repeated throughout Lévi-Strauss's works, i.e., in *Tristes Tropiques* (New York: Atheneum Publishers, 1963); *Structural Anthropology* (New York: Anchor Books, 1967), pp. 32, 39; and in *Myth and Meaning* (New York: Schocken Books, 1952).

7. Claude Lévi-Strauss, "The Structural Study of Myth," *Structural Anthropology*, p. 221.

8. Mark Poster, *Existentialism in Post-War France* (Princeton, N.J.: Princeton University Press, 1975), p. 70.

9. This is implied in *Tristes Tropiques*, pp. 60–63, and again in *The Savage Mind* (in the last chapter: "History and Dialectic"), and in the discussion with Sartre, pp. 245–69.

10. Lévi-Strauss, *Structural Anthropology*, pp. 329–30.

11. Ibid., p. 42.

12. Jean Pouillon, "Analyse dialectique d'une rélation du néant," in *Les Temps Modernes* 19 (July 1963), p. 81.

13. Michel Foucault, *The Archeology of Knowledge* (New York: Pantheon Books, 1974), p. 4.

14. Roger Fowler, "Language and the Reader," in *Style and Structure in Literature* (Ithaca, N.Y.: Cornell University Press, 1975), p. 87. Fowler discusses Riffaterre's introduction, in response to Roman Jakobson; of the superreader as a "tool of analysis."

15. Althusser used this run-of-the-mill play to show the dissociation between forty characters and the three main protagonists (parallel to the ruling class and the proletariat), and their false consciousness. Analyzing the structure of the misery of the masses through a critique of the "melodramatic consciousness," he illustrated the latent tragedy of the Milanese subproletariat and its inherent powerlessness. Whereas his neostructuralist mediations tied the social conditions on the stage to a "direct perception of this period, to the visual parallel between the 'wasteland' and the 'nonchalance of the unemployed,' " the technique, itself, reaffirmed Althusser's Marxism. And Bertolazzi (as well as Brecht) was tied to structuralist notions of time that "abolished the other time and the structure of its representation, and introduced a third dimension." In any event, *The Piccolo Teatro: Bertolazzi and Brecht* served as an illustration of Marxist-structuralist criticism in 1962, and as such was not a central concern to Althusser. In Louis Althusser, *For Marx* (New York: Pantheon Publishers, 1972), pp. 129–51.

16. Ibid., p. 38.

17. Norman Geras, "Althusser's Marxism: An Account and an Assessment," *New Left Review* (January-February 1972), pp. 57–86.

18. Althusser repeated this point many times, arguing that the later writings were based on economic realities and thereby refuted every notion rooted in idealism.

19. Roger Garaudy, an idealist Marxist, was Althusser's opponent within the party, until he broke with the party.

20. This quote from Marx's *A Contribution to the Critique of Political Economy* (1959) is frequently reiterated; Callinicos, for instance, leads off from it (correctly, I believe) as the basis of Althusser's thought.

21. Robin Blackburn and Gareth Stedman Jones, "Louis Althusser and the Struggle for Marxism," *The Unknown Dimension*, ed.

Dick Howard and Karl Klare (New York: Basic Books, 1972), pp. 347–68.

22. Ibid., p. 369. Blackburn and Jones explain particularly well how Marx's rejection of a human essence as the theoretical foundation of philosophy simultaneously rejects a whole organic set of postulates—in history, political economy, ethics, and philosophy itself.

23. Raymond Aron, *Marxismes Imaginaires* (Paris: Gallimard, 1970), pp. 196–97.

24. Ibid., p. 198.

25. Ibid., p. 199.

26. Michel Foucault, *The Archeology of Knowledge* (New York: Pantheon Publishers, 1974).

27. Michel Foucault, *Madness and Civilization* (New York: Pantheon Publishers, 1965), p. 91.

28. Ibid., p. 107.

29. Michel Foucault, *The Order of Things* (New York: Pantheon Publishers, 1970), p. 42.

30. Ibid., p. 34.

31. Michel Foucault, *The History of Sexuality, vol. 1* (New York: Pantheon Publishers, 1978), p. 3.

Marxian sociologists study the capitalist organization of production and its uses of a universal market to evaluate all things produced, exchanged, and consumed.

Capitalism encourages ideas that are compatible with its principles. Yet ideas also arise from capitalist contradictions to challenge the domination of capital. Michael Brown explores the effects of capitalism on the individual and groups as well as various forms of resistance to capitalism. New directions in Marxism are developed, including a Marxian social psychology to explain consumerism through the concepts of desire and need. The importance of the work of Erving Goffman and Harold Garfinkel for a Marxian theory of consciousness is discussed.

Michael Brown

NEW DIRECTIONS IN NEO-MARXISM: A MARXIST SOCIAL PSYCHOLOGY

INTRODUCTION

Marxian sociology, in one of its aspects, is the analysis of the social conditions (and their ramifications) of the attempt to organize production by classes. This involves the private accumulation of wealth, which is required to produce the conditions of continued production—what Marx called *reproduction*—and the establishment of a universe of exchange as the measure of all things. The chief metatheoretical claim of Marxian sociology is that we have to study society from this viewpoint in order to describe the historical conditions of the present as well as the ways in which social change can occur through the collective initiative. In other ways Marxism attempts to make manifest in all it studies the internal relationship between two inextricably intertwined aspects of social action: theory and practice.

The theory of Marxian sociology depends upon several concepts.

1. *Value* is seen as the difference something makes to the whole of which it is a part.

2. The *society of producers* is seen as the form of *sociality* in which action takes shape as something entirely different from exchange, and hence as something capable of displaying an internal relation of theory and practice.

3. *Opposition* exists between the social action of producing something in such a way as to conserve the possibility of that production and the historically limited form in which the product is removed from the sphere of production and placed within the sphere of exchange of circulation (that is, of *exploitation*).

4. The ways in which the difference between the activity of re-creating the social conditions of production and the momentary appearance of that activity as something fixed or a system are seen to show themselves as a history-making relationship between *subject* and *object*.

Therefore, among many other things, Marxist research deals with the composition and constant reorganization of the populations corresponding to the major classes, which Marx calls *capital* and *labor*. It deals with subsidiary social formations and projects, which sociologists often call *institutions*, which correspond to the divisions within and outside economic relations—political and cultural—between the classes. These include collective bargaining, elections, education, religion, the family, and the city. They also include such forms of collective behavior as popular protest, mass action, strikes, insurrections, and riots as well as other movements beyond and in opposition to capital-sponsored arrangements. Such forms are unconscious forms of resistance to the alienation of work, leisure, and sociality, the coordination of life by need-denying market considerations, and the calculated isolation of all social and personal forms that cannot, taken in combination, be integrated into capitalist production and exchange.

It is in the context of these topics, given the concepts that make them understandable as aspects of theory and practice, that Marxian sociology studies the primary objects of its concrete analyses of societal change—the consciousness, organization, and forms of action intrinsic to the development of labor (variously seen by Marx as the *working class* and the *society of the producers*) as an effective force for change. Heuristically, Marxian sociology deals with the whole of human affairs to the extent to which those affairs are organized by the intentions and practices instituted within the capitalist mode of production. It deals with those affairs historically, that is, in terms of the development and interactions of those interests directed toward and capable of organizing society as a whole. Its methodological hallmark is its emphasis on relations of opposition (exploitation, power, social organization as competing projects, culture as competing ideologies,

and conflict) in regard to the history of society as a whole.

WAYS OF THINKING UNDER CAPITALISM

Marxist literature lists at least two sources of ideas under capitalism. First, the fact that capitalism operates across the whole spectrum of social life encourages ways of thinking and acting that are compatible with its operative principles, and discourages thought that does not challenge the dominance of capital within the contradictory relations of production that make it possible and vulnerable. Second, the fact that capitalism consists of contradictory operations (that is, labor and capital) makes every expression of capitalist domination simultaneously an expression of resistance. Research has emphasized primarily the ways in which capital tends to dominate thought. This is illustrated in the following sections.

It should be clear that capitalism implicates a market that encompasses virtually all that is produced. This price-making money market grades everything against a standard and measures all things as if they were to be subject to exchange. However, what is especially important to the ways people think, in general and in common, is the fact that this market and its logic know no exception and exempt nothing from the requirement of comparability and the process of comparison. It is to be expected, then, that thought in one of its aspects will reflect this universalization of exchange. But in doing so, it must also represent all things, human and nonhuman, as if they were no more than commodities. Marx referred to this representation of social relations as *things*, and human beings and their needs as subordinate to the things of the market as a *fetishism*.

Things are thought to have a higher, more personal or voluntary, or even a more social, reality than people. The value of people lies in those properties that make them comparable to things. But the same applies to human products and affairs. They appear not as expressions of human intention, but as things commanding and commanded by the market, independent of the labor that made them and the purpose without which they would not have been made. So we speak of *the* economy instead of the *capitalist* economy; of the *occurrence* of fiscal crisis rather than of the contradictions of capitalist exploitation; of the *flow* of goods and money rather than of the expropriation of the surplus and the realization of value by members of the capitalist class; and of the *true* market value rather than of the level of profitability currently reflecting capital's power. Finally, moral persuasion loses its hold on the imagination altogether. This is illustrated by a report that appeared in a New York newspaper during the 1970s. Oil companies had raised their prices exorbitantly. As a result, many people who could not pay their increases in fuel cost found themselves without heat during a bitter winter. Several died. An executive of one of the oil companies was asked to comment. His response was identical to the responses of companies leasing slaves from the German government during the Second World War when asked to account for their behavior and its results: "That's business." Similarly, in 1980 David Rockefeller carried the following message to Argentina and other governments that use terror to control their populations: the United States will not condemn anything you choose to do to keep your people in line; trade will continue; there will be business as usual. The torture of people is of little significance alongside the motions of the market and the profits of the capitalist.

The generation of ideologies through the mass media, educational facilities, and special events, such as ceremonies, cold wars, etc., provides advertisements for capital and slogans that can achieve currency in other sectors—political, interpersonal—of the public sphere. Of course, they provide

even more since they have the advantage of the authority of their sources and the capacity to invade all the spaces of the settings in which they are received. These ideologies are displayed rather formalistically as artful expressions of collective life, and their presentations appear on otherwise sanctioned occasions so that it is difficult to untangle their significance from that of those occasions as such—the news, school, shopping, reading, and leisure.

We can trace the history of ideologies, their forms of display, their occasions of presentation, their origins, and their impact. This history of mass communications points, as does all Marxist sociology, to the situation of what it studies, the conflicts and intentions governing the course of development and deployment of various media and their content. That this is indeed a history of ideology and class strategies is indicated by one of its landmarks: the conflicts at the end of the eighteenth century over whether or not literacy should be encouraged among the poor. This conflict involved several arguments, each of which corresponded to the class-oriented character of the debate. One side argued that increased literacy would increase the level of dissatisfaction among "the dangerous classes." Another side pointed out that if the working class was ever to know its place in relation to its betters, it would have to be informed by correct literature.

The same undercurrent of interest can be found by tracing the history of the press, radio, and television: in all cases entertainment and information are coupled to the interests of class and of the state, though this coupling takes a variety of forms and contains its own contradictory impulses. We might well conclude after a provisional reading of this history that the mass media, more often than not, have successfully constrained thought and discourse within the framework of an ideology that discourages criticism, protest, and the acknowledgment of class and class interest. At the same time, however, the deployment of messages through the social media (radio and television—media that are consumed collectively rather than individually) has reinforced the social character of discourse and offered the possibility of successful movements to recapture the media for "the society of producers." The proliferation of underground media during the 1960s was a response to the demand for relevant news, and was instrumental in breaking the ideological hold on news about social protest against the American invasion of Vietnam. Thus, in the mass media as in all other sectors of capitalism, we find contradictory impulses and the class struggle.

It is possible to indicate more concretely the relevant topics for a Marxist study of communication. The important aspects of the transmission of ideology are the origin of the messages; their internal structure, context, and referents; the imagery that emerges with a proliferation of ideological material; and the character of public life, which ensures that what is presented formally is retransmitted informally, from person to person, with an air of improvisation and conversational validity. *Origin* refers to the particular authority of competence attributed to the source; the *structure* of messages refers to the ways in which what is shown, said, or written encompasses its subject matter without at the same time exposing the message or its origin to criticism; *context* refers to the whole collection of words whose convenient and easy use provides a background for messages that draw upon it for a sense of the commonness of their meaning; *referents* of ideology refers to recurring objects that make any act of communication appear relevant to public concern; *emergent imagery* is an epiphenomenon of communication, the sense of things (as dangerous, scarce, urgent, global, in good hands, etc.) that arises in thought as communication proceeds; and the *establishment of a public sphere* for the casual and therefore interpersonally reinforced reproduction of what had been initially presented formally guarantees that the ideology will persist beyond the instances of its presentation.

The generation of ideologies places limits on public debate over issues of public concern; and because of their dependence on the public sphere, the academic disciplines, too, reflect these limits. However, the very explicitness of such ideologies tends to engage an opposition which, if it gains access to official channels or finds its own medium, can introduce the possibility of an alternate perspective on society. But it should not be assumed that dialogue characterizes the field of ideological expression. Typically in American history, opposition is tolerated only to the extent to which it lacks power and an organizational base. Otherwise, it is denied adequate access to publication, or it is actively suppressed through such means as restricting expression, limiting political activities designed to provide a base for oppositional points of view, harassment by official agencies, and censorship of the left within the media. Despite the fact, then, that opposition has occasionally found its issues and its voice—small though that has been—the overall result remains the same: a public sphere dominated by official ideologies favorable to the interest of capital.

There is an even more pervasive effect of capitalism on culture. This occurs because of capital's tendency and capacity to universalize its own conditions, and thus to invade every situation with material that is compelling to thought and speech. In this sense of a pervasive set of conceptual tendencies and ways of thinking under capitalism, the logic of private property and privately conducted exchange becomes the basis for even the most mundane thought and discourse. This observation has produced one of the largest bodies of literature on culture in the history of Marxism. It has provided a way in which Marxism has achieved a genuinely interdisciplinary reach in our time. The recognition that capitalism involves a detailed, though contradictory, organization of society has engaged Marxist scholars in studies of language, cognition, literature, art, film criticism, urbanization, the socialization of children, the family, and religion. The result is a rich documentation of the pervasiveness of the logic of capitalist expansion and the beginnings of research on the role of oppositional culture and organization in the development of class consciousness.

The Prevalence of Consumerism

The universal market—that is, the overwhelming orientation of exchange in daily life—has provided much of the basic empirical material for a Marxist social psychology that challenges the rationalistic theories of consumer behavior still taken for granted by many economists. On the one hand, this social psychology documents the molding of every form of life to the logic of exchange, and with it to the contradictions of exchange. Human interaction becomes, under the auspices of the market, a round of evaluating, bargaining, negotiating, calculating, choosing, and accounting. Yet this interaction imposes market criteria upon processes and values that can only be measured if their personal and social significance is denied or suppressed. The result of the imposition of such criteria is that people are motivationally most uneasy at precisely the moment that they appear most rational. An even more important consequence is that expressive behavior loses its reference to needs as it comes to be predicated upon abstract comparisons among behaviors and objects. It follows that people become more perceptive of the quantitative aspects of judgment than of emotion, and less able to appreciate the self-defining quality of action rather than its position in the social market of behavior. Even traditional practices and intimacies take on the properties of relations of exchange under the impact of the market. Religion becomes the processes of grading conduct, honoring a hierarchy, and negotiating with God. The

ideas of sin and sacrifice lose their critical bearing on ordinary life, and nothing fills the gap they leave in the domain of moral experience.

Similarly, the intimacy of the family is distorted by the persistent appeals of commodities. Family life comes to be organized as a mixed market in which each member, defined through advertisement, film, and fashion as a member of a particular market, appeals for increasing or total control over the family budget. The results are processes of compromise and conflict more characteristic of haggling in the marketplace than of social cohesion, empathy, and mutuality. Every consumer good stands, in the political economy of the family, as a cost to all for the benefit of some, rather than a provision for the family as a group. The upshot, or at least one upshot, is that what has been called the *generation gap* can be seen as a difference created by the appeals of different markets, each of which commands its individual subjects to expend an increasing portion of an inflexible family budget, thereby undermining whatever unity and solidarity of domestic life is otherwise possible and reducing the sphere of privacy that has always depended upon that life for its protection.

Another body of literature has attempted to provide a psychodynamics of personality based on the Marxian analysis of consumerism. The main point of this literature is that individuals who are governed by market considerations are confronted with appeals to *desire* rather than to *need*. Desire refers to conventionally established wishes directed at what is commercially available. It gauges satisfaction quantitatively, in terms of amount. Need, on the other hand, refers to purposes that express self or identity. It points to the moral and interpersonal dimensions of individual life. The market appeals to and creates desires, and the prospect of satisfying those desires places the individual within the transactions of the market. But this reduces self-awareness, the perception of one's own and others' needs, and the sense of purpose that is essential for socially responsive personal development.

The result is that at each moment of choice, each moment of possible self-determination and self-awareness, we cannot know whether the choice has been made freely in relation to a felt need or under external control and obligation. This confusion is resolved by a constant reentering of the market, an obsessive seeking of new objects, and a compulsive vigilance against obsolescence and toward novelty. The distractions of these reactions disguise the problem and leave ungovernable traces of the confusion of need and control—guilt, self-doubt, etc.—operating at the margins of personality. More than this, it leaves needs active and yet lacking in personal and interpersonal significance. It insulates them from the practical and instructive world of daily experience, and consigns them to an unsocialized preconscious or unconscious, where they return only as sources of danger or threat. Such unsocialized needs nevertheless press for expression. When they finally achieve their release, it is only as addiction—unrefined, obsessive, and, above all, unable to be presented in the socially responsive way that is essential for adequate gratification and subsequent modification (learning).

Thus the transformation of society by capital includes the transformation of institutions, traditions, daily life, and personality, all of which are influenced by the market of goods as they are influenced as well by the market for people—labor power. Research on this secondary transformation of society by capital remains largely scattered and as yet not theoretically integrated with the aspects of Marxist theory that clarify the contradictory and progressive aspects of capitalism. At this point it is suggestive but not decisive. Its full incorporation into Marxism may well require attention to several other critical disciplines, including psychoanalysis, language studies, phenomenology, ethnomethodology, and symbolic interactionism.

Erving Goffman's work, which intersects several of these disciplines, provides an illustration of this possibility. Goffman has analyzed the interaction of people when they take for granted that their performances will be evaluated, and that the evaluation will bear on their acceptance by others. He argues that we enter groups and social settings uneasily, with an awareness that certain of our characteristics might, if disclosed, discredit us as participants. This is complicated by the fact that a considerable amount of the information we inevitably convey to others is nonverbal and therefore difficult to control. This means that we are apt, despite ourselves, to make damaging disclosures threatening our continued acceptance as members of the group. In order to deal with this predicament, and because there is a certain degree of tension in any gathering as a result of the mutual vulnerability of members to possible discreditation, individuals tend to present themselves in ways that conceal their defects or deny the significance of such defects. They also look for deviant patterns or traits in others in order to direct tension away from themselves, and they draw social boundaries that indicate possible alliances among similarly discreditable members. The result of Goffman's analysis is a picture of ordinary interaction that is uneasy, that involves more calculation than we would otherwise have supposed, and that is laced with the prospect of rejection systemic to every encounter.

If Goffman's work is to be appropriate to a Marxian sociology, it must not be taken as a study of the inevitable features of social life in all places and at all times. That sort of generalization is not defensible. Rather, we must ask under what conditions the attitude of calculation and self-advertisement does prevail as he describes it. It is clear from our discussion of exploitation, commodities, and exchange that he has described alienated interaction of the sort we might expect to find in a developed capitalist society. Goffman's value to Marxian sociology depends on the introduction of this historical dimension to his work. With it, we can see in his work a perceptive and useful description of daily life; what is missing is an elaboration sufficient to reveal the *critical* aspect of interaction, that aspect directed against precisely the alienation that his analysis has brought to our notice.

SOCIAL PSYCHOLOGY OF PROTEST MOVEMENTS

Non-Marxist sociologies have never been able adequately to explain organized protest. When they have tried to do so, they have had to introduce the idea of exceptional conditions in the light of which old patterns of behavior become irrelevant and human action becomes disorganized and volatile. For such explanations volatility is an effect of social disorganization induced by certain externally imposed strains on the social order. The Marxist approach begins with a level of disorder that is intrinsic to capitalism. It conceives of capitalist society not as a balanced and complete system of orderly relations, but as a systematic contradiction of interests characteristic of social action at all times and in all places. Volatility is built into the exploitative economy so that the emergence of organized protest and opposition, including insurrection and revolution, is not something that is an exception to the social order but an extension of what is already established as a given.

For this reason Marxist theories of collective behavior—riot, protest, and the like—find it possible to identify in most instances some relation to the class character of capitalism. At the same time, they find it necessary to deny the possibility of a general theory of mass behavior that can apply to all historical periods and all forms of society. For this reason, too, such theories can identify what have been called *commodity riots* not as reactions to deprivation but as generalized responses, collectively instituted, to contradiction between the society of pro-

ducers and private ownership. Maldistribution is experienced in the riot as an inevitable feature of private control and the expropriation of the socially essential surplus of production by a privileged class. When official control appears at the same time to be weak, power shifts not to individuals but to individuals as members of collectivities. The weakening of official power is a sign of the opposition of forces, class-based or only vaguely class-oriented, and not simply as an opening for individual expressiveness, as was posited by older theories of *the crowd*.

Thus the Marxist theory of revolution does not simply preview empirical cases of exceptional action directed against the state but also the development of the working class in the midst of the contradictions of capitalism. And it encompasses a great deal of what has in traditional sociological texts been called *collective behavior* as well as the whole range of activities shown by symbolic interactionist and ethnomethodological studies to involve attempts to resolve the unresolvable, to reconcile the unreconcilable, and to reproduce what has already irrevocably changed.

It is a theory of prospects *and* parameters rather than of merely one *or* the other; and it is part of a total view of political action rather than, as in the case of much of political science, an attempt to establish natural boundaries between rational, institutional action and nonrational, antiprogressive, noninstitutional conflict and mass behavior. In a phrase it holds that revolution (resistance and opposition in the historical contexts established as concrete manifestations of the contradictions of capitalism) is intrinsic to every process, arrangement, and event that can be identified as a feature of capitalist development.

Expansion of the Sociophysical, Political, and Economic Terrain of Capitalism

Karl Marx and Friedrich Engels made the following comment on capitalist expansion:

The need of a constantly expanding market for its products chases the bourgeoisie over the whole surface of the globe. It must nestle everywhere, settle everywhere, establish connections everywhere.

The bourgeoisie has through its exploitation of the world market given a cosmopolitan character to production and consumption in every country. To the great chagrin of reactionaries, it has drawn from under the feet of industry the national ground on which it stood.

This analysis attempts to establish that both the expansion of capital and the class struggle must now be understood on a global scale, and much of the history of the transition from feudalism to capitalism attempts to show precursors to precisely that development. The key to that analysis is the relationship between capital's inevitable expansionism, which utilized resources that were provided by national polities that expansionism must ultimately subvert, and the historically established territorial and political limits to the expression of class interests. The present age, seen in those terms, points to the limitations and ultimate futility of any large-scale struggle by labor that does not, in one way or another, take account of the internationalization of the labor market and the new weapon of investment mobility that capital can exercise on its own behalf. We can now indicate some of the sociological implications of this development.

The confrontation of national governments with international capital reduces the prospects of democracy by rendering local decisions and popular will impotent in the face of the supervening demands of big business. The result is an increased administrative order nationally, with electoral politics bearing more on transitions in top governmental personnel than on actual policy. We expect to find, and perhaps the United States is itself a case in point, less participation in national electoral processes and greater appeals during elections to patriotism, fear, and ethnic and sectarian hatreds, as well as a greater moralism in the ideologies of authority. We might expect, then, the beginning of breakdowns in representative organizations such as unions and parties; the development of new organized forms of protest (insurgent movements within unions, large-scale popular movements, etc.); realignments among those for whom the integrity of the nation-state is still important (relatively small businesses merely national in scope, older labor union leadership whose successes can only be measured on the scale of specific territories, and segments of the military for whom national production is still the basis for position and power); and realignments among those who must recognize and acknowledge, as a practical matter, the global sphere (large corporations, banks, and segments of the labor force whose wage fate is dependent upon the relative cheapness of foreign labor).

The establishment of satellites as means of communication provides bases for the instantaneous transfer of capital from one territory to another, for new and anticultural forms of marketing and advertisement, for corporate control over what can be known by the widest publics in any given area, and for military and political surveillance in the interest of political control over possibly intransigent governments and oppositional movements. At the same time the new technology provides new opportunities for interference and perhaps for a certain amount of power in those areas in which there is sufficient wealth and organization to establish local means of communication, though these possibilities remain in the realm of speculation.

The development of labor power in an international pool from which capital can draw according to costs and therefore according to degrees of impoverishment offers two possibilities for which there is some evidence. First, there is the possibility of cross-national labor movements, unions, and strikes, corresponding to corporate investment in various places and industries controlled by a single corporate structure no matter how diversified and stratified by the establishment of subsidiaries. This is limited by the extent to which governmental cooperation with those struggles can be secured. Second, local or national labor movements may either accommodate to capital's global reach by retreating in their demands for a social distribution of the surplus, or they may develop the issues of struggle around demands for redistribution without corresponding increases in productivity. This move represents a break with the logic of collective bargaining within the wage system since it offers nothing but social order in exchange for a more socially responsive division of the surplus. Welfare movements at present carry the burden of this possibility, but there is evidence that workers in highly unionized industries are becoming restive under the burdens of an inflation that they suspect is the creation of capital.

The point is that attention is again being drawn to the composition and recomposition of the work force, its internal divisions (men-women, black-white, national-foreign), and its extent. Attention is also being drawn again to the limitations of older forms of labor organization since the classical unions are at present limited in what they have gained and what they apparently can gain by their commitment to legally instituted collective bargaining, the wage system, and limited jurisdictions and spheres of control. Collective bargaining tends to dampen militancy by shifting control over the struggle to bureaucratic mechanisms; and the wage system leaves workers helpless to shifts in the value of money and competition from poorer workers in less developed regions. Because unions have typically bargained *within* specific regions, industries, and political areas (cities, states or nations) this limits their ability to make demands on capital since those demands can be confronted with threats by large corporations to take their business elsewhere and to move to a more "favorable business climate."

A service economy poses somewhat different, though related, problems than does the economy of exchange as such. The fact that productivity cannot be gauged when services are provided means that no adequate system of accounting can be devised in order to rationalize investment. Government appears, in its vacillations between providing services to a demanding public and cutting them back in the interest of speculative investment opportunities for capital elsewhere, to be the enemy or to be simply incompetent.

Antigovernment movements reflect this, revealing incompatibility of the service economy with capitalism, and hence, too, the contradiction of the socialization of production and private control over production and the surplus. Thus struggles for services confront the inability of the government to guarantee resources and the vulnerability of government and local economies to movements of capital. At the same time, those struggles are responsive to the relationship between capitalism and the personal and group experience. For these reasons Marxist theory is, as yet, indecisive about the relationship between those struggles and an effective reorganization of labor for the purpose of limiting and then ending exploitation. In addition, this indecisiveness reflects the fact that there are no clear models of socialism and its historical development that could provide clues as to the political significance of struggles over state-provided services, even though a great deal of attention has been given to this problem by European Marxists.

These struggles, the struggles for national liberation, the movements against racism, and feminism, have all raised several issues for Marxist sociology beyond those already mentioned. Among them are the relationship between class consciousness and class organization, the relative significance of production and distribution for the class struggle, and the role of culture in the development of class consciousness and class organization.

Class Consciousness

The very use of the term *consciousness* seems to require attention to mental phenomena and thus to the general psychology of individuals. If we follow this lead, *class consciousness* either refers to the prevalence of a certain type of awareness among the individuals making up a class or it refers to an individual's awareness that he or she is a member of a class—that he or she shares a certain predicament with others similarly located in production and dependent upon the exploitative and class character of that production. The first interpretation requires us to pay attention to the processes by which public opinion is formed, including propaganda, mass communication, and the informal transmission of news. It also requires us to define class not as an operative principle of capitalist production but as a particular collection of individuals, the overall historical significance of whom depends upon how many there are in the class.

The second interpretation requires us to pay attention to many of the topics ordinarily identified as social-psychological—the socialization of children, the role of language in thought, the relationship between motivation and reality encompassed by what psychologists occasionally call *personality* and *the learning process*.

However, each of these interpretations assumes something more than and something different from what is required or possible of Marxism. The problem is, essentially, that the term *class* is used by Marx and has its theoretical significance as a concept in connection with production. It refers to a particular operative principle of capitalist production, and thus to a relation among operative principles. Clearly someone must work and someone must invest. Thus the connection of class with social groups is obvious. But class should not be confused with the specific individuals or groups identified at one time or another as *the* workers or *the* capitalists. It follows that the term *class consciousness* is a curious one

because an operative principle, an agency, cannot have consciousness in the sense of being aware and self-responsive. It cannot have a psychology.

Certainly, individuals have experience and self-knowledge, and this is not simply the automatic *effect* of what they, as individuals, do or encounter in the world. But Marxism is not a general theory of human affairs, and its hostility to psychology is merely a result of the failure of psychology to understand the social dimension of individual life and experience, and the occasional demand that psychology be recognized as a generally relevant discipline describing a reality (a purely personal order) that all other disciplines must take into account. Marxism requires, but does not determine, a type of psychology that does not abstract individuals from their situations and situations from society. The content of such a psychology, however, is not an issue on which Marxism needs to stand or fall.

To return to our problem, what sense can be made of the notion of class consciousness if it is to apply either to an operative principle or to persons and groups taken in their concrete capacities as bearers of labor power? Perhaps it would be advisable to begin by removing the term *consciousness* since it is so laden with excess meaning that any use whatsoever would imperil the point to be made by using it in the first place. What is of importance is a certain reflexivity within an operative principle. If the principle is *labor power*, then class consciousness would consist of the reflexivity of labor power. By reflexivity is meant an inevitable self-reference to form: in the course of any activity whatsoever, we might witness a division within the activity such that its elements are both necessary to each other and incompatible. In that case each operates within the activity as a check on or, we might say, as a critique of the other. The reflexivity of the activity is the simultaneous operation of these elements so that no one can be seen without reference to the other and yet they cannot be seen as mutually stabilizing at the same time. The activity points to itself (is reflexive) because it can only be identified in regard to its own internal limits and therefore as taking those limits into account. Thus the characterization of any activity is a characterization of it as reflexive. But this means, since an activity is reflexive only in terms of alternative perspectives (each of which reflects a term of its internal contradiction), that any characterization can be challenged by another, and thus we cannot know an activity as such but only this or that sort of activity.

When this is applied to production, we speak of capitalist production because we know it in terms of two operations and the dominance of the whole by one of them. We speak of class struggle when we think again of the two productive operations but from the standpoint of the dominance of one over the other. The political significance of capitalist production or class struggle depends upon human beings living out the reflexivity of the activities they perform as productive agents. This may or may not depend upon their emotional development, personality, attitude, education, etc. What is important is that they do or do not. Whether they do or do not is dependent upon changeable conditions and not upon universal causes of behavior. What is important to Marxism is to establish the reflexivity of the operative principles of capitalist production—what Marx calls the *value aspects*—so that there will be a political development of labor.

Thus the first thing that Marxism might suggest is that class consciousness is present in production and available for human beings to grasp it. Its presence lies precisely in the contradictions of production that make the exercise of labor power and incomplete activity (requiring direction, investment, etc.) an activity that constantly confronts itself as incomplete, dependent, and the like. Whether any body of workers understands, intellectually, the operations of capitalism, they are in a position to be aware of and to respond to their situation.

This characterization of class consciousness merely establishes it as a resource for class politics, one that depends upon whether or not the reflexivity of labor power becomes an expansive principle of understanding among individuals, a way of talking about their condition and envisioning solutions to the problems of that condition. But this, in turn, is a problem that cannot be addressed unless we first of all say something about working-class organizations and the whole order of capitalist society in which those organizations have developed.

What this characterization of class consciousness does allow, however, is an understanding of the problem of class organization. The issue is not simply whether the establishment or maintenance of unions or parties or leadership tends to divorce politics from individuals' daily experience—an issue raised by a number of writers—but the relationship between organization and its content. That is, the issue of attempting to understand the development of political power within labor is whether or not organization retains a constant reference to the class character of capitalism and the class struggle. This will only occur if organization continues to change to accommodate the changing conditions of class struggle generated from within the expansion of capital itself.

This consideration, in turn, raises a problem. For a changing organization, whose resources for struggle are never as great as those of the opposition and whose composition is always diverse because of the factors discussed above, is an endangered organization. This is why working-class organizations have alternated between democracy as an internal principle and stable leadership and discipline. It is why some organizations have alternated between providing open forums on theoretical issues of practical concern and limiting the work of intellectuals, theoreticians, and planners by criteria derived from the immediate terms of conflict at a particular time. Any sociology of political organization, then, must deal with the class character of capitalism as a vital feature of organization, but one that is as complex as the differences represented by the organization. It must also deal with the development of political organization, in part, as a constant internal struggle to reconcile the class character of its orientation and the need for solidarity, strength, and discipline. This suggests that any particular glance at an organization will only show compromises provisionally attained and not a clarification of the nature of the organization or evidence of its fate.

Another issue related to class consciousness comes up in the context of political struggle, namely, why do people resist participation in protest movements even when conditions seem obviously to require them? Occasionally the term *false consciousness* is used as a shorthand way of speaking to this issue. Resistance to self-criticism has been discussed by psychoanalysts, who regard it as one of their most important topics. Freud concluded that we resist close examination of ourselves because dangerous needs might become apparent, because resistance itself provides some gain or pleasure, and because the dynamic relation of the ego to the id involves resistance in any case. Some Marxist psychoanalysts have argued that this "natural" resistance to self-knowledge becomes politically detrimental to our involvement in class movements because of the incorporation of capitalist ideology or ways of thinking and feeling into our personality through the socializing agencies of capitalism—the authoritarian, paternalistic, and male-dominated family, the models provided through the media and by educational institutions and the like. False consciousness is, in this account, both natural to human beings and a disorder that can only be overcome by fairly deep therapeutic appeals and a sensitivity by left organizations to individuals' needs and to the difficulty of expressing such needs.

While the issue of false consciousness has been approached psychoanalytically with some profit and considerable interest, a problem still remains. False consciousness moves us back to a sense of consciousness not entirely appropriate to the Marxian project. Moreover, it involves the use of a whole set of concepts, procedures, and ideas that are otherwise objectionable or at least subject to criticism on other grounds.

There are several recent bodies of literature that seem to have little to do with Marxism that shed a different light on the subject. Of these, we have already seen the possibility of symbolic interactionism as a way to understand human activity compatible with, and perhaps expressive of, Marxism. (Later on we'll consider in this regard ethnomethodology.) Most important in this context is the possible bearing of such literature on the problem of resistance to participation in movements against exploitation. We need to note that these disciplines have provided insight into issues connected with feminism that have to do with the ways in which power makes itself felt in groups; the content implications of structure and form; the characterization of male-supremacist interaction cycles; hidden ideologies; and covert and invidious representations of gender types. In fact, and this point would have to be defended, we might argue that these disciplines have found their voices only with the development of feminist politics, anti-colonial movements, and movements for human and civil rights as the expressions of an interest in how people are represented in the media and other discourse by one sort of image or another.

The attempt to politicize communication itself is part of the necessary effort of such movements to gain control over imagery that has ordinarily served the invidiousness of the distinctions by which people are known. It is notable, then, that symbolic interactionism and ethnomethodology have originated as studies of communication and have taken so many of their examples from the predicaments of "deviants" and others normally called upon to account for themselves in terms of abstract standards, the applications of which deny their accountability in the first place and altogether.

Harold Garfinkel's ethnomethodology can be understood, in part, as aimed at constructing instances of human interaction focused on some problem or common topic in such a way that it would not be sensible for an interacting party to ask the question: "Why aren't we doing other than what we are doing?" By describing the ways in which what is said at any particular moment can be seen as directed toward providing an occasion for something to be said at the next moment, Garfinkel and his students present a texture of social activity in which each gesture, phrase, and comment refers to something immediately preceding or subsequent in a line of discourse, thereby displaying accountability while avoiding it as an explicit issue. Each gesture is limited in its intention and never refers specifically to the setting as a whole, though it uses the setting as a resource.

In this way Garfinkel provides Marxism with cases of false consciousness—that is, repeatable, self-reproducing, or serialized interactions, in which people cannot, by virtue of their own activity, make sense of the question: "Why aren't we doing other than what we are doing?" This also suggests that the introduction of an overall critical principle to such a texture involves something more than and different from simply changing people's minds or trying to get them to attend to their settings. (Garfinkel points out that their activity precludes such attention or at least precludes their taking seriously attempts to draw attention to the setting.) It involves finding a principle *within* the interaction setting that not only reflects upon the setting as a whole but also does so from the standpoint of that setting's incorporation into more inclusive settings. Garfinkel himself has made a few suggestions along those lines. For example, he notes that when we speak with another person, we are establishing meanings that cannot be understood out of context, even though we are using words that have universal meanings—meanings that go beyond that context. That is, conversation is both interpersonally intimate and directed toward any possible listener. The recipient of a message is both *this* listener and *any* listener, and the speaker is both intimate, or intersubjectively involved, with the listener *and* indifferent to him or her as a particular individual. In speaking, we must address a particular other and, in responding to him or her, we construct meanings that are bound to the setting and limited by its own development. Yet if we are to remember and share the meanings of this setting with others, we must use abstract terms that convey meanings presumably independent of any particular setting. This contradiction of social intimacy as basic to communication—the abstractness of its terms as necessary for the memory and transmissibility of content—cannot be resolved within the exclusive domain of any given setting. The upshot is that interaction is motivated by the contradiction and represents both a compromise with it and a disguise of the fact that it is only a compromise. But this means—and Goffman has pointed it out in related work—that the intrinsic incompleteness of the setting is both a problem for interactants and an occasion for the development of interactions critical of themselves. This finding does not dispose individuals toward the clarification and critique of capitalism or toward the political struggles against exploitation. But it provides a certain unavoidable uneasiness in interaction that might be responsive to the sort of unease on which such movements must build. What is impressive in Garfinkel's work is his attempt to identify a realm of discourse, namely, conversation, as the place where we must look for *consciousness* in the sense that the term is of conceptual relevance to Marxism.

Sociobiology emerged as a social theory in the 1970s in the United States and Britain. It had its roots in social Darwinism, as outlined by Herbert Spencer and Thomas Henry Huxley. However, social Darwinism was plagued with racism and became discredited. Unfortunately, similar charges have been leveled against modern sociobiology.

Racism aside, sociobiology is controversial for its theoretical reliance on *genetic* causality for human action patterns. Few sociologists today would accept genetic explanations for complex social behavior. Yet sociobiology has much to offer. For, after all, the "animal" nature of humans has been neglected in sociological theory, and who can deny that so much of social life is linked to sex and aggression, child rearing, territorial defense, and the production of food, shelter, and clothing?

Given these biological realities, sociobiology—if separated from its biases and biological reductionism—could lend important insights to the study of humans in groups.

Walda Katz Fishman

SOCIOBIOLOGY: THEORY
AND CONTROVERSY

INTRODUCTION

Increasing attention, particularly in the last decade or so, is being focused on the biological and genetic bases of human social behavior.[1] Within the biological and social sciences large volumes of research are being conducted to take a fresh look at the old *nature-nurture debate*. The most recent comprehensive theory of the biological base of human behavior and social structure is sociobiology.

The concept and theory of sociobiology entered our consciousness in 1975 when E. O. Wilson, Harvard zoology professor, published his now famous and controversial tome *Sociobiology: The New Synthesis*. The vast bulk of this 700-page volume Wilson devotes to his explication of the theory of sociobiology and its illustration by and application to various species of insects, birds, and mammals. In the first and final chapters Wilson ventures into the virgin and highly uncharted territory of human

sociobiology—the application of sociobiological principles to human social behavior, culture, and society. It is this speculative and controversial analysis which became the storm center of a continuing and heated debate and which is the sole substance of Wilson's 1978 Pulitzer Prize–winning book *On Human Nature*.

Since 1975 those sociobiologists closest to Wilson—e.g., W. D. Hamilton, Robert Trivers, David Barash—whose own work had, in fact, laid the foundation for Wilson's synthesis have continued to research and publish in the "discipline" of sociobiology.[2] They have been joined by hundreds of other scholars. Numerous books have been written: *The Sociobiology Debate* by Arthur Caplan, *Sociobiology Examined* by Ashley Montagu, and *Human Sociobiology* by Derek Freeman, to name a few.[3] New journals dealing exclusively with sociobiological issues have appeared, e.g., *Ethology and Sociobiology* (Elsevier North-Holland, 1980). And many sociobiological

335

articles have found their way into print in academic journals in the biological and social sciences and in the popular press, e.g., *The New York Times, Time, Newsweek, Business Week,* and *People.*[4]

Sociobiological proponents and enthusiasts claimed that Wilson's "new synthesis" would indeed biologize and revolutionize our understanding of human social life. Others found sociobiology wanting in a variety of ways and were critical of it as "bad science" and "bad politics." Sociobiologists were charged with employing an outmoded and simplistic view of evolutionary and genetic theory[5]; with being reductionistic and insufficiently informed by the unique qualities of human intelligence and cultural development[6]; with having no data base[7]; and with presenting a highly politicized view of human nature and social relations in which aggression and inequities based on class, sex, and minority status are seen as "natural." [8]

What is this theory of human life which has attracted so much attention and generated so much controversy among biologists, social scientists, and the lay public? How does it portray human nature, the environment, society and culture, and the relations among these? How has it been evaluated in terms of its philosophical assumptions and methodology? What are its political implications and why have the popular media been so fascinated by sociobiology?

THE THEORY OF SOCIOBIOLOGY

Sociobiology Defined

Wilson defines sociobiology as:

the systematic study of the biological basis of all social behavior. For the present it focuses on animal societies. . . . But the discipline is also concerned with the social behavior of early man and the adaptive features of organization in the more primitive contemporary human societies.[9]

It is clear, however, that sociobiology is concerned with far more than early humans and primitive contemporary societies. Wilson pursues sociobiology precisely to learn of the biological constraints of present human societies and the biological destiny of the future of humankind.

According to Wilson:

The biologist. . . realizes that self-knowledge is constrained and shaped by the emotional control centers in the hypothalamus and limbic system of the brain. These centers flood our consciousness with all the emotions—hate, love, guilt, fear, and others—that are consulted by ethical philosophers who wish to intuit standards of good and evil. . . . [The hypothalamus and limbic system] evolved by natural selection. That simple biological statement must be pursued to explain ethics and ethical philosophers, if not epistemology and epistemologists, at all depths.[10]

Wilson concludes, therefore, that the meaning of human existence inheres solely in the fact that the human being, as a biological organism, reproduces and transmits its genes to the next generation through natural selection:

[I]n evolutionary time the individual organism counts for almost nothing. In a Darwinian sense the organism does not live for itself. Its primary function is not even to reproduce other organisms; it reproduces genes, and it serves as their temporary carrier.[11]

The concern of sociobiology, indeed its obsession, seems to be the development of a genetically based ethical system. This view of sociobiology is reiterated by Wilson in *On Human Nature,* not a work "of science," but a work "about science." [12] Here Wilson opens with the assertion that:

if the brain is a machine of ten million nerve cells and the mind can somehow be explained as the summed activity of a finite number of chemical and electrical reactions, boundaries limit the human prospect—we are biological and our souls cannot fly free.[13]

From this perspective of humankind stem two great dilemmas: meaning and choice. For sociobiology all species, including the human species, possess no purpose and no goals "beyond the imperatives created by [their] genetic history."[14] Second, choices must be made among the ethical premises inherent in human biological nature.[15]

Wilson sees the three great mythologies of Marxism ("sociobiology without biology"), traditional religion, and scientific materialism as competing intellectually and politically to offer the resolutions to these dilemmas. Traditional religion has lost its appeal since its beliefs themselves can be understood as mechanisms enabling human survival.[16] Marxism Wilson dismisses by asserting, but not demonstrating, that it embodies an inaccurate interpretation of human nature and history.[17]

The only viable contender among the three mythologies is thus scientific materialism, which, of course, means sociobiology and includes a biologized ethics and morality for humankind. In Wilson's words:

Thus does ideology bow to its hidden masters the genes, and the highest impulses seem upon closer examination to be metamorphosed into biological activity.[18]

More specifically, we learn that our ethical premises are formed through the deep and unconscious action of innate censors and motivators contained within our brains; and that "morality evolved as instinct."[19] Finally, Wilson anticipates that science may soon be positioned "to investigate the very origin and meaning of human values, from which all ethical pronouncements and much of political practice flow."[20]

The science of sociobiology is that science. Sociobiology's program and mandate have profound implications not only for morality and politics but also for intellectual activity. Wilson "codif[ies] sociobiology into a branch of evolutionary biology and particularly of modern population biology."[21] The goal of sociobiology with regard to human beings and human societies—ancient and modern, preliterate and postindustrial—"is to place the social sciences within a biological framework, a

framework constructed from a synthesis of evolutionary studies, genetics, population biology, ecology, animal behaviour, psychology and anthropology."[22] In a somewhat more ominous tone Wilson writes:

It may not be too much to say that sociology and the other social sciences, as well as the humanities, are the last branches of biology waiting to be included in the Modern Synthesis. . . . Whether the social sciences can be truly biologized in this fashion remains to be seen.[23]

Wilson singles out sociology for special mention. He maintains that sociology currently, because of its structuralist and nongenetic approach, is able merely to provide descriptive classifications and ecological correlations of surface phenotypes (the observable characteristics of organisms produced by the interaction of genetic constitution and environmental factors). Sociology could yield much richer findings and directives if it would become part of a neo-Darwinist evolutionary theory. Wilson notes:

The transition from purely phenomenological to fundamental theory in sociology must await a full, neuronal explanation of the human brain. Only when the machinery can be torn down on paper at the level of the cell and put together again will the properties of emotion and ethical judgement come clear.[24]

Sociobiology has gained a following among some social scientists and ethologists (for example, Robin Fox, Lionel Tiger, David Barash, Robert Trivers, Irven De Vore, and Pierre van den Berghe), though others have joined the chorus of criticism (for example, Marvin Harris, Marshall Sahlins, Ashley Montagu, Jerome Barkow, Derek Freeman, and S. L. Washburn).

The program of the new science of sociobiology, as revealed in the works of Wilson, van den Berghe, and other proponents, calls for the reduction of all behavior and social formations of all animals, including humans, to the genetic and biological substrate, as modulated by the evolutionary pressures of environment and natural selection. Further, for Wilson a driving force underlying this scientific endeavor is the attempt to derive a "more truthful" genetically based morality to guide the affairs of humankind. The linkage between science, morality, and politics is key to understanding the intensity of the criticism and controversy surrounding sociobiology.

Principles and Concepts: The Evolutionary Paradigm and Natural Selection

The question of the relationship among human biological nature, the environment, culture, and society has been with us for at least two thousand years. With the development of the social sciences in the last two hundred years, the common wisdom has stressed the importance of environmental factors—culture, human intelligence, and learning—in understanding the development both of human behavior and of social formations.[25]

Today sociobiology, a branch of evolutionary biology, is being offered by Wilson, Dawkins, Barash, van den Berghe, Ellis, Tiger and Fox, Fox, and others as an alternative paradigm for the understanding of human social life.[26] In essence, sociobiology offers the explanation of the behavior of all animals, including humans, in terms of a genetically based evolutionary process through natural selection. Thus the genotype (the genetic constitution of the organism) becomes the critical factor in explaining all aspects of the organism's phenotype (the observable characteristics of the organism, including anatomy, physiology, and behavior developed through interaction between the genotype and the environment).

The Darwinian theory of evolution places natural selection, genetic fitness, and adaptation at the center of the evolutionary process. Adaptation refers to any structure, physiological process, or behavioral sequence which enhances the organism's ability to survive and thereby to reproduce and

to pass its genes to the next generation. The organism's genetic fitness, then, is the degree of its contribution of its genes to the next generation. Individuals within a population or species will vary in their degree of adaptation, genetic fitness, and reproductive success. This will result, through the mechanism of natural selection, in those individuals more adapted having more offspring and greater representation of their genes in the next generation than less adapted individuals.

Adaptation and natural selection are always in relation to the environment. Changes in the environment will result in differential survival and differential reproduction. Biological evolution is simply the change, over time, of the genetic composition of populations stemming from these forces and processes.

However, Darwin and later evolutionary theorists, e.g., J. B. S. Haldane, V. C. Wynne-Edwards, and Sewall Wright, never perfected the articulation between these processes and the evolutionary paradigm.[27]

These difficulties, however, have not prevented social and biological scientists from applying the evolutionary paradigm to social behavior, including that of humans. Herbert Spencer is the most notable among sociologists who modified Darwinian evolutionary theory to explain and justify the existence of social differences and especially social inequality. Like Wilson who followed him, Spencer was concerned with putting morality and ethics on a scientific basis and, in particular, on a biological evolutionary basis.

Spencer's theory of social Darwinism has, in the ensuing years, been discredited as a scientific theory of society. It did, however, gain popular support among the ruling class in the nascent British Empire and burgeoning American capitalism for its ideological role in explaining inequality and the *status quo* in terms of natural rather than political and economic forces.

The next historic attempt to place human

social behavior within the genetic evolutionary paradigm came in 1975 with Wilson's proffering of sociobiology.

Altruism, Inclusive Fitness, and Kin Selection

This behavior—termed *self-destructive* by Wilson—which lessens one's own chances for survival and reproductive success while enhancing those chances for another is called altruistic behavior.[28] Examples of altruism include helping in times of danger; sharing food; helping the sick and the wounded, or the very young and old; sharing implements; and sharing knowledge.[29] The central theoretical problem of sociobiology is the explanation of altruism.[30]

A breakthrough in the explanation of altruism within the neo-Darwinian evolutionary paradigm was made in 1964 by W. D. Hamilton. Hamilton's solution to this puzzle involved the replacement of Darwinian individual fitness with inclusive fitness, a group-based unit for determining fitness, and elaborate mathematical formulations to support his theory of *kin selection*. According to the Darwinian notion of fitness, the individual is the unit of selection; any behavior (or gene), e.g., sterility, or any actions which threaten the life of the performer (though they may be livesaving to others), and thus reduce the individual's chances of survival and reproduction, also reduce that individual's fitness and the chances of his (or her) genes being represented in the next generation.

Hamilton suggested that the locus of selection be expanded to include the reproductive consequences of behaviors or traits for the individual and for those who are genetically similar to the individual.[31] Since those with whom the individual has the greatest probability of sharing genes are siblings, parents, children, and immediate relatives, Hamilton's theory was dubbed *kin selection*. Through the mechanisms of kin selection and inclusive fitness, it was now

possible to account for how behaviors and genes detrimental to the individual's personal reproductive success could be selected for and transmitted to the next generation through the individual's enhancement of the reproductive success of its kin. Hamilton, in providing the answer to the dilemma of altruism plaguing evolutionists since Darwin's day, facilitated the development of sociobiology and its application to human behavior.

Sociobiological Vision of Human Nature and Social Relations

Sociobiologists were now free to proceed in the construction of hypotheses and theories of the genetic basis of human nature and social action to explain human phenotypic features and behaviors and relationships in terms of their underlying genotypes resulting from environmental pressures and natural selection.

A problem still remained, however. Humans often exhibit altruistic behavior toward nonrelatives and strangers. Trivers addressed this dilemma by coining the concept of reciprocal altruism—doing good acts for others if it is felt there is a high probability the others will return the favor, where the cost to the altruist is much lower than the benefit (in survival and reproductive success terms) derived from the reciprocity.[32] Trivers explains with an example: if you rescue a drowning person who has a 50 percent probability of dying without your help at a small (e.g., 5 percent) risk to your own mortality, and if this person at some future time saves you from a similar situation where the chances of living and dying are reversed, then both people have increased their long-term chances for survival by 40 percent.[33]

There are a number of difficulties with both the sociobiological rendition of altruism and reciprocal altruism, especially the latter. Here the whole genetic foundation of human relations begins to be eroded since there are no biological ties between the helping parties. And as Sahlins wryly observes, the example of reciprocal altruism involving a drowning person is unfortunate "because after all it would be evolutionarily short-sighted to save a man who can't swim on the supposition that he will later rescue you from drowning. . . ." [34] He has further argued for the unlikelihood of people going around and before every act performing complex genetic computations to determine if the behavior in question is in their genetic self-interest, individually or inclusively. Most of us lack the requisite information for such genetic calculations, especially since much of even kinship structure is based on social rather than biological relationships.

These and other problems at the core of sociobiology have not daunted sociobiologists in their efforts to discover the human *biogram,* that pattern of traits and behaviors of the human species rooted in our genetic constitution. Human sociobiology, even for its strongest enthusiasts, is an admittedly recent and highly tentative discipline. Barash entitles his last chapter on human sociobiology "The Sociobiology of Human Behavior: *Extrapolations* and *Speculations*" (my emphasis). [35] Surely the inclusion of terms such as *extrapolations* and *speculations* is indicative of the dearth of data and evidence in this new and controversial area. Barash continues:

This chapter will be especially concerned with exploring possible implications for human social behavior, *assuming* that our species follows these same general rules [that we act to maximize personal and inclusiveness fitness]. This caveat is important. We are going to play "Let's Pretend." [36]

Sociobiologists have sought to identify those traits in the human repertoire common to people in all cultures and which are the "most general," "least rational," and "furthest removed from the influence of day-to-day reflection and the distracting vicissitudes of culture." [37] The assumption is that such universal traits exist and are in-

nate or genetic in nature. According to Wilson, the data to test the premises of human sociobiology must come from anthropological studies of "hunter-gatherer societies and the most persistent preliterate herding and agricultural societies." [38] The reason is that humans today are genetically very similar to our hunting and gathering ancestors who lived over 5 million years ago. The genetic evolution of human social behavior took place mostly in the 5 million years before civilization and agriculture, while most of cultural evolution has occurred in the last 10,000 years since the development of agriculture and cities. Thus, sociobiologists posit, traits which contemporary industrial societies share with hunter-gatherer societies are primarily of genetic rather than of cultural origin.

As further substantiation of the genetic basis of human universals, sociobiologists have focused on conservative traits, i.e., those characteristics which are constant throughout the order Primates and are "the ones most likely to have persisted in relatively unaltered form into the evolution of *Homo.*" [39] The human biogram developed by sociobiology includes universal human traits, some of which we share with our primate relatives and others which are unique among humans.

Comparative studies of Old World monkeys and the great apes have yielded a list of traits considered part of "human nature" which humans share with their closest living evolutionary relatives. These include:

- Aggressive dominance systems, with males dominant over females.
- Males larger than females, and a resulting mating system of polygyny (males taking two or more female mates).
- Long period of socialization of the young, first by close association with the mother and then by association with age- and sex-peer groups.
- Behavioral scaling of responses, especially in aggressive interactions (behavioral

scaling refers to genetic coding for variable phenotypic or behavioral responses in relation to varying environmental conditions.

- Intimate social groupings ranging in size from 10 to 100 adults.
- Social play emphasizing role practice, mock aggression, exploration, and sex practice.
- Matrilineal organization.[40]

Wilson also lists a series of features unique to human beings. Among these are:

- Erect posture, striding, the perfection of bipedal locomotion, molding of hands for precision grip, and the development of an extraordinary brain capacity.
- True language and an elaborate culture.
- Sexual activity continuous through the menstrual cycle.
- Formalized incest taboos and marriage exchange rules with the recognition of kinship networks.
- Cooperative division of labor among adult males and females.
- Facial expressions.
- Close sexual bonding (bonding refers to a close relationship between two or more individuals).
- Parent/offspring bonding.
- Male bonding.
- Territoriality.[41]

Wilson argues that "to socialize a human being out of such species-specific traits would be very difficult if not impossible, and almost certainly destructive to mental development."[42]

In addition, Wilson posits a number of highly controversial derivative universals of human nature which stem from those already noted.

- *Tribalism (and Territoriality).* "Each species is characterized by its own particular behavioral scale. In extreme cases the scale may run from open hostility, say, during the breeding season or when the population density is high, to oblique forms of advertisement or no territorial behavior at

all. . . . Systematic overt aggression has been reported in a minority of hunter-gatherer peoples."[43]

- *Xenophobia (Fear of Outsiders).* "Human behavior provides some of the best exemplification of the xenophobia principle. Outsiders are almost always a source of tension. If they pose a physical threat, especially to territorial integrity, they loom in our vision as an evil, monolithic force. Efforts are then made to reduce them to subhuman status, so that they can be treated without conscience. They are the gooks, the wogs, the krauts, the commies—not like us, another subspecies surely, a force remorselessly dedicated to our destruction who must be met with equal ruthlessness if we are to survive. . . . At this level of 'gut feeling,' the mental processes of a human being and a rhesus monkey may well be neurophysiologically homologous."[44]

- *Warfare and Genocide.* "Throughout recorded history the conduct of war has been common among tribes and nearly universal among chiefdoms and states. . . . The spread of genes has always been of paramount importance. For example, after the conquest of the Midianites Moses gave instructions identical in result to the aggression and genetic usurpation by male langur monkeys:

Now kill every male dependent, and kill every woman who has had intercourse with a man, but spare for yourselves every woman among them who has not had intercourse (Num. 31).

"By current theory, genocide or genosorption strongly favoring the aggressor need take place only once every few generations to direct evolution."[45]

- *Spite and Family Chauvinism.* "True spite is commonplace in human societies, undoubtedly because human beings are keenly aware of their own blood lines and have intelligence to plot intrigue. Human beings are unique in the degree of their capacity to lie to other members of their own species. They typically do so in a way that deliberately diminishes outsiders while promoting relatives, even at the risk of their own personal welfare." [46]

▪ *Blind Faith (e.g., in Religion)*. "The enduring paradox of religion is that so much of its substance is demonstrably false, yet it remains a driving force in all societies. Men would rather believe than know, have the void as purpose, as Nietzsche said, than the void of purpose." [47]

"The predisposition to religious belief is the most complex and powerful force in the human mind and in all probability an ineradicable part of human nature. . . . Today as always before, the mind cannot comprehend the meaning of the collision between irresistible scientific materialism and immovable religious faith. . . . I believe that religious practices can be mapped onto the two dimensions of genetic advantage and evolutionary change. . . . By traditional methods of reduction and analysis science can explain religion but cannot diminish the importance of its substance." [48]

▪ *Indoctrinability*. "Human beings are absurdly easy to indoctrinate—they *seek* it." [49]

▪ *Selfishness*. "Human beings appear to be sufficiently selfish and calculating to be capable of indefinitely greater harmony and social homeostasis. . . . True selfishness, if obedient to the other constraints of mammalian biology, is the key to a more nearly perfect social contract. . . . Imagine a spectrum of self-serving behavior. At one extreme only the individual is meant to benefit, then the nuclear family, next the extended family (including cousins, grandparents, and others who might play a role in kin selection), then the band, the tribe, chiefdoms, and finally, at the other extreme, the highest sociopolitical units. Which units along this spectrum are most favored by the innate predispositions of human social behavior? . . .

"Individual behavior, including seemingly altruistic acts bestowed on tribe and nation [e.g., ethnic allegiance or "racial" consciousness], are directed, sometimes very circuitously, toward the Darwinian advantage of the solitary human being and his closest relatives." [50]

▪ *Hard-Core Altruism*. "The altruistic impulse can be irrational and unilaterally directed at others; the bestower expresses no desire for equal return and performs no unconscious actions leading to the same end. . . . Where such behavior exists, it is likely to have evolved through kin selection or natural selection operating on entire, competing family or tribal units. We would expect hard-core altruism to serve the altruist's closest relatives and to decline steeply in frequency and intensity as relationship becomes more distant. . . .

"[P]ure hard-core altruism based on kin selection is the enemy of civilization. If human beings are to a large extent guided by programmed learning rules and canalized emotional development to favor their own relatives and tribe, only a limited amount of global harmony is possible. . . . The imperatives of blood and territory will be the passions to which reason is slave." [51]

▪ *Soft-Core or Reciprocal Altruism*. "'Soft-core' altruism . . . is ultimately selfish. The 'altruist' expects reciprocation from society for himself or his closest relatives. His good behavior is calculating, often in a wholly conscious way, and his maneuvers are orchestrated by the excruciatingly intricate sanctions and demands of society. The capacity for soft-core altruism can be expected to have evolved primarily by selection of individuals and to be deeply influenced by the vagaries of cultural evolution. Its psychological vehicles are lying, pretense, and deceit, including self-deceit, because the actor is most convincing who believes that his performance is real. . . . Reciprocation among distantly related or unrelated individuals is the key to human society." [52]

"Aggressively moralistic behavior, for example, keeps would-be cheaters in line. . . . Self-righteousness, gratitude, and sympathy enhance the probability of receiving an altruistic act by virtue of implying reciprocation." [53]

Human Sexual Reproduction and Male/Female Differences

Human sociobiology is a theory based on reproduction rather than social production (i.e., the use of human labor and tools to generate the necessary material goods for social life—food, shelter, clothing). Because human reproduction is sexual, the human male and female exhibit differing structures and functions with regard to the reproductive process. Sociobiologists, however, go far beyond the reproductive process and attempt to explain male/female differences in temperament, in the social division of labor, the double standard (monogamy for women and polygyny for men), and hypergamy (women marrying up in the status hierarchy) in terms of the biological differences of men and women. As Barash notes: "Sociobiology relies heavily upon the biology of male-female differences and upon the adaptive behavioral differences that have evolved accordingly. Ironically, mother nature appears to be a sexist." [54]

Let us recall that sociobiology posits the ultimate purpose of human existence as genetic fitness, and such fitness can be assured most directly through successful sexual reproduction and care of offspring. The human female produces only about four hundred eggs during her lifetime, while the human male produces 100 million sperm in each ejaculation. According to sociobiological theory, women have a "greater investment" in their sex cells than men and experience a higher cost than men in bringing the infant to term and caring for it. For women, then, "it is more profitable. . .to be coy, to hold back until they can identify males with the best genes. . . [and] who are more likely to stay with them after insemination." [55]

In contrast, the male investment in reproduction is considerably less—merely the physical act of insemination—unless the female can convince him to help in child care. Theoretically, sociobiologists reason, men can inseminate thousands of women and it

is to the man's advantage to do so as much as possible so his genes will be represented in the children of many women. This is, of course, the explanation for polygyny, or the practice of men taking many mates. This difference in investment and self-interest between men and women in reproduction and genetic fitness is also the proffered explanation for the "conflict of interest between the sexes."

For example, Barash argues that "in terms of Darwinian fitness, men *are* threatened more than women by out-of-pair bond copulations by their partner." [56] Sociobiology predicts that men will be significantly more intolerant of sexual infidelity by their female mates than women will be if their male partners engage in outside sexual relations. The reason is that women are sure that their offspring share 50 percent of their genes with them while men have no such assurance. The philandering husband is no real disgrace, assuming he is an adequate provider in the domestic arena. And his fitness is likely high. However, the cuckolded husband, writes Barash, "is an object of ridicule" and probably has a low degree of fitness. [57]

Sociobiologists also suggest that the intensity and variety of human sexual activity and "sex for its own sake" are the cement necessary to hold the pair bond together in the family unit to provide for the arduous task of human child rearing. [58]

Sociobiological theory adds yet another twist to the relations between the sexes. The Darwinian theory of sexual selection on which it is premised requires that all healthy females be reproductively active, but only that the "fittest" males contribute their sperm (and thus their genes) to produce the fittest offspring. In terms of evolutionary biology, fitness is measured solely as reproductive success—the propagation of one's genes in the next generation. It is inevitable, therefore, that males must compete for the available females. This necessity for competition forms the biological basis for male aggression, the formation of aggressive dominance systems in which males are dominant over females, territoriality, and entrepreneurship.[59]

In the sociobiological version of the relations between the sexes, men are bigger, stronger, quicker, more assertive, more aggressive, and more dominant. However, because humans reproduce sexually, men need women and are in competition for women in order to mate and produce offspring who will have their genes and pass them on. Women are thus a limiting resource and a valued property. Hence they benefit from the practice of hypergamy, or of marrying men of higher social status than themselves. Wilson suggests that hypergamy and polyandry are "complementary strategies."[60] Regardless of diversity in culture, he claims that "men pursue and acquire" and women are "protected and bartered."

Sociobiologists have freely extrapolated from the biological differences between men and women and the division of labor in sexual reproduction to the division of labor in the social sphere and production itself. Barash states that sociobiology can help us understand the different parental strategies and roles adopted by women and men.[61] Women, as mothers, are certain that their offspring possess 50 percent of their own genes, making it profitable in terms of selfish Darwinian fitness for mothers to invest in the nurturing of their children. On the other hand, men cannot be sure that they are the biological fathers of the offspring born to their wives, so it is less adaptive for men to invest heavily in the care and well-being of infants and children. These factors may explain, according to Barash, why women have primary child-care responsibilities and are almost universally relegated to the nursery, and why men, who are less involved in child care, obtain greatest satisfaction from their jobs. Unfortunately, this theory does not aid our understanding of such things as parental and especially maternal abandonment of children or child abuse. It also leaves unclear how it is that women of the wealthy classes have turned over the care of their children to nurses, nannies, and governesses, why some men are assuming child custody in divorce cases and others are devoting greater attention to child care, why the women of Betty Friedan's *Feminine Mystique* were not fully satisfied by their role as wife-mother, and why many women in recent years also find "greatest satisfaction" in their jobs.

Critics have concluded that sociobiology is sexist—not only because of the unsupported assertions by Wilson, Barash, and others. More important, the critics have claimed that it is inherently sexist because it posits the primacy of Darwinian fitness through sexual selection. Reproductive success is the ultimate explanation of all social life; biology and the sexual division of labor in reproduction are paramount, and all else recedes into the background. The fact is that those universal human traits selected for in evolutionary history are, indeed, male traits—aggressiveness, territoriality, and dominance. Sociobiology contends that only males need compete; so natural selection operates essentially on genetic variability among males. For females genetic variability through evolution becomes an issue only if women must choose from among competing men. Females are the passive recipients and carriers of selected male genes.[62]

Parent-Child Relations

Because of the centrality of altruism and kin selection to human sociobiology, parent-child relations—in addition to human universals, mating, and the sexual division of labor—have been the focus of early work in the area.[63] Just as the introduction of sexual reproduction and the development of genetically dissimilar group members was invoked to explain the conflict between the sexes, it is offered to account for parent-child conflict as well. Robert Trivers views parent-child conflict during the weaning period as the result of natural selection operating in opposing directions for the parent and offspring generations.[64]

Let us recall that the purpose of human life is reproductive success, and that parents and offspring share half of their genes. It is, therefore, to the parent's advantage to successfully produce and care for as many offspring as possible, while it is to the child's advantage, in terms of fitness, to receive the greatest care and protection and nurturing from its parents that it can secure. The concept of *parental investment* is used to illuminate the dynamics of parent-child conflict. Parental investment refers to "any behavior toward offspring that increases the chances of the offspring's survival at the cost of the parent's ability to invest in other offspring."[65] This notion of parental investment highlights again the competitive nature of social relations as presented in sociobiological theorizing.

EVALUATION OF SOCIOBIOLOGY: SCIENCE OR IDEOLOGY?

A Critique of Sociobiology

In the final analysis, sociobiology posits that the ultimate causation of all human behavior and social relations is our genetic constitution. This may be selected for and influenced by the environment, and modified, mediated, and made variable by culture. But in the end our genes are in control and the only meaning of our lives is the transmission of our genes or similar genes carried by close kin to subsequent generations. Wilson cautions that we may try to environmentally and culturally divert our innate predispositions, but *always* at some *cost*. "To whom?" of course is the critical question never raised by Wilson. If there is peace and not war, who gains and who loses? If women are no longer dominated by men, do men lose power and economic control? If workers and ethnic minorities gain equality through unity, and nationalism and racism are eliminated, is

there a corresponding loss in political and economic resources for industrialists, bankers, and whites? The answers to these questions are premised upon certain assumptions about human nature, social relations, and the linkages among these and various political-economic and cultural systems.

The most general, inclusive, and encompassing criticism of sociobiology is precisely that sociobiology embodies an inadequate and inaccurate formulation of the relationships among holders of the human genetic makeup, and the context of the environment, culture, and political economy. It is important to note that the criticisms of sociobiology have not been knee-jerk reactions or simple-minded rejections; they are not from philistine intellectuals trying to protect their turf. To be sure, criticism has come from sociologists and anthropologists responding to Wilson's claims that sociobiology will subsume them, or that they are waiting to be incorporated into the final synthesis. But very significantly, critics have also come from the philosophy of science and natural sciences and include geneticists and evolutionary biologists who are among Wilson's colleagues at Harvard.

Concrete charges have been lodged against sociobiologists for their unwarranted philosophical, methodological, and theoretical assumptions and their faulty conceptualization, interpretation, and rendering of evolutionary theory and genetic transmission. The critics of sociobiology have, for example, challenged the legitimacy, validity, and scientific status of sociobiology for the following reasons:

- Its positivistic, mechanistic, and reductionistic orientation.
- Its tautological and circular reasoning.
- Its specious argumentation for the similarity between animals and humans based on analogy (a similarity due to a convergence in evolutionary pressures) rather than on homology (a similarity due to a common ancestry).
- Its simplistic theory of genetic trans-

mission through single genes, especially given the virtual impossibility, with present technology and research ethics, of identifying the purely genetic as opposed to the environmental component of behavior and social relations.

■ Its assumptions regarding human nature and the distorted version of human nature which emerges from the selection of "universals" of the human biogram.

■ Its reification of human qualities and relations, the attribution of them to animals, and then the argumentation of a similarity between animals and humans based on them.

■ Its lack of an adequate data base, coupled with the selective use of data—cross-cultural, historical, and animal—and the omission of contradictory evidence.

■ Its political and moral content and implications in favor of the status quo of capitalism and imperialism and against movements for the equality and human rights of workers, women, ethnic minorities, and nations.

The question of the relationship, in humans, among genes, culture, and social relations goes to the heart of the controversy surrounding sociobiology. Qualifications and hedges notwithstanding, the sociobiological program outlined by Wilson and others is one of biological or genetic determinism of human behavior, of social relations and, indeed, of much of culture. Wilson's chapter in *Sociobiology* on humans and the entirety of *On Human Nature* is an extended speculation on the existence of isolated, individual genes for specific and variable human behavioral traits, including, e.g., aggression, spite, xenophobia, incest, homosexuality, conformity, and characteristic male-female behavioral difference. Wilson writes: "Although the genes have given away most of their sovereignty, they maintain a certain amount of influence in at least the behavioral qualities that underlie variations between cultures." [66] Later, in *On Human Nature*, Wilson asks:

Can culture alter human behavior to approach altruistic perfection? . . . The answer is no. . . .

The genes hold culture on a leash. The leash is very long, but inevitably values will be constrained in accordance with their effects on the human gene pool. [67]

Wilson's reduction of human life, values, and morality to the genetic material and the effort to perpetuate it and the very rote and mechanical fashion in which this occurs is illuminated in the continuation of the above passage:

The brain is a product of evolution. Human behavior—like the deepest capacities for emotional response which drive and guide it—is the circuitous technique by which human genetic material has been and will be kept intact. Morality has no other demonstrable ultimate function. [68]

Wilson himself is propelled by the desire to explain traditional religion in terms of the "mechanistic models of evolutionary biology," and particularly of the evolution of the brain. He explains: "I consider the scientific ethos superior to religion." [69] And if sociobiology can reduce religion to genetic causation, religion's "power as an external source of morality will be gone forever," to be replaced by Wilson's biologized morality. [70]

Finally, Wilson depicts the broad sweep of his positivistic program of reducing all phenomena, including art, religion, and morality, to the action of our genetic material destined to preserve itself for posterity. As all of social existence is reduced to the universal laws of the genetics of evolutionary biology, so all the social sciences and humanities are swallowed up by the biological sciences. Wilson elucidates:

The discipline abuts the antidiscipline; the antidiscipline succeeds in reordering the phenomena of the discipline by reduction to its more fundamental laws; but the new synthesis created in the discipline profoundly alters the antidiscipline as the interaction widens. I suggest that biology, and especially neurobiology and sociobiology, will serve as the antidiscipline of the social sciences. I will now go further and suggest that the scientific materialism embodied in biology will, through a reexamination of the mind and the foundations of social behavior, serve as a kind of antidiscipline to the humanities.[71]

This sociobiological scenario, in which human behavior, social relations and institutions, material culture, and now art and literature are reduced to and explained in terms of the mechanical action of our genetic material, has been at the storm center of the sociobiology debate. Is it possible to understand human social life in terms of the same universal laws of evolutionary biology by which we understand other animals?

Ethel Tobach notes that sociobiology, like all hereditarian theories, embodies a reductionism in which "the genes are the ultimate unit of living matter and as such offer the ultimate explanation of all phenomena of living matter."[72]

Further, James King has criticized the genetics of sociobiology as simplistic and outmoded.[73] The genetic thinking of Wilson, Dawkins, Hamilton, and Trivers, which has its origin in the Mendelian tradition, stresses the action of single, hard, and discrete gene units in selection and in the identifiable contribution to the observed characteristics of the organism. Those in this tradition usually think in terms of there being one "best genotype." King notes, however, the existence of another view of genetic phenomena "which many geneticists believe is closer to reality."[74] This view, which comes from the work of Theodosius Dobzhansky and others and is currently represented in Richard Lewontin's work, stresses interaction between genes and the principle of multiple gene inheritance. Those of this persuasion express great doubt about the possibility of determining the contribution of discrete genes to the individual phenotype and see "selection as acting on groups of coadapted alleles rather than on exhibitionistic, selfish genes."[75] In light of these developments, the critics of sociobiology view as absurd the claim of Wilson and others that discrete genes do or even might exist for such traits as homosexuality, conformity, spite, xenophobia, incest, and male-female differences in temperament.

Similar observations have been forthcoming from S. L. Washburn, a noted anthropologist who has conducted significant primate studies. Washburn contends that the state of our knowledge regarding genes and behavior in nonhuman primates is so slight that efforts to extend this knowledge to humans is surely unjustified scientifically.[76] It would simply result in a repetition of the errors of past generations of evolutionists, social Darwinists, eugenicists, and racists. Washburn also takes exception to the "weird set of behaviors" which sociobiologists claim is human nature and finds it extraordinary that in this purportedly "new science" not one gene accounting for any of these behaviors has been produced.[77]

The absence of data supporting the universal of male dominance has already been discussed. Nor has any evidence been brought forth in support of the numerous other postulated traits comprising the human biogram—such traits as conformity, spite, homosexuality, indoctrinability, altruism, selfishness, etc. In the words of the Sociobiology Study Group: "We can dispense with the direct evidence for a genetic basis of various human social forms in a single word: *none.*"[78]

Lacking such data as evidence for the genetic control of human relations, sociobiologists have devised several strategies—all problematical—by which they simply *infer* genetic determination. Universality of behaviors and social forms is the basis of the first inference for genetic control. Wilson and others simply assume that cultural invariants—e.g., calendars, weaving, weather control, the increasing division of labor, economic inequality, the growth of bureaucracies, and the perfection of agriculture—are necessarily programmed by our genes.

Tobach, Burian, and Lewontin have commented upon sociobiology's conceptual and logical confusion between the characteristics of humans and other animals.[79] These scholars charge that sociobiologists are guilty of the fallacies of both anthropomorphism—the attribution of human qualities to nonhuman animals—and zoomorphism—the equation of human behavior with that of other animals. Lewontin explains: "Animal behavior is described by a metaphorical carry-over from human social behavior, and then human institutions are rederived, by a kind of back-etymology, as a special case of the more general animal behavior."[80] Two obvious cases in point are sociobiological accounts of caste and slavery systems in insects and humans.

Caste, class structures, and slavery are all human social formations evolving under particular historical circumstances and designed to regulate the social, economic, and political relations of individuals and groups and bear no significant resemblance to their claimed counterparts in the insect community. The ant queen "a totally captive egg-producing machine, force-fed by the workers," does not resemble Elizabeth I, Catherine the Great, or even the politically powerless, but multimillionaire, Elizabeth II. "Ants do not know commodities, nor capital investment, nor rates of interest, nor slave revolts, nor the anguish of mothers and fathers torn from their children and spouses on auction blocks."[81] However, the false metaphor and faulty logic embodied in the application of human social relations to explain insect and animal behavior lends great legitimacy to the notion that castes and slavery among humans are just another instance of a phenomenon generalized throughout the animal world.

Conceptual confusion further confounds sociobiologists' efforts to reduce human mating behavior to a genetic base. As Washburn suggests, the term *monogamy* encompasses a host of different behaviors—continuing and temporary relationships, relations with spouses, concubines, slaves,

and mistresses—which could not possibly be accounted for in terms of a gene.[82] Identical problems exist for other concepts such as polygamy and parental investment. The point is that among humans monogamy and polygamy describe systems of marriage—institutionalized patterns of rights and duties involving much more than sexual behavior—and not mating. Mating outside of marriage has been known to occur in all societies. Washburn accuses sociobiologists of totally ignoring these fundamental differences between human marriage systems and animal mating behaviors, of misusing these concepts and of misunderstanding social science.[83] He states that human sociobiology "continues a history of scientific error . . . [and] renews the mistakes of social Darwinism, early evolutionism, eugenics, and racial interpretations of history. Such thinking is what Medawar and Medawar have called geneticism—the enthusiastic misapplication of not fully understood genetic principles in situations to which they do not apply."[84] Sociobiology, in defense of its position, must engage in scientific imperialism by attacking the social sciences; it must minimize the differences between learning and culture as opposed to inheritance; and it must posit genes for a "very odd assortment of behaviors." This negative evaluation is shared by virtually all of sociobiology's critics. They are in unanimous agreement that sociobiology does not adequately reflect the complex and dialectical relationships among human biology, human culture, and social forms, especially ignoring the importance of the human brain, language, and cultural evolution in distinguishing humans from other animals and marking a qualitative change in evolution with human development.

Another factor that disturbs the critics of sociobiology is not only that sociobiology assumes the adaptiveness of such behaviors as war, aggression, male dominance, tribalism, and others, that is, it assumes their genetic determination, but further that it prescribes that there are limits within which these innate behaviors can be altered and modified by culture and learning without also destroying human society. Such a position states that war and inequality based on class, sex, and ethnic nationality are biologically adaptive and natural and can be changed at great risk. What's more, this is all mere speculation and conjecture, unsupported by evidence of genetic control and untestable as well.

Xenophobia, coupled with aggression, territoriality, and war, is of special concern since it lends itself to an account of warfare between ethnic nationalities (races) as biological in origin, inevitable, natural, and adaptive. Wilson identifies circumstances under which "xenophobia becomes a political virtue." [85] Intergroup tension escalates "naturally" into warfare. Alper cautions that once races (ethnic nationalities or minorities) are considered types of groups, then warfare between these racial (national and minority) groups is seen as "natural" and "adaptive." [86] At a time when the Ku Klux Klan is preparing for such warfare in paramilitary training camps throughout the United States and Nazi groups are escalating their activities in Europe and America, pronouncements by Harvard professors about xenophobia and war cannot be taken lightly. The ideas of sociobiology can easily be used to support doctrines of discrimination and hostility between groups. [87] That these ideas do not have a scientific base in their conceptualization and in the evidence available is all the more vexing and troublesome. As many critics have claimed, it suggests that Wilsonian sociobiology is a pseudoscience and a political ideology rather than a legitimate scientific endeavor.

Another criticism focuses on the fact that sociobiologists, building on the fallacy of the "best" or "most natural" genotype, have committed the fallacy of human nature. This doctrine of human nature presumes that regardless of variations in human cultures, all human cultures contain a tendency to exhibit a similar structure and

content. Accordingly, so the sociobiologists argue, all men tend to be aggressive, territorial, entrepreneurial, polygamous, and to dominate women, while all women tend to be submissive, passive, monogamous, and "maternal." Individuals and cultures which do not clearly manifest these characteristics are said to "be in a state of temporary aberration or else to express the tendencies in a disguised or sublimated form." [88]

Marvin Harris rejects the notion that the human species can be characterized as "polygynous," arguing, instead, that our sexual behavior is so diverse that it defies species-specific characterization. [89] While more human females than males may be monogamous, millions of women do, in fact, have a plurality of sexual partners, and these women may be more sexually active than the most active men of other societies. Such is the case with de facto polyandry among matrifocal households in the Caribbean and northeast Brazil, as well as in southwest India and Tibet. As Harris puts it:

The idea that males naturally desire a plurality of sexual experiences while women are satisfied by one mate at a time is entirely a product of the political-economic domination males have exerted over women as part of the culturally created, warfare-related male supremacy complex. Sexually adventurous women are severely punished in male-dominated cultures. Wherever women have enjoyed independent wealth and power, however, they have sought to fulfill themselves sexually with multiple mates with no less vigor than males in comparable situations. I cannot imagine a weaker instance of genetic programming than the polygyny of *Homo sapiens*. Sexuality is something people can be socialized out of only at great cost. But people can be socialized into and out of promiscuity, polygyny, polyandry, and monogamy with conspicuous ease, once the appropriate infrastructural conditions are present. [90]

What about territoriality? Harris reports recent findings on hunter gatherers which "support the theory that the primordial units of human social life were open camp groups whose membership fluctuated from season to season and whose territories were not sharply defined." [91] It is likely that strong territorial interests came with changes in the modes of production, sedentary villages, and reproductive pressure. Harris flatly rejects Wilson's assertion that it is difficult to socialize people out of ownership of territory and that lack of territorial interests is "destructive of mental development." [92] He adds, "Indeed, one might argue more cogently that the territorial interests of modern states are destructive not only of mental development but of physical existence as well."

Sociobiology, divested of its scientific trappings, offers merely an *assumed* version of human nature and societal forms which carry a strong political and ideological message. The world and its inhabitants, according to Wilson, are characterized by an "economy of scarcity" and a resultant "unequal distribution of rewards."

> The members of human societies sometimes cooperate closely in *insectan* fashion, but more frequently they compete for the limited resources allocated to their role sector. The best and most entrepreneurial of the role-actors usually gain a disproportionate share of the rewards, while the least successful are displaced to other, less desirable positions. [93]

By *assuming* scarcity, Wilson is able to explain and justify existing inequalities as mandated by nature and to derive the necessity and adaptiveness of competition, struggle, individualism, selfishness, aggression, and dominance which give the successful an edge over nature's losers. In Wilson's words:

> In the language of sociobiology, to dominate is to possess priority of access to the necessities of life and reproduction. This is not a circular definition, it is a statement of a strong correlation observed in nature. With rare exceptions, the aggressively superior animal displaces the subordinate from food, from mates, and from nest sites. It only remains to be established that this power actually raises the genetic fitness of the animals possessing it. On this point the evidence is completely clear. [It does.] [94]

With this understanding we return to our beginning. The only purpose of our existence is to perpetuate our genes through our progeny. If, as is typical of human social relations but problematic for sociobiological theory, our competitive and aggressive struggles are moderated by displays of altruism, not to worry—sociobiology assures us this, too, is ultimately selfish. Lewontin concludes that in attempting "total explanatory power over all human social phenomena . . . [sociobiology] makes itself . . . into a vulgar caricature of Darwinian explanation." [95]

Is the rejection of sociobiological theory as an accurate and adequate scientific account of the relationships among biology, society, and culture at the same time a rejection of the biological and material aspect of human existence? The answer must be a resounding no.

Human organisms are material beings; thought is based on a material process; and social relations and institutions are constructed out of our thinking and material activity. But it has long been understood that meaning in human activity cannot be derived from complete knowledge of biology or of quantum mechanics. To be sure, human cultural evolution, the human self, and the human mind do have a genetic base; but at the same time they represent a qualitatively new force in evolution responsible for uncoupling cultural evolution from genetic evolution and uncoupling human social and cultural forms from specific controlling genes. [96] The human brain and its capacity for intelligence and language enable humans to think, to comprehend and give meaning to their existence, and to change and modify the natural forces and social relations affecting the quality of their lives. It is precisely this qualitative transformation contained within the biology of "human nature" which is the crux of human existence and human potentiality and which eludes sociobiological reductionism.

Sociobiology ignores the richness and variety, the plasticity and flexibility of human history and social formations. It overlooks the significance of human consciousness and choice in the evolution of culture and the adaptation of humans to their ecological niches. Humans have been selected precisely for their openness and flexibility rather than for specific behaviors under the direct control of isolated specific genes. This flexibility enables humans to be peaceful as well as aggressive, submissive as well as dominant, cooperative as well as competitive, and kind as well as spiteful. And all of these behaviors are equally biological in that they represent subsets of a possible range of behaviors. In criticizing the biological determinism of Wilsonian sociobiology, we do not need to invoke a nonbiological environmentalism. Such criticism "merely pits the concept of biological potentiality, with a brain capable of the full range of human behaviors and predisposed toward none, against the idea of biological determinism, with specific genes for specific behavioral traits." [97] As Gould explains, peacefulness, equality and kindness are also biological "and we may see their influence increase if we can create social structures that permit them to flourish." [98] It is precisely this understanding of the dialectical relationship among biological potential, social structure, and culture, rather than the biological determinism of sociobiology, which can profitably inform the work of sociologists and others who are genuinely seeking to explain the nature of human societies.

NOTES

1. Throughout the history of sociology there have been a number of sociologists, among them such luminaries as Talcott Parsons and George Homans, both of whom shared a Harvard address with E. O. Wilson, who have been drawn to biology. For Parsons there existed a basic compatibility between his system image and neo-Darwinian evolutionary theory, which allowed him to rectify the stasis of his social system by positing social evolution. Wallace and Wolf report that Parsons studied biology as an undergraduate. And, of course, the biological system is one of his four systems and he gives "optimization of gratification" as the basic motivating drive of human existence. Parsons was interested in and working on sociobiology until his death in 1979.

Homans offered a biologized and reductionistic program for sociology by which social behavior and social structure would be explained in terms of variables explicitly derived from biology.

Today Pierre van den Berghe is perhaps the most enthusiastic follower of Wilsonian sociobiology.

2. See W. D. Hamilton, "The Evolution of Social Behavior," *Journal of Theoretical Biology* 7 (1964), pp. 1–52; Robert Trivers, "The Evolution of Reciprocal Altruism," *Quarterly Review of Biology* 46 (March 1971), pp. 35–39, 45–47; David Barash, *Sociology and Behavior* (New York: Elsevier Science Publishing, 1977).

3. Arthur Caplan, ed., *The Sociology Debate* (New York: Harper & Row, 1978); Ashley Montagu, ed., *Sociobiology Examined* (New York: Oxford University Press, 1980); Derek Freeman, *Human Sociobiology*, "Sociobiology: The 'Antidiscipline' of Anthropology," in Montagu, ed., *Sociobiology Examined*, pp. 198–219.

4. Walda Katz-Fishman and Jan Fritz, "The Politics of Sociobiology," *Insurgent Sociologist* 10, no. 1 (Summer 1980), pp. 32–37.

5. See Richard Lewontin, "Biological Determinism as a Social Weapon," in Ann Arbor Science for the People Editorial Collective, eds., *Biology as a Social Weapon* (Edina, Minn.: Burgess International Group, 1977), pp. 6–20; Stephen Jay Gould, "Sociobiology and Human Nature: A Postpanglossian Vision," *Human Nature* 1, no. 10 (October 1978), pp. 1283–90; James King, "The Genetics of Sociobiology," in Montagu, ed., *Sociobiology Examined;* Mary Miggley, "Gene-Juggling," in Montagu, ed., *Sociobiology Examined*, pp. 108–34.

6. Montagu ed., *Sociobiology Examined;* Marvin Harris, *Cultural Materialism* (New York: Vintage Books, 1979); Jerome Barkow,

"Sociobiology: Is This the New Theory of Human Nature?" in Montagu, ed., *Sociobiology Examined;* S. L. Washburn, "What We Can't Learn about People from Apes," *Human Nature* (November 1978), pp. 70–75; Freeman, "Sociobiology"; and Richard Lewontin, "Sociobiology—A Caricature of Darwinism," in F. Suppe and P. D. Asquith, eds., *PSA 1976,* vol. 2 (East Lansing, Mich.: Philosophy of Science Association, 1976), pp. 22–31; Lewontin, "Sociobiology."

7. Gould, "Sociobiology and Human Nature"; Lewontin, "Sociobiology" and "Biological Determinism as a Social Weapon"; Michael Simon, "Biology, Sociobiology, and the Understanding of Human Social Behavior," in Montagu, ed., *Sociobiology Examined,* pp. 291–310; Sociobiology Study Group, "Sociobiology."

8. Montagu, ed., *Sociobiology Examined;* Gould, "Sociobiology"; Lewontin, "Sociobiology"; Sociobiology Study Group, "Sociobiology"; Joseph Alper, "The Ethical and Social Implications of Sociobiology" (1977) *Science for the People;* Joseph Alper, "Sociobiology Is a Political Issue," in Arthur Caplan, ed., *The Sociobiology Debate* (New York: Harper & Row, 1978); Barbara Chasin, "Sociobiology: A Sexist Synthesis," *Science for the People* (May/June 1977), pp. 27–31; S. L. Washburn, "What We Can't Learn about People from Apes" and "Human Behavior and the Behavior of Other Animals."

9. Edward O. Wilson, *Sociobiology: The New Synthesis* (Cambridge, Mass.: Harvard University Press, Belnap Press, 1975), p. 4.

10. Ibid., p. 3.

11. Ibid.

12. Edward O. Wilson, *On Human Nature* (Cambridge, Mass.: Harvard University Press, 1978).

13. Ibid., p. 1.

14. Ibid., p. 2.

15. Ibid., p. 5.

16. Ibid., p. 4.

17. Ibid., p. 199.

18. Ibid., p. 4.

19. Ibid., p. 5.

20. Ibid.

21. Wilson, *Sociobiology: The New Synthesis,* p. 4.

22. Edward O. Wilson, "Sociobiology: A New Approach to Understanding the Basis of Human Nature," *New Scientist,* May 13, 1976, p. 342.

23. Wilson, *Sociobiology: The New Synthesis,* p. 4.

24. Ibid., p. 575.

25. Within the social sciences there are a variety and multiplicity of theories to explain human social and cultural life. These theories can be seen as falling into one of two broad categories: materialist theories which stress the primacy of material reality and the economic foundation of society (following the lead of Marx); and idealist theories which emphasize the primacy of ideas, values, and norms in the shaping of social life and its material forms (e.g., functionalism).

26. Wilson, *Sociobiology: The New Synthesis* and *On Human Nature;* Richard Dawkins, *The Selfish Gene* (New York: Oxford University Press, 1976); Barash, *Sociobiology and Behavior;* Pierre van den Berghe, "Les Animaux Dénaturés," *Contemporary Sociology* 8, no. 3 (May 1979), pp. 348–50; Lee Ellis, "The Decline and Fall of Sociology, 1975–2000," *American Sociologist* 12, no. 2 (May 1977), pp. 56–65; Lionel Tiger and Robin Fox, "The Zoological Perspective in Social Science," *Man* 1 (1966), pp. 75–81; Robin Fox, "The Cultural Animal," *Encounter* 35, no. 1 (July 1970), pp. 32–39.

27. J. B. S. Haldane, "Population Genetics," *New Biology* 18 (1955), pp. 34–45; V. C. Wynne-Edwards, *Animal Dispersion in Relation to Social Behavior* (Edinburgh: Oliver and Boyd, 1962); Sewall Wright, "The Roles of Mutation, Inbreeding, Crossbreeding, and Selection in Evolution," in G. E. Brousseau, Jr., ed., *Evolution* (Dubuque, Iowa: Wm. C. Brown, 1962).

28. Wilson, *Sociobiology: The New Synthesis,* p. 578.

29. Robert Trivers, "The Evolution of Reciprocal Altruism," *Quarterly Review of Biology* 46 (March 1971), pp. 45–47.

30. Wilson, *Sociobiology: The New Synthesis,* p. 3.

31. W. D. Hamilton, "The Evolution of Social Behavior," *Journal of Theoretical Biology* 7 (1964), pp. 1–52.

32. Trivers, "The Evolution of Reciprocal Altruism."

33. Ibid., p. 36.

34. Marshall Sahlins, *The Use and Abuse of Biology* (Ann Arbor, Mich.: University of Michigan Press, 1977), p. 85.

35. Barash, *Sociobiology and Behavior,* p. 276.

36. Ibid., p. 277.

37. Wilson, *On Human Nature,* pp. 36–37.

38. Ibid., p. 36.

39. Wilson, *Sociobiology: The New Synthesis,* p. 551.
40. Wilson, ibid., p. 552; Edward O. Wilson, "Sociobiology: A New Approach to Understand the Basis of Human Nature," *New Scientist,* May 13, 1976, p. 13.
41. Wilson, *Sociobiology: The New Synthesis,* p. 552, and *On Human Nature,* p. 132.
42. Ibid.
43. Wilson, *Sociobiology: The New Synthesis.*
44. Ibid., pp. 286–87.
45. Ibid., pp. 572–73.
46. Ibid., p. 119.
47. Ibid., p. 561.
48. Wilson, *On Human Nature,* p. 176.
49. Wilson, *Sociobiology: The New Synthesis,* p. 562.
50. Wilson, *On Human Nature,* pp. 164–65.
51. Ibid., pp. 162–64.
52. Ibid.
53. Wilson, *Sociobiology: The New Synthesis,* p. 120.
54. Barash, *Sociobiology and Behavior,* p. 283.
55. Wilson, *On Human Nature,* p. 129.
56. Barash, *Sociobiology and Behavior,* p. 293.
57. Ibid., p. 296.
58. Wilson, *On Human Nature,* pp. 143–45.
59. Alper et al., "Sociobiology Is a Political Issue," p. 484.
60. Wilson, *On Human Nature,* p. 130.
61. Barash, *Sociobiology and Behavior,* p. 300.
62. Alper et al., "Sociobiology Is a Political Issue," pp. 484–85.
63. Barash, *Sociobiology and Behavior;* Trivers, "The Evolution of Reciprocal Altruism"; Wilson, *Sociobiology: The New Synthesis.*
64. Trivers, "The Evolution of Reciprocal Altruism."
65. Wilson, *Sociobiology: The New Synthesis,* p. 325.
66. Ibid., p. 550.
67. Wilson, *On Human Nature,* pp. 172, 175.
68. Ibid., p. 175.
69. Ibid., p. 208.
70. Ibid.
71. Ibid., pp. 211–12.
72. Ethel Tolbach, "The Methodology of Sociobiology from the Viewpoint of a Comparative Psychologist," in Arthur Caplan, ed., *The Sociobiology Debate* (New York: Harper & Row, 1978), p. 414.
73. James King, "The Genetics of Sociobiology," in Montagu, ed., *Sociobiology Examined,* pp. 86–87.
74. Ibid., p. 87.
75. Ibid.
76. Washburn, "What We Can't Learn about People from Apes," pp. 70–75.
77. S. L. Washburn, quoted in Myra Pines, "Is Sociobiology All Wet?" *Psychology Today* (May 1978), p. 24.
78. Sociobiology Study Group, "Sociobiology—A New Biological Determinism," p. 141.
79. Tobach, "The Methodology of Sociobiology"; Richard Burian, "A Methodological Critique of Sociobiology," in Caplan, ed., *The Sociobiology Debate*; Lewontin, "Sociobiology."
80. Lewontin, "Sociobiology," p. 23.
81. Ibid., p. 26.
82. Washburn, "Human Behavior and the Behavior of Other Animals," p. 260.
83. Ibid., p. 261.
84. Ibid., p. 256.
85. Wilson, *Sociobiology: The New Synthesis,* p. 565.
86. Alper, "Sociobiology Is a Political Issue," pp. 13–16.
87. Ibid.
88. Lewontin, "Biological Determinism as a Social Weapon," p. 11.
89. Marvin Harris, *Cultural Materialism* (New York: Vintage Books, 1979), p. 129.
90. Ibid.
91. Ibid., p. 133.
92. Ibid.
93. Wilson, *Sociobiology: The New Synthesis,* p. 554.
94. Ibid., p. 287.
95. Lewontin, "Sociobiology—A Caricature of Darwinism," p. 30.
96. See, for example, Montagu, ed., *Sociobiology Examined;* Derek Freeman, "The Evolutionary Theories of Charles Darwin and Herbert Spencer," *Current Anthropology* 15 (1974), pp. 211–37; David Layzer, "On the Evolution of Intelligence and Social Behavior," in Montagu, ed., *Sociobiology Examined.*
97. Stephen Jay Gould, "Biological Potential vs. Biological Determinism," *Natural History Magazine* (May 1976), pp. 12–21.
98. Ibid., p. 21.

Until quite recently technological development was, on the one hand, the object of celebratory treatment of individual achievements in elementary school textbooks, such as the invention of the cotton gin by Eli Whitney or the electric light by Thomas Alva Edison, and, on the other, a relatively obscure area of economic and sociological scholarship concerning the sources of invention and the relative contribution of technological change to economic growth.[1] An underlying hidden assumption of both perspectives was that technology was an autonomous force with a purpose and direction of its own.

The received view of technology has been challenged dramatically during the past two decades, although old forms of discourse persist alongside new concerns for the environment and international competitiveness. Moving from a discourse on inventive genius at varying intellectual levels of complication, technological development has become a controversial public issue in two apparently contradictory respects. The new questions concerning technology can be formulated as follows. Is there:

- Too much technological development, causing unacceptable damage to the environment and public health?
- Too little technological development, lessening productivity and creating an imbalance in trade due to increased imports?

Reconciling these two concerns theoretically and substantively is the fundamental problem facing theorists and practitioners of technological development. The issues that arise from these concerns provide the subject matter for this essay.

Henry Etzkowitz

TECHNOLOGY AND SOCIAL CHANGE: ALTERNATIVE PATHS

INTRODUCTION

In the course of the twentieth century, economic growth has increasingly become associated with technological development.[2] Formerly, the control of natural resources, access to capital, and skilled labor were believed to be the surest impetuses to economic development. While these factors are still important, especially as components of the process of developing new technology, technological development itself has increasingly become recognized as playing a central role in future economic growth. Understanding the economic conditions that foster or inhibit technological development has become an increasing concern of economists.[3] Companies are forming alliances to establish new research ventures, such as the SEMATECH project in the semiconductor industry, to improve the general level of their industry's technology. National and local governments are also searching for new ways to foster tech-

nological development in order to improve economic development in the face of evidence that small high-tech firms produce jobs at a high rate.[4]

The amount of money spent on research and development (R&D) has been a traditional indicator of a company or a nation's commitment to technological development.[5] However, the total amount spent, while providing a rough measure of commitment of resources to develop new technology, does not tell the story by itself. In many companies R&D funds are almost entirely devoted to maintaining and improving existing products, not to developing new ones. A large, and in recent years an increasing, proportion of federal R&D funds is devoted to weapons research that only sometimes has a spillover into the civilian economy.[6] Even when significant funds are devoted to developing a new technology, the outcome may not be successful as in the postwar effort to develop nuclear reactor technology to produce electricity economi-

355

cally and safely.[7] Or even when a technology is technically feasible, the funds may not be readily available to make it economical, especially if the time perspective for achievement of the goal is relatively long as with solar electricity technology.[8] At other times, of course, the commitment of resources brings a technology to fruition; witness duPont's success with nylon and the Manhattan Project to develop the atomic bomb during the Second World War. What these examples suggest is that while R&D funding does not guarantee a result, the commitment of resources allows a result to be achieved if it is technically feasible. It certainly shows the direction that its sponsors wish to take the development of new technology.

The increasing amount of funds devoted to R&D also highlights the social nature of technological development, i.e., that it is not a phenomenon that occurs autonomously, directed by an invisible internal gyroscope, but a phenomenon whose course and direction is influenced by identifiable people and institutions. The variable nature of technology has also been revealed by problems found in technologies that could either have been foreseen or, once found, resolved by changing the technology or selecting an alternative.

During the past two decades people's expectation that the development of new technology would benefit humanity, already shaken by the specter of the atomic bomb, received repeated blows from revelations about the environmental and safety hazards of many sophisticated technologies. The failure of nuclear power plants at Three Mile Island and Chernobyl, the harmful side effects of industrial processes revealed in the burial of hazardous wastes at Love Canal, dioxins inadvertently spread on the ground at Times Beach, Missouri, and the oil spill in the Santa Barbara Channel all combined to create a new consciousness of technological danger. During the same era computers were introduced into general use, and new electronic visual tech-

nologies such as VCRs became widely available, reinforcing existing beliefs in technological progress. These contrasting sets of events have created a Janus-faced, two-sided image of technology as a destructive force and hidden danger, on the one hand, and as a helpful aide and provider of entertainment on the other.

One consequence of this new image is that a cost/benefit calculation has replaced the previous virtually automatic acceptance of technology in the early post-World War II era. At the very least recognition of problems with technology has meant that the criteria for a successful technology have been subject to considerable change. Thus recognition of environmental effects has changed not only the way we view technology but also how it is developed. For example, the internal combustion engine used in automobiles has been recognized as a primary cause of smog. While such engines are still the most common way to power vehicles, they have been extensively modified to reduce harmful emissions. Our accumulated experience with technologies that have been recognized as problematic and then were discarded or changed in important respects has called into question taken-for-granted assumptions that technology develops according to an internal logic of its own that is beyond human control.

The social theory of technology has lagged behind this everyday life experience of technology. A systematic, clearly defined framework to articulate the distinctions among alternative forms of technology is a necessary first step. Part of this project is the development of a taxonomy of technological sophistication. Currently the spectrum is divided into polar opposites. At one extreme are highly sophisticated, multisystem technologies such as space shuttles and nuclear power plants. At the other pole are simple, individualized, and decentralized technologies such as family gardens and solar heating and cooling. In between these opposites lies an alternative approach which combines sophistication in technique with smallness in scale, leaving open the choice between centralization or decentralization.

DEFINITIONS

The physical universe provides a broad but by no means unlimited range of possibilities for the development of technology. Within the constraints of physical, chemical, and biological laws and the state of our knowledge of them, some subsets of physical phenomena rather than others are selected for utilization. However, these limits are not irrevocably fixed. New possibilities continually appear. Phenomena that were previously considered impossible become possible; for example, levitation with advances in the understanding of superconductivity. Nevertheless, alchemy, astrology, and the search for a perpetual motion machine are, at present, considered to be beyond the realm of what the physical universe will allow.

Technology is often defined only in terms of the physical means of performing a task.[9] A riveting machine, a chemical process that produces sulfuric acid, or a telephone are all physical objects that enable people to accomplish specific goals. However, physical objects by themselves do not constitute a technology. The purpose that the physical means are used to achieve must be stated to complete the description of any technology. For example, the communication of people over distance is part of the purpose of the telephone, and destruction or the threat of destruction is the purpose of a bomb. These goals are implicit in the material objects that constitute a bomb or a telephone and are as much a part of technology as the material used to build a machine.[10]

Thus values are an essential part of any technology, whether they are overtly built in by designers or appear as an emergent phenomenon. For example, centralized control was a deliberate intention of the designers of numerically controlled machine tools, while decentralized control appeared as a byproduct of record-playback

equipment.[11] Explicating the values involved in a technology is the first step to the formulation of an ethics of responsibility for the development and use of technology which, in one view, "has opened up a whole new dimension of ethical relevance for which there is no precedent in the standards and canons of traditional ethics."[12]

Technology can also be defined in terms of its relationship to social organization. Jacques Ellul has suggested the term *technique* to denote the efficient relationship of means to ends.[13] The model for technique is the machine. Yet although technique is embodied in technology, not all technique is technological. While some subset of non-machine technique is related to technology, such as the placement of workers in relation to machines so that the simplest and easiest physical exertions will be made, and even directs it, another subset is not machine-based. Thus technique also exists independently of physical means as a form of social organization used to accomplish the relationship of means to ends. Technique, then, is the social means to accomplish a specific goal such as a bureaucratic organization to ensure common standards in the issuance of licenses.

Ellul also argues that technique, a mode of procedure, has become an "end in itself," superseding other ultimate ends and values. Certainly this has happened to a great extent in modern society. It is our goal to show the existence of countertrends in which technique, and even technology, can be directed by other values or forms of social organization.

As a physical means, a given technology allows certain patterns of social relationships to exist among its users and disallows others. Technologies vary greatly in the range and type of social relations that they allow. The hydraulic civilizations of ancient China, with their huge waterworks, required an elaborate bureaucratic structure to operate.[14] On the other hand, a wide variety of social structures have been identified among many societies utilizing simple agricultural tools.[15] Some technologies are *fixed* and allow only a very narrow range of social relations. For example, a nuclear reactor is a fixed technology requiring a rigid hierarchical bureaucracy to operate. Other technologies are variable and allow a wide range of social relationships. For example, eighteenth-century textile manufacturing technology, as portrayed by Marx in *Capital*, could be carried on by families as a cottage industry or centralized in factories. The original motive for moving production from home to factory was to take control of the production process away from workers. It was not due to technological necessity since the instruments of production were the same.

Technology, then, is a physical embodiment of nature, social organization, and human purpose, and technologies are unique combinations of material goods, social activity, and ends. Particular technologies include means (physical and social) and ends that can be defined in terms of their value implications. Some technologies incorporate a broad range of ends and are multivalent, while others express only a few and are value-specific. Value-specific technology can be used to achieve only a narrow range of goals. For example, a bomb is used for destruction and a plow for breaking the earth. Other technologies are multivalent and can be used for a broad range of purposes. Thus an electric motor can be used to power a submarine, a hair dryer, or a sewing machine, achieving goals as diverse as national security, personal beautification, and the production of goods. Since technology consists of physical means, social relations, and human purpose, a change in any one or more of these factors can affect the direction of technological change.

HISTORICAL BACKGROUND OF IDEAS ABOUT TECHNOLOGY

From the inception of the Industrial Revolution in England, the development of new technologies has been recognized as an important contributing factor to economic growth.[16] At the same time workers in traditional crafts recognized that the productivity growth of new technologies could cost them their jobs and some took to breaking machines.[17] During the eighteenth century technological development was a public issue in the United States. During this era the United States, an underdeveloped country, was attempting to gain access to advanced technologies from England by luring skilled workers, among other stratagems. However, the issue during this period was whether industrial development based on new technology should be encouraged in the first place. There were justifiable fears during the early nineteenth century that industrial technology located in factories would disrupt the social structure based on crafts and farming.[18] The primary justification for accepting the change was that these new technologies would bring increased productivity and higher living standards. Once the decision was taken to accept textile mills and the machine industries that grew up to support them in Lowell, Massachussetts, and Boston, the United States rapidly industrialized.

Although concerns surfaced again in the late nineteenth and early twentieth centuries over the poor quality of manufactured goods and unsafe working conditions, leading to governmental regulation, technological development in itself remained an unquestioned goal of American society. Only during the depression of the 1930s when it was questioned whether too many labor-saving technologies might have cost some people their jobs did the social effects of technological development come to the fore. However, United States successes in World War II, partly based on industrial production capabilities and the research and development of new weapons, relegitimated technological development. During the early postwar era when the United States was the world leader in technology, technological development appeared to follow an inexorable course and, except for celebratory paeans, fell from public attention. For example, the development of atomic reactors seemed to lead unquestionably to a nuclear industry in popular predictions, even though behind-the-scenes, experts questioned its economic feasibility.[19] However, in recent years Japanese success in producing and marketing technologies such as the VCR, which was originally developed in the United States, has focused attention on the role of technological development in the economy, a process that was largely taken for granted when the United States was preeminent. A theoretical debate over the role of technology in society has raged behind these popular perceptions. Whether technology should be viewed as a positive or negative force is at the heart of the issue between Marx and Weber.

Weberian Paradox and Marxian Lemma

Marx viewed the development of large-scale industrial technology as deleterious in the short run and positive in the long run. In his analysis of the British parliamentary reports, Marx noted repeatedly that as new machines were introduced, wages were driven down. Nevertheless, the abundance of material goods created through machine production would eventually create the conditions for the elimination of capitalism. Moreover, Marx's vision of the future involved a reversal of the division of labor, although he could not at the time specify how this would be possible. However, at present we can identify trends in technological development in the computer and electronics industries which are moving toward a decrease in scale.

For Weber, until the modern era social change occurred through a shift from one type of organization to another such as from a patrimonial to a monocratic bureaucracy. The mechanism of change is ideas and emotions that are strongly believed and felt. The initiators of these subjective waves are charismatic leaders who are able to move people to break with existing organizational forms. Through the trust placed in them, they are able to initiate new patterns and get people to follow them. Until the modern era social change was a series of recurring patterns—not really change at all, but a recursive movement from personalized individual leadership to rigidified organizational structures.

In the modern era a cultural pattern that had been slowly gathering momentum in the West disrupted the cyclical pattern of charismatic upheaval and bureaucratization. Originating in magical thought, rationalization, the ever more efficient coupling of means to an end, became preeminent. Its acceptance in everyday life accelerated in the course of the Reformation as an unintended consequence of the calculus of intentions, actions, and rewards that Protestantism encouraged among its followers during the sixteenth century. Rationalization came to full flower, beginning in the seventeenth century, through the growth of science into a major institutional area of contemporary society. During the eighteenth century the interaction of scientists with industry began to make the development of technology part of the scientific project, while also making science part of the development of capitalism. The development of science and technology within universities and corporations during the late nineteenth and twentieth centuries resulted in ever larger scale and seemingly more efficient technologies.

This was the phenomenon that Marx also focused upon in its very early manifestations in the mid-nineteenth century in his analysis of the relationship of science to capitalism. Marx saw that the transmutation of science into capital made science one of the forces of production. According to Marx, "It is, firstly the analysis and application of mechanical and chemical laws, arising directly out of science, which enables the machine to perform the same labor as that previously performed by the worker."[20] "Invention then becomes a business, and the application of science to direct production itself becomes a prospect which determines and solicits it." [21] Science, in the service of capital, transforms "the production process from the simple labor process into a scientific process...." [22] Marx delineated the place of technology in this social relationship under the formulation, "In machinery objectified labor materially confronts living labor as a ruling power...." [23] Nevertheless, within this oppressive force there was a liberative potential. For the increase in productivity of technology under capitalism could be expected to result in an overwhelming material abundance. The end of scarcity made the continuation of capitalism ultimately untenable since it was a social system based on the principle of scarcity.

Although technology made available additional power to the capitalist class, Marx suggested how their control could be broken. Such a transformation would occur as a result of the growth of consciousness among a working class gathered together into factories from their previously isolated home workplaces. Politically conscious workers would organize and take power, redressing the theft of labor power represented by the earlier substitution of capitalist-controlled machines for worker-controlled tools. It was the subordinate role of workers in operating the technology owned and controlled by factory owners that was expected to induce this new consciousness and the resulting political movement. This thesis was in contrast to Marx's theory of the transition from previous stages of history, which involved the innovation of new forces of production by an emerging class. Thus in Marx's theory of social change, the weight of influence shifts from the relationship of technology to economic organization to the relationship between consciousness and political organization under capitalism.

The succeeding worker-controlled socialist society, using the technology developed under capitalism, would provide the means for all people to live a creative, free, and abundant life based on "the mastery by the whole society of society's mastery over nature." [24] For Marx, technology was neutral in itself, and could be used to achieve different purposes, given a change in ownership and control. Thus the tremendous productivity of technology under capitalism, utilized to create disparities of wealth and power, could be turned to egalitarian ends under socialism. The development of a highly productive technology was a necessary but not sufficient condition for the achievement of socialism. The productivity of modern technology was a prerequisite for the ending of scarcity. But scarcity could be artificially maintained under the social relations through which technology was operated under capitalism. Changing the control of that technology, but not necessarily changing the technology itself, was the project of creating a socialist society. Marx underestimated the ability of capitalists to build their ideology into machines as well as to embed it into workers' consciousness, making his project of social transformation more extensive and daunting.

Weber was more cautious about future possibilities for social transformation. He argued that "the expropriation of the individual worker from ownership of the means of production is in part determined by... purely technical factors...." [25] This condition would hold "in any rationally organized socialistic economy." Large-scale capital-intensive technologies would be the primary mode of economic and technical organization, and such technologies by their very nature require for their operation a hierarchical bureaucratic management. Irrespective of entrepreneurial or worker ownership—capitalism or socialism—bureaucracy would be the inevitable mode of social organization in advanced industrial societies. For Weber, the direction of technological development into ever larger-scale and more efficient production processes mandated bureaucratization. The self-organized decentralized society dreamed about by Marx was simply impossible, given the dictates of modern technology.

Even if a revolution took place and an industrial society was taken over in the name of socialism, the very nature of that industrial technology would force socialists to continue to maintain bureaucratic structures. Weber would seem to have interred socialism in the dustbin of history, having found the vital flaw in Marx's analysis of the development of large-scale machinery. Workers' consciousness might change so that they would act in their own interest, create political movements, and even make revolutions. But having done so, they would find themselves bound by technology to re-create bureaucracy. The post-1917 history of the Soviet Union provides a case history of this process of rebureaucratization anticipated by Weber. Taylorism was imported into the Soviet Union under the guise of the Stakhanovite system, and the workers' councils were disbanded.

Their differing definitions of the essential characteristics of the factory form the basis of Marx and Weber's theoretical disagreements on the issue of technology. For Weber, the mere gathering together of workers under a single roof by a capitalist did not make a workshop a factory. The essential characteristic of the factory was the use of mechanically powered machines. First, there is an improvement at the technical level in the process of production. Such improvements result in jobs being broken down into simpler forms, thus increasing the division of labor. As the process of production becomes more technically complicated, there is an increased need for managerial expertise. Separate classes of capitalists and workers are thus institutionalized on a technical basis. Even when the ownership relationship is removed, mechanical complexity requires a technically competent authority. Thus the role of the manager, who is not necessarily an owner, arises from the mechanization of the work process.

For Marx, of course, it is the gathering together of workers and their tools under a single roof that constitutes the factory. Only after workers have been so organized can their jobs be analyzed into their simplest components and machines devised to perform their tasks. Machines were part of the process by which capitalists increased their control over workers. Technologies were chosen not only for their economic efficiency but also for their utility in placing control of the work process in the hands of the capitalist. Technological development was part of a social process simultaneously directed toward the twin goals of increasing productivity and ensuring the control of capital over labor.

In the language of social research, technology is a dependent variable shaped by social forces for Marx, whereas for Weber technology is the independent variable that shapes social relationships. In Marx's view new technology was created in the context of changes in the balance of power between workers and capitalists. For Weber, scientifically based technological development creates a division of labor. The increase in scale of industry that initially took place in telegraphy and the railroad, required coordination that could only be achieved through bureaucracy. Although bureaucratic centralization also existed in earlier civilizations such as Egypt and Mesopotamia, "essentially technical factors...enter the picture as pacemakers of bureaucratization" in the West.[26]

Thus Marx was the idealist and Weber the materialist in their visions of the future. Both believed that the futures they projected were inevitable, given the development of industrial technology in the form that they specified. There is no way out of Weber's vision, given the development of technology into ever larger-scale forms, for they require bureaucratic coordination. Nor is there any way to achieve Marx's vision given this technological trend toward increase in scale. However, implicit in Marx's analysis of technology as socially influenced by the goals of capital is the conclusion that other technologies are possible that would serve different goals. Given other social inputs, different forms of technology could be developed. These technologies could involve a recombination of labor and a decrease in the need for bureaucracy. Marx did not pursue this line of analysis, given his optimistic expectations for change on the level of social relations. Indeed, the analysis of the potential for achieving social change through deliberately affecting the course of technological development has only begun to be undertaken,[27] even though developments in technology are one of the most utilized historical explanations of the appearance of unintended social consequences.

EXPLANATIONS OF TECHNOLOGICAL DEVELOPMENT

Most theories of technological development assume that the technologies developed and used are the most efficient and effective ones that could have been chosen. In other words "what is" is equated with "what ought to be" in both neoclassical economic and neo-Marxist theories of technology.[28] In both of these views, ironically, the maximization of profits is held to coincide with the development of the best technologies.

Traditionally economists viewed land, labor, and capital as the sources of economic productivity. During the post-World War II era economists began to view technological change as an important factor in the creation of economic productivity. Technological change was a major component of a "residual" variable consisting of what could not be explained by the three traditional factors of production. A strong relationship was identified between the amount of resources committed to research in an area of technology and the rate of technological advance. The amount of expenditure for research and development was identified as the best indicator of technological change. However, this finding of a strong relationship between resources

committed and rate of technological development does not by itself explain why one area of technology is developed and another left underdeveloped.

Four major hypotheses have been offered to answer this question:

- The generation of technology from previously developed technology according to an internal logic.
- The generation of technology from scientific advance.
- Economic demand exercised through the marketplace.
- Organizational pressures from governments, corporations and social movements.

The traditional process of technological development occurred apart from science and even engineering. It involved manufacturers and workers who were intimately familiar with a particular production process and who, over time, made small improvements based on their craft knowledge. Engineering disciplines began by organizing and systematizing this craft knowledge. Engineers then developed improvements in technology by extending the principles that were developed into new areas but were still closely tied to craft knowledge. The transformation of engineering into applied science occurred as engineers used scientific knowledge gained from chemical and mathematical research to develop production processes. Finally, scientists themselves became involved in translating basic research into working devices.

The invention of the transistor is perhaps the most well-known example of the development of a technology from scientific knowledge. During the early 1940s the leadership of Bell Laboratories determined that the expansion of knowledge in solid state physics provided the best opportunity to develop new amplifying devices that could improve upon the vacuum tube.[29] An interdisciplinary research group was established to develop solid state theory, with an eye to producing a working device. An initial device was produced through accidental circumstances, the point contact transistor, while a second device was produced as a direct result of theoretical prediction, the junction transistor. In any case the close connection between seeking theoretical knowledge and producing a working device in Bell Labs was highly productive. A parallel research effort at Purdue University focused exclusively on solid state theory barely missed inventing the transistor.

Another approach has been that technology drives itself through a cumulative and self-generating dynamic.[30] Thus the imbalance between a highly productive machine in one part of a manufacturing process and a less productive machine in another part of the same manufacturing process is a strong incentive to the development of new techniques. For example, "Ray's flying shuttle led to the need for speeding up spinning operations; the eventual innovations in spinning in turn created the shortage of weaving capacity which finally culminated in Cartwright's introduction of the power loom."[31] Other examples of imbalance among interdependent processes that led to technical advance include bicycle manufacture, steel production, and rifle ordnance. However, these instances of one highly productive component in a technological complex stimulating innovations elsewhere in an interdependent system occurred only after the key element in the technology was already established. Thus, metal-forming tools for bicycle manufacture and the Bessemer process of steel production were already widely used before they created an imbalance that stimulated innovation in related technical areas. However, the Bessemer process itself only slowly replaced previous processes of steel production, even though it was more efficient and available. Thus, while the thesis of technical imbalance helps explain the creation of additional advances once an element of a new technology is in place, it does not explain the origination of the initial element of a technology.

Technological progress has also been held to be the result of the need for new and/or improved products. Corporations fund industrial research to develop them, and such investment in research takes place in the expectation that profits will result. Most industrial research focuses on the existing products or processes of a company.[32] However, in a few large corporations the following three conditions hold:

1. Availability of resources to support basic research.
2. A business strategy that includes the introduction of new products that are clearly differentiated from the existing product line.
3. A close coordination between research laboratories, development groups, and manufacturing facilities.

Thus research in large industrial laboratories is most likely to lead to major technical advance. The alternative model is the small high-tech company operating as part of a technical community of similar companies in a geographical region. Most new products, even of such companies, involve recombining existing technological elements in a new format, such as the portable personal computer introduced by the Compaq Corporation. However, there have been significant instances of the development of new technologies by new small companies, often based on relationships with university researchers, such as the origins of the Digital Equipment Corporation from MIT and the development of the minicomputer. On the whole, industrial research is a "supply side" form of technological advance. A technology is developed on the basis of perceptions of what is needed and can be marketed rather than as an outgrowth of consumer demand.

Social Influences on Technological Development

Social influences on technological development occur through choice among alternative technologies, funding availability, and citizen pressures for new criteria. These can result in the pursuit of one line of technological development and the suppression of another by large corporations[33]; the skewing of technological development in one direction rather than another for political reasons, for example toward military rather than civilian objectives[34]; the passage of laws mandating as development objectives such considerations as safety and health-requirements[35] or the support of social movements.

David Noble's account of the development of computerized machine tools shows that two alternative courses of technological development were possible. One was based on so-called record playback equipment in which the motions of an experienced machinist manipulating the machine tool to produce a device were electronically recorded and then played back through the equipment to produce additional devices without the presence of the worker. The other was based on so-called numerical control, a theoretically conceived computer program designed to operate the machine tool equipment. The first was suitable to small companies and worker control; the second to large corporations and control by engineering experts. Record playback was a relatively simple device, whereas numerical control was a highly complicated procedure requiring a significant input of research to make it practicable. Noble argues that the large scale of the latter process with its requirement for technical expertise made it more compatible with organizations that were large and highly technical than the alternative process. This is similar to the remark by the director of a large national laboratory that his lab could switch from military to peacetime research but that the peacetime projects would have to be large in order for the lab to survive. The availability of research funds from the military encouraged large corporations to become involved in computerized machine tool design. Since there was an organizational fit with numerical control, this was the technology that was adopted.

Sociologist of technology Bernhard Stern in a series of articles and reports in the 1930s and 40s developed the most comprehensive analysis of corporate restrictions on technological development. Stern argued that large corporations in stable industries preferred to limit innovations that would increase productivity or lower prices, fearing that their control over an industry would be diluted. For example, the commercialization of fluorescent lights was held back for decades by existing corporations in the electric light industry. The patent system, designed to encourage the utilization of new technology by conferring exclusive rights to develop and license inventions, has been misused to delay their use. A firm may develop or purchase an invention for the specific purpose of tying up a device that would compete with one that it already uses. A Federal Communications Commission study of the Bell Telephone Company found that 1,307 patents were deliberately held and not used for competitive purposes.[36]

Stern argues that the *frustration of technology* takes place through direct acts affecting the particular technology itself such as use of patents to withhold a technology from the marketplace. I have argued that there is also a repression of technology that takes place through encouraging one line of technological development and indirectly repressing another. For example, heavy government subsidies to the oil, coal, and nuclear industries had the side effect of slowing the development of solar energy, a technology much less supported by government.[37] Such policies have the effect of supporting the introduction of new technologies that replicate the existing social structure and suppressing alternatives that do not.

Technology and Social Change

The ability to choose the direction of technological development, rather than accepting it as an inevitable fixed feature of the social universe, gives technology a political character. Conflicts over the direction of technological development increasingly emerge as public issues and are resolved as such.

The environmental, consumers, antinuclear, and feminist social movements have created an awareness of problematic technologies. As a result of controversies over the Corvair and Pinto automobiles, the supertampon, and D.E.S., significant segments of the population began to question the beneficence of technology in general as a result of repeated problems with individual products and processes. In recent years the development of a consumer and environmental critique of technology has brought forth additional factors that affect the development of technology, such as the control of markets, according to Barry Commoner.[38]

The Environmental Movement. The environmentalist critique of technology is exemplified by the work of ecologist Barry Commoner. For example, he has argued that the paper diaper was developed by a large corporation to enable it to displace an area of small business—the diaper laundry and delivery services. Commoner shows that the paper diaper, marketed through national advertising, has no greater efficiency than the cloth diaper that it displaced. This analysis suggests that the increase in technological scale associated with the production and marketing of the paper diaper was not accompanied by an increase in productivity. Instead a large-scale technology was introduced to allow a large-scale organization to subsume an area of activity. Moreover, the disposable diaper created an environmental problem since its plastic components were not biodegradable. While the environmental critique of technology was developed to call attention to issues of public health and safety, it also has implications for technological development. By explicating the motives behind the development of a technology, it calls into question the assumption that technological development proceeds according to

an internal logic, and it forces consideration of social influences on the development of technology.

The Consumers Movement. The contemporary consumers' movement grew out of Ralph Nader's critique of the automobile industry in the early 1960s, the industry's response to his criticism, and the subsequent growth of public awareness about problems with everyday products and government regulation. Nader's book *Unsafe at Any Speed* analyzed persisting safety defects in the Corvair automobile made by General Motors Corporation. Nader charged that General Motors was aware of the vehicle's flaws but ignored them because it was cheaper to pay occasional legal settlements for accidents than to remedy the defects. Moreover, the company received relatively few claims since at the time the tendency was to presume that accidents were the fault of the driver rather than of the automobile. Educational campaigns conducted through public service advertisements on radio and in newspapers placed the blame for virtually all accidents on drivers, ignoring the possibility that flaws in the vehicles themselves could be the at fault.

General Motors, nevertheless, was concerned enough about the potential impact of Nader's book to start a campaign to discredit him. The company hired detectives to investigate his life-style and went beyond mere observation by attempting to involve him in compromising situations. When these efforts were exposed in hearings before the United States Congress, Nader's analysis of the Corvair's defects simultaneously received nationwide publicity. Nader gained enormous credibility from the episode, and his name soon became a household word synonymous with consumer advocate as a result of subsequent investigations. With the aid of a small staff and volunteers Nader developed the technique of amassing facts about a specific issue, using his new status as a public figure to gain the attention of the mass media and thereby bring his analysis to the public. In addition to critiquing existing technologies, social movements have supported new directions of technological development.

The Feminist Movement. Birth control is a historical example of the influence of a social movement on the development of technology. In addition to lobbying for legislation and educating people to accept the goals of the movement, funds were raised to support research on birth control devices. In the early 1950s the birth control movement faced the fact that contraceptive technology had not advanced significantly since the perfection of the spring-loaded diaphragm in the 1920s. During that era two organizations, Planned Parenthood and the Population Council, played an important role in convincing many governments to recognize the value of contraception to both economic and public health policy. Resistance to birth control derived from a variety of religious beliefs, and the 1930s depression created fears of economic stagnation because of a low population growth.

An early twentieth-century feminist and crusader for contraceptive practice, Margaret Sanger, represented the aspirations of many women (radical feminists, middle-class club women, and working women) for whom autonomy, security, leisure, or an improved standard of living were dependent upon the success of female birth control methods. As founder of a network of birth control clinics that disseminated information and practical assistance, Sanger's organization, Planned Parenthood, was primarily supported by women, even as most of the doctors working in the clinics were female, although foundations and male admirers also made contributions. A parallel research effort, primarily supported by foundations and individual philanthropists, developed the contraceptive pill and the intrauterine device (IUD) by the early 1960s. Availability of these improved methods of birth control gave women an increased ability to control their reproductive

life. The research and development of these techniques was fostered by the work of the birth control movement in mobilizing and articulating a demand for them and in establishing criteria for researchers to aim for in developing birth control technologies that would be both effective and acceptable to their users.

The Appropriate Technology Movement. On the international level the United Nations has established an agency, United Nations Industrial Development Organization (UNIDO), to develop models of appropriate industrial development. Through a series of conferences bringing together technical experts from First, Second, and Third World countries, plans for using modern, but not necessarily the most advanced, industrial technology on a modest scale were developed for a number of industrial fields relevant to underdeveloped countries. UNIDO superseded the traditional notion of appropriate technology relying on labor-intensive, small-scale production, often "concerned with marginal improvements to traditional technologies used in developing countries." [39] Instead it was proposed that capital intensive technologies could be appropriate when they were "consistent with local resources and conditions." [40] Thus medium-scale projects using local raw materials and imported but easily maintainable technologies were to be distinguished from large-scale projects, technically dependent on outside sources on a continuing basis.

Indeed, a major purpose of these conferences was to effect the transfer of project models successfully attempted in one developing country to other countries where similar conditions obtained. For example, the working group on papermaking suggested that examples of small plants in Brazil, Egypt, and India using alternative fiber sources to coniferous wood pulp, such as reeds and paddy straw, could be duplicated in other developing countries with other potential papermaking resources such as banana stems and hemp. The papermaking processes typically involved low-heat chemical recovery systems, long discarded by large-scale capital-intensive manufacturers. Yet it was also expected that these older processes could be the subject of R&D improvements undertaken in research institutes in developing countries that would enhance their efficiency while retaining advantages of simplicity and scale. Thus one goal of the UNIDO effort was to shift technology transfer activities, wherever possible, from one developing country to another, replacing the usual pattern of relationship from developed to underdeveloped countries.

SOCIAL EFFECTS OF TECHNOLOGY

Our argument has been that there are alternative criteria for technological development, emanating from human values and social interests. On the one hand, there has been a contestation over whether to embody hierarchical or nonhierarchical modes of organizational structure within technology. On the other hand, there is a newer struggle over the weight to be given to protecting the environment or creating new economic wealth.

Large-Scale Technologies

Until quite recently technology has been presumed to follow a progression in which increase in scale was inexorable and brought with it an increase in efficiency. This assumption has come into question through the negative example of the nuclear reactor industry, where an increase in scale did not resolve the technical problems of light water reactor technology but, if it had any effect, exacerbated these problems. On the other hand, the transistorization of computers has resulted in a dramatic decrease in scale accompanied by equally remarkable increases in the efficiency of these devices. The underlying issue, however, is whether scale is totally related to technology as a physical phenomenon or whether scale also is affected by social choices and value preferences.

While the nature of the railroad industry with its stations spread over large distances required formal organizational methods to coordinate the movement of passengers and freight across a continent, the large scale of many other industrial organizations was not dictated by technological imperatives. Historically large corporations were typically founded to gain economic control over an industry. Thus the United States Steel Corporation and Standard Oil were organized in the late nineteenth century not as the result of technical necessity but of attempts to create monopolies. For example, prior to the creation of the Standard Oil Trust the various aspects of the production processes of the industry were being handled by numerous refining, pipeline, and drilling companies that were coordinated through market relationships rather than by bureaucratic mechanisms introduced as a means of coordinating a large-scale enterprise. More recently, the creation of so-called conglomerate corporations in the 1950s and 60s whose different lines of business are unrelated to each other demonstrates the financial rather than the technological imperative of much of the increase in corporate organizational scale.

The relationship between scale of technology and social organization has generally been presumed to be that size and complexity are associated with efficiency and productivity. For example, the space shuttle is a large and complex device that was expected to be able to move people and material into space with great efficiency. After serious problems in the United States space program emerged, such as the explosion of the *Challenger*, it was suggested that simpler rockets could have been used for most of the work of the shuttle.

Large-scale technologies are typically capital-intensive, complex, and inflexible. Facilities such as a nuclear power plant require hundreds of millions, even billions, of dollars to construct. A typical nuclear power plant consists of mammoth steel vessels encased in concrete, miles of piping, cooling towers, remote control devices, and elaborate electronic and computer systems to monitor and control the operation of the reactor. The delicate and unstable nature of reactor technology requires precise coordination and control of tasks. The misperformance of even a simple task can have catastrophic consequences. In one incident a worker, inspecting a pipeline for leaks by using a candle that would flicker in the presence of a leak, caused a fire resulting in millions of dollars of damage. Control over the reactor was almost lost when the fire affected the control systems. Other simple yet severe accidents illustrate the complex interdependence and fragility of such technology.[41]

A rigid and tightly organized bureaucracy is required to operate a nuclear power plant. The controls may not be left unattended at any time. A reactor cannot simply be shut down at the end of a shift; it is supposed to operate continuously except for periodic refueling and maintenance. Elaborate procedures have been conceived to guard against known possibilities of failure. Nevertheless, unforeseen events happen that require instant reaction and countermeasures if a nuclear power plant is not to go out of control.

Schumpter and John Kenneth Galbraith justify the existence of large corporations and oligopolies on the grounds that scale of operation is essential to provide sufficient resources to support research programs. On the other hand, Edward Mason argues that "in chemicals and allied products, machinery and electrical equipment, a firm engaging in R&D employing between 50 and 499 workers spent more on R&D as a percentage of their total assets than did bigger firms doing R&D."[42] He concludes that there is "no support for the notion that only big firms are research minded or can afford research." Mason goes further to argue that the protected oligopolistic position of large firms may even lead them to do less research. He cites the agreement between Standard Oil of New Jersey and I.G. Farbenindustrie of Germany in which Standard Oil agreed not to do research on synthetic rubber. Oil companies failed to do research on the chemical properties of oil, "apparently out of respect for the larger chemical firms."[43] Jacob Schmookler concludes that "some large firms—many of those in the railroad industry, for example—have done little or no research of any sort, probably because their large size and apparently protected position made research seem unnecessary."

The dilemma of modern technology is that while it has provided the means to increase the material resources available to society, it does not suggest an equitable method for distributing its benefits or directing its operation. Indeed the development of ever larger and more complicated machines and production processes appeared to require administration by an elite group. Even most plans for worker control of large-scale technology retain hierarchical administrative structures. Under such schemes workers typically elect their managers instead of having them appointed by the owners. In either system the very nature of large-scale technology appears to require a distinction between elite and mass.

However, in his classic article, "Metaphysical Pathos and the Social Theory of Bureaucracy," Alvin Gouldner questions the tendency of sociologists to assume that a highly specialized division of labor—a structure with many levels and rigid rules and procedures—is an inevitable feature of organizations that grow to any scale. Gouldner argues that these characteristics arise from the desire of organizational leaders to increase their power over what goes on in the organization and raise their prestige among its members. To increase control, jobs are broken down into their simplest components so that people can be easily replaced. A multiplicity of titles are given out to satisfy organizational members' desire for status within the group. These developments especially occur when members' commitment to organizational goals is low. When commitment is high, there is less need for supervision and reduced specialization is "not necessarily forbidden." [44]

Small-Scale Technologies

If technology is a complex process subject to numerous flaws, then an elaborate and even military form of bureaucracy may be necessary to ensure functioning of the system. However, if a technology is relatively simple and safe, elaborate organizational structures are superfluous. Bureaucracy may appear, but it is certainly not required. For example, small-scale technologies such as pottery kilns require relatively small amounts of capital to construct and very few persons or even one person to operate. A typical pottery workshop consists of storage containers for clay and other raw materials, a potter's wheel for shaping the clay, a kiln for firing the pots, and hand tools for working designs into the clay. The potter's skill is usually passed on through an apprenticeship relationship between an accomplished potter and a neophyte on a one-to-one basis. Individual skill is the major determinant of whether a lump of clay will be successfully transformed into a usable and esthetically pleasing form.

India's Independence leader, Mahatma Gandhi, recognized the relevance of technology to social change. A key element of his constructive program in India was the use of simple technologies as alternatives to large-scale Western technologies. This included the introduction of a simplified version of the spinning wheel to be used by villagers in their homes to make khadi, the local cloth. This spinning wheel would replace the production of cloth by machines in large factories. Gandhi viewed the introduction of large-scale Western technology into India as a development that would perpetuate the control of Indian society by an

elite. He felt that the control of such technology by a small group, added to the traditional caste distinctions in India, would further divide Indian society. Conversely, the introduction of a simple alternative technology available to all would be a means to reduce such divisions. Although Gandhi's technological program never became a major force in Indian society, he did provide an alternative model for the use of technology as an instrument of social change. The failure of Gandhi's technological program to become a reality was that few could accept simple technologies such as the spinning wheel as a substitute for the production efficiencies promised by large-scale technologies. Despite Gandhi's failure to realize his program of social change through pursuing alternative technologies, his attempt inspired others.

Economist E. V. Schumacher in *Small Is Beautiful* argued that economic goods should be produced using small-scale technology. He believed that by reducing the scale of the technology, bureaucratic controls would no longer be necessary to organize production. Once technology was simplified, workers would be able to manage their own enterprises. Schumacher originally worked out his ideas as a strategy for the industrialization of underdeveloped countries. He believed that transferring large-scale industrial technology hurt these countries. It used up scarce resources; it did not employ large numbers of workers; it was difficult to maintain; and the rate of production was often much greater than could be used. Using simpler technologies, even technologies that had been superseded in industrialized countries, would avoid these problems.

Schumacher's ideas have been applied to technologically advanced countries by such theorists as Ivan Illich and Murray Bookchin, who wish to achieve the benefits of democratically controlled small-scale organizations while reducing negative effects on the environment. Their fundamental goal is to replace the assumption of economic growth as a goal with a new ethic of "less is better"—consumption for use rather than for the attainment of status. Illich offers one solution to the Weberian dilemma: give up large-scale industry in exchange for individual fulfillment.

Illich and Bookchin propose the reorganization of modern society into small-scale units in order to achieve an ideal community. According to Illich, "Tools foster conviviality to the extent which they can be easily used by anyone, as often or as seldom as desired. Anticonvivial or manipulative tools control people and produce...according to abstract plans." [45] These include "networks of multi-lane highways, long-range, wide band width transmitters, strip mines, or compulsory school systems." For Illich, all rationally designed devices are technologies, whether they are social forms such as bankruptcy laws or physical artifacts such as road systems. Industrial efficiency and productivity are to be subordinated to individual creativity and personal autonomy. To achieve these goals it is held to be worthwhile to replace more productive with less productive technologies. Illich and Bookchin argue that small-scale solar devices are among the liberatory technologies of a future society. Resource constraints and the elimination of environmental pollution make the development of small-scale communities based on these technologies a political and economic necessity.

A problem with this approach is that relatively few citizens of advanced industrial countries are willing to give up the benefits of mass-produced goods either to save the environment or to create democratically controlled workplaces. Many people who support the goals of the environmental movement are unwilling to commit themselves to a utopian life-style. This apparent contradiction in the environmentalist movement shows up when, on the one hand, polls show widespread popular opposition to nuclear power plants but, on the other hand, there is voter support of nuclear power in referenda where economic factors are made an issue. This dilemma appears because most people are unwilling to give up the benefits of a large-scale source of power on which the industrial society is based. Faced with an apparent choice between a highly industrialized society with environmental problems and a small-scale, low-technology, environmentally pure society, most people choose the former. However, it has also been argued that a shift to small-scale environmentally benign technologies and corresponding small-scale social structures is an inevitable concomitant of a declining resource base.

Technology and Dualism. Amory Lovins, physicist and director of the British branch of Friends of the Earth, a conservationist organization based in the United States, began his 1976 *Foreign Affairs* article, "Energy Strategy: A Road Not Taken," with a quote from a Robert Frost poem, "The Road Not Taken." Lovins developed the metaphor of two paths, "soft" and "hard," to conceptualize alternative energy policies. Hard-energy technologies are large-scale and capital-intensive. Soft-energy technologies are small-scale and matched to end-use needs.

Hard-energy technologies include oil and gas and nuclear fission. The need for their rapid development is based on the assumption that growth in GNP is based on increased energy consumption. According to Lovins, this policy will fail because of fuel shortages of gas and oil and the high cost of capital required to develop coal conversion technologies. Diversion of the required amount of capital to these centralized high technologies would deplete the amount of capital available to other areas of the economy, thus reducing the national wealth and causing inflation.

Soft-energy technologies, by contrast, are based on renewable energy sources such as sun, wind, and vegetation. They comprise a wide variety of flexible and relatively low technologies that are matched in scale and energy quality to end-use needs. Lovins uses the concept of end-use needs as the criterion for determining the utility of a particular energy technology. End uses are particular things such as light, comfortable rooms, and vehicular motion. An energy technology is properly matched to end-use requirements if it produces temperatures or levels of light close to the range actually utilized. If, for example, a technology produces heat thousands of degrees hotter than required, then it is mismatched and wasteful. Lovins concludes that since most energy needs are relatively low-grade, small technologies will suffice to meet these needs without waste. Matching scale to end use reduces both costs of conversion and distribution. Solar heating and cooling, conversion of agricultural wastes to methanol, and wind hydraulic systems are the prime soft technologies. According to Lovins, the social scale which these technologies best fit is the residential neighborhood of approximately one hundred to one thousand persons.

On its face Lovins's call for small-scale alternatives to large-scale technologies represents a voluntary invitation to rethink priorities, change values, and take a new course of action: i.e., to place environmental quality over growth, community over hierarchical organization, and frugality over consumerism. However, the arguments for choosing a soft over a hard path are backed up by strictures of necessity. For while "enlightened" individuals would want to change their values and life-style to fit small-scale models, other who do not share soft views will have to learn to make the adjustment as well. According to Lovins, a society cannot exceed its energy income for long. While centralized systems could be kept going for a while, sooner or later they will have to be replaced by small-scale alternatives so that the society can live within its energy income. With careful planning and conservation present standards of living can be maintained although future improvements should not be expected.

Lovins's goal is to gain our acquiescence

to his political goal of a Jeffersonian, decentralized society not simply by convincing us of its virtues but by demonstrating to us its inevitability. Technological determinism, even in its low-tech form, implies that society is not open to change by human agency. Change will occur and indeed is to be expected, but we cannot affect its course and direction. Indeed, the appropriate response is to adapt ourselves to new techniques. According to Lovins, we should learn to like soft technology, for we shall have to accept it in any event.

Forced Choices. High and low technologies appear to present us with a choice between two alternative futures. High-technology advocates promise us a continued high standard of living if we support the continued development of nuclear power. We are told that if we do not implement this large-scale technology, jobs will be lost and poverty will increase. Such were the stark alternatives presented to voters by advocates of nuclear power in referendums such as the one held in Maine in November 1980. By using this argument, the local electric utility was able to persuade many voters otherwise opposed to nuclear power to vote for it out of fear of risking their jobs or losing their standard of living. Many advocates of small-scale technology also present us with a stark choice. They warn us that the resources to support large-scale technology will not be available for much longer. Even if we do not wish to reduce our use of energy and other resources, we will be forced, by a declining resource base, to adopt a simpler life-style.

Technological determinism in both its high and low forms suffers from the fallacy of the excluded middle. By positing technological choices as consisting only of extreme alternatives, we remove other possibilities from consideration. While each position appears to pose critical choices, the opposite alternative is posed only to show us that no alternative to high or low technologies exists.

Mesotechnology: A Third Way

Until recently modern technology appeared to be developing in a single direction. Technological innovation seemed to be inevitably associated with an increase in scale and complexity. Recently, however, new technologies have been invented that promise a new direction for technology. Arising from research in solid state physics transistors, integrated circuits and photovoltaic solar cells have made possible such developments as the miniaturization of computers and other electronic equipment, and opened the way to decentralized energy production. The reduction in cost and complexity of electronic devices has served to make them available to a broader range of organizations and individuals. For example, the ability to store and control large computerized databases, heretofore virtually limited to large organizations such as government bureaucracies and corporations which could afford mainframe computers, has now become available to small groups and individuals. Computers, formerly associated with the centralizing tendencies seemingly inherent in modern technology, have, as less costly and smaller devices were made available, become an instrument for the democratization of information.

Until recently, largeness of scale and technical sophistication have been features associated with highly productive technologies. Conversely, archaic and inefficient technologies have been characterized by a smallness of scale and technical unsophistication. Technical sophistication combined with moderation in scale and high productivity is the defining characteristic of a new form of technology that I call *mesotechnology*. Mesotechnology is technically sophisticated but not capital-intensive. It is neither a simple device such as a solar collector nor a complicated technology such as a breeder reactor. Mesotechnology is the development of devices that are at the edge of the scientific and technological frontier. Relatively sophisticated equipment and knowledge are required to develop such technologies but not enormous funds or huge laboratories. Mesotechnologies must also meet the requirements of environmental safety and high productivity necessary to sustain an industrial society. Mesotechnologies are variable and thus not deterministic. They may be organized on a small, medium, or large scale.

The development of mesotechnology dissolves the seemingly inevitable connection between productivity and largeness of scale. Low-technology characteristics such as smallness of scale and high-tech characteristics such as technical sophistication are now embodied in microcomputers and photovoltaics. The photovoltaic solar cell that produces electricity from sunlight is a model mesotechnology. For example, the thin film deposition process used to produce a new generation of solar cells is not a particularly sophisticated technique, although hardly a backyard craft.[46]

CONCLUSION

The confrontation of multiple, contrasting lines of technological development suggests that the current trend of technological development in large-scale forms is not inevitable, that is, it is not determined by some logic inherent within technology itself. While the range of possibilities is limited by physical and biological laws and the stock of knowledge of a society, alternative courses of technological development are ascertainable. While the range of possibilities allowed by nature is considerably less than infinite, there is certainly room for more than a single route to the utilization of nature. The ability of human beings to transform nature, including human nature, in more than one direction is a basic premise of Marxian theory. The multilinear or unilinear capacity of nature and the resulting multilinear or unilinear capacity of technological development are at the root of divergent Marxian and Weberian views of technology.

Technology is not a self-evolving process with a single possible result as suggested by Weber, but a socially determined process with multiple possible outcomes, as implied by Marx. The choice of a technology for development and utilization can extend an existing social trend and reinforce the status quo. The struggle to develop an alternative technology can lend weight to efforts to shift social structures to operate on alternative principles. The current controversy over nuclear and solar energy can be viewed as an exemplar of this thesis. Received notions of technological determinism begin to wither, and new ideas about the social shaping of technological development have begun to be explored.[47]

NOTES

1. Jacob Schmookler, *Invention and Economic Growth* (Cambridge, Mass.: Harvard University Press, 1966); S. C. Gilfilan, *The Sociology of Invention* (Cambridge, Mass.: MIT Press, 1970; first published in 1935).
2. Joseph Schumpeter, *Capitalism, Socialism, and Democracy* (New York: Harper & Brothers, 1942).
3. Ralph Landau, "Technology and U.S. Competitiveness" (Address to New York Science Policy Association, March 23, 1989).
4. National Science Board, *Science and Engineering Indicators* (Washington, D.C.: National Science Foundation, 1987).
5. Ibid.
6. John Irvine and John Martin, *Foresight in Science: Picking the Winners* (London: F. Pinter, 1984).
7. John Campbell, *Collapse of an Industry: Nuclear Industry and the Contradictions of U.S. Policy* (Ithaca, N.Y.: Cornell University Press, 1988).
8. Henry Etzkowitz, "Solar versus Nuclear Energy: Autonomous or Dependent Technology," *Social Problems* 31, no. 4 (April 1984), pp. 417-34.
9. Arthur Bright, *The Electric Lamp Industry: Technological Change and Economic Development from 1800 to 1947* (New York: Macmillan, 1949).
10. Paul Goodman, "Can Technology be Humane?" *New York Review of Books*, November 20, 1969, pp. 27-34.
11. David Noble, *Forces of Production: A Social History of Automation* (New York: Alfred A. Knopf, 1984).
12. Hans Jonas, "Technology and Responsibility: Reflections on the New Tasks of Ethics," *Social Research* 40, no. 1 (Spring 1973), pp. 31-54.
13. Jacques Ellul, *The Technological Society* (New York: Alfred A. Knopf, 1964).
14. Karl Wittfogel, *Oriental Despotism: A Comparative Study of Total Power* (New Haven, Conn.: Yale University Press, 1957).
15. George Murdock, *Social Structure* (New York: Macmillan, 1949).
16. David Landes, *The Unbound Prometheus: Technological Change and Industrial Development in Western Europe from 1750* (Cambridge: Cambridge University Press, 1969).
17. Malcolm Thomis, *The Luddites: Machine Breaking in Regency England* (New York: Schocken Books, 1970).
18. John Kasson, *Civilizing the Machine: Technology and Republican Values in America, 1776–1900* (New York: Grossman, 1976).
19. Etzkowitz, "Solar versus Nuclear Energy."
20. Karl Marx, *Grundrisse* (New York: Vintage Books, 1973), p. 704.
21. Ibid.
22. Ibid., p. 700.
23. Ibid., p. 693.
24. Alfred Schmidt, *The Concept of Nature in Marx* (London: New Left Books, 1971), p. 13.
25. Max Weber, "Social Categories of Economic Action," in Guenther Roth and Claus Wittich, eds., *Max Weber on Economics and Society* (New York: Bedminster Press, 1968).
26. Hans Gerth and C. Wright Mills, *From Max Weber* (New York: Oxford University Press, 1946), p. 213.
27. David Dickson, *The New Politics of Science* (New York: Pantheon Books, 1984).
28. Ernest Mandel, *Marxist Economic Theory* (New York: Monthly Review Press, 1968).
29. Richard Nelson, "The Link between Science and Invention: The Case of the Transistor," in *The Rate and Direction of Inventive Activity* (Princeton, N.J.: National Bureau of Economic Research, 1962).
30. Nathan Rosenberg, *Perspectives on Technology*

(Cambridge: Cambridge University Press, 1976), p. 110.

31. Ibid., p. 112.
32. Herbert Fusfeld, *The Technical Enterprise: Present and Future Trends* (Cambridge, Mass.: Ballinger Publishing, 1986).
33. Bernhard Stern, *Historical Sociology* (New York: Citadel Press, 1957).
34. Seymour Melman, *Pentagon Capitalism: The Political Economy of War* (New York: McGraw-Hill, 1970).
35. Allan Schnaiberg, Nicholas Watts, and Klaus Zimmerman, eds., *Distributional Conflicts in Environmental Resource Policy* (New York: St. Martin's Press, 1986).
36. Federal Communications Commission, Engineering Department, Telephone Investigation, Docket No. 1, *Report on Patent Structure of Bell Telephone System* (Washington, D.C.: Government Printing Office, 1937).
37. Etzkowitz, "Solar versus Nuclear Energy."
38. Barry Commoner, *The Closing Circle: Nature, Man, and Technology* (New York: Alfred A. Knopf, 1971).
39. United Nations Industrial Development Organization, *Conceptual and Policy Framework for Appropriate Industrial Technology* (New York: United Nations, 1979), p. 17.
40. Ibid.
41. Charles Perrow, *Normal Accidents: Living with High Risk Technologies* (New York: Basic Books, 1984).
42. Jacob Schmookler, "Technology and Progress," in Edward Mason, ed., *The Corporation in Modern Society* (New York: Atheneum Publishers, 1973), p. 162.
43. Ibid., p. 164.
44. Alvin Gouldner, "The Metaphysical Pathos and the Theory of Bureaucracy," *American Political Science Review* (June 1955), pp. 496–507.
45. Ivan Illich, *Tools for Conviviality* (New York: Harper & Row, 1973), p. 26.
46. Dave Elliot, "Soft Technology for Hard Times—Back to the Drawing Board," *Undercurrents* 13 (November-December 1975), pp. 15–20.
47. Wiebe E. Bijker et al., eds., *The Social Construction of Technological Systems: New Directions in the Sociology and History of Technology* (Cambridge, Mass.: MIT Press, 1987).

NAME INDEX

Adorno, Theodor W., 230, 289
Alexander, Jeffrey C., 267
Almond, Gabriel, 32
Althusser, Louis, 305, 310-12
Apel, Karl-Otto, 192-94
Appel, Otto, 291
Arcana, Judith, 261-62
Atkinson, D., 270

Baran, Paul, 100, 103
Bart, Pauline, B., 249
Barthes, Roland, 305, 306
Bauman, Zygmunt, 277
Beauvoir, Simone de, 248, 249
Berger, Bennett, 277
Berger, Peter, 41, 43
Betti, Emilio, 190-92
Blumberg, Rae Lesser, 254
Blumer, Herbert, 151, 152, 154, 157, 158
Bookchin, Murray, 369, 370
Brown, Michael, 227, 321

Chodorow, Nancy, 261-62
Chomsky, Noam, 221, 305
Clarke, Lorene M. G., 255
Coleman, James S., 29
Commoner, Barry, 365
Comte, August, 5, 69, 70, 73
Cooley, Charles Horton, 42, 151, 156, 157
Coser, Lewis A., 32, 51
Courbet, Gustave, 242

Darwin, Charles, 6
de Coulange, Fustel, 70
Dilthey, Wilhelm, 188
Dinnerstein, Dorothy, 261-62
Djilas, Milovan, 44
Duchamp, Marcel, 236, 238, 240
Durkheim, Emile, 6-11, 68-94

Echols, James C., 565
Eisenstadt, S. N., 32, 51, 272, 273
Ellul, Jacques, 357

Engels, Friedrich, 99, 101, 282
Ernst, Max, 236, 238, 240
Etzkowitz, Henry, 1, 355

Ferraro, Geraldine, 260
Fischer, George, 227
Fishman, Walda Katz, 335
Foucault, Michel, 47, 305, 312-15
Freedman, Marcia, 262-63
Freud, Sigmund, 38-39, 294-95
Friedan, Betty, 260-61
Frye, Marilyn, 250, 256

Gadamer, Hans-Georg, 188-93, 196-97, 220, 221
Galbraith, John Kenneth, 368
Garfinkel, Harold, 41, 168, 333
Ghandi, Mahatma, 369
Giddens, A., 48, 50, 51
Glassman, Ronald M., 1, 69, 125
Goffman, Erving, 42-43, 326
Goodall, Jane, 49, 52
Goode, William J., 268
Gouldner, Alvin, 1, 2, 33, 272, 273, 368

Habermas, Jurgen, 46, 192-95, 230, 231, 270, 271, 291, 293, 296, 302
Halley, Jeffrey A., 227
Haritos, Rosa, 69
Harris, Marvin, 349-50
Hartsock, Nancy C., 262
Hegel, Frederick, 14-17, 282
Heilbroner, Robert L., 101, 105
Heraclitus, 14-15
Hirsch, E. D., Jr., 190-92
Hochschild, Arlie Russell, 249
Horkheimer, Max, 230, 231, 288, 291, 292
Husserl, Edmund, 167, 168, 219

Illich, Ivan, 369, 370

Jakobson, Roman, 307
Jung, Karl, 239

Kant, Immanuel, 12-13, 28, 278
Kautsky, John, 44
Keller, Suzanne, 32
Kennedy, John F., 45
Kennedy, Robert, 45
King, James, 347
King, Martin Luther, 45
Kuhn, Thomas S., 2
Kurzweil, Edith, 321

Lacan, Jacques, 309, 316
Lazarsfeld, Paul F., 29, 33
Leakey, Louis, 49, 52
Lechner, Norbert, 272
Lenin, 120-21
Lévi-Strauss, Claude, 305, 307-10
Lipset, Seymour M., 29, 33
Lorde, Audre, 263
Lovins, Amory, 370, 371
Lukacs, Georg, 27, 46, 47, 100, 136, 227,
    228, 230
Lynd, Helen, 27
Lynd, Robert, 27

MacKinnon, Catharine A., 249, 250, 256-59
Malinowski, Bronislaw, 10, 11
Mandel, Ernest, 108
Mao Zedong, 144-45
Marcuse, Herbert, 38-39, 214-15, 230, 231,
    302
Marx, Karl, 17-23, 70, 99-123, 270, 294,
    310-12
Mason, Edward, 368
Mauss, Marcel, 47
Mayer, Tom, 99
Mead, George Herbert, 27, 42, 151, 153, 156,
    159
Merton, Robert K., 3, 31, 80, 89-90, 267-68
Michels, Robert, 26
Miliband, Ralph, 44, 51
Mill, John Stuart, 296
Mills, C. Wright, 33, 36-37
Moore, Barrington, 51, 284, 302

Nader, Ralph, 365
Newton, Isaac, 5
Nisbet, R., 8
Noble, David, 364

O'Brien, Mary, 254-55
Orleans, Myron, 167

Parsons, Talcott, 30-34, 46, 267-74
Plato, 12
Popper, Karl, 2

Poulantzas, Nicos, 47
Prager, Jeffrey, 272

Radcliffe-Brown, A. R., 11
Renan, Ernest, 70
Rich, Adrienne, 249, 256, 259-60, 261-62
Richter, Hans, 238, 239
Ricoeur, Paul, 192-94
Riesman, David, 34
Rose, Gillian, 302
Rossi, Alice, 262
Rossi, Peter H., 273
Rothman, Barbara Katz, 151
Russell, Bertrand, 48

Saint-Simon, C., 69-70, 85
Sanger, Margaret, 366
Sartre, Jean Paul, 309, 310
Saussure, Ferdinand de, 306-7
Schäffle, Albert, 7, 70
Schroyer, Troy, 302
Schumacher, E. V., 369
Schumpeter, Joseph, 368
Schutz, Alfred, 41, 168
Scuilli, D., 272
Seator, Penelope, 263
Seeley, John R., 34
Shumway, Loren, 227
Skocpol, Theda, 51
Smith, Adam, 282
Smith, Dorothy, 250-51, 254
Spencer, Herbert, 6, 71, 338
Starr, Jerold, 227
Stein, Maurice, 37
Stern, Bernhard, 364
Stimpson, Catharine, 249
Strauss, Anselm, 157

Tobach, Ethel, 347
Tonnies, Ferdinand, 9, 70
Tzara, Tristan, 236, 237, 238

Vidich, Arthur, 37

Wallerstein, Immanuel, 44, 51
Washburn, S. L., 347
Weber, Max, 23-25, 28, 44-46, 125-46, 228,
    229-30
Whitehead, Alfred North, 48
Whitehead, Marybeth, 261
Whyte, William H., 34
Wilson, E. O., 335-50
Wolff, Janet, 187
Wolff, Kurt H., 201
Wright, Eric Olin, 51

SUBJECT INDEX

Adaptation, 338
AIDS (Acquired Immune Deficiency
  Syndrome) case study, 91
American sociology, *see* United States sociology
Anomie, 10, 79-80, 86, 87, 89-91
  case study, 91-94
  positive and negative qualities, 88-91, 93-94
  working class, 83
Avant garde art, 228

Bureaucracy, Weber's theory, 126-27

Capitalism, 106-11
  business cycle, 108-9
  Marxist view
    exploitive nature, 106-8
    laws of capitalist accumulation, 108
  Weber's views, 127
Charisma, 128-30
  humanistic and evil, 129
  mass media, 129-30
  routinization of, 128
  social change, 128-29, 134, 144
Charismatic leader concept, 24
China, Weber's analysis of its transition, 139
Civilizational uniqueness, concept of, 143-44
Class
  based on mode of production, 135
  Marxist theory of conflict, 100-101, 105-6,
    112-13
Collective conscience, 9-10, 79, 80-83
Combahee River Collective, 263
Communicative action, theory of, 270
Communism, 111-14
  Russian Revolution, 114-22
Comparative method in sociology, 76-77
Concept, 155
Consciousness raising (CR) groups, 250
Conceptualizing, 155
Critical theory, 39, 46, 277
  basic concepts, 284-95
  compared to existential philosophy, 287
  compared to phenomenology, 286-87

creation of rational society, 298-300
cultural mode versus natural mode of
  interpretation, 282-84, 291
definition, 277
elitist view of, 290-91
emancipatory knowledge, 288, 289, 293-94
knowledge of fact versus knowledge of
  reality, 278
legitimation of state, 298-300
mastery and cooperation, 292-93
mode of theorizing, 277, 297
natural law, 282
nature mode interpretation leading to
  oppression, 285, 288
rational discourse, 296-97
relation of critical theory to critical practice,
  280, 291-92, 295
self-reflection, 286-88
sociological applications, 296-301
surrender and catch, 219
test of truth of theory, 296
Cultural mode of cognitive attitude, 282-87
Cultural politics, 241
Culture, 227
  resistance to rationalization, 228, 231

Dada art avant garde, 228-40
  attack on legitimacy of social order, 240-41
  counterideology, 232, 240
  critical accomplishments, 240-43
  cultural politics, 241
  delegitimation, 233-34
  disenchantment, 237
  example of, 236
  ideology, 232
  legitimation, 233
  randomization, 235, 239
  rationalization and resistance, 228-32
  reenchantment, 232-33
Darwinian theory of evolution, 338
Deviance, theory of, 79-80, 86, 90-91
Dialectics, 101-3

Division of Labor (Durkheim) 8, 78-79, 83-84, 89
Durkheim's sociological theories, 69-94
  collective conscience, 80
  functional analysis, 75-77
  influences on, 69-72
  Marxian theory contrasted, 83-85
  norms, 75
  organic solidarity, 77
  political sociology, 86-87
  scientific method, 73

Egoistic isolation, 79-80
Eidetic reduction, 177
Elementary Forms of Religious Life (Durkheim), 68-70
Empiricism, 5-6, 25-26, 52
Epistemology, 279
An Essay on Liberation (Marcuse), 231
Ethnomethodology, 168, 179-80, 332-33
Existentialist philosophy, 220
  compared to critical theory, 287

Feminist theories, 49
  black women's input, 263
  capitalism as cause of oppression, 250-51
  consciousness-raising, 250-51
  gender hierarchy, 256
  lesbianism, 259-60
  liberal feminism, 260-62
  radical feminism
    Adrienne Rich's theories, 259-60
    Catharine McKinnon's theories, 256-59
  rape, 258-59
Roe v. *Wade*, 257
sexuality, 256
socialist/Marxist theorists, 250-56
  Dorothy Smith's views, 250-51, 254
  Lorenne M. G. Clarke's theories, 255-56
  Mary O'Brien's views, 254-55
Forced division of labor, 83-85
Formal rationality, 228-29
Frankfurt school of sociology, 39, 46, 227-28
Functional analysis theory of Durkheim, 75-77
Functionalism, 1-2, 27, 30-35, 37, 40, 41, 75-76, 267
  characteristics of theory, 268-69
  concept of action, 268
  left-functionalism, 268
  neofunctionalism, *see* Neofunctionalism

Generalized other, 159
Germany
  historical summary, 11-12

ideology, 26-27
school of sociology, 13-26

Hermeneutics, 187
  critical, 193-94
  definition, 188
  explanation versus understanding, 189
  hermeneutical autonomy, 191
  interpretation, 188-90, 192-93
  objective, 188, 190-92, 196
  philosophy of, 188
  prejudices, 189
  relativism, 190-92
  sociology, 194-96
  structural, 192-93
  surrender and catch, 220-21
  theory, 188-89
Heroic pessimism, 127, 146
Hippie subculture, 39
Historic materialism, 103-6
Human biogram, 340, 347
Human society, 156-58

Ideal typification, 137, 229-30
Ideology, 133
  legitimating social order, 233
  rationality and resistance, 232-33
Individual isolation, 70
Instrumental rationalization, 230-31
Intermediary occupational associations, 86-87

Kinship structure theory, 305

Language
  Dadaism, 237-38
  medium of hermeneutics, 189, 196
  structuralism, 306-7
  surrender and catch, 221
Legal-rational authority, 130
Legitimate domination categories of Weber, 130-31
Legitimation Crisis (Habermas), 298, 300
Linguistic theory, 305-6, *see also* Language
Looking-glass self, 42, 156

Macrophenomenology, 168, 173
Madness and Civilization (Foucault), 313
Marxism, 17-23, 99-123
  capitalism, 106-11
  communism, 111-14
  definition, 99-101
  dialectics, 101-3
  historical materialism, 103-6
  ideology, 232

political action, 99
Russian Revolution, 114-22
stages of history theory, 18-19
theory of social change, 22-23, 131-32
U.S. sociology influenced by, 37-40, 44, 47
see also Neo-Marxism
Mesotechnology, 372
Microphenomenology, 173
Mind, 154-55
Monogamy, polygamy and polyandry, 348-49
Myths, structural theories of, 307-9

National Organization for Women (NOW),
  260
Natural mode of cognitive attitude, 282-87
Natural science, 281
Nature-nurture debate, 225
Neofunctionalism, 50, 267-74
  conflict theory, 273
  democratic thrust, 272
  ideological critique of Parson's functionalism,
  272
  reconstructionists attempts to alter Parson's
  theories, 272
  reinterpretation of functionalist tradition,
  270
Neo-Marxism, 50, 270, 271
  class consciousness, 330-31
  consumerism, 325
  desires versus needs, 325-26
  expansion of capital on global scale, 328
  false consciousness, 332-33
  limitations of collective bargaining, 329
  Marxian sociology, 321-22
  protest movements, psychology of, 327-29
  sources of ideas under capitalism, 322
  study of communication, 304, 332
  U.S. sociology, 37-40, 44
Nomos (social cohesion), 74
Norms, Durkheim's theory of, 8, 75

Occupational-role interdependence theory, 71
On Human Nature (Wilson), 335, 336
Ontology, 279
Organic solidarity, theory of, 77-79

Phenomenologophobia, 168
Phenomenology, 25, 40-43, 52, 67-82
  alternation, 181
  application to social life, 180-82
  approach to social analysis, 169-75
    empathic, 173, 175
    introspection, 173
  compared to conventional sociology, 175

definition, 169
distinguished from critical theory, 286
founders of theory, 167-69
method of social analysis, 175-80
objective consciousness, 174
paramount reality, 176
reduction, 177
subjective experiences, 175
surrender and catch, 219
Political legitimacy, 130-31
Political sociology, 86-87
Positivism, 5, 25, 27-30, 36, 52
The Power Elite (Mills), 36
Production in Marxist theory, 103-4
Proletariat
  class struggle, 112
  revolutionary consciousness, 109-10

Rationalization
  China in transition, 139
  cultural resistance to, 228, 231
    art, 231, 232
  defined, 228
  delegitimation of, 234
  of the economy, 126-27
  extension of capitalism, 230
  of social structure, 126-27
  of thought, 125-26
Reduction concept in phenomenological
  sociology, 177
Reference group concept, 42, 156
Religion, theories of
  Christianity, 17
  Durkheim's theories, 9-10, 68, 71-72, 73,
    80-82
  Greeks, 16-17
  Jewish, 16
  Marx's theories, 81-82
  Oriental religion, 16
  Weber's theories, 82, 125-26
  Wilson's theories, 342
Russian Revolution, 114-22

Scientific materialism, 337
Scientific socialism, 101
Scientific sociology, 5-11
Self, theory of, 155-56, 158-60
Self-indication, 154-55
Social causality theory, 72
Social change, theory of
  Durkheim's theory, 87-88
  Marxian theory, 131-32
  Weber's theory, 131-35
Social classes, 104-5

Social Darwinism, 6, 49, 338
Socialism
  Durkheim's views, 85
  Marxism, 77, 101, 113
Socialization, 158-60
Social psychology, 82, 151
Social structure, Weber's conception of, 135-36
Society, theories of, 156-58
Sociobiology, 49, 52, 335-51
  altruism, 339-40
  defined, 336
  evaluation of, 345-51
  evolutionary paradigm, 338-39
  genetic-based ethical system, 336-38
  human biogram, 340, 347
  inclusive fitness, 339
  kin selection, 339
  parent-child relations, 344-45
  sexual reproduction of male/female
    differences, 343
  social Darwinism, 338
  universal human traits, 341-42
Sociobiology: The New Synthesis (Wilson), 335
Sociological analysis theory of Durkheim, 69
Sociology
  basic theoretical systems, 3
  epistemology, 2
    phenomenology, 2-3
    positivist, 2-3
  French school, 6-11
  German tradition, 11-27
  multiparadigmatic, 3
  preparadigmatic, 2
  renascence, 50-54
  scientific school, 5-11
  U.S. after World War II, 27-46
Sociology of art, 227
  research, 242
Structuralism, 47-48, 220, 305-12
  Althusser's theories, 310-12
  definition, 306
  kinship theories, 305
  language, 306-7
  Lévi-Strass' theories, 307-10
  myths, 307-9
Structural linguistics, 305, 310, 312-13
Subjective experience, 175
Substantive rationality, 228, 229, 231, 232
Suicide: A Study in Sociology (Durkheim), 7, 72,
  79-80, 88-89
Surrender and catch, 201-21
  connection with sociology, 209-19
  community study, 209-11
  prerequisites to possibility of surrender, 212

  radicalism of, 213, 218
  critical theory, 219-20
  existentialism, 220
  linguistic theories, 221
  meaning of, 203-8
  hermeneutics, 220
  origin of, 203
  phenomenology, 219
  response to crisis, 202
  structuralism, 220-21
Symbol, 152-54
Symbolic interaction, 27, 42-43, 151-64
  basic premises, 152-54
  communication by gestures, 153
  definition of situation, 160-61
  looking-glass self, 42, 156
  meanings, 152-53
  mind, 154-55
  reference group concept, 42, 156
  research, 161-64
  self, 155-56, 158-60
  socialization, 158-60
  society, 156-58
Systems theory, 30

Technology, 355-72
  definitions, 357
  frustration of, 364
  Marx's view, 359-62
  mesotechnology, 372
  social change, 364-65
    consumer movement, 365-66
    environmental movement, 365
    feminist movement, 366
    underdeveloped countries, 366-67
  social effects of, 367-72
    dualism, 370
    large and small scale technologies, 367-71
  social influences on technological
    development, 363
  theories of technology development, 362-63
  Weber's theories, 359, 360, 361
Territoriality, 341

United States sociology
  functionalism, 30-36
  positivism, 28
  revival of Marxism, 37-40, 44, 47
  sociological theory after World War II, 27-49
Unintended effects, theory of, 134-35

White Collar (Mills), 36

Xenophobia, 341, 349

THE RENASCENCE OF SOCIOLOGICAL THEORY

Composition by Point West, Carol Stream, Illinois
Printed and bound by Arcata Graphics, Kingsport, Tennessee
Designed by Willis Proudfoot, Mt. Prospect, Illinois
Production supervision by Robert H. Grigg, Chicago, Illinois
The text is set in Galliard, with Optima display